AMERICAN ERAS

THE
REVOLUTIONARY ERA
1 7 5 4 - 1 7 8 3

AMERICAN ERAS

THE REVOLUTIONARY ERA

1 7 5 4 - 1 7 8 3

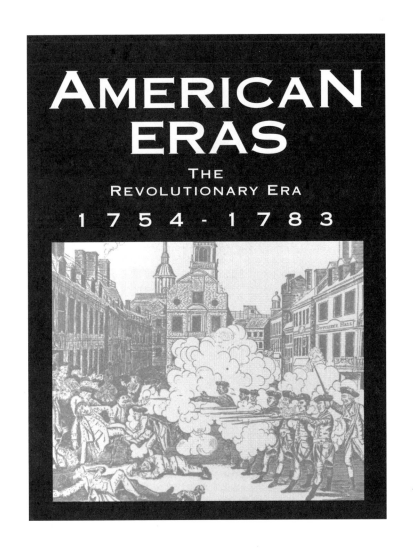

EDITED BY

ROBERT J. ALLISON

A MANLY, INC. BOOK

GALE

DETROIT LONDON

AMERICAN ERAS

REVOLUTIONARY ERA, 1754-1783

Matthew J. Bruccoli and Richard Layman, Editorial Directors
Karen L. Rood, Senior Editor

Copyright ©1998 by Gale Research
ISBN 0-7876-1480-7

CONTENTS

INTRODUCTION

Solon and Sophocles. As the secretary to the French Academy of Sciences reported on recently deceased members in April 1778, a general murmur and then a cry went up from the audience, which saw an opportunity to witness a rare encounter. Present at the meeting were Voltaire, recently returned to Paris from a long Genevan exile, and Benjamin Franklin, American envoy to France whose sojourn had made him one of the most famous men in the city. Monsieur Voltaire and Monsieur Franklin must be introduced, the crowd demanded. The two men, who in fact had met some days earlier, rose from their chairs and bowed to one another. But this was not enough—the crowd insisted on more. Franklin and Voltaire seemed puzzled and amused, but graciously shook hands. Still the crowd was not satisfied, and began to call, "Il faut s'embrasser, a la francoise," (They must embrace in the French style). Franklin and Voltaire understood, and to great applause they embraced and kissed one another's cheeks. How charming it was, those in attendance would say later, how enchanting to see "Solon and Sophocles embracing."

Connections Between Worlds. John Adams, who witnessed the scene, was not nearly as impressed as the French audience. He knew Franklin as a wily diplomat and shrewd politician; Voltaire, like Franklin, was a writer with skeptical philosophical convictions. But for the audience at the French Academy the two men represented the heights of human achievement. Voltaire, who would die just a few weeks after the encounter at the Academy, was the greatest of the French philosophes, writers who argued for human freedom against the constraints of church and state. Franklin, famous for his experiments with lightning, had arrived in France to help destroy the power of the British monarchy. French philosophe Anne-Robert-Jacques Turgot, Baron de l'Aulne provided Franklin with a Latin epigram, *Eripuit caelo fulmen sceptrumque tyrannis* (He snatched lightning from the sky and the scepter from tyrants). The meeting of the two men at the French Academy was a meeting between the American and French Enlightenments, showing to all the unity of the various intellectual currents of the age: the quest for scientific knowledge, for intellectual freedom, and for political liberty.

Age of Revolutions. It was an age of revolutions, but no other revolutions have had such a profoundly intellectual grounding. The American war, the revolutionaries never tired of pointing out, was only a small part of their revolution: the real revolution had taken place in the minds and hearts of the people. In the Declaration of Independence in 1776 Congress had explained that governments were created to secure certain rights that all men and women had been granted not by government but by "the laws of Nature and of Nature's God." These inalienable rights included "life, liberty, and the pursuit of happiness." Thomas Jefferson, who drafted the Declaration of Independence, insisted he had not said anything particularly new, he had merely written down what every American believed. The wonder is that so many Americans regarded these ideas as self-evident truths.

Seven Years' War. The revolution had, in fact, begun for much less lofty reasons. In 1754 delegates from England's North American colonies, Massachusetts, New York, and Pennsylvania met at Albany to improve their troubled relationship with the Iroquois confederation. Rivalries among the colonies had led the Iroquois to consider a closer relationship with the French colonists in Canada, who were extending their fur-trading operations into the Ohio River valley. The skirmishes along the Ohio were part of the broader imperial ambitions of England and France and ultimately would lead to a worldwide war fought in North America, Europe, the Caribbean, the Mediterranean, Africa and India. England would triumph, negotiating a treaty in Paris to end the war and secure England's primacy among nations.

Debts and Taxes. But the French and Indian War left England in debt, and to pay the debt England imposed taxes on the colonists, who had benefited from her military power. The colonists resisted the taxes but not simply because they did not want to pay. Instead, the colonists insisted, they could not be taxed by Parliament because they were not represented in Parliament. It was an argument that made no sense in England, but to the colonists it was plain that taxation without representation was tyranny. If the colonists could be taxed by men whom they had not elected, they would lose their liberty in other areas, and they would eventually be nothing more than slaves. For the British this seemed like exaggerated rhetoric, but to the colonists it was apparent that British tax policies were but the first step on a road to oppression.

Creating Political Societies. The colonists resisted the Sugar Act, the Stamp Act, and the Tea Act, organizing themselves into political communities to oppose British policies. These new political organizations created networks of informed and active citizens who joined together for common purposes. Even if the Revolution had been avoided, the creation of the Sons of Liberty and committees of correspondence would have made the American colonies much different places than they had been before. The resistance to the British acts also convinced the colonists of their mutual identity: they were not Virginians or New Englanders or British subjects living in a colony—they regarded themselves as Americans. Even though South Carolina had more in common with Barbados than it did with Massachusetts, and Massachusetts had closer ties to London than it did to Pennsylvania, by 1776 leaders in the colonies regarded themselves as members of one political society, and when they decided to declare their independence, they did so as the United States of America.

Experiments in Government. The revolutionary enlightenment ideas helped Americans shape their new political societies. Relying on the works of philosophes such as Montesquieu and Cesare Bonesana Beccaria, Marchese di Beccaria, Americans rewrote their basic laws and changed their governments to best fit their societies and their ideas of public order. It was an age of experiments in government, and virtually every state began its constitution with a declaration of rights. The government existed to protect the liberties of the governed, not to enhance the wealth of the governors. Pennsylvania experimented with a simple democracy while Massachusetts created a balanced political system that would protect both the rich and poor from the tyranny of each other. To hold the union together the states created a Confederation that could borrow money and negotiate treaties but could not tax the American people. That the Confederation was a failure should not detract from the notable success Americans had in constructing state governments. Philosophers such as John Locke and Montesquieu had speculated on the best kinds of government; the Americans had an opportunity to put theories into action, and their experiments are well worth studying.

Wealth of Nations. The Revolution began in response to British trade policies. In 1776 Scottish philosopher Adam Smith published *Wealth of Nations,* changing the standard perceptions of economic activity. England and France had come to dominate the world's economy through a tight control of markets and protection of their own manufactures. Smith argued that this mercanitilist policy was wrong; in the long run free trade would produce more wealth for a nation than would protection. Though England was slow to embrace this new political theory, in America the doctrine of free trade was

warmly received, both because it challenged British attempts to restrict American trade and offered a theory to map the American road to wealth and prosperity. For Americans the idea of free trade was another fundamental point of political philosophy that would become a staple of their economic thought and commercial practice.

Education. But their belief in free trade and limited government did not mean Americans wanted governments that would do nothing. In his constitution for Massachusetts, John Adams insisted that "Wisdom and knowledge . . . diffused generally among the body of the people" were necessary to preserve their rights and liberties. The newly independent states called for spreading the benefits of education through society. Thomas Jefferson was unsuccessful in persuading Virginians to adopt a system of public education, but virtually every state created colleges, and the Revolution made education more accessible to many.

Slavery. "How is it," Samuel Johnson asked in response to the American literature of revolution, "that we hear the loudest yelps for liberty from the drivers of negroes?" Thomas Jefferson, George Mason, and George Washington all owned slaves, and slavery as an institution flourished in all of the American colonies. How could the Americans justify a revolution for liberty, and how could Americans make pronouncements on human equality, when they owned men, women, and children as chattel? The Revolution challenged Americans to rethink their attitudes on slavery. Before the Revolution, Congress had voted to bar imports of slaves as part of the general campaign against British imports. Jefferson's draft of the Declaration of Independence included an attack on Britain for supporting the slave trade but also criticized England for encouraging slaves to revolt against their masters. In 1780 Pennsylvania voted to end slavery gradually, freeing slaves born after a certain date. In 1783 a Massachusetts court ruled that slavery was incompatible with the state constitution, which said "All men are born free and equal. . . ." Other states equivocated: Virginia amended its initial declaration of equality so that men became equal when they entered into a state of society. The Revolution forced all to rethink their attitudes on slavery, but not all came to the same conclusions. Some African Americans fought along with whites for political independence from England; others remained loyal to the British Crown or fought with the British to subdue their former masters. When the British abandoned the North American colonies, they took with them some African Americans who had won their freedom by fighting against the American revolutionaries who had enslaved them.

World Turned Upside Down. The American Revolution was more than a war, and it was more than a struggle for self-government. It opened a new world. This concept was best captured by the British musicians at Yorktown in October 1781. As the British army surrendered its arms to the American victors, their musicians played

"The World Turned Upside Down." It had been turned upside down and would never be the same again. Americans had begun the Revolution not merely to free themselves but to free their children to have better lives. As John Adams wrote, "I must study politics and war that my sons may have the liberty to study math and philosophy. My sons ought to study math and philosophy, geology, natural history and naval architecture, navigation, commerce and agriculture, in order to give their children a right to study painting, poetry, music, architecture, statuary, tapestry and porcelain." As Ralph Waldo Emerson would later say, the revolutionaries dared to die to leave their children free.

Starting the World Anew. Thomas Paine declared in *Common Sense* (1776) that Americans had it in their power to start the world anew. They not only had it in their power, but they also had a duty to do so. The cause was not merely that of thirteen colonies in North America, it was the cause of the whole world, as he wrote, "Oh ye that love mankind! Ye that dare oppose not only the tyranny but the tyrant, stand forth! Every spot of the old world is overrun with oppression. Freedom hath been hunted round the globe. Asia and Africa have long expelled her. Europe regards her like a stranger, and England hath given her warning to depart. O! receive the fugitive, and prepare in time an asylum for mankind."

ACKNOWLEDGMENTS

This book was produced by Manly, Inc. Anthony J. Scotti was the in-house editor.

Production and systems manager is Marie L. Parker.

Administrative support was provided by Ann M. Cheschi, Beverly Dill, Renita Hickman, and Tenesha S. Lee.

Bookkeeper is Neil Senol.

Copyediting supervisor is Phyllis A. Avant. The copyediting staff includes Samuel W. Bruce, Christine Copeland, Jannette L. Giles, Thom Harman, Melissa D. Hinton, Nicole M. Nichols, and Raegan E. Quinn. Freelance copyeditors are Rebecca Mayo and Jennie Williamson.

Editorial associate is Jeff Miller.

Layout and graphics staff includes Janet E. Hill, Mark J. McEwan, and Alison Smith.

Office manager is Kathy Lawler Merlette.

Photography editors are Margo Dowling, Margaret Meriwether, and Paul Talbot. Photographic copy work was performed by Joseph M. Bruccoli.

SGML supervisor is Cory McNair. The SGML staff includes Linda Drake, Frank Graham, Jennifer Harwell, and Alex Snead.

Software support was provided by Stephen Rahe. Database manager is Javed Nurani. Kim Kelly performed data entry.

Typesetting supervisor is Kathleen M. Flanagan. The typesetting staff includes Karla Corley Brown, Pamela D. Norton, and Patricia Flanagan Salisbury.

Walter W. Ross and Steven Gross did library research. They were assisted by the following librarians at the Thomas Cooper Library of the University of South Carolina: Linda Holderfield and the interlibrary-loan staff; reference-department head Virginia Weathers; reference librarians Marilee Birchfield, Stefanie Buck, Stefanie DuBose, Rebecca Feind, Karen Joseph, Donna Lehman, Charlene Loope, Anthony McKissick, Jean Rhyne, and Kwamine Simpson; circulation-department head Caroline Taylor; and acquisitions-searching supervisor David Haggard.

AMERICAN ERAS

REVOLUTIONARY ERA,

1754–1783

WORLD EVENTS:

SELECTED OCCURRENCES OUTSIDE NORTH AMERICA

MAJOR POWERS AND LEADERS

Austria—Queen Maria Theresa (1740–1780); King Joseph II (1780–1790).

China—Emperor Qianlong (1735–1796).

France—King Louis XV (1715–1774); Louis XVI (1774–1793).

Great Britain—King George II (1727–1760); George III (1760–1820); Prime Ministers: Henry Pelham (1746–1754); Thomas Pelham Holles, duke of Newcastle, (1754–1756; June 1757–1761); William Cavendish, duke of Devonshire (Nov.–Dec. 1756); William Pitt, earl of Chatham after August 1766 (Dec. 1756–June 1757; secretary of state, 1757–1761; prime minister, July 1766–Dec. 1767); John Stuart, earl of Bute (May 1762–April 1763); George Grenville (April 1763–July 1765); Charles Watson-Wentworth, marquess of Rockingham (July 1765–July 1766; March–July 1782); Augustus Henry Fitzroy, duke of Grafton (Dec. 1767–1770); Frederick Lord North, later earl of Guilford (Jan. 1770–March 1782); William Petty, earl of Shelburne (March 1782–April 1783); William Henry Bentinck, duke of Portland, with Charles James Fox and Lord North (April–Dec. 1783); William Pitt the Younger (Dec. 1783–1801).

Japan—Emperor Sakuramachi (1735–1747); Momozono (1747–1762); Go-Sakuramachi II (1762–1771); Go-Momozono II (1771–1779); Kokaku (1779–1817); Shoguns Ieshige (1745–1760) and Ieharu (1760–1786).

Ottoman Empire—Uthman III (1754–1757); Mustafa III (1757–1774); Abd al-Hamid I (1774–1789).

Portugal—King Joseph I (1750–1777); Queen Maria I (1777–1792).

Prussia—King Frederick II, the Great (1740–1786).

Russia—Czarina Elizabeth Petrovna (1741–1762); Czar Peter III (1762); Catherine II, the Great (1762–1796).

Spain—King Ferdinand VI (1746–1759); Charles III (1759–1788).

MAJOR CONFLICTS

1756–1763 — Seven Years War: England and Prussia versus Austria, France, Russia, Saxony, Spain, and Sweden

1763–1764—Pontiac's War: Coalition of Ohio River Valley Indian tribes versus Britain

1756–1764—East India Company wars against Bengal and Mughals

1757–1761—Afghani war against Marathas in India

1765–1768—Chinese war against Burma

1768–1774—Russian war against Turkey

1770–1772—Spanish and English war over the Falkland Islands

1775–1783—American Revolution

1775–1783—Spanish war against Algiers

1778–1783—French war against England in support of Americans

1778–1779—Prussian war against Austria

1779–1783—Spanish war against England in support of France

1779–1790—East India Company wars against Marathas in India

1780–1782—British-Dutch war in West Africa and Ceylon

1781—Oyo war against Dahomey in Africa

1754

- The Royal and Ancient Golf Club is founded at St. Andrew's, Scotland.

- France recalls its governor general from India, leaving the subcontinent to English control.

6 Mar. British prime minister Henry Pelham dies and is succeeded by Thomas Pelham Holles, duke of Newcastle.

1755

- Burmese king Aloung P'Houra, allied with the British East India Company against the French, founds the city of Rangoon.

- Samuel Johnson begins publishing *A Dictionary of the English Language.*

- Moscow University is founded, making it the first higher education institution in Russia.

13 Feb. A treaty arranged by the Dutch East India Company ends the Javanese war of succession, dividing Mataram into Surakarta and Jogyakarta.

7 June An earthquake in Persia kills forty thousand.

19 Sept. England and Russia form a convention at St. Petersburg; in exchange for an annual subsidy of £500,000, Russia agrees to use troops against Prussia in the event of war with England.

Sept.–Oct. Approximately eleven thousand Acadians are deported from Cape Breton Island by British authorities.

1 Nov. An earthquake in Lisbon, Portugal, followed by a tidal wave flooding the Tagus River, kills between ten thousand and sixty thousand people.

1756

- England and France declare war on one another.

- The Duc de Richelieu invents mayonnaise.

2 Jan. The Austrian composer Wolfgang Amadeus Mozart is born.

16 Jan. The Convention of Westminster between England and Frederick II of Prussia guarantees the neutrality of George II's German territories.

Apr. The nawab of Bengal, Ali Verdi Khan, dies, and is succeeded by Siraj al-Duala, who orders the British and French to stop fortifying their trading posts.

17 May French and Austrian representatives sign the Treaty of Versailles.

20–21 June Siraj al-Duala seizes Calcutta from the British. He forces 146 British prisoners into an eighteen-foot-by-ten-foot guard room; by morning all but twenty-three are dead. The "Black Hole of Calcutta" enrages the British public.

26 June French forces capture Minorca from the English.

29 Aug. Frederick II of Prussia invades Saxony, beginning a general war in Europe.

1 Oct. Frederick II defeats the Austrians at Lobositz in Saxony.

31 Dec. Russia accedes to the Treaty of Versailles and agrees to support France against England.

1757

•	James Lind prints second edition of *Treatise*, reporting that citrus fruit helps prevent scurvy.
Jan.	Ahmad Shah of Afghanistan sacks Delhi.
Jan.–Feb.	Robert Clive and a British naval force recapture Calcutta and seize Hoogly and Chandernagore.
9 Feb.	Clive and Siraj al-Duala sign a peace treaty.
14 Mar.	A British firing squad executes Adm. John Byng, whose failure to relieve the garrison of Minorca had allowed the French to capture the island in 1756.
Apr.	Frederick II invades Bohemia.
1 May	France and Austria sign the Treaty of Versailles, agreeing to a partition of Prussia.
6 May	Frederick II captures Prague.
18 June	Frederick II is defeated at Kolin and forced to evacuate Bohemia.
23 June	At the Battle of Plassey in India, Robert Clive defeats a Bengali force under Siraj al-Duala. Afterward Clive proclaims his ally Mir Jafar the new Nawab of Bengal.
26 July	The French defeat the British at the Battle of Hastenbeck in Saxony.
30 July	Russian forces defeat the Prussians at the Battle of Gross-Jägerndorf in East Prussia.
8 Sept.	In the Convention of Kloster-Zeven, a British army under the Duke of Cumberland capitulates to the French who then occupy Hanover; the treaty is later rejected by the British Parliament.
5 Nov.	Prussian forces defeat the French and Austrians at Rossbach, Saxony.
5 Dec.	Prussians defeat the Austrians in the Battle of Leuthen in southwestern Poland.

1758

•	Robert Clive becomes governor of Bengal.
•	Swedish scientist Emmanuel Swedenborg publishes a religious treatise, *The New Jerusalem*.
15 May	The Jesuits are ordered to cease preaching in Portuguese dominions.
25 Aug.	The Prussians defeat an invading Russian army at the Battle of Zorndorf in western Poland.
3 Sept.	An unsuccessful attempt to assassinate King Joseph I of Portugal leads to the arrest and execution of influential Portuguese aristocrats.
14 Oct.	Austrian forces defeat the Prussians at the Battle of Hochkirch in Saxony.

1759

•	The German composer Georg Friedrich Handel dies.

- Franz Joseph Haydn composes Symphony No. 1 in D major.

- The Jesuits are expelled from Portugal and Brazil.

- Arthur Guinness establishes a brewery in Dublin.

10 Aug. Ferdinand VI of Spain dies and Charles III becomes king.

1760

- Joseph Merlin, a Belgian musical instrument maker, plays a violin while demonstrating the first pair of roller skates.

- Laurence Sterne publishes *Sermons of Mr. Yorick* and *Life and Opinions of Tristram Shandy.*

23 June The Austrians defeat a Prussian army at Landshut, Bavaria.

15 Aug. The Prussians defeat the Austrians at Liegnitz, Poland.

9–12 Oct. A Russian army loots and burns Berlin.

25 Oct. George II of Great Britain dies; his grandson, George III, becomes king.

1761

- Spain invades Portugal.

- London doctor John Hill publishes "Cautions against the Immoderate Uses of Snuff," which for the first time links tobacco and cancer.

14 Jan. An Afghan army led by Amad Shah Abdali defeats the Marathas at Panipat. Afterward the Afghanis withdraw, leaving India in the control of the British East India Company.

May Franz Joseph Haydn signs a contract to be vice capellmeister to Hungarian prince Miklos Joszef Esterhazy.

15 Aug. In the Treaty of San Ildefonso, France, Spain, and several Italian states form an alliance against England.

5 Oct. William Pitt resigns as British prime minister when Parliament refuses to declare war on Spain.

1762

- Jean-Jacques Rousseau publishes *Emile* and *The Social Contract.*

4 Jan. England declares war on Spain.

5 Jan. Czarina Elizabeth of Russia, daughter of Peter the Great, dies; she is succeeded by her son, Peter III.

Feb. The British capture the island of Martinique.

5 May Peter III of Russia concludes a peace treaty with Frederick II of Prussia.

9 July Russian czar Peter III is deposed by his wife, Catherine, who reigns as Catherine II, the Great.

17 July	Deposed czar Peter III is murdered.	
13 Aug.	The British capture Havana, Cuba.	
Oct.	The British capture Manila in the Philippines.	

1763

- Cao Xueqin, author of the novel *Dream of the Red Chamber,* dies.
- Prussia establishes compulsory primary education.

10 Feb.	The Peace of Paris ends the Seven Years' War. France loses Canada, Senegal, and the West Indian islands to England and also cedes Louisiana to Spain.
23 Apr.	*North Briton* publishes issue no. 45, containing John Wilkes's criticism of King George III's speech.

1764

- At age eight, Mozart writes his first symphony.
- Haydn composes Symphony No. 22 in E-flat *(The Philosopher).*
- Parliament passes the Sugar Act to raise revenue and control smuggling in the empire.
- James Watt invents the condenser and air pump, improvements to the steam engine.
- French officer Louis Antoine de Bougainville lands a party of Acadian refugees on the Falkland Islands.

19 Jan.	John Wilkes is accused of libel and expelled from Parliament.

1765

- James Hargreaves invents the spinning jenny.

Jan.	British commodore John Byron claims the Falkland Islands for England.
23 Mar.	Parliament passes the Stamp Act to raise revenue from printed material in the colonies.
May	Robert Clive returns to India as governor of Bengal.

1766

- Rousseau publishes *Confessions.*

Jan.	The British fortify Port Egmont in the Falkland Islands.
11 Mar.	Parliament repeals the Stamp Act while simultaneously passing the Declaratory Act which maintains the power to tax British colonists.
12 Nov.	Nizam Ali of Hyderabad cedes territories to the East India Company.

1767

27 Feb.	Spain expels the Jesuits.
Mar.	Spanish and French forces arrive at the Falklands.
1 Apr.	France cedes its Falkland colony to Spain.
May	France expels the Jesuits.

1768

- Wolfgang Amadeus Mozart's first produced opera, *Bastien and Bastienne,* is performed in Vienna.

- Joshua Reynolds founds the Royal Academy of Art in London.

  James Bruce discovers the Blue Nile, a tributary of the Nile River.

- Russia invades Poland.

- Turkey declares war on Russia.

- Benjamin Franklin publishes maps showing the course of the Gulf Stream.

10 May	Several people are killed when British troops fire on a crowd of demonstrators at St. George's Fields, London, protesting imprisonment of political leader John Wilkes.
25 May	James Cook sails for the Pacific Ocean in the *Endeavor* to establish observatory at Tahiti.

1769

- British philanthropist Granville Sharpe publishes an antislavery tract, *A Representation of the Injustices and Dangerous Tendencies of Tolerating Slavery.*

- Mozart receives an honorary appointment as concertmaster to the archbishop of Salzburg.

- Famine in Bengal kills ten million people.

- David Garrick opens the first Shakespeare Festival at Stratford-on-Avon.

- James Watt patents the steam engine, which he had invented in 1765.

- Ali Bey, viceroy of Egypt, declares independence from the Ottoman Empire and makes a pact with Russia against Turkey.

- Spain occupies California, founding missions at Los Angeles and San Diego.

Jan.	The first "Letter of Junius" appears in the British press, attacking the government for silencing John Wilkes.
4 Feb.	Parliament expels John Wilkes, who is again reelected, but he is declared incapable of serving.
Nov.	The English warn the Spanish to evacuate the Falklands.
19 Dec.	Another "Letter of Junius" appears in three London papers arraigning King George III as the mastermind behind the attacks on John Wilkes; the British government charges the three newspaper publishers with sedition.

1770

- German composer Ludwig van Beethoven is born.
- Capt. James Cook maps the east coast of Australia.
- Ali Bey, governor of Egypt, captures Syria and Hijaz.
- Mozart's opera *Mitridate, rè di Ponto* is produced in Milan.

20 Feb. Spanish officials warn British colonists to leave the Falkland Islands.

10 June The Spanish attack Port Egmont in the Falkland Islands, forcing the British to evacuate.

13 June In a case arising from "Letters of Junius," a British jury finds a publisher "guilty of printing and publishing only," not of sedition.

5–6 July The Russians defeat a Turkish fleet in the Battle of Tchesmé.

1771

- *Encyclopedia Brittanica* is published for the first time.
- The Russians occupy the Crimea.
- Haydn writes his Sun quartets (nos. 25–30).

Jan. The British contemplate an assault on New Orleans and Spanish territories in North America in retaliation for the attack on the Falklands.

20 Jan. King Louis XV dismisses the Parliament of Paris.

July Turkey and Austria form an alliance against Russia.

1772

- In the *Somerset* case in England, Lord Chief Justice William Murray, earl of Manfield, rules that a slave who arrives in England is free.
- The final volume of Denis Diderot's *Encyclopedie* is published in Paris.

Jan. Spain returns the Falkland Islands to Britain.

Apr. Abu al-Dhahab supplants Ali Bey in Egypt and becomes viceroy the next year.

5 Aug. Austria, Prussia, and Russia partition Poland.

19 Aug. Gustavus III of Sweden abolishes the parliament and council, and institutes a series of reforms to encourage trade.

1773

2 Mar. The East India Company applies to Parliament for a loan of £1,500,000.

19 Apr. The Polish Diet is forced to accept the partition of the country.

10 May Parliament passes the Tea Act, giving the East India Company a monopoly on tea sold in the British colonies. The Company plans to ship six hundred thousand pounds of tea to American ports.

21 July The Pope suppresses the Society of Jesus, and Josef II expels the Jesuits from Austria.

1774

- Morocco liberates its Christian slaves.

- Hungary grants religious toleration to non-Catholics.

- John Wesley publishes *Thoughts on Slavery.*

- Joseph Priestley discovers oxygen.

10 May Louis XV of France dies and is succeeded by his grandson, Louis XVI.

21 July Russia and Turkey agree to a treaty, giving Russians the right to navigate the Black Sea and pass through the Dardenalles, and the freedom to make pilgrimages to Jerusalem.

2 Nov. Robert Clive, in poor health since his return to England in 1767 and facing parliamentary inquiries into his governorship of India, commits suicide.

12 Nov. Louis XVI restores the Parliament of Paris.

1775

- The Society of White Lotus organizes a rebellion in the Honan Province of China, beginning a twenty-seven-year uprising.

- The first Thames Regatta is held.

1776

- Adam Smith publishes the *Wealth of Nations.*

- Edward Gibbon publishes the first volume of *Decline and Fall of the Roman Empire.*

- John Wilkes proposes reforms in the British electoral system to make Parliament more representative of the people.

- The Dutch in South Africa make the first European contact with the Xhosa tribe on the Zeekee River.

1777

- Antoine-Laurent Lavoisier proves that air consists mainly of oxygen and nitrogen.

1 May The premiere of Richard Brinsley Sheridan's "School for Scandal" occurs in London.

1778

- The Dutch and Xhosa agree to a boundary on the Fish River in South Africa.

Jan. Capt. James Cook lands on the island of Kauai; he names the present-day Hawaiian Island chain after John Montagu, fourth earl of Sandwich.

6 Feb. France becomes the first European power to recognize the independence of the United States, and signs a commercial and military treaty with the new nation.

	11 May	William Pitt, earl of Chatham, dies.
	17 June	France declares war on England.
	18 June	Wolfgang Amadeus Mozart's Symphony 31, *(Paris Symphony),* premieres in Paris.

1779

	•	The first iron bridge is built in England.
	•	David Hume's *Dialogues Concerning Natural Religion* is published posthumously.
	14 Feb.	Capt. James Cook is killed by Hawaiians at Kealakekua Bay.
	16 June	Spain forms an alliance with France and declares war on England.

1780

	•	The *Bengal Gazette,* the first newspaper in India, is published by the British.
	•	The screwdriver and fountain pen are invented.
	•	Franz Joseph Haydn writes the *Toy Symphony.*
	10 Mar.	Catherine the Great proclaims Russia's armed neutrality, prohibiting the British from searching neutral ships.
	2–8 June	The Gordon Riots occur in London in protest of the Catholic Relief Act.
	Nov.	Descendants of the Incas rebel against Spanish rule and gain control of southern Peru, Bolivia, and Argentina.
	20 Nov.	Great Britain declares war on the Netherlands.

1781

	•	Immanuel Kant publishes *Critique of Pure Reason* and *Critique of Practical Reason.*
	•	Richard Arkwright opens a water-powered cotton factory.
	•	Austria liberates its serfs.
	31 Mar.	Sir William Herschel discovers the planet Uranus.

1782

	•	Spain suppresses the rebellion in Peru.
	•	Mozart's opera *Die Entführung aus dem Serail* (The Abduction from the Seraglio) opens in Vienna.
	4 Mar.	Despite the king's and prime minister's desire to continue the war in America, the British House of Commons rejects further military attempts against the former colonies.

9 Mar.	Parliament dismisses Prime Minister Lord North after a twelve-year administration.
Oct.	The British relieve the besieged fortress at Gibraltar.
30 Nov.	British and American negotiators accept a preliminary peace agreement.

1783

•	The French launch the first steam-powered vessel.
•	Mozart writes Mass in C minor.
6 Feb.	Spain ends its siege of Gibraltar.
13 Sept.	The peace treaty of Versailles goes into effect, recognizing the independence of the United States.
21 Nov.	Joseph-Michel and Jacques-Etienne Montgolfier make the first manned ascent in a hot-air balloon over Paris.

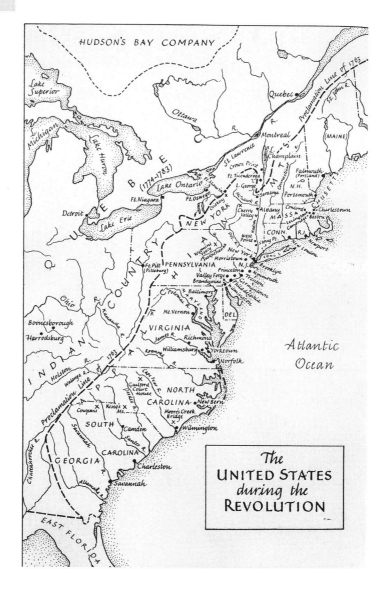

The UNITED STATES during the REVOLUTION

THE ARTS

by THOMAS E. AUGST

CONTENTS

Sidebars and tables are listed in italics.

1754

Literature   Jonathan Edwards, *Freedom of the Will;* Samuel Bownas, *God's Mercy Surmounting God's Cruelty, Exemplified in the Captivity and Redemption of Elizabeth Hanson;* Benjamin Franklin, *Poor Richard Improved: Being an Almanack and Ephemeris;* John Woolman, *Some Considerations on the Keeping of Negroes.*

- The poet Joel Barlow is born in Connecticut.

1755

Music   Thomas Johnson, *Rules for Singing, with a collection of about fifty tunes, for psalms and hymns.*

1756

Literature   Duncan Cameron, *The Life, Adventures, and Surprising Deliverances, of Duncan Cameron, Private Soldier;* Jacob Duché, *Pennsylvania: A Poem;* William and Elizabeth Fleming, *A Narrative of the Sufferings and Surprising Deliverance of William and Elizabeth Fleming;* Stephen Tilden, *Tilden's Miscellaneous Poems, On Divers Occasions; Chiefly to animate and rouse the soldiers.*

1757

Literature   Martha Brewster, *Poems on Divers Subjects;* Benjamin Church, *The Choice: A poem, after the manner of Mr. Pomfret.*

Music   Isaac Watts, *The Psalms of David imitated in the language of the New Testament* (seventeenth edition); *Divine Songs, attempted in easy language, for the use of children.*

- *The American Magazine and Monthly Chronicle* begins publication.

1758

Literature   Benjamin Franklin, "The Way to Wealth"; Anne Bradstreet, *Several Poems Compiled with Great Variety of Wit and Learning, Full of Delight;* John Brown, *An Estimate of the manners and Principles of the Times;* David Fordyce, *The Temple of Virtue. A Dream;* Jonathan Swift, *The Journal of a Gaming Lady of Quality;* John Williams, *The Redeemed Captive, Returning to Zion.*

- *The American Magazine and Monthly Chronicle* stops publication.

- The lexicographer and author Noah Webster is born in Connecticut.

1759

Music   *Marburg Hymn Book* (the first Lutheran Hymn book printed in the colonies).

1760

Literature Jean Lowry, *A Journal of the Captivity of Jean Lowry and her children.*

Music *The American Mock-bird. A Collection of the most familiar Songs now in vogue;* James Otis, *The Principles of Latin Prosody.*

1761

Literature John Banks, *Cyrus the Great: A Tragedy;* Richard Barford, *The Virgin Queen: A Tragedy;* Susannah Centlivre, *The Basset-Table: A Comedy;* Samuel Davies, *An Ode on the Prospect of Peace;* Samuel Nevill, *The History of North America.*

Music Francis Hopkinson, *An Exercise, Containing a Dialogue and Ode Sacred to the memory of his late gracious Majesty, George II;* James Lyon, *Urania. Or a choice Collection of Psalm Tunes, Anthems, and Hymns, from the most approv'd authors.*

- The St. Cecilia Society, the oldest musical society in the United States, is founded in Charleston, South Carolina.

1762

Literature Thomas Godfrey, *The Court of Fancy;* James Forrester, *The Polite Philosopher;* Benjamin Franklin, *Advice to a Young Tradesman;* Solomon Gesner, *The Death of Abel;* Frances Hopkinson, *Science: A Poem;* William Livingston, *Philosophic Solitude.*

Music Robert Lloyd, *Arcadia: or the Shepard's Wedding;* Benjamin Wallin, *Evangelical hymns and Songs;* Jemmy Carson, *Jemmy Carson's Collection of Ballads.*

- The novelist Susanna Rowson is born in Portsmouth, England.

1763

Literature *The New England Primer Enlarged.*

Music Frances Hopkinson, *A Collection of Psalm Tunes, with a few anthems and Hymns;* James Lyons, *The Lawfulness, Excellency, and Advantage of Instrumental Musick.*

- James Bremer opens a music school in Philadelphia; his pupils include Francis Hopkinson, the future political leader and writer.

20 June Benjamin West arrives in London.

3 Aug. The poet and playwright Thomas Godfrey dies.

1764

Literature Thomas Hutchinson, *History of the Colony of Massachusetts Bay;* James Otis, *Rights of British Colonies.*

Music Josiah Flagg, *A Collection of the Best Psalm Tunes* (engraved by Paul Revere); *The American Cock Robin: Or, A choice collection of English Songs . . . agreeable to the North-American Taste;* Daniel Bayley, *A New and Complete Introduction to the Grounds and Rules of Music.*

- Johann Snetzler sends an organ to Trinity Church in New York City.

1765

Literature	*Oppression: A Poem;* Samuel Adams, *Resolutions;* Thomas Godfrey, *Prince of Parthia* and *Juvenile Poems on Various Subjects.*
Music	*The Whiteoak Anthem,* taken from John Bunyan's *Pilgrim's Progress.*
•	Charles Willson Peale arrives in Boston.
•	John Singleton Copley submits his *Boy with Squirrel* for exhibition in London.
•	David Douglass arrives in Charleston with his theatrical company.

1766

Literature	Robert Rogers, *Ponteach.*
Music	Martin Madan, *A Collection of Hymns, for Social Worship.*
•	The first "Concert of Musick" is performed in Savannah, Georgia.
•	David Douglass opens the new Southwark Theater in Philadelphia.
•	William Dunlap, the painter, playwright, and historian, is born in Perth Amboy, New Jersey.

1767

Literature	Elizabeth Rowe, *The History of Joseph: A Poem, in Ten Books.*
Music	*The Masque, A New Song Book;* Andrew Barton, *The Disappointment, or the Force of Credulity* (the first American comic ballad libretto); William Tansur, *The Royal Melody Complete* (first American edition).
•	Benjamin West exhibits *Agrippina Landing at Brundisium with the Ashes of Germanicus.*
Jan.	Samuel Greville, the first professional American actor, makes his debut in Nicholas Rowe's play *Tamerlane* (1702).
•	David Douglass produces *The Prince of Parthia* in Philadelphia, the first American drama to be professionally produced on the American stage.

1768

Literature	John Dickinson, *Letters from a Farmer in Pennsylvania;* "Rusticus," *Liberty. A Poem.*
Music	George Whitefield, *A Collection of Hymns, for social worship.*
July	The Virginia Gazette prints John Dickinson's "Liberty Song."

1769

Literature	Thomas Hopkinson, *Liberty, A Poem;* Alexander Martin, *America, A Poem.*
Music	John Mason, *Spiritual Songs.*

1769

- The first known American sculptor, Mrs. Patricia Lovell Wright of New Jersey, leaves America for London.

- The first issue of *The American Magazine* (Philadelphia) appears.

Mar.   British troops riot at James Joan's concert in Boston.

June   Charles Willson Peale returns from England to Maryland.

Sept.   The *Boston Gazette* advertises "a very curious spinnet, being the first ever made in America," by John Harris.

1770

Literature   William Livingston, *America: Or, a Poem on the Settlement of the British Colonies;* John Trumbull, *An Essay on the Use and Advantages of the Fine Arts.*

Music   William Billings, *The New England Psalm Singer.*

The *Massachusetts Spy* begins publication.

16 Jan.   William Tuckey gives an overture and sixteen pieces from Handel's *Messiah* (1742), in New York.

26 Mar.   Boston newspapers advertise Paul Revere's engraving of the Boston Massacre.

10 July   A pipe organ is played for the first time in an American Congregational church in Providence.

1771

Literature   Mary Somerville, *A Tale.*

Music   Miss Ashmore, *The New Song Book Being Miss Ashmore's Favorite Collection of Songs, As Sung in the Theatres and Public Gardens in London.*

- Benjamin Franklin begins writing his *Autobiography.*

- The novelist Charles Brockden Brown is born in Philadelphia.

- Benjamin West's *Death of General Wolfe* is exhibited to critical acclaim at the Society of Artists in London.

1772

Literature   Philip Freneau, *The American Village, A Poem;* Freneau and Henry Brackenridge, *The Rising Glory of America;* Jonathan Trumbull, *Progress of Dulness;* Richard Cumberland, *The Fashionable Lover. A Comedy;* Samson Occom, *A Sermon, Preached at the Execution of Moses Paul, An Indian.*

Music   Lemuel Hedge, *The Duty and Manner of Singing in Christian Churches Considered and Illustrated;* John Willison, *Scripture Songs for Zion's Travellers.*

1773

Literature   Mercy Otis Warren, *The Adulateur;* Hannah More, *Search After Happiness: A Pastoral Drama;* Phillis Wheatley, *Poems on Various Subjects, Religious and Moral.*

•   James Rivington's *New York Gazetteer* begins publication.

1774

Literature   *The Child of Nature, a Philosophical Novel;* Alexander Dow, *Sethona, A Tragedy;* Robert Hitchcock, *The Macaroni, A Comedy;* Hugh Kelly, *The School for Wives;* Frances Lopkinson, *A Pretty Story;* Jacob Duché, *Caspipina's Letters;* John Trumbull, *An Elegy on the Times;* Robert Wells, *The Story of Aeneas and Dido Burlesqued.*

Music   Samson Occom, *A Choice Collection of Hymns and Spiritual Songs;* John Stickney, *The Gentleman and Ladies Musical Companion.*

10 June   John Singleton Copley sails for Europe.

1775

Literature   John Burgoyne, *The Blockade;* Philip Freneau, *American Liberty, A Poem;* Mercy Otis Warren, *The Group;* Jonathan Sewell, *Cure for the Spleen.*

Music   Samuel Mills, *The Nature and Importance of Singing Praise to God.*

•   John Behrent makes the first piano in America.

•   The first architecture book published in America is Abraham Swann's *A Collection of Designs in Architecture.*

•   *Yankee Doodle, or (as now Christened by the Saints of New England) The Lexington March* is published in London.

1776

Literature   Hugh Henry Brackenridge, *Battle of Bunkers-Hill;* Philip Freneau, "The Beauties of Santa Cruz"; John Leacock, *The Fall of British Tyranny;* Thomas Paine, *Common Sense;* Jonathan Trumbull, *M'Fingal: A Modern Epic Poem;* Elisha Rich, *A Poem on the Late Distress of the Town of Boston;* Mercy Otis Warren, *The Blockheads: Or, the Affrighted Officers. A Farce.*

Music   *A Complet Tutor for the Fife.*

8 Jan.   A British performance of *The Blockade of Boston* is interrupted by news of an American raid on Charlestown, Massahusetts.

Feb.   *The Farmer and his Son's Return from a visit to the CAMP,* the classic text of the song "Yankee Doodle," is published.

May   The Continental Congress commissions Charles Willson Peale to paint a portrait of George Washington.

1777

Literature Hugh Henry Brackenridge, *The Death of General Montgomery;* John Burgoyne, *The Maid of the Oaks: A New Dramatic Entertainment;* Robert Dodsley, *The Blind Beggar of Bethal Green;* Jane Marshall, *Sir Harry Gaylove, or Comedy in Embryo;* Hugh Kelly, *The Romance of an Hour; a New Comedy.*

Music George Stevens, *Songs, Comic, Satyrical, and Sentimental.*

• A British military theater opens in occupied New York and operates until 1783.

Oct. Fifers and drummers of Gen. John Burgoyne's army play "Yankee Doodle" during surrender ceremonies at Saratoga, New York.

1778

Literature Francis Hopkinson, "The Battle of the Kegs"; Joel Barlow, *The Prospect of Peace;* Wheeler Case, *Poems, Occasioned by Several Circumstances and Occurences in the Present Grand Struggle of America for Liberty.*

Music William Billings, *The Singing Master's Assistant.*

Jan. British officers begin their first play at the Southwark Theater in occupied Philadelphia.

May American troops at Valley Forge stage Joseph Addison's *Cato* (1713).

1779

Literature Jupiter Hammon, *An Essay on the Ten Virgins;* Mercy Otis Warren, *The Motley Assembly, A Farce;* Philip Freneau, "The House of Night."

Music William Billings, *Music in Miniature, Containing a Collection of Psalm Tunes; A Collection of the Most Approved Tunes and Anthems, for the Promotion of Psalmody; Loyal and Humorous Songs, on Recent Occasions;* "The Liberty Song."

• The lawyer and poet Francis Scott Key is born in Maryland.

• The Supreme Council of Pennsylvania commissions Charles Willson Peale to paint a portrait of George Washington.

Jan. The first issue appears of the *United States Magazine,* edited by Philip Freneau and Hugh Henry Brackenridge.

1780

Literature Ethan Allen, *A Narrative of Colonel Ethan Allen's Captivity;* Timothy Dwight, *America;* David Humphreys, *A Poem, Addressed to the Armies of the United States of America.*

1781

Literature Philip Freneau, *The British Prison Ship;* William Hayley, *The Triumphs of Temper; A Poem (with Plates);* Abbe Raynal, *The Revolution in America.*

Music William Billings, *The Psalm-Singer's Amusement.*

11 Dec. Francis Hopkinson's, *The Temple of Minerva,* the first grand opera staged in America, is performed in Philadelphia.

1782

Literature   J. Hector St. John de Crèvecoeur, *Letters from an American Farmer;* Jupiter Hammon, *A Winter Piece: Being a Serious Exhortation;* Thomas Mercer, *The Sentimental Sailor;* Samuel Pratt, *Emma Corbett: Exhibiting Henry and Emma, the Faithful Modern Lovers.*

Music   James Hart, *Hymns, composed on various subjects;* Simeon Jocelin, *The Chorister's Companion; Or, Church Music Revised;* Andrew Law, *A Collection of Hymns for Social Worship;* James and John Relly, *Christian Hymns, Poems, and Spiritual Songs.*

- The Aitken Bible becomes the first complete English Bible to be printed in America.

1783

Literature   Jupiter Hammon, *An Evening's Improvement.*

Music   Oliver Brownson, *Select Harmony: Containing the Necessary Rules of Psalmody;* Andrew Law, *The Rudiments of Music.*

- The *Boston Magazine* begins publication.

- The author Washington Irving is born in New York City.

- Noah Webster publishes his *American Spelling Book.*

A desk made by a Pennsylvania craftsman (Smithsonian Institution, Washington, D.C.)

OVERVIEW

Provincial versus Cosmopolitan. Before the Revolutionary era, men and women living in the British Colonies did not think of themselves as "Americans" but rather as British citizens and colonists. They imagined that they were ambassadors of culture, bringing European civilization to the wilderness of the new world. In *Verses on the Prospect of Planting Arts and Learning in America* (1725), first printed in America in 1752 and reprinted dozens of times in the third-quarter of the eighteenth-century, the English bishop George Berkeley described an ideal of *translatio,* the transmission of the highest expressions of human development—arts, letters, music, and all those forms of culture—which testified to the moral superiority of Anglo-European character and society to all other peoples. History showed that the great achievements of ancient Greece and Rome had eventually given way to barbarism and ignorance, but perhaps in these colonies to the West this cycle of empire and decline might be broken. America, Bishop Berkeley wrote, was like a rising sun, a growing plant, the final act in the epic history of mankind, the place where the progress of human reason and culture might find their highest realization and their lasting home.

Pursuit of Culture. Even in a society where living conditions were "rude" compared to London's refinements, colonists aspired to a cosmopolitan cultural standard. Americans imitated the fashions and manners of the civilized world that lay across the Atlantic. Wealthy Virginia planters attended balls, where humble young men might use their skills in dancing to win prestige and perhaps marry into the gentry. Maryland gentlemen gathered together for the conversation and pleasure of society in the Tuesday Club of Dr. Alexander Hamilton. Even middling folk hung prints by British artists such as William Hogarth, or read gossip about British actors in their local newspapers. The mass circulation of printed sheet music, lithographs, and books of all sorts put many forms of culture in reach of colonial Americans, helping them to identify themselves as members of the British world, while also reminding them of the provincial quality of life in colonial cities and towns.

Cosmopolitan Standards. The Enlightenment concept of culture that Bishop Berkeley and so many others celebrated in the eighteenth century assumed a difference between cosmopolitan and provincial ways that was both fixed in time and place, but which could also move. Patriot propaganda before the Revolution attacked the cultural refinements of England being imported into the colonies as decadent and corrupt luxuries that proved the mother country's civilization was already in decline. At the same time they pointed to provincial simplicity of colonial ways as evidence that the new United States might allow the rebirth of the civilization and civic virtues of the ancient republics. The arts of the Revolutionary era are particularly interesting because they express the inherent tensions of this enlightenment conception of culture *in translatio* from the old, cosmopolitan world to the new, provincial world. Especially during the Revolution, the question of how to define this distinction, and what social and political meanings to invest in them, became of crucial importance. Were the British innately superior to colonial Americans? Or were the artistic forms of civilization things that could be imitated, in the same way that one learned to wear a new suit of clothes or that genteel character could be practiced through the repetition of refined speech, movement, and other acquired habits of elegance?

The Politics of Culture. The distinction between politics and culture did not exist for colonial Americans. Eighteenth-century politics gave ample opportunity to indulge in satire, hyperbole, and sensationalism. The thoughts of radical Whig thinkers such as John Trenchard and Thomas Gordon, for example, profoundly influenced the literature as well as the politics of the Revolutionary era. Well before the Revolution the anonymous use of newspapers and pamphlets for the spirited expression of dissent were an accepted and pervasive feature of civic life. Attacking opponents in the mass media of the day, writers questioned the public fitness of leaders by pointing to the corruption of their private character or predicting dire consequences from their actions. Because politics was the preserve of educated gentlemen, this public debate tended to be governed by the stylistic conventions that displayed one's wit and erudition. Benjamin Franklin, for example, taught himself how to write by copying the artful rhetoric of Gordon and Trenchard's *Cato's Letters* (1723). Politics was a literary game governed by formal conventions of politeness and civility:

the acceptance of one's political views depended on one's mastery of a certain style of writing and argument that expressed the character of cultivated gentlemen in print. One's right to speak as a citizen was justified by demonstrating an ability to play this game by its literary rules; with few exceptions the literature, no less than the politics, of the Revolutionary era was a club that excluded those women, working-class men, and non-Englishmen who were denied the privilege of advanced learning and the social authority that came with it.

Enlightenment. The most educated Americans of the Revolutionary era were part of a transatlantic culture that debated questions of politics, philosophy, and science throughout the eighteenth century, and that was committed to a set of values derived from the Enlightenment: the importance of secular learning; faith in man's capacity to know and define the laws of nature, society, and history; and the power of reason to control the human passions and perfect the institutions of public life. The leaders who declared American independence and drafted a new government developed theories of natural right, the social contract, and civic virtue, which they learned as members of this international network of ideas and intellectuals. At the same time, however, the particular circumstances of political protest before and during the Revolution encouraged the emergence of different styles of thinking and writing, in which reside the beginnings of a new American literature. Political tracts by John Dickinson and Thomas Paine, as well as the poetry of Philip Freneau, explored themes and issues faced by the colonies and promoted an awareness of American identity. American writers imitated, but also transformed, the cultural forms they had inherited from Britain. Americans learned to imagine their political independence not only through Whig-Republican ideology and the values of the European enlightenment but also through homegrown styles of political activism and evangelical religion.

War and Propaganda. During the crises created by the Stamp and Townsend acts, many colonists boycotted British imports. It was common during these crises to denounce all consumer goods from abroad—whether musical instruments, clothing, or tea—not only as symptoms of European cultural corruption but also as tools of political tyranny: by leading patriots into debt and dissipation, the habits of "luxury" would undermine the moral discipline, manly strength, and Spartan simplicity of Americans. Independence was not only a political goal but a cultural ideal. To exercise disinterested civic virtue depended on being free from external obligations, which would be impossible if Americans slavishly imitated British refinement. While boycotts typically are economic and political means to mobilize a population against external threats or to conserve scarce resources in times of war, they also have a symbolic function. Theater in the colonies, for example, was both a vehicle for propaganda and a symbol of the political conflict with

Britain. Theater was banned in Massachusetts and Rhode Island in the 1750s and 1760s and outlawed by the Continental Congress in 1774 because it was viewed as a cultural import that threatened to undermine colonial character with European refinements. At the same time, both Patriots such as Royall Tyler and Mercy Otis Warren and Loyalists such as Jonathan Sewall and General John Burgoyne used satirical drama to promote or attack the patriot cause.

Rising Glory of America. Before and during the Revolution, literature and arts became forms of propaganda, used to incite hostility towards the Empire and to generate a new sense of cultural identity amongst people who had considered themselves British subjects. The nonimportation agreements encouraged the growth of cultural institutions in the colonies: printers, instrument makers, and activity in all the arts were stimulated by the boycotts. Of more importance, however, was the emergence of a new, self-conscious awareness of cultural difference, of the "Rising Glory of America," as Philip Freneau and Henry Brackenridge titled their 1772 poem. It was impossible for the colonists to go to war with Britain without inventing a morally charged sense of national purpose that defined the stakes of indepedence in the most ideological and dramatic terms. The self-sufficient Yeoman farmer became less a mark of American backwardness than a symbol of virtuous freedom. Even when anonymous poets published their attacks on British policies in colonial newspapers in the 1760s, or when Freneau, Brackenridge, and Jonathan Trumbull developed the first significant body of poetry about American culture in the 1770s and 1780s, they continued to rely on the allegorical and neoclassical forms of British literature of the era.

Myths of American Virtue. Before and during the Revolution, artists and writers began to think about what it might mean to be American rather than British. During this period two distinctive myths emerged that would become major touchstones for how future Americans would understand their values and define their culture as truly independent from the old world of Europe. In his *Autobiography* (1868), which he began writing in 1770, Benjamin Franklin turned his own life into a humorous and inspiring story of the "self-made man." A boy born into a large and modest household without the privilege of formal education leaves Boston in order to make a name and a life for himself in Philadelphia. Through his own hard work, his will to "improve" himself, and his careful management of the impressions he makes on people a provincial working-class youth finds success, happiness, and fame in his own land and the capitals of Europe. In writing about his own life Franklin was offering advice on how one ought to live, making himself into an example that other Americans might follow. Published in hundreds of editions over the last two hundred years, Franklin's *Autobiography* has been one of the most popular and enduring sources for the ideals of American culture in which individual character counts for more than heredity.

People of Nature. Living in a society that was overwhelmingly rural, Franklin's contemporaries in the Revolutionary era embraced another myth, of American's special relationship to nature, which also celebrated the opportunities and virtues that this new world made possible for ordinary individuals. J. Hector St. John de Crèvecoeur, a French immigrant who settled in New York, portrayed rural life in the colonies as a place where oppressed peoples of Europe could pursue their own self-interests, free from the tryanny of European monarchy, the Catholic church, and feudal society. Told from the point of view of a farmer and informed by European philosophy about the "noble savage," *Letters from an American Farmer* (1793) is the first America text to explore the question, "What is an American?" Like Franklin, de Crèvecoeur idealized American character in terms of simplicity, sobriety, and frugality, but he linked these values not with the individual powers of self-invention in the city, but with the discovery of an innate, universal goodness through life on the soil. Like Philip Freneau's poems such as "The Wild Honey Suckle" or James Fennimore Cooper's nineteenth-century novels about the wilderness, *Letters* offers a romantic vision of European culture being redeemed and purified through the absence of refinement in America. In this new Eden, through the struggle of families to cultivate their land and become self-sufficient, away from the corruptions and distractions of civilization, Americans would discover the true meaning of independence and realize the universal human rights to property, liberty, and happiness.

TOPICS IN THE NEWS

ARCHITECTURE

Amateurs and Imitators. Architecture in colonial America was the work of amateurs. Most buildings were built to serve practical functions rather than aesthetic ideals. The cost of building materials made it difficult to execute elaborate designs and purely decorative ornaments. In the third quarter of the eighteenth-century, more public buildings, usually churches, were built and their builders showed more interest in aesthetics. Because such projects were so infrequent, it is difficult to identify any architect who achieved a career in the colonies without devoting most of his time to other forms of work. Given the scarcity of architectural projects, it should not be surprising that colonial architecture tends to be noteworthy less for originality than for novelty. Most colonial buildings imitated particular buildings in London. St. Paul's Chapel in New York City, for example, imitated the interior of London's St. Martin in the Fields.

Domestic Architecture. The most important change in colonial architecture was in domestic styles. As Northern merchants, Southern planters, and imperial administrators grew wealthy, they sought to display their genteel status through the consumption of imported goods and the display of cosmopolitan tastes in clothing, furniture, books, and especially their houses. If architecture in the colonies did not have the status of a professional art, it nevertheless reveals the pervasive influence of cosmopolitan tastes in the New World. British influence in colonial culture came from recent immigrants, from travel to Europe, or more commonly through books and prints imported from England. Books were particularly important for bringing British tastes, especially in homebuilding and interior decoration, to the colonies. By the end of 1750, there were eighteen different architecture books circulating in the colonies, but by 1760 there were fifty-one. These books account for not only the sometimes remarkable sophistication of particular elements of colonial mansions, but also the eclectic confusion of their overall design. George Mason's Gunston Hall (1755-1759), for example, drew on five different books for its details of woodworking, plaster, and doorframes. Designer William Buckland used two books that had not even been published when he started building. The end result was a purely classical drawing room, Gothic Rococo arches in another room, and the first expression in American architecture of Chinese taste in the dining room. Like other impressive houses built in the late colonial era, Gunston Hall was built to showcase the latest tastes in architecture.

Harrison and Palladio. Peter Harrison, the first architect in the colonies who had more than one building to his credit, spent the majority of his life working as a customs official in New Haven. He designed the first

Monticello, circa 1825, watercolor by Jefferson Vail (Musée de Blérancourt, Pairs)

public synagogue (1759–1763) in Newport, Rhode Island, as well as Christ Church in Cambridge, Massachusetts (1760–1761). In these buildings and others, Harrison introduced elements of classical design that came to be known as Anglo-Palladianism. When he died in 1775, Harrison had a library of twenty-seven architecture books, the largest collection in the colonies. Andrea Palladio, an Italian architect during the Renaissance, had led the revival of Roman architecture, writing an influential book based on his intensive studies of the ancient ruins. Building Venetian palazzos and villas in the surrounding countryside, Palladio followed the classical example closely, using stately symmetrical logic and rectangular serenity. He used creative grouping and combination of columns and arches to achieve unity in his designs, which became a trademark of the Palladian influence so evident in the neoclassical architecture in Britain and America in the eighteenth century. The flowering of classical archaeology in Greece in the 1750s and 1760s provided new inspiration to architects on both sides of the Atlantic.

Monticello. Thomas Jefferson was the most talented and accomplished architect in Revolutionary America. For his home at Monticello he managed to draw myriad classical elements together in an overall innovative design. Begun in 1771 and built over the course of Jefferson's life, Monticello used a hilltop site typical of Roman country homes, but it reversed the usual Palladian scheme, in which service wings flanked a central en-

trance court. By extending and lowering these wings to the back of the main building, Jefferson used the slopes of the site to transform the flat roofs of the wings into terrace walks. The interior paraded a series of Roman-inspired details, with each room including a frieze from an ancient temple and educated the visitor in the variations of classical orders. "The Hall is in the Ionic, the Dining Room in the Doric, the Parlor is in the Corinthian, and the Dome in the Attic," Jefferson wrote. "In the other rooms are introduced several different forms of these orders, all in the truest proportions according to Palladio." Jefferson tinkered with and added to the building over forty years, and in this way it was much like the government he had helped design for the new nation—an ongoing experiment that self-consciously drew on the true, rational proportions of the ancient Republics but which in its eclectic and ahistorical combination of elements and values defied precedent. Monticello was a beautiful and awkward structure that was much more than the sum of its parts, a testament to the ongong idealism by which Jefferson and others of the founding generation sought to give form to timeless laws of nature, to adapt their prodigious learning and study to the practical problems of living.

Sources:

Robert Hughes, *American Visions: The Epic History of Art in America* (New York: Knopf, 1997);

G. E. Kidder-Smith, *Source Book of American Architecture: 500 Notable Buildings from the 10th Century to the Present* (New York: Princeton Architectural Press, 1996);

PATIENCE WRIGHT, SCULPTOR AND SPY

The first known American sculptor was a woman, Patience Lovell Wright. Wright molded busts and figures in wax, specializing in the sort of realistic wax tableaux that were made famous by Madame Tussaud in the nineteenth century. Wright turned to sculpture after she was left a widow with five children in 1769. Wright's life-size portraits of hands and faces were so detailed and accurate that when they were attached to clothed figures, she seemed to have captured people in suspended animation. After touring the colonies Wright moved to London, where she became known not only for her artistic skill but also for her charismatic personality, and in polite society she became notorious for her slightly wild manner of speaking and looking upon her subjects. A major personality during the Revolutionary War, Wright was also a spy who passed on any information that she gleaned from her influential and wealthy circle of patrons. She often hid messages in wax heads of Lord North and various British celebrities that she sent to her sister Rachel in Philadelphia, who would then pass them on to Washington.

Source: Wayne Craven, *Sculpture in America* (New York: Crowell, 1968).

Fiske Kimball, *Domestic Architecture in Colonial America and the Early Republic* (New York: Scribners, 1922);

Marcus Whiffen and Frederick Koeper, *American Architecture 1607-1976* (Cambridge, Mass.: MIT Press, 1981).

ART I: PROFESSIONALS FROM THE PROVINCES

West and Copley. Only in painting did Americans prove that they could compete with the finest artists of Europe, achieving an international reputation and financial success equal to that of any of their peers working in Britain, Italy, or France. The success of Benjamin West and John Singleton Copley, while noteworthy in itself for their innovations in artistic style, genre, and themes, reveals a great deal about the cosmopolitan ideal against which American arts and letters proved, to colonists and foreigners alike, so inferior and provincial. To begin with, they were among the few artists born in the colonies who can accurately be called professionals, supporting themselves (quite handsomely) from the sale of their art alone. In defying the expectation that American artists had little to contribute to the international development of arts and letters, however, their careers ironically reinforced the idea that America should measure its achievements by European standards of artistic taste. While both Copley and West began in the colonies, they only realized the height of their critical and commercial success by going to Europe at crucial points in their development and spending the remainder of their lives there. As the British painter Sir Joshua Reynolds advised Copley, "the example and instruction which you could have in Europe" would make Copley "one of the first

Agrippina landing at Brundisium with the Ashes of Germanicus (1767); painting by Benjamin West
(Yale University Art Gallery)

The Death of General Wolfe (1771); painting by Benjamin West (National Gallery of Canada, Ottawa)

Painters in the world"—but only if he received this assistance "before your Manner and Taste were corrupted or fixed by working in your little way in Boston." No one working in their "little way" in Boston, Philadelphia, or New York could entertain serious hopes of becoming a great artist.

Training. The success of West and Copley seems all the more remarkable given their lack of early training. Painters in colonial America were self-taught, and they learned their basic skills from imported engravings and primitive limner portraits. The limner style, influenced by Puritan hostility to ornament, tended toward two dimensional, maplike faces with symmetrical patterning that tended to undermine pretensions to realism. While the demand for personal portraits to mark one's social status stimulated a competitive market for commissions among a crowd of itinerant painters, only a few artists such as the Maryland painter John Hesselius managed to accumulate wealth from their work. John Wollaston, who came to the colonies in 1749 and worked throughout the colonies, left some three hundred portraits at his death. These artists mostly used a few conventional poses, expressions, and props drawn from the English court painter Godfrey Kneller and evoked little of their subject's individuality. West met Wollaston and copied his skills in capturing the shimmer of satin and silk, but he quickly left for Rome to study the Old Masters.

An American in Rome and London. Leaving for Rome in 1760, West was the first of many Americans to go to Europe to get an artistic education they could not find at home. In many ways his career and his work alike came to resemble that of any young European artist equipped with his talent and ambition. In Rome, West saw the Apollo Belvedere at the Vatican—in its day the most important surviving antique statue—and became friends with Johann Winkelmann, a founder of neoclassical art theory. He copied the history paintings of another German expatriate, Anton Raphael Mengs. West arrived in London in 1763, equipped with his own skills with color and composition and a thorough training in the conventions and themes of neoclassical painting. In *Aggrippina Landing at Brundisium with the Ashes of Germanicus* (1767), for example, West painted a theme taken from the Roman writer Tacitus. As with many neoclassical history canvases, West used classical buildings in the background to create a theatrical backdrop, against which a scene from a larger epic unfolds. The figures crowding the historical stage have stylized and unrealistic gestures and postures, and West used elaborate togas to show off his painting skill in the rendering of folds and the reflection of light. With this painting and many others that would follow, West demonstrated that artistic success in the later eighteenth century was not achieved through originality of style or theme but rather through the imitation of prevailing styles and tastes. One was not considered an artist unless one had acquired the cosmopolitan taste that was the proof of a truly international education.

Death of the Earl of Chatham in the House of Lords (1779–1781); painting by John Singleton Copley
(Tate Gallery, London)

Royal Patronage and the American School. By his example and his influence, West almost single-handedly paved the way for other American's artistic success in painting. West's later success with *The Death of General Wolfe* (1771) led him to the apex of the European art world. King George III, who became his friend, gave him a huge royal commission for a massive series of works, never to be completed, called *The History of Revealed Religion*. The size of his paintings, his income, and his reputation grew together, and after Sir Joshua Reynold's tenure, West was named the second head of the prestigious Royal Academy of Art. West became not only the major recipient of the king's patronage but almost a member of his family and kept work rooms in royal palaces while George III waged war on the American colonies. With this success West also became a mentor to several American artists seeking advice, employment, and instruction. His studio in London became "the American school," where West advised and trained three generations of American painters, including Mathew Pratt, Charles Willson Peale, Gilbert Stuart, John Trumbull, Washington Allston, Thomas Sully, and Samuel F. B. Morse. West influenced the development of American art perhaps less through his own painting than by teaching and guiding young men who would become the leading painters in the following generation. With his international training, his importance in Britain's art institutions for over forty years, and his influence on subsequent landscape and history painters in America, West established that Americans might become serious artists.

Sources:

R. C. Alberts, *Benjamin West: A Biography* (Boston: Houghton Mifflin, 1978);

Dorinda Evans, *Benjamin West and His American Students* (Washington, D.C.: Smithsonian Institution Press, 1980);

James Thomas Flexner, *America's Old Masters: First Artists of the New World* (New York: Viking, 1939);

Robert Hughes, *American Visions: The Epic History of Art in America* (New York: Knopf, 1997);

Kenneth Silverman, *A Cultural History of the American Revolution* (New York: Columbia University Press, 1987).

ART II: AMERICAN HISTORY PAINTING

Innovations. As successful and wealthy artists, both Benjamin West and John Singleton Copley turned to history painting, which was considered the highest branch of art, where ambitious artists might secure their critical reputation and financial success. Over the last decades of their careers they completed many large, impressive canvases depicting scenes from English history. History paintings portrayed real persons and events, but they typically did so by using neoclassical conventions to transform historical moments into timeless lessons that taught ideal behavior: characters would wear Roman and Greek costumes while impersonating the stoic attitude and heroic virtues exemplified by the ancients. In mas-

Signing the Preliminary Articles of Peace, 30 November 1782, an unfinished oil painting by Benjamin West, 1784 (Henry Francis du Pont Winterthur Museum, Winterthur, Delaware); the four British representatives refused to sit for the painting; the Americans (l-r) are Henry Laurens, John Jay, Benjamin Franklin, William Temple Franklin, and John Adams.

tering a genre of painting already weighed down by stylistic and thematic traditions, West and Copley's most noteworthy works are striking for their modification of reigning precepts and ideals of European history painting. Coming from provincial colonies that seemed devoid of history, they helped to bring a freshness, energy, and innovation to history painting that now seem peculiarly American and at the time profoundly changed the manner and themes that Western painters had brought to the genre.

The Death of General Wolfe. One of the most significant paintings by an American was completed in 1771 and exhibited in London to immediate critical and popular success. Benjamin West's scene portrays the last moments of the British hero's life, which coincided with Anglo-American victory in the French and Indian War. West dressed his hero in then-current fashion, and for the first time he invested a contemporary event on the American continent with historical significance. Equally as daring was the pose and expression of General Wolfe in the painting, which emphasized the hero's particular experience and humanity: this was a hero with whom

late-eighteenth-century people could identify, whose suffering invited viewers to sympathize with Wolfe's personal feelings of pain and dejection instead of teaching them to face death stoically and without self-pity. West revolutionized history painting by portraying the nobility of an ordinary mortal in real circumstances and giving an event of modern history a moral drama and epic dignity that had previously been reserved for biblical, mythological, or classical figures and stories. With West's paintings, contemporary events and people, as well as the American past itself, became legitimate subjects for the realistic portrayal of historical truths—models of timeless virtues and values to whom future generations would look for guidance and inspiration.

Copley in England. Copley's innovations in history painting were also significant. After he came to London in 1775 seeking to escape the political tensions in Boston and to perfect his technique, he completed a series of history paintings that continued the break with the tradition begun by West. In *Watson and the Shark* (1778) Copley portrayed recent events with human figures in contemporary dress. In *Death of the Earl of Chatham* (1779–

1781) Copley brought history painting together with portraiture, recording a scene for posterity that included the portraits of fifty-five of England's leading aristocrats. Copley's finest history painting was the *Death of Major Peirson* (1782–1784), which like West's *General Wolfe* depicted the tragic moment of a military hero's death in the midst of victory. This scene is especially striking for its contrasts of light and dark and for its composition, with an especially dramatic focus and clarity to the extraordinary energies being expressed in the scene. While Copley did not have students, his large history paintings influenced John Trumbull's series of war scenes of the American Revolution. They may have also influenced the French Neoclassicism of Jacques-Louis David, whose *Oath of the Tennis Court* (1790–1791) also records a contemporary moment by including dozens of individual portraits.

Sources:

James Thomas Flexner, *America's Old Masters: First Artists of the New World* (New York: Viking, 1939);

Robert Hughes, *American Visions: The Epic History of Art in America* (New York: Knopf, 1997);

Jules D. Prown, *John Singleton Copley* (Cambridge, Mass.: Harvard University Press, 1966);

Kenneth Silverman, *A Cultural History of the American Revolution* (New York: Columbia University Press, 1987).

DRAMA I: COLONIAL ERA

Moral Objections. Many colonial Americans viewed the professional theater with deep suspicion. Especially during tough economic times, Quakers and Congregationalists, for example, argued that the stage distracted people from their work, wasted scarce money, and promoted dissipation. Much of this moral suspicion of the theater was informed by Protestant religious beliefs that, in associating spiritual devotion with self-denial, were inherently conservative: any forms of levity and mirth led easily to sin, and the toleration of public amusements could infect an entire community with the corrupt tastes of a few individuals. Graven images and secular music, no less than the theater, were condemned by Puritan ministers because they interfered with spiritual devotion and religious duty. Theater, however, was unlike the other arts an unqualified evil in Elizabethan and Puritan culture alike. In part this was because the theater became so popular among working-class peoples. The specific objections to the stage were often repeated and lasted until the end of the eighteenth century: theater did not, like "improving" forms of recreation, let one return to work refreshed, but rather exhausted actors and audience alike; it promoted sexual adultery or deviance among actors; acting encouraged deceit and hypocrisy; because it appealed vividly to the senses, theater could exert a powerful influence on spectators that rivaled religious worship, promoting a false, if not heretical, view of life; and it encouraged public disorder by gathering people from all walks of life together in large crowds for the purpose of amusement. Some of the condemnation of the theater was rooted in an elitist disdain for "rude and riotous" working-class amusements in general, such as cockfighting and boxing matches, with which it was often linked.

Bans on Theater. The fate of professional theater in the colonies was affected by debates about its moral legitimacy that were mainly regional in scope. A few theatrical troops managed to perform in taverns, private houses, or warehouses, but they were short lived. A 1750 law simply prohibited theatre in Boston. Rhode Island passed a law in 1762 that punished actors and the renters of stage space with heavy fines. Citizens in New York and Philadelphia signed petitions and passed laws to prevent the building of theaters. The Massachusetts Assembly outlawed theater in 1767, so there were no productions in the state throughout the Revolutionary era. That these measures were needed suggests that there was a small but growing acceptance of the theater in public opinion, particularly among the southern colonies, college men, and others seeking to emulate the urbane and aristocratic refinements of London.

The Theater of Politics. If the professional stage struggled to gain a foothold in the colonies, the amateur theater of the Revolutionary era was vibrantly alive and, more than any of the other arts, central to the political upheavals leading to independence. This theater took place in the streets of Boston, Philadelphia, New York, and other cities rather than on a stage; the performers were colonial patriots expressing themselves as political actors through rituals and ceremonies charged with allegorical significance. The Sons of Liberty, for example, were artisans and shopkeepers who organized mass demonstrations to protest the Stamp Act; such demonstrations included burning effigies of colonial administrators. Each of the crises in the 1760s and early 1770s provoked mock funerals to "Fair Liberty," which involved thousands of ordinary people in symbolic dramas. To protest taxes on tea in 1773, patriots in Boston and New York dressed in Indian costume and sang odes to the king while dumping cargoes into the ocean. These actions grew from the European tradition of popular urban protest, in which traditional festival days provided illiterate masses with a "safe" means of challenging authority under the guise of holiday play. Dramatic performances of political protest gave colonists a means of expressing their emotions and opinions on current events, but they also allowed aggrieved British subjects to assume new political roles as patriots and citizens, to rehearse a new cultural identity as Americans. Contemporary reports frequently invoked theater as a metaphor for the political conflict in general, as when a New York writer described the tea embargo as a "curious East Indian farce, lately prepared in England to be played in America for the entertainment of the British Colonies. . . . It was intended only as a kind of an overture, prelude, or introduction to a grand performance (I don't know whether to call it Comedy or Tragedy)."

Sources:

Kenneth Silverman, *A Cultural History of the American Revolution* (New York: Columbia University Press, 1987);

Gordon Wood, ed., *The Rising Glory of America 1760–1820* (New York: Braziller, 1971).

DRAMA II: THE FIRST PROFESSIONAL THEATER

American Company of Comedians. Despite continuing hostility to the stage, one itinerant group—The American Company of Comedians—brought the first professional theater to the colonies, monopolizing a modest audience for hundreds of productions throughout the 1760s and the early 1770s. They typically performed plays that were popular in London; the most popular playwright was William Shakespeare, whose work (especially *Romeo and Juliet*) was performed from 180 to 500 times. To attract a reputable audience, or at least diffuse criticism, the American Company often advertised its plays as "moral dialogues" and printed testimonials to its "genteel" actors in newspapers.

The Prince of Parthia. After opening a new theater in Philadelphia in 1766, the company produced the first American play to be professionally performed in the colonies. *The Prince of Parthia* was a five-act tragedy first written in 1759 that was loosely based on an episode of classical history. Its author, Thomas Godfrey, borrowed from *King Lear, Macbeth,* and *Othello* as well as character types from the contemporary novel of seduction, sentimental drama, and revenge plays. While indulging a frenzy of rapes, suicides, insanity, sadism, and incest, the play's references to slave and tyrants echoed the Whig political thinking about despotism and ambition that surfaced in contemporary protests to the Stamp Act. An evening at the theater typically lasted four or five hours. Lighted by candles, with painted backdrops, wigs, and costumes, the performance of a long play such as *The Prince of Parthia* was accompanied by interludes of vocal or instrumental music, as well as an afterpiece—a short ballad, opera, farce, or masque. *The Prince of Parthia* appeared with more than forty full-length plays performed over one hundred nights from 1766 to 1767. This season also featured Samuel Greville, the first American to become a professional actor, as Horatio in *Hamlet*. The performances sparked a tremendous public debate in local newspapers, with twenty essays considering whether the stage could inspire virtue and airing familiar moral complaints. Despite strong opposition from the Quakers, the American Company managed to complete its season, thanks largely to the patronage of Governor Penn.

Theater and Political Crisis. Struggling against innumerable setbacks, the company's director, David Douglass managed to build the first permanent, brick theater in the colonies at Annapolis in 1771. Douglass's efforts to build an audience for the professional theater in colonial cities ended once he became embroiled in the political crises of the mid 1770s. The Tea Act was passed just

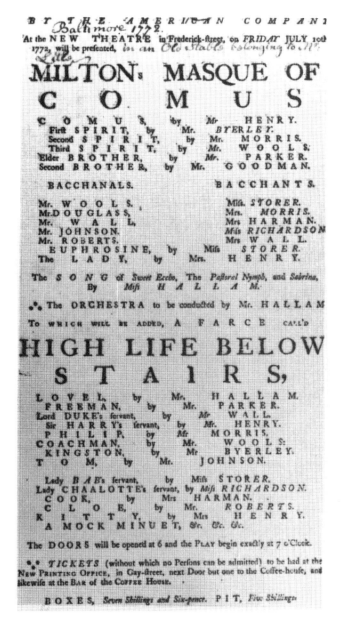

A colonial theater announcement (New-York Historical Society, New York)

as he was planning to build another brick theater in Charleston. Newspaper writers attacked once again the moral propriety of amusements at a time of crisis. With pressure from patriots to meet British trade policy with resolute and united action, the American Company was easily lumped with British luxury goods such as tea, and the aristocratic decadence of the gentry as part of a large conspiracy to seduce colonists into "slavery," or economic and cultural dependence. While these charges were not new, the context in which they circulated was fresh; putting on plays hardly seemed to be a way to encourage manly independence and other Republican virtues to which Patriot propaganda appealed in building popular support for boycotts against the mother country.

Congress and the Theater. Although the company completed its season in Charleston, the grievances

KING'S ARMS TAVERN—NEWPORT—RHODE ISLAND

On Monday, June 10th, at the Public Room of the above Inn, will be delivered a series of MORAL DIALOGUES, in five parts.

Depicting the evil effects of jealousy, and other bad passions, and proving that happiness can only spring from the pursuit of virtue.

Mr. Douglas—will represent a noble and magnanimous Moor, called Othello, who loves a young lady named Desdemona, and after he has married her, harbors (as in too many cases) the dreadful passion of jealousy.

> Of jealously, our being's bane,
> Mark the small cause, and the most dreadful pain.

Mr. Allyn—will depict the character of a specious villain, in the regiment of Othello, who is so base as to hate his commander on mere suspicion, and to impose on his best friend. Of such characters, it is to be feared, there are thousands in the world, and the one in question may present to us a salutary warning.

> the man that wrongs his master and his friend,
> What can he come to but a shameful end?

Mr. Hallam—will represent a young and thoughtful officer, who is traduced by Mr. Allyn, and getting drunk, loses his situation and his general's esteem. All young men, whatsoever, take example from Cassio.

> The ill effects of drinking would you see?
> Be warn'd, and fly from evil company.

Mr. Morris—will represent an old gentleman, the father of Desdemona, who is not cruel or covetous, but is foolish enough to dislike the noble Moor, his son-in-law, because his face is not white, forgetting that we all spring from one root. Such prejudices are very numerous, and very wrong.

Source: William W. Clapp Jr., *A Record of the Boston Stage* (Boston & Cambridge: J. Munroe, 1853), pp. 8–10.

Congress moved to shut down cultural trade with Britain as well with a sumptuary measure in which the delegates resolved to "discountenance and discourage every species of extravagance and dissipation, especially horse racing, and all kinds of gaming, cockfighting, exhibition of shews, plays, and other expensive diversions and entertainments." Having targeted the American Company in particular, Congress sent the resolution to Douglass in a personal letter. A few months later Douglass's company of actors dispersed, and he moved to Jamaica, never to return to America.

Sources:

Kenneth Silverman, *A Cultural History of the American Revolution* (New York: Columbia University Press, 1987);

Gordon Wood, ed., *The Rising Glory of America 1760–1820* (New York: Braziller, 1971).

LITERATURE I: LITERARY FORM AND POLITICS

Political Debate. Revolutionary era literature was written in the context of political conflict. In thousands of columns of colonial newspapers, hundreds of published pamphlets, and countless topical poems this polemical writing addressed particular issues and events that led to war with the mother country. While this literature typically concerned itself with the details of imperial policy—virtual and actual representation, taxation—it also grappled with questions that continue to be central to democratic life. What is the proper source of political authority? What should be the basis of individuals rights, and how far should those rights extend? If a government's success depends on the virtue of its citizens, what are the limits and possibilities of human nature? In exploring these questions writers drew on two distinct eighteenth-century literary traditions—the secular, Whig tradition in which critics had voiced opposition to the abuse of political power in England and a religious tradition of moral exhortation that developed out of colonial society's evangelical Protestantism. Involvement in political debate had been a privilege of educated gentlemen that depended on the importation of expensive books and access to private libraries. From the 1760s, with new newspapers and magazines, an increase in printing in the colonies, and the growth of colleges and "seminaries of learning," more Americans found the opportunity to publish their views. The Stamp Act, the Townsend duties, the burning of the *Gaspee,* and the Boston Massacre each provoked a storm of poetry and prose.

Pamphlet Wars. Literary protest in the colonies adapted the imagery and ideas of eighteenth-century English political radicalism. The ideas of John Trenchard and Thomas Gordon were repeatedly used on both sides of the Atlantic. A pastoral image of rural contentment highlighted the rampant corruption of city politics. Liberty was linked with the progress of civilization while the fate of the ancient empires of Greece and Rome warned how quickly a relaxing of moral discipline could

against it were still fresh when the Continental Congress met in 1774 and created the Continental Association, which provided for nonimportation, nonconsumption, and nonexportation. Between 1774 and 1775 the value of English imports fell by 90 percent. In October 1774

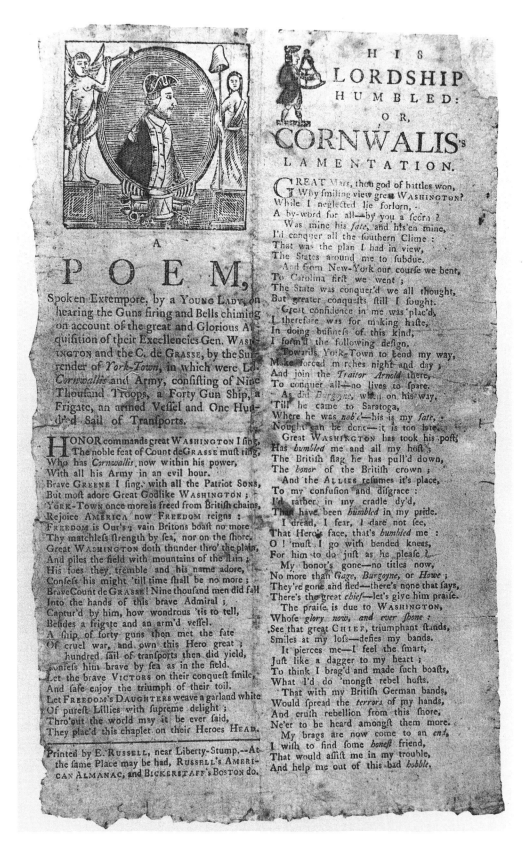

Verse celebrating the British defeat at Yorktown, Virginia, in October 1781 (American Antiquarian Society, Worcester, Massachusetts)

bring the most brilliant of societies to ruin. Joseph Addison's popular play *Cato* (1713) depicted the martyr of Republican Rome who stood against corruption and killed himself rather than submit to the tyranny of Julius Caesar; the play's lines, celebrating freedom and patriotism were quoted everywhere during the Stamp Act. James Burgh's *Britain's Remembrancer: or, The Danger Not Yet Over* (1746) and Dr. John Brown's *Estimate of the Manners and Principles of the Times* (1757) portrayed the decadence and luxury of the aristocratic class and linked the moral decadence of the Court Ministry with the political tyranny and conspiracy.

Virtue and Simplicity. Finding a wide readership in the colonies, such works furnished Americans with a vocabulary—images of corruption and virtue, phrases such as "inalienable right" and "sons of liberty," and allegories about the goddess Libertas. In "Letters from a Farmer in Pennsylvania to the Inhabitants of the British Colonies," published in newspapers from 1767 to 1768 and as a pamphlet in 1768, the lawyer John Dickinson assumed the persona of a simple farmer, a type that recurs frequently in Revolutionary poetry and prose. The narrator's humble simplicity and rustic virtues lent a tone of moderation and caution to Dickinson's otherwise seditious advice; although written in reaction to the Townshend duties, "Letters" did more than object to taxation. Imitate ancient Spartans, Dickinson wrote, and the virtues of prudence, bravery, justice, and humanity would allow America to triumph over the "ambitious, artful men" who governed Britain. In exploring the moral requirements for freedom Dickinson's writing, like most of the polemical literature of the 1760s, retained the learned and legalistic style of rational enlightenment—invoking proportion and balance, appealing to law and history, and assuming that the orderly exchange of ideas might resolve the political issues at hand. Like Dickinson's "Letters," the most influential work before the war, revolutionary literature translated theories of government and rights into compelling moral dramas and vivid metaphors, while restraining potentially raw political sentiments within the predictable style of neoclassical literary convention.

Religious Background. While pamphlet literature owed its emphasis on logic and reason to a transatlantic tradition of secular learning in science and moral philosophy, it drew on the native influence of evangelical Protestantism for its emotional appeal. Beginning with the Great Awakening, religious revivalism became the primary arena in which Americans questioned the authority of existing institutions (the clergy and orthodox doctrines) by appealing to the rights, obligations, and freedoms of popular piety. The Puritan Jeremiad furnished a powerful literary tradition of dissent, which made the immediacy of personal danger and collective crisis apparent. In colonial sermons of the 1760s religious faith and political liberty became intertwined with a millennial vision of American history. Commenting on

the book of Revelation, Joseph Bellamy's extremely popular *The Millenium* (1758) narrates the Second Coming as a peculiarly national deliverance: *"a nation shall be born in a day,* and *all the people shall be righteous."* These sermons taught colonists to associate "salvation" with a general well-being that all citizens would share once their sudden "awakening" led to a sudden liberation from the bondage of corruption into future glories of prosperity. Sermons were clearly the most influential kind of literature that helped to shape Americans' response to the crises of the Revolutionary era: while some four hundred political pamphlets appeared in the colonies at this time, more than eighteen hundred sermons were printed in Massachusetts and Connecticut alone.

Common Sense. Religious evangelism contributed to the dramatic change in literary tone and style of Revolutionary prose in the 1770s. Thomas Paine's *Common Sense,* published in January 1776 and selling more than 120,000 copies in three months, had a unique, overwhelming, and immediate impact in the colonies. No literary work had a greater influence in the political affairs of the day, and yet no other piece of writing from the Revolutionary era managed to transcend so successfully its historical moment and become a founding document of the emergence of an American literature. Ironically Paine was an immigrant from England who arrived in Philadelphia in 1774—a fact that perhaps explains his willingness to argue without apology for a complete break with Britain and with the customs of the past in general. Unlike the Whig lawyers who kept their treason within the decorum of erudite learning, Paine dispensed with traditional conceits such as the farmer-narrator and addressed himself directly to ordinary people in the simple and emotional fervor of righteous anger. Independence was no longer an abstract principle to be debated by gentlemen but a birthright of ordinary citizens, and it was to be seized without hesitation or regret.

A New Voice. Blending political and scientific ideas about natural rights and universal laws with millennial urgency, *Common Sense* describes independence as an accomplished fact and enlists the reader's patriotism in the most sensational and melodramatic terms. Writing in the wake of the British occupation of Boston, Paine declares that it is too late to turn back from the quest for independence.

But if you say, you can still pass the violations over, then I ask, Hath your house been burnt? Hath your property been destroyed before your face? Are your wife and children destitute of a bed to lie on, on bread to live on? Have you lost a parent of a child by their hands, and your self the ruined and wretched survivor. If you have not, then you are not a judge of those who have. But if you have, and can still shake hands with the murderers, then you are unworthy of the name of husband, father, friend, or lover, and whatever may be your rank or title in life, you have the heart of a coward, and the spirit of a sycophant.

A folk artist's drawing of the American commander in chief and his wife (Abby Aldrich Rockefeller Collection, Williamsburg, Virginia)

Importing Literature. From the founding of the colonies until the nineteenth century the great majority of books that circulated in the colonies were printed in Britain. Although by the late eighteenth century there were printers in the major American cities as well as in many towns, local presses could not print works cheaply enough or in enough quantity to satisfy the demands of the American reading public. As advertisements in colonial newspapers demonstrate, the urban bookseller was the means through which Americans maintained their cultural identity as Britons, keeping up with the latest fashions and developments in all of the arts. Some of the most important philosophical developments of the Enlightenment had their largest influence in the colonies through advice books and novels—new genres of literature that continue to be staples in American bookstores. John Locke's new educational psychology, organized around individual experience, and the Common Sense ideas about the moral sense both taught colonial readers to imagine a less coercive, more "liberal" ideal of childhood, in which trust of one's own innate capacity for sympathy and reason was more important than obedience to external authority.

American Editions. When a colonial printer chose to publish an American edition of a British work, it had important consequences for the development of culture on this side of the Atlantic. Colonial printers developed the reading tastes of Americans, helping both to supply domestic demands for cultural enlightenment and stimulating the local production of writers and composers. Before the invention of modern forms of mechanical production, printing was a time-consuming and labor-intensive process, and early America depended on the importation of costly materials such as type. It cost a great deal merely to print a book, and books were so expensive that most families would never own more than a few. For this reason printers were conservative in what they decided to publish: they could not afford to produce even one book that would not sell at least enough to cover the cost of printing. Most of what was published in colonial America were "safe" bets, such as bibles and versions of the psalms. *Poor Richard's Almanac,* first published by Benjamin Franklin in 1732, was another popular kind of book and might sell as many as ten thousand copies a year. British advice books such as Philip Dormer Stanhope, Lord Chesterfield's *Letters to his Son* (1774) were also dependable best-sellers throughout the later eighteenth century, and its American editions, beginning in 1775, helped to shape a less religious, more cosmopolitan culture in America. Especially in the case of the novel, colonial editions of British works helped to create an entirely new literary taste in America. Although Americans did not write novels before the Revolution, they certainly read them.

Paine speaks, in print, to the temper of the urban mobs that, during each crisis from the 1760s, played a dominant role in the colonial challenge to imperial authority. After years of genteel appeals to rational moderation, *Common Sense* makes the sentiments that circulated in taverns and streets the true source of colonial identity and cultural salvation. In asking every citizen to respond to such outrages, Paine promises like the evangelists that a providential glory awaits the colonies' break with the king. God will reign over the new republic as "the king of America." With a confident optimism that anticipates Walt Whitman's celebration of an American Adam, Paine's pamphlet convinced many people that "We have it in our power to begin the world over again." The radical defiance of existing authority, the demagogic appeal to the crowd, the absolute faith in reinvention, the dignity of common language and experience: these qualities made *Common Sense* a seminal work in the expression of a new literary voice of democracy.

Sources:

Bernard Bailyn, *The Ideological Origins of the American Revolution* (Cambridge, Mass.: Harvard University Press, 1967);

Emory Elliot, ed., *Columbia Literary History of the United States* (New York: Columbia University Press, 1988);

Robert Ferguson, *The American Enlightenment 1750–1820* (Cambridge, Mass.: Harvard University Press, 1997);

Gary B. Nash, *The Urban Crucible: The Northern Seaports and the Origins of the American Revolution* (Cambridge, Mass.: Harvard University Press, 1979).

The Novel in America. Many of the best-selling books of the Revolutionary era were editions of popular British novels printed in New York, Philadelphia, and Boston: Oliver Goldsmith's *The Vicar of Wakefield* (1772), Laurence Stern's *The Life and Opinions of Tristram Shandy* (1774), Daniel Defoe's *Robinson Crusoe* (1775), Samuel Richardson's *Clarissa* (1786), and Jonathan Swift's *Gulliver's Travels* (1793) all sold more than twenty thousand copies. On both sides of the Atlantic, fiction in the eighteenth century was only accepted as a tool for education that demonstrated new psychological ideas. For this reason American editions of British novels were always adaptations, ranging from chapbook versions for children to adult versions that were abridged or even rewritten to emphasize particular themes. *Robinson Crusoe*, for example, appeared in 125 editions in the United States between 1775 and 1825, and none of them were faithful to the original British text, first published in 1719. American editions of *Clarissa* changed the novel's title to emphasize a contemporary political message: "wherein the arts of a Designing Villain and the Rigours of Parental Authority conspired to complete the Ruin of a virtuous daughter." Americans interpreted the novel as a political allegory about a martyred heroine leading a revolutionary cause. "The Ministry are Lovelace and the People are Clarissa," John Adams later said, and the "artful villain will pursue the innocent lovely girl to her ruin and her death." His comments suggest not only how pervasive the taste for particular British novels had become in the young nation but also the extent to which American printers subtly reshaped imported literature according to local circumstances and values. Their success in making novels about the seduction and ruin of young women look like "improving" means of moral and political education paved the way for the success in the later 1780s and 1790s of American novelists such as Susanna Rowson, Hannah Foster, William Hill Brown and Charles Brockden Brown, and in general helped to make the novel the most popular literary genre of the nineteenth century.

Sources:

Cathy Davidson, *Revolution and the Word: The Rise of the Novel in America* (New York: Oxford University Press, 1986);

Jay Fliegelman, *Prodigals and Pilgrims: The Revolt Against Patriarchal Authority, 1750–1800* (New York: Cambridge University Press, 1982);

Frank Luther Mott, *Golden Multitudes: The Story of Bestsellers in the United States* (New York: Macmillan, 1947).

MUSIC

Institutions of Musical Life. Like the other arts in the colonies, music before the Revolution had a limited institutional base: there was almost no opportunity for the professional training and performance of musicians and composers. For this reason Americans acquired their taste for music through amateur performance, which relied almost entirely on the importation of sheet music of European composers such as Antonio Lucio Vivaldi and

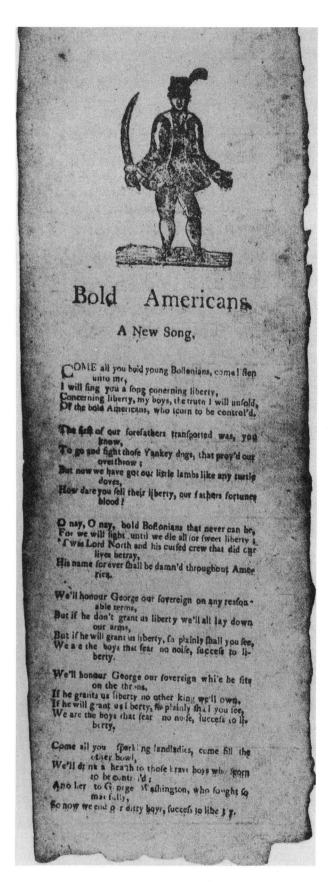

A late-eighteeth-century broadside paying tribute to American courage and fortitude (Bostonian Society, Boston, Massachusetts)

George Frideric Handel and instruments such as the spinet and harpsichord. Emulating the habits of the British gentry, fashionable men and women on this side of the Atlantic used their leisure time to practice "accomplishments" that they could share with other members of respectable "society." Most musical activity centered around concerts in the home, where genteel women sang and played guitar, for example, while men played violin and flute. The most accomplished musicians of the day were some of the wealthy Southerners—Thomas Jefferson, for example, collected musical instruments such as the pianoforte and performed in amateur concerts at the governor's mansion at Williamsburg—or the planter families who came to Charleston to escape the summer heat and take part in "public times," when concerts and plays were sponsored by the St. Cecilia society.

Church Singing. In church singing the new music of James Lyons and William Billings would not have been possible without changes that made vocal training more accessible and popular and helped to disseminate a taste for music as an art, separate from the needs of religious devotion. The musical life of the colonies prior to and during the Revolutionary era was dominated by psalms. Psalms were part of the larger democratizing of scripture that the Protestant Reformation had set in motion with its commitment to reading and devotion in vernacular languages rather than in Latin. Furnishing common people with simple religious ballads to be used in worship, psalms translated scripture from the Old Testament into metrical verses that were easy to remember and perform by nonliterate and literate people alike. In the eighteenth century alone more than 250 publications were devoted to psalmody, making such popular works as the *Bay Psalm Book* (1640) and Isaac Watts's *Psalm of David Imitated in the Language of the New Testament* (1719) as common in the colonies as almanacs and spellers. The English composer William Tansur was the most widely known psalmodist before the Revolution through compilations such as *Royal Melody Complete,* first published in Boston in 1767, but selections from which were being sung in America shortly after its printing in Britain in 1755.

Singing Schools. Singing schools brought young men and women together and became a primary means of keeping youths interested in church. Taught by itinerant musicians, singing schools trained young people in basic rules of vocal performance, typically meeting two or three times a week for three months, and concluding with a public performance of newly learned selections. Paul Revere's engraving at the front of William Billings's *The New England Psalm Singer* (1770), depicts a leader and six male singers seated around a table in a home or perhaps an inn but not a church. This engraving illustrates the way that psalmody increasingly served a social function instead of being confined to churches. Psalms were sung for recreation at various places where people gathered, and with the proliferation of singing masters

and new kinds of psalms that introduced national and secular themes there was obviously worry that people were performing sacred music as a form of social entertainment instead of assisting believers in religious worship. In the preface to his *The Singing Master's Assistant* (1778) Billings included advice on how to run a singing school. Although these schools were often sponsored by churches and sometimes held on church property, Billing's warnings to other singing masters suggests that the young adults and teenage boys and girls who attended them had other things besides solemn piety on their minds: "4. No unnecessary conversation, whispering, or laughing, to be practiced . . . and above all I enjoin it upon you to refrain from all levity, both in conduct and in conversation, while singing sacred words."

Profane Amusements. Teaching vocal skills that students used outside of church—at spinning bees, funerals, and Election Days—the schools spread a taste for music as a form of social recreation and secular entertainment. Like itinerant singing masters, roving musicians brought a wider range of music lessons to students throughout the colonies. The increased number of skilled singers led to the introduction of choirs in churches, which in turn led to the introduction of instrumental accompaniment on pitch pipes, bass viols, and small orchestras with wind and string instruments by the 1790s. As a result services increasingly resembled concerts. Singing had been an active means of participation in religious devotion for all church members, but it increasingly became an occasion for aesthetic appreciation, where members passively listened to virtuoso performances by their more skilled brethren. By meeting and stimulating a demand for musical training, these new institutions helped to build cultural support for professional composition and performance that blurred the distinction between sacred and secular. By the 1770s organists played both in church services and in public concerts.

From Sacred to Secular. The development of new institutions in the musical life of the colonies during the 1760s and 1770s both contributed to and expressed profound changes taking place in colonial music. The publication of two works of vocal music in this period illustrates the growth of secular composition styles and the improved quality of musical performance. In 1763 the publication of James Lyon's *Urania* introduced the colonies to more sophisticated compositions in psalm singing that had become fashionable in Britain. Especially in New England, conservative religious tradition had emphasized the sacred purpose of vocal music and discouraged instrumental performances as a distraction to spiritual devotion and, like theatre, a danger to public morality. Congregational and Presbyterian churches focused their singing on scripture, such as the use of David's psalms for the praise of God, and relied on "lining-out," having a deacon lead the congregation by reading the psalm line by line. As the first American tunebook to contain "ornaments," *Urania* moved colonial tastes towards neoclassical eloquence and paved the way for secu-

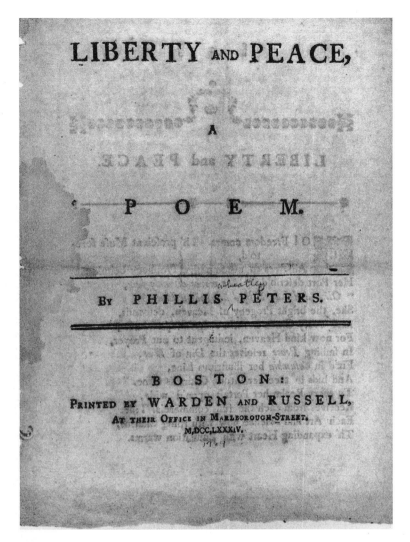

LIBERTY AND PEACE,

A

POEM.

By PHILLIS PETERS.

BOSTON:
PRINTED BY WARDEN AND RUSSELL,
AT THEIR OFFICE IN MARLBOROUGH-STREET.
M,DCC,LXXXIV.

Verse written by Phillis Wheatley, the first published African American poet. She married John Peters in 1778. (American Antiquarian Society, Worcester, Massachusetts)

lar modifications of sacred music through hymns, anthems, and fuguing tunes. These compositions were more complex than psalms, requiring singers to master trills and graces, lengthy four-part choruses and other kinds of aesthetic embellishment. Containing detailed explanations of tempo and rhythm and printing words under notes, *Urania* helped to improve the quality of musical performance in the colonies by introducing variety into psalmody and inviting vocal training amongst a wide audience.

William Billings. The publication of *Urania* and other European compositions spurred a revival of colonial singing. In 1770 *The New England Psalm Singer: or, American Chorister,* the first volume of music composed by an American, was published in Boston. Its author, twenty-four-year-old William Billings, was the first American composer of great importance, and as the title of his work indicates, he stood at the beginning of a new tradition and was concerned with developing an indigenous musical idiom. Rejecting European models of composition, Billings intro-

duced innovations in form that expressed something of a declaration of musical independence. His second published work, *The Singing Master's Assistant* (1778), was the first tunebook published after the outbreak of war and included musical settings of patriotic texts written by Billings himself that dealt explicitly with the war. It was also the only American tunebook of the eighteenth century by a composer that included many tunes already familiar to the public, and more than fifty of its tunes appeared in later compliations published by others. Billings's music was reprinted and performed throughout the 1780s and 1790s and was so popular that one Philadelphia critic declared in 1788 that Billings was "the rival of Handel."

Sources:

Gilbert Chase, *America's Music from the Pilgrims to the Present* (Urbana: University of Illinois Press, 1987);

Charles Hamm, *Music in the New World* (New York: Norton, 1983);

David P. McKay and Richard Crawford, *Willing Billing of Boston: Eighteenth-Century Composer* (Princeton, N.J.: Princeton University Press, 1975);

Kenneth Silverman, *A Cultural History of the American Revolution* (New York: Columbia University Press, 1987).

THE POETRY OF INDEPENDENCE

Imitation. Artists and critics would not value originality until the Romantic era transformed arts and letters in the late eighteenth and early nineteenth centuries. During the Revolutionary era colonial writers absorbed a cosmopolitan ideal of belles lettres both through their reading of English literature and through their training in the classics at colleges such as Princeton. The rational aesthetic ideals of the enlightenment were developed in art criticism and literary essays, now referred to as term belles lettres, by educated men of letters. Belles lettres distrusted the expression of strong passions and the experience of subjective feeling that would come to dominate the Romantic vision of the artist as an isolated, inspired genius. Instead, like the philosophy of natural law that influenced Thomas Jefferson in his writing of the Declaration of Independence, enlightenment philosophy of aesthetics proposed that truth was universally valid, and that reason was an objective demonstration of human nature, which was uniformly consistent in all times and places. If later Romantic artists such as William Wordsworth, Nathaniel Hawthorne, and Walt Whitman would justify their artistic originality on the basis of their private intuitions and subjective interpretations, eighteenth-century artistic thinkers such as Alexander Pope, Samuel Johnson, and many American poets valued instead the imitation of classical models and the repetition of aesthetic standards.

Politics of Style. Classical Greece and Rome had mastered the aesthetic rules of proportion and balance that remained as true for Anglo-America in the eighteenth century as they had been for ancient times, so men of letters felt that they could not do better than follow the Augustan themes and neoclassical forms that represented for them the height of civilized, cosmopolitan taste. Poets Phyllis Wheatley and Jupiter Hammon, among the first African American writers to publish in the Western world, were both slaves who used their mastery of neoclassical poetic conventions to defy ideas of racial inferiority. Both learned to read and write and gave literary form to their devout Christian piety and wide learning in the classics. Their literary works demonstrated that civilized character could be acquired through religion and learning and told colonial readers, "Remember, *Christians, Negroes,* black as *Cain,* May be refin'd, and join th'angelic train," as Phyllis Wheatley noted in "On Being Brought from Africa to America" (1773). In a similar way the poets known as the Hartford Wits adopted cosmopolitan conventions of neoclassical epic poetry in order to invest themes and events of the Revolution with heroic stature. Educated in the oratory of Cicero and the odes of Horace, Philip Freneau, Henry Brackenridge, and other college-educated writers sought in their poetry to give public testimony to the abstract ideals of republicanism to demonstrate that America might properly become the new capital of civilized, cosmopolitan culture. As with the piety of Hammon and Wheatley, the Augustan declamatory style of the early national poets appropriated an existing language in order to convince their colonial audience of the truth of new ideas.

American Identity. The events of the Revolution provoked one of the first substantial bodies of secular poetry in American literature. The disruption that political crisis brought to the lives of Americans tended, on the one hand, to inhibit activity in the arts generally. On the other hand, the urgency of events demanded that writers speak in the most immediate and forceful terms to their audience. The struggle for independence often made literature inseparable from propaganda, but this situation had the benefit of encouraging writers to move beyond the neoclassical conventions and formulas of English literature that had prevented colonial artists from realizing a distinctive American voice. The Revolution gave writers a topic that was unique to the historical, geographic, and moral situation of the colonies; aroused a range of emotional interest that was both diverse and profound; and invited speculation of what it might mean to be "American."

Philip Freneau. While at Princeton, Philip Freneau joined the American Whig Society, a student club. In this club he taught himself to be a poet by writing satire and preparing verses for the commencement exercises that, through the 1760s, had become a major showcase for native literary achievement. Freneau's first published piece was the graduation poem he wrote in 1771 with Hugh Henry Brackenridge, *A Poem, on The Rising Glory of America,* which reflected on the westward course of the empire and concluded with a millennial vision of America as a new Canaan that "shall excel the old." With his club fellows Brackenridge and James Madison, he composed a farcical romance, *Father Bombo's Pilgrimmage to Mecca* (1770), which some scholars have identified as the first American novel. He published his first collection of poems, *The American Village,* in 1772. While these poems show Freneau's facility with the conventions of pastoral verse, they also point toward a romantic idealization of American nature that would become a major theme for American writers in the nineteenth century. His later poem, "The Wild Honey Suckle" (1786), secured his reputation as a lyric poet of nature:

> Smit with those charms, that must decay,
> I grieve to see your future doom;
> They died—nor were those flowers more gay,
> The flowers that did in eden Bloom;
> Unpitying frosts, and Autumn's power
> Shall leave no vestige of this flower.

Pursuing a natural metaphor and elegiac tone for the transience and innocence of beauty, this poem is now seen as the first in the American Romantic tradition that would be developed by William Cullen Bryant and the Transcendentalists in the nineteenth century. Like many of his contemporaries in Revolutionary America, Freneau moved away from an orthodox Calvinist heritage toward a more secular devotion to the political life of the new nation. Not only did he use poetry as a weapon in the struggle for independence, but he also helped to invent a language and a set of topics suited to a democratic literature.

Poet of the Revolution. As the most prolific poet of early America, Freneau played an important role in the development of a national literature. Employing the newspapers and magazines to address a wide popular audience of engaged citizens, Freneau became the first of many writers to strive for a poetry that embodied American identity and to self-consciously pursue a career as a public poet. Unlike some writers who confined their activities to the refined and private world of genteel salons and clubs, Freneau published everything he wrote in magazines, newspapers, and inexpensive book editions. He also was one of the more vitriolic of the patriot poets, and his eagerness to be topical outweighed his desire to emulate the neoclassical finish of polite literature; he would revise many of his poems in later versions. While living in New York, Freneau captured an audience for his poetry with some burlesques of British officials, such as *General Gage's Confession* (1775), written in heroic couplets, as well as "Libera Nos, Domine," which parodies the liturgy of the mass. After living in the West Indies to avoid the war from 1776 to 1778 and stints as a blockade runner in the West Indies and as a captive in a British prison vessel, Freneau joined the *Freeman's Journal* in Philadelphia, from which he attacked the British and the Tories with a torrent of satirical and patriotic poetry. The humor and zeal of this work won him his reputation as "The Poet of the Revolution."

Satire. The best poetry of the Revolution is primarily satirical. John Trumbull, who graduated from Yale College in 1767 with two other members of the Connecticut Wits, Timothy Dwight and David Humphreys, published *M'Fingal* in 1776 and an expanded revision in 1782. In fifteen hundred couplets the poem describes a town meeting in which a Tory is tarred and feathered after coming into conflict with local Whigs. Trumbull managed to move beyond mere imitation of British satirists such as Samuel Butler and Charles Churchill, adapting native subject matter to an imported mock-epic genre of poetry. The poem is also notable for its detached humor and comic violence in a conflict that, for most writers, invited more bitterness and rage:

> The deadly spade discharg'd a blow
> Trememdous on his rear below
> His bent knee fail'd, and void of strength
> Stretch'd on the ground his manly length
> Like ancient oak overturned he lay,
> Or Tow'rs to tempests fall' a prey,
> And more things else—but all men know 'em
> If slightly vers'd in Epic.

Like Philip Freneau and other Patriot poets, Loyalists such as Jonathan Odell wield their verses like blunt instruments—their moves are often clumsy and unfinished, but meant to inflict quick injury. Odell's satires *The Congratulation* (1779) and *The American Times* (1780) brought to his attack on American leaders some of the precision of Alexander Pope.

Protest Poetry. The learned poets of the Revolution resorted to predictable poetic conventions as a response to an uncertain future, using blank verse and poetic couplets to invest their work with a civic importance. At the same time, however, the volatile political emotions of the colonial era nourished a less polished form of poetry that reached a larger audience through popular songs. In its raw humor, simple language, and obvious rhymes these lyrics did not rely on one's familiarity with cosmopolitan literary tastes and avoided abstract themes and classical references. Some of these songs were written by educated men of letters, such as "The Liberty Song" (1768), by the Philadelphia lawyer John Dickinson. Published in newspapers and sung during mock funerals for the Goddess of Liberty and various protest rallies staged by the Sons of Liberty and others, "The Liberty Song" was intended to incite patriotic fervor. Like many cartoons, parades, and political texts of the colonial rebellion, these songs helped to disseminate the themes and heroes of the Patriotic struggle for freedom against tyranny and were the means by which Republicanism became popularized as a civil religion. As the poet Joel Barlow, upon entering the Patriot Army, commented, "One good song is worth a dozen addresses or proclamations."

Yankee Doodle. Another sort of democratic poetry emerging from the folk culture of protest was more plebeian in its themes and was an important contribution to a vernacular comic tradition that would later also include the frontier humor of the Crockett Almanacs and Mark Twain in the nineteenth century. Although there are conflicting stories about the origins of the song "Yankee Doodle," it appears that the tune was based on a British drinking song. The words were originally intended as a satire of the motley American troops, meant to ridicule the colonials as provincial country bumpkins. The term "Yankee" was itself a contemptuous insult used by the British during the Revolution until Patriot troops used it as a positive emblem of their rebel pride. In April 1775 the redcoats marched to the battle of Concord singing "Yankee Doodle" but were badly beaten. From then on the Yankees would taunt British troops by singing the doggerel, turning the image of the provincial clown into a national symbol. Mocking their own rustic and ragtag simplicity, the rebels used the song in the same way J. Hector St. John de Crèvecoeur and others used the persona of the simple colonial farmer: they showed that a lack of cosmopolitan cultivation allowed the rebels to defeat British formality and pretention with shrewd practicality and natural sincerity. Many other stories and songs celebrating Patriot triumphs came out of the war, which could be sung to the tune of "Yankee Doodle." By transforming cultural backwardness into a new form of national identity, Revolutionary Americans invented a truly new and democratic definition of culture.

Sources:

William C. Dowling, *Poetry and Ideology in Revolutionary America* (Athens: University of Georgia Press, 1990);

Emory Elliot, *Columbia History of American Literature* (New York: Columbia University Press, 1986);

Elliot, ed., *Dictionary of Literary Biography*, volume 31: *American Colonial Writers, 1735–1781* (Columbia, S.C.: Bruccoli Clark / Detroit: Gale Research, 1984);

F. Leon Howard, *The Connecticut Wits* (Chicago: University of Chicago Press, 1976);

Oscar Sonneck, *Report on "The Star Spangled Banner," "Hail Columbia," "America," "Yankee Doodle"* (Washington, D.C.: U.S. Government Printing Office, 1909).

HEADLINE MAKERS

WILLIAM BILLINGS

1746-1800
COMPOSER

Beginnings. Born in Boston on 7 October 1746, William Billings was the first American composer. Like Copley, William Billings was a son of the colonial working class. Without the benefit of much formal education, let alone the chance of attending college (which remained a privilege of the genteel class), both men nevertheless managed to realize some remarkable artistic talents. Unlike Copley, however, Billings gave expression to a provincial, American culture instead of aspiring to the cosmopolitan ideal of British culture. At no time in his life would Billings ever achieve the social and economic success accorded to gentlemen, but given his fervent patriotism he may have regarded his artisanal background with pride. From his early teens Billings supported himself as a tanner. Like most colonial musicians, he apparently received his first musical education at singing schools; in 1769 he advertised the opening of his first singing school with John Barry, a former choir director at the New South Church who was probably Billings's main teacher. Billings never mastered any instrument but instead made the psalm the object of his musical innovations. Because it was integral to religious worship and supported by churches throughout the colonies, the psalm was the most common and important musical form in America before the nineteenth century.

Accomplishments. At the age of twenty-three Billings had already composed more than one hundred original pieces of sacred music, and in 1770 he published his first tunebook, *The New England Psalm Singer.* Only a dozen or so American-composed tunes had previously been published. Collecting more than 120 new compositions, *The New England Psalm Singer* was the first published compilation of entirely American music and the first tunebook composed by one American composer. Perhaps even more significant as a sign of both Billings's intentions and the times in which he lived, he advertised the work as "never before published" and stressed that it was composed by "a native of Boston"—made in America by an American. Published by Benjamin Edes and John Gill, who also published *The Boston Gazette and Country Journal,* a major Patriot newspaper, and including an engraving by Paul Revere, the book suggested that Billings was strongly aligned with the Rebels. His tunebook is striking for the manner in which it boldly signals these nationalist sentiments. For example, Billings's best-known tune, "Chester," declares:

> Let tyrant shake their iron rod
> And slav'ry Clank her galling Chains
> We fear them not we trust in God
> New Englands God for ever reigns.

His second published tunebook, *The Singing Master's Assistant* (1778), includes a paraphrase of Psalm 137 that refers to the occupation of Boston in 1775–1776. These selections captured the mood of confident defiance with which New England patriots entered the new era.

Innovations. For modern readers what makes the Billings compositions so striking is the manner in which he dispensed with conventions that had dominated the Anglo-American Psalm tradition. His tunes feature dance-like rhythms drawn from the popular music of the colonies, such as the Irish Jig; his melodies are borrowed from traditional Anglo-Irish folk songs such as "Greensleeves"; and his texts are more secular than literary. His tunes include a four-voice structure—tenor, treble, counter tenor, and bass—and they developed increasing coordination of texts and music by including printed words with the tunes. He also pioneered the fuguing tune, which involved successive vocal entries and an overlapping of sung texts. The end result was a dissonant sound, stripped of European refinements. Before his death in 1800 Billings had published a total of six collections of tunes, which moved toward more-involved musical forms such as the anthem and explored more complex musical textures. *The Psalm-Singer's Amusement* (1781) includes two extended concert pieces, which in their unusual choice of keys, variety of effects, and technical virtuosity represent some of Billings's most polished works. A separately published piece, "An Anthem for Easter," remains the most popular anthem by an eighteenth-century American.

Impact. Although his music was reprinted by others dozens of times and performed throughout the new United States, Billings died in poverty. His visibility within American music did much to transform music from anonymous aids to religious devotion to an artistic medium, by which composers might project their own distinctive ethos and individual personality. In his prefaces, joke-tunes, and commentary Billings assumed a self-deprecating intimacy (Billings addressed the tune "Jargon" "To the goddess of discord" as a way of answering critics of his music) that helped further to make singing a truly popular art. In its playful exploration of a more natural and primitive wildness, Billings's music became a model for later American composers, such as Charles Ives, who would also experiment with received European conventions and use popular culture in their search for a distinctive American sound.

Sources:

David P. McKay and Richard Crawford, *William Billing of Boston: Eighteenth-Century Composer* (Princeton, N.J.: Princeton University Press, 1975);

Kenneth Silverman, *A Cultural History of the American Revolution* (New York: Columbia University Press, 1987).

ROBERT BOLLING

1738-1775
POET

Significance. Bolling was the most eminent Southern poet before the Revolution, and his writing and his life demonstrate some of the profound problems of cultural identity faced by even the wealthiest members of the colonial gentry. Like other sons of the Virginia gentry such as the playwright Robert Munford and the Patriot writer Robert Bland, he attended a prestigious school at Wakefield in England (1751–1755), where he acquired a thorough knowledge of the classics. Bolling's life and the role that literature played in it were typical of Virginia gentlemen of the colonial era, who cultivated hobbies of writing history, poetry, and belles lettres both as proof of

their cultivation and refinement and as a central occasion for friendship and sociability with their peers. Writing for Bolling was not a vocation but an amusing and improving diversion from his main duties as one of Virginia's major landholders, and the minor political roles he assumed after inheriting plantations upon his father's death in 1757. His poems were published in English journals and newspapers throughout the 1760s and celebrated by patriots as evidence that culture in America could be homegrown and not just imported.

Commentary. Bolling's earlier poetry imitated the Italian lyrics of Torquato Tasso, Ludovico Ariosto, Gabriello Chiabrera, and Pietro Metastasio. Among the British elite these poets represented a fashionable ideal of metropolitan taste, and they provided Bolling with a model of lyrical conventions and a perspective of aristocratic refinement from which to depict and lament colonial backwardness. "The Exile," for example, offers a comic account of the alienation that a colonial sophisticate experiences in comparing his primitive Virginia home to the true charms of English society. By the second half of the 1760s Bolling increasingly used the pages of the *Virginia Gazette* to comment in satirical verse on the political fortunes of his colony. His frustration with the colonial government and his outrage at the infringements on individual rights produced some of the most original verse of the colonial era. Bolling's poems about the Chiswell scandal of 1766, in which Loyalist and rebel factions first became apparent among the Virginia elite, nearly got him indicted for treason against the Crown. Two other poems, "Civil Dudgeon" and "A Canzonet," dealt with the Norfolk smallpox inoculation, which Bolling interpreted as a rehearsal of Whig and Tory conflicts that would erupt with the Revolution.

Marriage. Although Bolling became well known to his contemporaries through the poems he published in newspapers in England as well as in the colonies, he is probably better remembered now for private poetry, which then had few readers outside his closest friends but today demonstrates the profound conflicts colonial gentlemen felt as they sought to transcend their provincial origins. Virginia gentlemen such as Bolling sought to identify with the cosmopolitan habits of the English gentry, but the wealth needed for the consumption and genteel display lay beyond the grasp of all but the largest landowners and political powers, such as the Byrds. For young Virginia gentry such as Thomas Jefferson and Bolling the main avenue for social and economic mobility was marriage. Bolling's courtship of Anne Miller promised to unite him not only with wealth but also with an English aristocratic family of high standing; his rejection by her father, and the frequent failure of these courtships in general, made such ambitious colonial men aware of their cultural inadequacy in an especially humiliating way. Although Bolling did have later success in marrying a wealthy woman (who died a year later), the path toward the modest success he achieved as Virginia's foremost poet and a leading squire before his death in 1775 was difficult. His case in particular reveals a gap between the myth of a Virginia gentry class celebrated in the public writings by Bolling, Jefferson, and William Byrd II and the private realities of colonial resentments and self-hatred that lay behind it.

Hatred of Women. In "Neanthe" Bolling wrote a mock epic about about the courtship of a lustful, fat daughter of a newly rich gentlemen by two friends who are after her estate. One suitor kills the other; the survivor is hanged; and the woman, "Neanthe," hangs herself. Perhaps the most vicious satire in American literature, Bolling's poem shows young gentry reducing themselves to the most grotesque behavior out of their crude drives for sex and money. Like his collection of poems, writings, and often obscene drawings in "Hilarodia," "Neanthe" seethes with hatred of women. The disgusting object of this courtship has been interpreted as a symbol for the ideal of British, metropolitan gentility. Young gentlemen chased this ideal through rituals of courtship that were a sham disguise for the degrading pursuit of primitive desires. Bolling's writings suggest in particular how the seemingly unattainable standards of cosmopolitan culture inspired among ambitious colonial men a deeply felt but rarely expressed cynicism about their provincial status and desperation about their seeming inability to ever transcend it.

Sources:

Emory Elliot, ed., *Dictionary of Literary Biography*, volume 31, *American Colonial Writers, 1735-1781* (Columbia, S.C.: Bruccoli Clark / Detroit: Gale Research, 1984);

J. A. Leo Lemay, *Robert Bolling Woos Anne Miller* (Charlottesville: University Press of Virginia, 1990);

Kenneth Lockridge, "Colonial Self-Fashioning: Paradoxes and Pathologies in the Construction of Genteel Identity in Eighteenth-Century America," in *Through a Glass Darkly: Reflections on Personal Identity in Early America,* edited by Ronald Hoffman, Mechal Sobel, and Frederika Teute (Chapel Hill: University of North Carolina Press, 1997).

JOHN SINGLETON COPLEY

1738-1815
PAINTER

Early Years. Copley was born in 1738 to poor and uncultured parents who had emigrated from Ireland. Growing up in a house on Long Wharf in Boston, Copley was at one of the wealthiest centers of commercial trade in the colonies. After his father's death Copley's mother married Peter Pelham, a noted engraver who introduced Copley to the artistic culture of England and America. Copley's first paintings were mythological works such as *The Return of Neptune,* based on European prints that were consistent with Pelham's baroque tastes and English training. Pelham's more lasting influence was to teach Copley that the successful artist had to be an entrepreneur and, like the traders and artisans of Long Wharf, had to create a desire for his commodities amongst an expanding group of affluent, upwardly mobile merchant and professional class, for whom Copley painted more than 60 percent of his pictures. This small group dominated the social, political, and economic world of provincial Boston. In contrast to their forbears, who might have been content to save their money, this group avidly bought luxury goods that had no practical function but which expressed their cosmopolitan tastes and their aspiration to English gentility. Along with silversmiths such as Paul Revere, furniture makers and portrait painters sought to gratify this fad for English style in consumer goods. Portraits in particular offered a vehicle through which the provincial, newly rich bourgeois class could acquire an illusion of aristocratic character.

Success. Copley was so successful in appreciating the desires of his patrons and in fueling demand for his services that his portraits became major status symbols, the possession of which signaled one's membership in a cultural elite. Despite his own humble origins, Copley turned himself into a gentlemen, sharing the expensive tastes and the self-conscious Englishness of his patrons. In 1769 he married Susanna Farnham Clark, and with the largest annual income of any artist or artisan he was able to build a mansion on exclusive Beacon Hill. Perhaps because Copley was so savvy as an entrepreneur, seeking to give his customers exactly what they wanted, or because he shared their aristocratic ambitions, his portraits offer precise depictions of the materialistic values of his patrons. The lace on a dress, the glint of a button, the polish of a tabletop, the softness of the subject's hands, the shine of the sitter's hair: no detail is more important than another, or as his fellow American painter Benjamin West phrased it, the different parts were not subordinated to the face and hands of the sitter but instead competed with them for the viewer's interest. Objects and persons become interchangeable, fields of contrasting texture, color and light that draw the viewer's attention not to one central point of interest but all over the canvas.

England. Given the overwhelming importance of English taste as an aesthetic and cultural ideal for ambitious and genteel Americans in the late colonial era, it is not surprising that Copley, like Benjamin West, should have gone to Britain. Copley's ambition to master an English style of painting led him in 1765 to send a painting of his stepbrother Henry Pelham, *Boy with Squirrel,* to London for an exhibition at the Society of Artists. While this and later submissions were highly praised by critics and painters, the advice that they offered inevitably concluded that Copley needed to study in England to properly conform to English manner—in his case, to soften and polish the hard lines that now make his

American portraits so oddly striking in their sharp contrasts, minute details, and indivisible brush strokes. Another consideration influenced Copley's eventual move to England: even though he had cornered the portait market in America, he would always remain merely an artisan there, someone who worked with his hands. In Europe, however, as West demonstrated to his peers, an artist might attain the status of a gentleman. The hostilities that followed the Boston Tea Party made the city an unfriendly place for Copley's Loyalist patrons. A radical activist even defaced Copley's portrait of Gov. Francis Bernard during the Townshend duties crisis, cutting out the heart area of the governor; Copley repaired the damage, which did not endear him to the Patriots. Although Copley struggled to remain neutral in the political crisis, his art was rightly linked with Tory values of luxury, idleness, and self-gratification that seemed treasonous to the Republican campaign for frugality, industry, and sacrifice.

Exile. Copley went to London in November 1775, where he spent the rest of his life living in and working for polite society. Since no artist could attain true greatness by confining himself to portraits, Copley began painting large history scenes. In 1778 Copley exhibited *Watson and the Shark,* which won him membership in the prestigious Royal Academy and secured his reputation as an English painter. It shares a familiar, sharp realism of visual details and, like Copley's portrait of Paul Revere, shows a democratic interest in plebeian characters: it includes the first sympathetic depiction of a black man by an American artist. Without resorting to caricature Copley paints a heroic sailor standing heroically at the center of the canvas, staring in mute horror at the primal conflict between man and nature, a theme that would be taken up by later American writers such as Herman Melville, William Faulkner, Winslow Homer, and Ernest Hemingway. In its style and composition, however, it marked a major departure from Copley's American works. The triangular arrangement of figures and collision of horizontal and vertical movement, combined with subtler brushwork throughout, keeps the viewer's attention firmly on the dramatic event at hand. His next history painting, *Death of the Earl of Chatham* (1779–1781), was huge in both size and appeal: more than seven by ten feet, the canvas attacted twenty thousand people to a private exhibition.

Importance. While Benjamin West was more successful in his day, Copley has, with the judgment of hindsight, proved to be the most original painter of Revolutionary America. And although Copley moved to Great Britain at the age of thirty-three to complete his rise to stardom and finish his training as an artist, it is mostly the startling, brilliant portraits he did before leaving the colonies for which he is now remembered. Postwar national pride in all things American fueled the reputations of Copley and other expatriates and secured steady commissions from diplomats and other Americans travelling abroad. Copley's success, like that of West, in guiding his art and career towards the ideal of English taste and ambition had the ironic result of making the paintings of his last decades more conventional. It is in the practical, focused gaze of Copley's colonial faces, in the seductive textures of the material world itself in which individuals reinvent themselves, where the viewer confronts a peculiarly American personality staring back.

Sources:

Robert Hughes, *American Visions: The Epic History of Art in America* (New York: Knopf, 1997);

Jules D. Prown, *John Singleton Copley* (Cambridge, Mass.: Harvard University Press, 1966);

Carrie Rebora, Pault Staiti, Erica Hirschler, Theodore E. Stebbins Jr., and Carol Troyen, *John Singleton Copley in America* (New York: Harry Abrams, 1995);

Kenneth Silverman, *A Cultural History of the American Revolution* (New York: Columbia University Press, 1987).

PHILLIS WHEATLEY

1754-1784
AFRICAN-AMERICAN POET

Beginnings. Born in West Africa, Wheatley was seized in 1761 and brought to the colonies when she was seven years old. Too young for the grueling labor of the West Indies or the southern colonies, where slave traders stopped first after the Atlantic crossing, she was brought to Boston. Phillis was purchased by John Wheatley, a well-known tailor, and his wife Susanna, who were looking for a domestic servant. Unlike the vast majority of Africans held in bondage in the colonies, Phillis was taught to read and write by the Wheatley family. While continuing in her domestic duties, she studied geography, history, astronomy, and Alexander Pope and John Milton as well as Virgil, Homer, Ovid, and other Greek and Latin classics. In 1767, at the age of thirteen, Phillis published her first poem in the *Newport Mercury,* "On Messrs. Hussey and Coffin." She achieved national and international attention when her elegy for the famed revival minister George Whitefield was published as a broadside and pamplet in Boston, Newport, and Philadelphia in 1770 and in London in 1771. With the help of Susanna Wheatley and the patronage of Selna Hastings, Countess of Huntingdon, a wealthy supporter of abolitionist and evangelical causes, Phillis traveled to England, where she met major dignitaries, including Benjamin Franklin.

Importance. In her day Wheatley was famous because she demonstrated that blacks could achieve intellectual and artistic distinction. As a representative of her race this poet was a powerful symbol for the abolitionist movement. For modern critics she occupies an important place at the beginning of a distinctive African American literary tradition. When her collection *Poems on Various Subjects, Religious and Moral* was published in London in

1773, it revealed a writer of remarkable breadth and so-phistication. The volume included Christian elegies, an original translation of Ovid from the Latin, Biblical paraphrases, and poems on nature, memory, and imagi-nation, typically composed in iambic pentameter and he-roic couplets. In her best-known poem, "On Being Brought from Africa to America," Wheatley applied bib-lical imagery to the issue of slavery:

> 'Twas mercy brought me from my Pagan land,
> Taught my benighted soul to understand
> That there's a God, that there's a Saviour too:
> Once I redemption neither sought nor knew.
> Some view our sable race with scornful eye,
> "Their colour is a diabolic die."
> Remember, *Christians, Negroes,* black as *Cain,*
> May be refin'd, and join th'angelic train.

Her kidnaping from Africa brought her a salvation she had not even sought, but Wheatley must remind her Christian audience that blacks "May be refin'd, and join th'angelic train." In this and other poems as well as in some of the thirty letters published after her death, Wheatley commented on her unique situation as an edu-cated slave, but she understood her own identity less in terms of race than in religious and intellectual terms— she was a Christian and a civilized person of classical learning.

Later Life. In 1784 Wheatley published a sixty-four line poem in a pamphlet called *Liberty and Peace* in which she was the first writer to hail the new nation as Colum-bia, linking the colonies' triumph in the War for Inde-pendence with a struggle for spiritual freedom. Her pa-triotism and faith in America's future, however, was not justified by the response of colonial Americans to her work, who had difficulty seeing beyond Wheatley's color. She advertised in Boston for subscribers to her first volume of poems but met with no success. While *Poems on Various Subjects* in its London edition sold twelve hundred copies in four printings, it could not sell most of the first printing of the American edition. In 1779 and 1784 Wheatley's appeal for subscribers to an-other volume of poetry was rejected by Bostonians. The failure of Americans to support one of their most noted poets perhaps had much to do with the short and sad re-mainder of her life. As a domestic for the Wheatleys, Phillis had suffered few of the hardships of slavery and had been sheltered from the harsh realities faced by free blacks in the colonies. She was freed by the Wheatleys in 1774, a few months before Susanna's death, and in 1778 she married John Peters, a free black man whose desire to be a gentleman and a merchant found no better success than Phillis's artistic ambitions. The couple had three children, all of whom died in infancy, and then drifted into poverty. Phillis's death in Boston in 1784 became, among nineteenth-century Americans who celebrated her work, a lesson in racial injustice. As Margaretta Od-ell described it: "The woman who had stood honored and respected in the presence of the wise and good . . . was numbering the last hours of life in a state of the most ab-ject misery, surrounded by all the emblems of a squalid poverty!"

Sources:

Emory Elliot, ed., *Dictionary of Literary Biography*, volume 31, *Ameri-can Colonial Writers, 1735–1781* (Columbia, S.C.: Bruccoli Clark / Detroit: Gale Research, 1984);

William H. Robinson, *Phillis Wheatley and Her Writings* (New York: Garland, 1984).

PUBLICATIONS

William Billings, *The Singing Master's Assistant* (Boston: Printed by Draper & Folsom, 1778);

Jonathan Trumbull, *M'Fingal: A Modern Epic Poem. Canto First, or The Town-Meeting* (Philadelphia: Printed and sold by William & Thomas Bradford, 1776);

Trumbull, *M'Fingal: A Modern Epic Poem, in Four Cantos* (Hartford, Conn.: Hudson & Goodwin, 1782);

Phillis Wheatley, *An Elegiac Poem, on the Death of that Celebrated Divine, and Eminent Servant of Jesus Christ, the Reverend and Learned George Whitefield . . .* (Bos-ton: Printed and sold by Ezekiel Russell & John Boy-les, 1770);

Wheatley, *Poems on Various Subjects, Religious and Moral* (London: Printed for Archibald Bell and sold in Bos-ton by Cox & Berry, 1773).

CHAPTER THREE

BUSINESS AND THE ECONOMY

by ROWENA OLEGARIO

CONTENTS

Sidebars and tables are listed in italics.

1754

- A board of brokers is formed to supervise the financial activities at the London Coffee-House for Merchants and Traders in Philadelphia.

1756

- A stagecoach line begins operating between Philadelphia and New York City.
- Parliament allows duty-free imports of American iron into England.

1759

- Virginia forms a public corporation to encourage the growth of manufacturing.

1760

- Benjamin Franklin publishes *The Interests of Great Britain Considered*, arguing that colonial manufactures will not hurt the mother country.
- Boston, Providence, New York City, Philadelphia, Baltimore, and Charleston are connected by a rough road.

1761

- Boston merchants oppose in Massachusetts court the use of general warrants by English customs officials. These warrants allow the authorities to search anywhere and at any time for smuggled goods.
- The United Company of Spermaceti Candle Manufacturers of Providence and Newport is formed to fix prices, limit dealers, and ban new candle companies.

1762

- Anthracite coal is discovered in Pennsylvania.

1763

- Parliament reduces bounties on indigo.
- Chambers of commerce are established in New York and New Jersey.
- Boston forms the Society for Encouraging Trade and Commerce.
- In Lancaster, Pennsylvania, Henry Williams unsuccessfully attempts to navigate a steamboat on Conestoga Creek.
- The Proclamation of 1763 places the Indian trade under royal control and temporarily bans new settlements west of the Appalachian Mountains.

9 Sept. The English Crown grants George Washington and associates 2.5 million acres at the junction of the Ohio and Mississippi Rivers.

1764

- New York City businessmen and merchants form the Society for the Promotion of Arts, Agriculture, and Economy.
- Parliament bans the immigration of skilled workers to the colonies.
- German-born Heinrich Stiegel founds a glass factory in Pennsylvania and staffs it with foreign glassmakers.
- Peter Hasenclever starts two industrial complexes, including blast furnaces, forges, stamping mills, and grist and steel mills, in northern New Jersey.

5 Apr.   Parliament passes the Sugar Act.

19 Apr.   Parliament passes the Currency Act forbidding colonies, particularly Virginia, from issuing paper money.

May–June   Boston merchants and mechanics begin to boycott English luxury goods.

1765

- John Harmon manufactures the first chocolate in North America, in Dorchester Lower Mills, Massachusetts.

22 Mar.   Parliament passes the Stamp Act.

19 Oct.   The Stamp Act Congress in New York City resolves not to import goods that require payment of the stamp duty.

1766

- London merchants, fearful of losing business, petition Parliament to repeal the Stamp Act.
- The Flying Machine, a wagon running from Camden, New Jersey, to present-day Jersey City, offers passengers a service faster than any currently available.

18 Mar.   The Stamp Act is repealed, but Parliament's Declaratory Act affirms its right to make any law for the American colonies.

1767

29 June   The Townshend Revenue Act imposes taxes on tea, glass, paper, and dyestuffs.

- Public protest meetings in Massachusetts and Virginia result in nonimportation agreements.
- A committee is formed in New York City to develop native industries.

1768

- The proclamation line of 1763 is redrawn to accommodate land companies.
- Twenty journeymen tailors strike for higher wages in New York City.
- The New York City Chamber of Commerce is formed in Fraunces' Tavern.

10 June	John Hancock's *Liberty* is seized by customs officials for transporting illicit wine, but the authorities release it when a mob forms.
1 Aug.	Boston and New York merchants boycott English goods.

1769

- Heinrich Stiegel opens a second American glassmaking plant at Manheim, Pennsylvania; his name becomes identified with a type of American glassware.
- Anthracite coal is used for the first time in Wilkes-Barre, Pennsylvania.
- The Grand Ohio Company is formed in England to buy twenty million acres in the Ohio River valley for settlement.
- New Jersey grants the Hibernian Ironworks seven years' exemption from taxes.
- A guild of building trades workers is founded in New York City.
- The Boston Society for Encouraging Industry and Employing the Poor builds a spinning school.

Mar.	Philadelphia and Baltimore merchants join the nonimportation association.

1770

31 Jan.	Five hundred Boston women agree to support a boycott of tea.
12 Apr.	Parliament repeals the Townshend duties but retains the tax on tea. In response the colonies lift their embargo of British goods except tea.

1772

July	A crisis in the English banking system reduces the credit available to colonial merchants, forcing them to sell their inventories at low prices.

1773

- Tailors in Philadelphia form a company to fix prices and limit journeymen's wages.
- Phillip Mazzei of Virginia imports workers and materials from Italy to start silk production.

27 Apr.	Parliament passes the Tea Act to save the British East India Company from bankruptcy. The company's resulting monopoly puts American tea merchants out of business.
16 Dec.	The Boston Tea Party occurs.

1774

- Parliament bans exports of textile machinery, including plans and models, to the American colonies; additional acts are passed in 1781 and 1782.

- The Transylvania Company is formed by land speculators in Kentucky. The Illinois and Wabash Land companies are formed to buy tracts of western territory.

19 Apr. Edmund Burke writes *On American Taxation.*

20 Oct. The Continental Association, a committee of the Continental Congress, bars the importation of British goods.

25 Oct. Fifty-one women in Edenton, North Carolina, sign an antitea declaration.

1775

- The English Board of Trade approves the Vandalia Company's request to buy 2.4 million acres of land in eastern Kentucky. (Benjamin Franklin is among the members of the company.)

- Samuel Wetherill starts a cloth factory with spinning jennies in Philadelphia.

20 Feb. The first joint-stock manufacturing company, the American Manufactory of Woolens, Linens, and Cottons, is established. Shares of the company sell at ten pounds apiece.

10 Mar. Daniel Boone begins blazing the Wilderness Road westward from Virginia's Shenandoah Valley. It was improved for wagon traffic in 1795.

22 Mar. Burke gives his *Speech on Conciliation with the Colonies* to Parliament.

May Congress establishes a postal system with Benjamin Franklin as postmaster.

15 July Congress authorizes foreign vessels to import essential war materials and to export American products.

19 Sept. Congress appoints a Secret Committee to make contracts for the purchase of foreign war supplies.

8 Nov. Congress empowers the Secret Committee to export American products to the West Indies in exchange for arms, ammunition, and saltpeter.

1776

- Congress institutes a national lottery.

- Paul Revere starts a gunpowder factory at Canton, Massachusetts.

- John Sears builds a saltworks on Cape Cod to evaporate salt from seawater.

- Adam Smith publishes *The Wealth of Nations.*

- Congress authorizes a loan of $5 million to finance the war.

6 Apr. Congress declares American ports open to all marine traffic except that from England.

26 Sept. Congress appoints commissioners to negotiate commercial treaties with European nations.

1777

- Oliver Evans invents a machine that improves the productivity of wool manufacturing.

- Congress establishes a cannon manufactory in Springfield, Massachusetts.

July   After declaring itself an independent state in January, Vermont adopts a constitution that abolishes slavery and adopts universal male suffrage without regard to property.

1778

- Congress prohibits the importation of slaves into the United States.

6 Feb.   A French-American commercial treaty is signed in Paris.

1779

- Peletiah Webster writes *Essay on Free Trade and Finance,* opposing regulations on prices and wages.

1780

25 Feb.   Congress requisitions the states to provide specific supplies to the Continental Army.

1 Mar.   Pennsylvania becomes the first state to abolish slavery. (Vermont does not join the Union until 1791.) All children born after the law's passage are free citizens.

18 Mar.   Congress passes an act to redeem Continental paper money at one-fortieth of the face value.

1781

- The first American pharmaceutical firm is founded.

- The Mutual Assurance Company is formed in Philadelphia to provide fire insurance on houses.

- Robert Morris and associates form the North American Land Company, the first American trust, to sell nearly six million acres of western lands in six states.

- France extends a large loan to the United States.

20 Feb.   Congress appoints Robert Morris as superintendent of finance.

31 Dec.   The Bank of North America is established by Congress.

1782

- The United States and the Netherlands sign a commercial treaty.

1783

3 Sept.   The Treaty of Paris is signed, ending the Revolutionary War.

•   Britain closes the West Indian trade to the United States but permits it to export manufactured goods to England.

•   The *Empress of China*, financed by Robert Morris and partners, is the first U.S. vessel to visit Canton, China.

Pennsylvania currency depicting the Philadelphia jail to discourage counterfeiters (Historical Society of Pennsylvania, Philadelphia)

OVERVIEW

Mercantilism and Empire. On the eve of the American Revolution, London was the metropolitan center of an empire that included Ireland, India, Ceylon (present-day Sri Lanka), the African Gold Coast (present-day Ghana), Newfoundland, Hudson Bay, Nova Scotia, Quebec, the thirteen American mainland colonies, east and west Florida, several Caribbean islands, and Belize in Central America. These colonies were important economically to Britain as sources of raw materials, foodstuffs, and semifinished goods. By the mid 1770s Britain imported more than £5 million worth of goods annually from its North American and West Indian colonies, which in turn served as markets for the processed and manufactured products that Britain exported. This arrangement—whereby colonies furnished resources to and markets for an imperial power—was part of a system known as mercantilism. People in the eighteenth century assumed that the world had a limited supply of wealth. The goal of nations, therefore, was to garner as much of this wealth as possible. They did this by selling their goods to other countries in exchange for gold and silver and then hoarding these precious metals. The imperial governments jealously protected their markets from foreign competitors and regulated the economic activities of their colonies. The most successful—Britain, France, Spain, and the Netherlands—reaped huge amounts of wealth and prestige. By the late eighteenth century mercantilism was being challenged within Britain itself. Scottish economist Adam Smith called such policies the "impertinent badges of slavery" and argued that free trade, rather than protected markets, would result in more wealth. Smith published his most important work, *The Wealth of Nations,* in 1776, the same year that the American revolutionary leaders signed the Declaration of Independence. Yet Smith was in the minority. Most people, including the colonists, continued to accept the necessity of regulated markets. Even Smith admitted that the colonies benefited from importing most of their manufactured goods from Britain. Because the colonies had relatively fewer workers, wages there were much higher. Manufactured goods would have cost more if they were made in the colonies rather than imported from the mother country.

Commercial Regulations. Beginning in 1660 Parliament passed a series of navigation acts to regulate the flow of goods from the British colonies. These regulations originally covered only a few products, most of them from the West Indies. But by the early eighteenth century the list of regulated (or enumerated) items included some goods produced by the American mainland colonies, including tar, pitch, turpentine, resin, hemp (all important to the British navy), tobacco, indigo, beaver skins, furs, and copper ore. By then Britain's imperial system had become a complicated series of commercial regulations. These specified the destination to which certain goods could be shipped, imposed tariffs in order to promote specific industries, and prohibited the colonists from engaging in industries that competed with ones that the British authorities were trying to protect. The Southern colonies were the most affected by the constraints because they produced a high portion of the important enumerated items, including rice, tobacco, and indigo. All tobacco and rice shipments were required to go to Britain, where English and Scottish merchants reexported up to 85 percent of the crops to buyers in Europe. If Southern planters had been allowed to send their crops directly to other European ports, their revenues from foreign trade would have been substantially higher. However, not all of the regulations hurt the colonists; even Southern planters benefited from them. Tobacco growers reaped huge rewards when British authorities gave them a monopoly of the market in Great Britain. Southerners who grew indigo, a plant used by the British textile industry to make dyes, also profited from the sixpence-per-pound bounty placed on this plant. (Bounties were financial rewards, that encouraged people to produce items that the British deemed important.) The imperial authorities prevented French, Dutch, and Spanish shippers from competing with the colonists. Thanks in part to this protection, shipbuilding became a tremendously profitable industry, especially in New England. So on balance, the commercial system that tied Great Britain to its American colonies worked well for both sides. The various regulations could be annoying, and the colonists protested against them from time to time. Yet overall the regulations affected only about 15 percent of all colonial goods and cost the colonists less than 3 percent of their total yearly income and sometimes the colonists simply ignored the regulations, or they negotiated with the customs officials to reduce the duties by a substantial amount. It was widely known, for example, that American merchants were smuggling large amounts of molasses from the West Indies. Molasses was used widely in the colonies for cooking and for brewing homemade beer. The Sugar Act of 1764, the first of the imperial decrees that attempted to reform the system, was designed in part to stop the colonists from avoiding customs duties.

Profitable Colonial Markets. By the 1770s the American mainland colonies had become important markets for British products. The statistics tell the story. In 1701 the American colonies (including the West Indies) absorbed only 10 percent of England's exports. By 1774 these colonies were buying more than 40 percent of all British-made goods, mostly textiles and metal hardware. America bought one-third of all West Indian refined sugar; one-half of all English exports of earthenware, ironware, copperware, glassware, and silk, cotton, and linen textiles; and between two-thirds and three-quarters of all British-exported iron nails, beaver hats, cordage, and Spanish woolen goods. American markets kept many Britons employed as farmers, artisans, merchants, sailors, dockworkers, shippers, carters, and warehouse men. The British pumped millions of pounds of capital into the colonies, particularly those south of Pennsylvania. Much of this investment was in the form of credit granted to colonial merchants and planters who bought British goods and sold them to colonial customers.

American Prosperity. American markets were so profitable because the standard of living in the colonies was high. Compared to most people in Europe, the colonists were able to meet their basic needs fairly easily, so they could afford to buy goods that were considered luxuries. In 1700 colonial output had been only about 4 percent as large as England's; by the 1760s the colonies' £35 million annual output was 40 percent as large as the mother country's. The population of the mainland colonies was one-third that of Britain and growing at a higher rate. Although the colonial population multiplied tenfold during the eighteenth century, average living standards remained high. During this period only two other countries, Britain and Holland, were able to maintain their living standards despite a rising population. The rate of population growth in the American colonies was much higher than in these two countries, so relatively speaking the American achievement was the most impressive of all. American prosperity was the result of several factors, including abundant land and resources, the resourcefulness of the people themselves, and the absence of widespread crop failures of the sort that sometimes devastated Europe. As the population increased, the colonists moved westward. Thanks to the fertility and availability of new land, they were able to export surplus foodstuffs such as wheat and rice to Europe. Observing these developments, optimistic thinkers such as Benjamin Franklin believed that in time the colonies would outstrip Britain in population. In fact Franklin's own city of Philadelphia, with about thirty thousand inhabitants in the 1770s, was already among the largest in the British Empire. The great British statesman Edmund Burke also recognized the colonies' growing economic strength. In a speech to Parliament in March 1775, Burke stated that all of England's increase "of seventeen hundred years" would be achieved "by America in the course of a single life!" He added that at "the beginning of the century some of these Colonies imported corn from the Mother Country," but for "some time past, the Old World has been fed from the New."

Wealth and Income. The typical laborer in Philadelphia had an annual income of about sixty pounds, only if he could find year-round work. This was just enough to keep a family of four decently housed, fed, clothed, warm in the winter, and able to meet their tax obligations of two to three pounds a year. Any disruption to the laborer's source of income could result in deprivation and hardship for his family. But even so, wages were relatively high in the colonies. Because labor was nearly always scarce, average wages were from 30 to 100 percent higher than those paid for similar work in Britain. The average annual income per free person was the equivalent of about $845 in 1980 prices, and tax burdens were much lower than those in England or in the late-twentieth-century United States. Per-capita wealth was also high: about £252 ($16,000 in 1980 dollars) for every free wealth holder in the colonies. (The figure is much lower if the calculation includes all colonists, not just the wealthy.) These figures may not sound like much, but they were higher than the per-capita income and wealth of China, India, and most of Africa during the late twentieth century. Colonial wealth was not evenly distributed, however. The top 20 percent of wealth holders held 68 percent of the colonies' total assets, and men owned about 90 percent. The few women who owned property nearly always inherited it from husbands or male family members, and few of these women owned land. Because there was such a high overseas demand for their staple crops, the Southern colonies possessed the largest share of per-capita wealth and income even when we exclude the wealth held in slaves and their contribution to income. The Middle colonies had the next highest share and New England the lowest. A high proportion of individuals who may be termed the "super-rich"—those who made up the top 1 percent of wealth holders—lived in the South, and nearly all of them were planters. The average value of these individuals' estates was £2,646, or more than twice the value of the largest estates in the Northern colonies. (To put this in perspective remember that the per-capita wealth for all free wealth holders was only about £252.) South Carolina's peculiar demographic and economic characteristics made it the richest of all, at least from the point of view of its white inhabitants. Whites made up only 30 percent of the population, so when the colony's total wealth is devided by the small number of whites, the resulting figures are enormous. Not surprisingly, white South Carolinians had the highest standard of living among all the colonists.

Consumer Goods. By the late colonial period British Americans spent as much as one-fourth of their total income on imported products, mostly consumer goods. These included cloth, ceramics (dishes), cutlery, notions (buttons and other trimmings), spices, wine, tea, and coffee. Because Great Britain forbade the colonists from engaging in most manufacturing activities, America provided an important market for goods manufactured in the mother country. Great Britain's pioneering role in the Industrial Revolution was due in part to these healthy colonial markets. By the 1770s the northern English industrial towns of Manchester, Sheffield, Leeds, and Birmingham sent nearly one-half of their products to the American colonies. Newspapers in Philadelphia and other towns regularly advertised for sale thousands of different items, especially textiles and ceramic products. Costly imported silks and velvets filled the stores in the American port cities. Inexpensive goods such as cotton cloth became available in more sizes, colors, and patterns. These items reached even the farmers in rural and frontier areas supplied by colonial merchants and peddlers. Rural customers spent a large part of their income on consumer goods, especially cloth. It was not unusual for a farm family living outside of Philadelphia to spend twelve pounds per year on goods imported from Europe. This represented a substantial portion of the typical family's yearly cash income, which was anywhere from eight pounds to forty pounds a year. Poorer people also desired items such as store-bought dishes, cutlery, and linens. By the mid eighteenth century these people were even drinking tea and doing it out of more-elaborate tea services. Previously the practice of drinking tea was confined to wealthier households. Some writers became concerned by this demand for what they considered luxuries. Newspaper articles and sermons warned against the effects that so many luxury goods would have on society. But they could not stop the flood of goods. Between 1720 and 1770 the amount of imports per person in the colonies rose by about 50 percent. Imported goods were so much a part of daily life that they became the focus of the colonists' early acts of resistance. Beginning in 1764 many colonists participated in nonimportation and nonconsumption agreements in order to pressure Britain to give in to their demands. Many patriotic colonists began to wear homespun instead of the fancier cloth made in British factories. In 1773 a group of colonists dumped tea into Boston harbor to protest the tax on this popular beverage.

Economic Diversity. Part of the colonial economy's strength lay in its diversity. Each region specialized in particular products and services for export abroad and to the other colonies. Within each region the local economies were further diversified. Instead of just farming, the colonists were able to engage in different kinds of work. They could do this because the population increased so rapidly, creating larger markets for more and different kinds of goods and services. The economy was broadly divided into three regions: New England, the Middle colonies, and the Southern colonies. New England—Massachusetts, New Hampshire, Connecticut, and Rhode Island— produced lumber, ships, fish, furs, rum, whale products, and potash, a forest product used in making soap and candles. New England also excelled in services such as shipping. The region bought many British goods, but in 1769 only about one-third of its overall foreign trade was with Britain itself. The rest was conducted directly with the West Indies, southern Europe, and to a much lesser extent Africa. The Middle colonies of New York, New Jersey, Pennsylvania, and Delaware produced grains such as wheat, rye, oats, and barley. These colonies exported large quantities of flour and bread mostly to the West Indies and southern Europe. By 1770 the Middle colonies handled nearly one-quarter of the colonies' foreign trade. Its foremost city, Philadelphia, became the colonies' largest and among the most populous city in the entire British Empire. From the British point of view the Southern colonies of Maryland, Virginia, North and South Carolina, and Georgia best fulfilled the mercantilist ideal. They provided British industry with raw materials and imported the manufactured goods that Britain produced. And, unlike the other two regions, the Southern colonies traded mostly with Britain itself. Virginia and Maryland produced the tobacco that British merchants sold to European customers. South Carolina exported large amounts of rice and indigo, nearly all of it through Charleston. That city became the most important commercial center in the South. But, unlike the merchants in Northern ports, Charleston's had limited clout. British representatives of firms based in London and Liverpool handled nearly all of South Carolina's trade in rice and indigo.

Trade and Society. The colonists exported only 9 to 12 percent of what they produced. They themselves consumed the rest, or about 90 percent of the total. However, overseas trade had social and political consequences for the colonies far in excess of what these numbers indicate. Although typical colonial farmers and artisans may not have felt the effects of foreign trade too greatly, their societies were decidedly shaped by it. For example, the huge overseas demand for rice, indigo, and tobacco spurred the spread of slavery from the West Indies into the Southern colonies. Had it not been for the immense profitability of these exportable staple crops and the South's heavy dependence on slave labor in order to produce them, the region would probably not have developed its peculiar economy and culture. Foreign trade also brought about the existence of particular economic elites. Because the social structure of the American colonies was looser than Great Britain's, foreign trade became an important avenue to power in colonial life. The urban merchants and Southern planters who were the most dependent on foreign trade for their livelihoods—men such as Boston merchant John Hancock and South Carolina planter Henry Laurens—were among the colonies' richest individuals. They also made up a disproportionately large part of the colonies' politicians. In the mid eighteenth century fully one-half the members of the Massachusetts lower assembly were merchants. Yet the merchants did not form a stable "class." Because fortunes in the colonies could be made and lost quickly, the men in power changed too. Political leadership, like business fortunes, was much more fluid than was the case in Britain and Europe.

New Commercial Regulations. The new regulations imposed by the British authorities beginning in 1763 had significant economic consequences for some segments of the colonial population. The Proclamation of 1763, the first of the new imperial regulations, prohibited people from purchasing Indian lands west of the Appalachians. The act angered frontier farmers, colonies with claims on western lands, and speculators such as George Washington. The Sugar Act of 1764, with its new regulations, customs duties, and tightened enforcement, made overseas trading more complicated and imperiled the colonies' trade with the West Indies. The Currency Act of 1764 declared colonial paper money illegal for paying public and private debts, a move that threatened to disrupt the colonial economy. In 1767–1768 the British created a board of customs and three new vice-admiralty courts in Boston, Philadelphia, and Charleston. These new bodies had the job of tightening up the customs service and increasing revenues for the British Treasury, objectives that they pursued with more zeal than Americans were used to. As Parliament passed these and various other new regulations—among them the Stamp Act (1765), the Townshend duties (1767), and the Tea Act (1773)—the colonists wondered where the British authorities would draw the line. Would Parliament eventually destroy the trading patterns that had evolved over the course of nearly a century and had brought the colonists so much prosperity? The colonials were further disturbed by the behavior of some British merchants who successfully petitioned Parliament to keep colonial merchants out of certain areas of the imperial trade. These perceived abuses and the fears of a British conspiracy to reduce them to "slavery" persuaded many colonists that they would be better off outside of the British Empire.

Conclusion. The American Revolution dismantled the imperial structures that had existed for more than a century and a half. After the Declaration of Independence most American merchants no longer considered themselves a part of Britain's hugely successful commercial empire. They paid a price for their resistance to British authority. Many merchants lost the highly profitable trade with Britain. But others benefited by gaining the freedom to trade with other countries, a privilege that had largely been denied to them during the colonial era. In the long run these new benefits were of great importance to the prosperity of the new American republic. But in the short run the price of independence—including a long and disruptive war—was steep. To achieve independence Americans fought an eight-year war with the world's richest nation. Why did Americans engage in revolution? And once they did, why did they continue fighting a costly war that disrupted the lives of so many for so long? The answers to these questions are not simple. A combination of reasons, many discussed in other chapters of this volume, contributed to the American determination to break free from the British imperial structure. It is clear, however, that economic factors played a decisive role. The colonists' relatively high standard of living and their bright economic prospects contributed to their self-confidence and convinced many that their future lay outside of the British Empire. Economic consideration played into the British calculations as well. Observing and perhaps envying the colonists' high standards of living, British administrators concluded that the colonists could afford to pay a larger share of the overall costs of administering and protecting them.

AGRICULTURE

An Agricultural Economy. America in the eighteenth century was an overwhelmingly agricultural economy. Most colonists spent the bulk of their working hours growing food plants and other crops, raising livestock, or hunting, fishing, fur trapping, and timbering. About 80 to 85 percent of colonial working men were farmers. Few white women worked in the fields to the same extent as men; only slave women did extensive agricultural work. Even in early colonial times a division of labor between the sexes emerged among whites, with men responsible for most agricultural production and women for domestic gardening, housekeeping, and some home manufactures. Colonial farms, at 75 to 125 acres, were much larger than those in Britain and Europe; however, few were fully cultivated. Instead the typical colonial farm household cultivated only a portion—about 15 to 35 acres—of its landholdings and consumed most of what it raised. Most farms did not specialize in particular crops, nor did farmers often purchase what they needed from the market. Instead they diversified their crops and devoted most of their resources to activities that met the needs of their own household. Because agriculture was seasonal, farmers also diversified their activities. They worked part-time as coopers (barrel makers), blacksmiths, millers, and in other artisinal or processing activities or gathered wood and other forest products for sale. By the end of the colonial period a higher proportion of farmers produced more than enough for their own needs, and they sold the surpluses in the market. How

A painting of a typical Northern farm in the mid eighteenth century (Abby Aldrich Rockefeller Folk Art Center, Williamsburg, Virginia)

Advertisement for an eighteenth-century English tobacco merchant

much they sold depended on where they lived. In the less fertile region of New England and in areas far from commercial centers and good transportation, farmers produced less for the market. But in areas where the land was fertile or that were close to an active commercial center, farmers sold their surplus in the market to a greater extent. Those living in the Philadelphia hinterlands at times sold nearly half of what they produced. Wheat farmers in this area even hired extra hands during the harvest season. Virginia farmers sold about 15 percent of their corn and wheat.

Staple Crops. Although North American farmers were primarily concerned with feeding their own households, they still managed to export significant amounts of agricultural products. The most important of these staple crops were grown in the regions south of Pennsylvania: tobacco in the Chesapeake and rice and indigo in the lower South. Tobacco was cultivated by large planters who depended on slave labor, but smaller farmers also

grew the crop. Typically, these farm households provided all of their own labor and planted only three acres or so of tobacco. Even with such a small acreage, though, the average farm produced some twenty-four hundred pounds of tobacco per year. Members of the family grew the crop, cut it, hung the leaves in the barn to dry, and then sorted and packed the leaves for shipment to a warehouse downriver. After 1720 Chesapeake families earned about £10 to £20 annually ($650 to $1,300 in 1980 prices), or about 10 to 25 percent of their income, from tobacco. Beginning around 1740 Scottish tobacco merchants began paying farmers cash on the spot for their crop. The Scots opened stores for this purpose along the shores of the major rivers, mostly in Virginia. By the 1770s they were the most important middlemen between the Chesapeake farmers and the European markets. Tobacco dominated the economy of the Chesapeake throughout the colonial period, but its importance diminished somewhat in the first decades of the eighteenth century when the worldwide price of wheat rose relative to tobacco's. More Chesapeake farmers switched to growing foodstuffs for the domestic, southern European, and West Indian markets, and by 1770 these crops accounted for nearly 20 percent of the region's export earnings. With the rising importance of nontobacco crops the Chesapeake began to develop urban commercial centers similar to those in the North. Baltimore and Norfolk, Virginia, became more important commercial centers, and an extensive network of small backcountry towns emerged. The lower South's prosperity also rested on staple crops and was even more dependent on an exploitative system of slavery. Rice was the region's most important export crop, and it shaped the region's economy and social structure to an even greater extent than tobacco did the Chesapeake. Unlike tobacco, which was grown in small farm households and large plantations alike, rice tended to be grown only in large plantations using many slaves. Successful rice planters in South Carolina became extremely wealthy, and they dominated their societies to a greater degree than did the planters of the Chesapeake and upper South. The slave population was also proportionately larger in South Carolina than in any other colony.

Planters. In order to qualify as a successful planter a man had to accumulate about five hundred acres of land and twenty slaves. With these assets a planter did not need to do the hard physical work himself but could delegate it to his slaves and perhaps an overseer. However, relatively few individuals in the South managed to own any slaves at all. Those who did typically owned only a small number. Rather than a life of leisure, these small slaveholders continued to do manual labor, even at times working side by side in the field with their slaves. Unlike the great British landowners, even the largest colonial planters were roll-up-your-sleeves businessmen who were deeply involved in all aspects of managing their estates. They performed several diverse occupations connected to the business of growing their crops, including lending money and working as part-time lawyers. Because there were few urban areas in the South, planters frequently also functioned as merchants: they bought the crops grown by local farmers and supplied their communities with goods from overseas suppliers. Like Northerners, enterprising men in the South aimed to have enough property to become financially independent. Most set their sights on becoming planters because such men occupied the highest positions in the Southern social structure. They were among the richest men in the colonies and made up a large portion of the top 1 percent of all wealth holders. Even successful merchants such as South Carolina's Henry Laurens chose to become planters after they had accumulated enough capital from trade.

Conservative Practices. Colonial farmers appeared wasteful, inefficient, and slovenly compared to their British counterparts. The Americans did not place a high premium on innovation, nor did they try hard to increase the productivity of their land and equipment. Sometimes the introduction of a new seed type quickly resulted in more and better crops, but improvements overall were gradual: the average output per farm increased by only about 7 percent between the first and third quarters of the eighteenth century. The New England agricultural writer Samuel Deane observed in 1790 that American farmers "usually give themselves little or no trouble in . . . examining their methods of agriculture, which have been handed down from father to son, from time immemorial." The farmers' behavior was probably not the result of laziness. Instead it was a reasonable response to American circumstances. In an environment where land was plentiful and cheap but labor and capital were scarce and expensive, there was little incentive to increase the land's productivity. As Thomas Jefferson explained: "We can buy an acre of new land cheaper than we can manure an old acre." The Americans' conservative practices were a prudent response to risk. Markets for most farm products were small; transportation was inadequate; and prices fluctuated too much. Because elaborate government welfare and subsidy programs did not exist, farmers could not afford to risk their whole crop by experimenting with newfangled methods. Instead they diversified their crops and livestock and engaged in a variety of activities. These practices spread the risk and distributed work requirements more evenly throughout the year. A few farmers such as Jefferson experimented with new techniques, but they tended to be well-to-do men who pursued innovations as a hobby. Gentlemen farmers founded the country's first agricultural societies, including the Philadelphia Society for Promoting Agriculture in 1785. Similar organizations were founded in South Carolina, Maryland, and New Jersey at about the same time. These societies did not immediately affect farming practices in the United States, where productivity gains continued to be small until the nineteenth century.

Millers. Milling was an extension of the colonists' heavy focus on agricultural products. Crude gristmills that ground wheat into flour and corn into meal could be found everywhere in the colonies throughout the eighteenth century. Eventually specialized milling firms using more-advanced technologies emerged to take advantage of the increased scale of agricultural commodities, especially those that were bound for overseas markets. These firms ground the farmers' grain and corn in exchange for a portion of the milled products, which the millers then sold either locally or overseas. Because of their contact with local and outside markets, some millers became merchants, and vice versa. A few opened small general stores that sold their surplus grain, flour, and meal to the local population. These merchant-millers became conduits of information about the local and overseas market prices for farmers' products. Until about the middle of the eighteenth century, mills were small operations that were run by water or animal power. Just before the Revolution, however, larger dams and canals were built that improved the application of water power along the Delaware River and Chesapeake Bay. The mills in these areas became among the most advanced in the world, capable of grinding one hundred bushels of corn or wheat a day. The largest of these could turn out about seventy-five thousand bushels annually. An entrepreneurial miller, Oliver Evans, invented a process that allowed him to process grain on a continuous basis. He opened his mill in 1782. With only six workers Evans was soon able to produce one hundred thousand bushels of grain a year. Mills such as Evans's became the basis for industrialization in the United States, a process that accelerated in the first decades of the next century.

Sources:

Percy W. Bidwell and John I. Falconer, *History of Agriculture in the Northern United States, 1620–1860* (Washington, D.C.: Carnegie Institution of Washington, 1925);

Lewis C. Gray, *History of Agriculture in the Southern United States to 1860*, 2 volumes (Washington, D.C.: Carnegie Institution of Washington, 1933);

John J. McCusker and Russell R. Menard, *The Economy of British America, 1607–1789* (Chapel Hill: University of North Carolina Press, 1985);

Edwin J. Perkins, *The Economy of Colonial America* (New York: Columbia University Press, 1980).

BUSINESS STRUCTURES

Small Scale. The corporate structure, which became tremendously popular in the nineteenth century, separates a business from its owners so that it can go on even when owners die or sell their shares. In the eighteenth century, however, few businesses continued to exist separately from the people who owned and operated them. Some partnerships lasted only as long as a particular venture, and merchants could belong to several partnerships simultaneously. These were fairly easy to form and manage because all businesses were small in scale, and they were organized simply. Even the largest had only a few employees. In addition to the owner himself there were a few clerks and perhaps an apprentice or two. There was no need for the sophisticated systems that characterize modern business corporations. Bookkeeping was simple and was done by the owners or their clerks. Nor was there much need for business service providers, other than some lawyers and a few insurance associations. So although colonial merchants performed a wide array of activities, they did not work too hard by modern standards. Letters were the primary form of communication, but merchants wrote only a few of these a week. And although large-scale importers dealt with many different customers, they usually had a core group of customers numbering only between ten and forty. In the countryside, stores handled fewer than twenty sales per day, and most of these were for only a few items.

Importance of Trust. The businesses of the period were frequently owned and operated by people who were related by blood or marriage. Family and religious connections were especially important for people who worked in long-distance trade. There were many risks to doing this type of business, and merchants had to be reasonably certain that their trading partners were reliable. Merchants extended large amounts of credit to each other, and creditors had to be confident that their debtors would pay bills when they came due. They had to be sure that distant merchants would not shortchange them or adulterate the merchandise. Although standards for measurement and quality could be enforced among people living in the same town or village, there were no mechanisms for doing so among merchants living in different places. Terms such as *hogshead, barrel,* and *bale* had various meanings depending on the country or port. Merchants also had to be confident that their trading partners would do a good job in packing and handling the merchandise so that breakage and loss were kept to a minimum. Because merchants could seldom accompany their cargoes to distant ports, they relied on trusted agents or ship captains to dispose of the goods for them. These individuals worked on a commission basis, earning between 3 to 10 percent of the total profit. Commission agents had autonomy to make decisions because prices in faraway ports could rise or drop unexpectedly, and slow communication prevented these agents from checking with their clients before responding to sudden developments.

Apprenticeships. The apprenticeship system was another way of cultivating trusting relationships. Several revolutionary leaders served as apprentices in their youth. For example, as a young man on the Caribbean island of Nevis, Alexander Hamilton, who later became the country's first secretary of the Treasury, was apprenticed to Nicholas Cruger, who ran a general store. Apprentices often were related to the merchants for whom they worked or were recommended by someone the merchant knew. The young men lived in the merchants' homes and became an extension of their families. Apprentices learned how to write business letters, maintain accounts, keep the workplace tidy, and a variety of other routine tasks. When the apprentice was ready, the merchant entrusted him with more responsibility, such as accompanying a cargo to its destination and selling the goods on behalf of his employer. The most able apprentices accumulated enough capital to set up business for themselves. Some of them became junior partners of their firm, eventually taking over when the senior partner retired. A few spent time in distant ports as resident agents for their firms before returning home to set up their own businesses.

The Quaker Network. Quakers, or the Society of Friends, as they called themselves, became successful overseas traders because they could rely on fellow members of their sect to transact business for them. The Quakers had established Pennsylvania in 1681–1682, and they dominated Philadelphia's economic life until the Revolution. The Society of Friends had a strong tradition of mutual aid and community as well as a shared

A British depiction of industrious colonials (Granger Collection, New York City)

sense of being a "peculiar people" who were different from their non-Quaker neighbors. So it was only natural for Quakers to rely on one another in their business dealings and to set up businesses with relatives and other members of their sect. Quaker merchants frequently combined trading voyages with religious visits to other communities of the Society of Friends. They developed commercial, religious, family, and personal relationships throughout the entire north Atlantic trading economy that stretched from Nova Scotia in the north to Curacao in the Caribbean and east to the European cities of Hamburg and Lisbon. In London the Philadelphia Friends dealt almost exclusively with fellow Quakers. Some of the most prominent Quaker merchants in the Atlantic trading community were related by marriage to leading Quaker families in Philadelphia. Among these were the Hills in Madeira, Portugal, the Lloyds in London, the Callenders in Barbados, the Wantons in Newport, and the Franklins in New York. The Society of Friends became less prominent in the merchant community after the Revolution. But for nearly a century their far-flung business networks allowed Philadelphia Quakers to conduct trade with greater confidence, and this gave them a competitive advantage over other colonial merchants.

Risk and Insurance. Another way to decrease the risks in overseas trade was to spread it among several partners, each of whom took a fractional interest in a ship or cargo. That way an accidental loss would not ruin any one merchant but would instead be shared among all of the partners. Insurance was yet another way of dealing with risk,

and it was already fairly common by the end of the colonial period. Merchants could buy it from government-approved English firms or from fellow merchants, who usually formed a partnership for each separate policy. Merchants about to embark on a venture went to a broker, usually a fellow merchant, who wrote a policy and set a premium. The policy was then signed by other merchants who agreed to underwrite a portion of the venture. Rates varied depending on the circumstances. Shipping along the colonies' Atlantic coastline was deemed relatively safe, so premiums were only 1 or 2 percent of the value of the goods. In contrast, insurance for vessels involved in the African trade cost 8 or 9 percent, and premiums during wartime were even higher. In 1757 a group of Philadelphia merchants formed the colonies' first formal insurance association. Thomas Willing, who later became the first president of the Bank of North America, led the effort, and other merchants soon imitated it. By 1783 these associations supported a semimonthly paper reporting on insurance news. Yet most American merchants had limited resources, so they were unable to insure large ventures. It was only in 1792 that the Insurance Company of North America was incorporated in Philadelphia with a capitalization of $600,000.

Business and Government. The colonists did not accept the concept of laissez-faire, which held that businesses function best when left alone by the government. That idea became more popularly accepted only in the nineteenth century. Instead colonists expected governments to be involved in nearly all areas of private economic behavior. This mixed economy, as it would later be called, had a long history. The settlement of the colonies had been a mix of private initiative and public incentives. The British government gave trading monopolies and land grants to private investors, who then recruited settlers such as those who came on the *Mayflower*. Mercantilism, practiced by all of the great European powers, was also based on the idea that governments should direct the flow of trade and regulate the economic activities of colonies. Mercantilism operated through government regulations that by the mid eighteenth century controlled a wide array of colonial products. The provincial and municipal colonial governments also regulated economic activities. Responding to public demand, they established town markets and passed regulations that maintained the just price of certain goods. These governments guaranteed the right of people to make contracts with each other, granted licenses to shopkeepers and peddlers, administered land sales, operated schools and land banks, and printed money. They taxed their residents to pay for roads, bridges, and wharves or required able-bodied men to help build them. In this way colonial governments helped to increase trade by linking farms, villages, and towns. Sometimes these governments even passed measures that discriminated against British merchants. For example, Virginia passed a law that favored locally owned vessels despite the strong protest of British traders. The protection provided by the Virginia assembly encouraged colonial capital to stay in local hands.

Sources:

Arthur H. Cole, "The Tempo of Mercantile Life in Colonial America," *Business History Review*, 33 (1959): 277–299;

Robert A. East, *Business Enterprise in the American Revolutionary Era* (New York: Columbia University Press, 1938);

Frederick B. Tolles, *Meeting House and Counting House: The Quaker Merchants of Colonial Philadelphia, 1682–1763* (Chapel Hill: University of North Carolina Press, 1948).

MANUFACTURING AND PROCESSING

Restrictions on Manufacturing. The vast majority of colonists worked in the agricultural sector as farmers and planters, yet they were familiar with a wide array of manufactured goods. The colonists themselves had no large factories for manufacturing many of the products they used every day. British regulations forbade most manufactures in the colonies because the authorities wanted to prevent any competition with English industries. But there were other obstacles too, and in the end these probably were more significant. For one, manufacturing required a large labor force. Compared to agriculture, it also demanded a large amount of capital. Both of these factors of production, as economists call them, were relatively scarce and expensive in the colonies. Besides, the colonists could not protect their domestic industries by imposing tariffs on British goods, so the colonial-made products would have had to compete with affordable, well-made, and high-quality ones from Britain. Not surprisingly, most colonists concluded that it

was not worth the effort to manufacture such goods on a large scale.

Successes. Even so, there were some significant exceptions. Imperial authorities encouraged the colonists to produce iron although they were only allowed to produce the raw iron, not the finished goods. In 1645 John Winthrop Jr., the son of the governor of Massachusetts Bay, established the first iron furnace in Saugus, Massachusetts. His venture did not last, but many later ones did. By 1775 at least 82 furnaces and 175 forges operated in the colonies, mainly in Pennsylvania, Maryland, and New Jersey. The colonial iron industry was larger than that of England and Wales, and it accounted for a full 15 percent of the total world output. Shipbuilding was another manufacturing success story. The vast supply of timber available in the colonies made shipbuilding there relatively cheaper than in Europe. In the 1770s nearly half of the ships built in the colonies were sold to overseas buyers, sometimes as part of the cargo. Up to 10 percent of workers in Boston and Philadelphia were involved directly in shipbuilding. Colonial merchants also had some success in manufacturing consumer products. Among the most prominent were the four Brown brothers of Providence, Rhode Island. In the early 1760s the Browns produced high-quality spermaceti candles made from the oil of the sperm whale. The Browns packaged these candles in a distinctive box with their company's logo, one of the earliest examples of a recognizable brand in American history. Colonial manufacturers succeeded in establishing cottage industries—wherein goods are produced in households rather than factories—for earthenware, nails, footwear, and textiles. Women made a large proportion of the textile products, including table linens, blankets, undershirts, shawls, and hosiery. Their contribution was significant: even in the early nineteenth century, the total value of homemade cloth was ten times that of cloth manufactured outside the home.

Artisans. Most colonial manufacturing was not done in factories. Instead it was done primarily in small workshops or households by artisans, farmers, women, children, and slaves. The term *artisan* encompassed many occupations, including coopers, tailors, cordwainers (shoemakers), weavers, and silversmiths. Men who made their living primarily by doing artisinal work headed from 7 to 10 percent of all colonial households; most lived in villages and towns. They were self-employed, owned their own tools, did their own accounts, and worked at home or in small workshops attached to their homes. All of these shops produced goods in small quantities or made them to order for a few customers. Wives, children, and a few apprentices contributed to the artisan's work, and sometimes two or more artisans pooled their resources to form a joint workshop. Although few artisans became wealthy, most owned enough property to qualify as voters. Because of their numbers and their ability to influence the outcome of elections, colonial artisans played a larger social and political role than did

COLONIAL MANUFACTURED AND PROCESSED GOODS

Although the colonies depended on the mother country for many of their manufactured products, they engaged in a substantial amount of manufacturing and processing activities themselves. By the 1760s the colonial economy had become large and diversified.

Food and related products:
Wheat flour
Tobacco
Animal products:
Meatpacking
Leather goods:
Shoes
Whale products:
Lighting Oil
Candles
Fermented and distilled beverages
Refined sugar
Other food products

Textiles and textile products:
Woolen
Cotton
Linen
Other textile goods

Forest products:
Sawmill products
Casks and other wooden containers
Masts, spars, and other ship timbers
Pitch, tar, and turpentine
Furniture
Other forest products

Paper and printed materials:
Paper
Newspaper and other periodicals
Books
Other paper products

Chemicals and allied substances:
Industrial chemicals
Consumer chemicals:
Salt
Other chemical products

Stone, clay, and glass products:
Construction materials
Domestic utensils
Other stone, clay, and glass products

Metals:
Precious metals
Iron and steel products
Other metal products

Equipment and apparatus:
Machinery, agricultural and nonagricultural
Tools
Guns
Waterborne vessels
Land vehicles
Other equipment

Source: John J. McCusker and Russell R. Menard, *The Economy of British America, 1607–1789* (Chapel Hill: University of North Carolina Press, 1985), pp. 328–329.

---

their European counterparts. Disruptions in local politics during the Revolution gave artisans even greater opportunity to participate in the political process. They formed mechanics committees to discuss and act upon issues that were important to them. In Boston, New York, and Philadelphia artisans organized or joined with other patriots to force reluctant merchants to abide by nonimportation agreements.

Processing. Mills, distilleries, and refineries used some of the colonies' most advanced technologies to transform raw and semifinished products. Sawmills—the largest of them located in Pennsylvania, Delaware, and New Jersey—cut lumber into boards. Mills processed iron into the pigs and bars that were turned into finished goods by some colonial artisans but mostly shipped to Britain. Tanneries, as well as papermaking and textile establishments, also used mills extensively. Sometimes mills were clustered near sources of water power. Wilmington, Delaware, emerged as a milling center that by the 1790s processed large volumes of cloth, lumber, paper, snuff, cotton, and iron. Distilling and refining also were important processing activities. From the mid seventeenth century the colonists had distilled molasses imported from the West Indies into rum. Domestic rum was a cheaper alternative to imported rum and brandy, and colonial demand for it remained high over the next century and a half. In 1770 about 140 rum distilleries, most of them run by merchants in the northern port towns, were in operation. Colonial distilleries produced nearly five million gallons of rum that year, or about 60 percent of the 8.5 million that the mainland colonies consumed annually. The colonists also processed large amounts of another West Indian product: muscovado sugar, which they refined into the more costly white sugar that colonial consumers had come to prefer. The colonists used the sugar to sweeten their imported tea, coffee, and chocolate drinks. Some twenty-six sugar refineries were in operation in 1770, and they met about 75 percent of the rising domestic demand. Like the distilleries, most sugar refineries were run by Northern merchants as adjuncts to their West Indian importing business.

Self-Sufficiency. Beginning in the 1760s the colonists tried to decrease their dependence on Great Britain by becoming more self-sufficient in manufacturing. They formed various organizations for this purpose. After the Sugar Act was passed in 1764 New York established the Society for the Promotion of Arts, Agriculture, and Economy. The colonists' resolve intensified when Parliament imposed the Townshend duties in 1767. Colonial governments and eventually the Continental Congress began offering inducements to support native industry. These included bounties, loans, guaranteed markets at set prices, monopoly privileges, tax exemptions, and land grants. The Americans succeeded best in producing cloth, especially linens and woolens, made mostly by women working at home. In 1775 the United Company of Philadelphia for Promoting American Manufactures was formed to encourage textile production. Philadelphians established a manufactory that became among America's largest enterprises, eventually employing hundreds, perhaps even thousands, of women. The home manufacture of cloth became a celebrated activity during the early years of the Revolution, and spinning schools were established in cities and villages. In 1769 the women of Middletown, Massachusetts, wove 20,522 yards of cloth. Women in Lancaster, Pennsylvania, produced 35,000 yards. Spinning bees became popular, and entire communities sometimes turned out for these events. Ezra Stiles estimated that the spinning bee held at his house in 1769 drew some six hundred spectators. Newspapers cheered on these patriotic women by referring to them as the "Daughters of Liberty" and reporting on their achievements. At times the newspapers used harsher tactics to encourage production. One newspaper in 1774 lectured women to "cease trifling their time away [and] prudently employ it in learning the use of the spinning wheel." In the end the value of the formal spinning groups and spinning bees was more symbolic than real. Most did not even meet regularly. But they focused public attention on the importance of supporting native industry and allowed many women to make a political statement in support of the Revolution.

War Industries. The colonists tried to manufacture items other than cloth, but many of these could be produced only in households using inefficient tools and methods. Nevertheless several industries succeeded in becoming more permanently productive and efficient, especially when the colonies declared their independence and broke away from imperial restrictions. The war stimulated the domestic manufacturing sector as the demand for war matériel and other products that the colonists could no longer get directly from Britain increased. Armies on both sides bought locally produced items such as shoes—which became a major enterprise in Massachusetts and New Jersey—tents, clothing, and other military supplies. Great Britain prohibited the exportation of gunpowder, firearms, and other military stores, so the Americans had to produce these items locally. Maryland, located far from most of the fighting, became a center for gun making; Connecticut farmers produced saltpeter for gunpowder. In 1777 Congress established an armory in Springfield, Massachusetts. War supplies had to be transported, and this led to some permanent enhancements of the road network. The military demand for munitions stimulated the development of the iron and steel industries, and Americans erected new forges, mills, foundries, and shops. From 1775 to 1783 Pennsylvania alone built at least eleven new forges and furnaces. Along with the improvements in inland transportation the invigorated manufacturing sector allowed Pennsylvanians to enlarge their markets in the South. The war also proved a boon for paper mills because the number of newspapers rose from only thirty-seven in 1776 to more than a hundred by 1789.

Sources:

Victor S. Clark, *History of Manufactures in the United States*, 3 volumes (Washington, D.C.: Carnegie Institution of Washington, 1929);

John J. McCusker and Russell R. Menard, *The Economy of British America, 1607–1789* (Chapel Hill: University of North Carolina Press, 1985);

Edwin J. Perkins, *The Economy of Colonial America* (New York: Columbia University Press, 1980).

MERCHANTS

Activities. In the large port cities of New York, Boston, and Philadelphia merchants were the individuals who imported or exported goods in bulk. Usually they also owned or rented a warehouse. In contrast, shopkeepers sold only a limited amount of goods at retail— that is, to ordinary customers rather than to other merchants. In areas outside of the port cities, however, *merchant* became a generic term that referred to any individual who bought and sold goods. By the time of the Revolution the largest of the mercantile businesses specialized in importing and wholesaling, but most merchants did not confine themselves to particular goods or functions. The colonial market was simply too small and scattered, and

The Society of Patriotic Ladies at Edenton, North Carolina, signing an agreement not to drink tea (engraving by Philip Dawe, 1775)

transportation and communication too primitive to allow for the kind of large-scale specialists that emerged in the nineteenth century. Instead most colonial merchants in the port cities made a living by diversifying their activities. They worked as middlemen, coordinating the buying and selling of goods between overseas suppliers and the numerous storekeepers and farmers who lived outside of the main cities. A few merchants also invested their excess capital in manufacturing. Others functioned as bankers during a time when the colonies lacked banks (except for land banks, discussed below). These merchants accepted deposits and honored checks drawn on these funds, just like modern banks do today. Some merchants made additional money by buying shares in ships and cargoes. Retail stores were also largely unspecialized. The older commercial centers had a few specialty stores for books, wine, medicine, tobacco, groceries, and millinery. However, most retail establishments, especially those in rural and frontier areas, were general stores that sold a wide variety of goods. Country storekeepers became important figures in their communities because they were the primary source for goods and information about the outside world. They acted as middlemen, buying the farmers' surplus products and extending credit so that farmers could afford to buy supplies. In areas that were remote, small trading posts and a few peddlers supplied the inhabitants with the goods they needed.

She-Merchants. A few women participated in trade. In England some had done so since at least the four-

teenth century, and a small number even belonged to guilds. Most colonial businesswomen were widows who had taken over upon the death of their husbands or single women forced to support themselves and perhaps a few dependents. But working for pay was hardly typical for women, and operating as a merchant was even rarer. During the revolutionary era women made up less than 10 percent of all the traders in Boston. At most, only about 2 percent of New York's substantial merchants were women. One was Mary Alexander, who was born Mary Spratt in 1693. In 1711 she married merchant Samuel Provoost, and when he died in 1719, Mary took over his dry goods business. In 1721 she married James Alexander, a prominent attorney and member of the New York Council, with whom she had seven children in addition to the three that she had with her first husband. According to James Alexander, Mary did not let childbearing stop her from continuing her business; in fact she was back at the store the day after giving birth to one of her daughters, selling goods worth some thirty pounds. When James died in 1754, Mary was named the executrix of his estate. Yet no matter how large their businesses might be, female merchants rarely sought political clout. The New York Chamber of Commerce, founded in 1768, had no female members, and none seemed interested in joining.

Nonimportation Agreements. During the Revolution many merchants signed nonimportation agreements to force Britain into rescinding its new regulations. Some

Just prior to the War of Independence tobacco, grown in the Chesapeake and marketed in Europe by British merchants, was the most important of the British continental colonies' export crops. These colonies (including Newfoundland, the Bahamas, and Bermuda) also exported substantial amounts of foodstuffs such as bread, flour, fish, rice, and wheat.

Export Commodity	Value (£ sterling)	Great Britain and Ireland %	Southern Europe %	W. Indies and Africa %
Tobacco*	£906,638	99.8%	0%	0.2%
Bread, flour	504,553	8.4	40.3	51.3
Fish	397.945	3.2	61.7	35.0
Rice*	340,693	48.9	24.0	27.1
Wheat, oats, maize	176,086	12.0	56.6	31.4
Timber	171,737	——	——	——
(wood products consisting of):				
Masts, yards, etc.*	16,630	99.9	0	0
Pine, etc. boards	58,618	14.8	1.1	84.0
Staves, heading	61,619	37.7	8.2	54.1
Furs, skins*	149,326	100.0	0	0
Indigo*	131,552	99.0	0	0
Whale oil, fins*	104,134	92.3	3.1	4.7
Horses, livestock	80,212	0	0	100.0
Iron*	70,250	96.6	0.1	3.3
Beef, pork	66,035	0	1.4	98.5
Potash, pearl ash*	64,661	100.0	0	0
Flaxseed	35,169	99.8	0.2	0
Tar, turpentine, etc	35,076	94.4	0	5.7
Other native products	122,094			
Re-exports	81,555			
TOTAL EXPORTS	£3,437,715			

* Enumerated products

Sources: Jacob M. Price, "The Transatlantic Economy," in *Colonial British America: Essays in the New History of the Early Modern Era,* edited by Jack P. Greene and J. R. Pole (Baltimore: Johns Hopkins University Press, 1984), p. 27;

U.S. Bureau of the Census, *Historical Statistics of the United States, Colonial Times to 1970,* 2 volumes (Washington, D.C.: U.S. Government Printing Office, 1975), 2:1,183–1,184.

joined voluntarily while others succumbed to pressure from patriots. The colonists first used nonimportation to protest the Sugar Act in 1764, and they turned to it again when the Townshend duties were passed in 1767. Although some merchants, especially those in Philadelphia, resisted these agreements, nearly every colony eventually signed them. Nonimportation affected merchants and artisans in opposite ways. Artisans benefited because the ban on British goods enlarged the market for domestic-made products. In contrast, the movement divided merchants. Those who dealt primarily in dry goods from Britain believed that they were being unfairly singled out. They complained that the boycotts left virtually unaffected the merchants who dealt in West Indian molasses and rum. Nonofficial bodies, called committees of inspection and headed by merchants, planters, and artisans, took on the responsibility of enforcing the agreements. Patriotic newspapers did their part by publishing the names of merchants who continued to import from British suppliers. Mobs sometimes exerted pressure by tarring and feathering those who refused to honor the agreements. A few merchants were driven out of town or had their warehouses damaged and looted. In 1769 an angry mob confronted the Boston shopkeepers Betsy and Anne Cuming for continuing to import British goods. "I told them we have never antred into eney agreement not to import for it was verry trifling owr Business," Betsy wrote to a friend. The committeemen threatened to publish the sisters' names in the newspaper, but Betsy claimed that the publicity only "Spirits up our Friends to Purchess from us." The Cumings could not long resist the Patriots' pressure, however, and the sisters immigrated to Nova Scotia when the British army evacuated Boston in 1776.

Consumer Boycotts. Because almost everyone was a consumer to some degree, many individuals and groups participated in the patriot cause by resolving not to consume British-made products. Merchants dealing in imported luxury items were hurt by these movements. Women vowed to stop serving tea and refrained from wearing clothes made with fabrics imported from Britain. A widely reprinted appeal that first appeared in 1767 urged them to "Wear none but your own country linen / Of economy boast. Let your pride be the most / To show cloaths of your make and spinning." College students also, participated in the boycotts. They abstained from drinking foreign wines, and the Harvard graduating class of 1770 wore black cloth that was manufactured entirely in America. At least one wedding received publicity because, as one newspaper reported, "the bride and two of her sisters appeared in very genteel-like gowns, and others of the family in handsome apparel, with sundry silk handkerchiefs, &c., entirely of their own manufacture." A few women's groups even formalized their agreements, to much fanfare. In February 1770 the *Boston Evening Post* reported that more than three hundred "Mistresses of Families" had vowed to "totally abstain" from serving tea, "Sickness excepted" as an expression of their desire to save the "Country from Ruin and Slavery." Another group in North Carolina signed an agreement in October 1774 proclaiming it their "duty" to do "every thing as far as lies in our power" to support the "publick good." Most of the shunned items were luxuries, not necessities. In addition to tea, wine, and fancy textiles patriotic Americans gave up their coaches and carriages, gold and silver buttons, diamonds, clocks, watches, and jewelry. Poor consumers had fewer opportunities to express their support of the Revolution through nonconsumption. Nevertheless these boycotts allowed participation in public affairs to those, especially women, who had few other channels for expressing their political sentiments.

Quartermasters and Commissary Officers. During the War of Independence merchants played the key role

THE COLONISTS' TRADING PARTNERS, 1768–1772

Mercantilism was a system of political economy wherein the imperial powers strictly regulated their colonies' trade. Britain provided the bulk of its colonies' imports (mostly manufactured products) and received more than half of their exports (mostly raw and semifinished goods.) The system helped to make Britain a pioneer of the Industrial Revolution and one of the world's richest nations.

Proportion imported from:

Great Britain	80 percent
West Indies	18
Southern Europe	2
Africa	1

Proportion exported to:

Great Britain	56 percent
West Indies	26
Southern Europe	18
Africa	less than 1

Source: James F. Shepherd and Gary M. Walton, *Shipping, Maritime Trade, and the Economic Development of North America* (Cambridge: Cambridge University Press, 1972), pp. 160–161.

in organizing supplies for the Continental Army. They filled nearly all of the posts within the new Congress's quartermaster and commissary departments. Thomas Mifflin of Pennsylvania was named the army's first quartermaster general in August 1775. In addition to procuring supplies his job included maintaining the roads and bridges traveled by the army, furnishing the wagons and boats they needed, and constructing camps. In 1776 the first chairman of the Secret Committee of Trade, responsible for purchasing foreign goods, was another prominent Philadelphia merchant—Robert Morris, who became superintendent of finance in 1781. Supplying the Continental Army was a public enterprise much larger than anything merchants had run before. The deputy quartermaster of Philadelphia, John Mitchell, supervised more than three hundred workers, a number three times the size of the largest businesses of the period. Procuring supplies also proved difficult because Congress made many bureaucratic and tactical blunders. For example, Congress set payment rates for some items below what the market was paying, so the procurement officials had a hard time finding people willing to sell to them. Knowing the army's predicament, speculators and other suppliers tried to force the government to pay the highest prices possible. The officials frequently could not wait for prices to drop but had to buy whatever was available. Merchants John Chaloner and James White, who bought supplies in Philadelphia after the British left the city in 1778, came to regard the speculators there as "monsters

An American teapot used to express defiance of imperial policy (Colonial Williamsburg Foundation, Williamsburg, Virginia)

in human shape" because of the excessive prices they charged. Yet despite their indispensable expertise, merchants working for Congress aroused public resentment because they mixed public obligations with their private business. Because Congress neither supervised them too closely nor required them to separate their public and private functions, merchants frequently used public funds and resources to their advantage. Many found it more convenient, or at least more profitable, to purchase supplies from their own firms or those of their partners: for example, about one-fourth of the Secret Committee's expenditures from 1775 to 1777 went to its chairman's firm, Willing and Morris. A scandalized Congress learned in 1779 that while the army had been short of supplies, public wagons had been transporting merchants' private goods to New York and New England. The commissions earned by quartermasters—1 percent of all monies spent—also infuriated some members of the public, with some justification. Nathanael Greene, who succeeded Thomas Mifflin as quartermaster general in March 1778, admitted that the profit he made from the post "is flattering to my fortune." Throughout the war many patriotic merchants performed their duties honorably and well, given the circumstances. However, most Americans distrusted them and believed that the merchants' corruption worsened wartime inflation. In 1780, alarmed by the amount of money that was being spent and the general demoralization of both the citizenry and the army, Congress decided to reorganize its departments. Characteristically it turned for help to a merchant, Robert Morris, who himself had frequently been charged with corruption during his stint as chairman of the Secret Committee of Trade.

Beneficiaries of War. During the war some merchants, including New York's James Beekman and some loyalist Quakers in Philadelphia, chose to withdraw from business and wait for peaceful times to return. But the war benefited others who took advantage of the peculiar opportunities it offered. The war's disruptions broke the hold of established merchants and allowed new ones to emerge. Traders and storekeepers who operated on only a small scale substantially enlarged their businesses when they became military contractors. Older laws that discouraged competition from smaller traders became unenforceable. For example, New York merchants in 1766 had sponsored legislation prohibiting peddlers, but the law disappeared during the war. Merchants doing business for the government benefited by having access to public resources. The war gave them new contacts in Europe, and some set up branch houses there or entered into partnership with Europeans. In 1781 Congress established the Bank of North America in Philadelphia to help finance the war, a move that led to a boom in that city. Entrepreneurs from Scotland, Ireland, and France immigrated to Philadelphia, and many of the city's resident merchants became wealthy. Baltimore and Alexandria, Virginia, served an area that was relatively untouched by fighting, and many of the region's merchants profited from the wheat and flour trade. New opportunities inspired some to take greater risks. Entrepreneurs traded with the enemy, whose goods fetched high prices among American consumers. Many other entrepreneurs profited handsomely from privateering. Still others speculated on the paper money printed by the states and Congress. In 1781 Maryland merchants sold goods to soldiers in exchange for currency and Western land patents, which the soldiers received as pay from the government. The merchants accepted these at only one-seventh their face value and then resold them later at a higher price. Of course, not all merchants were successful. The war disrupted the economy, causing a number of merchants to go out of business, retire, or see their capital shrink. On average, Philadelphia merchants' wealth grew more slowly during the period 1776 to 1789 than in the previous twenty years. Nevertheless the merchants who managed to prosper during the war years were in a good position to capitalize on the huge amount of commercial credit that flowed into America from Europe after the war ended.

Sources:

Thomas M. Doerflinger, *A Vigorous Spirit of Enterprise: Merchants and Economic Development in Revolutionary Philadelphia* (Chapel Hill: University of North Carolina Press, 1986);

E. James Ferguson, *The Power of the Purse: A History of American Public Finance, 1776–1790* (Chapel Hill: University of North Carolina Press, 1961);

Jean P. Jordan, "Women Merchants in Colonial New York," *New York History,* 58 (October 1977): 412–439.

PAYING FOR GOODS AND SERVICES

Business and Consumer Credit. In the colonies the shortage of specie (gold and silver coin) made credit an important means of paying for goods. About 80 percent of the goods purchased from Britain was bought on credit. Credit also functioned as a kind of seed capital: it allowed farmers to grow and harvest their products before selling them, a process that could take months and

An example of Continental currency (New York Public Library)

even years to complete. Local storekeepers extended up to nine months' worth of credit to farmers for seed and supplies. The storekeeper, in his turn, depended on about twelve months' credit from merchants in the large cities, who were also given credit by their British suppliers. Southern planters also relied on credit. They extended it to one another or obtained it from English and Scottish merchants. In the late colonial period the British merchants extended increasingly liberal credit terms to thirty-five thousand planters in Virginia alone. A Glasgow merchant operating in the Chesapeake in 1766 observed that young men in that area "must have some household furniture and working tools. With these, they are supplied upon Credit, by some Factor or Storekeeper." He concluded that credit was granted on the basis of the young men's "labor, industry and honesty" rather than on their "real property." Most of these accounts were for the relatively small amount of under £100, but collectively they totaled about £2 million worth of credit. The increased indebtedness of planters did not necessarily mean that they were in economic trouble. On the contrary, going into debt often meant that planters were optimistic about the economy and the future, so they borrowed to buy more land and slaves. Credit was a valuable asset in the developing colonial economy because it allowed individuals to do business across vast distances, from the British ports all the way to the most remote trading outpost on the frontier. But credit also made people extremely vulnerable to economic downturns. When prices for crops were good, everyone got paid quickly. But during a downturn, such as the one that hit tobacco prices during the early 1770s, the whole process slowed down. A lot of people were unable to pay their debts and became insolvent.

Paper Currency. People of the eighteenth century believed that specie was the safest and best form of money. Unfortunately the colonists' supply of specie tended to flow to Britain because of the huge amount of British-made goods that the colonies bought. In order to compensate for this loss and to pay for government expenses, most colonies printed their own paper money, especially during wartime. The paper money took the form of "bills of credit." Rather than levying additional taxes, which would have been unpopular with voters, the colonial governments simply issued these bills to pay for the supplies they bought. In effect the government borrowed from their suppliers by giving them a kind of IOU that circulated as paper money among the populace. The bills were later retired—that is, taken out of circulation—when the governments accepted them as payment for taxes. At a time when few colonists had much liquid wealth (specie), this method was often the only way that colonial governments could get people to pay for public expenditures. The paper money issued by colonial governments and land banks generally worked well, especially in the Middle colonies. Prior to the War of Independence the currencies usually held their value, and people used them as readily as they did specie. Many currencies even circulated outside of the colonies that issued them. But the paper money caused problems with Parliament. Colonial creditors and British traders complained whenever the bills of credit lost their value, as they sometimes did in New England and the Southern colonies. The Currency Act of 1751 ordered the New England colonies to retire their bills of credit within two years after they had been issued and prohibited the use of paper money in the settlement of private debts. In 1764 Parliament prohibited all of the colonies from using paper money to pay any kind of debt, public or private. Both acts caused great re-

COINS	Weights			Value	Lawfull Money
	OZ	dw	Gr	OLD TENOR	£ s
Guinea	0	5	9	16.10.0	28/
Half D.		2	16½	5..5	14/
Moidore		6	22	13..10	36/
Half D.		3	11	6.15	18/
Dubloon or Pistole Piece		17	8	33	88/
Half D.		8	16	16.10	44/
Pistole		4	8	8.5	22/
Half D.		2	4	4.2.6	11/
Double Joannes or £3 14 Sterl Piece		18	10	36	96/
Single Joannes or 36/ Sterl Piece		9	5	18	48/
Half D.		4	14½	9	24/
Quarter D.		2	7¼	4.10	12/

Silver Coins	Weights			Value
	oz	dw	Gr	£ s d
Eng Crown	0	19	8½	.2.10
Half Ditto		9	16¼	1.5
Dollar		17	12	.2.5
Half Ditto		8	18	1 2 6
Quarter D.		4	9	.11.3

oz	dw	Gr	GOLD p oz	SILVER p oz
1	0	0	£38.0.0	2.10.0
	10	0	19	1.5
	5	0	9.10	12.6
	2	0	3.16	5
	1	0	1.18	2.6
	0	12	19	1.3
	0	6	9.6	0.7½
	0	3	4.9	0.3¾
	0	1	1.7	0.1¼

NB 24 Grains is one penny wt 20 Penny wt one Ounce.

A table of exchange rates for colonial currency, circa 1775 (American Antiquarian Society, Worcester, Massachusetts)

sentment among the colonists, and they often broke the law. In 1773 Parliament relented and allowed colonial paper money to be used for paying taxes. A year later an estimated $12 million was in circulation throughout the colonies. Some colonists, including Benjamin Franklin, believed that plentiful paper money was good for the economy so long as it was carefully monitored by the colonial governments.

Other Ways to Pay. Merchants living far away from one another used an instrument called a "bill of exchange" to pay for goods. They used it instead of specie, which was in short supply and dangerous to transport. This method of payment had originated in the Middle Ages and was widely used by Venetian merchants. A bill of exchange was similar to a modern-day check except that it was used exclusively by merchants, and it was drawn on other merchants rather than on a bank. Each merchant who received a bill of exchange as payment for goods imposed a service fee for accepting it. In business parlance the bills of exchange made the value of the goods they represented liquid and therefore capable of being traded more easily and quickly. By the seventeenth

century the bills functioned as a kind of currency within the merchant community. Ordinary consumers also had other means of paying for goods whenever specie and paper money were in short supply. Storekeepers accepted all sorts of "country produce" as payment, and rural customers brought in eggs, chickens, wheat, corn, deerskins, furs, and butter (made mostly by the women of the house) to exchange for store-bought goods. Storekeepers sold the perishable items such as butter locally. They shipped the rest of the country produce to nearby cities, either for consumption there or for export overseas.

Land Banks. The colonists did not have banks in the modern sense. Theirs did not accept deposits from customers, clear checks, or buy and sell foreign currencies. Instead the colonial governments chartered banks that functioned essentially as loan offices. They were called land banks because land was used as collateral for the loans. This way the colonists used their most plentiful asset—land—as the basis for money and credit. In the eighteenth century every colony except Virginia had land banks that made loans in the form of bills of credit. People used these bills as a kind of paper money, in the same

WEALTH DISTRIBUTION: AVERAGE FOR ALL WEALTH HOLDERS, 1774

Free white colonists were well-off compared to their European counterparts. Probate records—lists of people's assets that were made upon their deaths—show that in 1774 the average wealth holder owned about £252 worth of assets. (Wealth holders made up about one-quarter of the total free population.) Land accounted for the largest portion of these people's assets, followed by slaves. Wealth was not evenly distributed. Then as now, the top 20 percent of wealth holders owned a disproportionately large share.

	All Colonies	New England	Middle Colonies	South
Average wealth	£252	£161	£189	£395
Distribution:				
Bottom 20%	0.8%	1.0%	1.2%	0.7%
Top 20%	67.3%	65.9%	52.7%	69.6%
Composition:				
Land	53.0%	71.4%	60.5%	45.9%
Slaves & servants	22.1%	0.5%	4.1%	33.6%
Livestock	9.2%	7.5%	11.3%	8.8%
Personal	6.7%	11.2%	8.4%	5.1%

Source: Alice H. Jones, *American Colonial Wealth: Documents and Methods*, 3 volumes (New York: Arno, 1978).

way that they used the bills issued by colonial governments. In the Middle colonies the loans issued by public land banks served as a substitute for taxes because the government received interest on the loans. Pennsylvania operated a land bank almost continuously after 1723. The land banks became popular with the colonists. According to John Adams the Currency Act of 1751, which prohibited private land banks in New England, "raised a greater ferment" in Massachusetts "than the Stamp-Act did." The first true commercial bank was established only in 1781 with the Bank of North America. Afterward other commercial banks appeared that bought—or "discounted"—commercial bills and notes from merchants and created deposits, similar to modern-day checking accounts, on which they could draw.

Sources:
Bray Hammond, *Banks and Politics in America from the Revolution to the Civil War* (Princeton, N.J.: Princeton University Press, 1957);

Jacob Price, *Capital and Credit in Birtish Overseas Trade: The View from the Chesapeake, 1700–1776* (Cambridge, Mass.: Harvard University Press, 1980).

SLAVERY

The Slave Trade. The enterprising spirit that was evident throughout the British Empire and that produced the high standard of living in the colonies also led to the horrifying trade in human beings. England became the most important slaving nation during the eighteenth century, establishing trading posts in Gambia and the lower Guinea coast in Africa. From there English merchants transported slaves to the cities and plantations of the Caribbean and mainland colonies. The Caribbean was by far the larger market for slaves, and by the late colonial period about 90 percent of the population there was black. A substantial proportion of the mainland colonies' population was also enslaved: about one in five during the 1770s. From 1761 to 1810 more than three hundred thousand slaves were imported into the colonies. An estimated 12 percent of those brought over by American traders did not survive the voyage. Even so, the slave population on the American mainland rose rapidly due as much to natural increase as to the trade itself. In South Carolina blacks outnumbered whites as early as 1708 and continued to do so throughout the eighteenth century. In the plantation districts along the colony's tidewater, blacks comprised nearly 90 percent of the population by 1740.

Colonial Participation. Colonial merchants participated in the slave trade, although on a much smaller scale than the British. With its excellent bay, tiny Rhode Island became the center of the North American trade. In 1764 the colony's merchants argued that poor farmlands left them no choice but to turn to slaving so that they could afford to buy British manufactured goods and food from the Middle and Southern colonies. Ships originating from Rhode Island eventually transported more than one hundred thousand Africans to the New World. The colony's trade was suspended when the British occupied the town of Newport during the Revolutionary War, but the trade thrived again after the war ended and continued until the slave trade was made illegal in 1808. New Yorkers and even some Quaker merchants also were active in the trade. Apart from the merchants of South Carolina, Southerners were much less so even though that region was most heavily dependent on slave labor. Many prominent colonial merchants who became strong supporters of the Revolution were directly or indirectly involved in the slave trade. Robert Morris, the "financier of the Revolution" and the founder of the Bank of North America, had participated in the trade during the 1760s. The revolutionary statesman Henry Laurens had been a prominent slave merchant in his native South Carolina.

Slave Labor. By 1770 slaves made up one-fifth of the colonial population and were the second-largest occupational group after farmers. Most slaves grew staple crops while others worked as house servants or did full- or part-time artisinal work. In 1780 four states—Virginia, South Carolina, North Carolina, and Maryland—held 85 percent of all the slaves on the mainland. New York,

A commemorative painting of the slave ship *Marie Séraphique* anchored off Haiti following a transatlantic voyage in 1772–1773 (Musee des Beaux Arts, Nantes)

whose metropolis was active in the slave trade, was fifth. It had the highest proportion of blacks—about 12 percent—of all the Northern states, and its slaves worked as house servants, in urban occupations, and on small farms scattered throughout the countryside. Slavery became much more deeply entrenched in the South because of the profitability and labor requirements of staple crops, especially tobacco and rice. Tobacco was grown extensively in the Chesapeake by both small farmers and large planters. The planters preferred to use slave labor because tobacco required only a few hours' work a day during most of the growing season; thus it would have been significantly more expensive to hire free white laborers, who often demanded a full day's pay. In contrast, wheat was labor-intensive only during the planting and harvest seasons, so it made sense to hire free laborers to work for several full days during those peak times. The differences in the two crops' growing requirements perhaps explain why tobacco, but not wheat, tended to rely on slave labor. In the lower South slavery became an even more important component of the economy. Rice was the region's

primary export crop, and it relied on slavery even more than did tobacco. The reasons for this appear to lie in the economies of scale—that is, the higher productivity of large plantations versus small farms—for this crop. Several groups of laborers working in one large plantation were able to cultivate rice more effectively than could small farm households working separately. This may explain why rice plantations tended to be large, with slave populations of fifty to one hundred. The unhealthy climate of the region also contributed to planters' heavy dependence on slaves, who seemed better able than their white masters to withstand the diseases associated with rice plantations. Unlike tobacco, rice was cultivated using the task system, whereby slaves were required to finish a prescribed amount of work per day, after which their time was essentially their own. According to a Scottish observer writing in 1773, lowcountry slaves generally were done with their assigned tasks "by one or two o'clock in the afternoon, and have the rest of the day for themselves, which they spend in working in their own private fields, consisting of 5 or 6 acres of ground, allowed them by their masters, for planting of rice, corn, potatoes, tobacco, &c. for their own use and profit, of which the industrious among them make a great deal." The task system suited white planters, who preferred not to have to supervise their slaves too closely and to spend a portion of the year in Charleston, where they could escape from the dullness and diseases of their plantations.

Effects of the Revolution. The slave trade became a casualty of the nonimportation agreements and the overall disruption in overseas trade. During the nonimportation movement of 1769 Virginia, North Carolina, and South Carolina prohibited the importation of slaves. In October 1774 the Continental Congress prohibited slaves from entering the United States and forbade any commercial dealings with nations that engaged in slave trading. The decision was met with strong objections by the merchants of Liverpool and Bristol and by the Board of Trade in London, which declared that Britain "cannot allow the colonists to check or discourage in any degree a traffic so beneficial to the nation." In 1776 Thomas Jefferson inserted a passage in the Declaration of Independence condemning the trade. The Continental Congress deleted it, but the passage had by then become unnecessary because most state constitutions had abolished the slave trade. The relative importance of slaves in the economy diminished as importations ceased and the British army freed thousands of Southern slaves. South Carolina, the state most dependent on slave labor, lost twenty-five thousand of its bondsmen during the war, while Virginia lost about thirty thousand. Once the war ended, however, the trade revived. Thousands of Africans were transported to the colonies between 1783 and 1787, the year the Constitution was written. By 1787 New England, the Middle states, and Maryland once again ceased importing slaves. South Carolina and Georgia, however, managed to insert a clause ensuring that the slave trade would remain open for at least twenty years. Those two states imported more than forty thousand African slaves before Congress made the trade illegal in 1808. Ironically slavery gained in strength after the trade was made illegal. The invention of the cotton gin in 1794 made the cotten crop immensely profitable and helped to entrench slavery even more deeply in the Southern economy throughout the first half of the nineteenth century.

Sources:

Philip D. Morgan, "Work and Culture: The Task System and the World of Lowcountry Blacks, 1700 to 1880," *William and Mary Quarterly*, 39 (1982): 563–599;

James A. Rawley, *The Transatlantic Slave Trade: A History* (New York: Norton, 1981).

WAR AND THE ECONOMY

War's Effects. The Revolutionary War did not significantly affect all Americans. Even at its peak in 1776, the American army numbered fewer than ninety thou-

---

SLAVE IMPORTS INTO BRITISH AMERICA AND THE UNITED STATES, 1626-1810

The number of Africans forcibly removed from their homeland during the four-hundred-year period of the Atlantic slave trade is a matter of debate. Many historians agree that approximately 10 million slaves were imported into the Americas and other parts of the Atlantic basin from 1451 to 1870, but some argue that the numbers were considerably higher. One historian made the following estimates of slave imports into British America and the United States from 1626 to just after the trade was made illegal in 1808:

Period	Barbados	Jamaica	Other British Caribbean	British N. America
1626–1650	18,700	------	2,000	1,600
1651–1675	51,100	8,000	10,100	3,900
1676–1700	64,700	77,100	32,000	23,000
1701–1720	67,800	53,500	8,800	19,800
1721–1740	55,300	90,100	8,800	50,400
1741–1760	57,300	120,200	22,000	100,400
1761–1780	49,300	149,600	67,000	85,800
1781–1810	22,700	248,900	76,300	91,600
Total	386,900	747,400	227,500	376,500

Source: James Rawley, *The Transatlantic Slave Trade: A History* (New York: Norton, 1981), p. 167.

sand men, or only about one-eighth of the total number of military-age men. In 1779 and 1780 the army shrank to about half that size. Many people felt no strong loyalty either to the patriotic or the British cause. Some were opportunistic, selling to whichever side happened to be buying or paying the best prices. The war did not affect the rate of population growth either. Owing to Americans' high rate of natural increase, the population grew by 83 percent between 1770 and 1790, a rate nearly identical to the one for the period 1750 to 1770. Nevertheless, the War of Independence was different from previous colonial wars, in which the colonists participated as British subjects. This time the Americans were fighting their old protector with the backing of a former enemy, France. Although France provided important support to the American cause, the French entered the war for their own, and not the Americans', benefit. The French were never as successful at defending their new ally as the British had been. These dramatically changed circumstances meant that the War of Independence disrupted the American economy more severely than had previous wars.

Overseas Trade. By January 1776, nine months after the fighting began, both Congress and Great Britain had prohibited all trade between the mother country and its former mainland colonies. The disruption of overseas trade had serious effects on the American economy. With independence, American merchants lost their large and lucrative markets in Great Britain and the Caribbean. They also forfeited the British bounties on goods that had made products such as indigo and naval stores so profitable. Overall earnings from the export sector fell dramatically, with the trade in foodstuffs and shipbuilding particularly hard hit. Although large quantities of American tobacco, flour, and a few other foodstuffs made it to foreign ports, the overall levels remained well below those of the early 1770s. Americans offset some of the losses in income by engaging in privateering, through loans and subsidies from European allies, especially France, and by selling goods and services to the British and French military. Despite these alternative sources, the disruption in overseas trade sharply curtailed the incomes of many Americans. They also had to get by with much smaller quantities of foreign-made goods and paid higher prices for them. Lower-quality textiles from France and Germany, for example, sold at double or triple the prices of prewar English imports. Recovery occurred slowly, and the American economy probably did not regain its former levels of income and wealth until the end of the eighteenth century. The level of deprivation varied throughout the course of the war because American policies and tactics went through several different stages. From late 1774 to April 1776 the colonies engaged in nonimportation agreements that resulted in serious shortages of imported goods. Congress allowed a limited amount of trade with foreign nations once fighting began in April 1775, and in April 1776 it removed all

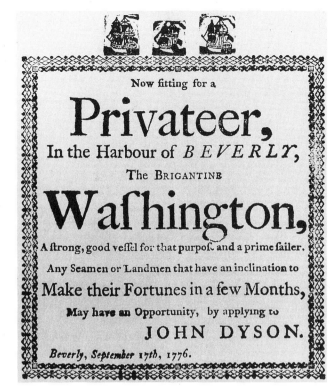

A Massachusetts broadside recruiting crew members on an American warship

restrictions on foreign trade. Until the middle of 1778 the British navy largely succeeded in blocking shipments from France and the West Indies. However, the situation for the Americans brightened from mid 1778 to early 1782, when the French, Spanish, and Dutch entered the war and the Royal Navy's attention shifted to the fighting itself. During this period Americans were able to obtain significant quantities of British-made goods from Dutch traders who ran the blockades. The Royal Navy could not mount an effective blockade because it did not have sufficient troops to occupy simultaneously the major ports of Halifax, Boston, Newport, New York, Philadelphia, Norfolk, and Charleston. Besides, the Americans' trading partners in Europe and in the French, Spanish, and Dutch West Indies were themselves either hostile or indifferent to Great Britain. In 1782 overseas trade suffered again, as the British turned their attention to intercepting American shipments. By then, however, the war had turned to favor the Americans, and shortages never again became severe.

Other Disruptions. Fighting occurred in many densely populated areas and interfered with farming and production. Warfare in frontier regions destroyed the Indian trade; maritime fighting weakened New England's commerce in fish; and ships and other peacetime resources were converted into war matériel. Southern farmers generally felt the effects more acutely than did their Northern brethren. During the 1781 campaign British soldiers destroyed thousands of hogsheads of Virginia tobacco and freed slaves in an attempt to disrupt

An engraving by Paul Revere of workers refining saltpeter used in the manufacture of gunpowder (*Royal American Magazine,* 1 August 1774)

the Southern economy. Virginia estimated that it lost thirty thousand slaves, and South Carolina claimed losses totaling twenty-five thousand. The supply of labor, already inadequate, shrank further as men were called into military service. Many American women were forced to take over the responsibilities of operating farms, businesses, and plantations from absent husbands, fathers, and brothers. "I find it necessary to be the directress of our husbandry," Abigail Adams wrote to her husband, John, who was frequently in Philadelphia and abroad during the war. "I hope in time to have the reputation of being as good a *farmeress* as my partner had of being a good statesman." The war also interfered with normal mercantile activities. Commercial credit from England and Europe, formerly generous, became more difficult to obtain. The war disrupted the court system, so debts became harder to collect. One Philadelphia merchant wrote in 1783 that the "Face of trade has greatly altered here in the Course of the war, many people are ruined & others next door to it." Ordinary people suffered when both British and American troops stripped the countryside of food and fuel. The Continental Army requisitioned goods from farmers and paid with currency whose value shrank dramatically and wreaked havoc on local economies. Despite the bravado of women such as Abigail Adams, many people found themselves in desperate straits. In 1777 a newspaper reported that twenty women in East Hartford, Connecticut, "attacked and carried without opposition from powder, law or conscience, Mr. Perkin's store, in which was lodged a quantity of sugar designed for the army of which they plundered and bore away in triumph 218 lb."

Privateering. Finding themselves shut out of the imperial trade, Americans turned to other means of securing income. They hired privateers, merchant-ship cap-tains who received a letter of marque from state or national authorities that allowed them to raid enemy shipping, strip the vessels of their cargo, and then sell the goods. Privateering became a major American enterprise during the war, and Britain lost some two thousand vessels (worth an estimated £18 million sterling) to these predators. Overall the privateers' successes surpassed those of the government's vessels and took a greater toll on the enemy. Privateers captured enemy ships off the coast of North America and in the Caribbean Sea. They preyed upon British shipping in the English Channel and in the waters between Britain and Ireland. Some privateers went as far as the Spanish port of Bilbao and the French coastal towns of Brest, Le Havre, Nantes, and Bordeaux. In addition to capturing enemy ships and diverting the British Navy away from military action, privateering stimulated the economy. Privateers made scarce imported goods available to American consumers, who eagerly bought them. The activity employed many commercial vessels that would otherwise have remained idle, and it helped to sustain the American shipbuilding industry. Privateering gave employment to seamen and fishermen, especially those in New England, whose trade had been disrupted by the war. In 1778 alone an estimated ten thousand men were employed in privateering, nearly as many as served in the army. Enterprising merchants, sea captains, and even entire towns made substantial profits from the activity. In a twelve-month period Providence, Rhode Island, earned about £300,000 from privateering and shipbuilding—about double the total value of the town's property in 1774. John Adams wrote in 1776 that "Thousands of schemes of privateering are afloat in American imaginations." Wealthy individuals treated it as a business investment. A group bought shares in a vessel, sometimes even trading the shares with each other much like stocks are traded today. The investors took on all the expenses and gave a bond to a Continental or state agent as assurance that they would capture only enemy ships. Nearly seventeen hundred of these bonds were issued during the war. Prominent Americans eagerly joined in these ventures. While serving as ambassador to France, Benjamin Franklin commissioned three raiders: the *Black Prince*, the *Black Princess*, and the *Fearnot*. Philadelphia merchant and congressional leader Robert Morris reportedly made between £300,000 and £400,000 by such ventures.

Sources:

Elizabeth Cometti, "Women in the American Revolution," in *Women and War*, volume 15 of *History of Women in the United States*, edited by Nancy F. Cott (Munich: K. G. Saur, 1993), pp. 3–20;

Robert Middlekauff, *The Glorious Cause: The American Revolution, 1763–1789* (New York: Oxford University Press, 1982);

Curtis P. Nettels, *The Emergence of a National Economy, 1775–1815* (New York: Holt, Rinehart & Winston, 1962);

Jacob M. Price, "Reflections on the Economy of Revolutionary America," in *The Economy of Early America: The Revolutionary Period, 1763–1790*, edited by Ronald Hoffman and others (Charlottesville: University Press of Virginia, 1988), pp. 303–322.

DEPRECIATION OF OLD CONTINENTAL CURRENCY

From January 1777 to April 1781 the value of the Continental currency dropped precipitously, especially after January 1779. At the beginning of this period, it cost $1.25 of Continental money to purchase $1.00 worth of specie (gold or silver coin). A little more than two years later, it took $167.50 of Continental money to purchase $1.00 worth of specie.

January 1777	1.25	October 1779	30.00
October 1777	3.00	January 1780	42.50
January 1778	4.00	October 1780	77.50
October 1778	5.00	January 1781	100.00
January 1779	8.00	April 1781	167.50

Source: E. James Ferguson, *The Power of the Purse* (Chapel Hill: University of North Carolina Press, 1961), p. 32.

WAR AND GOVERNMENT

Role of Government. The colonists were used to governments regulating their economic behavior. Even so, the government's presence in people's lives increased during the Revolution. In order to fight the war Congress and the new state governments intervened in the economy to a greater extent than they ever had previously. Although in the beginning the Continental Congress had little real power, it issued several resolutions. In 1777 Congress recommended that the state governments fix the value of most services and commodities. It resolved that the states should pass laws authorizing the seizure of goods for use by the Continental Army. Congress also suggested that the states control retailers by limiting their number and obliging them to obtain licenses. Beginning in 1780 a nearly bankrupt Congress turned to the states for specific supplies, to pay soldiers, and to take the severely depreciated currency out of circulation. The states responded with new laws governing taxation, land, business, labor, and the relationship between debtors and creditors. They confiscated items from their citizens in order to meet congressional requisitions. Congress's most significant measure was to issue paper currency that rapidly depreciated during the course of the war. Because the money was used so extensively by the populace, it had a greater impact on people's daily lives than did any other single act of the Continental Congress.

Supplying the Continental Army. The new Congress and the state governments mobilized the society's resources in order to supply the Continental Army. In doing so these governments profoundly affected local economies. Connecticut's requisition system was among the most intricate and successful. In July 1776 the state's governor and council of safety required Hartford's citizens to provide one thousand coats, one thousand vests, and sixteen hundred shirts. Smaller towns were also obliged to contribute on a proportionate basis. The council authorized the purchase of hats, blankets, shoes, tents, wooden bowls, canteens, and iron pots, and it placed an embargo on the export of cloth, tanned leather, and shoes. In 1777 the Connecticut government again required towns to supply additional items. The state did such a good job that Connecticut merchant Joseph Trumbull, Congress's first commissary general, relied mainly on his own state for supplies. In 1780 the near-bankrupt Congress decided to rely more heavily on the states. It requisitioned specific supplies and made the states responsible for paying the army. The states were themselves short of money, and they went into debt to pay their soldiers. Toward the end of the war the states resorted to collecting supplies forcibly from their citizens. Most states abandoned their procurement systems by 1781. Although many citizens were patriotic, they were reluctant to accept depreciating currency and worthless certificates as payment, and their state governments were equally reluctant to force them.

Impressments. Congress, the state governments, and the army also intervened in local economies by impressing, or confiscating, supplies. They used impressment as early as December 1776, and they continued to rely heavily on the practice, especially when the currency rapidly lost its value, beginning in 1779. From that time forward impressment was the primary means of support for the army's field operations. States passed laws empowering government agents to seize specific goods. New York, for example, stated that its citizens had to sell their surplus products to the army. The state declared that since farm-

STATE OF NEW-HAMPSHIRE.

In the HOUSE of REPRESENTATIVES,
July 3, 1781.

THE Committee to form a Table or Scale of Depreciation for this State, reported as their Opinion, That all Contracts previous to the last Day of January 1777, shall be considered as Silver and Gold; and all Contracts for Paper Money from the last Day of January 1777, to the last day of June 1781, to be computed in the following Manner.

	Continental Paper in 1777.		Continental Paper 1778		Continental Paper 1779.		Continental Paper 1780.		Continental Paper 1781.	
	£	£	£	£	£	£	£	£	£	£
January,	Equal.		325	100	742	100	2234	100	7500	100
February,	104	100	350	Ditto	868	Ditto	3322	Ditto	7500	Ditto
March,	106	Ditto	375	Ditto	1000	Ditto	3736	Ditto	7500	Ditto
April,	110	Ditto	400	Ditto	1104	Ditto	4000	Ditto	7500	Ditto
May,	114	Ditto	400	Ditto	1215	Ditto	4800	Ditto	7500	Ditto
June,	120	Ditto	400	Ditto	1342	Ditto	5700	Ditto	12000	Ditto
July,	125	Ditto	425	Ditto	1477	Ditto	6000	Ditto		
August,	150	Ditto	450	Ditto	1630	Ditto	6300	Ditto		
September,	175	Ditto	475	Ditto	1800	Ditto	6500	Ditto		
October,	275	Ditto	500	Ditto	2030	Ditto	6700	Ditto		
November,	300	Ditto	545	Ditto	2308	Ditto	7000	Ditto		
December,	310	Ditto	634	Ditto	2393	Ditto	7300	Ditto		

Which Report being read and considered, VOTED, That it be received and accepted.

Sent up for Concurrence.

JOHN LANGDON, Speaker.

In COUNCIL, the same Day read and concurred.

E. THOMPSON, Secretary.

Copy examined by

J. PEARSON, D. Secretary.

A colonial legislative report on the depreciation of Continental currency
(Library of Congress)

ers were withholding wheat from the market, the entire crop was subject to confiscation. Pennsylvania citizens became so disgruntled that they threatened not to plant any crops beyond what they themselves needed because the surplus would be confiscated anyway. Whenever possible, officials seized goods from Loyalists, people known to be hoarding goods, and speculators. But officials frequently had no choice but to impress the goods of Patriots too. At times the line between purchase and confiscation became vague. Government officials started out paying with paper currency, but eventually both the Continental agents and state officials relied more heavily on certificates or simply on impressment. Because they were poorly administered, the federal certificates that were issued before 1780 resulted in nearly total loss to those who received them. People who were forced to accept the certificates later experienced great difficulty in getting paid, and they received no interest. Meanwhile inflation steadily decreased the certificates' value. By 1781 most states had stopped impressing their citizens' products. The army continued doing so although George Washington was careful to use it only as a last resort.

Continental Currency. The state governments and Congress devised various ways to pay for the war. During the first five years issuing paper money was by far the government's most important tactic for raising revenue. Foreign loans from France and Holland and taxation of the American populace became more important only after 1780. Americans resorted first to paper money because of their long experience with it during the colonial period, when they had used bills of credit to finance the needs both of governments and business. Besides, they had no real alternatives. Until the Bank of North America began operation in January 1782, there were no banks in America that could have advanced large loans. Nor could Congress borrow from citizens, many of whom supported Britain or were suspicious of lending to a new government that was likely to renege on its financial obligations. From 1777 to 1780 the depreciating currencies allowed Congress and the states to pay for a war that would otherwise have been difficult to fund. As Benjamin Franklin remarked in 1779, the currency "is a wonderful Machine. It performs its Office when we issue it; it pays and clothes Troops, and provides Victuals and Ammunition; and when we are obliged to issue a Quantity excessive, it pays itself off by Depreciation." Franklin had a point: the high rate of depreciation meant that at the end of the war some $226 million worth of government-issued currency had shrunk to almost nothing. Had the government borrowed that amount, it would have been left with a huge debt. Instead citizens were stuck holding the worthless paper, so in effect the currency amounted to a tax on the American population.

Inflation. Nothing in their previous experience with paper money prepared Americans for the devastating effects of depreciation during the war, when hyperinflation rose to the highest level in all of American history. As the need for funds grew, Congress and the states simply printed bills without first withdrawing those that had been printed earlier. The states had the responsibility of retiring the bills, but they failed to collect the taxes that were necessary to do it. As the quantity of money in circulation grew, and as wartime shortages of goods continued, the prices of nearly all commodities soared. In the Delaware River valley one hundred pounds in paper currency bought 143.3 hundredweight of flour in 1776, but only 83.8 in 1777, and an almost unbelievably trifling 0.71 by 1781. Soldiers' pay did not rise along with the inflated goods, and their families were frequently devastated. One soldier complained that "Four months' pay of a private will not procure his wretched wife and children a single bushel of wheat." Joshua Huntington, who left Yale College just before graduation to join the army, wrote a bitter letter to the Connecticut assembly, reporting that "not a Day Passes . . . but some Soldier with Tears in his Eyes, hands me a letter to read from his Wife Painting forth the Distresses of his Family in such strains as these 'I am without bread, & cannot get any, the Committee will not supply me, my Children will Starve, or if they do not, they must freeze, we have no wood, neither Can we get any—*Pray Come Home*.'" States could do nothing to stop the runaway inflation although they tried various legislative measures to control the prices of goods, wages, transportation rates, and other basic services. These codes made mandatory the acceptance of paper money at its face value, but people either ignored the laws or found ways to get around them. Merchants increased prices in order to compensate for the greater risks, and they sent their goods to wherever the prices were highest. The merchants who bought farmers' produce were especially hurt by inflation. Farmers held back their produce in anticipation of higher prices in the future, but merchants had to sell their goods quickly in order to make a profit, and they were forced to accept rapidly depreciating currency as payment. In desperation people resorted to hoarding goods and bartering; farmers threatened not to plant any crops at all. Ironically some relief arrived when the British army bought local goods and paid for them in specie rather than paper money. Farmers and merchants near the British camps in Newport, New York, Philadelphia, Savannah, and other areas frequently traded with the enemy. These entrepreneurs were accused of treason by their patriotic neighbors, but their activities yielded some benefit. Eventually, Patriot merchants received the hard currency paid by the British, and these merchants used it to purchase desperately needed supplies in Europe. The Continental currency finally expired in 1781, by which time it was deemed worthless, "viler than the Rags" on which it was printed.

Financial Crisis. By early 1781 Congress faced a financial crisis. The Continental currency had depreciated to a state of worthlessness, and Congress could not compensate by obtaining substantial loans from abroad. The states, themselves exhausted by the war effort, stopped supplying their allotted contributions. Congress suspended payment on its public debt, thereby destroying its credit with investors. The army was in severe distress, and the bankrupt Congress could do little to provide adequate supplies, much less guarantee that soldiers would be paid. Alarmed by Congress's ineffectiveness, a faction began agitating to increase Congress's powers. Philadelphia merchant Robert Morris emerged as the faction's leader, and he was named superintendent of finance in the spring of 1781. Morris eventually became involved in nearly every congressional department, and it was said that he had more power than anyone except the head of the army, George Washington.

Bank of North America. Morris's main objectives were to reorganize the country's finances and strengthen the national government's powers. One important element of his overall plan was the establishment of a private institution that would function as the government's bank. Morris believed that such a bank would not only put the government's finances in order but also provide an attractive investment for investors, whose interests would thereby become tied to the national government's. The bank would also provide a stable currency that could be used to pay state taxes and in business transactions. Congress quickly approved the plan, but initial subscriptions from investors proved inadequate. Undeterred, Morris arranged for the government to subscribe $254,000 of hard money that it had received as a loan from France. He used his considerable business connections to attract the remaining $146,000 needed for incorporation, and the bank opened its doors in January 1782. Under Morris's direction the Bank of North America proceeded to make loans to the government eventually totaling some $1.2 million. In addition it advanced loans to merchants who were contracted to supply the army and issued notes that were readily accepted as a medium of exchange. People trusted the bank's notes in part because Morris's own financial standing was so high. The Bank of North America functioned as the country's first commercial bank. It lost its charter in 1785 but was rechartered in 1787 as a private bank run for and by merchants. Morris's bank allowed Congress to run its fiscal affairs more smoothly. It also provided a model for Alex-

ander Hamilton's even more ambitious Bank of the United States, incorporated in 1791.

Sources:

E. James Ferguson, *The Power of the Purse: A History of American Public Finance, 1776–1790* (Chapel Hill: University of North Carolina Press, 1961);

James A. Henretta, "The War for Independence and American Economic Development," *The Economy of Early America: The Revolutionary Period, 1763–1790*, edited by Ronald Hoffman and others (Charlottesville: University Press of Virginia, 1988), pp. 45–87.

HEADLINE MAKERS

JOHN HANCOCK

1737-1793

MERCHANT AND STATESMAN

The House of Hancock. John Hancock was born in Braintree, Massachusetts, a son of the Reverend John Hancock and the former Mary Hawke. When his father died, the boy was adopted by his childless uncle, Thomas, Boston's richest merchant. After graduating from Harvard College in 1754, John entered his uncle's mercantile firm. Like many young merchants being groomed to take over the family business, John was sent for a short period to England to complete his commercial education. John returned to Boston in 1761 and two years later became a partner in Thomas Hancock and Company. In 1764 Thomas Hancock died, leaving the twenty-seven-year-old John as head of the firm and heir to the bulk of his uncle's £70,000 fortune.

Revolutionary Leader. The wealthy young merchant led a life of ease and luxury. He traveled with six horses and several servants, set a fine table, and was partial to imported goods such as Madeira wine. Like many commercial men, he became involved in Massachusetts politics, which in the 1760s revolved around the colony's discontent with Parliament. In 1765 Hancock protested to his English correspondents against the Stamp Act. When Parliament's new commissioners arrived in late 1767 to tighten enforcement of the customs laws, Hancock refused to allow the militia unit that he commanded to participate in the welcoming ceremonies. He became even more of a public patriotic figure in 1768, when Massachusetts was in the midst of mob violence following the imposition of the Townshend duties. Tensions with the customs officials worsened, and in April, Hancock had his men forcibly remove two minor officials from his brig *Lydia* for going below decks without a warrant. In response the commissioners instructed the Massachusetts attorney general to file a criminal charge against Hancock, but the charges were eventually dropped. Meanwhile customs officials, harassed by the colonial mobs, had sent a plea to England for military help. When the British warship *Romney* arrived in June, the officials saw their chance to send a clear message that they would no longer tolerate smuggling and other acts of noncompliance. The authorities tried to make an example of Hancock by seizing another of his ships, the *Liberty*, and charging him with a technical violation of the Sugar Act of 1764. Instead of subduing the colonists, however, the action provoked one of the worst riots in Boston's history. A mob of several hundred roamed the town's streets hunting for and harassing customs officials. Hancock refused to capitulate. He was defended in court by his friend John Adams, and the suit was dropped after a few months. The incident convinced Parliament to send troops into Boston; it also enhanced Hancock's prestige among patriots. In 1769 Hancock was elected to the Massachusetts General Court and following the Boston Massacre in 1770 was appointed head of the town committee. As relations with Britain improved in the early 1770s, Hancock's radicalism subsided somewhat. But in 1773 the Tea Act once again threw Boston into an uproar. Hancock was one of the few substantial merchants who supported radical action, and he was elected chairman of the town meeting protesting the new tax. In 1774 Hancock was chosen to deliver the oration on the fourth anniversary of the Boston Massacre. He exhorted his listeners "if necessary" to "fight and even die for the prosperity of our Jerusalem." Later that year Hancock was elected president of the new Massachusetts provincial Congress and chairman of the committee of safety.

Congress. In late 1774 Hancock was made a delegate to the Second Continental Congress that was to meet in Philadelphia the following June. Hancock's radicalism marked him as a serious troublemaker in the eyes of the British, and in April 1775 Gen. Thomas Gage attempted to seize him and Samuel Adams for high treason. Both men were staying in Thomas Hancock's former home in Lexington, Massachusetts, along with Dorothy Quincy, whom John Hancock married later that year. Warned by Paul Revere, Hancock and Adams escaped just as the battles of Lexington and Concord began. They made their way to Philadelphia to attend the Second Continental Congress and were cheered as heroes in towns along the way. Adams and Hancock had become so notorious that General Gage specifically exempted them from the British offer of general amnesty, part of an attempt to restore peace. Hancock later became president of Congress, and he was the first to sign the Declaration of Independence on 4 July 1776. He did it boldly and with characteristic flourish, and today his signature is recognized the world over as a symbol of the American Revolution. Hancock hoped to be made commander in chief of the army, but Congress chose George Washington instead. Feeling slighted and perhaps sensing that other political figures were overshadowing him, Hancock resigned as president in October 1777 and was succeeded by Henry Laurens of South Carolina.

Massachusetts Politics. Hancock had ceased to be actively involved in his firm's business upon being elected to the Massachusetts provincial congress in 1774. After resigning from the Continental Congress in 1777, he began to spend much of his time in Boston devoting himself to Massachusetts politics and expending his money on public works. In 1780 he was a member of the Massachusetts constitutional convention and later that year was elected the first governor of the state. He served until early 1785, when an attack of gout forced him to resign just when rural debtors were revolting against the government. Hancock stood for the governorship again after the trouble subsided, eventually serving a total of nine terms. In 1788 he presided at the state convention that ratified the U.S. Constitution. Hancock had been reluctant to support the Constitution, but at a crucial moment he offered amendments that satisfied the Anti-Federalists, and Massachusetts ratified. Hancock never matched the business talents of his uncle. Upon his death the fortune left to him by Thomas Hancock was considerably diminished by years of inattention to the firm's business. Yet it was a respectable fortune, having been considerably augmented by large tracts of frontier land given to John Hancock in recognition of his services to the new country. He was serving as governor of Massachusetts when he died in 1793 at age fifty-six.

Sources:

W. T. Baxter, *The House of Hancock: Business in Boston, 1724–1775* (Cambridge, Mass.: Harvard University Press, 1945);

William M. Fowler, *The Baron of Beacon Hill: A Biography of John Hancock* (Boston: Houghton Mifflin, 1980).

HENRY LAURENS

1724-1792
MERCHANT, PLANTER, AND STATESMAN

Early Career. Henry Laurens's forebears were Huguenots, Protestants who fled France after the Edict of Nantes was revoked in 1685. Henry's grandfather Andre Laurens left earlier, in 1682, and eventually made his way to America, settling first in New York City and then Charleston, South Carolina. Andre's son John married Hester (or Esther) Grasset, also a Huguenot refugee. Henry was their third child and eldest son. John Laurens became a saddler, and his business eventually grew to be the largest of its kind in the colonies. In 1744 he sent Henry to London to augment the young man's business training. John Laurens died in 1747, bequeathing twenty-three-year-old Henry a considerable estate. In July 1750 Henry married Eleanor Ball; they eventually had at least a dozen children, but only four survived into adulthood. Laurens became a partner of Charleston merchant George Austin and for the next several decades developed a reputation for scrupulous honesty, industry, and business sagacity. Most of his firm's trade was with England, but it also dealt with firms in Glasgow, Rotterdam, Oporto, Lisbon, Madrid, and the West Indies. The firm's most common—and most profitable—transaction was exchanging rice for slaves. Because the slave trade was considered risky, it paid a 10 percent commission versus only 5 percent for other goods. Laurens later lamented that abandoning the trade cost him "many Thousands of pounds." In 1762 he continued the firm alone, and it was among Charleston's leading establishments when Laurens withdrew from active participation in 1764.

Planter and Politician. Planters were the most respected men in the Southern social hierarchy. Like many of his cohorts, Laurens aspired to owning plantations rather than simply being a merchant. After 1764 he began acquiring and managing a collection of rice and indigo plantations. These eventually included a three-thousand-acre estate near Charleston called Mepkin, two others called Mt. Tacitus and Wambaw, and several plantations on the Georgia coast. In total, Laurens acquired some twenty thousand acres. At the outbreak of the Revolution his plantations were becoming profitable, and he was one of the province's wealthiest men. Laurens was reputed to be a humane creditor and slaveholder. In 1757 he was elected to the South Carolina assembly and was regularly re-elected to that post until the Revolution.

Revolutionary Statesman. Laurens participated in the events of the Revolution from an early date. He generally took a middle course, fearing the colonial mob element but also resenting the new regulations imposed by what he regarded as a corrupt British administration. In 1764 he refused a seat in the provincial council as a protest against the inclusion of royal placemen. Laurens supported South Carolina's nonimportation agreements of 1769 and published several pamphlets decrying parliamentary measures. Extremely sensitive to slights, he became involved in several duels, once even challenging a vice-admiralty court judge when Laurens's ships were seized on suspicion of smuggling. His wife, Eleanor, died in 1770, and the following year Laurens went to London to supervise the education of their sons, John and Henry. He became so disturbed by the corruption of the English ruling classes that he transferred his sons to schools in Geneva, Switzerland. While in England he joined a group of thirty-eight Americans who petitioned Parliament not to pass the Boston Port Bill, a measure designed to punish the town by closing its harbor following the Boston Tea Party. Various business opportunities were offered to him in England, but Laurens opted to return to America, stating that although he was "resolved still to labor for peace," he was "determined in the last event to stand or fall with my country." Shortly after returning to Charleston in December 1774, Laurens was elected to the new Congress of South Carolina. He became president of that body and of the Council of Safety. In February 1776 Laurens helped draft South Carolina's temporary constitution. In January 1777 he was elected to the Continental Congress and participated in several committees, becoming president of Congress when John Hancock resigned later that year. Laurens was intolerant of what he considered the corrupt practices of some congressional delegates. In December 1778 he resigned in protest and was succeeded by John Jay. Laurens remained in Congress through most of 1779, when he called for an investigation of Robert Morris, the acting banker and financier of Congress.

Diplomatic Missions. In 1779 Congress sent Laurens to negotiate a treaty with the Dutch. He left Philadelphia in August 1780 and was captured by the British off of Newfoundland. Laurens threw his papers overboard, but the British succeeded in fishing out a draft of the treaty. They charged Laurens with high treason and took him to England, where he was confined in the Tower of London from October 1780 until December 1781. Although the fifty-six-year-old Laurens was ill, the English officials gave him no medical attention. They charged him for all of his upkeep at the tower, even including the salaries of his warders (a common practice at the time). Laurens was placed in solitary confinement and was not allowed writing materials. Even so, he frequently managed to smuggle out letters to the American press. Laurens resisted the efforts of his Brit-

ish friends to bring him to their side, but at the same time he felt neglected by Congress. While in the tower he wrote two petitions to the English authorities that were considered too submissive by some Americans back home, including James Madison, who called for an annulment of Laurens's diplomatic commission. Benjamin Franklin and the British statesman Edmund Burke fought to secure his release, and in December 1781 Laurens was freed in exchange for Gen. Charles Cornwallis, who had surrendered to George Washington at Yorktown, Virginia. In November 1782 Laurens received instructions from Congress to join Franklin, Jay, and John Adams in Paris to negotiate a peace treaty with the British. Laurens was also acting as an unofficial minister to England, so he was not present when the final peace treaty was signed on 3 September 1783.

Later Years. Henry Laurens arrived back in New York in 1784, four years after leaving the United States. He reached Charleston in early 1785 and retired to his plantation Mepkin for the remaining seven years of his life. The war had cost him dearly: he estimated his losses at around 40,000 guineas. His time in the Tower of London ruined his health, and he remained a semi-invalid the rest of his life. Ill and saddened by the death of his son John, who was killed in action in August 1782, Laurens refused all political posts offered to him. He was elected a delegate to the Constitutional Convention in Philadelphia in 1787 but declined to go. In his will he stipulated that his body be cremated, an unusual practice at the time. His wishes were carried out upon his death in 1792.

Source:
David D. Wallace, *Life of Henry Laurens* (New York: Putnam, 1915).

ROBERT MORRIS

1734-1806

MERCHANT, FINANCIER, AND STATESMAN

Early Career. Robert Morris was born in Liverpool, England. His father, also called Robert, was engaged in exporting tobacco, and at the age of thirteen young Robert left England to join his father in Maryland. After a brief period in a Philadelphia school the boy started work for the Willings, a firm of substantial shipping merchants. At the age of fifteen Morris inherited a modest estate when his father was accidentally killed. Four years later the young man entered into partnership with his former employer's son, Thomas. Morris kept an interest in the firm of Willing and Morris for thirty-nine years and was an active director for much of that time. In 1769 he married Mary White of Maryland, a sister of William

White, who became bishop in the American Episcopal Church. They had five sons and two daughters.

Revolutionary Career. Robert Morris served the Revolution in many financial, administrative, and political capacities. After the Stamp Act of 1765 he participated in Philadelphia's nonimportation agreement even though his firm did substantial business with British traders. He joined a committee of citizens that forced the city's stamp tax collector to cease performing his duties. Morris was not fully committed to the patriot cause when the First Continental Congress met in 1774 but became fully so after the Battle of Lexington in April 1775. From 1775 to 1778 Morris was a delegate to the Continental Congress, where he served on several important committees including the Committee of Secret Correspondence (later called the Foreign Affairs Committee and then the Committee of Commerce). He was also in charge of procuring munitions and frequently acted as a banker of Congress, both of which he accomplished to his advantage primarily through his firm, Willing and Morris. Although his mercantile activities were widely known, many members of Congress admired his financial and administrative abilities and overlooked the conflict of interest. "He has vast designs in the mercantile way," John Adams wrote of him, "And no doubt pursues mercantile ends, which are always gain; but he is an excellent Member of our Body." In 1776 Morris initially voted against the Declaration of Independence because he still hoped for a reconciliation with Great Britain, but he signed it a month later. When Congress fled Philadelphia for Baltimore in December of that year, Morris stayed behind to carry on his committee work. Despite grave difficulties, he managed to buy supplies for the army and sent funds borrowed in his own name to George Washington. Morris retired from Congress in 1778 but remained active in the Pennsylvania assembly. His frequent mixing of private gain and public duty angered some of his congressional colleagues and members of the public. In January 1779 Thomas Paine publicly criticized him, and later that year Henry Laurens, the former president of the Congress, charged Willing and Morris with conducting fraudulent transactions. A congressional committee investigated Morris and cleared him of all charges. In May 1779 a mass meeting in Philadelphia appointed a committee to investigate his conduct; again he was cleared of all charges. Although he lost some of his former popularity, Morris was re-elected to the Pennsylvania assembly in November 1780 and served until June 1781.

Financier of Congress. With the collapse of the currency, military defeats in the South, and Congress's inability to raise adequate supplies for the army, many delegates began to feel that the Articles of Confederation (adopted in 1777) were inadequate. Something had to be done to make Congress more effective. In September 1780 Alexander Hamilton suggested that all of the committees charged with handling the country's finances be consolidated and that Morris be appointed the superintendent of finance. Congress reorganized its committees in early 1781 and appointed Morris to the new and uniquely powerful position. Before agreeing to fill the post, Morris stipulated that Congress recognize his right to continue operating as a private trader and to have primary control over his personnel. Congress hesitated but eventually approved Morris's request. Once in office, Morris used his considerable commercial reputation to save that of the bankrupt Congress. In January 1782 he declared that his "personal Credit, which thank Heaven I have preserved throughout all the tempests of the War, has been substituted for that which the Country lost . . . if I can regain for the United States the Confidence of Individuals so as that they will trust their property and exertions in the hands of Government, our Independence and Success are certain but without that Confidence we are nothing."

Reforms. Morris attempted both short-term fixes and longer-term reforms. He imposed thrift on the executive departments by abolishing the system of commissaries and buying supplies for the army himself. In order to keep the government running he issued $1.4 million of "Morris notes" backed by his own credit and borrowed substantial amounts from his business acquaintances. He took great financial risks in order to fund the Yorktown campaign that ended in Gen. Charles Cornwallis's defeat. Just as important, Morris set about reorganizing the country's finances by proposing a series of permanent reforms. He sought to fund the country's outstanding debt by issuing bonds to investors. Morris proposed levying taxes on the states to be paid in specie that would in turn be used to pay interest on the debt. He also tried to have the articles amended so that the Confederation could levy a 5-percent duty on imports. Thanks to a loan from France, Morris was able to accomplish one of his goals, the formation of the Bank of North America, which began operations in January 1782. Morris reasoned that once Congress's finances were on a secure footing, it would have less trouble borrowing money and would attract investors to its bonds. But except for the bank Morris's ambitious program for strengthening the national government failed. Despite his efforts to convince them, the states did not contribute their share and would not agree to his funding plan for Congress. In 1783 Morris was still unable to pay off Congress's debts. Discouraged, he offered his resignation, but Congress ordered it to be kept secret until January 1784. Although Morris assured the public that he would be personally responsible for all liabilities assumed during his administration, he was severely criticized in the press for resigning. Morris stayed on because no one else could fill his role. A loan from the Netherlands negotiated by Adams carried the government through until Morris finally left in November 1784.

Political Legacy. Morris had a talent for serving both his country and himself and was frequently criticized for mixing his public duties with private interests. Nevertheless Morris succeeded in leaving a distinctive mark on the American political system. He and Roger Sherman of Connecticut were the only men to sign all three revolutionary documents: the Declaration of Independence, the Articles of Confederation, and the Constitution. Along with the first two secretaries of the Treasury, Alexander Hamilton and Albert Gallatin, Morris helped to lay the financial and political foundations of the United States. Throughout his administration he tried to strengthen the powers of the national government and to tie the interests of business people more closely to it. Unlike men such as Thomas Jefferson, Morris did not subscribe to the prevailing republican belief that there was an inherent conflict between public and private interest and between business and government. Instead he sought to tie these interests together through deal making and by appealing to people's monetary self-interest. Although Morris's nationalizing program failed to accomplish the constitutional reform he wanted, his policies helped to galvanize a coalition of leaders who agreed with his political and commercial vision. In 1786 Morris was a delegate to the Annapolis convention that met to discuss interstate trade regulations. The following year he sat in the Constitutional Convention in Philadelphia. Morris was offered but declined the position of secretary of the treasury. Instead he recommended Alexander Hamilton, who shared and successfully implemented many of Morris's political ideas. Morris was elected one of Pennsylvania's first two senators, and he served in the new Congress from 1789 to 1795. During that time he supported most of Hamilton's financial programs. In 1790 Morris helped to broker the political deal wherein Virginia voted for the federal resumption of state debts in exchange for locating the permanent national capital on the Potomac River, the site of present-day Washington, D.C.

Later Mercantile Career. On his retirement from the Continental Congress in 1784, Morris continued to take large business risks. He engaged in trade with the East Indies and China, sending the first American ship to the port of Canton. Morris also continued to expand the French and Dutch ties he had established during the war. In 1785 he negotiated a contract with the French Farmers-General that gave him the monopoly of the American tobacco trade with France. The move aroused considerable antagonism among Virginia tobacco traders, and Morris suffered large financial losses when the Marquis de Lafayette and Jefferson, the minister to France, intervened to nullify the contract. Morris also speculated on great tracts of land in western New York and elsewhere, including (with a partner) a large portion of present-day Washington, D.C. He was building a mansion designed by Pierre L'Enfant, the architect of the new capital, when the market collapsed. Morris could not meet interest payments and taxes, and in February 1798 a small creditor had him arrested. He was incarcerated in Prune Street, Philadelphia's debtors prison, for three-and-one-half years. In 1801 he was released following the passage of a federal bankruptcy law. For the remaining five years of his life he lived on a small pension that his cousin, Gouverneur Morris, had arranged for his wife, Mary. The financier of the Revolution ended his days in a small house in Philadelphia, where he died at age seventy-three.

Sources:

E. James Ferguson, *The Power of the Purse* (Chapel Hill: University of North Carolina Press, 1961);

Clarence L. Ver Steeg, *Robert Morris, Revolutionary Financier* (Philadelphia: University of Pennsylvania Press, 1954).

PUBLICATIONS

William Barton, *Observations on the Nature and Use of Paper Credit* (Philadelphia: Printed by R. Aitken, 1781)—a Philadelphia lawyer urges the establishment of a national bank funded by specie. Barton believed that the scheme would allow Congress to pay its debts and thereby restore public confidence in the government;

Edmund Burke, *Speech on Conciliation with the Colonies* (New York: Printed by J. Rivington, 1775)—in his speech to Parliament a prominent political thinker and Whig spokesman outlines the astonishing economic growth of the American colonies and argues that British sovereignty and American liberty must be reconciled;

Michel Guillaume Jean (J. Hector St. John) de Crèvecoeur, "What is an American?," in *Letters from an American Farmer* (London: Printed for Davies & Davis, 1782)—a French immigrant to New York reflects on how the country's fertile land and plentiful resources produced a distinctly American character;

Benjamin Franklin, *Advice to a Young Tradesman, Written by an Old One* (Boston: Printed by B. Mecom, 1762)—one of several pieces by Franklin advising young men on how to be successful in business. These works were among the first examples of the "success manual" genre, which became extremely popular in the nineteenth century and into our own time;

Franklin, *The Interest of Great Britain Considered, With Regard to Her Colonies* (Boston: Printed by B. Mecom, 1760)—Franklin reassures the British that American manufactures will not soon replace the products imported from the mother country. Instead Great Britain and America will continue to grow together, with Britain maintaining its economic lead;

Richard Price, *An Appeal to the Public on the Subject of the National Debt* (London: T. Cadell, 1772)—a radical English Whig explains how Britain could retire its enormous public debt. Some Americans, including Alexander Hamilton, were fascinated by Price's theories;

Pelatiah Webster, *An Essay on Free Trade and Finance* (Philadelphia: Printed and sold by Thomas Bradford, 1779)—in the face of crippling wartime inflation, a prominent financial theorist in Philadelphia analyzes the role of money in the economy.

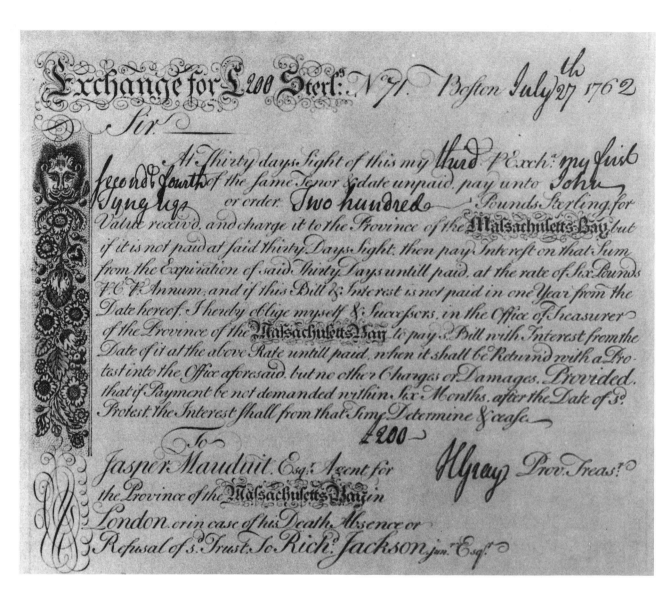

A colonial bill of exchange (American Antiquarian Society, Worcester, Massachusetts)

COMMUNICATIONS

by ANTHONY J. SCOTTI

CONTENTS

Sidebars and tables are listed in italics.

1754

- As postmaster general, Benjamin Franklin makes an inspection of branch offices in British North America, instructing local postmasters in how to improve mail delivery.

- William Bradford III, editor of the *Pennsylvania Journal and Weekly Advertiser,* opens the London Coffee-House for Merchants and Traders at the corner of Front and Market Streets in Philadelphia. Here newspapers are filed, letters posted, ships chartered, sailing dates announced, and auctions held.

1755

- A monthly packet service begins between Falmouth, England, and New York City.

7 Apr. Benjamin Edes and John Gill take over the *Boston Gazette and Country Journal.*

12 Apr. James Parker, a close associate of Benjamin Franklin, begins publishing the *Connecticut Gazette* in New Haven; John Holt acts as manager and silent partner of the colony's first newspaper.

1756

- A stage route opens linking Philadelphia and New York City. Jersey Wagons, vehicles without spring suspension, operate in relays between the two cities.

1757

- At a cost of £3,000 city officials authorize the paving of sixteen thousand yards of roadway on Boston Neck.

1758

Jan. James Parker begins publishing the *New American Magazine* in Woodbridge, New Jersey.

26 Sept. The New Jersey assembly makes James Parker public printer.

1759

Sept.–Oct. Colonial newspapers carry the story of Gen. James Wolfe's stunning victory over the French on the Plains of Abraham, outside of Quebec.

1760

- The Conestoga wagon is the primary means by which settlers of the Allegheny Mountains move their goods and possessions. Each wagon is usually pulled by four to seven horses and can carry four to six tons. The bottom is curved to keep loads in place as the wagon goes up and down hills.

Mar. James Parker stops publication of the *New American Magazine.*

25 Sept. The *Pennsylvania Gazette,* published by Benjamin Franklin and David Hall in Philadelphia, carries news of the British capture of Montreal.

1761

- *Poor Richard's Almanack* sells an average of ten thousand copies.

1762

- William Goddard starts the *Providence (R.I.) Gazette and Country Journal.*

6 May   John Holt becomes the sole publisher of the *New-York Gazette and Weekly Post-Boy;* he leases the shop and presses from James Parker.

1763

- The packet service from England extends to Boston and Charleston.

1764

- The *Connecticut Courant* begins circulation as a weekly newspaper in Hartford, Connecticut; later renamed the *Hartford Daily Courant,* it is the oldest continuously published newspaper in the United States.

1765

- There are twenty-three newspapers in North America.
- James Parker starts the *Constitutional Courant* in Woodbridge, New Jersey.

22 Mar.   Parliament passes the Stamp Act, which authorizes revenue stamps (costing anywhere from a halfpenny to £10) to be affixed to all commercial and legal documents, licenses, newspapers, broadsides, almanacs, pamphlets, playing cards, and dice.

7–25 Oct.   The Stamp Act Congress meets in City Hall, New York City. Twenty-eight delegates, representing nine colonies, are present.

31 Oct.   In protest of the Stamp Act, William Bradford III publishes the *Pennsylvania Journal and Weekly Advertiser* with a black border resembling a tombstone on the front page.

1 Nov.   The Stamp Act goes into effect. Despite the heavy penalties, many leading newspapers, including the *New-London Gazette, (New Haven) Connecticut Gazette, (Portsmouth) New-Hampshire Gazette,* and *New-York Gazette and Weekly Post-Boy,* appear on unstamped paper.

1766

- The Flying Machine, a box wagon that runs from Camden, New Jersey, to what is now Jersey City, makes the nintey-mile trip every two days.
- John Holt changes the name of his paper to the *New-York Journal or General Advertiser.*

17 Mar.   The Stamp Act is repealed. King George III approves the measure the next day, but it will not become effective until 1 May.

1767

- William Goddard starts the *Pennsylvania Chronicle and Universal Advertiser Journal* in Philadelphia.

2 Dec. The *Pennsylvania Chronicle and Universal Advertiser Journal* prints the first of John Dickinson's "Letters from a Farmer in Pennsylvania to the Inhabitants of the British Colonies," an argument against the Townshend duties. The letters are reprinted in many other colonial newspapers.

1768

- Hugh Gaine becomes the public printer of the province of New York. As printer and editor of the *New-York Mercury*, he renames it the *New-York Gazette; and the Weekly Mercury*.

1769

Dec. James Parker prints an essay titled "To the Betrayed Inhabitants of New York" and signs it "A Son of Liberty." He is charged with sedition and libel by the General Assembly, but dies the next year while the case is still pending.

1770

12 Mar. The *Boston Gazette* prints an inflammatory account of the Boston Massacre, complete with heavy black borders and a picture of four large coffins.

1771

Nov. John Dunlap begins publication of the weekly *Pennsylvania Packet, or the General Advertiser* in Philadelphia.

1772

- Thomas Paine writes an essay, "The Case of the Officers of the Excise," and as a result loses his position as a customs officer.

Nov. Samuel Adams organizes the first committee of correspondence in Boston.

1773

- William Goddard begins the *Maryland Journal; and the Baltimore Advertiser*.

- James Rivington begins *Rivington's New York Gazetteer or the Connecticut, Hudson's River, New-Jersey, and Quebec Weekly Advertiser*.

Jan. There are more than eighty committees of correspondence throughout Massachusetts.

Sept. Hugh Finlay begins a nine-month inspection of post roads and offices from Falmouth, Maine, to Savannah, Georgia.

16 Dec. The Sons of Liberty gather at Benjamin Edes's house on Brattle Street and plan the Boston Tea Party. Afterwards the *Boston Gazette* prints a warning to royal officials not to arrest Edes and his associate John Gill, or they would fall "into the pit they are digging for others."

1774

• Until April of the next year the *Boston Gazette* reports a weekly circulation of two thousand copies.

20 May The Massachusetts Government Act forbids public meetings unless sanctioned by the governor.

1775

24 Jan. Benjamin Towne, a former journeyman for William Goddard, publishes the first issue of the triweekly *Pennsylvania Evening Post*.

10 Mar. Daniel Boone begins to blaze the Wilderness Road from Fort Chiswell in the Shenandoah Valley of Virginia, through the Cumberland Gap, and into Kentucky. It is not improved for wagon traffic until 1795.

19 Apr. The battles of Lexington and Concord occur in Massachusetts. By the beginning of the next month news of the fighting will spread as far as Charleston, South Carolina.

10 May Isaac Sears and the Sons of Liberty wreck James Rivington's presses. Rivington flees to the safety of a British warship. He soon receives an appointment as His Majesty's printer in New York and reopens his printing shop.

5 June Benjamin Edes flees Boston with a press and types and resumes publishing the *Boston Gazette* in Watertown, Massachusetts; royal authorities arrest his son Peter and hold him in Boston.

20 Nov. Sears and the Sons of Liberty again wreck Rivington's presses, and they carry his type back to Connecticut.

1776

• Of the original thirteen states only Delaware lacks at least one newspaper. There are thirty-nine newspapers being published in twenty-three locations in the new United States.

Jan. James Rivington flees to the British warship *Sansom* and eventually to England; he does not return to New York for more than eighteen months.

10 Jan. Thomas Paine publishes *Common Sense,* and in less than three months 120,000 copies are sold.

6 July The *Pennsylvania Evening Post* becomes the first newspaper to print the Declaration of Independence. A four-page paper, it devotes the entire front page and the first column of the second page to the declaration.

2 Aug. All the delegates officially sign the Declaration of Independence. However, their names are withheld from the public for six months because the signers fear royal prosecution.

19 Dec. The first number of *The American Crisis,* a series of essays written by Thomas Paine to bolster the morale of the Continental Army, is issued in William Bradford III's *Pennsylvania Journal and Weekly Advertiser.* Three other essays appear over the course of the next year.

1777

- The first American edition of the Bible in English is published, but only the New Testament; a complete version does not appear until 1782.

- Peter Timothy, editor and publisher of the *(Charleston) South Carolina Gazette,* renames it the *Gazette of the State of South Carolina.*

Sept. James Rivington returns to New York City as the king's printer.

4 Oct. Rivington begins to publish his newspaper again, calling it *Rivington's New-York Loyal Gazette.*

13 Dec. Rivington changes the name of his paper to the *Royal Gazette.*

1778

- Numbers 5, 6, and 7 of *The American Crisis* appear.

1779

7 Jan. Thomas Paine resigns his position as secretary of the Committee of Foreign Affairs amid accusations that he revealed information concerning French arms shipments to the United States.

1780

- Numbers 8 and 9 of *The American Crisis* appear.

May After the fall of Charleston, British authorities arrest Peter Timothy but quickly parole him. When he refuses to take the oath of allegiance, he is imprisoned in St. Augustine, Florida, for a year.

1781

- Benjamin Edes publishes a broadside titled "CORNWALLIS TAKEN!" in celebration of the Franco-American victory at Yorktown, Virginia.

1782

- Numbers 10, 11, and 12 of *The American Crisis* appear.

1783

- There are fifty-eight newspapers published in twenty-six places in the United States.

- James Rivington renames his newspaper *Rivington's New-York Gazette and Universal Advertiser.*

15 Apr. Congress ratifies the preliminary peace treaty signed on 30 November 1782.

19 Apr. *The American Crisis,* number 13, is printed. Meanwhile, Gen. George Washington announces to the Continental Army the end of hostilities.

30 May   The *Pennsylvania Evening Post* becomes the first daily newspaper in the United States.

10 Nov.   Hugh Gaine prints the final issue of the *New-York Gazette; and the Weekly Mercury.*

4 Dec.   George Washington delivers his farewell address to his officers at Fraunces' Tavern in New York City.

31 Dec.   The last issue of James Rivington's paper appears.

Title page for James Parker's short-lived journal

OVERVIEW

A Revolutionary People. The period 1754 to 1783 not only witnessed a political revolution but one in communications as well. In 1754 most inhabitants of British North America would readily call themselves Britons and would also identify themselves with their resident colonies as Virginians, New Yorkers, or Rhode Islanders, for example. By 1783, even though local identity was still important, they also thought of themselves as Americans. In a letter to Hezekiah Niles on 15 February 1818, colonial statesman and former president John Adams asserted that the American Revolution was effected long before the war commenced. "The Revolution was in the minds and hearts of the people." This sentiment developed in colonial America partially through an enhanced system of communications.

Transportation. Colonial America was an ever-expanding, mobile society. The population doubled every twenty years, and the economy grew faster than in England. American attempts to facilitate trade, travel, and dissemination of information contributed to the communications revolution. Although transatlantic voyages still took approximately eight weeks, more ships made the trip than in the previous century. Land travel was greatly aided by improved road networks, including the Great Wagon Road connecting western Pennsylvania with Georgia. Military expeditions such as Maj. Gen. Edward Braddock's against French posts in the interior cut pathways through the forests, helping open the West to settlement. And Daniel Boone blazed the Wilderness Road through the Cumberland Gap and into Kentucky. The refinement of the Conestoga wagon during this era allowed travelers to move large amounts of freight and personal possessions. By 1775 British North America had achieved integration in an economic empire, and most colonies enjoyed a reliable if not swift means of transportation.

The Printed Word. American provincials were probably the most literate people of the eighteenth century. In New England approximately 90 percent of the adult white men and 40 percent of the adult white women could read and write. In other colonies the literacy rate among white males varied from 35 to more than 50 percent. (Only 33 percent of males in England were liter-

ate.) Most of what Americans read was religious though the Enlightenment encouraged inquiry into man's scientific as well as social and political environment.

Postal Service. An organized post office helped spread ideas and information. Packet ships (small, fast vessels designed specifically to carry the mail) provided regular deliveries from England, but once the mail reached the colonies, it encountered delays caused by unreliable post riders, circuitous routes, and occasionally severe weather. As deputy postmaster general, Benjamin Franklin introduced a series of reforms that improved service and increased profits for the Crown through standardized rates. Since many local postmasters were also printers, the bulk of the correspondence in the mail bags of post riders was newspapers. With the approaching conflict with the mother country, intercolonial committees of correspondence arranged for their own mail deliveries through specially appointed couriers.

Newspapers and Pamphlets. The revolutionary crisis increased the power and prestige of the press. There were twenty-one newspapers published in America in 1763. By 1775 there were forty-two: fifteen in New England, thirteen in the Middle colonies, and fourteen in the Southern colonies. An average of one paper was published for every sixty thousand to sixty-five thousand people. Colonial newspapers were weeklies (unlike modern papers that are generally dailies), and circulation figures are hard to determine for them. Benjamin Edes of the *Boston Gazette and Country Journal* claimed two thousand copies weekly from mid 1774 to mid 1775, and James Rivington of *Rivington's New York Gazetteer or the Connecticut, Hudson's River, New-Jersey, and Quebec Weekly Advertiser* maintained he sold thirty-six hundred copies in seven days in October 1774. Such figures are unusual, however, and the weekly average for a colonial newspaper was probably closer to three hundred copies. The revolutionary crisis also sparked a tremendous increase in political pamphlets. More than one-half of the non-newspaper imprints from American presses between 1639 and 1783 were concentrated in the twenty years after 1763. Thomas Paine's *Common Sense* (1776) and *The American Crisis* (1776–1783) were probably the most influential pamphlets of the revolutionary era.

Printers. One of the most striking features of this period is the extent to which the Whigs controlled the press. The Stamp Act of 1765 confronted printers with a challenge to both their economic livelihood and traditional political neutrality. Although virtually all printers opposed the statute out of self-interest, only a few initially issued strong statements of protest. Gradually popular opinion forced them to take sides and abandon their objectivity. While some entered the Loyalist camp, the majority went to the Patriot side. The latter group soon controlled public opinion through propaganda, and their stature rose in the eyes of Americans as the guardians of virtue. Indeed, until the early nineteenth century a partisan press was the norm in the United States.

Word of Mouth. Although a literate people, most Americans preferred face-to-face communication. They lived in a world of oral culture, in which ideas and information passed through the spoken word. By the 1750s Boston, New York, and Philadelphia had dozens of taverns, where patrons exchanged news, gossiped, or discussed business. Sunday mornings presented a time to converse as community members gathered to worship at the local church. Similar opportunities occurred at markets, fairs, militia musters, and elections. On the frontiers people eagerly awaited the arrival of traders and peddlers.

Language. The Revolution created not only a new nation but also a new variety of English. The moment the first settlers landed at Jamestown, Virginia, in 1607, the new physical and social environment plus contacts with foreign peoples caused a language drift from parent English. The affirmation of American English as an official variety of the language, however, did not occur until the Revolution and the creation of a culturally and politically independent society.

TOPICS IN THE NEWS

BRITISH PROCLAMATIONS OF MAY AND JUNE 1780

Southern Colonies. Following the Franco-American alliance of February 1778, King George III and his military advisors devised a new strategy to subdue the rebellious North American colonies. Until this time the British army had concentrated its activities in the Northern provinces; now the major theater of operations would be the South. Royal officials believed that a majority of the people in the Southern colonies remained loyal to the king and would flock to His Majesty's standard upon sight. However, this proved to be a serious overestimation. Scholars today believe that John Adams's estimate indicating the American population as one-third Patriot (Whig), one-third Loyalist (Tory), and one-third neutral is too high for the last two categories. Historians assert that Loyalists comprised only 16 percent (513,000 out of 3,210,000) of the total colonial population, or 19.8 percent of white Americans.

Civil War. In addition the British were unprepared for the vicious civil war plaguing the South since 1775. The Whig versus Tory conflict, found in all the colonies, seems to have been most intense and ferocious in the Southern provinces. Tories regarded Whigs as traitors despicable in their perfidy. Meanwhile, Whigs saw Tories as cowards who lacked the courage to defend their nation's rights and as collaborators willing to sell themselves and fellow countrymen into slavery. One side rarely granted mercy to the other. Whig Dr. David Ramsay stated that the countryside "exhibited scenes of distress which were shocking to humanity." The Ninety-Six District of South Carolina alone supposedly contained fourteen hundred widows and orphans at the war's end. By 1780 the bulk of the Southern Loyalist population had fled to Florida or New York while the remainder hid out in the forests and swamps waiting for the appearance of the British army.

Invasion. On 29 December 1778 a British expedition captured Savannah, Georgia. An American attempt to recapture the city the following October failed. Charleston, South Carolina, fell to the British on 12 May 1780, and later in the summer Charles, Earl Cornwallis, completely routed an American army at Camden. Nevertheless the British presence in the South only inflamed the bitterness between Whigs and Tories. "King's Men" came out in full force after the royal victories, perpetuating "rapine, outrage and murder." Many joined the Loyalist regiments attached to the British army, such as the New York Volunteers, Ferguson's American Volunteers, and the British Legion. Meanwhile, Patriot guerrilla bands led by Francis Marion ("Swamp Fox"), Thomas Sumter ("Carolina Gamecock"), and Andrew Pickens harassed the English. The Patriots also committed the most heinous acts; indeed, their innocence and nobility have been much exaggerated by historians.

Clinton's Decrees. Immediately after the fall of Charleston the British commander in chief in North America, Gen. Sir Henry Clinton, issued three decrees that had a profound effect upon the Southern populace. His rationale for doing so was to facilitate the restoration of "tranquillity and order to the country." On 22 May 1780 Clinton declared that anyone taking up arms or persuading "faithful and peaceable subjects" to rebel would suffer imprisonment and confiscation of property. In the second proclamation on 1 June, Clinton granted a full pardon to those individuals who returned to their allegiance. However, two days later the third decree proclaimed that all paroled civilians had to sign an oath of allegiance to the Crown within seventeen days; if not, they would be considered rebels. (A paroled individual was someone who had been released from imprisonment with the pledge not to bear arms again for a set period of time.)

Ramifications. The last decree, according to historian Charles Stedman, initiated a "counter-revolution." Paroled Whigs viewed it as treachery, for they could not now live as neutrals. Taking the oath meant resuming the duties of British citizenship, including service in Loyalist militia units. Many had no desire to take up arms against their former comrades, and as a result they fled to the backcountry in order to resume the fight against the redcoats. Others, meanwhile, took the oath without any intention of obeying it. This last group gained the King's protection and disgusted many authentic Loyalists in the process. The mood in the South changed overnight from one of resignation under British occupation to suspicion with this "arbitrary fiat of the commander-in-chief."

Friend or Foe. By this time in the war the British could not easily differentiate between friend or foe. For instance, Sumter had resigned his commission in the American army in 1778, returning to his estate and the life of a simple country gentleman. When British soldiers burnt his home in May 1780, he decided to rejoin the Patriot army. Another American soldier named John Postell received a parole after the fall of Charleston, but this did not prevent Loyalist cavalrymen from confiscating his horses and slaves and plundering his house. As a result Postell decided to "seek refuge" with Marion's partisans, feeling that his treatment at the hands of the British released him from all obligations concerning his parole.

Significance. In hindsight the three British proclamations of May and June 1780 can be viewed as serious mistakes. Royal authorities communicated an ambiguous message about their allegiance policy and in turn alienated a large segment of the population. As a result for the rest of the war in the South, Whig opposition stiffened while many Loyalists became neutrals, left the region, or even joined the Patriot cause.

Sources:

Robert D. Bass, *Ninety-Six: The Struggle for the South Carolina Back Country* (Lexington, S.C.: Sandlapper, 1978);

John S. Pancake, *This Destructive War: The British Campaign in the Carolinas, 1780–1782* (Tuscaloosa & London: University of Alabama Press, 1985);

John Shy, "British Strategy for Pacifying the Southern Colonies, 1778–1781," in *The Southern Experience in the American Revolution*, edited by Jeffrey J. Crow and Larry E. Tise (Chapel Hill: University of North Carolina Press, 1978), pp. 155–173;

Charles Stedman, *The History of the Origin, Progress, and Termination of the American War,* 2 volumes (New York: New York Times & Arno Press, 1969);

Robert M. Weir, *Colonial South Carolina: A History* (Millwood, N.Y.: KTO Press, 1983).

COMMITTEES OF CORRESPONDENCE

Unity. In the 1760s Patriot leaders discovered that the key to resisting imperial policy was unity. Instigating popular outrage proved effective during the controversy surrounding the Stamp Act and Townshend duties. However, by 1770 the nonimportation associations had disbanded, and the only significant grievance to complain about was the tax on tea. Radical leaders such as Samuel Adams of Boston expected Parliament to resume taxing at anytime, especially since it had never surrendered the right to do so. Adams despaired of keeping the quarrel with Britain alive and fresh, but he did not have to wait long for a new crisis to emerge. Tension mounted following the *Gaspee* incident of 9 June 1772, when inhabitants of Providence, Rhode Island, burnt a customs schooner to its waterline. When royal authorities attempted to apprehend the culprits, propagandists filled the newspapers with cries of oppression. Meanwhile the Boston town meeting unsuccessfully petitioned Lt. Gov. Thomas Hutchinson for a session of the Massachusetts General Assembly to look into the salaries of provincial judges. (Henceforth they would receive their salaries directly from the Crown.)

Function. After Hutchinson refused to comply, Adams on 2 November 1772 proposed an official network of corresponding societies to keep the public notified of political developments. These committees of correspondence would disseminate information and promote unity through formal expressions of support from the various towns in Massachusetts. The objective was "to state the rights of the Colonists and of this province in particular, as men, as Christians, and as subjects, to communicate and publish the same to the several towns in this province and to the world as the sense of this town, with the infringements and violations thereof that have been, or from time may be made—also requesting of each town a free communication of their sentiments on this subject." The idea for such committees was not new, having been previously recommended by Adams in 1764 and Richard Henry Lee of Virginia in 1768. In fact, during the Stamp

The following is a compilation of Paul Revere's activities as an express rider for a two-year period. All the rides originated and ended in Boston:

Date	Destination	Purpose
17 Dec. 1773	1,2	News of Tea Party
14 May 1774	1,2,3	News of Intolerable Acts
Summer 1774	1	Meetings with Whig leaders "for calling a Congress"
11 Sept. 1774	1,2	Deliver Suffolk Resolves
29 Sept. 1774	2	Response to British measures
12 Dec. 1774	4	Warning of British attack
26 Jan. 1775	5	Liaison with N.H. assembly
7 Apr. 1775	7	Warning to move stores
16 Apr. 1775	6	Meeting with town leaders
18 Apr. 1775	6,7	Warning of British march; captured in Lincoln
20 Apr. 1775	8	"Out of door work" for the Committee of Safety
12 Nov. 1775	2	Studying methods for the manufacture of munitions

Key:
1-New York City   5-Exeter, N.H.
2-Philadelphia   6-Lexington, Mass.
3-Hartford, Conn.   7-Concord, Mass.
4-Portsmouth, N.H.   8-Various Places

Source: David Hackett Fischer, *Paul Revere's Ride* (New York & Oxford: Oxford University Press, 1994), pp. 299–301.

Act crisis the Sons of Liberty formed correspondence circles among several towns, counties, and provinces. Yet it was through the efforts of Adams that the committees of correspondence became "a powerful political weapon for revolutionary action."

Decision to Commit. At first other leading Bostonians gave a lukewarm response to Adams's idea. Thomas Cushing, Samuel Phillips, and John Hancock all declined to serve on the committee because of business obligations. Eventually the Boston town meeting created a committee of twenty-one individuals chaired by James Otis to draft a statement of colonial rights and to list violations. On 20 November the Boston Committee of Correspondence presented a circular to the Massachusetts towns written by Adams, Joseph Warren, and Benjamin Church. It addressed the state of the imperial controversy and invited towns to form their own groups. Fifty-eight towns responded and set up committees on the Boston model. Many wrote their own declarations of co-

lonial rights and printed them in newspapers. By January 1773, according to Hutchinson, more than eighty such organizations existed throughout the province. Special couriers carried dispatches between the various towns. Boston silversmith Paul Revere made approximately twenty rides for the Boston Committee of Correspondence between December 1773 and November 1775.

Network. By a resolution of the Virginia House of Burgesses on 12 March 1773, the movement to form committees of correspondence became intercolonial. While House members discussed the fallout of the *Gaspee* incident, Thomas Jefferson remembered that "We were all sensible that the most urgent of all measures [was] that of coming to an understanding with all the other colonies, to consider the British claims as a common cause of all, and to produce a unity of action. . . ." As a result the House of Burgesses formed a committee "whose business it shall be to obtain the most early and authentic intelligence of all such acts and resolutions of the British Parliament . . . as may relate to or effect the British colonies in *America,* and to keep up and maintain a correspondence and communication with our sister colonies. . . ." A group of eleven then sent copies of this statement to the other colonial legislatures; all but New Jersey's assembly replied favorably. By the end of 1773 committees of correspondence had spread all the way to Charleston, South Carolina.

Worth. Many Loyalists saw the committees as treasonous. Hutchinson called them a "contagion" while Daniel Leonard of Taunton, Massachusetts, called them "the foulest, subtlest, and most venomous serpent ever issued from the eggs of sedition." Following the passage of the Coercive Acts, the committees proved their worth to the Whig cause. When the port of Boston was closed, the Newport, Rhode Island, committee reported in the *Newport Mercury* that "the insult and indignity" to Boston "ought to be viewed in the same odious light as a direct, hostile, invasion of every province on the continent."

Significance. In late March 1774 Adams confidently wrote that "Colony communicates with colony" and that "the whole continent is now become united in sentiment and in opposition to tyranny." Although his assessment was a bit overoptimistic, Adams correctly identified the value of committees of correspondence in fostering intercolonial solidarity. Many committee members served in their respective colonies' elected assemblies, a fact that gave them strong credence when the legislatures appointed delegates to attend the First Continental Congress in Philadelphia. By 1775 the committees of correspondence had been supplanted in importance by the committees of safety, the paramilitary bodies that secured arms and munitions and trained local militia in preparation for hostilities.

Sources:

Richard D. Brown, *Revolutionary Politics in Massachusetts: The Boston Committee of Correspondence and the Towns, 1772–1774* (Cambridge, Mass.: Harvard University Press, 1970);

John R. Galvin, *Three Men of Boston* (New York: Thomas Y. Crowell, 1976);

John C. Miller, *Origins of the American Revolution* (Boston: Little, Brown, 1943);

Francis G. Walett, *Patriots, Loyalists, and Printers: Bicentennial Articles on the American Revolution* (Worcester, Mass.: American Antiquarian Society, 1976).

THE CULPER RING

Significance. The code name for an American spy network during the Revolutionary War, the Culper Ring, proved to be the most effective espionage service employed by either side during the whole conflict. The ring successfully operated in the New York City area for almost six years, sustaining only one major reversal in 1780. Its history entails many hair-raising episodes, and James Fenimore Cooper used the ring as a basis for his 1821 novel *The Spy.*

Members of the Boston Committee of Correspondence conferring on the news of the Coercive Acts

Origins. Early in the war George Washington recognized the need for good intelligence concerning enemy troop dispositions and movements. In 1776 Nathan Hale was captured in New York City and hanged as a spy. During the Pennsylvania campaign of 1777 and subsequent British occupation of Philadelphia, various individuals supplied American forces with information. However, not until after the Battle of Monmouth Courthouse in June 1778, when the British reestablished their headquarters in New York City, was the American commander in chief able to construct a reliable, systematic intelligence service.

Tallmadge. Washington preferred to act as his own head of the secret service. He alone determined policy and paid his spies with hard specie derived from a special fund provided by Congress. However, in late 1778 he needed a new deputy intelligence chief because the current one, Brig. Gen. Charles Scott, was in poor health and requested to be relieved of duty. Scott suggested one John Bolton, a man highly recommended by Maj. Benjamin Tallmadge. (Little did Scott know that John Bolton was the code name for none other than Tallmadge.) A dedicated dragoon officer, Tallmadge had once lived in Brookhaven, Long Island, a fact that made him invaluable to Washington.

Chain of Correspondence. The young officer was entrusted with the correspondence of an individual named

A letter written in code from Benedict Arnold to John André, 12 July 1780

Samuel Culper. Tallmadge apparently utilized his Long Island connections to establish a viable secret service. All the initial members of the Culper Ring were Tallmadge's friends or neighbors prior to the war. Caleb Brewster, a blacksmith and lieutenant in the Continental Army; Austin Roe, a tavern keeper; and Abraham Woodhull (alias Samuel Culper), a prosperous farmer, all hailed from Setauket, Long Island. At this time, the British not only occupied Manhattan, but Staten Island, Westchester County, and Long Island as well. The chain of correspondence that developed was as follows: Woodhull would pay frequent visits to his sister, Mary, who with her husband ran the Underhill Boardinghouse on Queen Street in New York City. There, Woodhull would gather information concerning enemy troop movements, shipping, and supplies. When Roe came into the city on the pretense of buying goods for his tavern, Woodhull would pass him this information. When Roe returned to Setauket, he would give the dispatches to Brewster. In 1779 Woodhull returned to his Long Island farm; his place in New York was taken by Robert Townsend, alias Samuel Culper, Junior. Townsend would pass the information to Roe, who would bury the secret messages in a meadow near Woodhull's home. They were hidden there until Woodhull observed a black petticoat hanging on the clothesline of Anna Strong (whose sister was Tallmadge's stepmother). The Strong residence commanded a panoramic view of nearby Setauket Harbor, and the black petticoat indicated that Brewster had crossed Long Island Sound from Connecticut in a whaleboat. The number of handkerchiefs hanging next to the petticoat indicated at which inlet Brewster waited. Woodhull

A pen-and-ink self-portrait of John André, 1 October 1780
(Library of Congress)

would then retrieve the intelligence and bring it to the lieutenant, who would recross the Sound, land at Fairfield, Connecticut, and deliver the information to Tallmadge, who would dispatch dragoon couriers to carry the news to Washington.

Frayed Nerves. This undercover operation worked in absolute secrecy, supplying the American commander in chief with accurate intelligence. Nevertheless, Samuel Culper, Senior feared capture on a daily basis, and in April 1779 he had a severe fright when two female relatives burst into his room while he was composing a secret message. (British officers occupied the adjacent quarters.) Tallmadge reported to Washington that "such an excessive fright and so great a turbulence of passions so wrought on poor C. that he has hardly been in tolerable health since."

Culper Junior. In June, Woodhull requested to be relieved of his duties in the city; he found a trustworthy replacement in Townsend. A young Quaker merchant from Oyster Bay, Long Island, he made Woodhull pledge to never reveal his identity. (Apparently Woodhull did tell Tallmadge.) Culper Junior proved to be a most enterprising spy. In order to conceal his activities, he opened a dry goods business with Henry Oakman and occasionally contributed articles to James Rivington's Tory newspaper, the *Royal Gazette.* Rivington's printing house and coffee shop afforded Townsend the opportunity to mingle with British officers, especially Maj. John André. As the newly appointed adjutant general to General Sir Henry Clinton, André coordinated British intelligence-gathering efforts.

More Contacts. By October 1779 the Culpers employed a whole crew of seemingly innocent civilians. Joseph Lawrence, whose son married Townsend's niece, helped the spies on several occasions. James Townsend, a younger cousin of Culper Junior, once carried a message across the Hudson River to Washington's headquarters. Sarah Townsend frequently provided her brother Robert with information obtained from conversations with enemy officers staying at the Townsend house. Meanwhile, Hercules Mulligan, a prominent tailor, sent reports on troop movements. An unidentified woman simply known as 355 also supplied the Culpers with information.

Code. In order to transmit messages, Tallmadge in July 1779 devised a code based on John Entick's *New Latin and English Dictionary* (1771). He made only four copies of the code book, keeping one for himself and giving the others to Washington and the Culpers. Words that were most apt to be utilized in secret correspondence were assigned numbers. However, Tallmadge inadvertently numbered the words in nearly alphabetical order and with little variation (they, 629; there, 630; thing, 631). As a result, words beginning with *a, b,* or *c* had low numbers while words beginning with *x, y,* or *z* had high numbers. The code could have been easily broken but fortunately this never occurred. Proper names also received numbers: 711 (Washington), 712 (Clinton), 721 (Bolton), 722 (Culper Senior), 723 (Culper Junior), 724 (Roe), 725 (Brewster), and 726 (Rivington).

Invisible Ink. More important than the code was an invisible ink developed by James and John (future chief justice of the U.S. Supreme Court) Jay before the war. Called "white ink" or "stain," its exact composition is unknown. James Jay claimed that "if one writes on the whitest paper, the letters immediately become invisible." In order to become legible the writing needed to be brushed with a "sympathetic" developer. The Culpers wrote invisible dispatches on preselected sheets in a ream of paper and on the leaves of pamphlets, registers, and almanacs. Even private correspondence was a practical vehicle for secret information: stained messages were written between the lines, at the end of the letter, or on the reverse side.

Valuable Information. The Culper network may have passed along valuable information to the American army, but it was usually a slow process. The distance from Manhattan to Setauket is fifty miles. In summer 1779 Culper Junior warned of an imminent attack upon the French army at Newport, Rhode Island. Information supplied through Culper Senior enabled Tallmadge and one hundred dragoons to raid Fort St. George on South Bay, Long Island, in November 1780.

The Arnold Conspiracy. The treason of American general Benedict Arnold and the subsequent execution of André involve the most perplexing secrets of the Culper espionage network. Tallmadge in his *Memoir* (1858) stated that he purposely omitted "some things relating to the detention of André." What these "things" are will never be known, but evidence suggests Sarah Townsend had overheard André at her house mention West Point (a post commanded by Arnold) in a conversation with another officer. On 23 September 1780 an

American patrol captured André in Westchester County with the plans of West Point. After Arnold fled to the enemy, the members of the ring scattered for several weeks, but in November several of them were imprisoned and questioned by British authorities.

Other Close Calls. Aside from the Arnold-André affair, the Culper Ring was almost exposed on several other occasions. In a skirmish with enemy cavalry Tallmadge lost some Washington missives addressed to the Culpers. British sentries searched Woodhull at the Brooklyn ferry in May 1781 because "some villain" was carrying messages out of the city and to the American army. Brewster's frequent trips across Long Island Sound attracted the attention of the enemy from the start, but all attempts to capture him proved fruitless.

End of Service. When hostilities ceased in 1783, the need for the Culper Ring came to an end. Washington had a high opinion of the Culpers but never met either man. Although he knew Culper Senior's real name, Tallmadge and Woodhull kept Culper Junior's identity a secret. In fact, Culper Junior's identity was not revealed until 1939, when the Long Island historian Morton Pennypacker noticed a fascinating resemblance between the handwriting of Culper Junior and Robert Townsend. Tallmadge and the Culpers had no desire for public recognition and never publicly discussed their activities during the war.

Sources:

Corey Ford, *A Peculiar Service* (Boston: Little, Brown, 1965);

Memoir of Colonel Benjamin Tallmadge (New York: Thomas Holman, 1858);

Morton Pennypacker, *General Washington's Spies on Long Island and in New York,* 2 volumes (Volume 1, Brooklyn, N.Y.: Long Island Historical Society, 1939; Volume 2, East Hampton, N.Y.: East Hampton Free Library, 1948);

Carl Van Doren, *Secret History of the American Revolution* (New York: Viking, 1941).

THE LOYALIST PRESS

Definition. Anti-Whig newspapers and pamphlets began to appear in 1774 and existed in British-held regions until 1783. Unlike the rhetoric generated by the Patriot press, Loyalist propaganda had a more difficult time in achieving its goals: maintaining the morale of loyal colonists and demoralizing the enemy. In the end the pro-British press failed to win the hearts and minds of the American people.

Prewar Sparring. By the early 1770s royal officials recognized the power of colonial printers in fomenting discontent among the American people. Although Loyalist postmasters destroyed publications they deemed to be seditious, such as William Goddard's *(Philadelphia) Pennsylvania Chronicle and Universal Advertiser Journal,* these efforts were not enough to stop the flood of anti-British material. Tory writers exchanged verbal attacks with their Whig counterparts in the newspapers. Jonathan Sewall published five series of anonymous essays

---

THE LEADING AMERICAN PRINTERS OF ORIGINAL POLITICAL PAMPHLETS, 1764-1776	
Edes & Gill (Boston)	34
James Rivington (New York)	20
William & Thomas Bradford (Philadelphia)	9
Robert Bell (Philadelphia)	5
Thomas & John Fleet (Boston)	5
John Dunlap (Philadelphia)	4
John Holt (New York)	4
Total	81

Source: G. Thomas Tanselle, "Some Statistics on American Printing, 1764–1783," in *The Press and the American Revolution,* edited by Bernard Bailyn and John B. Hench (Worcester, Mass.: American Antiquarian Society, 1980), p. 354.

---

between 1763 and 1775, refuting the criticism heaped on the Massachusetts royal governor. One of the most famous exchanges involved John Adams ("Novanglus") and Daniel Leonard ("Massachusettensis") in the *Boston Gazette and Country Journal* and the *Massachusetts Gazette and Boston Post-Boy and Advertiser* in 1774–1775. While Adams emphasized "liberty and innovation," Leonard extolled "order and imperial stability."

Disadvantage. Once the war commenced in April 1775, it became clearly evident that the Whigs dominated the press and postal networks and could use those advantages to crush Tory polemics. As a result Loyalist propaganda was circumscribed, limited in time and place to those areas under direct British military control, usually major cities and the surrounding communities. During the course of the Revolutionary War, the cities occupied by royal troops for an extended period of time included New York, Newport, Philadelphia, Savannah, and Charleston.

Newspapers. Fifteen Loyalist newspapers appeared at various times following the Declaration of Independence, but not a single one published continuously from 1776 to the end of the war. The largest number in any one year was eight in 1778 while the smallest was five in 1779. New York City had the longest-lived and most-popular Loyalist papers, including Hugh Gaine's *New-York Gazette; and the Weekly Mercury,* Alexander Robertson's *The Royal American Gazette,* James Rivington's *Royal Gazette,* and William Lewis's *New York Mercury.* Because of the abundance of city newspapers, the British in 1779 organized the following daily schedule: Gaine published on Mondays, Rivington on Wednesdays and Saturdays, Robertson on Thursdays, and Lewis on Fridays. The *Newport Gazette* in Rhode Island ran from January 1777 to October 1779 while Philadelphia had three Tory newspapers during the British occupation from Septem-

ber 1777 to June 1778: the *Pennsylvania Evening Post,
Pennsylvania Ledger,* and *Royal Pennyslvania Gazette.*
There were also two German-language newspapers with
pro-British slants, but they lasted only a few months.
Charleston had three pro-British newspapers between
May 1780 and December 1782: the *South-Carolina and
American General Gazette, The Royal Gazette,* and *Royal
South-Carolina Gazette.* The *Royal Georgia Gazette* ap-
peared in Savannah (1779–1782) and the *East Florida
Gazette* in St. Augustine (1783–1784).

Function. These newspapers served the royal cause
on several levels. They acted in a psychological capacity,
providing a semblance of normality for areas under British military and civil control. They also stimulated the
economy by running advertisements and other information useful to consumers and merchants. Moreover, the
papers announced British victories and published the
decrees of army commanders and magistrates. Probably
their greatest purpose was to provide a useful means by
which Loyalists could lambast the Patriots and express
the needs of "King's Men" to the Crown.

Themes. Loyalist propaganda addressed various
themes when attacking the Patriot cause. First and foremost, the legal justification (both civil and biblical) of
suppressing the rebellion was not lost on the Loyalist
propagandists who urged "that obedience to legal
authority is the positive command of God, and the constant doctrine of his word." On 28 November 1776, 948
persons signed the Loyalist Declaration of Dependence,
expressing their dedication to British constitutional supremacy. In *The Christian Soldier's Duty briefly Delineated* (1777), Charles Inglis appealed to soldiers "to assert the just rights of your amiable, insulted Sovereign
— a Sovereign whose numerous Virtues add Lustre to
his Throne." Warnings of Patriot "illusions of victory"
also surfaced. On 3 October 1778 "Concord" wrote the
following admonishment in Rivington's *Royal Gazette:*
"Look forward, Americans! Compare the secure, prosperous, and truly free and independent state which is
now most certainly and immediately in your offer, to the
hazards, intermediate distresses, and probably consequences of the projects into which the Congress wish to
plunge you." By the same token Tory writers down-
played the defeat of British redcoats by remembering
how the martial prowess of England had reigned supreme in previous conflicts. And like all propagandists
they spread rumor and falsehoods whenever to their advantage. For example, on 13 February 1781 Gaine reported the defeat of British lieutenant colonel Banastre
Tarleton at the Cowpens, South Carolina. Simultaneously he printed an extract of a letter that claimed Lord
Charles Cornwallis had defeated Gen. Nathanael
Greene and taken sixteen hundred prisoners. Although
Greene's defeat later proved to be false, Gaine maintained that the news "arrived last Evening from Jersey
from a Person who saw the Letter, and who may be relied on." Pro-British writers also focused on the deprav-

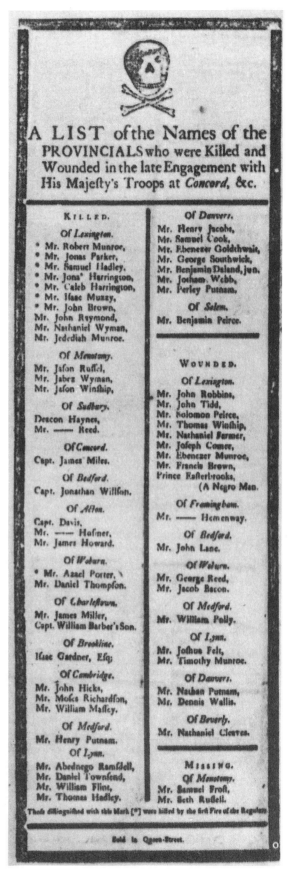

An unofficial list of the Patriot casualties sustained
on 19 April 1775

The Retreat

From Concord to Lexington of the Army of Wild Irish Asses Defeated by the Brave American Militia
M'r Deacon M'r Leenings M'r Hulchens M'r Bonds Houses and Barn all Plunderd and Burnt on April 19th

An American cartoon depicting the first battle of the Revolutionary War (British Museum)

ity of the enemy, reporting on the depredations of rebel troops and the arrogance of Congress to deny overtures made by the Carlisle Peace Commission in 1778. "It is as near the truth to say," wrote Leonard, that the enemy leadership displayed serious character flaws, especially "disaffection, petulance, ingratitude, and disloyalty." In addition Leonard hinted at their ultimate moral shortcoming by stating that "the annals of the world have not yet been deformed with a single instance of so unnatural, so causeless, so wanton, so wicked a rebellion." "Grotius" in a January 1775 letter summarized the Loyalist point of view on the rebellion when he asked Virginia lawyer Peyton Randolph how "could you thus attempt to make blind eyes blinder, to make the mad Americans rage, and the deceived people imagine vain things."

Assessment. The Loyalist press ultimately failed in its mission to undermine the Patriot cause. Although it took the moral high ground by appealing to the colonials' sense of loyalty to a gracious king, the press never presented a fully developed alternative and, for that matter, appealing, solution to the political crisis. The Loyalist press existed as long as the presence of British redcoats made it possible.

Sources:

Catherine S. Crary, ed., *The Price of Loyalty: Tory Writings from the Revolutionary Era* (New York: McGraw-Hill, 1973);

Philip Davidson, *Propaganda and the American Revolution 1763–1783* (Chapel Hill: University of North Carolina Press, 1941);

Janice Potter and Robert M. Calhoon, "The Character and Coherence of the Loyalist Press," in *The Press and the American Revolution*, edited by Bernard Bailyn and John B. Hench (Worcester, Mass.: American Antiquarian Society, 1980), pp. 229–272.

THE PATRIOT PRESS

Importance. The term *Patriot press* refers to those newspapers and pamphlets after 1765 that ran essays, editorials, and articles critical of the king and Parliament. The impact that these periodicals had on American society was indeed significant. They stimulated the

SWEET LIBERTY

These are the times that try men's souls: The summer soldier and the sunshine patriot will, in this crisis, shrink from the service of his country; but he that stands it NOW, deserves the love and thanks of man and woman. Tyranny, like hell, is not easily conquered; yet we have this consolation with us, that the harder the conflict, the more glorious the triumph. What we obtain too cheap, we esteem too lightly: 'Tis dearness only that gives every thing its value. Heaven knows how to put a proper price upon its goods; and it would be strange indeed, if so celestial an article as FREEDOM should not be highly rated. Britain, with an army to enforce her tyranny, has declared that she has a right (*not only to* TAX) but "to BIND *us in* ALL CASES WHATSOEVER," and if being *bound in that manner*, is not slavery, then is there not such a thing as slavery upon earth. Even the expression is impious, for so unlimited a power can belong only to GOD.

Source: Thomas Paine, *The American Crisis*, no. 1 (Philadelphia: Printed & sold by Styner & Cist, 1776–1777).

people's outrage by the principal means of opinion control: propaganda, or the spreading of ideas, information, and rumor for the purpose of aiding or undermining a cause, institution, or person.

Dominance. Whig control of the colonial communication network on the eve of the war with Britain was a significant feature of the revolutionary movement. Prominent printers such as Benjamin Edes, Isaiah Thomas, William Goddard, John Holt, William Bradford III, and Peter Timothy were early instigators of the Patriot press. In fact, prior to 1774 not a single newspaper was exclusively pro-British. There are several reasons for this. First the Stamp Act bound many printers to the Patriot side at the beginning of the controversy with England. It infringed on both the printers' profits and their rights. Meanwhile, Loyalist publishers were slow to come to the defense of the British government, finding it safer to remain neutral until British military and civil authorities could protect them.

Postmasters. What made the Patriot press even more effective was the fact that many Whig newspaper editors such as Goddard and James Parker were also local postmasters. Until 1773 printers used the official mails, causing Postal Inspector Hugh Finlay to note that couriers were overburdened with newspapers. After this point some publishers, especially Goddard, employed their own riders to deliver papers. Moreover, the committees of correspondence began operating an intercolonial news exchange through the use of special post riders such as Paul Revere of Boston. Even when the British-sponsored General Post Office closed in late December 1775, news of the signing of the Declaration of Independence spread like wildfire.

Political Pamphlets. Between 1764 and 1776 approximately 195 pamphlets addressing the issue of independence appeared in North America. Thomas Paine's *Common Sense* (1776), undoubtedly the most reprinted pamphlet of the era, sold more than 120,000 copies in less than three months. Eventually it went through twenty-five American and five foreign editions. It passionately stated the grievances against the king and Parliament and was greatly instrumental in uniting public sentiment.

Virtue. The dominant theme of Patriot propaganda was virtue. In the eighteenth century *virtue* was a vogue word, so widely used that it had no precise meaning. However, its main qualities seem to have been self-restraint and self-sacrifice. A virtuous person did not engage in excess during times of plenty and certainly did not betray his cause in times of adversity. Virtue was in essence the desire to put the public good ahead of personal interest. A person had to daily make steady self-conscious choices in order to maintain his or her virtue and to check any of the more-base human desires. Moreover, the virtuous person acted with courage no matter what the circumstances.

The Death of Jane McCrea; painting by John Vanderlyn, 1803 (Wadsworth Atheneum, Hartford, Connecticut)

Other Themes. Americans believed they had a moral as well as legal responsibility to themselves to defend their hearths and homes against tyranny. Prewar propaganda had long established the notion that England had violated the rights of the people. Reverend Jacob Green stated in a 1778 sermon: "We are contending for liberty. Our cause is just — is glorious; more glorious than to contend for a kingdom." Another minister noted that "This land is God's possession, given to us to inherit, and England herself recognized the grant by the charters granted the settlers; no one else has any right to it; therefore British attempts to take it by force are unjust and barbarous." Self-interest played a role in continuing the war as well. The consequences of having participated in a failed rebellion were never far from the thoughts of Patriot soldiers and statesmen alike. Reverend Phillips Payson intoned that "the subjugation of these States would be followed with the most shocking scenes of hanging and gibbeting." In *The Crisis Extraordinary* (1780) Paine focused on economic considerations, warning that the cost of British taxation (£6 million) outweighed the total price tag of waging war (£2.75 million). The newspapers and pamphlets emphasized the positive features of the rebellion by addressing the advantages of victory. Propagandists purposely wrote in terms of generalities so as to not alienate large groups. Commerce, freedom, and happiness were the key words employed in many Whig polemics. And like Loyalists, Patriots focused on the depravity of their enemy, who "by fire, sword and famine spread destruction and desolation around them." The

Massachusetts Spy (Boston), *New York Journal, Connecticut Journal* (New Haven), *Freeman's Journal* (Exeter and Portsmouth, New Hampshire), *Pennsylvania Evening Post* (Philadelphia), and *Pennsylvania Packet* (Philadelphia) all ran accounts describing desecrated graves, burned libraries, and defiled women.

Propaganda Coups. There is no doubt that the Patriot press waged a more effective propaganda campaign than did the Loyalist press. One of the finest examples concerns the rapidity in which news spread of the fighting at Lexington and Concord: within four days word of the battles reached New York City; five days, Philadelphia; nine days, Williamsburg, Virginia; and twenty days, Charleston. The Declaration of Independence and *Common Sense* were read to American troops and also made readily available in printed form. After composing *Common Sense* Paine served in the American army as a private and wrote his first series of *Crisis* papers (1776–1783) on a drumhead. These essays appealed directly to the emotions of American men, women, and children and helped rouse flagging spirits during the bleak winter of 1776–1777. He assured his audiences that "by perseverance and fortitude we have the prospect of a glorious issue; by cowardice and submission, the sad choice of a variety of evils" including "slavery without hope."

McCrea. Probably the greatest propaganda coup of the war concerned the murder of Jane (Jenny) McCrea. During British general John Burgoyne's expedition in July 1777 to seize Albany, New York, some of his Native American scouts raided near Fort Edward and brought in the scalp of a young woman. Ironically, McCrea was the fiancée of Lt. David Jones, one of Burgoyne's Tory militia officers. American general Horatio Gates quickly saw the propaganda value of this incident (regardless of McCrea's political affiliation) and wrote a letter designed for publication "in every Gazette," describing "a Young Lady lovely to sight, of virtuous Character, and amiable Disposition" murdered "and mangled in a most shocking Manner." As a result thousands of American

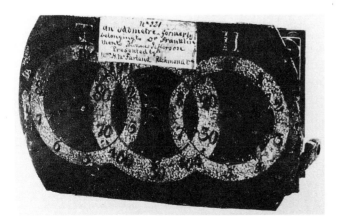

Benjamin Franklin's odometer used to measure the distances of postal routes; it was attached to the wheel of a carriage (Franklin Institute, Philadelphia)

militiamen flocked to Gates's army, "inflamed with such wrath as had not filled their bosoms" since Lexington and Concord. By October the name Jane McCrea had become a watchword, and Gates had enough troops to surround Burgoyne and defeat him in one of the most stunning American victories of the war.

Significance. The Patriot press helped keep the Revolution alive in the hearts and souls of the American populace until the war was finally won. After 1783 newspapers maintained their position as guardian of the public good and safeguard against tyranny. Indeed a vigorous partisan press was the norm in the United States for several more decades.

Sources:

"The Colonial Press," in *Encyclopedia of the North American Colonies*, volume 3, edited by Jacob E. Cooke (New York: Scribners, 1993), pp. 111–122;

Philip Davidson, *Propaganda and the American Revolution 1763–1783* (Chapel Hill: University of North Carolina Press, 1941);

Richard B. Kielbowicz, *News in the Mail: The Press, Post Office, and Public Information, 1700–1860s* (Westport, Conn.: Greenwood, 1989);

Arthur M. Schlesinger, *Prelude to Independence: The Newspaper War on Britain, 1764–1776* (New York: Knopf, 1957);

Christopher Ward, *The War of the Revolution*, 2 volumes (New York: Macmillan, 1952).

POSTAL SERVICE

Packet Service. In the early colonial period transatlantic news and mail usually came aboard merchant vessels. Caribbean islands received the news first, as ship captains sailed there first, then to the North or South American mainland colonies. To improve communications with its colonies during the War of Spanish Succession, England established a packet service to the West Indies in 1702. Packets were small armed vessels that carried only the mail. During the initial phases of the French and Indian War, the English government began a direct packet service to the North American mainland. In 1755 a monthly packet commenced operations between Falmouth, England, and New York City; by 1763 service had extended to Boston and Charleston. Intercolonial packet routes also linked such places as Charleston with Pensacola and St. Augustine, Florida.

Problems on Land. After a packet docked at a port, post riders delivered the mail to various destinations. The arrival of a post rider in a colonial American community was usually a significant event, as people anxiously awaited letters from loved ones, overseas business correspondence, newspapers, or even the latest rumors from the post rider himself. By the early 1750s a coastal post road connected Boston, New York, Philadelphia, Williamsburg, Charleston, and Savannah, but because of the great distances involved and insufficient demand, postal service was sporadic and undependable. Through the efforts of Deputy Postmaster Andrew Hamilton in the late seventeenth century, mail service had improved in the Northern colonies, but the South lagged behind.

SPREADING THE WORD: NEWS OF LEXINGTON AND CONCORD

Day	Hour	Place	Means
19 Apr.	10 a.m.	Watertown, Mass.	
		Boston, Mass.	
	12 p.m.	Worcester, Mass.	express rider
	afternoon	Newburyport, Mass.	express rider
	evening	Providence, R.I.	letter
20 Apr.	early morn.	Portsmouth, N.H.	express rider
	11 a.m.	Brooklyn, Conn.	express rider
	2 p.m.	Woodstock, Conn.	
	3 p.m.	Pomfret, Conn.	
	4 p.m.	Norwich, Conn.	express rider
	7 p.m.	New London, Conn.	
21 Apr.	1 a.m.	Lyme, Conn.	
	4 a.m.	Saybrook, Conn.	
	7 a.m.	Killingsworth, Conn.	
	8 a.m.	East Guilford, Conn.	
	10 a.m.	Guilford, Conn.	
	12 p.m.	Branford, Conn.	
		New Haven, Conn.	
22 Apr.	8 a.m.	Fairfield, Conn.	
23 Apr.	4 p.m.	New York, N.Y.	
	evening	Elizabeth, N.J.	
		Woodbridge, N.J.	
24 Apr.	2 a.m.	New Brunswick, N.J.	
	6 a.m.	Princeton, N.J.	
	9 a.m.	Trenton, N.J.	
		Philadelphia, Pa.	
		Chester, Pa.	
		Newcastle, Del.	
25 Apr.		Christiana, Del.	
		Head of Elk, Md.	
26 Apr.		Baltimore, Md.	
		Annapolis, Md.	handbill
		Alexandria, Va.	
28 Apr.	late night	Williamsburg, Va.	express rider
30 Apr.		Dumfries, Va.	
		Fredericksburg, Va.	
1 May		King William, Va.	
2 May		Surry, Va.	
3 May		Smithfield, Va.	
		Nansemond, Va.	
		Chowan, N.C.	
		New Bern, N.C.	ship
4 May		Edenton, N.C.	
5 May		Bath, N.C.	
7 May		Onslow, N.C.	
8 May		Wilmington, N.C.	
9 May		Brunswick, N.C.	
		Charleston, S.C.	ship
		Shenandoah Valley, Va.	
10 May		Georgetown, S.C.	

Source: David Hackett Fischer, *Paul Revere's Ride* (New York & Oxford: Oxford University Press, 1994), pp. 324–325.

The seasons and weather presented the greatest challenges to post riders, who worked in relays. While some operated under a royal warrant, others, especially in the Carolinas and Georgia, were employed by private companies. An express rider from New York to Virginia could seldom accomplish his trip in less than three weeks. Low wages caused some riders to supplement their income by selling household goods or cattle along the routes. As a result mail was frequently delayed. Postal rates varied from colony to colony, from as low as two pence per letter to as high as three shillings per newspaper.

Franklin. Postal deliveries were more frequent and reliable after Benjamin Franklin became deputy postmaster general for the American colonies in 1753. (He served with William Hunter until 1761; Hunter was replaced after his death by John Foxcroft.) Franklin had lobbied for two years to receive this position, having acted as postmaster of Philadelphia since 1737. As a prominent printer he had an interest in creating an efficient postal system that could deliver newspapers to larger colonial audiences. In 1754, 1755, 1756, and 1763 Franklin made inspection tours of branch offices, recommending to local postmasters ways to improve speed and frequency of delivery. Franklin and Hunter standardized rates and approved the free exchange of newspapers between publishers (long a custom in England), a practice that remained unchanged in the United States until the 1870s. Post riders received 80 percent of the revenue from newspaper postage while the other 20 percent went to the postmasters. Consequently the post office became the agent of newspaper publishers.

Results. By 1770 there were sixty-five post offices in the Thirteen Colonies. Careful record-keeping, increased responsibility of post riders (now traveling by day and night), consistent rates, shorter routes, and advertising of undelivered letters in the newspapers all encouraged confidence in the system. The important postal artery between Boston and Philadelphia saw the most improvement: it no longer took twenty-one days but six days for a letter and response between the two cities. Mail was sent three times a week from New York to Philadelphia in about thirty-three hours, ensuring a fairly constant stream of up-to-date news in the weekly papers. Nevertheless, Franklin's reforms had little impact in the Southern colonies, where delivery remained haphazard and postmasters operated in chronic deficit.

Profit. Because of the reforms introduced by Franklin, the postal service made a profit each year for the Crown although critics noted that he appointed his son William, brother John, and New York business associate James Parker to postal positions. In 1774 royal officials "found it necessary" to remove Franklin from his position as deputy postmaster general of North America because of his involvement in obtaining private letters of Massachusetts governor Thomas Hutchinson. Foxcroft then managed the General Post Office on his own, but with less-profitable results.

Finlay. On the eve of the Revolutionary War royal officials made another inspection of the colonial postal network. They appointed Hugh Finlay, who made a nine-month tour of post offices and roads from Falmouth, Maine, to Savannah, Georgia. In the North he found a reliable system with good roads but recommended alternative routes to avoid ferries. (He also noted the abundance of newspapers in the mail, which attested to the growing propaganda campaign against British rule.) In the South, Finlay discovered poor management and deplorable roads. Heavy sand and mud in some places quickly tired horses. The road from Charleston, South Carolina, to Wilmington, North Carolina, he said was "certainly the most tedious and disagreeable of any on the continent of North America."

Revolutionary War. With the approach of an open breach with England, Patriot leaders used their own mail couriers and relied less on the "Parliamentary Post" as they called it. In 1772 the various committees of correspondence had installed a system of intercolonial news exchange. On 25 December 1775 the General Post Office ceased operating in the colonies. American officials attempted to utilize the system already in place, but with mixed results. While news of the Declaration of Independence spread fairly quickly (it was printed in Philadelphia two days after its passage; New York City, six days; and Boston, fourteen days), the war disrupted the collection of newspaper subscription fees. As a result some riders before setting out on their routes had to buy copies of newspapers themselves and find their own subscribers. Franklin served the United Colonies as postmaster general from late 1775 to 1776 and then resigned

A tax stamp affixed to a business document (American Antiquarian Society, Worcester, Massachusetts)

to become U.S. commissioner to France. He was replaced by his son-in-law Richard Bache, who served until 1782, when he was replaced by Ebenezer Hazard. In October and December of that year Congress acted on Hazard's recommendations and revised and codified postal regulations. Largely a continuation of the existing system, these regulations stayed in effect until 1792.

Sources:

Ronald W. Clark, *Benjamin Franklin: A Biography* (New York: Random House, 1983);

Richard B. Kielbowicz, *News in the Mail: The Press, Post Office, and Public Information, 1700–1860s* (Westport, Conn.: Greenwood Press, 1989);

Ian K. Steele, *The English Atlantic, 1675–1740: An Exploration of Communication and Community* (New York: Oxford University Press, 1986).

THE STAMP ACT

Crisis. The Stamp Act in 1765 not only provoked an imperial crisis but also illustrated the power of the colonial press. More than any other group in eighteenth-century America, printers were capable of having their opinions heard near and far. They controlled the volume and intensity of news coverage, and by working in conjunction with the Sons of Liberty, newspaper editors and pamphleteers instigated opposition to the parliamentary statute and contributed to its repeal in 1766.

Bone of Contention. Lord George Grenville introduced the Stamp Act resolution in Parliament on 6 February 1765. A revenue-raising measure, it imposed taxes on a whole range of official and unofficial documents such as court papers, licenses, college diplomas, commis-

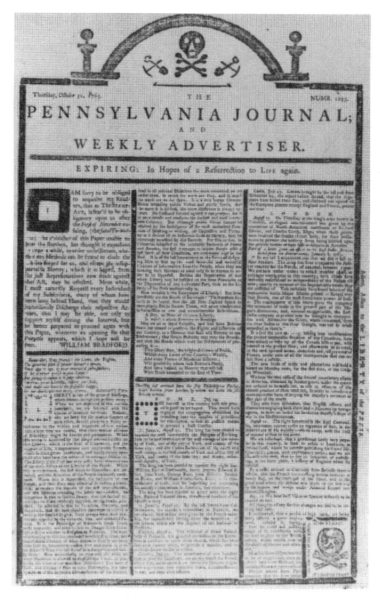

The front page of William Bradford III's newspaper the day before the Stamp Act went into effect; the black borders were designed to make the page resemble a tombstone (New York Public Library)

sions to public office, ship manifests, land titles, mortgages, bills of sale, contracts, indentures, articles of apprenticeship, playing cards, dice, pamphlets, almanacs, and newspapers (including the advertisements contained therein). The stamps cost anywhere from one halfpenny to ten pounds, depending on the document. Appointed officials distributed the paper already carrying a stamp embossed by the Treasury Office. Payment of the tax had to be in sterling, not colonial currency, and in most cases it did not represent a hardship. (The colonials were fortunate enough not to be included in the more harsh stamp act then enforced in the British Isles). The Stamp Act passed Parliament in March, and news of it first reached the colonies the following month.

Initial Response. Contrary to popular belief, the colonies reacted at first with resignation. Although royal of-

ficials noted some anger, no one predicted any major problems. The statute would become effective on 1 November 1765, and Lt. Gov. Thomas Hutchinson of Massachusetts wrote that "the Stamp Act is received among us with as much decency as could be expected. We shall execute it."

Henry. In late May the young lawyer Patrick Henry rose in the Virginia House of Burgesses and proposed seven resolutions asserting the doctrine of no taxation without representation. Although the assembly endorsed only four of these resolves, local newspapers conveyed the impression it had passed all seven by printing Henry's proposals. Moreover, Henry was reported as making a fiery speech, including the statement "In former times Tarquin and Julius had their Brutus, Charles had his

Cromwell, and he did not doubt but some good American would stand up in favour of his Country."

Sons of Liberty. The publicity afforded the Virginia resolves in the colonial press changed the mood in America from bitter acceptance to one of open defiance. "No taxation without representation" became the cry of opponents to the new imperial measure, especially after Maryland lawyer Daniel Dulany wrote the pamphlet *Considerations on the Propriety of Imposing Taxes in the British Colonies, for the Purpose of Raising a Revenue, by Act of Parliament* (1765). In Boston, Massachusetts, the Sons of Liberty, a secret organization of artisans and shopkeepers, emerged and fomented ways in which to thwart collection of the duties. The targets of its campaign were the distributors of the stamped paper. These individuals were local appointees, and if they could be intimidated, then the whole taxation measure would be crushed. On 8 August, Boston newspapers published the names of those designated to distribute the news stamps. Andrew Oliver was one of the first to resign after a mob destroyed his home and burned him in effigy. (In fact he resigned even before receiving his commission.) The same scene repeated itself in other colonies as new cells of the Sons of Liberty arose and "persuaded" the distributors not to fulfill their duties. By 1 November, the date it was to take effect, the Stamp Act had essentially been nullified by the resignation of most distributors, including George Meserve of New Hampshire, Augustus Johnston of Rhode Island, James McEvers of New York, William Coxe of New Jersey, Zachariah Hood of Maryland, George Mercer of Virginia, and Caleb Lloyd of South Carolina.

Printers Protest. Of all groups affected by the Stamp Act, newspaper and pamphlet publishers had the most to lose. Although the tax varied from one penny to one shilling per page depending on the size and number of sheets, newspapers and pamphlets incurred multiple penalties with each printing on unstamped paper. Nevertheless publishers had no intention of paying the duties although many cautiously suspended publication on 1 November. Only eight of the twenty-three colonial newspapers continued publishing without interruption, and only by changing titles or appearing anonymously. Some of the more popular newspapers that defied "the fatal Black-Act" were Benjamin Edes and John Gill's *Boston Gazette and Country Journal,* William Bradford III's *Pennsylvania Journal and Weekly Advertiser* (Philadelphia), Hugh Gaine's *New-York Gazette; and the Weekly Mercury,* and William Goddard's *Providence (R.I.) Gazette and Country Journal.* In the case of Edes, Bradford, and Goddard, they were members of the Sons of Liberty who printed incendiary articles denouncing the parliamentary statute. For them it was not so much the tax as the perceived infringement on and ultimate death of their rights as Englishmen. As a result Edes and Gill printed their paper with a skull and crossbones while Bradford made his front page resemble a tombstone.

In Need of Inspiration. The protest quickly spread among printers throughout the colonies. Lt. Gov. William Bull called the *Charleston South Carolina Gazette* the "conduit Pipe" for poisoned "principles . . . imbibed and propagated from Boston and Rhode Island." Yet not all were brave enough to defy Crown law, and reluctant printers felt the same pressure used on stamp distributors. John Holt, publisher of the *New-York Gazette and Weekly Post-Boy,* received a warning from the Sons of Liberty that "should you at this critical time shut up the press, and basely desert us, depend upon it, your house, person, and effects, will be in imminent danger." Andrew Steuart of the *North Carolina Gazette* resumed printing in mid November following a visit from a mob, but when he ran an article by a parliamentary supporter, he was threatened with a horsewhipping. He appealed to his readers: "What part is he now to act? — Continue to keep his Press open and free, and be in danger of corporal punishment, or bloque it up and run the risk of having his brains knocked out?" Although Peter Timothy closed his Charleston paper as a form of protest, he found himself reduced to "the most unpopular man" in South Carolina; three years later he still felt the loss of business because of the hostility of Patriot leaders. In fact the fear of losing customers greatly influenced printers' decisions to continue their operations, especially after four new newspapers arose during the crisis to fill the market void. As a result most newspapers gradually resumed publication long before news of the law's repeal arrived in the Thirteen Colonies.

Sources:

Lawrence Henry Gipson, *The Coming of the Revolution, 1763–1775* (New York: Harper, 1954);

Edmund S. Morgan and Helen M. Morgan, *The Stamp Act Crisis: Prologue to Revolution* (Chapel Hill & London: University of North Carolina Press, 1953);

Peter D. G. Thomas, "The Stamp Act Crisis and its Repercussions, Including the Quartering Act Controversy," in *The Blackwell Encyclopedia of the American Revolution,* edited by Jack P. Greene and J. R. Pole (Cambridge, Mass.: Basil Blackwell, 1991), pp. 113–125.

TRANSPORTATION

Sea Travel. Before the advent of the steam engine in the nineteenth century, mariners had to depend on sail power in order to propel their vessels. In the mid 1700s a ship leaving London could make the transatlantic crossing to Boston in less than eight weeks. The currents, prevailing winds, storms, and skill of the ship's captain factored in the length of a voyage. A typical deep-sea ship had three masts and square sails and displaced between three hundred to four hundred tons. Although faster than ships in the previous century, these vessels averaged only two to five knots (a knot is one nautical mile per hour). In contrast an American destroyer in World War II could travel thirty-seven knots. Life aboard an eighteenth-century ship was anything but ideal, with cramped conditions, salt provisions, occasional tainted water, and the possibility of illnesses, especially dysentery, smallpox, typhoid fever, and typhus.

To the PUBLIC.

THAT the Stage Waggons, kept by John Barnhill, in Elm-Street, in Philadelphia, and John Mercereau, at the New Blazing-Star, near New-York, continues their Stages in two Days, from Powles-Hook Ferry, opposite New-York, to Philadelphia; returns from Philadelphia to Powles-Hook in two Days also: They will endeavour to oblige the Publick by keeping the best of Waggons and sober Drivers, and sets out from Powles-Hook and Philadelphia, on Mondays and Thursdays, punctually at Sun-rise, and meet at Prince-Town the same Night, to exchange Passengers, and each return the Day after: those who are kind enough to encourage the Undertaking, are desired to cross Powles-Hook Ferry the Evening before, as they must set off early. The Price for each Passenger is Ten Shillings to Prince-Town, and from thence to Philadelphia, Ten Shillings more, Ferriage free. There will be but two Waggons, but four Setts of fresh Horses; so it will be very safe for any Person to send Goods, as there are but two Drivers, they may exchange their Goods without any Mistake. Persons may now go from New-York to Philadelphia, and back again in five Days, and remain in Philadelphia two Nights and one Day to do their Business in. The Publick may be assured, that this Road is much the shortest, than any other to Philadelphia, and regular Stages will be kept by the Publick's obliged humble Servants,
JOHN MERCEREAU, and
JOHN BARNHILL.

An advertisement for two competing stagecoach operators (Library Company of Philadelphia)

Inland Waterways. The major river systems in British North America provided a valuable means of transportation. The Hudson, Susquehanna, Potomac, Roanoke, Pee Dee, and Savannah rivers provided access to the interior. River craft included canoes, pirogues or dugouts, bateaux, barges, and rafts. Overall, transportation on rivers was slow. For instance, it took four to five days to travel from Augusta to Savannah, Georgia, a distance of 250 miles. Ice floe, rapids, sandbars, and floating debris represented obstacles to river travel. Yet for many colonial Americans water transportation was the only option available when it came to moving goods and produce. Especially in the South, where roads were scarce, farmers settled near streams.

Roads. The easiest means of travel in British North America was via roads. By 1717 a continuous road along the East coast connected all the Thirteen Colonies. Massachusetts, Connecticut, Pennsylvania, and Maryland possessed fairly good networks of major and ancillary roads, with the hub town of Boston connecting more than seventy inland and coastal towns. Meanwhile, in Georgia as late as 1750 few roads existed. In the 1770s thousands used the Great Wagon Road, the most traveled route in all the colonies. Begun in the 1730s, it extended eight hundred miles from Philadelphia to the backcountry of Georgia. Westward routes developed as well. During Maj. Gen. Edward Braddock's expedition to Fort Duquesne in the late spring and summer of 1755, British and colonial forces cut a road from Fort Cumberland, Maryland, to the Monongahela River in western Pennsylvania. Twenty years later Daniel Boone blazed the Wilderness Road from Fort Chiswell, Virginia, to Kentucky. Although hardly more than foot paths, Braddock's Road and the Wilderness Road helped open up the West to settlers.

Conditions. The Pennsylvania traveler Stephanie Grauman Wolf noted that the road linking Germantown with Philadelphia in the summertime was ground to "fine choking dust" while in the winter and spring it became nearly impassable "on account of the mud." Such an observation was fairly typical of road conditions in the era. Practically all country roads were ungraded and filled with ruts. Rocks, large tree stumps, and occasional fallen branches made travel difficult. Cost-conscious road builders adhered to a policy of the path of least resistance when planning routes and therefore avoided gullies, ravines, and creeks. In urban areas travelers enjoyed better road conditions, and by 1760 most city streets were paved, usually with cobblestones or bricks. Nevertheless road travel was slow. A rider on horseback averaged seven miles per hour while a fully loaded Conestoga wagon could manage thirty miles a day. In 1750 a coach ride from Philadelphia to Portsmouth, New Hampshire (approximately 375 miles), took eighteen days. In 1783 Thomas Jefferson complained that it took him five days to make the 104-mile journey from Philadelphia to Baltimore.

Maintenance. Roads varied in size and condition given the locale. The width of the roadbed between New York and Philadelphia fluctuated between ten and twenty feet while in Georgia it was thirty-three feet. The responsibility of maintaining roads fell to city and county officials, and they employed several means to obtain the funds needed for repairs. Aside from taxes and fines, they used lotteries, as occurred in Newport, Rhode Island, and Philadelphia. Some colonies, such as Georgia, made it compulsory for all males between the ages of sixteen and sixty to work six days a year on road maintenance. Local officials usually responded to petitions of the inhabitants in deciding the location of roads, ferries, and bridges. They frowned on ferries and bridges because of the expense and whenever possible encouraged the use of fords and corduroy roads, a series of twelve-foot logs laid side by side through marshy areas. As road networks expanded, road maps became more available. New York authorities had stone markers placed along routes to inform travelers of the distances to various destinations. Travelers also received aid in the guise of *The Vade Mecum for America; or, A Companion for Traders and Travellers,* written by Daniel Henchman and Thomas Hancock in 1732.

Modes. Aside from walking and riding a horse, a person in eighteenth-century America had other means of traveling. Farmers used two-wheeled carts while Indian traders frequently had packhorses. During this era, the Conestoga wagon came to the forefront. German craftsmen along Conestoga Creek near Lancaster, Pennsylvania, had first developed the wagon around 1725. A high-wheeled vehicle with a canvas cover, it had a curved bottom in order to keep its load from shifting. The Conestoga could carry up to six tons, four times the capacity of the average farmer's cart. (The famed prairie schooner was a lighter version developed later during the settlement of the trans-Mississippi West.) As may be expected, the Conestoga quickly became popular. By the 1770s more than ten thousand were in use in Pennsylvania while in the South Carolina backcountry there were an estimated three thousand. More-wealthy colonials living in Boston, Philadelphia, New York, or Charleston enjoyed the comfort (and status) of such vehicles as chaises, buggies, phaetons, and coaches. In fact, by the time of the American Revolution wheeled transport was available for anyone who could afford it. Several stagecoach lines operated between all the major cities in the North. The most heavily traveled route, that linking New York and Philadelphia, was served twice weekly by a stage between New Brunswick and Trenton, New Jersey.

Source:
"Transportation and Communication," in *Encyclopedia of the North American Colonies,* volume 1, edited by Jacob Ernest Cooke (New York: Scribners, 1993), pp. 495–510.

HEADLINE MAKERS

WILLIAM BRADFORD III

1719-1791
NEWSPAPER PUBLISHER

Relatives. William Bradford III was born on 19 January 1719 in Hanover Square, New York City. His grandfather, William Bradford I, had established a press in Pennsylvania, the second in America. Because of an argument with the ruling Quaker hierarchy (a rift that would plague the Bradford family for generations), he moved his print shop to New York in 1693 and founded that colony's first newspaper. In 1733 William Bradford III was apprenticed to his wealthy uncle Andrew Sowle Bradford, founder of the *American Weekly Mercury* in Philadelphia. Having no children of his own, Andrew looked upon William as a son and heir, providing him with fine clothes and a good education. At the age of twenty William became his uncle's partner, but when he refused to an arranged marriage with a cousin, his uncle wrote him out of the will.

Interlude in England. Bradford traveled to England in 1741 in order to distance himself from the family squabble and to establish his own business connections. Through the patronage of his great-aunt Tace Sowle Rayton he was able to return to Philadelphia the next year and establish in December his own newspaper. At first he called it the *Weekly Advertiser, or Philadelphia Journal* but after the third issue renamed it the *Pennsylvania Journal; and Weekly Advertiser.* He married Rachel Budd that year, and in 1754 he opened the London Coffee-House for Merchants and Traders. As a place to conduct business transactions and exchange gossip, the coffeehouse quickly became a commercial as well as social center of town.

Middling Sort. Unlike many other newspaper publishers, Bradford had an affiliation with the middling sort and demonstrated an early interest in the rights of colonists. During the French and Indian War, his *Pennsylvania Journal* took a strong stance on military preparedness, and to the chagrin of Quaker leaders he helped organize militia forces in Philadelphia. In October 1757 Bradford started the *American Magazine and Monthly Chronicle for the British Colonies.* The magazine was popular and had one thousand subscribers, including George Washington. It focused on the current state of American affairs and noted the accomplishments of colonial painters, writers, and scientists. Unfortunately it ceased publication after only one year because the editor, William Smith, departed for England following a four-month jail sentence for libel. (Smith and his father-in-law, Judge William Moore, had criticized the Pennsylvania assembly in the local press.)

Coming Crisis. The mounting tension with England caused Bradford to become even more firmly entrenched in his views on colonial rights. He was an early member of the Sons of Liberty and advocate of the creation of a continental congress. During the Stamp Act controversy Bradford, like many other printers, took great offense at the Crown's attempt to censor the press. As a result he made one of the more noticeable newspaper protests of the day. On 31 October 1765, the day before the act went into effect, the front page of the *Pennsylvania Journal* had black borders to make it look like a tombstone. A skull and crossbones with grave digger's tools appeared at the top while beneath the nameplate was the announcement: "EXPIRING: In Hopes of a Resurrection to Life again." Bradford also signed the nonimportation resolutions circulating at that time.

War Service. Politics did not occupy Bradford to the point that he ignored his press. During this period he published more than twenty volumes on politics, religion, and literature as well as his newspaper. He also attempted, unsuccessfully, to revive the *American Magazine* in 1769. With the outbreak of war he joined the American army and served during the winter campaign of 1776–1777. Severely wounded at the Battle of Princeton, he received a promotion to colonel. Meanwhile his paper had published the first of Thomas Paine's "Crisis" papers on 19 December 1776. During the British occupation of Philadelphia the *Pennsylvania Journal* suspended operations. Once enemy troops evacuated the city in June 1778, however, Bradford reopened his print shop and coffeehouse. His health had been greatly damaged by his wartime service, and he resigned his commission in 1780. His eldest son, Thomas, increasingly took on the responsibility of running the paper and continued to publish the *Journal* for two years after Bradford died on 25 September 1791. Isaiah Thomas wrote in *The History of Printing in America* (1810) that "in his most solitary hours" Bradford "reflected with pleasure, that he had done all in his power to secure for his country a name among independent nations; and he frequently said to his children, 'though I bequeath you no estate, I leave you in the enjoyment of liberty.'" Because of his devotion to the revolutionary movement, Bradford is known as the "Patriot Printer of '76."

Sources:

Henry Darrach, *Bradford Family, 1660–1906* (Philadelphia, 1906);

Isaiah Thomas, *The History of Printing in America. With a Biography of Printers, and an Account of Newspapers,* 2 volumes (Worcester, Mass.: Isaiah Thomas, 1810);

John William Wallace, *An Address Delivered at the Celebration by the New York Historical Society, May 20, 1863, of the Two Hundredth Birth Day of Mr. William Bradford, Who Introduced the Art of Printing into the Middle Colonies of British America* (Albany, N.Y.: J. Munsell, 1863).

BENJAMIN EDES

1732-1803
NEWSPAPER EDITOR

Significance. For forty-three years Benjamin Edes and his partner, John Gill, published the *Boston Gazette and Country Journal.* During the years preceding the Revolutionary War their paper served as the mouthpiece of the Patriot cause in Boston, and other colonial newspapers frequently reprinted stories from the *Boston Gazette.* Royal authorities continuously tried to silence the "trumpeters of sedition" but were never successful.

Beginnings. Edes was born on 14 October 1732 in Charlestown, Massachusetts, the son of Peter and Esther Hall Edes. As a boy he received some schooling. In 1754 he married Martha Starr, and in April of the next year Edes and Gill took over the *Boston Gazette.* The paper, established in December 1719 by William Brooker, had five other owners before Edes and Gill.

Political Commitment. The two young printers set up a shop at the corner of Court Street and Franklin Avenue. In 1765 they became embroiled in politics when they purposely violated the Stamp Act. This statute placed a tax of from a halfpenny to a penny on newspapers, depending on size. While some colonial papers ceased publication, others published issues without paying the tax and printing the publisher's name. Edes and Gill did not pay the tax and circulated the *Boston Gazette* with a skull and crossbones on the front page.

A Son of Liberty. The printers were not penalized for two reasons. First they conveniently did not use stamped paper in printing the *Boston Gazette.* (They had cut off the stamps in a cutter's binder.) Second, Edes's membership in the "Loyal Nine," a secret group of leading Bostonians who controlled the Sons of Liberty, intimidated the stamp distributor, Andrew Oliver. Frequent visitors to the printing shop of Edes and Gill included Samuel Adams, John Adams, Joseph Warren, Josiah Quincy, James Otis, and John Hancock, all of whom contributed articles to the *Boston Gazette.* In 1768 and 1769 the paper criticized Gov. Francis Bernard as a "scourge" and "plague" to the province. Bernard was recalled by Whitehall soon afterward.

Angry Bostonians. Between 1764 and 1776 Edes and Gill led colonial printers in the production of political pamphlets; indeed until 1783 their firm was the leading printer in America. The *Boston Gazette* had a record-breaking weekly circulation of two thousand papers between 1774 and 1775, evidence of its popularity among the mechanics, dockworkers, and other laborers of Boston. Seven days after the Boston Massacre in March 1770 the newspaper appeared with heavy black borders to mourn those killed. On the second page Paul Revere drew four large coffins with the initials of the deceased. The account of the event began

"The Town of Boston affords a recent and melancholy Demonstration of the destructive Consequences of quartering Troops among citizens in a Time of Peace." A special report covered the death of a fifth rioter several days later.

Tea Party. The coverage of the Boston Massacre aroused the Sons of Liberty to a fever pitch. Edes's home became the focal point of the next crisis, and it was here that the Boston Tea Party was conceived and organized. When the first tea ships arrived on November 1773, the *Boston Gazette* ran a protest, and Edes and Gill recruited armed men to patrol the docks twenty-four hours a day to ensure the cargo was not unloaded. Edes himself served on the guard. Governor Thomas Hutchinson remained steadfast that the tea be unloaded, and on 16 December leading Patriots met at Edes's house on Brattle Street. That night they disguised themselves as Indians and, joining others at the meetinghouse, boarded the ships and destroyed the tea.

Fallout. Neither the Patriot nor Loyalist press identified Edes as one of the participants. In fact the *Boston Gazette* published a warning that Edes and Gill were not to be arrested or the authorities would fall "into the pit they are digging for others." Nevertheless the threat of arrest remained, especially after Loyalists in the city requested that Gen. Thomas Gage apprehend certain individuals. Edes escaped from Boston with an old press and types, but his son Peter and Gill were arrested and jailed for several weeks. On 5 June 1775 the *Boston Gazette* resumed publication in Watertown.

Mission Accomplished. After the British evacuated Boston in March 1776, Edes returned to the city, but without the same popularity among readers and financial support of patrons; apparently the *Boston Gazette* had served its purpose. Gill started his own paper in May; the *Constitutional Journal* ran until 1787. The last issue of the *Boston Gazette* appeared on 17 September 1798. Edes spent his last years in ill health and poverty and died on 11 December 1803.

Source:
Sallie A. Whelan, "Benjamin Edes," in *American Newspaper Journalists, 1690–1872, Dictionary of Literary Biography*, volume 43, edited by Perry J. Ashley (Columbia, S.C.: Bruccoli Clark / Detroit: Gale Research, 1985), pp. 178–183.

HUGH GAINE

1726-1807
NEWSPAPER EDITOR

Irish Apprentice. Hugh Gaine is best remembered as "the turncoat printer of the American Revolution." Born near Belfast, Ireland, he became an apprentice to the printers Samuel Wilson and James Magee in 1740. Before his six years of servitude ended, however, young Gaine found himself unemployed when the Wilson-Magee partnership dissolved. As a result Gaine boarded a ship bound for America. Settling in New York, he became a journeyman for James Parker, printer-editor of the *New York Weekly Post-Boy* and an associate of Benjamin Franklin. Gaine worked at Parker's shop for seven years.

Making a Name. In 1752 Gaine started his own newspaper, the *New-York Mercury.* Its content soon made it one of the better papers in the colonies. Aside from the more-common stories on fires, robberies, and murders gleaned from other newspapers, the *Mercury* had essays on religion, philosophy, science, and love and marriage. Gaine focused on political issues and frequently printed the decrees of governors. The newspaper along with the proceeds earned from selling sundries at his print shop made Gaine a prosperous man. In 1759 he married Sarah Robbins and fathered three children: Elizabeth, John, and Anne. After his first wife died Gaine married Cornelia Wallace in 1769 and had two more children: Cornelia and Sarah.

Early Patriot. In the early 1760s Gaine protested the British mercantile policies, like many other colonial printers. When the Stamp Act became effective on 1 November 1765, the *Mercury* appeared on unstamped paper with the heading "No Stamped Paper to be Had," which appeared in place of the paper's title for the next two weeks. When the Townshend duties went into force in 1767, Gaine again joined the opposition; he endorsed colonial nonimportation and printed John Dickinson's "Letters from a Farmer in Pennsylvania."

Conservative Heart. After Parliament had recalled all the duties except the tax on tea, Gaine advocated that the Whigs end the colonial boycott as a measure of goodwill. Unlike many others, he wished to limit the opposition to British economic policies and did not see any reason to further antagonize the mother country. Perhaps Gaine's increasing wealth contributed to newfound conservatism. A 1768 appointment as public printer of the province of New York carried with it a government contract as well as a measure of prestige. (To mark the occasion Gaine changed his newspaper's name to *New-York Gazette; and the Weekly Mercury.*) In addition, by the late 1760s Gaine owned real estate, including his shop and house in Hanover Square and part of a farm in Albany County, and he had heavily invested in the construction of a Long Island paper mill.

Wavering Stance. Between 1768 and 1775 Gaine supported accommodation with the mother country. Although he sympathized with the Whig movement, he deplored violent acts such as the Boston Tea Party. Nevertheless, after the battles of Lexington and Concord in April 1775 Gaine joined the Patriot camp wholeheartedly. He enthusiastically accepted the Declaration of Independence, and before the British army captured New York in September, Gaine and his family fled to Newark, New Jersey, where the *Mercury* became an organ for the revolutionary cause.

Serle. All the printers had fled New York City, but royal authorities found Gaine's shop, the Bible and Crown, nearly intact. (When Gaine departed he left the paper's nameplate and most of his type in the care of a clerk.) Ambrose Serle, the secretary of Adm. Lord Richard Howe, began to publish a British version of the *Mercury.* Meanwhile, Gaine's operations in Newark were not bearing fruit. Subscribers were scattered and short of cash, and few advertisers were to be found. As a result, on 1 November 1776 Gaine returned to New York City. British officials quickly saw the propaganda value of his return and allowed him to resume printing the *Mercury,* but under Serle's editorial supervision. The Patriot press labeled Gaine "the greatest liar upon earth."

Tory Servant. After Serle returned to England in the summer of 1777, the *Mercury* reverted to Gaine's full control although the British still did not trust him. As a result the appointment of royal printer in the province went to another Tory editor, James Rivington, who had just returned from exile in England. Nevertheless, Gaine remained firmly in the royal camp for the next six years of British occupation. He boarded a naval officer in his home and even served in the city militia. Once British forces evacuated New York, however, he dropped the word *Crown* from the name of his shop and ran the last issue of the *Mercury* on 10 November 1783.

Last Years. For the remaining years of his life Gaine maintained his printing business, selling a variety of domestic and imported tomes. His former loyalism did not dissuade him from supporting the new federal Constitution in 1787. He also became active in civic affairs and helped found the American Booksellers Association, serving as its first president. Various real estate holdings ensured that his last years were financially comfortable. Gaine died at the age of eighty-one in 1807.

Significance. The common view of Hugh Gaine is that he surrendered his political convictions too readily, especially when his financial security was threatened. James Grant Wilson observed: "When with the Whigs, Hugh Gaine was a Whig; when with the Royalists, he was loyal; when the contest was doubtful, equally doubtful were the politics of Hugh Gaine." Yet, Gaine's *Mercury* made a lasting impact on American journalism, serving as a model for other newspapers during its thirty-year life.

Sources:

Paul Leicester Ford, ed., *The Journals of Hugh Gaine, Printer,* 2 volumes (New York: Dodd, Mead, 1902);

Alfred Lawrence Lorenz, *Hugh Gaine: A Colonial Printer-Editor's Odyssey to Loyalism* (Carbondale: Southern Illinois University Press, 1972).

WILLIAM GODDARD

1740-1817
NEWSPAPER PUBLISHER AND POSTMASTER

Family Affair. One of the most active publishers in the late colonial era, William Goddard had the aid of his mother, Sarah, and sister, Mary Katherine, in his newspaper ventures. Without their financial and managerial savvy it is unlikely that Goddard would have kept afloat any of his three newspapers. Although historians have traditionally focused on Goddard's career, they have ignored the fact that his mother and sister were accomplished printers in their own right.

Early Opportunities. William Goddard was born on 20 October 1740 in New London, Connecticut, and received some schooling during his youth. His father was a wealthy doctor and postmaster. In 1755 Goddard started an apprenticeship in the New Haven shop of James Parker, one of the most successful printers in the colonies and comptroller and general secretary of all the post offices in British North America. John Holt actually managed the shop where the *Connecticut Gazette* was published, and he became so impressed with Goddard's sense of responsibility that he sent him on a survey of local post offices. Three years later young Goddard went to work for the *New-York Weekly Post-Boy,* another Parker paper. In New York he learned the finer points of printing books and almanacs as well as postal administration.

Making a Name. When Goddard's apprenticeship expired in October 1761, he moved to Providence, Rhode Island, to seek his fortune. The city had a strong appeal to him. Not only was it a growing commercial center, but it was also home to some of his mother's wealthy relatives. Sarah Goddard advanced her son the money necessary to open his first shop and, along with his sister, came to Providence to assist him. On 20 October 1762 the three Goddards started the weekly newspaper *Providence Gazette and Country Journal,* the first in the city. They also printed almanacs and pamphlets, including one of the first verbal attacks on the Stamp Act. In 1764 William Goddard received an appointment as local postmaster.

Overcoming Disappointment. Despite their hard work the three Goddards suffered financial difficulties that ultimately caused them to suspend publication of the *Providence Gazette* on 4 May 1765. Part of the problem stemmed from a lack of subscribers and competition from rival newspapers in Newport. While Goddard went to New York and became the silent partner of his old employer Holt, his mother stayed on in Providence and managed the post office and print shop. In August 1766 she gathered enough subscribers and advertisers to successfully revive the *Providence Gazette.* Like her son, Sarah Goddard was strongly opposed to certain British government policies and soundly criticized the Townshend duties.

New Venture. Goddard stayed briefly in New York before starting anew in Philadelphia with Joseph Galloway and Thomas Wharton, two of the city's most influential citizens. There on 26 January 1767 they began the *Pennsylvania Chronicle and Universal Advertiser Journal.* The Whig Party used the paper as their mouthpiece against the proprietors of the colony. Although Goddard did not get along well with his partners, they managed to convince him to sell his Providence paper so that he could invest more in the Philadelphia one. Once again Sarah and Mary Katherine came to William's assistance and worked in his print shop. In fact they managed the paper on a day-to-day basis while he traveled to collect overdue subscription fees. When Sarah died on 5 January 1770, her obituary noted her "virtue, ingenuity and abilities."

Dispute. By 1770 the *Pennsylvania Chronicle* had a circulation of twenty-five hundred, making it one of the most successful colonial newspapers. Nevertheless, Goddard did have his problems. He and a rival Philadelphia printer, William Bradford III, conducted a newspaper war that degenerated into personal insults. Meanwhile, Galloway and Wharton, had sold their shares of the paper to Robert Towne, who in turn made every effort to make Goddard sell out. After Goddard publicly criticized Galloway and Wharton he found himself jailed for debt in September 1771. Upon his release three weeks later, he decided to leave the colony and start another paper elsewhere. While Mary Katherine continued to produce the *Pennsylvania Chronicle,* Goddard started the *Maryland Journal; and the Baltimore Advertiser* on 20 August 1773.

Rescued Again. For a third time Goddard started a newspaper and needed outside assistance to keep it in circulation. His frequent travels, poor health, and work for the local committees of correspondence kept him preoccupied. As a result he decided to close the *Pennsylvania Chronicle* on 8 February 1774 and bring his sister to Baltimore to work on the *Maryland Journal.*

Revolutionary Service. Goddard supported the revolutionary movement wholeheartedly but never received the recognition he thought he deserved. The Continental Congress used his suggestions in constructing a national postal network and appointed him surveyor but did not grant him the position of postmaster general as he had hoped. His attempts to obtain a colonelcy in the Continental Army also proved fruitless. Meanwhile, Mary Katherine was named postmistress of Baltimore, the first woman in the nation to be appointed to federal office.

Sibling Rivalry. Like her mother, Mary Katherine took a stagnant business and revived it. For three years she successfully ran the newspaper while her temperamental brother was kept busy with his duties as surveyor.

Once William returned to Baltimore, however, he embroiled the *Maryland Journal* in controversy by publishing two pieces local authorities considered unpatriotic. Nevertheless the Continental Congress recognized Mary Katherine's ability by appointing her chief printer in Baltimore after the Congress moved there following the British occupation of Philadelphia in September 1777. After the war Goddard took sole control of the paper and married Abigail Angell; together they had five children.

Falling Out. In 1784 William and Mary Katherine printed competing almanacs, and Goddard maintained that his sister's volume had been published "by a certain hypocritical Character for the dirty and mean Purpose of Fraud and DECEPTION." Consequently, Mary Katherine had no further contact with her brother. She hoped to continue in her position as postmistress, but in 1789 the new postmaster general replaced her with a man because "more travelling might be necessary than a woman could undertake." She appealed personally to President George Washington and the U.S. Senate, but her petition met with failure. She made a modest living as a bookseller and storekeeper until her death in 1816. William Goddard died the next year on 23 December 1817.

Source:
Ward L. Miner, *William Goddard, Newspaperman* (Durham, N.C.: Duke University Press, 1962).

JAMES PARKER

1714-1770
PRINTER, POSTMASTER, AND JOURNALIST

Dedication. James Parker dedicated a good part of his life to the written word, establishing printing houses in three colonies and founding several newspapers. Considered one of the best printers in colonial America, Parker gave a measure of respectability to the field of journalism and developed a reputation for accurate reporting. Some historians maintain that as a newspaper editor he was the superior of both William Bradford III and Benjamin Franklin.

Youth. Parker was born in Woodbridge, New Jersey, the son of a cooper. When his father died in 1727, Parker traveled to New York City to become the apprentice of Bradford, but he ran away from his master before his eight years of service had expired. Arriving in Philadelphia, the energetic youth impressed Franklin, who gave him a job in his printing establishment. In February 1742 the two men formed a six-year partnership, and Franklin supplied Parker with a press and type for starting a newspaper in New York.

New York. On 4 January 1743 Parker founded his first newspaper, the *New-York Weekly Post-Boy,* to compete with the *New-York Gazette,* published by his former master Bradford. The following December, Parker became public printer of New York, and when Bradford's publication ceased operations in November 1744, Parker renamed his paper the *New-York Gazette, Revived in the Weekly Post-Boy.* Over the next several years it grew in popularity until it became the foremost newspaper in the colony. Readers respected Parker's ethics and sense of honor, especially after he publicly apologized to some respectable Quakers for publishing two forged letters that criticized them. By 1746 Parker had become librarian of the Corporation of the City of New York. In 1753 he once again changed the name of his paper, calling it the *New-York Gazette; or, The Weekly Post-Boy.* He then turned the management of his New York press over to William Weyman and returned to New Jersey.

Connecticut. During this time Parker published four short-lived periodicals, became the printer to Yale College, and received an appointment (through his old friend Franklin) as postmaster of New Haven, Connecticut. On 12 April 1755 Parker and his silent partner, John Holt, established the *Connecticut Gazette,* the first newspaper in the colony. The next year Parker became comptroller and secretary of the general post offices of the British colonies, and in 1758 the New Jersey assembly made him public printer.

Apprentices and Journeymen. Almost everything Parker set out to do ended in success. Aside from his newspapers he tried his hand at printing almanacs as well as works of poetry, fiction, history, religion, and science. His only notable failure during this period was the *New American Magazine,* published in Woodbridge between January 1758 and March 1760. Nevertheless, Parker was undaunted; indeed, many of his apprentices and journeymen showed some of the same industriousness. Among these men were William Goddard, the first to establish a printing press in Providence, Rhode Island, and Hugh Gaine, editor of the *New-York Mercury.*

Illness. In his later years Parker suffered from severe gout, and he centered his activities more and more in New Jersey. In 1762 he terminated his partnership with Holt, who then became the sole publisher of the *Weekly Post-Boy.* Parker opposed the Stamp Act ("the fatal Black-Act") and began the first newspaper in New Jersey, the *Constitutional Courant,* on 21 September 1765 in protest. The paper bore the imprint "Printed by Andrew Marvel, at the Sign of the Bribe refused, on Constitution-Hill, North America."

Death. On 20 February 1770 Parker wrote to Franklin that his gout had become so debilitating he was "drawing nigh to the Grave with a good deal of Rapidity." Nevertheless he continued his course as a voice piece for the Patriot movement. Two months earlier he had printed an anonymous essay addressed "To the Betrayed Inhabitants of New York," which the General Assembly declared "a false, seditious, and infamous libel." Parker was charged, but he died on 2 July 1770 while the case was pending. He left his presses (two each in New York

and New Jersey and one in Connecticut) to his son, Samuel. His former partner, Holt, eulogized him as a man who "left a fair Character" and was "industrious in Business, upright in his Dealings, [and] charitable to the Distressed."

Sources:

William H. Benedict, "James Parker, the Printer, of Woodbridge," *Proceedings of the New Jersey Historical Society,* new series 8 (July 1923): 194–199;

Larry R. Gerlach, *Prologue to Independence: New Jersey in the Coming of the American Revolution* (New Brunswick, N.J.: Rutgers University Press, 1976);

Isaiah Thomas, *The History of Printing in America. With a Biography of Printers, and an Account of Newspapers,* 2 volumes (Worcester, Mass.: Isaiah Thomas, 1810).

JAMES RIVINGTON

1724?-1802
PRINTER

Man of Mystery. One of the most intriguing printers to come out of the Revolutionary era is James (Jemmy) Rivington. While Isaiah Thomas of the *Massachusetts Spy* stated that "few men, perhaps, were better qualified . . . to publish a newspaper," Ashbel Green described Rivington as "the greatest sycophant imaginable; very little under the influence of any principle but self-interest, yet of the most courteous manner to all." Moreover, his newspaper circulated some of the most vicious anti-Patriot propaganda of the war, yet there is reason to believe that Rivington was a spy in the pay of George Washington.

Origins. The son of prominent London publisher and book dealer Charles Rivington, James was born around 1724. After his father's death in 1742 Rivington and his brother John operated the family business. In 1752 Rivington married his first wife, Elizabeth Minshull, and four years later became the partner of James Fletcher. Together they printed Tobias Smollett's *History of England* (1757–1758) and made a profit of £10,000, considered a fortune at the time. After Rivington gambled away some of his share at the Newmarket racetrack, he decided to pay off his debts and sail to America. He still had enough money to start several new business ventures, including a bookstore in Philadelphia (1760) and New York City (1761). He also opened an art gallery in New York and a bookshop in Boston in 1763.

Giving Offense. Rivington lost another large sum of money by investing in a land scheme called the Maryland Lottery. However, he managed to recover once again and launched his most well-known endeavor in New York City in 1773, *Rivington's New-York Gazetteer or the Connecticut, Hudson's River, New-Jersey, and Quebec Weekly Advertiser.* The newspaper proved to be a huge success, with 55 percent of its contents devoted to advertisements. At first Rivington promised to please readers of all "Views and Inclinations," but as time went on, his Tory views became more audible. On 18 August 1774 the *Gazetteer* ran a letter signed "A Merchant of New-York." The missive incurred the wrath of Isaac "King" Sears, the local leader of the Sons of Liberty, by calling him "a *tool* of the lowest order." Rivington refused to reveal the identity of the author and continued to run stories critical of the Whigs. By 1775 Thomas referred to the Loyalist printer as "*that* JUDAS" while Benjamin Edes and John Gill of Boston called him "dirty" and "malicious." When a New Jersey mob on 13 April hanged him in effigy, Rivington labeled its members as "snarling curs" and lambasted Sears as "SIMPLETON SAP-SKULL." However, ten days later news of the battles of Lexington and Concord reached New York, and Rivington softened his tone by declaring that he would henceforth act from "such principles as shall not give offence."

Public Enemy. On 10 May, Sears and a mob wrecked Rivington's print shop while its owner fled to the safety of a British warship in the harbor. Rivington then petitioned the Second Continental Congress for a pardon, apologizing for his "wrong and mistaken" opinions. Congress referred the matter to the New York Provincial Congress, which granted Rivington's request. Once he became His Majesty's printer in New York, however, Rivington was emboldened and started anew with his verbal attacks upon the Patriots. On 20 November 1775 Sears and the Sons of Liberty again destroyed Rivington's presses but this time carried his type back to Connecticut. Although the New York Provincial Congress denounced this violence, Connecticut officials would not extradite Sears for prosecution. Rivington returned to England in January 1776.

Return. Rivington stayed in exile for eighteen months and then returned to New York in September 1777 as the king's printer. In order to show his support for the royal cause, on 4 October he renamed his newspaper *Rivington's New-York Loyal Gazette;* the name changed to the *Royal Gazette* on 13 December. Rivington delighted in publishing the most outrageous and unfounded rumors concerning the Patriots, causing George Washington himself to complain. Following the British defeat at Yorktown, Virginia, in October 1781 Rivington sensed the need to change his tone and asked the forgiveness of American military and civil authorities. New York officials allowed him to remain in the city after the British evacuation. Some historians speculate that the reason for such leniency was because Rivington was actually an American spy. A story circulated that Washington himself visited the printer immediately after the British evacuation and gave him a large purse of money. In 1783 he renamed his paper for the fourth time, calling it *Rivington's New-York Gazette and Universal Advertiser.* Nevertheless his apparent change of heart did not convince his old nemesis Sears, who warned Rivington not to print his paper anymore. On 31 December 1783 the last issue of the *New-York Gazette* appeared. Rivington continued as a bookseller and stationer for another nineteen years, but without much success. His second wife, Elizabeth Van Horne, whom he married in 1769, died in 1795, and he was placed in debtor's prison in 1797. Rivington's legacy lingered in New York for many years following his death on 4 July 1802. During the Civil War the *Boston Journal* stated that "Rivington lives in history as well as Arnold."

Sources:

Catherine Crary, "The Tory and the Spy: The Double Life of James Rivington," *William and Mary Quarterly,* 16 (January 1959): 61–72;

Michael Sewell, "James Rivington," in *American Newspaper Journalists, 1690-1872, Dictionary of Literary Biography,* volume 43, edited by Perry J. Ashley (Columbia, S.C.: Bruccoli Clark / Detroit: Gale Research, 1985), pp. 398–402.

PUBLICATIONS

Samuel Adams, *An Appeal to the World; or, A Vindication of the Town of Boston . . .* (Boston: Printed & sold by Edes & Gill, 1769)—a frequent contributor to the *Boston Gazette,* Adams airs his views concerning the military occupation of Boston;

William Bradford III, *Catalogue of Books Just Imported from London, and to Be Sold by William Bradford, at the London Coffee-House, Philadelphia. Wholesale And Retaile. With Good Allowance to Those That Take a Quantity* (Philadelphia: Printed by William Bradford, 1760?);

Daniel Dulany, *Considerations on the Propriety of Imposing Taxes in the British Colonies, for the Purpose of Raising a Revenue, by Act of Parliament* (Annapolis, Md.: Printed & sold by Jonas Green, 1765) — the most effective and popular of the colonial protests against the Stamp Act, this pamphlet appeared in five American editions. Dulany maintained that the statute was a violation of English common law because the colonists had no representation in Parliament, and he urged the American colonies to develop strong economies. In later years he became disillusioned by the violence of the American Revolution and opposed independence;

Benjamin Franklin, *Poor Richard improved: Being an Almanack and Ephemeris . . . For the Year of Our Lord 1755 . . . ,* as Richard Saunders, Philom. (Philadelphia: Printed & sold by B. Franklin & D. Hall, 1754)—during this period Benjamin Franklin's famous almanac sold on average of ten thousand copies per year. It represented an indispensable item to the colonial American, providing all sorts of practical information, including astrological forecasts, calendars, recipes, jokes, poems, essays, maxims, and moon and tide changes;

Hugh Gaine, *Gaine's Universal Register, or, American and British Kalendar for the Year 1777* (New York: H. Gaine, 1777);

William Goddard, *The Partnership: or the History of the Rise and Progress of the Pennsylvania Chronicle, &c.* (Philadelphia: Printed by William Goddard, 1770)

—a scathing account of how Goddard felt duped by his partners, Joseph Galloway and Thomas Wharton, into liquidating his Providence, Rhode Island, business so that he could invest more heavily in the Philadelphia newspaper;

Thomas Paine, *The American Crisis,* numbers 1–4 (Philadelphia: Printed & sold by Styner & Cist, 1776–1777); number 5 (Lancaster, Penn.: Printed by John Dunlap, 1778); numbers 6–7 (Philadelphia: Printed by John Dunlap, 1778); numbers 8–9 (Philadelphia: Printed by John Dunlap, 1780); numbers 10–12 (Philadelphia: Printed by John Dunlap?, 1782); number 13 (Philadelphia, 1783)—first written while Paine served as an aide to Gen. Nathanael Greene during the long, hard winter of 1776–1777. The *Crisis* papers are probably Paine's greatest contribution to the war effort because they roused the morale of soldier and citizen alike during critical times;

Paine, *Common Sense: Addressed to the Inhabitants of America . . .* (Philadelphia: Printed & sold by R. Bell, 1776)—initially published anonymously, this forty-seven-page pamphlet was variously attributed to Benjamin Franklin, Samuel Adams, and John Adams. By using simple language that the masses could understand, Paine helped unite Americans behind the independence movement;

James Parker, *Report of the Business of the Firm of B. Franklin & David Hall* (New York, 1766);

James Rivington, *A Catalogue of Books Sold by Rivington and Brown, Booksellers and Stationers from London, at Their Stores, over against the Golden Key* (Philadelphia: Heinrich Miller, 1762);

Rivington, *To the Public. Having Already Signed the Association, Recommended by the General Committee of New-York, Voluntarily and Freely;—For the Further Satisfaction of the Respectable Public, I Hereby Declare, That It Is My Unalterable Resolution Rigidly to Conform Myself to the Said Association; and I Humbly Intreat the Pardon of Those Whom I Have Offended by Any Ill Judged Publications . . .* (New York: Printed by James Rivington, 1775).

EDUCATION

by BARBARA DEWOLFE

CONTENTS

Sidebars and tables are listed in italics.

1754

- The Anglicans establish King's College (Columbia University) in New York City; Samuel Johnson, an Anglican clergyman, is the first president.

- Eleazar Wheelock founds the Indian Charity School in Lebanon, Connecticut, and receives funding from the Society for Promoting Christian Knowledge (S.P.C.K.).

- The Charleston Library Society is incorporated.

- The New York Society Library is established in New York City Hall by 140 wealthy citizens.

25 Apr. Anthony Benezet opens the Morning School for Girls in Philadelphia so that young women can learn reading, writing, arithmetic, and English grammar.

1755

- Georgia passes a law to prevent slaves from learning to write.

- According to the terms of the Additional Charter, the Academy of Philadelphia receives collegiate rank and becomes the Academy and College of Philadelphia (University of Pennsylvania).

- The Winyaw Indigo Society, founded in 1740 in Georgetown, South Carolina, receives a royal charter. In 1756 it starts an educational program by endowing apprenticeships and establishing a free school for poor children.

1756

- The College of New Jersey moves from Newark to Princeton, New Jersey, and is the largest college in the American colonies at this time.

- Daniel Dowle writes *A New Gift for Children*, the earliest known storybook for children published in America.

- The New York bar requires college education for admission.

1758

17 Apr. Francis Williams, the first black college graduate in the Western Hemisphere, publishes a collection of Latin poems.

20 Nov. Thomas Bray's Associates opens a trial school in Philadelphia for blacks, directed by the Reverend William Sturgeon, a Society for the Propagation of the Gospel catechist.

1760

- Thomas Bray's Associates opens schools for black children in New York City and Williamsburg, Virginia.

1762

- Thomas Bray's Associates opens a school for black children in Newport, Rhode Island.

1763

10 Feb.   William Rind of Annapolis, Maryland, starts the first circulating library in the colonies. In England fifty-three circulating libraries have been established by this time.

16 Feb.   George Wood advertises the opening of the first circulating library in Charleston, South Carolina.

29 Aug.   Bookseller Garrat Noel opens the first circulating library in New York with several thousand books.

1764

- The College of Rhode Island (Brown University) is founded in Providence. It is affiliated with the Baptist Church.

- Alexander Garden's school for black children, which was started in 1743 in Charleston, South Carolina, by Garden and the Society for the Propagation of the Gospel, closes.

26 Jan.   Harvard College Library is destroyed by fire, and only about four hundred books out on loan are saved.

1765

- At commencement exercises at the College of New Jersey, the senior class wears homespun clothing in support of the boycott of British goods.

- John Morgan establishes the first formal medical department in the American colonies at the College of Philadelphia.

- A school for black children is opened in Fredericksburg, Virginia, by Thomas Bray's Associates.

- Sodalitas, a voluntary society for the study of law and oratory, is founded in Boston.

31 Oct.   John Mein opens the first circulating library in Boston at his shop called the London Book-Store. He has twelve hundred books with seven hundred different titles.

1766

- Thomas Clap resigns as president of Yale College following student demonstrations.

10 Nov.   Queen's College in New Jersey (Rutgers University) is granted a charter. The college, named for Charlotte, the Queen Consort, is affiliated with the Dutch Reformed Church.

1767

- A medical department is established at King's College.

EDUCATION   119

	14 Sept.	Lewis Nicola opens the first circulating library in Philadelphia with approximately four hundred volumes.

1768

- Student unrest occurs at Harvard College, and pupils wear homespun clothing at commencement exercises in order to protest English duties.

1769

- The first commencement ceremonies at the College of Rhode Island are highly political, with disputations such as "Whether British America can under Present Circumstances Consistent with Good Policy, Affect to Become an Independent State?"

2 Jan. The American Society for Promoting and Propagating Useful Knowledge Held at Philadelphia merges with the American Philosophical Society to become the American Philosophical Society Held at Philadelphia for Promoting Useful Knowledge.

13 Dec. George III grants a royal charter to Eleazar Wheelock to found Dartmouth College in Hanover, New Hampshire. Wheelock becomes the first president of the school.

1770

- Christopher Dock's *Schulordnung* is published. It is the first book on school management published in America.

- Georgia outlaws the teaching of slaves to read.

- A voluntary society, the Moot Club, is founded in New York City for the study of law.

20 Mar. A new charter is granted for Queen's College.

28 June Anthony Benezet opens a free school for blacks in Philadelphia.

1771

- The first publication of the American Philosophical Society, *Transactions*, appears.

- The Massachusetts Poor Laws are revised to allow females to be taught writing as well as reading.

1773

- The Virginia Society for the Promotion of Useful Knowledge is established, with John Clayton as its first president.

1774

- The Abolition Society of Philadelphia starts a school for blacks, which flourishes for one hundred years.

- The first law school in the American colonies is established by Tapping Reeve in Litchfield, Connecticut.

- Students at the College of New Jersey burn tea on campus and in the streets of Princeton. They also burn Massachusetts governor Thomas Hutchinson in effigy, ceremoniously boycott the drinking of tea, and form a militia company. Other colleges participate in similar patriotic activities.

1775

- The minimal cost for annual college education ranges from £25 to £35 in the colonies, compared to more than £100 in England.

1776

- An academy in Virginia is established under the direction of Samuel Stanhope Smith and five trustees, all graduates of Princeton College. This academy receives degree-granting status in 1783 and becomes Hampden-Sydney College.

- Twenty-two students have graduated from the medical schools of the College of Philadelphia and King's College since their founding in 1765 and 1767, respectively.

1777

- New Jersey initiates the separation of blacks and whites in education.

- Quakers in Salem, New Jersey, approve the creation of schools for blacks.

1778

- Phillips Andover Academy, in Andover, Massachusetts, is founded.

1779

- Thomas Jefferson introduces a "Bill for the More General Diffusion of Knowledge" in the Virginia House of Burgesses, but the legislature rejects his proposal to establish the first free public school system in America.

- Jefferson also writes "A Bill Concerning Slaves," a plan to train slaves in agriculture and artisanship so that they can be prepared to live independently when they are freed.

11 May   Slaves in Connecticut petition the state for freedom. One of their grievances is the masters' "holding us in gross Ignorance, so as to render Our Subjection more easy and tolerable."

1780

- The American Academy of Arts and Sciences is chartered by the Massachusetts General Court. John Adams, James Bowdoin, and John Hancock are among the founding members.

1781

- Philips Exeter Academy is founded in Exeter, New Hampshire.
- The New Jersey Society for the Promotion of Agriculture, Commerce and Art is established.

1782

- Washington College in Chesterton, Maryland, is founded.
- Liberty Hall Academy (Washington and Lee University) in Lexington, Virginia, receives a charter from the state legislature.

1783

- Noah Webster publishes his popular "blue-backed speller," *A Grammatical Institute, of the English Language,* which he hopes will standardize the American language and instill republican virtue.
- Hampden-Sydney College in Virginia is chartered to grant degrees. As the first president, John Blair chooses a curriculum similar to that of the College of New Jersey.
- Transylvania Seminary in western Virginia (present-day Kentucky) is chartered to grant degrees.

A colonial schoolroom, circa 1770 (Bettmann Archive, New York)

OVERVIEW

Mixture. In colonial America education included many types of learning, with little emphasis placed on formal schooling. Parents were more involved in their children's learning than the government was, and schools received support from a great variety of places but were not accessible to all. Since the population of colonial America, especially south of New England, was widely scattered, the organization of a formal school system was also geographically demanding. Colonial education encompassed nearly every aspect of colonial society: families, communities, public and private schools, literary societies, churches, individual schoolteachers and tutors, missionary and philanthropic associations, and places of employment, including the household. Formal schooling existed primarily for wealthy males of European descent.

Religious Influence. In the seventeenth and early eighteenth centuries religion motivated most educational efforts. Literacy was the key to understanding the word of God, so most schools and colleges were organized by the clergy, missionaries, or some religious organization. Since 1642 New England had been under a mandate to establish schools because Puritans insisted that literacy was necessary to read the Bible. Primers and hornbooks were filled with religious and moral maxims and instructions. In the Middle colonies various denominations—German Pietists, Presbyterians, Dutch Reformed, and Quakers—created their own forms of schooling. The Quakers were unique in their inclusion of males, females, blacks, and Indians in their education system. In the South the Anglican Society for the Propagation of the Gospel in Foreign Parts and a few other religious organized schools.

Enlightenment. The early colonial college and grammar school curriculum was based on the European tradition of instruction in classical languages and literatures though other subjects such as politics, mathematics, divinity, and ethics were taught as well. The course of study was the same for everyone: Latin and Greek were necessary, not only for theology but also for law and medicine, and proficiency in these languages was a mark of the well-educated man. The classical curriculum predominated, but by the middle of the eighteenth century it had been expanded to include more mathematics, natural science, English literature, and modern languages—changes influenced by the spread of European Enlightenment ideas of the philosophes, who embraced the sciences, reason, and natural law and scorned institutional religion and the supernatural. In America the new science, which emanated from the works of men such as Sir Isaac Newton, René Descartes, Sir Francis Bacon, and John Locke, touched a society that was becoming more commercial. A more practical, vocational education appealed to a rapidly increasing middle class of artisans, merchants, and traders, who needed courses such as accounting, business, and writing. The introduction of Enlightenment ideas created a tension between classical and practical education that resulted in important curricular changes. Philadelphia became the center of the debate, largely because many of the men who were thinking and writing about the educational application of these ideas lived there—men such as Benjamin Franklin, William Smith, Francis Alison, and John Morgan.

Formal Secondary Schools. During the eighteenth century the number of secondary schools increased rapidly though mainly in the Northern and Middle colonies. In general three types of formally established schools existed. The earliest formal secondary school in the colonies was the Latin grammar school, open primarily to boys from the upper classes, but some poor boys were able to attend for free. Here students could prepare for higher education, particularly for the ministry; a grammar school and a college together formed a single education system. Latin grammar schools were run either privately by masters or were set up under town authority. The curriculum was based on classical languages and literatures, but reading, arithmetic, and writing were also taught. The English school evolved in the eighteenth century as a popular alternative to the Latin school. It offered a more practical course of study with more emphasis placed on reading, arithmetic, English grammar, history, and writing and less on the classics and religious instruction. Finally the youngest and least well-defined of the formally established secondary schools was the academy, which developed in the latter half of the eighteenth century. Its curriculum was a combination of Latin grammar and English school curricula, but college-level courses were added as well. For the next century the academy became the foremost secondary school.

Southern Schools. The Southern colonies had few grammar schools compared to New England, but they had other kinds of schools: charity, publicly endowed free, private, parish and church-sponsored, old-field, and tutorial. Private schools were run by individuals who charged fees and hoped to make a profit teaching the public. Parish schools were funded by parishes. Old-field schools were set up usually in one of the abandoned buildings on worn-out tobacco fields. These were usually in rural areas, organized by parents who hired a teacher and paid fees for their children to attend. The tutorial school was set up on a plantation for the education of a planter's children and his neighbors or relatives. The number of boys and girls could be twenty or thirty, all of different ages and educational levels. This kind of plantation school was most prevalent in the Chesapeake Bay area. Free schools and old-field schools could also be parish schools. Parish schools and church-related schools sometimes expanded to become academies and later colleges.

Colleges. By the beginning of the American Revolution nine colleges had been chartered to grant degrees: Harvard, Yale, William and Mary, the College of New Jersey (Princeton University), King's College (Columbia University), Queen's College (Rutgers University), the College of Rhode Island (Brown University), Dartmouth, and the College of Philadelphia (University of Pennsylvania). By 1784 four more had been established: Washington College in Maryland, Liberty Hall Academy (Washington and Lee University), Hampden-Sydney College in Virginia, and Transylvania Seminary in present-day Kentucky. In addition some academies provided students with college-level courses so that approximately twenty to twenty-five institutions offered collegiate instruction of some kind by the end of the Revolution. The early colonial degree-granting colleges modeled themselves after Harvard, which had faithfully tried to replicate the traditions of Emmanuel College at Cambridge University. However, by the middle of the eighteenth century certain changes in colonial society were beginning to have an impact on higher education. The population had grown in cities and in rural areas and had become more ethnically and religiously diverse. At the same time commercialism was expanding and bringing with it an interest in secular pursuits. Earlier colleges had required their board members to be clergymen of the same denomination as the college, but colleges established after 1750 also included board members who were laymen and clergy of different denominations. Franklin and others even proposed the establishment of secular colleges. Though this was never fully realized in the eighteenth century, the colleges did begin to de-emphasize clerical training and institute other intellectual disciplines, such as law, medicine, and agriculture. Until 1750 half of all college students trained to be clergymen, but by the end of the century only 22 percent of college students studied for the ministry.

Educating Females. In colonial society most formal secondary education and all higher education were open only to men. Women were regarded as helpmates of men, and their education was defined in terms of what would be most useful in making them good wives, mothers, and homemakers. Therefore they were not educated in the same manner as men, as this would be unnecessary preparation for their roles in society; they would for the most part not be involved in the public sphere of men but rather the private sphere of the home and family and as such were under the authority of their husbands unless the husbands were absent or deceased. A female's formal education was rudimentary, limited in general to instruction in reading and sewing. Though women had always had some occupations, such as midwifery, outside the home, by the mid eighteenth century their public roles expanded more in areas such as keeping inns, taverns, and small shops; printing or publishing; and assisting in or running family businesses. During the Revolution women's roles changed as wives were forced to assume their husbands' public responsibilities while the men were at war. Women participated in raising funds, in organizing protests, and in carrying out other duties related to the patriot cause. During the 1770s some of the upper-class, better-educated women challenged the educational limit imposed on females. Two of these were Abigail Smith Adams, wife of John Adams, and Mercy Warren, wife of James Warren. Mercy Otis Warren wrote political satires and plays against the supporters of Britain, and Abigail Adams protested the lack of education for females. But though ideas about women's education were changing during this period, the world dominated by men was not ready to accept the need for the higher education of women until later in the nineteenth century, nor did it even find useful a complete secondary education for women. Domestic duties remained women's priority, and no one, including Mercy Warren and Abigail Adams, challenged this or advocated that women compete with men in law, medicine, or the ministry.

African Americans. Supporters of education for blacks in the colonial period fell generally into two categories: those who wanted to provide occupational training for economic benefit and those with religious and charitable goals such as missionaries, who regarded literacy or at least the ability to read the Bible as necessary for conversion. Since skilled labor was scarce in eighteenth-century America, masters found it necessary to train some of their slaves in a trade. Slave men and women either learned these skills from other slaves or served apprenticeships under white craftsmen. Some slaves received training in more than one trade, depending on the needs of the master. As far as reading and writing were concerned, slaves usually received these under the auspices of a religious group. While most religious denominations supported the education of free and enslaved blacks, two religious groups stood out as especially active in this area: the Society for the Preservation of the Gospel (S.P.G.), a missionary society run by the Anglican Church in England; and the Quakers. Both had been active in black education since the beginning of the eighteenth century, and both established schools for blacks. The S.P.G. also sent out missionaries to catechise African Americans in order to prepare them for conversion. But education for blacks was at best haphazard and ephemeral and at worst forbidden outright, and it was often met with resistance by white slave owners, who were afraid that literate slaves would organize protests against enslavement. In 1770 Georgia even went as far as making it unlawful for anyone to teach a slave to read or write and imposed a fine of twenty pounds for doing so.

Antislavery Advocates. Education for blacks had powerful advocates in the later eighteenth century, including such important colonial thinkers as Franklin, Thomas Jefferson, and Benjamin Rush. Franklin believed that the social condition of African Americans was the result of their lack of education, and in his essay "Negro Literature" he stated that blacks have "unusual intellectual power." He published antislavery pamphlets, supported schools for blacks in many of the colonies, and became a member of Thomas Bray's Associates, a society that endeavored to provide both formal and informal education for blacks in America. Franklin also became president of the Abolition Society of Philadelphia, which started a school for blacks in 1774. Samuel Davies, a Presbyterian minister in Virginia, who later became the president of the College of New Jersey (Princeton University), tried to convert and educate African Americans. Davies received aid from Great Britain in the form of spelling books and catechisms. He continued his instruction from 1748 to 1759 until he assumed his responsibilities as college president.

Native Americans. Education of Indians in colonial America was almost always the result of efforts of religious organizations to convert them to Christianity. Before conversion could take place, the ability at least to be able to read the Bible and religious literature was necessary, so education went hand in hand with conversion. Various approaches were used. Many missionaries went to Indian societies to teach reading and writing, thereby making it possible for the children to remain with their families and at the same time giving them skills to become interpreters. Some Indians, such as those recruited by Eleazar Wheelock for his Indian Charity School, were taken away from their homes to be educated in English settings. Most of these found the separation from their culture too difficult and went back to their old ways when they rejoined their native groups. However, some became cultural brokers and were able to live and communicate in both worlds. What the colonists considered success in educating Indians depended in large measure on the degree to which the Indians were acculturated or on the extent to which their culture had already been disrupted by the encroachment of the European population. Few Indians received the benefits of higher education. From as early as 1618, when the Virginia Company of London made plans for Henrico Indian College in Virginia, to the end of the eighteenth century various parties raised money to provide higher education for the Native Americans, though the actual numbers of Indian students were always low. In the middle of the eighteenth century, from the 1750s to the beginning of the Revolution, the College of William and Mary always had about three to five Indian students. The last such effort in the colonial period was Wheelock's establishment in 1754 of the Indian Charity School (later Dartmouth College). Wheelock's agents raised about £12,000 in Britain, which was, to that date, the largest fund collected solely for Indian education. However, Wheelock used the money to build the college mainly for the benefit of English scholars, and by 1774 the fund, out of which only the interest was to be used, had been completely expended. The basis of all these efforts was the pious commitment to convert Indians. However, even though large sums of money were raised to support Indian education, little of it was actually used for that purpose. Throughout the colonial period funds gathered abroad for Indian higher education were deceptively funneled to other areas of the colleges, which were always struggling to stay afloat.

TOPICS IN THE NEWS

THE ACADEMY AND COLLEGE OF PHILADELPHIA

Franklin's Proposals. Having been influenced by Enlightenment ideas, especially the writings of John Locke, Benjamin Franklin became the foremost proponent of utilitarianism in education in the eighteenth century. His background as a printer and his avid love for applied science formed his belief that learning should be useful for one's life and for society. To that end he envisioned a new kind of formal school that would educate America's future leaders. In 1749 he wrote *Proposals Relating to the Education of the Youth in Pennsylvania,* in which he described his model for an academy, and in 1751 added *Idea of the English School, Sketch'd Out for the Consideration of the Trustees of the Philadelphia Academy,* which included further details for the six-year curriculum. His ideas departed radically from the founding principles of earlier colonial American sectarian schools and colleges. *Proposals* advocated broadening and liberalizing the standard classical curriculum by de-emphasizing Latin, Greek, and modern foreign languages—subjects that he thought should be optional—and by requiring English to be the language of instruction. Franklin's new curriculum was based on practical rather than classical instruction, that is, an education that would train students for careers in commerce, manufactures, or some profession other than the ones classical education prepared them for, such as the ministry, law, medicine, and teaching.

Though Franklin considered it necessary to educate virtuous and moral citizens, religion was no longer to be the organizing focus of the curriculum.

The Academy of Philadelphia. Franklin's plans for an academy were realized in 1753, when the Academy and Charitable School of Philadelphia was chartered and opened with about 145 boys. The new academy introduced a dual school system: one school was a traditional Latin grammar school offering a classically based curriculum, and the other was an English grammar school, where students could take useful courses, such as English grammar, composition, handwriting, astronomy, science, natural history, writing, drawing, rhetoric, history, agriculture, accounting, and mechanics. For the English school, English grammar, composition, and writing formed the core of the program because Franklin wanted to educate students for the communities in which they lived and worked. He saw history as an equally important discipline to prepare students for civic and political duties in service to the state. Furthermore history would lead to other areas of study, such as geography, ancient culture, and eventually political theory. However, Franklin's ideas did not solidify in the new academy. Though he became its first president and sat on the Board of Trustees, he thereafter kept himself at a distance, rarely visited the school, and remained ignorant of its progress. He complained that the trustees had violated the original plans set forth in his 1749 "The Constitutions of the

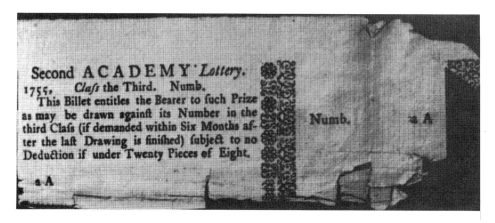

An unsold ticket for a lottery to raise money for the College, Academy, and Charitable School of Philadelphia (University of Pennsylvania, University Archives)

The 1755 charter of the College, Academy, and Charitable School of Philadelphia (University of Pennsylvania, University Archives)

Publick Academy in the City of Philadelphia," which had explained the purposes of the two academies. The Latin school was the favorite choice of many parents, who saw in its curriculum an opportunity for their children to advance in society, and of the school's influential subscribers, but Franklin was most interested in the English school, which he wanted most to succeed. However, public preference for the Latin school overpowered Franklin's premature education reforms, and the English School collapsed under the weight of the more popular Latin academy. In 1756 Franklin was removed as president of the board but remained a trustee for the rest of his life. It was not until twenty years later that his educational ideas influenced the founding of an academy: in 1778 Phillips Andover was founded in Andover, Massachusetts, the first of many academies to follow that based their curricula on some of Franklin's ideas for a practically oriented liberal arts education.

William Smith. About the same time that Franklin was creating his new academy William Smith was thinking and writing about new forms of curricula. Born in Scotland and educated at King's College of the University of Aberdeen, Smith arrived in America in 1751 and, while working as a tutor on Long Island in 1753, wrote a pamphlet titled *A General Idea of the College of Mirania,* in which he designed the ideal or utopian college of Mirania that offered two curricula. The classical curriculum was for men planning to be clergymen, lawyers, doctors, or government officials, and the practical curriculum was for students preparing for trades and the mechanic arts. Like Franklin's English school, this was a new idea. Smith also proposed to alter and expand Mirania's classical curriculum with courses such as science, surveying, history, and agriculture. Smith wrote this pamphlet with the hope that he would be considered a candidate for president of the newly proposed King's College in New York City, but since he was not an ordained clergyman, he was not eligible. However, he sent a copy to Franklin, who was so impressed with it that he invited Smith to head the Academy and Charitable School of Philadelphia. Smith accepted the position. In 1755, under the terms of the Additional Charter, the academy was granted collegiate rank and became the College, Academy and Charitable School of Philadelphia in the Province of Pennsylvania, otherwise called the College of Philadelphia. Smith became the college's first provost.

College of Philadelphia. In 1756 Smith took the idea for the college of Mirania and wrote a "scheme of Liberal Education" for the College of Philadelphia, adapting some of the ideas put forth in *Mirania* for a more secular and pragmatic curriculum for the new college. Parts of his plan such as the creation of a separate college of "mechanical arts" never received approval from the trustees. Nevertheless some significant changes were made to the classical curriculum: to the sciences were added more practical courses, including agricultural chemistry, surveying, navigation, and mechanics. Also new were history, political science, and commerce. To the College of Philadelphia belonged the distinction that it became the first college in North America to place emphasis on the study of science and the first to institute a department of medicine. Though smaller and much newer than Yale, Harvard, and the College of New Jersey, its curriculum was the most comprehensive and innovative and anticipated the reforms later proposed by Horace Mann in the nineteenth century.

Sources:

Douglas Anderson, *The Radical Enlightenments of Benjamin Franklin* (Baltimore: Johns Hopkins University Press, 1997);

John S. Brubacher and Willis Rudy, *Higher Education in Transition: A History of American Colleges and Universities* (New Brunswick, N.J.: Transaction, 1997);

Lawrence Cremin, *American Education: The Colonial Experience, 1607–1783* (New York: Harper & Row, 1970);

Lorraine Smith Pangle and Thomas L. Pangle, *The Learning of Liberty: The Educational Ideas of the American Founders* (Lawrence: University Press of Kansas, 1993);

Meyer Reinhold, "Opponents of Classical Learning in America During the Revolutionary Period," *Proceedings of the American Philosophical Society*, 112 (1968): 221–234;

Lawrence C. Wroth, *An American Bookshelf: 1755* (Philadelphia: Publications of the Rosenbach Fellowship, 1934).

APPRENTICESHIP

Anglo-American System. Apprenticeships were labor contracts between two parties. One party was the master craftsman or artisan knowledgeable about a trade or business, and the other was a young boy or girl, often an orphan or a child from a poor family, who wanted to prepare for that trade. The Statute of Artificers in 1562 had standardized the institutional regulation of apprenticeship in England. The Poor Laws in 1601 had opened apprenticeships to the poorer classes. The American colonies imitated the formal English institution of apprenticeship in many respects, especially the careful moral and occupational supervision, but had modified the system to suit the needs of the colonial economy. Craft guilds, crucial to the system in Britain, never took hold in America. Regulations governing terms of service, entry fees, ages of entry into service, training, and property restrictions were loosened or ignored altogether, largely as a result of the shortage of labor. Apprentices in England would normally be required to serve seven years. In

A hand press from James Franklin's Boston print shop (Franklin Institute, Philadelphia, Pennsylvania)

America apprentices discovered that they could get employment without finishing their contracted time of service because their labor was needed, so apprenticeships of four years became more common. In the colonies boys could be apprenticed until they were twenty-one and girls until they were eighteen or until they married, but these terms varied. Females served apprenticeships under similar regulations as their male counterparts but had fewer occupational choices.

Terms of Contract. Apprenticeships could be either voluntary, with a young person choosing his or her master and negotiating a contract, or compulsory, as arranged by parents, guardians, or governing officers. The training was lengthy and expensive but virtually guaranteed the apprentice a useful skill for life, one that he or she had learned by example and participation. The indenture of apprenticeship was a legally binding document, spelling out the responsibilities of both parties. For example, certain exemplary behavior was expected of apprentices, who usually lived with their masters. They were not allowed to reveal "trade secrets" or misuse the master's goods. They could not marry, play illegal games, or frequent taverns and playhouses, nor could they be away from their places of work without permission from the master. The master, for his or her part, agreed to instruct the apprentice in a trade and to feed, clothe, lodge, and perhaps educate the youth. But terms could be negotiated. In eighteenth-century America, since labor was scarce, prospective voluntary apprentices were able to bargain with masters for more favorable contract terms, one of which was the education clause, which allowed

A printer's type cases, chase or letterpress frame, and composing sticks

them some form of free basic education outside the workplace. They learned their reading and writing during hours when they were not working for their masters, usually at evening schools. Involuntary apprentices and females had less bargaining power in regard to the education clauses of their contracts. In any case boys received more education than girls. However, emphasis on education for apprentices was not uniform throughout the colonies. The Southern colonies were not as concerned about the formal education of apprentices, and by the middle of the eighteenth century slave apprenticeships were curtailed or outlawed in some colonies such as Georgia, which allowed blacks to be apprenticed only to coopers.

Rural v. Urban. Urban areas were filled with craftsmen of all sorts. Trades for males fell into different categories of difficulty and prestige. Among the easiest to learn and the lowest in terms of status were the shoemakers, tailors, and candlemakers. Those ranking somewhere in the middle were carpenters and blacksmiths. At the elite end of the artisan scale, and the most expensive in which to get apprenticed, were trades such as silversmithing and printing. Females chose among limited options. They were most often apprenticed in another household to learn domestic skills, but some received training in a craft or trade, such as spinning, dressmaking, hairdressing, millinery work, or embroidery. In rural areas apprenticeship choices for males and females were much narrower. They did not have the wide variety of specialized crafts that the cities and larger towns had but only those that supplied the

needs of the community, such as shoemakers, blacksmiths, and carpenters. Furthermore, the demands of the rural agricultural economy meant that most children had to spend much of their time farming or doing farm chores. Their education choices were constricted as well. In mid-eighteenth-century cities and towns apprentices could meet their basic education needs, guaranteed by their contracts, in one of the numerous evening schools. But for rural apprentices most training and education took place in the home or from plantation tutors in their spare time. Boys learned crafts from their fathers, and girls learned housewifery from their mothers. Whatever reading and writing they learned was often provided informally by family members.

Opportunity. Apprenticeships provided an opportunity for children and adolescents to receive training in a craft or skill and at the same time to learn the basics of reading, writing, and sometimes ciphering. This was particularly important for poor children who usually had no other means of obtaining a formal education unless they could attend one or more years of a free school, set up by charitable means for the purpose of teaching children who could not afford schooling. But apprenticeships ideally offered a dual education: training in a skill as well as the rudiments of education, both of which were protected by law. In this way apprenticeship became an important vehicle for educating colonists in an era when formal education was neither required nor regulated.

Sources:

Richard Beale Davis, *Intellectual Life in the Colonial South, 1585–1763* (Knoxville: University of Tennessee Press, 1978);

On 4 January 1757, John Waring, an Anglican clergyman in London and secretary for the Associates of Thomas Bray, wrote a letter to Benjamin Franklin, asking his opinion about the Associates' plans to start a school for black children in Philadelphia. The following letter is Franklin's response.

Cravenstreet, Jan. 3. 58.

I send you herewith the Extract of Mr. Sturgeon's Letter, which I mentioned to you. He is, among us, esteemed a good Man, one that makes a Conscience of the Duties of his Office, in which he is very diligent; and has behaved with so much Discretion, as to gain the general Respect and Good-will of the People. If the Associates of Dr. Bray should think fit to make Tryal of a School for Negro Children in Philadelphia, I know no Person under whose Care it would be more likely to succeed. At present few or none give their Negro Children any Schooling, partly from a Prejudice that Reading and Knowledge in a Slave are both useless and dangerous; and partly from an Unwillingness in the Masters and Mistresses of common Schools to take black Scholars, lest the Parents of the white Children should be disgusted and take them away, not chusing to have their Children mix'd with Slaves in Education, Play, &c. But a separate School for Blacks, under the Care of One, of whom People should have an Opinion that he would be careful to imbue the Minds of their young Slaves with good Principles, might probably have a Number of Blacks sent to it; and if on Experience it should be found useful, and not attended with the ill Consequences commonly apprehended, the Example might be followed in the other Colonies, and encouraged by the Inhabitants in general. I am, Sir, Your most humble Servant.

B FRANKLIN

Source: Leonard W. Labaree, ed., *The Papers of Benjamin Franklin*, volume 7 (New Haven, Conn.: Yale University Press, 1963), p. 356.

William E. Drake, *The American School in Transition* (New York: Prentice-Hall, 1955);

Huey B. Long, *Continuing Education of Adults in Colonial America* (Syracuse, N.Y.: Syracuse University Publications in Continuing Education, 1976);

W. J. Rorabaugh, *The Craft Apprentice: From Franklin to the Machine Age in America* (New York: Oxford University Press, 1986);

Harold W. Stubblefield and Patrick Keane, *Adult Education in the American Experience: From the Colonial Period to the Present* (San Francisco, Cal.: Jossey-Bass, 1994).

DR. BRAY'S ASSOCIATES

Thomas Bray. Thomas Bray was an Anglican clergyman dedicated to missionary and philanthropic endeavors in England and its colonies, especially the education and conversion of American blacks. Trained in theology at Oxford, he served as an Anglican curate, chaplain, and vicar, but his real interests were in organizing missionary and philanthropic enterprises. He was a key figure in the founding of the Society for the Propagation of the Gospel in Foreign Parts (S.P.G.), the Society for Promoting Christian Knowledge (S.P.C.K.), and the Associates of Dr. Bray.

Early Years of the Associates. After a brief visit to America in 1699, Bray successfully petitioned the Crown for a charter for the S.P.G., which was established in 1701. Its purpose was to send missionaries to the colonies to minister to all people, but its outreach to the Native Americans and blacks was secondary to that regarding the European colonists. Therefore in 1724 the Associates of Dr. Bray was formed to minister to the spiritual and educational needs of the Native Americans and blacks. Shortly before his death Bray reorganized the Associates and expanded their number from four to about thirty. The new associates had several missions: to convert and educate blacks in America, to distribute books and create parochial libraries, and to establish a charitable colony (Georgia). One of the associates was James Oglethorpe, leader in the movement to found a charitable colony. Georgia was their first priority, but after the Georgia Charter was granted, the Associates of Dr. Bray ended their affiliation with the Georgia Trustees. With the colony founded, the Associates concentrated in the 1730s and 1740s on distributing books and founding parochial libraries. In the 1750s they turned their attention to the education and conversion of blacks. Early efforts included not only distributing books but also sending out missionaries as catechists to Georgia and South Carolina. When this proved unsuccessful, the Associates made plans for the formal education of blacks and the establishment of schools.

Schools. Bray's Associates began with the idea of sending itinerant schoolmasters to teach blacks, but they soon decided to open a school in Philadelphia. They sought the advice of Benjamin Franklin, who was enthusiastic and encouraging. He suggested that if it worked the Associates should start more schools in other colonies. The trial school opened in Philadelphia in 1758 under the directorship of the Reverend William Sturgeon, the S.P.G's catechist to Philadelphia's blacks. The trial period was to last three years at an expense of twenty pounds a year. The school started with one mistress and about thirty pupils. The venture was so successful that in 1760 the Associates established two similar schools in New York City and Williamsburg, Virginia, and another school in Newport, Rhode Island, in 1762. The Williamsburg school was perhaps the most successful. Franklin had recommended that Williamsburg's postmaster, William Hunter, and the president of William and Mary, William Dawson, supervise the organization of the school, hire the teacher, and order books. The first schoolmistress received twenty pounds and had twenty-four students. In 1765 the Associates opened a school in Fredericksburg, Virginia, but since the black population was so low there, the school closed in 1770. The begin-

A list of supporters of the colonial college that later became Columbia University (New-York Historical Society, New York)

ning of the Revolution interfered with the operation of the other schools, and all of them closed by 1775. However, in 1774 the Associates purchased land in Philadelphia for a school for blacks and after the war, in 1786, opened the Negro Charity School. Their other attempts to institute black schooling—in Chester, Maryland; Edenton, Wilmington, and Bath, North Carolina; and Yorktown and Norfolk, Virginia—failed, partly because teachers willing to teach blacks were difficult to find.

Impact. The Associates met with many obstacles in trying to carry out their plans for the Christianization and education of blacks: teachers were hard to find; some colonies outlawed the education of blacks; slave owners resisted; and fear of educated slaves causing rebellions slowed acceptance of the idea. Furthermore, African dialects made it hard for blacks to understand what they were learning and hard for teachers to instruct them. Perhaps the Associates in England were too naive about what they could accomplish in the racial environment in the colonies. Ultimately the Associates educated and converted only a small portion—perhaps two or three thousand—of the approximate five-hundred thousand African Americans in the prerevolutionary American colonies. However, they were successful in setting precedents, in drawing colonial support for black education from influential men such as Franklin, and in providing a counter ideology to the one held by slave owners and others opposed to literacy for blacks.

Sources:

Richard Beale Davis, *Intellectual Life in the Colonial South, 1585–1763* (Knoxville: University of Tennessee Press, 1978);

Edgar L. Pennington, "Dr. Thomas Bray's Associates and Their Work among the Negroes," *Proceedings of the American Antiquarian Society*, 48 (1938): 311–403;

John C. Van Horne, ed., *Religious Philanthropy and Colonial Slavery: The American Correspondence of the Associates of Dr. Bray, 1717–1777* (Urbana: University of Illinois Press, 1985).

COLLEGE STUDENT LIFE

Colonial Colleges. Colonial colleges were small. An estimate of the number of students in all nine colleges in 1775 was about 750. In 1775 Harvard had a graduating class of forty; Yale, thirty-five; Columbia, thirteen; Dartmouth, eleven; and the College of Philadelphia, eight. Most colleges had a grammar school that supplied students to the college, and these schools generally contained more students than the higher institutions. Not only were colleges small, but they were also poor, especially in comparison to English universities. College was expensive on the eve of the Revolution: tuition ranged from £9 to £20 per student, and with other costs such as books, clothing, travel, and spending money, a student's annual fees usually ran as high as £25 to £35. This was a high percentage of most annual salaries—a college instructor, for example, made about £100 annually—so most scholars came from wealthier families though some loans and charitable funds helped the poorer students. In spite of the high tuition, colleges could not meet expenses and had to depend on gifts, provincial subsidies, and lotteries. During the second half of the eighteenth century they raised funds by subscription, often by sending agents abroad to do so. Most of the operating expenses—which took about three-seventh's of a college's budget—were used for faculty salaries, which remained low until the nineteenth century.

Admissions. Higher education in the colonies was open to males who had received a classical education either in a Latin grammar school or privately by a clergyman or tutor. Even though all colonial colleges, with the exception of the College of Philadelphia, had been established by religious denominations, they did not exclude students affiliated with different religions. Every spring oral entrance exams were given to prospective students, and if the candidate passed the exam, he was admitted to the fall session. Until the middle of the eighteenth cen-

An embroidery of the main building at Harvard College, circa 1770 (Massachusetts Historical Society, Boston)

tury classical education was the major requirement for entrance. About midcentury the requirements changed, and Yale, for the first time, included an arithmetic requirement. All students who were admitted at the same time formed a class that continued through four years, and classes were ranked by seniority according to English custom. The ranking was rigidly maintained, especially by the upper classmen, who demanded petty and oppressive services from the freshmen, in ways similar to the English custom of fagging.

Daily Life. Most colonial college students shared simple, sparsely furnished rooms in the main building, or college hall. The college hall also contained the classrooms and the refectory, where students ate their meals. The food was generally poor and never plentiful—always a major cause of student protests. Some students who could afford it boarded with local families. A typical day began early with morning prayer followed by classes, then the main meal of the day and more classes, evening prayer, and study period. Professors seldom lectured; rather they required the students to recite passages from textbooks. Since the heart of the college life was religion, students were expected to attend morning and evening prayers and Sunday services and to enroll in theology courses.

Extracurricular Activities. Popular student activities outside class included oratory, singing, dramatics, verse writing, and various kinds of music, but literary societies (debating clubs), which began in the eighteenth century, were the most important. Here students could expound their ideas without the constraints imposed by classroom discipline. These societies competed with each other in heated debates over current political issues and decisions relevant to college life, such as the choice of commencement speakers. They had their own regulations, elected officers, and raised money for their libraries, clubrooms, and furnishings.

Student Rebellions. Faculty and students were frequently at odds with each other because the faculty had the responsibility of disciplining students and maintaining strict parental control over them, outside as well as inside the classroom. A long list of regulations governed all aspects of college life, including class attendance, idleness, clothing, dancing, drinking, and swearing. A tight rein was considered necessary in order to educate moral and religious gentlemen. To enforce the rules faculty imposed such punishments as fines, revocation of privileges, suspension from certain classes or from the college, and expulsion. One primary cause for student rebellion in the eighteenth century was the bad quality and meager quantity of food. Harvard's first revolt in 1766 was caused by rancid butter. In addition students at some of the more patriotic colleges, such as the College of New Jersey, Harvard, the College of Rhode Island, and Yale, rebelled against British policies by wearing homespun clothes to commencements, burning and boycott-

AMERICAN COLLEGES

The following is a list of American colleges that received charters to grant degrees before 1784:

Original Name	Modern Name	Date Chartered
Harvard College	Harvard University	1636
College of William and Mary	College of William and Mary	1693
Yale College	Yale University	1701
College of New Jersey	Princeton University	1746
Kings College	Columbia University	1754
College of Philadelphia	University of Pennsylvania	1755
College of Rhode Island	Brown University	1764
Queens College	Rutgers University	1766
Dartmouth College	Dartmouth College	1769
Washington College	Washington College	1782
Liberty Hall Academy	Washington and Lee University	1782
Hampden-Sydney College	Hampden-Sydney College	1783
Transylvania Seminary	Transylvania University	1783

Sources: Beverly McAnear, "College Founding in the American Colonies, 1745–1775," *Mississippi Valley Historical Review*, 42 (1955): 24–44;

David W. Robson, "College Founding in the New Republic, 1776–1800," *History of Education Quarterly*, 23 (1983): 323.

ing tea, forming militia companies, burning British leaders in effigy, and delivering heated patriotic orations.

Degrees. Colonial colleges conferred two degrees: the bachelor of arts and the master of arts. If after taking a four-year fixed curriculum a student could demonstrate his competence in the classical languages and literatures and logic, he would receive the bachelor of arts degree. In the middle of the eighteenth century these requirements changed to include proficiency in the newer courses of instruction, such as science. Achievement for the masters degree was a different matter since there was no fixed curriculum or plan of study nor any residence requirement. A masters was conferred after three years, sometimes as a matter of course and sometimes as the result of intensive study, particularly by clergy-in-training. By the end of the seventeenth century colleges were also granting honorary degrees, but for doctorates and advanced degrees not offered in colonial colleges, students had to travel abroad.

Changes. Colleges became more politically oriented during the revolutionary struggles. By the middle of the 1760s college leaders began to link education with the welfare of the state. Institutions of higher education founded during and after the revolution focused on the education of men for republican leadership on local, state, and national levels. Still embedded in religion, they began to put more emphasis on culture, public virtue, and education for practical purposes. However, the curricula for these new schools, two of which were established before the end of the war in 1783, were similar to those of the older colonial colleges: the classics, English and modern languages, mathematics, and sciences.

Sources:
John S. Brubacher & Willis Rudy, *Higher Education in Transition: A History of American Colleges and Universities* (New Brunswick, N.J.: Transaction, 1997);

Lawrence Cremin, *American Education: The Colonial Experience, 1607–1783* (New York: Harper & Row, 1970);

Beverly McAnear, "College Founding in the American Colonies, 1745–1775," *Mississippi Valley Historical Review*, 42 (1955): 24–44;

David W. Robson, "College Founding in the New Republic, 1776–1800," *History of Education Quarterly*, 23 (1983): 323–341;

Robson, *Educating Republicans: The College in the Era of the American Revolution, 1750–1800* (Westport, Conn.: Greenwood Press, 1985).

LIBRARIES

Public Libraries. Community tax-supported public libraries that were free and open to everyone did not take root until the nineteenth century. Most public libraries were actually book collections or private libraries open to the public. For example, the foundations of the Boston Public Library date from 1673 with the donation of Robert Keayne's private collection of books, which was administrated by the town of Boston. In the mid eighteenth century probably no more than about ten or twelve community-owned library collections such as this were founded. However, many other kinds of libraries were founded, some private or quasi-private, some by membership only and those accessible to people who could pay a rental fee.

Proprietor	Location	Founded	Annual Fee	Number of Vols.	Longevity (in months)
William Rind	Annapolis	1763	£11	150+	12
George Wood	Charleston	1763		1,000	48
Garrat Noel	New York	1763	$5	3,000?	12?
John Mein	Boston	1765	£1-8	1,200	
Lewis Nicola	Philadelphia	1767	$2-3	400–1,000	51+
Thomas Bradford	Philadelphia	1769			45+
Samuel Gifford	Charleston	1772	£1		
William Aikman	Annapolis	1773	£11	1,200	426
Joseph Rathell	Baltimore	1773	$4	800+	0
Samuel Loudon	New York	1774	£1	1,000–2,000	32+
Robert Bell	Philadelphia	1774		2,000	48+

Source: David Kaser, *A Book for a Sixpence: The Circulating Library in America* (Pittsburgh, Pa.: Beta Phi Mu, 1980).

Demand for Books. Throughout the colonial era educated people collected books and possessed their own libraries. Most individual libraries contained less than a dozen books, but collections ranged in the thousands, such as John Adams's library of five thousand volumes

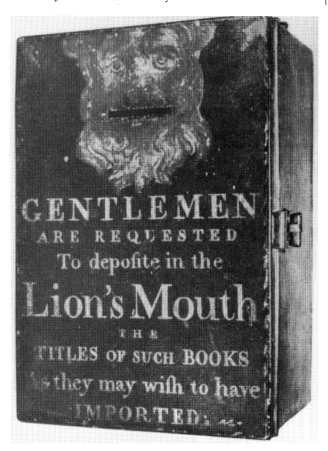

A book request box maintained by the Library Company of Philadelphia, circa 1732 (Library Company of Philadelphia, Pennsylvania)

and William Byrd II's twenty-three cases of three thousand books. Most libraries contained Bibles, almanacs, and devotional literature, but during the eighteenth century reading interests expanded to include books on science, politics, gardening, medicine, law, surveying, agriculture, conduct and civility, grammar, textbooks, drama, poetry, history, and education. Colonial booksellers stocked imprints from Britain as well as from colonial presses, which by 1762 numbered about 40. Between 1689 and 1783 colonial presses had printed, by one estimation, 100,000 titles. The proliferation of books and other printed items and the increase in literacy in the eighteenth century meant a surge of new booksellers in the colonies. By 1750, 121 booksellers had opened shops in five American cities: Boston, Charleston, Philadelphia, New York, and Newport. Between 1761 and 1776 the number had increased to 151.

College Libraries. College libraries built their early collections primarily through donations from philanthropists abroad and from colonial men of letters. Harvard's library began with the bequest of John Harvard's four hundred books. The College of William and Mary received donations from abroad and from prominent Virginia gentlemen, the largest of which was given by Gov. Francis Nicholson. In the eighteenth century, college libraries grew rapidly, though most suffered huge losses by fire or through the ravages of war. The largest of the libraries was at Harvard. From its modest beginnings in 1638 it grew to about 3,500 books in the eighteenth century before it was destroyed by fire in 1764. But two years later the library had grown from purchases and donations to 4,350 volumes, which doubled by 1783. William and Mary, Yale, and the College of New Jersey each had between 2,000 and 3,000 books before the Revolution, but many of these were destroyed during the war. King's College and the College of Philadelphia had small libraries, but students at these colleges had access to larger libraries nearby.

Parish Libraries. Thomas Bray, an Anglican minister and commissary to Maryland's Anglican parishes, is credited with planning the first parochial lending library. His purpose was to give poorer clergy the opportunity to educate themselves with theological, philosophical, and scientific books housed in nearby parish libraries. The first library, with 1,095 volumes, was created in 1696 in Annapolis, Maryland. With top priority given to the establishment of parish libraries by the Society for Promoting Christian Knowledge (S.P.C.K.), more than thirty were founded in Boston, Charleston, New York, Philadelphia, and Maryland in the following three years. However, they were created mainly for clergy, and the public could use them only on a limited basis.

Subscription Libraries. Two other kinds of libraries, the subscription and circulating libraries, were more accessible to the public. The subscription libraries, also known as social libraries, were formed as clubs or voluntary associations by individuals who contributed to a general fund that was supported by annual contributions or subscriptions for the purpose of buying and maintaining books. In 1731 Benjamin Franklin founded the first of its kind, called the Library Company of Philadelphia, with a plan to have subscribers pay an initial fee of forty shillings to buy books and an additional annual fee of ten shillings to maintain the collection and add new books. Rules determined hours of access, fines for overdue books, limits on the number of books that could be checked out, fees for damaged books, and other collection-related concerns. Sometimes educational activities such as lecture series were offered by these libraries. By 1775 there were about seventy subscription libraries in the colonies.

Circulating Libraries. The most publically accessible library was the circulating library, a popular institution at this time in England, where there were about fifty in existence before 1762, when the first known American circulating library was organized in Annapolis, Maryland. These lending libraries were attached to booksellers' shops or printing companies, and were places where readers rented books for a fee and for a certain period of time. Though the Annapolis library failed after a few months, eleven more successful replicas followed in urban areas such as Boston, Philadelphia, New York, and Charleston before the Revolution. The number of volumes in each ranged from 150 to 3,000. They catered to men and women in trying to fill the increasing demand for literature, history, biography, and travel books. However, since both the subscription and circulating libraries cost users money, they were not available to everyone and therefore not actually public. In addition the circulating libraries were located only in cities that had booksellers and printers. At least one colony, Virginia, had neither a circulating nor a subscription library.

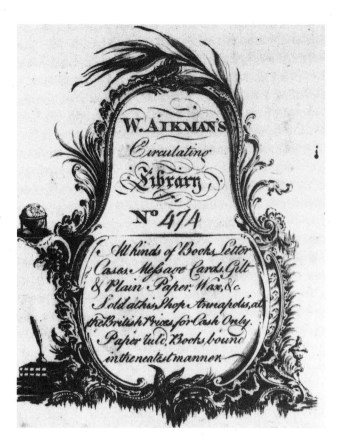

Bookplate from an Annapolis, Maryland, book company, 1773–1775 (American Antiquarian Society, Worcester, Mass.)

Sources:

David Kaser, *A Book for a Sixpence: The Circulating Library in America* (Pittsburgh, Pa: Beta Phi Mu, 1980);

Malcolm Knowles, *A History of the Adult Education Movement in the United States* (Huntington, N.Y.: R. E. Krieger, 1977);

Huey B. Long, *Continuing Education of Adults in Colonial America* (Syracuse, N.Y.: Syracuse University Publications in Continuing Education, 1976);

Jesse H. Shera, *Foundations of the Public Library: The Origins of the Public Library Movement in New England, 1629–1855* (Chicago: University of Chicago Press, 1949);

Harold W. Stubblefield and Patrick Keane, *Adult Education in the American Experience: From the Colonial Period to the Present* (San Francisco, Cal.: Jossey-Bass, 1994).

LITERACY

Skill. During the colonial period reading and writing were usually taught separately, with reading being first in order of instruction as it was considered essential for studying the Bible and religious literature. Writing, on the other hand, was regarded more as an art or as a technical skill for certain occupations such as bookkeeping and commerce. It was also more expensive: paper was scarce; writing texts were costly; and students had to purchase quills and powder ink. For many people, especially girls and boys from poor families, writing was not necessary for their future employment. Some females from wealthier families learned to write, but for most, writing was not deemed as useful as sewing. However, the inability of most colonists to write was not as much of an im-

Prior to the mid eighteenth century, children's reading consisted primarily of the Bible and religious material. The Bible remained the first book from which children learned to read, but gradually secular books became more common. The most prevalent of the secular books and almost as popular as the Bible were almanacs, printed in the colonies since the early seventeenth century. Children as well as adults enjoyed reading them for stories, weather forecasts, verses, events, advice, maxims, useful information, and, of course, the calendar. The most famous of these was Benjamin Franklin's *Poor Richard's Almanack* (first published in 1732). Children's books used by Americans were primarily English in origin. Even though by 1760 all colonies had printing presses, Americans continued to rely on England for almost all books bought for American children. Perhaps the greatest influence on children's literature was a London publisher by the name of John Newbery, who started publishing children's books in the 1740s. On 15 November 1750 he advertised some of these books, most of them educational, in the *Pennsylvania Gazette*. One was titled *A Museum for Young Gentlemen and Ladies or A private tutor for little Masters and Misses* (1750), which counseled children on how to behave properly. *The Pretty Book for Children* (1750) was a guide to the English language. In 1752 Newbery published a magazine for children, the *Lilliputian Magazine*, and filled it with stories, verses, and other entertaining miscellanea. Newbery died in 1767, but his firm continued to print children's recreational books, which by then were considered acceptable but not yet commonly owned—most children advanced from reading the Bible and religious verses to reading more-adult literature. Children's books became more universal in the nineteenth century, when they became more affordable.

Aside from Newbery and the almanacs, other types of reading matter available to children were songs and hymns, riddles, verses and nursery rhymes, religious literature, storybooks such as *Robinson Crusoe* (1719) and *Arabian Nights,* and schoolbooks. A common theme found in many of these works was that of self-improvement—diligence, frugality, and industry led to virtue, wealth, and success. This was the lesson to be learned from the popular storybook *Goody Two-Shoes: The Means by which she acquired her Learning and Wisdom, and in consequence thereof her Estate* (1765). Goody Two-Shoes was Margery Meanwell, an orphan who was once delighted to receive two shoes to replace her one shoe. From her humble beginnings she taught herself to read, started teaching, married a wealthy man, and became a "Lady" and a philanthropist.

Schoolbooks were available to a privileged few. Those used before the Revolution were generally from England, but after 1783 many were written by Americans. One commonly used English text was Thomas Dilworth's *A New Guide to the English Tongue*, a spelling book first printed in 1740 and used until the 1780s. It was replaced in popularity by Noah Webster's spelling book, *A Grammatical Institute, of the English Language* (1783), though this was not the first speller written by an American. In 1779 Anthony Benezet put his years of teaching experience into several publications, one of which was *The Pennsylvania Spelling Book*.

Source: Gillian Avery, *Behold the Child: American Children and Their Books, 1621–1922* (Baltimore: Johns Hopkins University Press, 1994).

---

pediment then as it would be today. Their society depended more on oral than written communication; information circulated by word of mouth, public readings, sermons, and oral performances.

Measuring Literacy. One way scholars measure literacy is by examining legal documents for the percentage of signatures versus marks. If someone could not write, he or she made a mark, sometimes with an *X* but more often with initials. This did not mean the person was unable to read since reading was taught before writing, as it was considered a more essential skill. But a person who signed his or her name could probably read as well, and though he or she might not have been able to write much, he or she at least knew how to write something. General literacy rates for mid-eighteenth-century America are hard to estimate since they varied widely according to place, socioeconomic status, gender, race, religion, and occupation. Port towns had a higher number of literates than rural areas, and professional and wealthy people were more literate than poor people. And only in New England did the law require that all children learn to read. This, combined with the prevalence of town schools, made New England the most literate population of any area in the colonies. Studies show that 80 percent of New England males were literate by 1760, with the highest percentage in Boston and densely populated rural areas. Only about 65 percent of females in Boston and about 30 to 40 percent in rural areas were literate, largely because education opportunities were fewer for girls. The increase in literacy in the Middle and Southern colonies was slower than in New England but varied by

A painting of men reading newspapers in a tavern

area and ethnic culture. In North Carolina only about 33 percent of women could sign their names before the Revolution. By this time at least 80 percent of men in all the colonies could sign their names.

Reading. The first book used to teach reading was usually the hornbook, followed in succession by the primer, Psalter, Testament, and finally the Bible. In the eighteenth century most literate Americans put religious literature at the top of their reading preferences, but increasingly secular material became more popular, especially as the Revolutionary War got closer and political issues became more newsworthy. People read not only for religious enhancement but also for entertainment, information about public issues, and knowledge about a wide variety of subjects. Newspapers, almanacs, pamphlets, and books began circulating to broader areas. The number of American-published books and pamphlets doubled between the 1740s and 1760s and increased by a third in the 1770s, at which time about 640 a year were printed in thirty-six places. The number of all imprints (excluding weekly newspapers) published by American presses jumped dramatically from 1,582 titles between 1704 and 1723 to 11,098 for the years 1764 to 1783, or one-half of all imprints produced in the colonial period. Almanacs, essential for their calendars, became almost as prevalent as the Bible in the homes of colonial Americans. Their production, which in the 1740s was about five editions a year, expanded to twenty a year in the 1770s. One of the most popular was Franklin's *Poor Richard's Almanack,* which sold 141,257 copies between 1752 and 1765.

Newspapers. Another indication that literacy was on the rise in colonial America at the middle of the eighteenth century was the increase in the number of newspapers after 1750. John Campbell's *Boston News-Letter* had an initial circulation of 250 copies when it was started in 1704, and it was the only newspaper in the colonies until 1719. In 1740 colonial newspapers numbered 12; by 1765 there were 25; in 1776, 39 newspapers were published in all colonies except Delaware; and by 1783 the total had jumped to 58. Two-thirds of the papers were printed in five cities: Boston, Philadelphia, Charleston, Newport, and New York, with New England taking the lead in the number of newspapers in operation. Though the average weekly circulation was about 600 papers, the larger papers had as many as 2,000 or 3,000 subscribers and during the war as many as 8,000. However, the readership was much broader than the number of subscriptions, especially considering the fact that a popular pastime was to gather at taverns and coffeehouses to read the latest news.

Summary. Reading and writing were taught separately, often by different instructors: women usually taught reading, and men taught writing. Reading was learned first, as it was necessary for religious education, but many children did not stay in school long enough to learn writing skills. Writing was a useful tool for employment and therefore taught mainly to boys, but exceptions to this pattern did exist. German sects and Quakers taught reading and writing to both sexes, as did plantation tutors. Throughout the early colonial period books were imported from England, but by the middle of the eighteenth century every colony had a printing press for

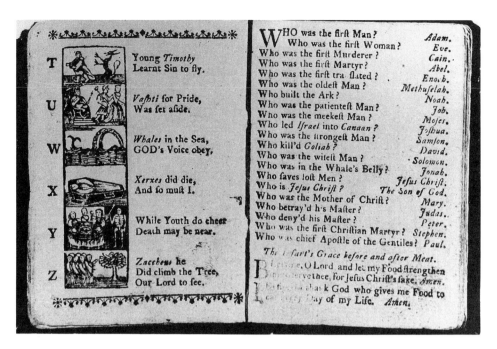

Two pages from the 1767 edition of the *New England Primer*

the production of newspapers, small books, textbooks, and almanacs. But even with the growth of printing in America, distribution networks were not well developed and were usually confined to areas near the presses. Private book ownership for most people meant possession of a Bible and perhaps an almanac and a few smaller books.

Sources:

Catherine Hobbs, ed., *Nineteenth-Century Women Learn to Write* (Charlottesville: University Press of Virginia, 1995);

Huey B. Long, *Continuing Education of Adults in Colonial America* (Syracuse, N.Y.: Syracuse University Publications in Continuing Education, 1976);

Averil Evans McClelland, *The Education of Women in the United States: A Guide to Theory, Teaching, and Research* (New York: Garland, 1992);

E. Jennifer Monaghan, "Literacy Instruction and Gender in Colonial New England," in *Reading in America: Literature and Social History*, edited by Cathy N. Davidson (Baltimore: Johns Hopkins University Press, 1989), pp. 53–80.

MOOR'S INDIAN CHARITY SCHOOL

"The Great Design." The Indian Charity School (later known as Moor's [More's] Indian Charity School) was founded in Lebanon, Connecticut, in 1754 by Eleazar Wheelock. His plan was to remove Indian children from their homelands in order to educate and convert them so that they could return to their societal groups and teach their own people. He believed his plan was divinely sanctioned as the best defense against hostilities between the Indians and colonists. All previous attempts at schooling Indians had been carried out by missionaries in Indian communities, and these efforts failed, Wheelock thought, because the children were easily distracted by friends, families, and duties. Education

away from home seemed to Wheelock to be the key to success. Some of the inspiration for the school had come from his experience tutoring a Mohegan named Samson Occom, who studied with Wheelock from 1743 to 1748 and had succeeded beyond his master's expectations. At the end of 1754 Wheelock opened his charity school in a house on two acres of land, a gift valued at about £500 from Col. Joshua More, a wealthy farmer from Mansfield, Connecticut.

Recruitment. At first Wheelock's field of recruitment was limited to New England and New Jersey. The French and Indian War (1754–1763) interfered with recruitment outside this area. The school's first pupils were two Delaware Indian boys, John Pumshire and Jacob Woolley, who arrived on 18 December 1754. By 1760 the male students included two more Delawares, a Pequot, several Mohegans, a Montauk, and a white student from Norwich, Connecticut. In 1761, when France was no longer in a position to encourage Indian hostilities against the English, Wheelock turned to the Iroquois in upstate New York, and that year five Mohawk boys came to his school, followed by three more in 1762. By 1765 fourteen Iroquois boys had entered the school. In 1761 the first two Indian girls enrolled: Amy Johnson, a Mohegan, and Miriam Storrs, a Delaware. By 1765 thirty-nine Indians (twenty-nine boys and ten girls) and seven white boys had studied at the school for varying lengths of time, from several months to six years, with an average enrollment in the 1760s of about eighteen pupils. All had been supported by charity.

Schooldays. The boys boarded in the upper story of the schoolhouse and attended classes on the first floor. They received a basic secular and religious education six days a week and were also trained in husbandry. Each day began with prayer and catechism before dawn. In morning classes the boys were taught Latin and Greek, with instruction continuing in the afternoon until supper. The evening hours were reserved for study. For the girls Wheelock's curriculum was similar to that for English girls in New England, that is, reading, writing, and domestic skills. He sent them to live in nearby homes, where they could learn housekeeping. Unlike the rigorous training the boys received, the girls' formal instruction took place just once a week in order to keep expenses down. In Wheelock's plan the girls were to be educated so they could help the boys in their mission. In 1765 Wheelock's first students were ready for examination by the Connecticut Board of Correspondents, one of several such colonial boards that represented the Society in Scotland for Propagating Christian Knowledge. They graduated eleven students: two white boys became missionaries; three Indian boys became schoolmasters to the Iroquois; and six Indians served as teaching assistants (ushers). Ten of them worked in various Iroquois schools, attended by 127 Indian children.

Fund-raising. Funds for the school came primarily from charity, and therefore much of Wheelock's time was spent fund-raising. Donations came from many sources, including the general assemblies of Massachusetts Bay and New Hampshire, and various churches and ministers in New England and New York as well as private citizens and prominent figures such as the marquis of Lothian. By 1760 the enterprise had cost £285.14.4, but revenues had amounted to only £156.9.6. In order to publicize the school and to avoid having to explain repeatedly the school's purpose in his numerous solicitations, Wheelock decided in 1763 to write a pamphlet that provided details of the school's history, plan, and progress. His *Plain and faithful Narrative of the Original Design, Rise, Progress and Present State of the Indian Charity-School at Lebanon, in Connecticut* was published in Boston in 1763 and was revised, updated, and republished eight times before the Revolution. In 1765 Wheelock calculated that he had spent £1,639 of charitable money on the school, but the school's expenditures had exceeded its income by £280, money that came directly from his personal funds. Continually squeezed for finances, Wheelock sent Nathaniel Whitaker and his former pupil Samson Occum to England in 1765 on an enormously successful fund-raising mission. No other college to date had collected that much charitable money abroad: more than £9,000 from England and £2,500 from Scotland, enough for Wheelock to consider expanding and moving to a larger site.

Dartmouth College. In the mid 1760s Wheelock realized that his original plan of sending Indians and English missionaries to the Indian homelands to educate and Christianize Native Americans was not working as well as he planned, so he decided he needed to change direction. Since 1760 he had wanted to move the school

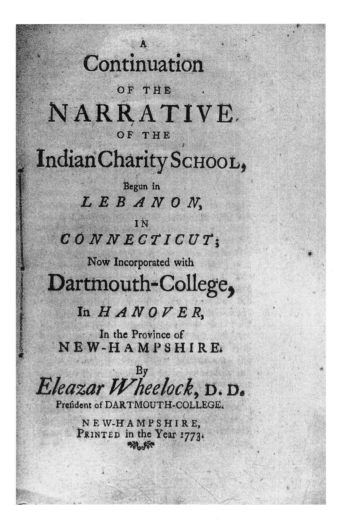

A

Continuation
OF THE
NARRATIVE
OF THE
Indian Charity School,
Begun in
LEBANON,
IN
CONNECTICUT;
Now Incorporated with
Dartmouth-College,
In *HANOVER*,
In the Province of
NEW-HAMPSHIRE.
By
Eleazar Wheelock, D. D.
President of DARTMOUTH-COLLEGE.

NEW-HAMPSHIRE,
PRINTED in the Year 1773.

Title page for an influential missionary's account of the school he founded

and add more white students to train as missionaries. With the more than £11,500 Whitaker and Occom raised in Britain, Wheelock received the encouragement he needed to expand, and he started looking for other locations. One possible site was in the Susquehanna valley in Pennsylvania. Another was offered by John Wentworth, governor of New Hampshire, who promised Wheelock a township grant and a charter. Still others were in Albany, New York, and the Berkshires, in western Massachusetts. In 1768 Wheelock sent two men to Portsmouth to discuss Wentworth's offer and to inspect the land in what would become the township of Hanover, New Hampshire, and to compare this with the sites in Albany and the Berkshires. In April 1769 the trustees chose the New Hampshire site and the following 13 December received the charter for the school, to be named for William, second Earl of Dartmouth, who was president of the trustees of the English Fund—the money that was raised by Occum and Whitaker in 1765. It was a liberal charter for the time because it did not require students or faculty to take religious tests, and of the twelve trustees seven were required to be laymen. Wheelock was appointed Dartmouth College's first president and at the same time continued to operate the charity school that he had moved to Hanover, where it was newly instituted as More's Indian Charity School in memory of Joshua More, the first donor. In the meantime, however, Wheelock and his school had fallen out of favor with the Iroquois, and he had lost all of his Iroquois students, so by 1772 he was left with only five students from New England. He started new recruitment efforts, this time in Canada, and by the end of the year, he had seventy students, thirty-nine of whom were charity students. The 1772 catalogue listed forty-one enrolled at the college, five of whom were Indians on charity. During the 1770s his missionary efforts decreased as the demands of the college increased, but he continued to recruit Indian students.

Impact. Wheelock had small successes according to his original plan. He was able to teach the Indian children how to read and write. The girls learned some domestic skills such as dairying, sewing, and spinning and the boys some husbandry skills. He sent his graduates out to teach in schools in Indian communities. But in a larger sense his plan failed because most of the students held onto their cultural values and were caught between two worlds: they were not able to assimilate into colonial society, yet they had learned enough of white culture to be uneasy in their native societies. His experiment represented a departure from the usual missionary work in Indian homelands, but it lasted only about fifteen years, with the most active years from 1761 to 1769. After Dartmouth was founded, Wheelock spent most of his time administering the new college.

Sources:

James Dow McCallum, ed., *The Letters of Eleazar Wheelock's Indians* (Hanover, N.H.: Dartmouth College Publications, 1932);

Leon Burr Richardson, *History of Dartmouth College,* 2 volumes (Hanover, N.H.: Dartmouth College Publications, 1932);

Margaret Connell Szasz, *Indian Education in the American Colonies, 1607–1783* (Albuquerque: University of New Mexico Press, 1988);

Bobby Wright, "'For the Children of the Infidels'?: American Indian Education in the Colonial Colleges," *American Indian Culture and Research Journal,* 12 (1988): 1–14.

PRIVATE SCHOOLS

Popularity. Private schools, also called venture, adventure, or evening schools, first appeared about 1660 in New Netherland and by the beginning of the eighteenth century were found in most cities and towns in America. Colonial private schools were organized by individual schoolteachers who thought they could make a living or at least supplement their incomes by teaching adults and older children in the evenings or at times convenient to the student. The terms were usually short, perhaps six or seven weeks, and the fees were low enough to attract a sufficient number of students to make the teacher's effort worthwhile. In the seventeenth century these schools helped to satisfy the educational needs of apprentices, whose contracts often contained an education clause allowing them to take courses during times when they were not working for their masters. Between 1698 and 1727 at least one hundred apprentice contracts in New York City mentioned evening school education. By the beginning of the Revolution private schools were well attended by all types of individuals who could afford the fees.

Schoolteachers. The quality of the private school depended on the ability of the teacher. Since anyone could open a school by taking out an advertisement in the newspaper and since no regulatory agency or board of trustees controlled quality, some teachers were underqualified or self-serving. However, most had at least adequate credentials for the courses they offered—if not college degrees, then apprenticeship training or business experience. Many were schoolteachers in more formal secondary schools and colleges; for example, at least seven private teachers in Philadelphia also taught at the Academy and College of Philadelphia. Others had occupations such as surveying and bookbinding and by experience were qualified to teach these subjects. Some even wrote their own textbooks. The outside teaching added something to their meager incomes, and they were sometimes able to make a little more by selling school supplies to their students: slates, books, quills, ink powder, compasses, and stationery. Most teachers were men, but some women taught as well, especially wives who assisted or supplemented their husbands' courses.

Advertisements. Schoolmasters and mistresses attracted students by advertising in newspapers. About four hundred advertisements for private schools appeared in the *South-Carolina Gazette* between 1732 and 1775 and at least thirty-two in the *Boston Gazette and Country Journal* in the decade before the Revolution. Advertisements included information on the qualifications of the teacher, entrance fees for boys and girls, courses offered, times, and locations. Classes were offered most often at night or when people would not otherwise be busy, especially during the winter months. Fees varied according to the subject, demand, and gender of the student but probably did not exceed a shilling a week. Schools were located wherever schoolteachers could find an inexpensive place to hold classes, most often in their own residences, but rooms in taverns, other town buildings, and schoolhouses were also used. Occasionally teachers mentioned that they were willing to go to students' homes.

Curriculum. Seventeenth-century evening schools provided the basics of education—reading, writing, and arithmetic. During and after the first quarter of the eighteenth century the curricula changed, with more emphasis placed on courses geared toward commerce and business. By the middle of the eighteenth century, as commerce and merchandizing expanded, private schools increased to meet the demands of the public for practical subjects in addition to academic ones. Accounting and bookkeeping, particularly Italian bookkeeping, were popular choices. Among the long list of vocational subjects found in advertisements were business, navigation, surveying, leveling, mechanics, architecture, gunnery, drafting, construction, masonry, and weaving. More advanced academic subjects supplemented the classical curricula, with courses such as midwifery, offered by Dr. Shippen of Philadelphia in 1765. But curricular offerings were not limited to academic and vocational subjects. A third category was that of leisure education—dancing, singing, fencing, painting, and drawing.

Significance. In responding to the particular needs of local communities, private venture schools provided the public with the practical education or skills that primary and secondary schools did not. They were more ephemeral in nature than formally established schools, and the instructors were of mixed quality, but for those who did not generally receive more than elementary level schooling, especially females and apprentices, private schools enabled them to achieve a higher level of education.

Sources:

Lawrence Cremin, *American Education: The Colonial Experience, 1607–1783* (New York: Harper & Row, 1970);

Richard Beale Davis, *Intellectual Life in the Colonial South, 1585–1763* (Knoxville: University of Tennessee Press, 1978);

Malcolm S. Knowles, *A History of the Adult Education Movement in the United States* (Huntington, N.Y.: R. E. Krieger, 1977);

Huey B. Long, *Continuing Education of Adults in Colonial America* (Syracuse, N.Y.: Syracuse University Publications in Continuing Education, 1976);

Robert Middlekauff, *Ancients and Axioms: Secondary Education in Eighteenth-Century New England* (New Haven, Conn.: Yale University Press, 1963);

Harold W. Stubblefield and Patrick Keane, *Adult Education in the American Experience* (San Francisco, Cal.: Jossey-Bass, 1994);

Thomas Woody, *A History of Women's Education in the United States* (New York & Lancaster, Pa.: Science Press, 1929).

A portrait of Jane Beckman Van Cortlandt by John Durand, circa 1770 (New-York Historical Society, New York)

EDUCATION OF WOMEN

Women's Roles. The dearth of formal educational opportunities for women in the eighteenth century did not mean that women lacked education; they had an extensive and complex education that centered around managing a household and raising children. The skills necessary for this were daunting. A woman had to not only make the family's clothing but also to produce the cloth. She had to cook, process, and preserve food from crops she had planted and tended; to acquire at least a rudimentary knowledge of herbal medicines and how to apply them; to act either as a midwife or to assist midwives and know something about birthing; to tend the livestock and take care of the dairy; to educate young children; and sometimes to help with the family business. To master these skills young women learned from their mothers or served as apprentices or domestic servants to other families. Girls, like boys, were also educated in schools outside the home or by tutors who were hired by their families. Girls and boys went to dame schools up to the age of about seven. Most dame schools were private and taught by women (dames) in their own houses. After this some girls received a secondary education with the boys, were tutored at home, or went to private schools. However, educational opportunities for girls varied from colony to colony.

New England. In colonial New England young girls and boys attended dame schools for their first education. For many girls this would be the only formal education they would receive, but the boys were prepared here for the town schools. In the seventeenth and early eighteenth centuries some town schools were open to girls, but most were attended only by boys. After the middle of the eighteenth century female attendance at town schools became more common, but the quality and quantity of learning was not equal to that of boys until the nineteenth century. Typically during this time girls were taught separately from boys, usually after the boys had left for the day or during the summer months. There were no all-female town schools until 1773, when a Portsmouth, New Hampshire, teacher opened a school for girls to learn reading, writing, arithmetic, and geography. If girls wanted to supplement their rudimentary dame school education, they could pay a fee to attend a private school, sometimes called an adventure, venture, or evening school, taught by individual schoolmasters or mistresses. Before the Revolution some private schools for girls opened, a few of which later evolved into female academies.

THE MORAVIAN LITTLE GIRLS' SCHOOL IN SALEM

In 1753 the Moravians purchased one hundred thousand acres in North Carolina and called their tract Wachovia. During the next fifteen years they established several settlements there: Bethabara, Bethania, and finally Salem in 1766, which became the main town. In 1772 Salem was still small, with no more than twelve houses clustered near the large town square. Two larger buildings sat opposite each other on the square. One was the Single Brothers' House, and the other was the Gemein Haus, where the Moravian congregation met for services.

In 1766 a group of Single Sisters arrived in Bethabara from Bethlehem, Pennsylvania, where they started the first Single Sisters' choir. On 9 April 1772 many of the Single Sisters moved to Salem to live at the Gemein Haus. One of these was Elisabeth Oesterlein, who was chosen to open a school for girls in the Gemein Haus. Classes started at the end of April with only three girls, aged two and a half, four and a half, and eight. Moravians believed in starting education for their children early, and Oesterlein herself began her schooling at the age of two. She received a shilling a week for the two younger girls and six pence for the eight-year-old, who probably required less care. Two years later, in 1774, the school had seven girls of varying ages, who attended at irregular times and days. Some parents allowed their daughters to stay for only one hour a day, others for a few weeks at a time. If the parents needed

them at home, the girls were taken out of school and sent back later.

At first the curriculum was a simple one: reading, writing, sewing, and knitting. However, in 1779 the elders remarked that the girls were not learning arithmetic, probably because Sister Oesterlein did not know any. In 1780, when Sister Oesterlein married the town potter, Sister Catherine Sehner took over the girls' school and added arithmetic to the curriculum. Neither Sister Oesterlien nor Sister Sehner could afford to live on the meager salary afforded them as they were responsible for paying for their own room, board, and clothing. The elders agreed to pay the teachers in the girls' and boys' schools from the congregation treasury, which for Sister Sehner was four shillings a week. Even though the town and surrounding area suffered looting during the Revolutionary War, neither the girls' nor the boys' schools closed, even for a day.

The girls' school remained small during the 1780s, with no more than twelve girls in attendance at any one time, including one black girl from an outlying farm. The school remained at the Gemein Haus until the end of the century. In 1804 the school moved into new buildings and became a boarding school, which was the foundation of the Salem Female Academy and College.

Source: Frances Griffin, *Less Time for Meddling: A History of Salem Academy and College, 1772–1866* (Winston Salem, N.C.: J. F. Blair, 1979).

Middle Colonies. The Dutch Reformed Church in New York and the Quakers and various German sects in Pennsylvania and New Jersey were more liberal than the English colonists in New England in providing both boys and girls an equal elementary education, even though women's roles everywhere centered on the family and household. German schools were set up in churches, which administered them, though some German children were tutored in private homes. Moravians believed females had the same learning ability as males, so they established not only schools for boys and girls but also girls' schools. In the Dutch Reformed Church the sexes were not treated equally, but girls were provided with at least an elementary education. The church established various schools during the Revolutionary era; in Pennsylvania alone there were thirty-six Dutch Reformed Church–affiliated schools by 1783, attended by more than one thousand students. For Quaker children a practical education, such as an apprenticeship to a trade, was most important, but Quakers also started many schools for boys and girls and some for girls only. The most important of the girls' schools was the one founded in

Philadelphia by Anthony Benezet in 1754. Here girls could study reading, writing, arithmetic, and English grammar. Another Philadelphia school was opened by Mary McAllester in 1767 for girls who wanted to board. Females in the Middle colonies could also attend private or evening schools, which enabled them to achieve a higher level of education.

The South. The geography of the South, with its scattered farms and plantations, made a New England–style town school system difficult if not impossible to organize. Therefore the education of white females was not as advanced as it was in the Middle colonies and New England, and, as a result, the literacy rate was lower. Education of most children was a private family affair, with the exception of a few private schools in urban areas such as Charleston, South Carolina. Mothers taught their young children at home. After this rudimentary education wealthier families hired tutors for additional education, primarily for their sons. While daughters were also educated by their brothers' tutors, the purpose of education for them was to prepare for marriage and family and was more ornamental. Girls learned music, dancing, art,

The Mortalities, a silk and satin sampler by Prudence Punderson, circa 1770 (Anne S. K. Brown Collection, Brown University)

fancy needlework, conduct and etiquette, and perhaps conversational French in addition to whatever basic education they received in reading, writing, and arithmetic. The prevailing cultural attitude toward women's education was that it was not appropriate or necessary for women to pursue intellectual subjects. Girls from poorer families were educated according to the regulations of their apprenticeships or could attend free schools where available. The education clause in apprenticeships for girls in Virginia usually stipulated that they be taught to read, or to read the Bible, and learn household skills and sewing. In North Carolina the apprenticeship regulations for education were not always upheld, and though some girls were taught to read and even write, others were required to learn only spinning and other household duties. In Maryland and South Carolina, masters were not required to school apprentices. Free schools were free only to those children who could not afford to pay tuition; otherwise, parents paid tuition. Both boys and girls attended these schools but with different conditions; usually boys were required to attend for longer periods of time and were taught different subjects. Charitable organizations also set up schools and scholarships. Most poor children received no education at all, and those that did learned only the rudiments of reading and writing.

Sources:

Huey B. Long, *Continuing Education of Adults in Colonial America* (Syracuse, N.Y.: Syracuse University Publications in Continuing Education, 1976);

Averil Evans McClelland, *The Education of Women in the United States: A Guide to Theory, Teaching, and Research* (New York: Garland, 1992);

Daniel Blake Smith, *Inside the Great House: Planter Family Life in Eighteenth-Century Chesapeake Society* (Ithaca, N.Y.: Cornell University Press, 1980);

Barbara M. Solomon, *In the Company of Educated Women: A History of Women and Higher Education in America* (New Haven, Conn.: Yale University Press, 1985);

Julia Cherry Spruill, *Women's Life and Work in the Southern Colonies* (Chapel Hill: University of North Carolina Press, 1938);

Thomas Woody, *A History of Women's Education in the United States* (New York & Lancaster, Pa.: Science Press, 1929).

HEADLINE MAKERS

ANTHONY BENEZET

1713-1784
QUAKER REFORMER, EDUCATOR, AUTHOR

Background. Anthony Benezet was born on 31 January 1713 in Saint-Quentin, France, to Huguenot parents, Jean Etienne and Judith Benezet. In 1715 Jean Etienne took his family to London to avoid religious persecution. In London, where the Benezets remained for sixteen years, Anthony trained as an apprentice in a mercantile business but left his master to bind himself to a cooper. In 1731 the Benezet family of nine moved to Philadelphia, where Anthony worked as a commercial trader and started attending Quaker meetings. In 1736 Benezet married Joyce Marriott, a Quaker from Burlington, New Jersey, to whom he was married for forty-eight years. He and his wife moved around as Benezet tried to find a comfortable career in business, but he finally decided that business was not what he wanted. In 1739 he took his first teaching job as master of the Germantown Academy, where he succeeded Francis Daniel Pastorius.

Early Teaching Career. Benezet remained at the Germantown Academy until 1742, when he applied for a teaching position at the Friends' English Public School in Philadelphia (later the William Penn Charter School). The overseers agreed to hire him at fifty pounds for one year if he would teach fifteen poor children. He taught eight hours a day, six days a week, and was known as an unconventional schoolmaster because he treated his pupils with kindness rather than with harsh discipline. In 1754 he left the Friends' School to establish a Girls' School in Philadelphia. This morning school for about thirty girls was directed by the Society of Friends, who donated the building and equipment and drew up the regulations. Benezet agreed to teach reading, writing, arithmetic, Latin, French, and English grammar, but he stayed only a year. From 1755 to 1757 Ann Thornton took Benezet's place as teacher, but when she left, Benezet returned to the school. He taught classic and literary studies to the daughters of wealthy Philadelphians. In 1766, in poor health, he retired from the Girls' School to rest. In these months he wrote *A Caution and Warning to Great Britain,* a treatise on slavery. However, after only nine months of retirement he missed education, and in 1767 he went back to teaching classes for poor girls at an annual salary of twenty pounds.

Crusader against Slavery. In addition to his other duties in the early 1750s, Benezet started an evening school for blacks in his home that he continued for about twenty years without pay. By the 1760s he was an active abolitionist. His Quaker beliefs led him to condemn slavery as a sin, and he joined others in outlawing Quaker slaveholding. In 1776, with John Woolman, another prominent Quaker, he led the Quaker Yearly Meeting that ordered other local meetings to expel slave-owning Quakers. In addition he wrote newspaper articles and pamphlets opposing the slave trade. He corresponded with abolitionists William Wilberforce and Granville Sharp in England and the Abbé Raynal and Benjamin Franklin in France. A steady proponent of education for the poor, blacks, and girls, he encouraged the Society of Friends to build a school for blacks and solicited funds for it. In 1770 such a school was built in Philadelphia, but schoolmasters were hard to find. When the schoolmaster John Houghton resigned in 1782, no qualified replacement could be found, so Benezet spent the last two years of his life teaching at the school. When he died, he left his small estate to endow this school, which became a Quaker school with the Overseers of the Friends' Public Schools as trustees.

Publications. Benezet wrote against slavery, war, and inhumanity. Among the many publications Benezet wrote about slavery were *A Caution and Warning to Great Britain and her Colonies on the Calamitous State of the Enslaved Negroes* (1766) (perhaps his most important writing, approved by the Yearly Meeting in Philadelphia in 1766 and distributed in England), *A Caution to Great Britain and Her Colonies, in a Short Representation of the Calamitous State of the Enslaved Negroes in the British Dominion* (1767), and *Some Historical Account of Guinea, its Situation, Produce and the General Disposition of its Inhabitants. With an Inquiry into the Rise and Progress of the Slave-Trade its Nature and Lamentable Effects* (1771), which inspired the antislavery agitator Thomas Clarkson to begin his campaign against slavery in the 1780s. Benezet also wrote several educational books in response to the needs of his students. For young children he wrote *A First Book for Children* (1778), and for the older students he published *The Pennsylvania Spelling Book* (1776) and *An Essay on Grammar* (1779). His spelling book was unique in that it combined a primer with a spelling book so that they could be used together or separately. In 1782 Benezet revised and expanded the spelling book to 168 pages. More than just a book on spelling, it contained pronunciations, parables, maxims, poetry, catechism, and rules for behavior.

Social Reformer. Benezet's life and work were filled with Quaker principles. He worked for social justice in teaching all children regardless of race, age, physical limitations, and economic status; in helping French Acadians and Native Americans; and in crusading against slavery. He opposed the use of cruel teaching methods, preferring instead to use compassion and gentleness. He created his own primer, speller, and grammar books, including a curriculum for the deaf. He died on 3 May 1784 in Philadelphia.

Sources:

George S. Brookes, *Friend Anthony Benezet* (Philadelphia: University of Pennsylvania Press, 1937);

Lawrence Cremin, *American Education: The Colonial Experience, 1607–1783* (New York: Harper & Row, 1970).

CHRISTOPHER DOCK

1698?-1771
EDUCATOR, WRITER

Early Years. Christopher Dock was a Mennonite schoolteacher. Little is known of his geographical origin, family, and date of immigration to America. He was probably from the Rhenish Palatinate but left for America in 1718, having spent four years as a teacher in Germany. After his arrival in Philadelphia he went to Skippack in Montgomery County, an area of German settlements about twenty miles from Germantown. There he opened a Mennonite school, where he taught for ten years before taking up farming. In 1735 he bought one hundred acres in Salford Township and three years later went back to teaching, this time at two schools simultaneously: the school in Skippack and another in Salford. He split a six-day teaching week into three days at one school and three at the other, an arrangement that lasted until his death in 1771. He also spent four summers teaching in Germantown in the log meetinghouse where Francis Daniel Pastorius had taught. He excelled in the art of *Fractur-Schriften,* illuminated manuscripts of scriptural texts beautifully drawn in color. He used them to decorate the walls of his schoolhouse and gave them as rewards to his students.

Teacher. Education in Pennsylvania in the eighteenth century was left up to the local communities to organize. German pietists were strongly committed to education so that everyone would learn to read religious books and therefore preferred to establish their own schools so that parents would have control of their children's learning. Parents got together to find a place to house the school, then they set the tuition costs and hired the teacher. The school at Skippack was not free; the tuition cost about four to six shillings a week. But some people donated money to help pay the fees of the poorer children. Dock believed that no child should be denied an education because he or she could not afford it. An innovative teacher, Dock emphasized learning for the building of character rather than the accumulation of knowledge. This meant that in addition to the rudiments of reading, writing, and numbers he cared about religion and morals, singing, safety, physical and emotional health, and manners. In other words he sought to educate the whole child. He preferred not to use the harsh and arbitrary punishments that were common in other colonial schools but to control his classes instead by persuasion, discussion, understanding, and love. He made punishments suitable for the misdemeanors and rewarded student progress.

The *Schulordnung*. One of Dock's Germantown students was the son of printer Christopher Sauer. Sauer was so impressed with Dock's teaching style that in 1749 he asked Dock to write down his methods in a teaching guide that Sauer would publish. At first Dock declined the request, but when Sauer composed specific questions for Dock, the teacher complied with the understanding that nothing be published during his lifetime. The questions were put together in manuscript form and finished, but not published until 1769, while Dock was still alive. The topics include enrollment, beginning the school day, teaching prayer, grading, discipline, and the teaching of the alphabet, of numbers, of punctuation, and of love and respect. Two hymns were also added in a section called "Children's Songs or Encouragement for the Children." The *Schulordnung* (School Management) was the first publication in America on schoolkeeping. The book is important not only for its description of Dock's schoolteaching methods but also for what it reveals about colonial Mennonite family life.

Other Writings. Dock also wrote several articles for the religious magazine *Ein Geistliches Magazien* (A Spiritual Magazine) published by Christopher Sauer Jr., who succeeded his father. The most famous of these were "A Hundred Necessary Rules of Conduct for Children" and "A Hundred Christian Rules for Children." The rules of conduct covered appropriate behavior for children at home, school, church, and other public places, while the Christian rules advised children on their relationships to God, to their neighbors, and to themselves. Dock also wrote at least two hymns, possibly six, for the magazine. These were included in the 1803 Mennonite hymnal, *Kleine Geistliche Harfe,* and later editions.

Source:

Gerald C. Studer, *Christopher Dock: Colonial Schoolmaster: A Biography and Writings of Christopher Dock* (Scottsdale, Pa.: Herald Press, 1993).

SARAH HAGGAR WHEATEN OSBORN

1714-1796
TEACHER, RELIGIOUS LEADER, WRITER

Vocation. Sarah Haggar was born in London on 22 February 1714 to Benjamin and Susanna Guyse Haggar. Her family immigrated to New England in 1722 and settled permanently in Newport, Rhode Island, in 1729. When she was eighteen years old, Sarah married Samuel Wheaten, who died at sea two years later, leaving her with an infant son. Sarah took over a neighbor's school in order to earn a living. In 1737 she joined the First Congregational Church in Newport and became an active member. She was profoundly affected by the revivals during the Great Awakening in 1740 and 1741, especially by the preaching of George Whitefield and Gilbert Tennent. In 1742 Sarah married Henry Osborn, a widower with three children. But soon after their marriage her husband's business failed, and his health declined. Sarah had to go back to teaching school to support the family despite criticism from some people in her community that her teaching took her away from family responsibilities. By the middle of the 1760s the Osborn home was a center of education and spiritual guidance for Newport's poor people. By 1766, during a revival, more than 300 people came to one or more of her weekly meetings, and by January 1767 that number had increased to 525 men and women, blacks and whites. She was the first woman to be a leader at such a revival. Osborn also considered writing to be part of her vocation. She tracked her spiritual journey in fifty diaries and penned many letters and other miscellaneous writings. The diaries are filled with her own religious reflections as well as commentaries on theological writings, such as Jonathan Edwards's *Treatise concerning Religious Affections* (1746) and Joseph Alleine's *An Alarm to the Unconverted* (1672).

Schools. Osborn's schools struggled financially, and the family had to take in boarders in order to make enough money. On 5 December 1758 she placed an advertisement in the *Newport Mercury:* "Sarah Osborn, School-mistress in Newport, proposes to keep a boarding school. Any person desirous of sending children, may be accommodated, and have them instructed in reading, writing, plain work, embroidering, tent stitch, samplers, &c. on reasonable terms." The following May she confessed to her friend the Reverend Joseph Fish of Stonington, Connecticut, that her family was surviving as a result of the income from boarders. In her teaching Osborn was influenced by her minister, Nathaniel Clap, who believed that servants, blacks, and the poor should be educated. Osborn's school, which reached a total enrollment of seventy students, contained not only boys and girls from well-established Newport families but also blacks and children of the poor, whose mothers sometimes paid tuition by washing, ironing, and sewing for the Osborns.

Societies. One of the outcomes of her spiritual transformation at the time of the Great Awakening was her desire to help organize and lead a female society whose members would gather to support each other in their spiritual growth. At their weekly meetings in Osborn's home they read the Bible and other religious literature, prayed and meditated, and conversed about religious concerns. These women, many of them unmarried, were among the most faithful attendees of her various evening meetings. One of the members of the society was Susanna Anthony, who became Osborn's close friend and correspondent and the apparent inspiration for one of Osborn's letters that were published anonymously in 1755 as *The Nature, Certainty, and Evidence of True Christianity.* Osborn founded other societies. One, called the Ethiopian Society, met at her house on Tuesday evenings, and another group of forty-two slaves met on Sunday night. To the latter, neighborhood boys and girls also stopped by for singing and reading, sometimes making the total number of visitors about seventy. The blacks who came to her meetings were among the most faithful. They had no opportunities for formal schooling and therefore referred to her gatherings on Sunday night as their school. The spiritual activity encouraged them to learn to read. However, Osborn was careful not to disrupt community relations and allowed the black servants to attend her Sunday meeting only under certain conditions: they had to obey their masters and mistresses; they had to go home immediately after the meeting; and they could not bring her presents.

Criticism. Many women, especially single women, kept small schools to earn their livings. Nevertheless, Osborn was criticized for assuming the roles of teacher and spiritual leader. She was participating in activities that were beyond what she as a woman was supposed to be doing; she was, as she said, "Moving beyond My Line." In particular she was criticized for hosting the men and older boys who came to her weekly meetings, and she was even ostracized for the Sunday evenings she spent with the black slaves. In response she remarked, "O the bitters that lurk under the most splendid appearances." Even her friend and correspondent Fish advised her to curtail her activities, arguing that her work with blacks would threaten the social hierarchy, that others (men) were better suited to this work, and that she needed to concentrate her energy more on feminine interests, such as needlework. But her commitment to her work and her conviction that she was fulfilling God's purpose made her resolute in her vocation.

Sources:

Samuel Hopkins, *Memoirs of the Life of Mrs. Sarah Osborn* (Worcester, Mass.: Leonard Worcester, 1799);

Sheryl A. Kujawa, "The Great Awakening of Sarah Osborn and the Female Society of the First Congregational Church in Newport," *Newport History,* 65 (1994): 133–153;

Kujawa, "Religion, Education, and Gender in Eighteenth-Century Rhode Island: Sarah Haggar Wheaten Osborn, 1714–1796," *Rhode Island History,* 52 (1994): 35–47;

Mary Beth Norton, "'My Resting Reaping Times': Sarah Osborn's Defense of Her 'Unfeminine' Activities, 1767," *Signs: Journal of Women in Culture and Society*, 2 (1976): 515–529.

EZRA STILES

1727-1795

CONGREGATIONAL MINISTER, THEOLOGIAN, SCHOLAR, COLLEGE PRESIDENT

Education and Early Career. Ezra Stiles was born on 29 November 1727 in North Haven, Connecticut, to Isaac Stiles, a Congregational minister, and Kezia Taylor Stiles, who died five days after giving birth to Ezra. Isaac married Esther Hooker in 1728. Ezra received his early education at home and entered Yale College in 1742 with twelve other freshmen. He studied the classical curriculum of liberal arts: classical languages, logic, rhetoric, geometry, geography, natural philosophy, astronomy, mathematics, metaphysics, ethics, and divinity. After graduation in 1746 he stayed at Yale to study theology to prepare for the ministry, and in 1749 he received a masters degree. In April of that year he was appointed tutor at Yale for a salary of twenty-three pounds a year, and the following May he was licensed to preach by the New Haven County Association of Ministers. Stiles was hesitant to enter the ministry and thought he would like to study law, so he continued his job as tutor at Yale while reading law, and in November 1753 he was admitted to the New Haven bar. In 1755 he was asked to be the rector of the Second Congregational Church in Newport, Rhode Island, for an annual salary of about fifty pounds, barely enough to support himself. Still intent on practicing law, he hesitated to accept the offer but was greatly impressed with Newport, a large and beautiful seaport. He finally accepted the position for a salary of sixty-five pounds plus firewood and a house and gave up his tutorship at Yale. Two years later he married Elizabeth Hubbard from New Haven, with whom he had eight children. Elizabeth died in 1775, and Ezra married Mary Cranston Checkley in 1782.

Dedication to His Flock. Newport held many attractions for Stiles, one of which was the Redwood Library, for which he became librarian in 1756. In Newport his intellectual interests expanded. He observed natural phenomena, such as the comet of 1759; performed experiments in chemistry; studied Hebrew, Arabic, Syriac, Armenian, and French; raised silkworms; read through the entire Bible eight times with his family, and wrote voluminous correspondence as well as sermons and other works, most of which, including his diary, remained unpublished during his lifetime. All of this was in addition to his responsibilities as a minister. He made as many as 1,000 pastoral visits a year and also catechised children, held special monthly meetings for men and for women, and attended to the spiritual needs of slaves by inviting them to his home for Bible readings and singing. In 1762 Stiles began thinking about founding another college in New England and with James Manning formulated plans for a Baptist college. He drafted the charter, and in 1764 the College of Rhode Island (Brown University) was established. Stiles was a proponent of American liberty, and when the war broke out, he supported the American cause. In May 1775 his wife Elizabeth died, leaving him with the care of their children. This personal tragedy was followed by the rapid dispersal of his congregation following the start of the rebellion against Great Britain. One hundred of the 130 families in his church had fled in 1775, most of them Patriots like himself. By March 1776 Stiles and his children also decided to leave and moved to Dighton, Massachusetts, where they stayed about a year. In May 1777 he was offered the ministry of the First Congregational Church in Portsmouth, New Hampshire, which was one of the largest in New England, with a congregation of 230 families. Still hoping to return to his Newport congregation after the war, he accepted the position for a year.

College President. No sooner had Stiles and his family settled in Portsmouth than he received a new offer in September to serve as president of Yale College. He did not accept the position right away. He was eager to return to teaching but did not want the administrative problems of running the college and referred to the "Diadem of a President" as a "Crown of Thorns." Yale was almost depleted of funds and in a state of republican turmoil and student rebellion. He wondered if the college could afford to pay him a decent salary and worried because the corporation was divided in its choice for president. If he could have returned to Newport, he would have rejected the offer, but on 20 March 1778, after carefully weighing all arguments for and against, he sent his acceptance to the college board of directors and was installed on 8 July as president and professor of ecclesiastical history. His salary was set at £120 plus the president's house and other compensations—roughly the same as his last salary as a minister had been.

War. At the time Stiles assumed the presidency in 1778, he faced several problems. One issue was the potential loss of students to the army. When Stiles arrived, the enrollment of the college was 132, but when the Connecticut Assembly exempted college students from the militia, he no longer had to worry about administering an empty college. Also since the fees from students made up most of the revenue of the college, this was encouraging news. The students, who had been sent to three Connecticut towns in 1777 to remove them from possible dangers, had to be reassembled in New Haven even though the threat of attack and the food shortages were still troublesome. Stiles had to ask parents for food and even sent students home for vacation two weeks early because the college could not feed them. In July 1779, when a British fleet of forty vessels anchored off West Haven, Stiles sent the students home for an indefinite period. The British raided New Haven, and though they did not remain, they continued to harass other Connecticut towns, so Stiles did not reopen the college until October. He had other, internal problems at Yale, especially with the board of directors, but after the war, in 1784 the college was flourishing with an enrollment of 270 students, the largest of any American college. The income from student fees and tuition was about £1,200.

Assessment. Stiles not only strengthened Yale but also secularized it, took it through the war successfully, and saved it financially. One important accomplishment of his administration was a change in the charter that allowed several state officials to become college board members and ensured state financial aid for the college. He not only performed well as an administrator but also taught classes in Hebrew, ecclesiastical history, theology, philosophy, and science, and even though he was not a minister of a specific church, he continued to perform ministerial duties until his death on 12 May 1795.

Sources:

Franklin B. Dexter, ed., *The Literary Diary of Ezra Stiles* (New York: Scribners, 1901);

Edmund S. Morgan, *The Gentle Puritan: A Life of Ezra Stiles, 1727–1795* (New Haven, Conn.: Yale University Press, 1962);

Francis Parsons, *Six Men of Yale* (New Haven, Conn.: Yale University Press, 1939).

PUBLICATIONS

Anthony Benezet, *A First Book for Children* (Philadelphia: Printed by Joseph Crukshank, 1778)—an early American primer written by Benezet after almost forty years of teaching experience;

Benezet, *The Pennsylvania Spelling Book, or Youth's Friendly Instructor and Monitor* (Philadelphia: Printed by Joseph Crukshank, 1776)—this book went through six editions until 1800; it was used for spelling and reading instruction as well as orthography and was intended especially for private instruction for families who lived in areas that were inaccessible to schools;

Benezet, *Some Observations Relating to the Establishment of Schools* (Philadelphia, 1778)—recommendations for attracting quality teachers;

Samuel Blair, *An Account Of The College of New-Jersey. In which are Described the Methods of Governments, Modes of Instruction, Manner and Expences of Living in the Same, &c. with a Prospect of the College Neatly Engraved* (Woodbridge, N.J.: Printed by James Parker, 1764);

Thomas Clap, *The Annals or History of Yale-College, In New-Haven, In the Colony of Connecticut, From the First Founding Thereof, in the Year 1700, to the Year 1766; With an Appendix, Containing the Present State of the College, the Method of Instruction and Government, with the Officers, Benefactors and Graduates* (New Haven: John Hotchkiss & B. Mecom, 1766);

Clap, *An Essay On The Nature and Foundations of Moral Virtue And Obligations; Being A Short Introduction To The Study of Ethics; For the Use of the Students of Yale-College* (New Haven: B. Mecom, 1765);

Clap, *The Religious Constitution of Colleges* (New London, Conn.: Printed by T. Green, 1754)—Clap was president of Yale, and in this tract he explains that it is right that the only governing influence of the college should be Congregationalism;

The Countryman's Lamentation On The Neglect Of A Proper Education Of Children: With an Address to the Inhabitants of New-Jersey (Philadelphia: Printed by W. Dunlap, 1762)—an allegorical tract;

Christopher Dock, *Schul-Ordnung* (Germantown, Pa.: Printed by Christopher Sauer, 1769)—a Mennonite schoolteacher, Dock completed this volume in 1750; it was the first book about school management published in America;

Germantown Academy, *Certain Agreements And Concessions, Made Concluded and Agreed On By and Between the Contributors to a Sum of Money for Erecting and Establishing a School House and School in Germantown, . . .* (Germantown, Pa.: Printed by Christopher Sauer, 1760);

John Mein, *A Catalogue of Mein's Circulating Library; Consisting of Above Twelve Hundred Volumes, in Most Branches of Polite Literature, Arts and Sciences . . .* (Boston: Mein & Fleeming, 1765)—an example of several such catalogues that were printed at this time. Mein opened his circulating library on 31 October 1765 with about 1,200 volumes representing 700 titles and sold this catalogue for one shilling;

John Morgan, *A Discourse upon the Institution of Medical Schools in America* (Philadelphia: Printed by William Bradford, 1765)—a baccalaureate address of the 1765 commencement of the College of Philadelphia in which Morgan discusses the horrible state of the medical practice in America and proposes the establishment of a formal program of medical education. Today the address is known as the "charter" of medical education in America;

William Smith, *A Brief History of the Rise and Progress of the Charitable Scheme, Carrying on by a Society of Noblemen and Gentlemen in London for the Relief and Instruction of Poor Germans, and Their Adjacent British Colonies in North-America . . .* (Philadelphia: Printed by B. Franklin & D. Hall, 1755);

Smith, *A General Idea of the College of Mirania: With a Sketch of the Method of Teaching Science and Religion, in the Several Classes: And Some Account of Its Size, Establishement and Buildings. Address'd More Immediately to the Consideration of the Trustees Nominated, by the Legislature, to Receive Proposals, &c. Relating to the Establishment of a College in the Province of New-York* (New York: Printed by J. Parker & W. Weyman, 1753)—Mirania was a fictitious institution that embodied Smith's ideas of what a college should be like; Smith used these ideas to design the curriculum for the College of Philadelphia;

Society of Friends. Philadelphia Yearly Meeting. Boarding School Committee, *Some Observations Relating to the Establishment of Schools, Agreed to by the Committee, to be Laid for Consideration Before the Yearly Meeting* (Philadelphia, 1778)—proposals of the committee signed by Anthony Benezet and Isaac Zane;

John Trumbull, *The Progress of Dulness, Part First: Or the Rare Adventures of Tom Brainless; Shewing what His Father and Mother Said of Him; How He Went to College, and What He Learned There; How He Took His Degree, and Went to Keeping School; How Afterwards He Became a Great Man and Wore a Wig; And How Any Body Else May do the Same—The Like Never Before Published. Very Proper to be Kept in All Families . . .* (New Haven, Conn.: Printed by Thomas and Samuel Green, 1772)—a satire in verse that makes fun of contemporary education as well as a criticism of classical education in favor of a more useful education;

Noah Webster, *A Grammatical Institute, of the English Language. Comprising, an Easy, Concise, and Systematic Method of Education, Designed for the Use of English Schools in America. In Three Parts: Part I. Containing, a New and Accurate Standard of Pronunciation* (Hartford, Conn.: Printed by Hudson & Goodwin for the author, 1783)—a spelling and pronunciation book. The first edition of five thousand copies sold out in one year, and by 1837 an estimated fifteen million copies had been printed. It was referred to as the "blue-backed speller" and rapidly replaced Thomas Dilworth's *A New Guide to the English Tongue* (1770) in popularity; in 1778 the name was changed to *An American Spelling Book*;

Eleazar Wheelock, *A Plain and Faithful Narrative of the Original Design, Rise, Progress and Present State Of the Indian Charity-School at Lebanon, in Connecticut* (Boston: Printed by Richard & Samuel Draper, 1763)—the first edition was updated by eight successive narratives; it explained the history and purpose behind Moor's Indian Charity School that Wheelock established in 1754 for the education of Indian boys and girls;

John Woolman, *Some Considerations on the Keeping of Negroes: Recommended to the Professors of Christianity, of Every Denomination* (Philadelphia: Printed by James Chattin, 1754)—a Quaker teacher opposed to slavery who proposed manumission and education for slaves; a second volume appeared in 1762.

Drawing of an eighteenth-century hornbook

GOVERNMENT AND POLITICS

by ROBERT J. ALLISON

CONTENTS

Sidebars and tables are listed in italics.

1754

- The Philadelphia State House is completed.

9 May Benjamin Franklin draws a cartoon of a snake cut into eight pieces, representing the colonies, with the caption "Join or Die."

19 June Representatives from seven American colonies meet at Albany, New York, to work toward common defense against the French and to secure the support of the Iroquois Confederacy.

10 July The Albany conference approves Benjamin Franklin's plan to form a union of colonies.

17 Aug. Pennsylvania rejects the Albany Plan, and other colonies and the British government also refuse to support it.

1755

14 Apr. British general Edward Braddock meets with colonial governors at Alexandria, Virginia, to plan an attack on French fortifications.

1757

3 Feb. The Pennsylvania assembly appoints Benjamin Franklin their agent in dealing with the proprietary government.

1762

5 Nov. In the secret Treaty of San Ildefonso, France cedes Louisiana to Spain.

1763

- The Ottawa chief Pontiac leads an Indian uprising against the British in the Ohio River valley.

1764

5 Apr. Parliament passes the Sugar Act, reducing the tariff on molasses imported into North America and sending customs agents and collectors to the colonies.

1765

2 Feb. Benjamin Franklin and other colonial agents meet with Prime Minister George Grenville to protest the stamp tax.

22 Mar. King George III endorses the stamp tax, which Parliament had approved on 27 February; it will take effect in November.

15 May Parliament passes the Quartering Act, requiring the colonists to provide shelter and supplies to British soldiers.

13 Aug. A Boston mob destroys the office of stamp collector Andrew Oliver and attacks his house.

26 Aug. A Boston mob destroys the home of lieutenant governor and chief justice Thomas Hutchinson in protest of the Stamp Act.

16–17 Sept.	A Philadelphia mob attacks stamp distributors.
7–25 Oct.	Nine colonies represented at the Stamp Act Congress in New York protest Parliament's taxation of the colonies.
1 Nov.	The Stamp Act goes into effect, and colonial courts are shut down by angry mobs refusing to purchase stamps.

1766

17 Mar.	Parliament rescinds the stamp tax but insists it has power to tax the colonies.
16 May	Celebrations begin in America as news of the Stamp Act's repeal reaches the colonies.
July	The Treaty of Oswego ends Pontiac's War.
6 Dec.	The Massachusetts assembly votes to compensate victims of the Stamp Act riots but also pardons the rioters.

1767

•	John Dickinson begins publishing "Letters from a Farmer in Pennsylvania to the Inhabitants of the British Colonies," protesting Parliament's power to tax the colonies.
20 Jan.	The formal transfer of Louisiana to the Spanish governor Don Antonio de Ulloa occurs.
2 July	Parliament passes the Townshend duties, imposing taxes on tea, glass, paper, and other goods sold in the colonies.

1768

11 Feb.	Georgia appoints Benjamin Franklin its colonial agent in London.
10 Apr.	After inspecting all the Spanish presidios from Texas to Sonora, Mexico, Marques de Rubi recommends that Spain consolidate them into a line of seventeen sites, which will be done in 1772.
10 June	British authorities seize John Hancock's sloop *Liberty* for violating customs laws.
1 Aug.	Boston merchants adopt a nonimportation agreement.
22 Sept.	Delegates from twenty-six Massachusetts towns meet in a convention to draw up a protest against the Townshend duties.
Oct.	A rebellion by French colonists forces Spanish governor Ulloa to flee New Orleans for Havana.
1 Nov.	British troops arrive in Boston to enforce customs laws.
5 Nov.	In the Treaty of Fort Stanwix the Iroquois confirm the cession of territories in the Ohio and Tennessee River valleys to the British.

1769

16 May	After Virginia's House of Burgesses rejects Parliament's right to tax the colonies, the governor dissolves the assembly, which continues to meet privately, agreeing not to import British goods.
27 June	The Massachusetts House of Representatives petitions the king to remove Governor Francis Bernard from government.
18 Aug.	Gen. Alexandro O'Reilly suppresses the Louisiana rebellion and restores Spanish control.
19 Nov.	Inhabitants of the French settlement at St. Louis take the oath of allegiance to the king of Spain.

1770

Jan.	Lt. Gov. Thomas Hutchinson refuses to use military force to protect customs agents and merchants from Massachusetts protestors.
19–20 Jan.	The Battle of Golden Hill, New York, results in one death as the Sons of Liberty skirmish with British soldiers trying to remove liberty poles from Golden Hill, Manhattan.
5 Mar.	In the Boston Massacre five Bostonians are killed when British soldiers fire into a mob.
12 Apr.	Parliament repeals all the Townshend duties except the one on tea.

1771

3 Feb.	Pedro Fermin de Mendinueta, Spanish governor of New Mexico, makes peace with the Comanches.
14 Mar.	Thomas Hutchinson is commissioned as royal governor of Massachusetts.
23 Sept.	Antonio Maria Bucarely y Ursua becomes viceroy of New Spain and immediately advocates the Spanish settlement in California.

1772

28 Feb.	The Boston assembly threatens to secede from the British Empire unless its rights are protected.
9 June	The H.M.S. *Gaspee*, a British customs vessel, runs aground while chasing a suspected smuggler in Rhode Island; local citizens drive off the British sailors and burn the ship to the waterline.
2 Nov.	The Boston town meeting creates a twenty-one-member committee of correspondence to communicate with other towns in the colony and to defend the rights of colonists "as Men, as Christians, and as Subjects."
20 Nov.	The Boston committee of correspondence issues a declaration of rights and a list of grievances drafted by Samuel Adams.

1773

6 Jan. Gov. Thomas Hutchinson opens a session of the Massachusetts assembly with a speech outlining the proper constitutional roles of colonies and Parliament.

25–26 Jan. The Massachusetts assembly responds to Hutchinson's speech on proper constitutional roles.

12 Mar. The Virginia House of Burgesses creates an eleven-man committee of correspondence to obtain information about British actions and to keep other colonies informed of these developments.

May New York and Massachusetts resolve a border controversy.

7 May The Rhode Island assembly creates a committee of correspondence.

10 May The king approves the Tea Act, giving the British East India Company a monopoly on all tea sold in North America.

21 May Connecticut forms a committee of correspondence.

27 May The New Hampshire assembly forms a committee of correspondence.

28 May Massachusetts Bay forms a committee of correspondence.

2 June The Massachusetts assembly reads letters from Governor Hutchinson and Lt. Gov. Andrew Oliver to British authorities, advocating repression against rebellious colonists; the assembly calls for the removal of Hutchinson and Oliver.

7 July Governor Hutchinson learns that Benjamin Franklin had sent his letters to the assembly and calls for his prosecution for treason.

8 July South Carolina forms a committee of correspondence.

10 Sept. Georgia forms a committee of correspondence.

14 Oct. An Annapolis mob burns a cargo of tea.

15 Oct. A Philadelphia mass meeting denounces the Tea Act as an attack "upon the liberties of America which every American was . . . bound to oppose." Maryland forms a committee of correspondence.

16 Oct. The Pennsylvania assembly forms a committee of correspondence.

23 Oct. Delaware forms a committee of correspondence.

8 Dec. North Carolina forms a committee of correspondence.

16 Dec. A Boston mob disguised as Mohawk Indians dumps a cargo of tea into the harbor.

1774

20 Jan. The New York assembly forms a committee of correspondence.

29 Jan. Benjamin Franklin is examined by the Privy Council for Plantation Affairs and by Solicitor General Alexander Wedderburn, who is also representing Thomas Hutchinson and Andrew Oliver, on how he obtained Hutchinson's correspondence; the next day he is dismissed from his postmaster general position.

8 Feb. The New Jersey assembly forms a committee of correspondence.

31 Mar.	Parliament enacts the Boston Port Bill, closing the port of Boston in retaliation for the Tea Party.
3 May	Effigies of Thomas Hutchinson and British solicitor general Alexander Wedderburn are burned in Philadelphia.
13 May	Thomas Gage, commissioned governor of Massachusetts, arrives in Boston.
20 May	The king signs two statutes: the Massachusetts Government Act suspends the colony's charter and gives the royal governor the power to appoint local sheriffs and magistrates; the Administration of Justice Act allows the Crown to move trials in cases involving royal officials to Nova Scotia or England.
26 May	After reading the Virginia House of Burgesses' call for a day of fasting and prayer in support of the Massachusetts colonists, John Murray, Lord Dunmore, the Virginia governor, dissolves the assembly.
27 May	Eighty-nine members of the dissolved Virginia Assembly meet at the Raleigh Tavern and agree to support Massachusetts, call for a Continental Congress to consolidate action, and support economic pressure to force England to rescind the Massachusetts Government Act.
15 June	Twelve colonies begin choosing delegates to a Continental Congress.
17 June	After the Massachusetts House of Representatives meets behind locked doors to choose delegates to the Continental Congress, Gen. Thomas Gage dissolves the General Court.
22 June	The king signs the Quebec Act, establishing a government in the province of Quebec, extending its borders to the Mississippi and Ohio Rivers, and granting the Catholic Church power to collect tithes.
10 Aug.	Georgia adopts a declaration of rights but decides not to send delegates to the Continental Congress.
3 Sept.	General Gage begins fortifying the town of Boston.
5 Sept.– **16 Oct.**	The First Continental Congress meets in Philadelphia; each state has one vote in this body.
17 Sept.	Congress approves the Suffolk County Resolves.
28 Sept.	Joseph Galloway proposes a union of colonies with Great Britain, with the colonies choosing members of a grand council, which, with a president-general chosen by the king, could make laws for the colonies with the approval of Parliament; the proposal is defeated, six to five.
18 Oct.	Congress adopts the Continental Association, pledging to cease imports from England after 1 December 1774.
22 Oct.	Congress expunges Galloway's plan from its records.

1775

9 Feb.	The king declares Massachusetts to be in rebellion.
19 July	The Massachusetts legislature meets in Watertown.
21 July	Congress receives a plan of union prepared by Benjamin Franklin.
4 Nov.	Indians attack the Spanish mission at San Diego, California.

7 Nov.	Virginia governor John Murray, Earl of Dunmore, declares martial law, charging with treason all men eligible for military duty who do not serve "His Majesty's standard" and offering freedom to all slaves who join his forces.
21 Dec.	Parliament passes the Confiscation Act, allowing for the seizure of property belonging to rebels.

1776

5 Jan.	New Hampshire adopts a new constitution to create a stable government while British authority collapses.
9 Feb.	Juan Bautista de Anza leaves San Diego to explore the area of San Francisco Bay.
10 Feb.	The South Carolina provincial congress begins a debate on a new form of government.
5 Mar.	The *Pennsylvania Post* publishes the plan of union drafted the previous summer by Silas Deane.
26 Mar.	South Carolina adopts a new government to take the place of British authority.
27–29 Mar.	The Anza expedition determines that the San Francisco Bay area will be conducive to Spanish settlement.
4 May	Rhode Island removes the mention of royal authority from its charter, in effect renouncing allegiance to the king.
6 May	The final meeting of Virginia's House of Burgesses occurs; it is replaced by the Virginia Convention.
10 May	The Continental Congress calls on the colonies to form new governments.
15 May	The Virginia Convention instructs its representatives in Congress to declare independence from England.
8–10 June	George Mason presents a plan for state government to the Virginia Convention.
12 June	Congress appoints a committee led by John Dickinson to draw up a plan for confederation.
21 June	The New Jersey provincial congress votes to write a state constitution.
23 June	George Wythe presents the Virginia Convention with a draft constitution prepared by Thomas Jefferson.
29 June	The Virginia Convention adopts a new state government, and Patrick Henry is elected governor.
2 July	The Continental Congress votes unanimously that "these thirteen colonies are, and of right, ought to be, free and independent states."
•	New Jersey adopts a state constitution.
4 July	Congress adopts the Declaration of Independence.
9 July	The New York provincial congress begins work on a state constitution.
12 July	Adm. Lord Richard Howe arrives in New York as head of a peace commission; Howe's terms are not acceptable to the colonials.
15 Aug.	John Adams publishes *Thoughts on Government* anonymously.

20 Aug.	Congress has copies of the Articles of Confederation printed.
20 Sept.	Delaware adopts a state constitution.
28 Sept.	Pennsylvania adopts a state constitution.
Oct.	Concord, Massachusetts, protests the power of the Massachusetts General Court to write a state constitution, insisting that constitutions can only be created by the sovereign power of the people.
9 Nov.	Maryland adopts a state constitution.
18 Dec.	North Carolina adopts a state constitution.

1777

5 Feb.	Georgia adopts a state constitution.
20 Apr.	The New York provincial convention adopts a state constitution.
8 July	Vermont draws up a state constitution, but it will not officially become a state until 1791.
15 Nov.	The Continental Congress adopts the Articles of Confederation and Perpetual Union and sends it to the states for approval; it needs the endorsement of all state legislatures to take effect.
21 Nov.	Congress recalls Silas Deane from Paris.
17 Dec.	Louis XVI of France recognizes the independence of the United States.

1778

6 Feb.	France and the United States sign a treaty of mutual defense.
28 Feb.	The Massachusetts legislature submits a constitution to town meetings for ratification. The towns reject it by a vote of 9,972 to 2,083 and instruct the legislature to call a special convention to draw up a constitution.
19 Mar.	The South Carolina assembly approves a state constitution.
10 June	The New Hampshire state constitutional convention meets in Concord and is the first special convention called to draw up a constitution; its proposals, though, are rejected by town meetings.
19 June	The British evacuate Philadelphia.
22–25 June	Congress rejects thirty-seven changes to the Articles of Confederation proposed by the state legislatures.
9 July	Delegates from eight of the ten states that have ratified the Articles sign them.
4 Sept.	The city of Amsterdam in the Netherlands and Congress sign a treaty of amity and commerce.
20 Nov.	New Jersey adopts the Articles of Confederation.
Dec.	Maryland refuses to adopt the Articles of Confederation.
5 Dec.	Silas Deane publishes a defense of his conduct in the *Pennsylvania Packet*.

9 Dec.	Henry Laurens resigns as president of Congress because Congress refuses to censure Deane for publishing his defense.

1779

20 Jan.	Congress appoints a committee to investigate the Silas Deane affair.
1 Feb.	Delaware adopts the Articles of Confederation.
5 June	The New Hampshire town meetings reject a proposed state constitution.
21 June	Spain declares war on England although it does not recognize American independence.
1 Sept.	The Massachusetts state convention meets to draw up a constitution.
13 Sept.	John Jay, president of Congress, asks the states to collect taxes in order to pay requisitions to the federal treasury.

1780

19 Feb.	New York agrees to cede its western land claims to the United States.
1 Mar.	The Pennsylvania assembly approves a law abolishing slavery.
2 Mar.	The Massachusetts convention submits a state constitution to the towns for ratification.
12 May	The five-thousand-man garrison of Charleston, South Carolina, surrenders to the British.
25 Sept.	Benedict Arnold's plot to betray West Point to the British is discovered.
10 Oct.	Connecticut cedes its western land claims to the United States.
21 Oct.	Congress grants retiring Continental officers half-pay benefits for life.
25 Oct.	The Massachusetts state constitution takes effect.

1781

2 Jan.	Virginia cedes its territories north of the Ohio River to the United States on the condition that Congress establishes new states in the region and that land purchases from Indians be voided.
10 Jan.	Congress creates a ministry for foreign affairs.
1 Mar.	New York delegates present their land cession to Congress, and Maryland delegates ratify the Articles of Confederation on behalf of their state.
26 May	The Pennsylvania legislature charters the Bank of North America.

1782

Mar.	The British Parliament calls for an end to the war in America.
20 Mar.	Lord North resigns as prime minister, and the new government opens peace negotiations with the United States.

30 Nov.	Benjamin Franklin, John Adams, Henry Laurens, and John Jay sign the preliminary peace agreement with British emissaries.
30 Dec.	A congressional commission resolves the Connecticut and Pennsylvania dispute over the Wyoming River valley in Pennsylvania, maintaining that the land is within Pennsylvania's jurisdiction but that claims of Connecticut settlers should be honored. Meanwhile, Pennsylvania militiamen begin ejecting Connecticut settlers from their homes.

1783

15 Mar.	Gen. George Washington denounces the threat by some officers to force Congress to pay them. He promises to use his own influence with Congress to ensure officers are paid.
18 Apr.	Congress proposes a revenue system as a way of paying the national debt.
26 June	Mutinous soldiers from Pennsylvania march on Philadelphia, and Congress flees to Princeton, New Jersey.
2 July	The British close West Indian ports to American shipping.
7 Oct.	Congress votes to build a "federal town" on the banks of the Delaware River in New Jersey.
20 Oct.	Congress votes to build a second federal town on the Potomac River, alternating its sessions between the two sites.
31 Oct.	New Hampshire towns ratify the state constitution, having rejected three earlier proposals.
3 Sept.	British and American negotiators sign the Treaty of Paris, recognizing American independence and ending hostilities.
13 Nov.	The first and only meeting of the Pennsylvania Council of Censors occurs.
25 Nov.	The British evacuate New York City.
26 Nov.	Congress meets at Annapolis, Maryland, resolving to alternate meetings between Annapolis and Trenton until the new federal cities are built.
23 Dec.	George Washington resigns his commission as commander in chief of the Continental Army.

OVERVIEW

Structure of Colonial Government. The systems of government in the American colonies looked much like the British government. England and the colonies had executives (England had a king; each colony had a governor) and two-house legislatures (England had a Parliament with a House of Commons and a House of Lords; each colony had an assembly with a House of Representatives and an upper house, or council). Despite the similar structures, these governments were different. The king of England represented the nation's sovereign power, but since Parliament had beheaded Charles I in 1649 and deposed James II in 1688, kings had learned to govern with the support of Parliament. In Parliament the House of Lords represented England's aristocrats while the House of Commons represented the merchants or middle class. Members of Parliament did not represent local constituencies; their real job was to make laws for the good of the entire realm. In the colonies, on the other hand, the governor, appointed by the king, represented the king's interests and the interests of the empire while the assembly represented the local colonial interest. Members of the assembly had to live in the town they represented. As long as England and her colonies had similar interests, these two systems worked well. But when the interests of the British nation and her colonial subjects began to differ in the 1760s, the system fell apart.

Salutary Neglect. The American colonies had governed themselves for much of their history. The British nation, preoccupied with its own problems, had allowed the colonial assemblies to make their own rules. Parliament passed regulations to control all trade in the empire but had not enforced these rules, allowing the colonies to grow and prosper under a policy of salutary neglect. Governors, appointed by the king, would spend at most a few years in the colonies and then return home to a more lucrative position in England, having performed their duty of protecting the king's interest and advancing their own. The assemblies did the real work of governing, levying taxes to pay for local improvements and paying salaries of the governor and other civil officers. The assemblies jealously guarded their prerogatives and those of their own colony. Virtually every colony disputed its borders with every other colony and at times went to war over its

boundaries. The colonies were also threatened by Native Americans and by Spanish and French imperial ambitions. In these conflicts each colony looked to England for defense.

Plan for Union. In 1754 tensions with the Iroquois and French encroachments into the Ohio River valley prompted Benjamin Franklin to call for a union of the colonies, to be governed by a Grand Council chosen by the colonies and a governor general chosen by the king. This plan for a colonial union failed as the colonial assemblies, jealous of their individual interests, rejected the idea. Franklin remarked that the colonists would never unite unless the British forced them to do so.

French and Indian War. The tensions between the French and the English colonists escalated into the first global conflict, involving England and France and most of Europe, fought in the American colonies, the West Indies, the Mediterranean, India, and Indonesia. The British won the war, driving the French from North America and from India; wresting Havana, Cuba, from Spain; and establishing British control of the seas. But the war was expensive, costing Britain more than £122 million (close to £1 billion in today's currency). Since the British people were already heavily taxed and since the debt had been incurred in defending the American colonists, Parliament decided to tax the colonists. Colonists insisted that Parliament could regulate trade but could not tax them because they were not represented in Parliament. In 1765 Parliament passed the Stamp Act, requiring the colonists to pay a tax on all printed materials and legal documents. This provoked a near rebellion in the colonies, and most colonial leaders insisted that they could be taxed only by their own elected representatives.

Virtual and Actual Representation. The Stamp Act dispute showed how far apart colonial and British ideas about government were. The idea that no one could be taxed without his consent was a fundamental British principal, but Parliament did not represent the British people in the way the American colonists insisted they must be represented. Parliamentary boroughs had been created centuries earlier, and by 1760 some of England's largest cities did not have representatives in Parliament. However, according to British political theory all subjects were represented because members of Parliament were concerned with the good of the whole empire; they were not chosen to defend the petty local interests of a community but to make wise laws for the whole nation. Parliament represented the interests of all. In the American colonies, however, members of a colony's assembly were chosen to represent the local interests of a community; the good of the entire society would be advanced by a careful adherence to the good of each constituent part.

Montesquieu. The American perception of differences was sharpened by the publication in French of Charles de Secondat Baron de Montesquieu's *Spirit of the Laws* in 1748, which was translated into English by 1752 and regularly reprinted in London and Scotland throughout the century. Montesquieu's work, the first treatise on political theory since Aristotle, examined different forms of governments: tyrannical, aristocratic, and democratic. Each of these forms was suited to a particular kind of country, and each operated through different principles. While Montesquieu studied many different ancient and modern political societies, he admired eighteenth-century England the most. Its government balanced all three political forms: the king represented despotic power; the aristocracy was represented in the House of Lords; and the House of Commons was the democratic branch. Each part balanced the others, and each branch checked the other two, preventing the government from becoming completely tyrannical or disintegrating into democratic anarchy. It was vital to Montesquieu's theory that each branch's powers be strictly separated, otherwise the whole system would be corrupted and deteriorate. Montesquieu was a better political theorist than a student of English politics: in England the government's functioning powers were not separated at all but in fact were combined as the prime minister controlled the legislative branch through his power to appoint executive officers. While Montesquieu's *Spirit of the Laws* did not describe England, but it did describe the kinds of governments that had emerged in the American colonies. The colonists read *Spirit of the Laws* as a powerful defense of their forms of government, in which legislative and executive powers were separated, and the assemblies checked the governors.

Dickinson and Boycott. The British did not believe that the assemblies could check the governor, nor did Parliament accept the idea that assemblies had exclusive power to tax the American colonists; but leaders in Parliament did recognize that they could not enforce the unpopular Stamp Act. Rather than provoke a rebellion, Parliament bowed to political pressure and rescinded the law. Parliamentary leaders insisted that Parliament could tax the colonies but hoped the colonial assemblies would take the initiative to raise revenue for Britain. When this did not happen, in 1767 Parliament passed a new series of tariffs, the Townshend duties, on goods imported into the colonies. These duties were meant both to raise revenue and to protect English goods from colonial competi-

tion. Predictably, the colonists again objected. John Dickinson of Pennsylvania wrote a series of essays, *Letters from a Farmer in Pennsylvania to the Inhabitants of the British Colonies,* arguing that while Parliament could regulate external trade, only the colonial assemblies could tax the colonists. Parliament would never accept this idea, but the colonist's century and a half of experience convinced them of its legitimacy. To prove their point, colonists agreed not to import any British goods, which they knew would pressure British merchants to pressure Parliament to rescind the duties.

Crown Salaries. The boycott succeeded, and Parliament rescinded most of the Townshend duties. The colonists were convinced of their economic power though Parliament did not accept Dickinson's arguments. To prove its power Parliament maintained the three-penny-per-pound duty on tea. The colonists still were able evade this tax and get tea more cheaply from Dutch and Danish traders. For five years relations between the colonies and England were relatively tranquil, with the notable exception of the killing of five civilians in Boston by British troops in 1770. Charged with murder, the soldiers were ably and successfully defended by John Adams, one of the leaders in colonial opposition to Parliament's taxation powers. The soldiers were acquitted, and calm was restored until 1773, when a series of ill-advised British political moves provoked more colonial resistance. The British government proposed that the Crown, and not the assembly, should pay the governor, judges, and other civil officers in Massachusetts. The assembly reacted angrily to this threat to take away their control over these officers and moved to impeach Chief Justice Peter Oliver, who accepted his salary from the Crown.

The Quebec Act. In 1773 Parliament began debates on the Quebec Act to govern the vast province won from France ten years earlier. This act had something in it to offend most colonists. For New Englanders, overwhelmingly and fanatically Protestant, the Quebec Act protected the religious traditions of Roman Catholics, who were the majority of Quebec's Christian population. For colonists from Virginia, Pennsylvania, and New York, who all claimed the Ohio River valley, the Quebec Act granted title to this entire region to the former French province. These colonies had been bitterly divided over the Ohio country. Virginians had set up land companies to sell off the land to white farmers; Pennsylvanians hoped to open trade with the Wabashs, Miamis, and other native peoples; and New Yorkers threatened war against both Virginia and Pennsylvania to protect the claims of the Iroquois in the region. While the three colonies threatened war on each other to prevent their gaining an advantage in the region, they would cooperate to ensure that Quebec did not get control of the region.

Tea Act. Parliament passed the Tea Act in 1773 to revive the fortunes of the East India Company, on the verge of collapse after its conquest of India. The Tea Act gave the company a monopoly on all tea sold in the British empire and also promised the company a rebate on the taxes it would have to pay in England. American merchants, who could buy tea more cheaply from Dutch or Danish merchants, were angered by this act of favoritism. The fact that two sons of Massachusetts royal governor Thomas Hutchinson (brother-in-law of Andrew Oliver) were designated to sell the East India Company tea did nothing to appease the colonists. Sons of Liberty, political action groups formed during the Stamp Act controversy, organized to prevent the tea from being unloaded. When the first ship, the *Dartmouth*, reached Boston, the Sons of Liberty would not allow the tea to be unloaded while Hutchinson refused to allow it to sail until it had unloaded and paid the tax. This political standoff ended when a mob of colonists disguised as Mohawk Indians boarded the *Dartmouth* and dumped its cargo into the harbor.

Aftermath. When Parliament learned of the tea's destruction, it ordered the port of Boston closed until the colonists repaid the East India Company. It suspended the Massachusetts charter government, replacing it with one more amenable to British rule. It restricted the power of the town meetings, allowing them to meet only once a year and taking from them the power to choose sheriffs, magistrates, jurors, and judges. Gen. Thomas Gage, the military commander of British forces in North America, was sent to restore order in the troublesome province, which Parliament hoped to isolate. But these new laws, which the colonists called the Intolerable Acts, came too late. A Philadelphia mob used electricity to burn Hutchinson in effigy, and the Virginia House of Burgesses called for a day of fasting and prayer in support of the suspended Massachusetts government. When Virginia's governor, John Murray, Lord Dunmore, suspended the Burgesses for supporting Massachusetts, the Virginians met outside their assembly hall and called on the other colonies to choose delegates to a Continental Congress, which would seek redress for their common grievances against the British government.

The Suffolk Resolves. In Massachusetts, Gage found that it was easier for Parliament to order him to govern than it was for him to create a government. With the government that had operated since 1691 suspended, the people in the towns continued to govern themselves. In Suffolk County, which included Boston and the surrounding towns, a county convention met in September 1774. This convention acknowledged the colony's allegiance to George III but insisted that the Massachusetts Government Act and the closing of Boston harbor were "gross infractions" of natural law, the British constitution, and their colonial charter that the courts and other offices created under this act were unconstitutional. Suffolk County would support sheriffs and other officials who ignored these illegal courts, but officials of Gage's government would be considered "incorrigible enemies of the country." Suffolk county called on each town in the province to elect delegates to a Provincial Congress to meet in Salem in October, and it directed tax collectors to hold on to their receipts until the Provincial Congress could determine what to do. By the end of 1774 two governments operated in Massachusetts; one, commissioned by the king, led by General Gage, held power in Boston; the other, with neither commission nor charter, met in Salem. Those in the province who supported British authority found it prudent to move to Boston, which Gage now fortified; in the rest of Massachusetts the towns and county conventions governed.

First Continental Congress. Every colony except Georgia was represented in Philadelphia in the first Continental Congress, which met in September 1774. Joseph Galloway of Pennsylvania, who hoped the colonies would ultimately reconcile with England, proposed a union of the colonies, similar to what Franklin had proposed in 1754. From Boston, delegates John Adams and his cousin Samuel believed that independence was inevitable, and though they were joined by Virginia's Patrick Henry in espousing this, independence was still a "strange and terrible" idea for most of the delegates. The delegates rejected Galloway's proposal but were not ready to go along with the Adamses and Henry. Instead Congress called for a boycott of British goods to pressure British merchants to force Parliament to rescind the Intolerable Acts. Congress called on each colony to establish a committee of safety to enforce the boycott and to set prices. After petitioning the king, Congress adjourned, to meet again on 10 May 1775.

Outbreak of War. The political situation had changed dramatically when Congress met again in May. In February 1775 Parliament had declared Massachusetts to be in a state of rebellion. Gage was authorized to use force in suppressing the uprising. Prime Minister Lord North at the same time proposed a compromise: Parliament would refrain from taxing the colonies if the colonial assemblies would collect revenues and send them to England. Similar to the compromise proposal made in 1765, this one had less of a chance for success. In April, Gage received Parliament's proclamation of rebellion, and decided to arrest Samuel Adams and merchant John Hancock, whom he knew to be in Concord. He also knew that colonists were collecting and storing weapons in Concord, which he intended to seize along with the rebellion's leaders. Early on the morning of 19 April 1775, British regulars left Boston, reaching the town of Lexington at dawn. There they met a hastily assembled group of colonial minutemen. The regulars ordered the militia to disperse; the colonials refused; and the regulars fired. (The regulars expected that this mob would flee at the first sound of gunfire). The regulars then marched on to Concord. There they could not find either Adams or Hancock, but they did meet more militia, and this time the colonials were not overwhelmed by British power. When the minutemen stood their ground, the regulars panicked and began a long, disastrous retreat to Boston, with colonial militia chasing them, firing from behind rocks, trees, and walls. General Gage, fortified in Boston, could no longer maintain the pretense that he governed the province of Massachusetts.

Second Continental Congress. The outbreak of war changed the political situation. More colonial leaders were now certain that the Empire and the colonies could not be reconciled. Congress took a number of seemingly contradictory steps. In response to a query from the Massachusetts provincial congress about its legitimacy to govern, Congress told the provincial congress to operate under terms of the 1691 charter but to declare the office of governor vacant. Congress also created a Continental Army, and to demonstrate that the rebellion was not isolated to Massachusetts, appointed George Washington of Virginia to lead it. Congress authorized paper money to help pay for this army. In addition to these defensive measures, moderates still hoping for reconciliation pushed Congress to adopt the "Olive Branch petition," drafted by John Dickinson, which asked the king to reconsider the policies that had provoked the crisis. At the end of July, Congress rejected North's conciliatory proposal, and at the end of August, George III rejected the Olive Branch petition.

New Governments. When the New Hampshire and South Carolina provincial congresses asked for advice on how to govern, Congress recommended that each colony have a "full and free representation of the people, and that the Representatives if they think it necessary, establish such a form of Government, as in their judgment will best produce the happiness of the people." In each colony the Provincial Congress declared itself to be the House of Representatives, declared the office of governor vacant, and continued governing. By the end of 1775 royal authority had collapsed in most of the American colonies though what would replace that authority was very much in doubt. John Adams wanted Congress to recommend model constitutions to the colonies, but moderates in Congress did not want to suggest that the people of the colonies could form new governments, as this would mean that they aimed for independence, not reconciliation.

1776. In January 1776 Thomas Paine's *Common Sense* convinced Americans that they could be independent, that reconciliation would be impossible. When Washington forced Gage to evacuate Boston in March, it seemed that independence might even be easily obtained. Congress sent negotiators to Quebec to secure that colony's alliance, and on 10 May, Congress recommended that the colonies begin forming new governments. This was not independence, Joseph Duane said, but it was a "machine for fabricating independence." On 2 July, Congress declared that the thirteen colonies were free and independent states.

State Constitutions. Each state except Connecticut and Rhode Island, who simply eliminated the references to the monarch in their colonial charters, drew up new plans of government. Most of the new constitutions of 1776 and 1777 created systems that looked very much like the old charter governments though the governor would be almost completely under the assembly's control: he would be chosen by the assembly or by the people and would not have power to veto the assembly's actions. Virginia, which drew up the first constitution in June 1776, began its constitution with a declaration of rights, a model other states followed. By beginning with a Bill of Rights, the states showed that the purpose of government was to secure rights to citizens. Pennsylvania created a unique government, with a single-house legislature chosen every year by all adult male taxpayers, making the legislature the most representative body in the world.

Constitutional Conventions. The first constitutions were temporary measures; some of the men helping to write them, such as John Rutledge in South Carolina, hoped that ultimately the colonies could be reconciled with England; but by 1778 reconciliation was impossible, and problems were beginning to emerge from the hastily constructed state governments. Some states that now had more leisure to consider the best way to organize a government began to revise their state constitutions. One problem with these earlier constitutions was that they had been written by the state legislatures, which the constitutions were supposed to control. The idea emerged that a constitution could not be written by a legislature but had to emanate from a special convention which the people had chosen specifically to write a constitution. This convention would represent the sovereign power of the people and could create a fundamental law, delegating power to the legislature that the constitution created. When the Massachusetts legislature submitted a constitution to the people of the state in 1778, the people rejected it because the legislature did not have the power to write a constitution. New Hampshire held the first constitutional convention in June 1778 though the constitution this convention submitted to the people was also rejected. After 1778, states would use conventions, rather than the legislature, to draw up their fundamental laws.

Confederation. Though each state created a new government, the states were also members of a union, the United States of America. As the United States they would form treaties with other nations, maintain Washington's army, issue paper money, and borrow money to pay for the war. John Dickinson began drafting a plan of union in the weeks after independence was declared, and in the fall of 1777 Congress submitted the Articles of Confederation to the states. The Articles of Confederation was not a constitution since the Confederation was not an organic entity like a state. The articles were an agreement to cooperate, which the states would do in certain limited ways. Under the articles each state could choose no fewer than two and no more than seven delegates to Congress. No matter how many delegates a state sent, and no matter how many citizens a state had, each state would have only one vote in Congress. In order to do anything nine states would have to agree; to change the Articles every state would have to agree. Congress could not tax citizens or states, nor could it draft soldiers; to raise money Congress would have to determine the relative wealth or man power of each state and then request money or troops from the states accordingly. Approved by Congress in 1777, the articles were not ratified by all of the states until 1781. Maryland withheld support until New York and Virginia surrendered their western lands to the Confederation. As part of the British empire, the colonies had slowly and painfully learned the necessity to cooperate. Without this union the United States would not have won their independence. By 1787 they would discover the union they had created under the strain of war was not sufficient to maintain their liberty or independence in times of peace.

TOPICS IN THE NEWS

THE ALBANY CONFERENCE

Concerns of the Crown. In 1754 the British Board of Trade worried that disputes between Pennsylvania, New York, and Virginia over the Ohio River valley had nearly destroyed the British relationship with the Iroquois and that these disputes were allowing the French to move into the Ohio country. The Board of Trade encouraged colonists to meet at Albany, New York, to resolve their differences. In June and July 1754 delegates from New Hampshire, Massachusetts, Rhode Island, Connecticut, New York, Pennsylvania, and Maryland arrived in Albany, sent by their colonial assemblies. The Albany Conference, the Board of Trade hoped, would foster colonial unity and restore the "Covenant Chain," the relationship between the British colonial government and the Iroquois.

Covenant Chain. By the beginning of the century the Iroquois, the powerful confederation of Onondaga, Mohawk, Seneca, Oneida, and Cayuga tribes, had established the Covenant Chain with the New York colony. This agreement technically recognized English sovereignty over settled areas and Iroquois domination over all Indians between the Hudson and Mississippi Rivers. Though the Shawnees, Miamis, Wabashs, Delawares, Wyandots, and other native people of the Ohio River valley disputed Iroquois domination, they were not strong enough to resist the Iroquois confederation. New York's alliance gave the Iroquois even more power over their neighbors and diverted the fur trade, which the Ohio valley people had carried on with the French at Montreal, into Albany.

Iroquois Confederation. The Iroquois had formed their confederation in the fifteenth century under the leadership of the legendary Deganawida and Hiawatha.

Under the Iroquois system the five different nations of the Iroquois agreed not to fight with one another and to hold an annual council to resolve differences and form policy. This policy gave the Iroquois considerably more power than their neighbors, and when the Europeans had arrived in New England and in Canada, they found the Iroquois united and often at war with other native people.

The English and the Ohio. The Virginians, Pennsylvanians, and New Yorkers all greedily eyed the Ohio River valley, and each had a different agenda for it. Virginians, including George Mason and Lawrence and Augustine Washington, had formed the Ohio Company, which claimed title to five hundred thousand acres along the Ohio River. The Virginians hoped to sell this land to investors and to settlers, creating a new agricultural colony in the rich Ohio soil. Pennsylvania traders, meanwhile, had pushed across the mountains to the Ohio country and had begun a lucrative trade with the native people in the area. The furs that the Pennsylvanians bought, and the trade goods they sold, took business away from the New York traders and their Iroquois allies. These disputes permitted the French, who had easier access than the English to the Ohio by way of the Great Lakes, to move into the area and divert trade from both New York and Pennsylvania.

Franklin and Union. Benjamin Franklin saw the Iroquois confederation as a model for colonial unity. "It would be a strange thing if Six Nations of ignorant savages should be capable of forming a scheme for such a union, and be able to execute it in such a manner as that it has subsisted for ages and appears indissoluble; and yet that a like union should be impracticable for ten or a dozen English colonies, to whom it is more necessary, and must be more advantageous, and who cannot be supposed to want an equal understanding of their interests." By uniting and putting aside narrow differences, the Iroquois had come to dominate eastern North America. Their Algonquian neighbors had not united and now were either at the point of extinction or under Iroquois or European control. The lesson was plain for Franklin, who printed the first political cartoon in the American colonies: a snake cut into eight pieces, representing the colonies, with the caption "Join or Die."

The French Connection. The French had begun moving into the Ohio country, which formed a natural connection between the St. Lawrence River and the Great Lakes of French Canada and France's colonies on the Mississippi River. The Ohio River valley was more easily entered from the Great Lakes than it was from the eastern seaboard since the Appalachian Mountains formed a natural barrier between the ocean and the interior. The French established trading posts and forts in the territory, using these posts to secure trade with the Algonquian people, who resented Iroquoian domination. Detroit, Fort Duquesne, Terre Haute, and other posts connected Canada with the French trading posts at St. Louis and New Orleans. The English colonists disagreed too much among themselves about control of the Ohio country to make a common policy against the French.

Iroquois and English. The Iroquois noticed the English colonists' failure. Mohawk chief Hendrick told the commissioners at Albany, "Look at the French; they are men; they are fortifying everywhere. But, we are ashamed to say it, you are all like women, bare and open, without any fortifications." The British colonists, on the other hand, had grown complacent about their Iroquois allies, he told them, "You have . . . thrown us behind your backs and disregarded us; whereas the French are a subtile and ever vigilant people, ever using their utmost endeavors to seduce and bring our people over to them."

Restoring the Chain. The delegates did restore the Covenant Chain, but they could not resolve their own differences. In some ways the conference exacerbated the differences. Pennsylvania's delegation bought a huge tract of land from the Iroquois in an area also claimed by Virginia. Land disputes such as this would fester for a generation. As the delegates made their separate peaces with the Iroquois, they also discussed a plan for colonial unity presented by Franklin.

Franklin's Plan. Franklin's plan would unite the colonies for defensive purposes under a Grand Council chosen by the colonial assemblies and a governor general chosen by the king. Each colony would choose a number of delegates to the council based on the colony's contributions to the general treasury. The council would meet every year, and its meeting place would rotate among the colonial capitals. The governor and council would have power to make treaties and regulate trade with the Indi-

ans; to encourage new settlements; build forts and coast guard vessels; and to encourage new settlements. Money to do these things would come from taxes on liquor, on taverns, or on "superfluities, as tea, &c. &c." In an emergency, the council and governor could draw money from the colonial treasuries. The king and the Board of Trade could veto acts of the council, but the council for the most part would govern the American colonies in all internal matters.

The Fate of the Plan. The delegates to the Albany conference adopted Franklin's plan and submitted it to the colonial assemblies. Once the assemblies had approved it, the plan would be sent to the British government for approval; but each assembly rejected the plan, feeling it gave too much power to the other colonies, and all resented the power given the council and governor general. Many years later Franklin wrote that the colonies had rejected the plan because it gave too much power to the king's agent, the governor general; the British, he said, did not like the plan because it was too democratic. He speculated about what would have happened if the colonies had adopted his plan for union: they would have raised revenue for their own defence and would have united more effectively to fight the French in the Seven Years' War; Parliament would not have been forced to tax the colonists with the Stamp Act and Townshend duties; the colonists would not have united in protest against British policy; and the Americans would not have had a revolution. But in 1754, when the colonies rejected his plan, Franklin could not see all these future consequences. Franklin said in 1754 that the colonies would only unite if the British government forced them to do so.

Sources:

William N. Fenton, *The Great Law and the Longhouse: A Political History of the Iroquois Confederacy* (Norman: University of Oklahoma Press, 1998);

Carl Van Doren, *Benjamin Franklin* (New York: Viking, 1938).

CONTINENTAL CONGRESS

First Continental Congress. The Continental Congress became the government of the United States out of necessity, not design. The forty-five delegates who gathered in Philadelphia in September 1774 were not sure why they were there. Some members, such as Joseph Galloway, John Jay, and John Dickinson, thought their task was to propose common policies to pressure England to rescind its unreasonable policies. Their ultimate goal was to resolve the crisis and reconcile the colonies with England; they did not see the Congress as the beginning of a new, independent government. Some delegates, such as Patrick Henry and Samuel and John Adams, did. The reconcilers carried the day, and the first Congress rejected the idea of independence but called for a boycott of British goods to take effect in December 1774. The Congress also empowered local Committees of Safety to enforce this boycott and to set prices for goods in communities.

Choosing Delegates. Each colony had chosen its delegates to Congress in different ways. In four colonies, Rhode Island, Connecticut, Pennsylvania, and Massachusetts, the assembly chose its delegates to Congress. The Massachusetts assembly made its choices behind locked doors; outside, Governor Gage's secretary was proclaiming the legislature suspended. In Virginia, when the governor, Lord Dunmore, dissolved the assembly, it had reconvened in a nearby tavern to choose delegates; New York held a general election for delegates; and an open meeting in Charleston, South Carolina, chose that colony's delegation. In other colonies delegates were selected at provincial conventions that had not been called by the established authorities. This created a problem, made more acute by the colonists's grievances with England: the colonists were resisting what they regarded as unconstitutional British authority and objecting to British government policy that was contrary to their written charters. How, then, could the colonists have conventions or other meetings not authorized by charter or law to choose new governments or delegates to a Continental Congress? It was a difficult question, one the delegates did not have the leisure to consider though it restrained Congress from asserting more power.

Representation. Did the delegates represent the people of the colonies, or did they represent the colonies? Should the delegates vote according to their colony's relative population or according to its wealth? Or should each colony have one vote? As soon as Congress met, it had to grapple with these questions. At the Albany Conference each colony had one vote, and the roll was called from north to south, starting with New Hampshire. The Stamp Act Congress had followed this precedent. Congress continued the custom of voting geographically. But the problem of representation was less easy to solve. Virginia, the largest colony, believed it should have the most votes. Delegates from the smaller colonies believed each colony should have one vote. Samuel Chase of Maryland proposed a compromise: give each colony one vote except in cases involving money, then each would vote in proportion to its contributions to the cause. Ultimately the delegates agreed that each colony would have one vote. This was done both to appease the smaller colonies and because discovering a practical alternative was too difficult. Neither Virginia nor Massachusetts thought this solution either fair or reasonable.

Summer 1775. The Second Continental Congress met in May 1775. This time war had broken out in Massachusetts. British forces occupied Boston, and two governments attempted to govern the province. Moderates in Congress still resisted the ideas that the Congress was a government and that the colonies could become independent states. Congress voted to raise a Continental Army to defend the beleaguered citizens of Massachusetts and appointed George Washington, a delegate from Virginia, to be its commander. Congress also voted to print paper money to help pay for this army and to establish a post office and appoint commissioners to negotiate with Indians. John Dickinson drafted a conciliatory petition to the king, called the Olive Branch petition. The Congress considered the Prime Minister, Lord North's, conciliatory proposal: Parliament would not tax the colonies, but the colonial assemblies would tax the colonists and forward the receipts to London. This proposal might have averted the crisis in 1765, but by 1775 the colonial mood had shifted. After Congress learned of the Battle of Bunker Hill, it rejected North's proposal. At about the same time King George III rejected the Olive Branch petition and declared the colonies to be in a state of rebellion. In the fall, when South Carolina and New Hampshire requested instruction from Congress on what government was legitimate, Congress told each to have "full and free representation of the people, and that the Representatives if they think it necessary, establish such a form of Government, as in their judgment will best produce the happiness of the people."

Plans for Union. All delegates understood the importance of unity: in 1754, when the colonies were threatened by France, Benjamin Franklin proposed a plan of union that would have the colonies unite under a general council, with a governor appointed by the king. In 1774 Joseph Galloway proposed a similar plan of union, but by this time delegates from Massachusetts were not willing to support any concessions to British power. Galloway's plan was struck from the record, and he would remain loyal to the king while his colleagues in Congress drifted toward independence. In the summer of 1775 Franklin proposed another plan of union, with Congress serving as a governing body for the colonies. Silas Deane of Connecticut proposed a similar plan, but Congress was consumed with other problems and did not seriously consider either. Farsighted delegates such as Franklin, Deane, and John Adams realized that unity was essential, but at the moment they were also trying to convince delegates that independence was achievable.

Independence. The convincing arguments were made by Thomas Paine's *Common Sense* in January and by Washington's forcing the British out of Boston in March. In May, Congress called on all the colonies to form new governments: this was not independence but was, as delegate James Duane said, "a Machine for fabricating Independence." Five days later Virginia's new provincial congress, which had replaced the old House of Burgesses as the government, called on Congress to declare that the American colonies "are, and of right ought to be, free and independent states." This resolution, which Congress received on 7 June and approved on 2 July, changed the necessity for union. The Albany Plan, and all subsequent plans for union, envisioned the colonies cooperating for specific external objectives: either to protect the frontier or to make common cause against British attacks. With independence, though, the union

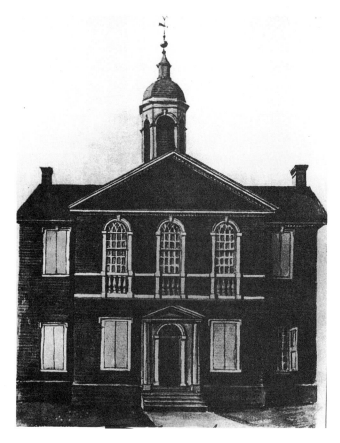

A drawing of Carpenters' Hall, Philadelphia, where the First Continental Congress met in 1775 (Bettmann Archive, New York City, New York)

would be a government. The problem in constructing a union would be to make a government that would govern but would not interfere with each state's power to govern itself.

Dickinson's Plan. Congress appointed a committee of thirteen to draw up a plan of confederation. John Dickinson took the lead in drawing up the plan of union, which he presented to the Congress on 12 July. South Carolina's Edward Rutledge complained to John Jay that Dickinson's plan "has the Vice of all his Productions . . . ; I mean the vice of Refining too much." Dickinson's plan created a confederation of states but left ambiguous how much power the states would retain. Debate centered on three issues: the division of powers between the states and the confederation, representation of states in Congress and and contributions of states to the union, and control of the western lands claimed by several states. After Dickinson left Congress, the debate continued on

his plan, and on 20 August a committee presented to Congress a somewhat amended plan of union, which Congress debated over the next year. Ultimately Congress decided to continue allowing each state one vote, making it clear that "Each state retains its sovereignty, freedom, and independence." Congress could not resolve the issue of land claims. On 15 November 1777 Congress approved the Articles of Confederation and submitted them to the states for approval.

The Articles. The Articles of Confederation created "a firm league of friendship. . . . For . . . common defence, the security of their liberties, and . . . mutual and general welfare" while each state remained sovereign and independent. Under the articles, each state could send between two and seven delegates to Congress, but each state would only have one vote. The delegates would be paid by their respective states. Because the Congress was not elected directly by the people, it could not tax the people, nor could it draft people into military service. Instead Congress could determine how much each state should send to the common treasury and how many men each state should contribute to the Continental Army, and then Congress could request each state to honor its commitments. No state could engage in foreign affairs, or tax goods sent into or out of other states, nor could any states enter into treaties or agreements with one another. Congress would be given the power to decide issues be-

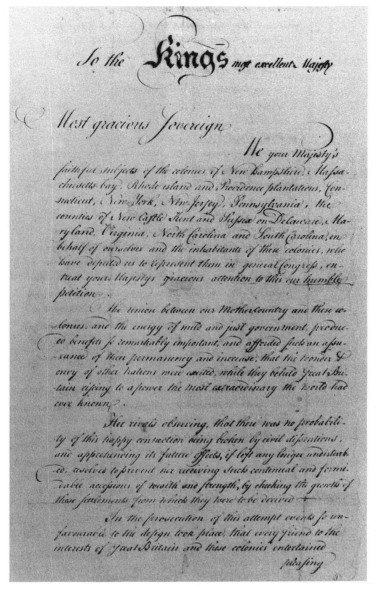

The first page of the "Olive Branch" Petition, written by John Dickinson in 1775 (Public Record Office, London)

tween states over land claims and other matters, as well as matters of foreign affairs and relations with Indians. Congress submitted the articles to the states for ratification, requesting that the states do so by 10 March 1778.

Awaiting Ratification. Only Virginia ratified by 10 March, but most of the states ratified by July 1778. New Jersey, Delaware, and Maryland held out because the articles did not give the union control of the Western lands. New Jersey (20 November 1778) and Delaware (1 February 1779) would ratify, but Maryland held out until both New York and Virginia agreed to cede their land claims to the union in 1781. Until the articles took effect, Congress continued to act, coordinating the military and attempting to raise money to pay for the army. But inflation skyrocketed, and the currency issued in 1777 became virtually worthless. In April 1780 one Spanish dol-

lar, the basic unit of value, was worth four hundred dollars in Continental currency.

Political Divisions. With no political parties, divisions occurred based on personality and regional differences, the most notable being an attempt by some members of Congress, after Horatio Gates's brilliant victory at Saratoga and George Washington's failure to prevent the British from capturing Philadelphia, to replace Washington with Gates. The controversy over Silas Deane also bitterly divided the Congress in 1779–1780. The problems of war prevented further political divisions though within the states there were controversies over paper money and raising troops.

Executive Government. When the articles came into effect in the spring of 1781, Congress was empowered to create executive boards to better manage affairs. Robert Morris was appointed minister for finance, and he immediately undertook to make sense of the country's debts and currency problems, which were immense. The country owed approximately $42 million, and the continental currency was virtually worthless. Morris proposed two solutions. First, he suggested creating a national bank. But since Congress did not have the power to charter a bank, Morris persuaded Pennsylvania's legislature to charter the Bank of North America. Second, to help Congress raise revenue, Morris and the reformers in Congress, led by Alexander Hamilton and James Madison, proposed amending the Articles to allow Congress to levy a 5 percent tax on imports. To change the Articles required the unanimous consent of the states, and Rhode Island's refusal killed the plan. Morris tried to use his considerable political skill in reorganizing the finances, but failed, in part because the war's end in September 1781 removed from the minds of many the pressing necessity to take action.

Woes. Congress's lack of power became too apparent after the war. In 1783 Congress could not pay the soldiers who had helped to win independence. Pennsylvania's soldiers mutinied, marched on Philadelphia, and surrounded Congress. State authorities would not call the militia to disperse the soldiers, and Congress was forced to flee the city, taking refuge in Princeton, then deciding to build two permanent capitals, one on the Delaware River in New Jersey, the other near Georgetown, Maryland, on the Potomac. Americans made fun of the powerless, wandering Congress, "not . . . stars of the *first* magnitude, but rather . . . *inferior* luminaries, or *wandering* comets, [who] again appear in their eccentric orb, assuming various directions and courses, sometimes regular and uniform, at other times, vain and retrograde." Another suggested putting Congress into a balloon, so the members could "float along from one end of the continent to the other, . . . and when occasion requires can suddenly pop down into any of the states they please." The Congress, called into existence to meet the crisis of British power, threatened to dissolve.

Sources:

Merrill Jensen, *The Articles of Confederation* (Madison: University of Wisconsin Press, 1940);

Andrew C. McLaughlin, *A Constitutional History of the United States* (New York: Appleton-Century, 1936);

Jack Rakove, *The Beginnings of National Politics: An Interpretive History of the Continental Congress* (Baltimore: Johns Hopkins University Press, 1979).

DECLARATION OF INDEPENDENCE

Richard Henry Lee's Resolution. On Friday, 7 June 1776, Richard Henry Lee of Virginia presented Congress with a resolution from Virginia's Convention "that these United colonies are & of right ought to be free & independent states, that they are absolved from all allegiance to the British crown, and that all political connection between them and the state of Great Britain is & ought to be totally dissolved. . . ." Lee's resolution called on Congress to begin taking measures to secure foreign assistance and to form a confederation to bind the colonies more closely together. The Congress, busy with other matters, put off discussion until the following day, which it spent debating independence. On the one side, James Wilson of Pennsylvania, John Dickinson of Delaware, Robert Livingston of New York, and the Rutledges of South Carolina, argued that the time was not right for independence. While New England and Virginia were united in support, the Middle colonies, New York, New Jersey, Pennsylvania, Maryland, and Delaware "were not yet ripe for bidding adieu to British connection." The delegates from these areas thought it better to wait until all the colonies were ready, and then act with unanimity, rather than force the issue. On the other side, Lee was joined by John Adams, Virginian George Wythe, and others in arguing that a declaration of independence would not "make ourselves what we are not," but would only "declare a fact which already exists." The contending sides could not agree. Congress decided to postpone action on Lee's resolution until 1 July, but also decided to appoint committees to consider the Virginia proposals on declaring independence, on foreign alliances, and on confederation.

Committee on Independence. Congress named five men to the committee on independence. John Adams, Benjamin Franklin, Roger Sherman, Robert Livingston, and Thomas Jefferson. Jefferson was chosen for two reasons: Virginia had sponsored the resolution, so a Virginian had to be on the committee. Richard Henry Lee should have been the representative, but he wanted to return to his state to create its new government. Jefferson was relatively new to Congress, having served in 1775, and though he never uttered a word in debate, he was known for his insightful contributions on committees and for his writing. In July 1774 he had written "A Summary View of the Rights of British America," a set of instructions to Virginia's delegates to Congress, and in 1775 he had drafted Congress's response to Lord Frederick North's offer of conciliation, and Congress's Declaration of the Causes and Necessity for Taking up Arms.

Jefferson is Chosen. Despite Jefferson's reputation as a writer, he expected John Adams to draw up the declaration. Adams was the foremost public leader for independence. But Adams, who was busy on the committees for foreign treaties and the Board of War, refused Jefferson's request to draft a declaration. "Why, will you not?," Jefferson said with surprise, "You ought to do it." "I will not," Adams said. "Why?" Jefferson asked. "Reasons enough," said Adams. "What can be your reasons[?]" "Reason first," Adams said, "Your are a Virginian, and a Virginian ought to appear at the head of this business. Reason second—I am obnoxious, suspected, and unpopular. You are very much otherwise. Reason third—You can write ten times better than I can." "Well, if you are decided," Jefferson said, "I will do as well as I can."

IN CONGRESS, JULY 4, 1776.

A DECLARATION

BY THE REPRESENTATIVES OF THE

UNITED STATES OF AMERICA,

IN GENERAL CONGRESS ASSEMBLED.

WHEN in the Courfe of human Events, it becomes neceffary for one People to diffolve the Political Bands which have connected them with another, and to affume among the Powers of the Earth, the feparate and equal Station to which the Laws of Nature and of Nature's God entitle them, a decent Refpect to the Opinions of Mankind requires that they fhould declare the caufes which impel them to the Separation.

We hold thefe Truths to be felf-evident, that all Men are created equal, that they are endowed by their Creator with certain unalienable Rights, that among thefe are Life, Liberty, and the Purfuit of Happinefs--That to fecure thefe Rights, Governments are inftituted among Men, deriving their juft Powers from the Confent of the Governed, that whenever any Form of Government becomes deftructive of thefe Ends, it is the Right of the People to alter or to abolifh it, and to inftitute new Government, laying its Foundation on fuch Principles, and organizing its Powers in fuch Form, as to them fhall feem moft likely to effect their Safety and Happinefs. Prudence, indeed, will dictate that Governments long eftablifhed fhould not be changed for light and tranfient Caufes; and accordingly all Experience hath fhewn, that Mankind are more difpofed to fuffer, while Evils are fufferable, than to right themfelves by abolifhing the Forms to which they are accuftomed. But when a long Train of Abufes and Ufurpations, purfuing invariably the fame Object, evinces a Defign to reduce them under abfolute Defpotifm, it is their Right, it is their Duty, to throw off fuch Government, and to provide new Guards for their future Security. Such has been the patient Sufferance of thefe Colonies; and fuch is now the Neceffity which conftrains them to alter their former Syftems of Government. The Hiftory of the prefent King of Great-Britain is a Hiftory of repeated Injuries and Ufurpations, all having in direct Object the Eftablifhment of an abfolute Tyranny over thefe States. To prove this, let Facts be fubmitted to a candid World.

He has refufed his Affent to Laws, the moft wholefome and neceffary for the public Good.

He has forbidden his Governors to pafs Laws of immediate and preffing Importance, unlefs fufpended in their Operation till his Affent fhould be obtained; and when fo fufpended, he has utterly neglected to attend to them.

He has refufed to pafs other Laws for the Accommodation of large Diftricts of People, unlefs thofe People would relinquifh the Right of Reprefentation in the Legiflature, a Right ineftimable to them, and formidable to Tyrants only.

He has called together Legiflative Bodies at Places unufual, uncomfortable, and diftant from the Depofitory of their public Records, for the fole Purpofe of fatiguing them into Compliance with his Meafures.

He has diffolved Reprefentative Houfes repeatedly, for oppofing with manly Firmnefs his Invafions on the Rights of the People.

He has refufed for a long Time, after fuch Diffolutions, to caufe others to be elected; whereby the Legiflative Powers, incapable of Annihilation, have returned to the People at large for their exercife; the State remaining in the mean time expofed to all the Dangers of Invafion from without, and Convulfions within.

He has endeavoured to prevent the Population of thefe States; for that Purpofe obftructing the Laws for Naturalization of Foreigners; refufing to pafs others to encourage their Migrations hither, and raifing the Conditions of new Appropriations of Lands.

He has obftructed the Adminiftration of Juftice, by refufing his Affent to Laws for eftablifhing Judiciary Powers.

He has made Judges dependent on his Will alone, for the Tenure of their Offices, and the Amount and Payment of their Salaries.

He has erected a Multitude of new Offices, and fent hither Swarms of Officers to harrafs our People, and eat out their Subftance.

He has kept among us, in Times of Peace, Standing Armies, without the confent of our Legiflatures.

He has affected to render the Military independent of and fuperior to the Civil Power.

He has combined with others to fubject us to a Jurifdiction foreign to our Conftitution, and unacknowledged by our Laws; giving his Affent to their Acts of pretended Legiflation:

For quartering large Bodies of Armed Troops among us:

For protecting them, by a mock Trial, from Punifhment for any Murders which they fhould commit on the Inhabitants of thefe States:

For cutting off our Trade with all Parts of the World:

For impofing Taxes on us without our Confent:

For depriving us, in many Cafes, of the Benefits of Trial by Jury:

For tranfporting us beyond Seas to be tried for pretended Offences:

For abolifhing the free Syftem of Englifh Laws in a neighbouring Province, eftablifhing therein an arbitrary Government, and enlarging its Boundaries, fo as to render it at once an Example and fit Inftrument for introducing the fame abfolute Rule into thefe Colonies:

For taking away our Charters, abolifhing our moft valuable Laws, and altering fundamentally the Forms of our Governments:

For fufpending our own Legiflatures, and declaring themfelves invefted with Power to legiflate for us in all Cafes whatfoever.

He has abdicated Government here, by declaring us out of his Protection and waging War againft us.

He has plundered our Seas, ravaged our Coafts, burnt our Towns, and deftroyed the Lives of our People.

He is, at this Time, tranfporting large Armies of foreign Mercenaries to compleat the Works of Death, Defolation, and Tyranny, already begun with circumftances of Cruelty and Perfidy, fcarcely paralleled in the moft barbarous Ages, and totally unworthy the Head of a civilized Nation.

He has conftrained our fellow Citizens taken Captive on the high Seas to bear Arms againft their Country, to become the Executioners of their Friends and Brethren, or to fall themfelves by their Hands.

He has excited domeftic Infurrections amongft us, and has endeavoured to bring on the Inhabitants of our Frontiers, the mercilefs Indian Savages, whofe known Rule of Warfare, is an undiftinguifhed Deftruction, of all Ages, Sexes and Conditions.

In every ftage of thefe Oppreffions we have Petitioned for Redrefs in the moft humble Terms: Our repeated Petitions have been anfwered only by repeated Injury. A Prince, whofe Character is thus marked by every act which may define a Tyrant, is unfit to be the Ruler of a free People.

Nor have we been wanting in Attentions to our Britifh Brethren. We have warned them from Time to Time of Attempts by their Legiflature to extend an unwarrantable Jurifdiction over us. We have reminded them of the Circumftances of our Emigration and Settlement here. We have appealed to their native Juftice and Magnanimity, and we have conjured them by the Ties of our common Kindred to difavow thefe Ufurpations, which, would inevitably interrupt our Connections and Correfpondence. They too have been deaf to the Voice of Juftice and of Confanguinity. We muft, therefore, acquiefce in the Neceffity, which denounces our Separation, and hold them, as we hold the reft of Mankind, Enemies in War, in Peace, Friends.

We, therefore, the Reprefentatives of the UNITED STATES OF AMERICA, in GENERAL CONGRESS, Affembled, appealing to the Supreme Judge of the World for the Rectitude of our Intentions, do, in the Name, and by Authority of the good People of thefe Colonies, folemnly Publifh and Declare, That thefe United Colonies are, and of Right ought to be, FREE AND INDEPENDENT STATES; that they are abfolved from all Allegiance to the Britifh Crown, and that all political Connection between them and the State of Great-Britain, is and ought to be totally diffolved; and that as FREE AND INDEPENDENT STATES, they have full Power to levy War, conclude Peace, contract Alliances, eftablifh Commerce, and to do all other Acts and Things which INDEPENDENT STATES may of right do. And for the fupport of this Declaration, with a firm Reliance on the Protection of divine Providence, we mutually pledge to each other our Lives, our Fortunes, and our facred Honor.

Signed by ORDER and in BEHALF of the CONGRESS,

JOHN HANCOCK, PRESIDENT.

ATTEST.
CHARLES THOMSON, SECRETARY.

PHILADELPHIA: PRINTED BY JOHN DUNLAP.

An official copy of the Declaration of Independence printed by John Dunlap on 5 July 1776 (American Philosophical Society Library, Philadelphia, Pennsylvania)

A painting of a New York mob pulling down a statue of King George III in
1776

Congress Debates. In drafting his work, Jefferson kept in mind all of the arguments made in support of independence over the previous years. At the end of June he presented his draft to Franklin and Adams, who made minor suggestions, and on Friday, 28 June, the committee reported its declaration to Congress. On Monday, 1 July, the delegates took up Lee's resolution, voting nine states to two in favor of independence. South Carolina and Pennsylvania both opposed the move, Delaware was divided, and New York's delegates could not vote for independence, though they supported it, because their instructions from the assembly required that they work toward reconciliation. John Rutledge of South Carolina moved that the Congress put off a final vote until the next day, as he believed by then his colleagues would support independence in the interest of unanimity. Overnight, a new delegate arrived from Delaware, and the reluctant members of the Pennsylvania delegation stayed away, making the vote twelve in favor, New York abstaining. On 2 July 1776, Congress declared independence.

The Second of July. On 3 July, as Congress debated the Declaration of Independence, John Adams wrote to his wife Abigail. He reflected on the train of events since 1761, when he heard James Otis make his argument against writs of assistance, and marvelled at the suddenness and "Greatness of this Revolution." He worried about the future, about the war England would fight against the colonies, but he was certain that right would prevail. "The Second Day of July 1776, will be the most memorable Epocha, in the History of America," he wrote. "I am apt to believe that it will be celebrated, by succeeding Generations, as the great anniversary Festival. It ought to be commemorated, as the Day of Deliverance by solemn Acts of Devotion to God Almighty. It ought to be solemnized with Pomp and Parade, with Shews, Games, Sports, Guns, Bells, Bonfires and Illuminations from one End of this Continent to the other from this Time forward forever more."

The Fourth of July. Adams had the right celebration, but the wrong date, according to popular American thought. Declaring independence was a revolutionary event but the reasons for the Declaration made it even more so. On 4 July Congress concluded its debate over the Declaration of Independence, and unanimously adopted it, with New York's delegates abstaining until after 9 July, when their state's provincial convention rescinded their instructions to work only for reconciliation. The Declaration of Independence, adopted on 4 July as "The Unanimous Declaration of the thirteen United States of America," begins with a preamble declaring its purpose to the world why Americans took such revolutionary measures. The Declaration also states a set of self-evident truths: all men are created equal; all men are endowed by their creator with inalienable rights, including the rights to life, liberty, and the pursuit of happiness. To help secure these rights, men establish governments, but when a government begins destroying, rather than protecting rights, the people have a right to alter or abolish the government, and to create a new one which will better protect their "safety and happiness." These were the basic premises of the declaration. Next, to prove that the British government had trampled on the rights of Americans, the Declaration listed the wrongs done them by the British government. But unlike previous colonial declarations, this one aimed directly at the King. Americans had been arguing for years that Parliament could not govern their political societies, and in 1775 Congress had insisted that Americans owed no allegiance to Parliament. Now, Congress had to shift its focus from Parliament to the King, as some Americans still might believe that they could create a system, such as the one proposed by Franklin in 1754 and Joseph Galloway in 1774, with colonies tied together by a common allegiance to the British Crown. So the list of grievances in the Declaration place the blame directly on the King, charging him with tyranny and cruelty "scarcely paralleled in the most barbarous ages" and declaring that "A prince whose character is thus marked by every act which may define a tyrant is unfit to be the ruler of a free people." The Declaration closes with a statement of disappointment in the British people, whom the Americans implored to disavow the King's tyrannic conduct, but as they had proved deaf to every entreaty, the Americans now would "hold them as we hold the rest of mankind, enemies in war, in peace friends." Concluding, the Declaration declared "that these United colonies are & of right ought to be free & independent states," and "with a firm reliance on the protection of divine providence we mutually pledge to each other our lives, our fortunes, & our sacred honour." Congress made some notable alterations in Jefferson's draft, omitting about one-fourth of the text, simplifying some clauses and removing others. One of the most notable omissions was Jefferson's charge that George III had encouraged the slave trade, that he had "waged cruel war against human nature itself, violating its most sacred rights of life and liberty in the persons of a distant people who never offended him," in carrying them across the Atlantic into slavery in America. Jefferson concluded this charge with another, that the King had also encouraged the slaves to rebel against their masters, "thus prying off former crimes committed against the *Liberties* of one people, with crimes which he urges them to commit against the *lives* of another." Congress dropped this whole section, according to Jefferson, because South Carolina and Georgia wanted to continue importing slaves, and because "our Northern brethren" had few slaves themselves, but were "pretty considerable carriers of them to others."

Signing the Declaration. Jefferson remembered that all of the delegates who were present, except John Dickinson, signed the Declaration on 4 July, but he may have been mistaken. No such copy exists. On 5 July, a broadside copy of the Declaration of Independence was published in Philadelphia, signed by John Hancock, the president of Congress, and Charles Thomson, the secretary of Congress. The next day it was printed for the first time in a newspaper, and on 8 July was publicly read to a large gathering in Philadelphia. The crowd responded by tearing down the royal arms and with bonfires and ringing bells. The same enthusiasm met the event in other colonies as copies of the Declaration were read publicly, announcing the fact of independence. On 19 July Congress voted to have the delegates sign an engrossed copy, possible now that New York had allowed its delegates to vote for independence. By 2 August, the parchment Declaration of Independence was formally signed by fifty-six delegates to Congress.

Sources:

Julian P. Boyd, ed., *The Papers of Thomas Jefferson*, volume 1, *1760–1776* (Princeton, N.J.: Princeton University Press, 1950);

Lyman H. Butterfield, ed., *The Adams Papers: Diary and Autobiography of John Adams*, volume 2, *1771–1781* (Cambridge, Mass.: Belknap Press of Harvard University Press, 1961);

Merrill Peterson, *Thomas Jefferson and the New Nation* (New York: Oxford University Press, 1970);

Garry Wills, Inventing America: *Jefferson's Declaration of Independence* (New York: Random House, 1978).

HUTCHINSON-WHATELY LETTERS

Background of Crisis. Less dramatic than the Boston Massacre or Boston Tea Party, the mysterious case of Thomas Hutchinson's letters to British political figures, meant to inform them of American affairs and to suggest ways to handle the crisis of the 1760s, led directly to the crisis of the 1770s. The episode also demonstrates the differences between American and English conceptions of politics.

Francis Bernard. Massachusetts governor Francis Bernard returned to England in 1769, determined to change the province's government, which gave too much power to the elected assembly. For example, the Governor's Council was elected by the assembly, and so instead of advising the governor, acted against him. The towns had far too much political power. Bernard wanted to reform this government, giving more power to the governor and less to the assembly and town meetings. In England, he found allies among the supporters of George Grenville, the former chancellor of the exchequer who had proposed the Stamp Act and who still smarted at the way the colonists had pressured Parliament to rescind that Act.

Charles DeWolf Brownell's 1892 painting "The Burning of the Gaspee" (Rhode Island Historical Society, Providence)

New Governor. One of Grenville's allies, Thomas Whately, opened correspondence in the 1760s with several American political leaders. He sought out Americans who had supported British policy, and their letters informed the British group pushing quietly to amend the colonial governments. Among Whately's correspondents was Hutchinson, who became acting governor when Bernard left for England and was elevated to governor in 1771. Hutchinson believed that Parliament could govern the colonies in all cases, but he also believed it was a mistake for Britain to try to impose its will on colonists who were used to governing themselves. Hutchinson believed that either Parliament governed the entire empire, or the component parts of the empire must be independent. As governor of Massachusetts, Hutchinson hoped to keep his colony within the empire and continue the prosperity it and the empire had enjoyed for generations. In his public statements Hutchinson never ceased making these same arguments; privately he believed that his opponents, the Otis family, John Hancock, and Samuel Adams, were motivated by self-interest and jealousy, and he feared that their attacks on him would damage the empire. His opponents believed that Hutchinson's passion for preserving the British empire came from his own self-interest: better than most colonial Americans, Hutchinson had managed to rise politically, using connections in the British bureaucracy to secure offices for himself and relations.

The Assembly. For most of his administration Hutchinson quarreled with the assembly over important issues as well as relatively insignificant ones. The British government thought it best to have the colony's government meet outside of Boston, which was coming to be dominated by Samuel Adams and the Sons of Liberty. The assembly balked at moving, but Hutchinson insisted

on British prerogative. The British government also decided to give the assembly less control over judges, magistrates, and even the governor by having them paid by the Crown rather than by the assembly. Hutchinson again agreed with the Crown and made his point in long speeches to the assembly. On 6 January 1773 Hutchinson opened the assembly's meeting by outlining Parliament's power to govern the empire. Parliament was supreme, he reminded the assembly, and to assert otherwise was to assert that the colonies were independent. The people of the colonies could not enjoy as much liberty as the people in England, Hutchinson argued, but still they enjoyed more than the people in Spain or France's American colonies. If the colonies became independent of Parliament, it was likely they would fall prey to Spain or France.

Reaction. In Massachusetts, Hutchinson's debate with the assembly united that body in opposition to him. The assembly responded unanimously to Hutchinson's constitutional argument, conceding that without Parliamentary supremacy the colonies might become independent, but what of it? "There is more reason to dread the consequences of absolute uncontrolled supreme power, whether of a nation or a monarch, than those of total independence." Hutchinson had drawn a line in the sand, and the assembly had crossed it. Parts of Hutchinson's exchange with the assembly were printed in newspapers throughout the colony. John Adams was amazed that Hutchinson had forced the controversy on the assembly and noted in his diary that Hutchinson "will not be thanked for this. This Ruin and Destruction must spring out of it, either from the Ministry and Parliament on one hand, or from his Countrymen, on the other. He has reduced himself to a most ridiculous State of Distress." In England, where Hutchinson might have ex-

Philip Dawe's 1774 cartoon, "The Bostonian's Paying the Excise-man, or Tarring & Feathering" (Library of Congress, Washington, D.C.)

pected his argument to be welcomed, news of his controversy with the assembly disturbed William Legge, Lord Dartmouth, the new colonial secretary. Dartmouth had hoped to calm the troubled colonists by not provoking controversy. But now, Dartmouth told Benjamin Franklin, the Massachusetts assembly's agent in London, Hutchinson had provoked the assembly to assert its independence of Parliament. Parliament could not possibly ignore that. Could Franklin convince the assembly to withdraw this declaration? No, Franklin told him, not unless Hutchinson withdrew his assertion of Parliamentary power. Dartmouth also wrote Thomas Cushing, speaker of the assembly, pledging to work to remedy "every real or imaginary evil of which the province may think she has reason to complain" if the assembly would retract its assertion of supremacy over Parliament. Speaker Cushing responded to Dartmouth, saying that "the eyes of the whole continent . . . are turned upon this province," and the assembly could not retract its position. Dartmouth, anxious to avert a crisis, privately and politely reprimanded Hutchinson for having provoked the assembly.

The Letters. For Hutchinson this private rebuke was devastating. What followed was even worse. In March a package arrived in Boston containing letters Hutchinson and four others had written to Whately in the 1760s.

Samuel Adams and James Otis had insisted for a decade that Hutchinson was the real architect of the Stamp Act and other odious measures; now the assembly read Hutchinson's private letters urging the British government to assert itself against the growing movement in Massachusetts for self-government. Hutchinson's letters were more moderate than those of other correspondents, but they were damaging enough. He had written that "there must be an abridgement of what are called English liberties" and "that a colony distant from the parent state cannot possibly enjoy all the liberty of the parent state." Though these passages were subject to different interpretations, the colonists interpreted them in one way, that Hutchinson had advised the British government to curtail colonial liberty. The astonished assembly read the letters and voted, 101 to 5, to form a committee to respond to Hutchinson's attempt "to overthrow the constitution of this government and to introduce arbitrary power."

Motives. Hutchinson had written the letters to help the British government heal the breach with the American colonies. Franklin, who had sent the letters to Massachusetts, had a similar motive. Franklin hoped to make Hutchinson the scapegoat and divert colonial anger from the British ministry to the governor. Hutchinson could be replaced with a governor the assembly would find acceptable. Franklin, who believed that the American colonies eventually would become independent, wanted them to remain part of a British commonwealth of nations. The break would come naturally, in the next century or so, Franklin believed, and in the meantime he wanted to avoid unnecessary political violence. By keeping calm and not provoking trouble, Franklin and Dartmouth both hoped to avoid a clash between the colonies and the empire.

Reaction. But the publication of the letters provoked a furious storm of outrage in both England and America. How Franklin had gotten the letters in the first place remains something of a mystery. Franklin took considerable abuse for his role in the affair, but he would insist that he alone was responsible for finding and releasing the letters. But their release provoked a duel in England between Whately's brother (Whately had died before Franklin received the letters) and John Temple, a former customs collector in Boston (and son-in-law of Massachusetts political leader James Bowdoin), whom Whately accused of stealing the letters. Temple escaped unscathed, Whately was wounded, and Franklin insisted on his sole responsibility. In Massachusetts, Hutchinson was ruined; in June he asked for a leave of absence, and the Massachusetts assembly petitioned to have him removed.

Privy Council. The Privy Council, a body of advisors to the king, received the assembly's petition and called for a hearing in January, 1774. Andrew Wedderburn, the English solicitor general, represented Hutchinson and his brother-in-law Andrew Oliver while Franklin was summoned to represent the assembly. The session convened just a few days after word reached London that a Boston mob had destroyed the East India Company's tea, and the city was in an uproar. Thirty-six privy councillors crowded the room, which was packed with spectators, including Edmund Burke, Joseph Priestley, Jeremy Bentham, and Prime Minister Lord North, who had to stand along with the other spectators. Wedderburn turned the hearing into an attack on Franklin, accusing him of stealing the Hutchinson letters and of exciting the colony's ill will against Hutchinson and Oliver. "I hope, my lords, you will mark and brand this man, for the honour of this country, of Europe, and of mankind. . . . He has forfeited all the respect of societies and of men. . . . Men will watch him with a jealous eye; they will hide their papers from him and lock up their excritoires. He will henceforth esteem it a libel to be called a man of letters. . . ." Wedderburn charged that Franklin had no moral scruples and had acted out of ambition: "My lords, Dr. Franklin's mind may have been so possessed with the idea of a Great American Republic that he may easily slide into the language of the minister of a foreign independent state." For an hour Franklin stood impassive and silent as Wedderburn abused him.

Whigs and Tories arguing in a local town meeting

INSIDE THE SMOKE-FILLED ROOM

Samuel Adams came to dominate Boston politics through the Caucus Club, or South End Caucus, which met in secret to choose candidates for town and provincial offices. His cousin, John Adams, recorded his observations of one of this club's secret meetings.

Boston. Feby. 1763.

This day learned that the Caucas Clubb meets at certain Times in the Garret of Tom Daws, the Adjutant of the Boston Regiment. He has a large House, and he has a moveable Partition in the Garrett, which he takes down and the whole Clubb meets in one Room. There they smoke tobacco till you cannot see from one End of the Garrett to the other. There they drink Phlip I suppose, and there they choose a Moderator, who puts Questions to the Vote regularly, and select Men, Assessors, Collectors, Wardens, Fire Wards, and Representatives are Regularly chosen before they are chosen in the Town. Uncle Fairfield, Story, Ruddock, Adams, Cooper, and a rudis indigestaque Moles of others are Members. They send Committees to wait on the Merchants Clubb and to propose, and join, in the choice of Men and Measures. Captn. Cunningham says they have often solicited him to go to these Caucas, they have assured him Benefit in his Business, &c.

Source: *Diary and Autobiography of John Adams*, volume 1, *1755–1770*, edited by Lyman H. Butterfield (Cambridge, Mass.: Belknap Press of Harvard University Press, 1961).

Aftermath. The next day Franklin was fired as deputy postmaster general. The episode of the letters may have ended Franklin's career as a London courtier. However, it launched his career as an American patriot. Before his humiliation in the cockpit, Franklin had hoped that England and the colonies could be reconciled. The torrent of abuse he endured convinced him that this would not happen. "When I see, that all petitions and complaints of grievances are so odious to government, that even the mere pipe which conveys them becomes obnoxious, I am at a loss to know how peace and union are to be maintained or restored between the different parts of the empire." Franklin had hoped to save the empire by destroying Hutchinson. The letters destroyed Hutchinson in America but could not save the empire. Wedderburn hoped to save the empire by destroying Franklin. Franklin was destroyed as a British courtier, and he put away the suit of Manchester velvet he had worn when he stood silently during his public humiliation. He put away his suit, but he did not forget the day he wore it. He would wear the suit twice more in his life: in 1778, when as a representative of the United States he signed an agreement on their behalf with the king of France, and in September 1783, when he signed the treaty with England recognizing the independence of the United States of America.

An accurate painting of the Boston Massacre in 1770

Sources:

Bernard Bailyn, *The Ordeal of Thomas Hutchinson* (Cambridge, Mass.: Belknap Press of Harvard University Press, 1974);

Carl Van Doren, *Benjamin Franklin* (New York: Viking, 1938).

MASSACHUSETTS GOVERNMENT

Collapse. In 1774 the king and Parliament suspended Massachusetts's government. The new royal governor, Thomas Gage, dissolved the assembly, restricted the town meetings, and replaced all elected sheriffs, magistrates, and other officials with his own appointees. But Gage found he could not govern by decree. In the late summer and fall of 1774 county conventions assembled throughout the colony, calling on citizens to choose their own officials and to pay taxes to collectors appointed by their county conventions and calling on all counties to choose members of a new legislative body to replace the dissolved General Court. The conventions asked the Continental Congress, which the colonies had formed in response to the attack on Massachusetts, for advice in how to proceed with framing a government, and in June 1775, after the battles of Lexington, Concord, and Bunker Hill, Congress recommended that Massachusetts choose an assembly and governor's council and declare the office of governor vacant until the king appointed a new governor, under the terms of the 1691 charter. By suspending the government, Massachusetts believed the king had acted illegally. The legal step for them to take would be simply to resume functioning under the charter.

Push for Change. The new elected assembly assumed the functions of the old charter government and governed the state, without a governor, for five years. When the British evacuated Boston in March 1776, and Congress declared independence in July, it became clear the king would not be appointing a new governor for Massachusetts. The twenty-eight member Governor's Council acted as an executive. The assembly expanded the right to vote, lowering the property qualifications of the old charter. However, some in Massachusetts began to argue that the new government did not have the legitimate power to govern. The old charter, they said, was a compact between the king and the people of the colony. The new government had been created by the legislature without the approval of the people. In September 1776 the legislature asked the towns if they would approve its conversion into a constitutional convention and if they would want the constitution this body wrote to be submitted to them before the legislature ratified it.

Writing a Constitution. The people in their town meetings overwhelmingly rejected the idea. A constitution, they said, was a fundamental law. It could only be created by the sovereign power of the state, which meant the people of the state, not their elected legislature. Since the constitution controlled and created the legislature, the legislature could not simply create the constitution.

In January 1777 a legislative committee recommended that the towns choose delegates to a special constitutional convention. The whole house rejected this idea, and in March asked the people to take special care in choosing their next representatives to the legislature, as they would not only make laws but would also write a new state constitution. This constitution would be submitted to the people of the state for ratification: when two-thirds of the adult freemen in the town meetings voted for ratification, it would take effect.

Document. Boston's town meeting rejected this idea and instructed her representatives not to participate in drawing up a constitution. Some western towns sent delegates to a meeting in Worcester to protest the legislature's acting as a constitutional convention; but the assembly went ahead with its work, and a committee led by Robert Treat Paine, James Warren, James Prescott, and Thomas Cushing drafted a constitution. The constitution created a legislature with two branches: the upper house, or Senate, would be chosen by the lower house, as would the governor, who would not be able to act without the advice and consent of the Senate. The constitution had no bill of rights and was so poorly written that the assembly's chaplain thought the assembly meant to have it rejected so they could govern under the old charter.

Rejection. The people did reject this constitution by a vote of 2,083 in favor, 9,972 against. Two-thirds of the voters would need to approve the constitution for it to become law; but more than three-fourths voted against it. The people, who voted in their town meetings, insisted that a fundamental law such as a constitution could only be created by a convention chosen specifically for that purpose.

Essex Result **vs. Democracy.** In Essex County a group of leading citizens published a call for a special convention and outlined the kind of government they would like to see created. The *Essex Result,* as their manifesto was called, proposed a bill of rights and a more clearly defined role, and more independence for the three branches of government. These men of wealth from Essex County wanted the government to be in the hands of other men of wealth, and they wanted to limit the lower class's power to interfere with property. On the other side citizens in the western part of the state feared the power of merchants such as these Essex men in Boston and Salem, whose wealth exaggerated their influence. These two very different groups, wealthy men pushing for an aristocratic government and westerners pushing for a more democratic one, joined together to force the legislature to call a special state convention. In June 1779 the people elected delegates to a special state convention to draft a constitution.

Convention. On 1 September 1779 the state convention opened in Cambridge. Its 293 delegates had been chosen by the adult freemen in the town meetings and thus were more representative than the legislature, which was elected by freemen who owned property that was worth £40 (about $2,300 today) or that provided an annual income of 40 shillings. The convention had two powerful factions: the Boston and Salem merchants, who wanted a state government to protect their property from oppressive taxation; and the proponents of democracy, consisting of the farmers of the west and the urban tradesmen and artisans, including patriot leader Samuel Adams of Boston. These two rival factions were conciliated by the able work of Samuel Adams's cousin, John Adams, representative from Braintree. John Adams had returned from Europe barely a month before the Convention met, but he had thought more about government than any other man in America. He was quickly named to a committee of thirty to draft a constitution. He wrote, "I was by the Convention put upon a Committee—by the Committee upon the Subcommittee—and by the Subcommittee appointed a Sub SubCommitee—so that I had the honour to be the principal Engineer."

Declaration of Rights. The constitution John Adams drafted began by explaining that a government existed "to secure the existence of the body politic, to protect it, and to furnish the individuals who compose it with the power of enjoying in safety and tranquility their natural rights, and the blessings of life." The constitution opened with a declaration of rights, which stated that "All men are born free and equal, and have certain natural, essential, and unalienable rights" and prohibited the legislature from exercising executive or judicial powers, or the executive interfering with the legislature or judiciary, or the judiciary exercising legislative or executive powers. This constitutional protection of the separation of powers would ensure that the government of Massachusetts would "be a government of laws and not of men."

Balanced Government. Adams was harshly critical of Pennsylvania's experiment with a unicameral legislature and no governor to check it. Adams believed society had natural divisions, that the division between rich and poor, between the Boston merchants and the western farmers and urban artisans was a natural development. For Adams an ideal government would balance these different social orders or classes so that both rich and poor could live in peace under one government. The government should prevent either from tyrannizing over the other. Adams's constitution for Massachusetts had a two-house legislature and gave the governor a veto over legislation. The two-house model was based partly on the British government, which has a House of Commons, representing common people, and a House of Lords, representing aristocracy. How could one create this kind of balance in a society without a titled, hereditary aristocracy?

Property Qualifications. In his constitution Adams required certain property qualifications for members of the different Houses. Members of the House of Repre-

A British revenue stamp (Bostonian Society, Boston, Massachusetts)

sentatives would have to own at least £100 ($5,700 today) worth of property in the town he represented; Senators would have either a freehold estate worth £300 ($17,000) or real property worth £600. Each town would have at least one representative while larger ones could have more (an additional representative for every 225 people). Senators would be chosen by districts, which would be created based on the amount of taxes paid by each area. Adams imagined that the state could be divided into thirteen Senate districts based on taxes, and thus Senators would represent property. The governor, who had to own an estate worth £1,000, would serve a one-year term and would be chosen directly by the people, who would also choose the lieutenant governor and the members of the governor's council. The governor would consult this council before choosing judges and magistrates, and he could veto laws passed by the legislature though the legislature by a two-thirds vote could override his veto. (No governor would use this veto before 1825). Adams completed his draft of the constitution, submitted it to the convention, and on November 13 sailed for Europe.

Ratification. The Convention made a few minor changes after Adams sailed and then submitted the con-

stitution to the people of Massachusetts for ratification. More than two-thirds of the voters in their town meetings approved the constitution, and on 15 June 1780 the new constitution took effect. By then Adams was back in Europe. In his three months at home he had written a new constitution for his state that would endure, with minor changes, for more than two centuries, making it the longest surviving written constitution in the history of the world.

Sources:

Diary and Autobiography of John Adams, 1771-1781, volume 2, edited by Lyman H. Butterfield (Cambridge, Mass.: Belknap Press of Harvard University Press, 1961);

Allan Nevins, *The American States During and After the Revolution, 1775-1789* (New York: Augustus M. Kelley, 1969).

PENNSYLVANIA GOVERNMENT

Pennsylvania Politics. In the 1770s the most troubling issue for Pennsylvanians was the control three counties—Philadelphia, Bucks, and Chester—had over the rest of the province. Though home to only one-third of the population, these three counties elected twenty-six of the thirty-six members of the assembly. Westerners and German immigrants, who were subject to strict naturalization laws, were effectively disenfranchised. Residents of the city of Philadelphia had fewer representatives than did residents of Philadelphia County, living beyond the city boundaries. In 1776 resentment against this domination erupted, and on 10 May, when Congress called on the states to form new governments, Philadelphians responded enthusiastically, calling for a general conference to meet in Philadelphia on 18 June. This conference called for a state convention in which each county and the city of Philadelphia would have an equal number of delegates. On 15 July the convention met and almost immediately proclaimed itself the new government of Pennsylvania, drawing up a new state constitution to break the former assembly's power.

Paine's Influence. Influenced by Thomas Paine's plan of government in *Common Sense* (1776), the Pennsylvania convention drew up one of the most radical constitutions ever to govern an American state. Because they believed it was unrepublican to have any check on the popular will, the convention created a single-house legislature that would be elected every year. Every man over twenty-one who paid a shilling in taxes could vote. This allowed virtually all adult men to vote, eliminating the kind of property qualifications that every other state considered necessary to protect property rights and political stability.

The Executive. Pennsylvania, along with New Hampshire, South Carolina, and Delaware, did not have a governor under its new constitution. These states instead gave executive power to a "president," one who would preside rather than govern. Colonial governors had been representatives of the king. With the king no longer part of the political system, he did not need a rep-

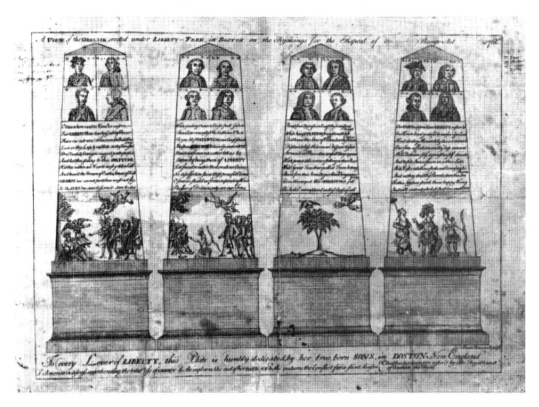

An engraving by Paul Revere of the obelisk built to celebrate the repeal of the Stamp Act (American Antiquarian Society, Worcester, Massachusetts)

resentative. It was not clear who the governor would represent, though, since Americans had not made up their minds about the proper role and structure of government. Pennsylvania's constitution put executive power in the hands of a council elected by the people of the state. This twelve-man executive board, with a president and vice president chosen from among them by the legislature, would have limited functions: it would choose judges (who would serve for seven-year terms) but would not have a veto over the assembly.

Checks on the Majority. Pennsylvanians understood that sometimes even the majority could be wrong. Their constitution provided two checks on potential tyranny. First, no law would take effect until one year after it was passed. This would give the people a chance to elect a new legislature, which could affirm or reject the last legislature's laws. The constitution also created an eighteen member Council of Censors (two representatives from each county and the city of Philadelphia) to be elected every seven years. This council would review all laws passed and all actions of the executive and determine if the constitution needed amending. If the council decided the constitution needed amending, it would call a state convention.

Critics. Though Pennsylvania promised to have the most direct democracy in America, not all thought this would be a good thing. John Adams exclaimed on reading the constitution, "Good God! The people of Penna will . . . fall upon their knees to the King of Great Britain to take them under his protection in order to deliver them from the tyranny of their government." The constitution's main flaw, as Adams saw it, was in giving too much power to the legislature and not leaving sufficient power anywhere else to check it. Adams believed that governments needed to balance the interests of various constituencies and that no branch of government should be able to overwhelm the others. This idea of separating the powers of government to prevent tyranny came from French writer Charles Secondat, Baron de Montesquieu's *Spirit of the Laws* (1748), a landmark work in political theory. Montesquieu praised the British constitution for its careful separation of executive and legislative functions, and colonists regarded the king's interference with the legislature as one of their primary grievances. Executive authority had overstepped its bounds before 1776, and the colonists responded with revolution. Now, in setting up new governments, the Americans limited the executive severely; to Adams the legislature now seemed the likely source of tyranny.

Violations of the Constitution. Pennsylvania's legislature did overstep its constitutional limits. Though the state Bill of Rights protected private property, the legislature had allowed property to be taken for military use and had set the price for the taking. The Bill of Rights protected citizens and their property from being searched or seized, yet the legislature permitted the military to search private property to determine how much a citizen owed in taxes and whether the property should be taken for military levies. The legislature also interfered with the judiciary: it voted to set aside fines imposed by judges; it settled civil cases despite the constitutional guarantee of jury trials; and it dissolved marriages.

Attacks on the Constitution. The constitution came under attack from the more conservative Pennsylvanians, who distrusted mass democracy. When the Council of Censors met for the first (and only) time in November 1783, the more conservative element had a small majority. Calling themselves "Republicans" (as they were opposed to the "democratic" constitution; its supporters called themselves "Constitutionalists"), this group tried to call for a state convention to change the constitution. They wanted to replace the executive council with a governor and add an upper house to the legislature as a check on the assembly. They wanted representation to be determined by taxable property rather than population. The Constitutionalists blocked the call for a convention in 1784, but the Pennsylvania constitution continued to be the state's central political issue. In 1789 the Republicans succeeded in calling a convention, and in 1790 Pennsylvania adopted a new constitution, with a popularly elected governor able to veto acts of the legislature, which was divided into a Senate and a House of Representatives. Judges, appointed by the governor, would serve during good behavior.

Sources:

Allan Nevins, *The American States During and After the Revolution, 1775-1789* (New York: Augustus M. Kelly, 1969);

Harry Marlin Tinkcom, *The Republicans and Federalists in Pennsylvania, 1790-1801* (Harrisburg: Pennsylvania Historical Museum and Commission, 1950);

Gordon S. Wood, *The Creation of the American Republic, 1776-1787* (New York & London: Norton, 1969).

STAMP ACT

New Tax. While New England merchants protested the Sugar Act, news arrived in April 1765 that Parliament had passed the Stamp Act. This act imposed an excise tax on all newspapers and pamphlets, legal documents, leases, deeds, licenses, playing cards, diplomas, broadsides, and other paper products. Once the tax had been paid (in gold or silver coin), a revenue officer would affix a stamp on the paper. The act would take effect on 1 November 1765.

Predictions of Reaction. The Stamp Act passed Parliament easily although the American colonies had warned that though they were loyal subjects of the king, they could be taxed only by their own assemblies. Col. Isaac Barre, a member of Parliament, warned that this revenue measure would cause "the blood of these sons of liberty to recoil within them." Massachusetts lieutenant governor Thomas Hutchinson wrote that "There is not a family between Canada and Pensacola that has not heard the name of the Stamp Act and but very few . . . but what have some formidable apprehensions of it." Hutchinson, who opposed the Stamp Act but believed Parliament had a right to levy it, told of a farmer whose servant was suddenly afraid to go to the barn at night. "Afraid of what?" the farmer asked. "Of the Stamp Act," the servant replied.

Sons of Liberty. Reaction to the Stamp Act was violent and widespread. Taking their name from Barre's speech, groups of colonists formed the Sons of Liberty, political action groups that channeled resistance to the Stamp Act. In Boston, Andrew Oliver, Hutchinson's brother-in-law, had been appointed stamp agent. On the night of 15 August a mob led by the Sons of Liberty attacked Oliver's office, where he stored the hated stamps. After destroying the office and stamps, they marched to his home, which they nearly completely destroyed. Two weeks later the mob descended on Hutchinson's home, regarding his moderate response as a sign of duplicity: James Otis charged Hutchinson with creating the idea of the Stamp Act. The mob destroyed Hutchinson's home and his papers, including documents Hutchinson was collecting for his history of Massachusetts. Similar violence in other colonies greeted the arrival of stamps and the appointment of stamp agents as the Sons of Liberty and an active press whipped the people into a frenzy.

Stamp Act Congress. Colonial leaders opposed the Stamp Act, but most also deplored the kind of violent action taken by the Sons of Liberty. To avoid tyranny and anarchy they called for a general meeting of delegates from all the colonies to make a united stand against the Stamp Act. In October 1765 delegates from nine colonies (Massachusetts, Rhode Island, Connecticut, New York, New Jersey, Pennsylvania, Delaware, Maryland, and South Carolina) met in New York to draw up a unified response. The Stamp Act Congress affirmed their loyalty to the king but insisted that they could be taxed only by their own representatives. They would gladly support the British government financially, but these levies could only be made by their own assemblies.

Actual versus Virtual Representation. The colonists and the British government had different ideas about the nature of representation. Members of Parliament did not represent specific locations or constituents. Members did not have to live in the boroughs they represented, and since most of the boroughs had been created centuries earlier, some of England's largest cities, such as Manchester, Birmingham, and Liverpool, were not represented at all. For the Americans to claim that because they had not voted for members of Parliament that Parliament could not tax them, was ridiculous. People in Manchester, Birmingham, and Liverpool had not voted for members of Parliament either. Parliament's job was to take care of the welfare of the whole realm, not to represent the interests of each locale. Members of Parliament were supposed to represent the good of the nation, not the interests of local constituency. In the American colonies, however, members of the colonial assemblies were chosen by towns or counties and were specifically chosen to represent their constituents. The Stamp Act, and England's attempt to tax the colonists, brought to light this fundamentally different approach to representation. Though the American colonists were asserting a fundamental right of English people, not to be taxed without their own consent, their experience as colonists had given them a different idea of the role of representatives and how consent was to be given.

Repeal. The British government would not accept the notion that the American colonists could be taxed only by their own representatives. The government insisted that because the Americans were British subjects, their interests were represented by Parliament. However, the British government recognized that enforcement of the Stamp Act would provoke continued violence in the American colonies. Opposition made the Stamp Act nearly impossible to enforce. Gov. Francis Bernard of Massachusetts wrote in December that "all real power in this town is in the hands of the people," and the Sons of Liberty threatened violence against any officials who dared use the stamps. "The time is come," Bernard wrote, "when even a nominal governor, though without authority or pretending to any, will not be allowed to reside here." In 1766 Parliament voted to rescind the act if the loyal colonial assemblies would raise money to meet royal requisitions, would volunteer to support British troops sent to protect the colonists, and would compensate those whose property had been destroyed by the mobs. At the same time Parliament passed the Declaratory Act, insisting that it had the power to tax the colonists for all purposes.

Aftermath. Parliament believed it had struck a bargain with the colonists, giving up a tax the colonists did not like in order to affirm the principle that Parliament could tax them. The colonists who had resisted the Stamp Act, however, interpreted the result differently. They had not wavered from the idea that only their own assemblies could tax them, and they had also learned that loud and sometimes violent opposition could force Parliament to back down. They also resisted the idea of paying the victims of the riots. In addition, the colonial assemblies and the Sons of Liberty had begun to learn the benefit of cooperation, seeing that the colonists had common interests that benefited from working together.

Source:
Edmund S. Morgan and Helen M. Morgan, *The Stamp Act Crisis: Prologue to Revolution* (Chapel Hill: Published for the Institute of Early American History and Culture by the University of North Carolina Press, 1953).

SUGAR ACT

War and Debt. The British Empire triumphed in the Seven Years' War, winning undisputed control of North America and control of the world's oceans. However, the war was extremely expensive, and maintaining the empire and the seas required a military force in North America and a navy. The war itself left England with a debt of £122,603,336, requiring an annual interest payment £4,409,797, or about half of the nation's annual budget. With the British people already heavily taxed, Parliament sought other sources of revenue.

Colonial Trade. One lucrative source of revenue, Parliament realized, would be the trade of the American colonies. Because the colonies benefited from British military power, and in fact the war had been fought to protect the colonists, it seemed only fair that the colonists share the burden of debt. Britain had never enforced regulations on colonial trade, and though the American colonists had a thriving commercial economy, their trade only contributed about £2,000 each year to the British treasury. In 1764 Parliament passed the Sugar Act, which actually reduced the tariff colonists would have to pay on sugar, but it increased enforcement. By having customs collectors in the colonies inspect ships and cargoes, Parliament could raise £78,000 each year from the intercolonial sugar trade.

Molasses and Rum. Britain's most lucrative colonies were in the West Indies. Barbados and Jamaica produced sugar, which would be shipped in the form of molasses to the North American mainland colonies, particularly Rhode Island and Massachusetts, where it would be refined into either sugar or rum. In return these colonies shipped food supplies to feed the slave laborers in the West Indies so that the sugar planters would not have to grow food for the labor force but could use every available bit of land to grow sugar. North American traders would also go to Africa to buy more slaves for the West Indian plantations, which absorbed about 40 percent of all Africans brought to the New World. Molasses and rum and slaves were making some of the American colonists wealthy, and it seemed only fair that they pay their share to the British treasury.

Enforcement. Parliament reduced the tariff on molasses from six pence per gallon to three pence; however, Parliament also sent customs collectors to the colonies to make sure this tax was collected. Parliament also gave the vice-admiralty courts more power to hear cases involving the trade laws and limited the power of other courts to hear related cases. Vice-admiralty courts, which did not have juries, had originally been established to hear cases involving sailors' wage disputes as well as cases involving trade laws. With one judge, who was often also the colony's chief justice, and no jury these courts could resolve disputes quickly. They were not, however, courts of record—their decisions were not binding on other courts. There were twelve vice-admiralty courts in British America (Quebec; Nova Scotia; Newfoundland; Massachusetts and New Hampshire; Rhode Island; Connecticut, New York and New Jersey; Pennsylvania and Delaware; Maryland; Virginia; North Carolina; and Georgia). The sugar act established a new vice-admiralty court in Halifax, Nova Scotia, and gave this court jurisdiction over all the local admiralty courts.

Newport. John Robinson arrived as customs collector in Newport, Rhode Island, determined to enforce the

A 1789 engraving of the Boston Tea Party (Library of Congress, Washington, D.C.)

law. On his arrival the merchants of Newport greeted him with an offer of a £70,000 bribe if he would look the other way when their ships reached port. Robinson was outraged, but he discovered that his own rectitude was not enough. The local merchants already had allies in the vice-admiralty judge and advocate, both consisting of local men. The judge would wait until Robinson was out of town to call his cases, so no evidence could be presented. Sometimes the case would be dismissed when the advocate, who was supposed to prosecute cases, would not show up in court. In the rare cases when the judge felt compelled to condemn a ship for violating the sugar act, Robinson would see the full extent of the community's support for its own merchants. The judge would order the condemned ship auctioned off, and no one would bid. The judge then, for a nominal sum, would sell the ship back to its original owner.

John Robinson and the *Polly*. In April 1765 John Robinson followed the ship *Polly* up the Taunton River from Newport, suspecting it had sailed past his customs office without reporting the molasses on board. When the ship docked at Dighton, Massachusetts, twenty miles from Newport, Robinson boarded it, discovered the molasses, and ordered the *Polly* seized; but no Dighton men were willing to execute his orders. He had to walk twenty miles back to Newport, where he hoped to find men willing to enforce His Majesty's customs laws. While Robinson was walking back to Newport, men from Dighton boarded the ship and removed all its cargo and equipment, stripped it to its frame, then drilled holes into its hull. When Robinson returned to Dighton, the *Polly* sat on the bottom of the Taunton river, and its owner charged Robinson with destroying his ship. The local sheriff arrested Robinson and marched him eight miles up river to Taunton. Though Robinson was ultimately

released, his arrest showed the difficulty a customs official would have in enforcing this unpopular law.

Unlikely Allies. The Sugar Act brought together unlikely allies: wealthy colonial merchants and the lawless lower orders of society. By convincing both that they had a common interest, and that this interest differed from the interests of Britain, Parliament had begun a process which would end in independence. Colonists also began to distinguish between acts passed to regulate trade, such as the 1690 Navigation Acts, and taxes passed to raise revenue. Parliament, they said, could regulate colonial trade, but only the colonial assemblies could tax the colonists. Eight colonial assemblies adopted protests against the Sugar Act, but because the Sugar Act mainly hurt New England merchants, and as it could be considered an act to regulate trade more than a revenue act, the protest was muted. But just as the colonial assemblies were drafting their protests, Parliament passed the Stamp Act, designed to raise revenues from all the colonists. Opposition to the Sugar Act was drowned out by the fierce opposition to the Stamp Act.

Sources:

Edmund S. Morgan and Helen M. Morgan, *The Stamp Act Crisis: Prologue to Revolution* (Chapel Hill: Published for the Institute of Early American History and Culture by the University of North Carolina Press, 1953);

Lawrence Henry Gipson, *The British Empire before the American Revolution,* volume 11, *The Triumphant Empire: The Rumbling of the Coming Storm, 1766-1770* (New York: Knopf, 1965).

TEA ACT

British Taxes on Tea. In 1721 Parliament had given the East India Company a virtual monopoly on the colonial tea market and had required a tea sold in the colonies to pass through England. The monopoly, however, was a paper one: in the late 1760s the American colonies imported an average of 562,281 pounds of tea each year from the East India Company, but they smuggled 900,000 pounds each year from French or Dutch sources. The Townshend duties had imposed a duty of three pence per pound on tea imported into the American colonies; in 1770 Parliament had repealed all of the Townshend duties except the duty on tea, which was maintained to prove the point that Parliament could tax the colonists.

Relief. In January 1773 the East India Company, heavily in debt from the conquest of Bengal and with more than ten million pounds of tea in its London warehouses, petitioned Parliament to remove the duty on tea, which they hoped would boost sales in America. Prime Minister Lord North was not willing to repeal the remaining duty; instead, Parliament would allow the East India Company to ship tea directly from India to the American colonies and would give the company a rebate on the tariff paid when the tea came to England. Member of Parliament Edmund Burke, colonial agent for New York, wrote to New York's Committee of Correspondence, "The East India Companys Political and Financial affairs are put into the hands of the Crown, but I am much afraid, with little Benefit either to the Crown or the Publick."

Shipments. In the fall the company sent seven ships, carrying nearly six hundred thousand pounds of tea, to the American colonies. Under terms of the law the company had designated thirteen colonial merchant firms to receive and sell the tea; in Massachusetts, Thomas and Elisha Hutchinson, Gov. Thomas Hutchinson's sons, were among the tea agents assigned to arrange public sales for the tea. For selling the tea and paying the import duty the agents would receive a 6 percent commission. When word of the act, and of the sailing of the tea ships, reached the colonies, the Sons of Liberty prepared to meet the new threat. Not only did the Tea Act give more force to the Townshend duty, but it also gave a monopoly to the British East India Company. On both grounds colonists would resist the importation of tea.

Pressuring the Tea Merchants. The first tactic, drawn from the colonists' experience with the Stamp Act, was to pressure the tea agents to resign their commissions. The tea agents in Charleston, South Carolina, and Philadelphia did resign under pressure from the local communities. In Charleston, with no agent to claim the tea or pay the duty, it was put into a warehouse (where it remained for three years, when the revolutionary government sold it). The tea ships that reached Philadelphia and New York never unloaded their cargoes. In Boston the town meeting on November 5 appointed a committee, chaired by John Hancock, to call on the tea merchants and demand their resignations. The merchants refused to resign, but one of them, Jonathan Clarke, promised not to unload the tea before he received orders from the company. On 28 November, when the first of the ships, the *Dartmouth,* appeared in Boston harbor, the tea merchants, along with the British customs commis-

sioners, fled to the safety of Castle Island, protected there by a British garrison. Members of the North End Caucus, a political group whose members included Paul Revere, guarded the *Dartmouth.*

Negotiations. The town committee and Governor Hutchinson began negotiations as the Committee of Correspondence called for mass meetings, which were too large to be held in Faneuil Hall, so they were moved to the Old South Meeting House. At the second meeting Francis Rotch, one of the owners of the *Dartmouth* promised to send the tea back to England, and John Singleton Copley, son-in-law of a tea agent, offered to store the tea on shore until the company sent new orders. The meeting rejected these proposals. In the next week two more ships reached Boston and were ordered docked next to the *Dartmouth* (a fourth ship wrecked off Cape Cod; its tea was salvaged and stored at Castle Island). Under British customs laws a ship had twenty days from arrival either to leave port or to pay duties on its cargo. The *Dartmouth* would have to sail by 18 December, or Governor Hutchinson could seize the cargo, which then would be sold to pay the duty. The ship's owner and the townspeople wanted the ship to leave, saving the cargo and not paying the tax. Governor Hutchinson, however, refused to allow the tea to leave port. Some townspeople believed Hutchinson and the British fleet would take the tea under their protection, pay the duty on it, and then sell it. Hutchinson instructed the British troops not to allow the vessels to leave port. On 16 December, Rotch met with Hutchinson to ask for a pass. Hutchinson refused, saying he would not allow the ship to leave until its cargo was unloaded. That evening in front of a huge mass meeting at Old South Meeting House, Rotch was questioned about his conversation with Hutchinson. As he finished, Samuel Adams rose and said, "This meeting can do nothing more to save the country."

The Tea Party. This was a prearranged signal. From taverns surrounding the docks a thousand people converged on the ship, and between thirty and fifty men disguised as Mohawk Indians boarded the *Dartmouth* and proceeded to unload the tea. With their hatchets they quickly opened the chests, and by 9 P.M. the entire cargo of tea had been dumped into the harbor. The men did no damage to the ship and did not take anything other than the tea, all of which was destroyed. One man seen with his pockets full of tea had them opened, and all the leaves were thrown into the water. Having destroyed a cargo of tea worth £9,659, the men retreated into the crowd and disappeared. None of the "Indians" would ever be identified.

Boston Port Act. When news of the tea party reached England on 20 January, the British government did not take the destruction of tea lightly. The solicitor general and attorney general both confirmed that the perpetrators had committed high treason, but since none could be identified, it was recommended that the leaders of the committee that had opposed the landing of the tea be prosecuted and that Samuel Adams, John Hancock, and many others be charged with high misdemeanors. By the end of March,

Parliament had closed the port of Boston, and on 2 April four new regiments of British troops were ordered to Boston. Hutchinson was replaced by Gen. Thomas Gage, commander in chief of all British forces in North America. Lord Dartmouth, in his instructions to Gage, told him that the "Sovereignty of the King in his Parliament over the Colonies requires a full and absolute submission," and until Boston, "where so much anarchy and confusion have prevailed," submitted absolutely, Gage and the government of the colony should move to Salem.

Reforming the Massachusetts Government. Gov. Francis Bernard in the 1760s, and Thomas Hutchinson in the early 1770s, had also proposed reforming the colony's 1691 charter government to give the troublesome colonists less room to make trouble. On 15 April, Lord North introduced a bill to regulate the Massachusetts government, providing that after 1 August 1774 the council, the upper house of the assembly, would no longer be chosen by the lower house but would be appointed by the king. After 1 July provincial judges, county sheriffs, justices of the peace, and the Attorney General, all appointed by the council, would be ap-

pointed by the governor, who could also dismiss them. Under the charter, town selectmen could call town meetings whenever the public business warranted it; in Boston the town meeting had been a regular source of opposition to the royal authorities. Under the charter the town meetings also elected grand jurors and drew lots for petit jurors. The new law limited town meetings to one each year and gave the sheriff, rather than the town meeting, the power to name jurors. Some members of Parliament, including Edmund Burke and Rose Fuller, opposed these acts as going too far. But Lord North disagreed. "Convince your Colonies that you are able and not afraid to controul them, and, depend upon it, obedience in them will be the result. . . ." Act with firmness and resolution, North said, and "peace and quietude will be restored." On 20 May the king approved the Massachusetts Regulating Act. Attempting to control the colonists and restore peace and order, Parliament instead made revolution inevitable.

Source:
Bernhard Knollenberg, *Growth of the American Revolution 1766-1775* (New York: Free Press, 1975).

HEADLINE MAKERS

SAMUEL ADAMS

1722-1803
REVOLUTIONARY LEADER

The Famous Adams. When John Adams arrived in France in 1778, he was greeted with a persistent question: was he "le fameaux Adams?" John Adams often bristled at the attention paid to others in the Patriot cause, such as James Otis, George Washington, and Thomas Jefferson. But in 1778 he acknowledged that he was not the famous Adams; that was his cousin, Samuel, leader of the Massachusetts Patriots, and the only American whom King George III exempted from a promise of amnesty. "If the American Revolution was a blessing, and not a curse," John Adams wrote later, "the name and character of Samuel Adams ought to be preserved. It will bear a strict and critical examination even by the inveterate malice of his enemies. . . . His merits and services and sacrifices and suffering are beyond all calculation."

Education. Samuel Adams was born in Boston on 27 September 1722. His father, Samuel, a successful brewer, had served as a deacon of both the Old South Church and New South Church and as a Boston selectman and representative to the assembly. Samuel's mother, Mary, was deeply religious, influenced by the preaching of Jonathan Edwards. Only three of their twelve children survived infancy. Samuel and his sister and brother were kept away from the influence of other children, instead instilled with deep feelings of personal responsiblity and isolation. At the age of fourteen Samuel entered Harvard. With class rank determined by a family's social position, he was ranked fifth in a class of twenty-two. At graduation (1740) he won the class debate on the subject of liberty, and in 1743 he was awarded a master's degree for his thesis "Whether It Be Lawful To Resist The Supreme Magistrate, If The Commonwealth Cannot Be Otherwise Preserved."

Entrance to Public Life. Adams studied for the bar briefly and then went into business. He was not a good businessman, and he quickly went bankrupt. His father paid off his debts and established Samuel as the manager of the brewery, which had grown so successful it needed little management. Father and son now had more time to devote to politics. In 1746 Governor Shirley vetoed the senior Adams's appointment to the Governor's Council, elevating Andrew Oliver instead. Young Samuel regarded this as an insult, and on 4 June 1746 he was elected by a special town meeting to fill Oliver's seat in the assembly. In his annual report Shirley reported to the king that the elder Adams, whom he said was a gentleman of great ability, was disgruntled by the veto of his appointment, but the younger Adams's "indefatigable zeal" made him more dangerous.

Political Career. In January 1748 Adams launched a newspaper, the *Independent Advertiser,* which he would publish until British authorities shut it down in 1775. The *Advertiser* was devoted entirely to politics, and Samuel Adams wrote most of the material, including the letters to the editor. His political position from the 1740s to the 1770s remained consistent: Massachusetts, or any political society, should be free to govern itself. These political essays attracted few readers, and the *Advertiser* never had a wide circulation. His father's sudden death in March 1748 left Samuel Adams responsible for the family brewery and other interests, and his brother and brother-in-law, better businessmen, handled most of the financial affairs. Political activity paid little, and Samuel Adams was not attentive to the businesses his father had left him. Adams spent most of his time talking, either with members of the Caucus Club, the leaders of Boston's business and political communities, or with the sailors and longshoremen who spent long hours in waterfront taverns. Adams would forget everything when he had a chance to talk politics, but if the conversation veered in another direction, Adams would leave in disgust. In 1749 he married Mary Checkley, the daughter of the New South pastor, with whom he had five children, two of whom survived infancy. Politics consumed Samuel Adams, and neither family nor business could distract him. The children especially suffered when Mary Checkley Adams died from a fever in 1757.

Political Passion. When his father died, Adams had been elected to the Caucus Club, a political group whose members were able to dominate the Boston town meeting. Because few men had the time to pay close attention to civic affairs, and few were willing to devote the hours necessary to attending such meetings, a handful of organized men were able to control the town meeting. In 1753 the town meeting elected Samuel an assessor, and in 1756 he was a Boston tax collector; but Adams was so lax in collecting taxes that in 1758 the sheriff gave notice that on 5 August his property, including his house and gardens, the brewery, a wharf, and several apartment buildings, would be auctioned off to pay Adams's outstanding debts. The day of the auction Adams responded with a public letter to the sheriff, threatening to sue anyone who took his property. He and the sheriff conducted a newspaper argument over the auction, which never took place. By 1765, when he was finally removed as tax collector, he had failed to collect more than £8,000 that was owed by his fellow citizens.

Breach with England. Though Adams devoted himself almost completely to politics, his career by 1764 had taken him nowhere. He was in debt; the house and businesses his father had left him were in ruins; and he seemed not the least concerned. In 1764 he married Elizabeth Wells, who was twenty years his junior. They would have no children, but Elizabeth would become responsible for the care of his son and daughter. Along with James Otis and John Hancock, Adams was one of the leaders of the group opposed to Thomas Hutchinson, but Hutchinson continued to rise in power while Adams, Otis, and Hancock were shut out. The Sugar Act, though, changed this. Hutchinson opposed the Sugar Act, but merely because it was unwise. For Adams the Sugar Act raised the same issue he had been writing about for twenty years: the right of the people of Massachusetts to govern themselves. Adams's long days and nights in political gatherings had also given him a new outlook on politics. Most opponents of the Sugar Act, wealthy merchants, expressed opposition in letters to men of influence in England. For Adams political action meant something more dramatic than writing letters. He would use mass protests against the political establishment, using public opinion, rather than private intrigue, to make policy. Parliament repealed the Sugar Act before Adams could completely bring his political theories into practice, and even his allies believed he had tried to carry things too far.

Stamp Act and Aftermath. But in 1765, when Parliament passed the Stamp Act, Adams was prepared with a campaign of massive public resistance. Able to mobilize both the merchant elite and the men of the lower orders, able to articulate the cause with both passion and eloquence, Adams became the leader of resistance. He was elected to the assembly in September and prepared both the House's answers to the governor's speech and resolutions asserting American rights. In 1766 the radical faction that looked to Adams as a leader took control of the assembly, and from 1766 until General Gage dissolved the assembly in 1774, Adams was its clerk. Adams used his position as spokesman for the House to harass every British official sent to the province. The colonial assemblies, Adams insisted, were not subject to Parliament. The colonial assemblies had the exclusive power to guarantee the natural and constitutional rights of Americans. These principals, Adams insisted, rested on the British Constitution, which was not, as English practice made it, subject to Parliamentary whim; instead, according to Adams, the British Constitution embodied the inherent and inalienable natural rights of men, which no legislative body could limit.

Committees of Correspondence. In 1770 the assembly appointed a committee of correspondence, of which

Adams was a member, to keep in contact with other colonies. In 1772 Adams, as leader of Boston's town meeting, moved that the town appoint a committee of correspondence to "state the rights of the Colonists . . . as men, as Christians, and as Subjects; and to communicate the same to the several towns and to the world." Adams drafted its declaration and privately urged other towns to form similar committees. When the British government in Massachusetts collapsed following the Boston Tea Party, these committees became the province's new government. When the British government closed the port of Boston, Adams called for an intercolonial Congress to unite all the colonies in opposition to British policy. Adams was chosen to the first Continental Congress, and he may have been the only delegate already thinking of independence. Before he left for Philadelphia, friends provided him with new clothes and a wig; while he was gone, other local supporters built a new barn and repaired his dilapidated house. Adams refrained from an active part in Congress's debates, but he used his influence in small informal meetings, successfully convincing the delegates to adopt the militant Suffolk Resolves and repudiate Joseph Galloway's plan for a colonial union under Parliamentary rule. Returning to Massachusetts, Adams narrowly escaped arrest when Gage's forces attacked Lexington and Concord, and in 1776 he returned to Congress publicly advocating independence. He signed the Declaration and continued to serve in Congress until 1781.

Covering his Tracks. His cousin John was the great speaker and public organizer; but Samuel Adams was the influential figure behind the scenes. As such, it is harder to trace all of his influence, but Adams is visible in the results. The committees of correspondence had operated with a large degree of secrecy; the planning for the Boston Tea Party also had to be done with great discretion since destroying the tea would be considered an act of treason. John Adams asked many years later, "The letters he wrote and received, where are they? I have seen him . . . in Philadelphia, when he was about to leave Congress, cut up with his scissors whole bundles of letters into atoms that could never be reunited, and throw them out the window, to be scattered by the winds. . . . In winter he threw whole handfuls into the fire. . . . I have joked him, perhaps rudely, upon his anxious caution. His answer was, 'Whatever becomes of me, my friends shall never suffer by my negligence.'"

Later Years. Adams, more than any other man, was responsible for independence, and more importantly, he was responsible for the particular causes for independence. Franklin believed that the colonies ultimately would be independent because of their demographic and geographic destiny; Adams believed the colonies would need to be independent because all men had the inalienable right to govern themselves. From 1746 until the end of his life he advocated this simple idea; and though his ideas found warm support in Boston after 1764, and in

the rest of the United States after 1776, he, as an admirer said, was an austere and distant man, feared by his enemies, but too secret to be loved by his friends. Once independence was declared, leadership passed to other hands, including those of John Hancock, whom Adams did not entirely trust. Adams continued to be active in Boston politics, continuing to lead the town meeting. In 1788 he served in the Massachusetts ratifying convention though his only son died as it met. At first he opposed the new Constitution since it created a distant government that the people would not be able to control. He was defeated for election to the first Congress under the Constitution, but he was elected lieutenant governor of Massachusetts in 1789, serving in that post until 1794, when he became governor on the death of Gov. John Hancock, serving in that office until 1797. In 1801 Thomas Jefferson wrote to Adams, "I addressed a letter to you, my very dear and ancient friend, on the 4th of March [the day Jefferson became president]; not indeed to you by name, but through the medium of my fellow citizens. . . . In meditating the matter of the [Inaugural] address, I often asked myself, Is this exactly in the spirit of the patriarch Samuel Adams? Will he approve of it?" After Adams's death on 2 October 1803 he was given a state funeral against his wishes, and members of the Massachusetts legislature and of the U.S. House of Representatives and Senate all wore mourning bands in his memory for the duration of the year.

Source:
Paul Lewis, *The Grand Incendiary: A Biography of Samuel Adams* (New York: Dial Press, 1973).

SILAS DEANE

1737-1789
DIPLOMAT

Scandal. Silas Deane was a rising star on the American political scene until he was destroyed in a political scandal that reshaped American politics and altered the course of American diplomacy. The scandal of 1778–1779 destroyed Deane's political and business career, left his chief detractor labeled as unstable and erratic, led the president of Congress to resign, and forced Congress to fire Thomas Paine as secretary to a congressional committee. The Deane scandal developed at the same time as other political disputes, involving issues as different as the structure of Pennsylvania's government and the proper nature of the new nation's relationship with France. The Deane scandal marked the first open breach among supporters of American independence and led these political leaders to turn to public opinion to secure support.

Man on the Make. Born in Groton, Connecticut, on 24 December 1737, Silas Deane, the son of a blacksmith, graduated from Yale College in 1758. He was admitted to the bar in 1761 and received a master's degree from

Yale in 1763. An ambitious young lawyer, in 1763 Deane married Mehitabel Webb, a widow with six children and a successful store, which helped launch Deane on the road to success. When Mehitabel died in 1767, Deane again married this time to Elizabeth Saltonstall, granddaughter of a former colonial governor. In 1769 he was named chairman of the local committee responsible for enforcing the nonimportation agreements, and in 1772 he was sent to the general assembly. Secretary to the assembly's committee of correspondence, Deane in 1774 and 1775 was sent to the Continental Congress. There he was actively involved in creating a Continental Navy, and with other Connecticut men Deane outfitted a military force to capture Fort Ticonderoga. Connecticut did not send Deane to Congress in 1776, but Congress sent him to France, the first representative of the united American colonies in Europe.

Commissioner. Deane carried secret instructions from two committees of Congress to France. One committee authorized Deane to sell American goods in France or in other countries; the other committee instructed him to buy guns, ammunition, and other military supplies. If possible he was to begin negotiations for French support of American independence. Deane did all these, with great success. Working with French playwright and political activist Pierre-Augustin Caron de Beaumarchais (author of *The Marriage of Figaro*, first performed in 1784), Deane sent eight ships loaded with military supplies to the colonies, which helped the poorly supplied American army win the Battle of Saratoga. Deane also sent French officers to join Washington's army.

French Officers. Deane reported on the "rage" among French gentlemen and officers for an American military adventure, and he obliged dozens of French officers with American commissions. Washington could not use all the officers Deane commissioned, but he had to make room for them, which might mean displacing his own commanders. After Congress voted not to commission French officers who did not understand English, Congress had to tell Deane this did not mean that he could commission any officer who did understand English. Finally Congress voted not to receive any more French officers, but those already in America insisted on keeping their positions. One French officer, the Irish-born general Thomas Conway, collaborated with other officers and with some Congressional supporters to try to replace Washington in 1778. Another French officer, Philippe Charles Tronson Du Coudray, arrived expecting to be given senior command of the American artillery. The prospect of Du Coudray's promotion prompted Henry Knox, Nathanael Greene, and John Sullivan to offer their resignations. Du Coudray's extravagant claims to honor and preference were ended when he tried to ride his horse on the ferry across the Schuylkill. Refusing to dismount, Du Coudray drowned when his panicked horse dove into the river, thus relieving "Congress from a very troublesome malcontent."

Recall. In 1776 Congress had dispatched Arthur Lee and Benjamin Franklin to join Deane as American commissioners to France. As the three worked on a treaty with the French government, members of Congress, along with Washington, grew frustrated with Deane's French officers, and in August 1777 Congress began to consider recalling Deane from France. In November 1777 Congress formally asked him to return home, but he would not receive the news before the commissioners signed the treaty with France in February 1778. Deane returned home to answer to Congress and to inform Congress that Arthur Lee's incompetence threatened to undermine the French alliance. Arthur Lee, for his part, had grown deeply suspicious of Deane and had told his brother Richard Henry Lee that the military aid Deane had sent from France in 1776, for which he had billed Congress, had been intended as a French gift to the Americans. The Lees, joined by Samuel Adams and Connecticut's Roger Sherman, with whom Deane had endured a frosty relationship (Deane called him "my old Colleague Roger the Jesuit"), suspected Deane of profiteering and corruption.

Deane and Congress. Deane demanded a quick investigation, but Congress did nothing in the fall of 1778. In October, Deane published a series of anonymous queries in the *Pennsylvania Packet,* charging Arthur Lee with close, traitorous communications with a British agent, and in December, Deane publicly blasted the Lees in a newspaper essay "To the Free and Virtuous Citizens of America." This marked the first open political dispute among the Patriots, and it caught the Lees off guard. To John Adams the publication of Deane's defense "appeared . . . like a dissolution of the Constitution." The Lees moved to have Congress censure Deane for his public breach, but they failed. Henry Laurens, president of Congress and a Lee ally, resigned to protest Congress's failure to censure Deane. The Lees then turned to Thomas Paine, secretary to Congress's Committee on Foreign Affairs, to come to their aid. Paine wrote a vigorous series of essays attacking Deane for profiteering. Deane had risen like a rocket, Paine said, and now he would fall like a stick. But in blasting Deane's connection with Beaumarchais, Paine revealed too much about French diplomacy, publicly acknowledging that France had supported the American colonies as early as 1776, when France insisted she was neutral. The French envoy to America forced Congress to fire Paine for publishing this information. "I did not see how they could ever trust any of Us again," John Adams wrote in his diary, saying the scandal "would have the worst Effects upon Spain, Holland, and in England, besides endangering a civil War in America."

Political Division. Congress divided between a Deane faction, led by Robert Morris and John Jay, and a Lee faction, led by Richard Henry Lee and Samuel Adams.

New England and the Lees joined together against Southern delegates and the New Yorkers, whom Adams called Deane's "Tory friends and Mercantile Abettors." The issue for Congress was public virtue: by mixing his diplomatic responsibilities with the pursuit of private profit, Deane had betrayed the public trust. On the other hand, Deane's defenders did not see why public servants such as he should go broke in serving their country. Civil war was averted, but while Congress and the newspapers debated charges and countercharges, Washington's army was dissolving. Deane had left France without the necessary paperwork to prove his case; to his supporters this was an honest mistake, but to his detractors it looked as though he had something to hide. In 1780 Deane returned to Europe as a private citizen, hoping to recover the small fortune he had spent in 1776 supplying the American army. In 1781, with the British in control of South Carolina and New York, Deane despaired of American victory, and wrote to American friends urging reconciliation. When the British intercepted these letters, and the Loyalist New York press published them, what little was left of Deane's public reputation was destroyed. He now seemed not only a profiteer but also a traitor. His health broken, his money gone, Deane lived in poverty in Belgium, then in England, where the British government gave him a small pension. In 1789 he tried to sail to Canada, but died just out of the port of Deal on 23 September 1789. In 1842 the United States government agreed that the 1779 audit had been "a gross injustice to Silas Deane" and awarded his heirs $37,000.

Sources:

Thomas Paine, "The Affair of Silas Deane," in *Complete Writings of Thomas Paine,* edited by Philip S. Foner (New York: Citadel Press, 1945);

Jack Rakove, *The Beginnings of National Politics: An Interpretive History of the Continental Congress* (Baltimore & London: Johns Hopkins University Press, 1979);

Gordon S. Wood, *The Creation of the American Republic 1776–1787* (New York: Norton, 1972).

JOSEPH GALLOWAY

1731-1803
PENNSYLVANIA LOYALIST

Career. Joseph Galloway was a born politician. By the 1760s he was perhaps the most powerful man in Pennsylvania after the proprietors, against whom Galloway made a direct attack. Though this failed, Galloway was speaker of the colonial assembly from 1766 to 1775, and in 1774 he was elected a member of the first Continental Congress. Galloway had too much faith that the disagreement between England and the colonies could be reconciled; in 1776 he broke with the patriot movement and joined British forces in New York. He returned to Philadelphia when British forces occupied the city, and he supervised the police and the port during the British occupation. When Philadelphia fell to the Patriots, Gal-

loway fled with the British and lived the rest of his life in exile.

Background. Joseph Galloway's father, Peter Galloway, was a wealthy Maryland merchant and farmer. A young boy when his father died, Joseph went to Philadelphia to be trained as a lawyer. By the 1750s he had acquired such a bright legal reputation that he was elected to the colonial assembly, and he married the daughter of the assembly's speaker, Lawrence Growden, one of Pennsylvania's wealthiest men. In the assembly Galloway joined with Benjamin Franklin and with the Quaker party in opposing the interests of the Penn family. With Franklin he pushed to have the Penn estates taxed, and he also called for Pennsylvania to become a royal colony, stripping the Penn family of their proprietary title. The assembly approved the bill, over the objections of John Dickinson, who did not defend the Penns but thought the British crown might not be the best protector of colonial liberty. The assembly's proposal was ignored in the midst of the Stamp Act controversy. Galloway and Franklin also proposed a bill to punish whites who murdered Indians, in the wake of the Paxton riots. The assembly killed the bill, and Galloway and Franklin were both defeated for reelection.

Quarrel with Dickinson. Galloway was not out of the assembly for long. He was reelected in 1765 and would serve as speaker for the next nine years. As the crisis with England worsened, Galloway became a voice of restraint. Though he was zealous in protecting Pennsylvania's liberties, he acknowledged Parliament's power to tax the colonies. He disagreed with John Dickinson, who argued in his "Letters from a Farmer in Pennsylvania to the Inhabitants of the British Colonies" (1767) that Parliament could not tax the colonies; Galloway insisted that Parliament had this power, but he believed colonial leaders such as himself could convince the British ministry not to exercise these powers. Dickinson became the more prominent leader in the growing Whig movement though when Pennsylvania chose delegates to a Continental Congress in 1774, Galloway made sure he, and not Dickinson, was sent.

First Continental Congress. Galloway believed that the growing rift with England could be mended if the colonies and mother country replaced the unwritten system under which they were governed with a written constitution. On 28 September 1774 he introduced into the Congress a "Plan of Union," which would guarantee to the colonists the "first and most excellent privileges of Englishmen," the right to representation in Parliament and to consent to the laws under which they lived. Galloway's plan would have created an American legislature, chosen by the colonial assemblies for three-year terms. The king would appoint a president general to administer the colonies and execute the laws. No law would take effect for the colonies without the approval of both Parliament and the American legislature; in this way the American colonists could protect their rights, and Parliament could continue to reign supreme in the British empire. Though Galloway believed this system would preserve both colonial liberty and the British empire, it did not receive wide support. "I stand here almost alone," he wrote to an English friend. By a vote of six states to five, Congress postponed consideration of Galloway's plan, endorsing instead the more militant Suffolk Resolves, which denied Parliament's power to tax the colonies and called for a boycott of British goods. In October, Dickinson was elected to Pennsylvania's assembly; Galloway was removed as speaker; and Dickinson was chosen to represent Pennsylvania in the Congress.

Break with Congress. Congress voted to expunge Galloway's plan from the journal, so he published it himself in 1775, chastising his readers and Congress for ignoring his correct analysis of Parliament's powers and colonial rights. "I have . . . deduced your rights, . . . and explained your duties," he wrote, and Congress should follow the line of conduct he laid down. But by 1775 resistance to Parliamentary authority had grown; with it, the idea grew that it was not for men such as Galloway to instruct the people in their proper conduct or in the limits of their rights; it was for the people to instruct their elected officials in these things. Galloway became disenchanted with the new mood of the Whig movement; though he signed the nonimportation agreement, by 1776 he had broken with Congress and moved out of Philadelphia. He hoped he could remain neutral, but he also believed that only he could repair the breach and rescue the impetuous Americans from their instinct for independence.

Occupied Philadelphia. Galloway went to New York to offer his services to the British army, commanded by Gen. Sir William Howe. On 26 September 1777 Howe's army occupied Philadelphia. Confident that Galloway could help restore order in the city and perhaps reconcile the second largest city in the empire to the British crown, Howe put Galloway in charge of policing the city, and of imports and exports. Galloway's real task was to prevent goods from reaching Washington's army and to suppress revolutionary activity. He hired spies and magistrates to root out disloyalty, but he also created an efficient and organized government for Philadelphia. Galloway believed that four out of every five Americans would prefer to remain loyal to the Crown if only they were given an effective government that could lead them to loyalty. He hoped that with an efficient system of government, Philadelphia could be a model for disaffected Americans of what they risked by rejecting British rule. Trade increased under his administration, and his troops prevented provisions from reaching Washington's camp at Valley Forge. But General Howe would not give Galloway a free hand, rejecting Galloway's proposal that British and loyalist forces kidnap New Jersey's governor and council. When the British decided abruptly to abandon Philadelphia in June 1778, they rejected Galloway's request to negotiate directly with Washington. The British knew that most of their soldiers in New York were Americans; if the Philadelphia loyalists made a separate peace with Washington, New York also might be lost.

Exile. With his daughter, Galloway fled Philadelphia for England in 1778. He would never return. In London he became a spokesman for other American exiles, continuing to argue for reconciliation based on his constitutional plans. The peace treaty in 1783 was a bitter shock, and the victorious patriots siezed Galloway's property in Pennsylvania. He became dependent on a British pension, and he argued that the British government, which had failed to heed the advice of Galloway and other Americans, and in ignoring them had lost their best chance to hold on to the colonies, should support the exiles. Some loyalists and British distrusted Galloway, who had early on supported the Whigs and been an ally of Franklin and Adams. He was rejected when he applied for a civil position in Nova Scotia, and in 1793 the Pennsylvania government rejected his petition to be allowed to return home. In his later years he wrote less about politics, more about religion. He died on 29 August 1803 and is buried in Watford, Hertfordshire.

Sources:

Robert M. Calhoon, *The Loyalists in Revolutionary America 1760–1781* (New York: Harcourt Brace Jovanavich, 1965);

Mary Beth Norton, *The British Americans: The Loyalist Exiles in England* (Boston: Little, Brown, 1972);

Lorenzo Sabine, *Biographical Sketches of Loyalists of the American Revolution*, 2 volumes (Boston: Little, Brown, 1864).

THOMAS HUTCHINSON

1711-1780
MASSACHUSETTS GOVERNOR

Education of a Public Man. Thomas Hutchinson could have been the most successful American political figure of the eighteenth century. The fifth generation of his family in Massachusetts, great-grandson of Anne Hutchinson, Thomas was an accomplished historian, businessman, and politician, cultivating the right connections in London to secure for himself a series of offices: chief justice, lieutenant governor, and in 1771 an appointment as governor of his native colony. But the skills that Hutchinson used to rise to the top were useless in the changing political climate of the 1770s, and as governor Hutchinson was unable to balance his prime political responsibility, representing the interests of the British crown in Massachusetts, and the growing unwillingness of his fellow colonials to obey British authority. In 1765, when Bostonians accused Hutchinson of supporting the Stamp Tax, they demolished his home; in 1773, when Hutchinson tried to articulate the position of the Crown in governing the American colonies, the Massachusetts assembly called for his removal. Hutchinson went to England in the summer of 1774 for what he hoped would be a temporary political visit; he would never return to his home, and in 1779 the Massachusetts assembly voted to banish him permanently. The greatest honor in his life was an honorary doctorate in civil laws from Oxford, which he received for his efforts to govern the recalcitrant colony. The degree was awarded on 4 July 1776.

Background. Thomas Hutchinson was born in Boston on 9 September 1711. His great-great-grandparents, Anne and William Hutchinson, had arrived in 1634 but had been exiled for Anne's outspoken views on religion. Since then the family had prospered within the colony; both his father and grandfather were members of the executive council. Thomas entered Harvard when he was twelve, graduated at sixteen, and at age nineteen earned a master's degree, after which he went to work in his father's counting house. He married Margaret Sanford in 1734, and they had five children. Thomas began his political career in 1737, when he was chosen both to represent Boston in the colonial assembly and to serve as a town selectman.

Political Rise. Hutchinson clearly stood out in the assembly; he was chosen to be Speaker for three terms, and in 1740–1741 he was sent to England to represent Massachusetts in its border dispute with New Hampshire. His mission failed, but he used his time in England to make connections with influential members of Parliament and to lobby against the Land Bank, a financially unsound venture that Parliament agreed to dissolve. One of the Land Bank's promoters was Boston businessman Samuel Adams, whose son Samuel, graduating from Harvard in 1740, would become Hutchinson's chief political enemy. Hutchinson's brother-in-law, Andrew Oliver, was chosen to the council instead of the senior Adams in 1746; three years later Hutchinson, who was not reelected to the assembly, was placed on the council, where he remained until 1766. In 1752 he was chosen to be a judge of probate and justice of common pleas for Suffolk County. In 1754 he represented Massachusetts at the Albany conference and was one of the strongest supporters of Franklin's plan of colonial union. In 1758 Hutchinson won appointment as lieutenant governor. Two years later, when the office of chief justice became vacant, James Otis Sr. was the leading candidate. However, the new royal governor, Francis Bernard, persuaded Hutchinson to accept the post. His appointment infuriated James Otis Jr. just as his earlier appointments had riled the younger Samuel Adams. They railed not only against what they perceived to be Hutchinson's political manipulation to secure offices but also against the idea that one man could simultaneously hold executive, legislative, and judicial offices. Montesquieu's theory of separation of powers was relatively new, but Otis and Adams and his supporters began to see Hutchinson as a dangerous threat to liberty.

Otis and Adams. By 1763 Hutchinson was the most influential man in the colony, but he had also become a target for James Otis and Samuel Adams. Hutchinson agreed with Adams and Otis on matters of policy; he did not think that the governor could issue writs of assistance, nor did he think Parliament should pass laws such as the Sugar Act or the stamp tax. In 1764 the assembly had tried to send Hutchinson to England to make its case against the Sugar Act. He believed these were unwise measures, but unlike Adams and Otis, Hutchinson insisted that Parliament had a right to tax the colonists. He would never agree with their assertion that Parliament's power did not extend beyond England. If that were the case, the colonies must become independent. Neither Otis nor Adams was willing to make the case for independence in the 1760s, but Hutchinson saw where their arguments were going. He wanted to avoid independence and have Massachusetts prosper as part of the British empire. Since Adams and Otis both denied that they were interested in independence, Hutchinson interpreted their almost violent opposition to his ideas and policies as motivated by political self-interest rather than political principle.

The Stamp Act. However, Otis and Adams believed that self-interest in fact motivated Hutchinson. His brother-in-law, Andrew Oliver, had been appointed to distribute the hated stamps; to Otis and Adams it was apparent that Hutchinson's support for the law came from his personal stake in it. On 13 August 1765 a mob destroyed Oliver's shop and the stamps; the next night the mob surrounded Hutchinson's house and demanded to know if he had written to England in support of the Stamp Act. Hutchinson had not, but he also did not feel he needed to "answer to all the questions that may be put me by every lawless person." The mob dispersed out of respect for Hutchinson's faithful public service, but two weeks later the mob returned. This time it destroyed Hutchinson's home and property, causing damage estimated at £3,000 ($122,000 today), tearing the eyes from Hutchinson's portrait, and, in a loss that cannot be calculated, scattering the manuscript for the second volume of his *History of the Colony of Massachusetts Bay* (1767). When Hutchinson appeared to preside in court the next morning, he had to apologize for his appearance: he had fled the mob with "no other shirt; no other garment but what I have on; and not one of my family in a better situation."

Political Tempers. Tempers cooled after Parliament rescinded the Stamp Act. "We have not been so quiet these five years," Hutchinson wrote in 1771, "if it were not for two or three Adamses we should do well enough." Otis's growing insanity and Samuel Adams's business failures did not make either an entirely credible opponent. Their ally, John Hancock, opposed Parliament's tax policies out of self-interest; a wealthy Boston merchant, Hancock did not want to pay taxes on goods he imported. Hutchinson regarded the three as political opportunists. He saw a role for the colonies in the empire similar to the role he and Franklin had envisioned with the Albany plan of 1754. He made this case in a series of letters to a British correspondent, insisting that the colonists could not enjoy all the liberties of British subjects while they relied on British power to protect them from the French and Native Americans. Parliament did have the power to legislate for the colonies in all cases; it was not up to the colonists to determine which laws they would obey.

Political Downfall. 1773, the year of Hutchinson's greatest political victory, would also be the year of his downfall. That year he successfully ended Massachusetts's long border dispute with New York, securing to his own colony undisputed title to the lands west of the Connecticut River; but in opening the assembly that year, Hutchinson provoked a debate that would lead inexorably to independence. In his opening speech to the assembly in January, Governor Hutchinson developed his ideas of Parliamentary supremacy. The assembly responded, feeling that Hutchinson forced it to make its own argument on the limits of Parliamentary authority.

Franklin and Tea. In London, Benjamin Franklin, acting as the assembly's agent and eager to have the colony reconcile with England, came to believe that a more conciliatory politician, who would not lecture the assembly on political theory, would be able to heal the rift. In order to save the empire Franklin determined to rid it of Hutchinson. He obtained copies of Hutchinson's private letters of the 1760s and sent them to the Massachusetts assembly. Samuel Adams had been charging Hutchinson with conspiring to destroy American liberty; the letters, carefully edited and published in the Boston press, seemed to confirm Adams's charges. Arriving in Massachusetts at about the same time as news that Parliament had passed the Tea Act and that Hutchinson's two sons had been chosen to sell the tea in Boston, the letters destroyed Hutchinson's political credibility. The assembly demanded his recall. When the tea ships reached Boston in December, Hutchinson's unwillingness to compromise and his adamant belief that the ships could not legally leave port until they had been unloaded provoked the Boston mob, disguised as Indians, to dump the tea into Boston harbor.

In England. Hutchinson asked leave to go to England to propose a solution to the crisis. In his absence Massachusetts would not get a more conciliatory governor; instead Gen. Thomas Gage, the commander in chief of the British forces in North America, was named to govern the province. Though Hutchinson urged conciliation, Parliament was now determined to get tough. Hutchinson spent his last years in England, helplessly watching as his native colony became an independent state, and the political connections he had carefully cultivated in England to secure his power in Massachusetts proved only good enough to sustain a meager livelihood in England. He died of a stroke on 3 June 1780. His country home in Milton, Massachusetts, was seized by the state

of Massachusetts and sold to revolutionary leader James Warren and his wife, Mercy Otis Warren, sister of Hutchinson's old nemesis. Arthur Lee, American commissioner to France, congratulated the Warrens that "It has not always happened . . . that the forfeited seats of the wicked have been filled with men of virtue. But in this corrupt world it is sufficient that we have some examples of it for our consolation."

Source:
Bernard Bailyn, *The Ordeal of Thomas Hutchinson* (Cambridge, Mass.: Belknap Press of Harvard University Press, 1974).

GEORGE MASON

1725-1792
VIRGINIA REVOLUTIONARY

Reluctant Statesman. George Mason was a private man devoted to his family and plantation, yet he was periodically called on by his community for advice and counsel. A slaveholder, Mason spent his public life attacking the institution of slavery, which violated his ideals of liberty and republican virtue. A leader in Virginia's break with England, Mason drafted the state's Declaration of Rights and called for a firm union of the states. In the 1780s Mason joined Washington and Madison in calling for a stronger union, and he helped draft the U.S. Constitution. Mason was horrified that the Constitution did not include a Bill of Rights and that it would allow the slave trade to continue for another twenty years. He opposed its ratification in 1788. The changes he proposed became the model for the Bill of Rights.

Family Life. When Mason was ten, his father, George Mason III, drowned in the Potomac. His mother, Ann Thomson Mason, managed the estate, instilling in her three children traits that became part of their character: an attention to detail, hard work, and the necessity to avoid extravagance and debt. Under Virginia law George, as oldest son, would inherit all of his father's estate, so his mother shrewdly added to her own holdings to give his younger sister and brother an inheritance. George's uncle, lawyer John Mercer, acted as a guardian to the Mason children, and in Mercer's extensive library George Mason studied law and political philosophy. Though he never went to college, he became one of the best-educated men in the American colonies. In 1750 he married Anne Eilbeck, with whom he would have nine children who survived to adulthood. In 1758 the Masons commissioned English architect William Buckland to design their home, Gunston Hall, which became a showplace. A dozen miles away young George Washington had inherited his half-brother's estate at Mount Vernon, and for the next forty years Mason and Washington would be close business partners and political allies. Mason managed his estate and attended to his family, reluctantly doing his civic duty as a parish vestryman and member of the colonial assembly. In 1772 Ann gave birth to twins who lived only a few hours; she never recovered from the difficult pregnancy, and she died in March 1773. In the crisis between England and the colonies Mason would play an important role, but his first duty was to his family.

The Fairfax Resolves. On 18 July 1774 the voters of Fairfax County elected George Washington and Maj. Charles Broadwater to the House of Burgesses, and Mason drew up the county's instructions to their representatives. These instructions, the Fairfax Resolves, declared that Virginians enjoyed all the rights of Englishmen and that the "most important and valuable Part of the British Constitution" is the "fundamental Principle" that the people can not be made to obey laws "to which they have not given their Consent, by Representatives freely chosen by themselves." The power to make laws governing the colonies could be exercised only by their own provincial assemblies. The Resolves called on all colonies to support Boston and urged every county in Virginia to send provisions to the town. While "our greatest Wish and Inclination" was to remain connected to the British government, the Virginians would "use every Means which Heaven hath given us to prevent our becoming it's Slaves." The Resolves asked the king not to reduce his subjects to desperation as "from our Sovereign there can be but one Appeal." Mason's Resolves called for a general boycott of British goods and for the colonists not to export any of their produce for sale in England until the crisis had been resolved. Mason chose not to be a candidate for the House of Burgesses or the Provincial Convention that replaced it. However, he remained active on his community's Committee of Safety, and, in Washington's absence, he chaired the Fairfax County Committee. In July 1775 Mason was elected to the Virginia Convention, and when Governor Dunmore fled the colony at the end of the year, Mason served on the committee of safety, which acted as the new executive power.

Declaration of Rights. James Madison called Mason the "master builder" of Virginia's 1776 constitution, and as its author Mason had a profound influence on all subsequent written constitutions. Mason began the new state constitution with a Declaration of Rights. The declaration declared "That all Men are born equally free and independent, and have certain inherent natural rights, of which they cannot by any Compact, deprive or divest their posterity; among which are the Enjoyment of Life and Liberty, with the means of acquiring and possessing Property, and pursueing and obtaining Happiness and Safety." The Declaration of Rights went on to guarantee protection of property, trial by jury, the right of the accused to face his accusers, religious toleration, freedom of the press, and separation of powers in government. This declaration was a model for Thomas Jefferson's Declaration of Independence, for other state constitutions, for France's 1789 Declaration of the Rights of Man, and for the first ten amendments to the U.S. Constitution.

Slavery and Liberty. The Virginia convention made one crucial change in Mason's declaration. Mason, and most of Virginia's political leaders, owned slaves. How could they declare that all men were born free and that they could not divest their posterity of liberty? What about slaves? Were they to be free? Robert Carter Nicholas warned that Mason's declaration would create "civil convulsion," and the convention amended the draft to say that men were "by nature" free, and that once they entered "into a state of society" they could not divest their posterity of liberty. This permitted the white men in the state to continue holding slaves. The tortured reasoning here had a profound result. The 1780 Massachusetts constitution began with a statement exactly like Mason's original draft. A Boston slave named Quok Walker sued for his freedom, arguing that this constitution prohibited slavery, and the Massachusetts courts agreed. Had Virginia's convention not amended Mason's draft, his constitution also might have ended slavery, a result he would have applauded. Mason regarded slavery as an evil that weakened society; he urged Virginia to stop importing slaves and blamed England for extending the slave trade. Mason called for gradual emancipation and for educating the freed people so they could become independent members of society.

Devoted Republican. Having launched an era of constitution writing, Mason retired to his family and plantation. In 1780 Mason married Sarah Brent, a fifty-year old spinster. In 1785 he participated in the Mount Vernon conference, and though he was chosen as a delegate to the Annapolis conference the next year, he did not go. He was elected to the legislature in 1785, over his objections, and in 1787 he represented Virginia in the Constitutional Convention at Philadelphia. Mason was an active delegate, and years later Madison recalled Mason at Philadelphia as a "powerful Reasoner, a profound Statesman and a devoted Republican." At the end, though, Mason refused to sign the constitution because it lacked a Bill of Rights and permitted the slave trade to continue until 1808. He left Philadelphia, Madison said, "in a very ill humor," returning home to oppose ratification. Mason failed to prevent his state from ratifying, but his opposition pushed Madison and the Federalists to propose a Bill of Rights.

Retirement. Mason had a profound influence on the public affairs of his day, and Virginia's Declaration of Rights that he drafted continues to be the basis for written constitutional guarantees of liberty. Though Mason left home reluctantly, his letters to Washington, Jefferson, and other men gave him great influence until his death on 7 October 1792.

Source:
Helen Hill Miller, *George Mason: Gentleman Revolutionary* (Chapel Hill: University of North Carolina Press, 1975).

THOMAS PAINE

1737-1809
REVOLUTIONARY WRITER

Background. Thomas Paine was born in Thetford, England, on 29 January 1737. The son of a corsetiere, he was apprenticed to his father for three years before running away at age 16 to sail on a British privateer in the Seven Years' War. Returning to London, he worked as a corsetiere, held a minor government post, and taught school briefly before securing a post as an excise officer. His first marriage ended with his wife's death; a second marriage ended in separation. Paine's wages as an excise officer were too low to support his family; the family shop barely kept them alive. At the request of other excise officers, Paine drew up a memorial urging Parliament to raise their wages, presenting it in 1773. Parliament was not persuaded, and Paine's superiors fired him. Paine had to sell the shop to escape imprisonment for debt.

Flight to America. He boldly called on Benjamin Franklin, who thought Paine might make a good "clerk, or assistant tutor in a school, or assistant surveyor" in Philadelphia. With this reference Paine landed in America in November 1774, determined to start his life anew. He found work with printer Robert Aitken, publisher of the *Pennsylvania Magazine,* which had six hundred subscribers. Within a few months Paine's vigorous literary style had attracted more readers, and circulation increased to more than fifteen hundred. Paine's essays called for an end not only to the slave trade but also to slavery, and he attacked British colonial policies both in America and in India. Encouraged by Franklin and Benjamin Rush to write a history of the dispute between England and her American colonies, Paine published *Common Sense,* on 10 January 1776.

Common Sense. More than one-half million copies of *Common Sense* circulated in the colonies, and long excerpts appeared in newspapers and magazines. The real importance of *Common Sense* lay not so much in its vigorous call for independence as in its call for leveling the old order and starting anew. Most Americans believed that governments evolved naturally from society, and the English government, for example, reflected the country's social organization. This, Paine said, was wrong. Society and government were two different things. "Society in every state is a blessing; but government, even in its best state, is but a necessary evil; in its worst state an intolerable one.... Government, like dress, is the badge of lost innocence; the palaces of kings are built upon the ruins of the bowers of paradise." Paine called for independence, but he also urged Americans to reject the British model of government, which gave too much power to the king and the aristocrats.

Model Governments. The whole premise of a balanced constitution, Paine said, was wrong. The British constitution worked only because the Commons were able to check the aristocrats and the king; if there were no king or aristocrats, it would be unnecessary to check the Commons. Americans should construct new governments that were not modeled on the British constitution: their governments should have a single-house legislature, and instead of having governors who could become tyrants, it should have the executive as a committee chosen by the legislature for a limited term. Pennsylvania adopted a government on Paine's model. *Common Sense* had a profound influence on American opinion, and it helped convince Americans that they were not simply fighting for home rule or for their rights as English people. Instead they were fighting for essential human rights that could only come with independence. The Americans could make a break with the past, and with the British empire, and they should do it immediately.

The Crisis. Paine published *Common Sense* at a highpoint of the American campaign. Though independence had not been declared, Washington had forced the British to evacuate Boston; royal authority was collapsing in all the American colonies; and an army led by Benedict Arnold was laying siege to Quebec. But by the end of 1776 the situation had changed. The Canadian expedition had failed; the British had captured New York; and Washington's army was driven through New Jersey and into Pennsylvania. In December 1776 the British fleet threatened Philadelphia, and Congress fled to Baltimore. Paine, enlisted in a Pennsylvania regiment, accompanying Washington's retreating army in what seemed to be the final moments of the struggle, sat by the campfire and wrote a new pamphlet addressed to the problems of this moment. On Christmas Eve, Washington had his troops assemble to listen to the first four essays of Paine's new pamphlet, *The American Crisis* (1776–1777), before they were rowed across the Delaware to surprise the British at Trenton.

The Times that Try Men's Souls. "These are the times that try men's souls," Paine began. "The summer soldier and the sunshine patriot will, in this crisis, shrink from the service of their country; but he that stands it now, deserves the love and thanks of man and woman. Tyranny, like hell, is not easily conquered; ... the harder the conflict, the more glorious the triumph. What we obtain too cheap, we esteem too lightly: it is dearness only that gives everything its value.... [I]t would be strange indeed if so celestial an article as FREEDOM should not be highly rated." Paine's pamphlet rallied Washington's troops, whose surprise victories at Trenton and Princeton in turn rallied public opinion. Paine would publish fourteen *Crisis* essays over the next seven years, all designed to strengthen American resolve and to comment on specific issues of a moment. His final number, published on the eighth anniversary of the battle of Lexington, 19 April 1783, declared that "'The times that tried mens souls,' are over—and the greatest and completest revolution the world ever knew, gloriously and happily accomplished." Paine urged the American people to adopt a stronger central government that could protect their liberty against a hostile world.

After the Revolution. During the war Paine served in a number of political positions, as secretary to Congress's Committee on Foreign Affairs, and as clerk of the Pennsylvania assembly. As clerk, in 1780 Paine drafted the preamble to Pennsylvania's law abolishing slavery, a cause he had advocated in his first months in America. Paine continued to write on political questions, defending the Bank of North America and criticizing the citizens of Rhode Island for scuttling the proposed five percent impost duty. Paine was committed to the independence of America, and he had little patience with local political grievances that he felt detracted from American unity and strength. Paine also turned more attention to scientific matters, trying to develop a smokeless candle and inventing an iron bridge that would not require piers to support its span. To perfect the bridge Paine sailed for Europe in April 1787. He expected to be gone for about one year, but he would not return to America until 1802. After visiting his mother and British Whigs Edmund Burke and Charles Fox, Paine was invited by the Marquis de Lafayette to visit France. Paine met with Thomas Jefferson, American minister to France, and Lafayette, offering advice on a new constitution for France, and Paine helped draft France's Declaration of the Rights of Man and of the Citizen. When the Bastille fell in 1789, Lafayette entrusted its key to Paine, who was to present it to George Washington (the key now hangs at Mount Vernon).

Paine and Burke. On a visit to London in 1790 Paine was stunned to read Edmund Burke's speech denouncing the French Revolution. Burke, who had warmly and bravely supported the American cause, believed that the French Revolution was a mistake. Governments, Burke believed, evolved from the social customs and traditions of a people. Without a government to restrain men from injuring one another, the French would collapse into anarchy and ultimately tyranny. Paine was outraged at Burke's attack, and later in the year, when Burke published his *Reflections on the French Revolution* (1790), Paine responded with a vigorous defense, *Rights of Man* (1791–1792). Paine not only vindicated the French Revolution but also argued for the power of all people to construct whatever kind of government they chose. This was the fundamental premise of *Common Sense,* and Paine held true to the revolutionary cause. Paine won the long-term historical argument: men and women can form their own governments. But for France, Burke was a far more able prophet since the French Revolution became a bloody reign of anarchy followed by military dictatorship.

Arrest. Paine was charged with seditious libel in England, and he fled to France, where he was elected to the French Convention. He arrived in September 1792, days before the Convention proclaimed France a republic. Paine welcomed this, but he opposed the execution of Louis XVI, fearing it would give England a pretext to declare war on France. When the radical Jacobins overthrew Paine's more moderate faction, he stopped attending the Convention, and he was arrested on 18 December 1793. He narrowly escaped the guillotine and nearly died in prison. The American minister to France, James Monroe, secured Paine's release in November 1794.

Final Pamphlets. Paine recovered from his imprisonment at Monroe's home, writing two more pamphlets: *The Age of Reason* (1794–1795), an attack on organized religion, and *Agrarian Justice* (1797), a call for the redistribution of wealth. *The Age of Reason* brought down on Paine the charge of atheism as he tried to demonstrate that the Bible was not divinely inspired but was the work of men intent on maintaining power. He tried to demolish the institutional church, which he felt had conspired with wealth and privilege to oppress humankind. The attack on religion alienated Paine from many Americans, including Samuel Adams, who supported his political views. He also criticized Presidents Washington and Adams for their pro-British and anti-French policies, which led to his further estrangement from many Americans. President Thomas Jefferson invited Paine to return to America in 1802, and Paine spent his last years on a farm in New Rochelle, New York. Paine died on 8 June 1809. Two decades later English journalist William Cobbett had Paine's body exhumed, to be reburied in England. Cobbett's plans for a suitable memorial to Paine fell through, and Paine's body disappeared.

Sources:

Bernard Bailyn, *Faces of Revolution: Personalities and Themes in the Struggle for American Independence* (New York: Vintage, 1992);

Philip S. Foner, editor, *The Complete Writings of Thomas Paine,* 2 volumes (New York: Citadel Press, 1945).

PUBLICATIONS

John Adams, *Thoughts on Government* (Philadelphia: Printed by John Dunlap, 1776)—in response to Thomas Paine's call for a single-house legislature, Adams calls for balanced government to protect different social classes;

Francis Bernard, *Select Letters on the Trade and Government of America; and the Principles of Law and Polity, Applied to the American Colonies* (London: Printed for T. Payne, 1774)—the former royal governor of Massachusetts urges Britain to take more responsibility for governing the American colonies;

Daniel Dulany, *Considerations on the Propriety of Imposing Taxes in the British Colonies, for the Purpose of Raising a Revenue, by Act of Parliament* (Annapolis, Md.: Printed & sold by Jonas Green, 1765);

William Hicks, *The Nature and Extent of Parliamentary Power Considered* (Philadelphia, 1768)—Hicks argues that the colonists had not delegated taxing power to Parliament;

Thomas Hutchinson, *Copy of Letters sent to Great-Britain, by His Excellency Thomas Hutchinson, . . . and Several Other Persons . . .* (Boston: Printed by Edes & Gill, 1773)—letters from Hutchinson, Andrew Oliver, and others to Thomas Whately urging a stronger hand against the colonists in the 1760s. The missives were sent to the Massachusetts assembly by Benjamin Franklin in December 1772, resulting in the legislature demanding Hutchinson's removal and Franklin being denounced in the Privy Council;

Hutchinson, *The Speeches of His Excellency Governor Hutchinson, to the General Assembly . . . with the Answers of His Majesty's Council and the House of Representatives* (Boston: Printed by Edes & Gill, 1773)—Hutchinson set out his views on constitutional order in a speech to the assembly on 6 January 1773. Samuel Adams and Joseph Hawley drafted a reply corrected by John Adams. Hutchinson retorted in one of the most significant constitutional debates before 1776;

Thomas Jefferson, *A Summary View of the Rights of British America* (Williamsburg, Va.: Printed for Clementina Rind, 1774)—in these instructions to Virginia's delegates to the First Continental Congress, Jefferson argued that Parliament and the king had little or no authority in the colonies;

Thomas Paine, *Common Sense* (Philadelphia: Printed & sold by R. Bell, 1776)—a scathing attack on royal power and the English constitution;

Allan Ramsay, *Thoughts on the Origin and Nature of Government. Occasioned by the Late Dispute between Great Britain and her American Colonies. Written in the Year 1766* (London: Printed for T. Becket, 1769)—an argument against the colonies' right not to be taxed because men gave up natural rights when they entered a state of society;

James Wilson, *Considerations on the Nature and Extent of the Legislative Authority of the British Parliament* (Philadelphia: Printed & sold by William & Thomas Bradford, 1774)—Wilson argued that the colonies owed loyalty to the king, but not to Parliament.

LAW AND JUSTICE

by ELI C. BORTMAN

CONTENTS

Sidebars and tables are listed in italics.

IMPORTANT EVENTS OF 1754-1783

1754	June	The Albany Congress proposes a plan of colonial union, but not one provincial assembly approves it.
1755	30 Nov.	Acadian refugees expelled from Nova Scotia by the British begin to arrive in Maryland.
1756	•	Peter Oliver receives an appointment as a justice of the superior court in Massachusetts.
1757	•	John Dickinson is admitted to the bar after completing his studies at the Inns of Court in London.
1758	•	Virginia passes the Twopenny Act, a temporary measure meant to regulate tobacco prices.
1759	•	Peter Oliver becomes a member of the governor's council in Massachusetts.
1760	•	Patrick Henry is admitted to the bar in Virginia.
1761	Feb.	James Otis argues in a Massachusetts court against the issuance of writs of assistance.
1762	•	John Dickinson is elected to the Pennsylvania assembly.
1763	Dec.	In the Parson's Cause, Patrick Henry argues that the King had no legal right to disallow the Twopenny Act.
1764	•	Parliament passes the Sugar Act.

1765

- Riots erupt in Boston and elsewhere following Parliament's passage of the Stamp Act and Mutiny or Quartering Act.

7–25 Oct. Twenty-eight delegates from nine colonies attend the Stamp Act Congress held at City Hall in New York City. The congress adopts the Declaration of Rights and Grievances, a series of resolutions that protest the duties imposed by the Stamp Act and implement a policy of nonimportation of British goods until the statute is repealed.

1766

Mar. Parliament repeals the Stamp Act but at the same time passes the Declaratory Act, asserting its power to tax the colonies.

1767

- Parliament passes the Townshend duties, imposing taxes on a wide range of imports including tea.

- Thomas Jefferson is admitted to the bar in Virginia.

Dec. "Letters from a Pennsylvania Farmer" begin to appear in colonial newspapers.

1768

June Customs officials impound John Hancock's ship *Liberty,* and sell its cargo.

Oct. At the request of the Massachusetts royal governor, British troops arrive in Boston in order to quell civil disturbances.

1769

Mar. Three hundred Philadelphia merchants agree to boycott all British goods until the Townshend duties are repealed.

1770

5 Mar. In what becomes known as the Boston Massacre, British troops fire on a crowd, killing five colonists.

Oct. The Boston Massacre trials occur; all but two British soldiers are acquitted of manslaughter.

1771

- Parliament decides to pay the salaries of Massachusetts judges with royal and not colonial funds.

1772

- William Cushing joins the Massachusetts Supreme Court and fills the vacancy left by his father.

1773

27 Apr. Parliament passes the Tea Act, giving the near-bankrupt East India Company a monopoly on the tea trade to America.

16 Dec. In the Boston Tea Party colonists disguised as Indians board three merchant vessels and dump 342 chests of tea into Boston Harbor.

1774

May Parliament passes the Coercive Acts, four punitive measures against Massachusetts for the Boston Tea Party. Meanwhile the Virginia assembly calls for a continental congress to "consult upon the present unpleasant state of the colonies."

Sept. The First Continental Congress meets in Philadelphia.

1775

23 Mar. In an address to the second Virginia convention in Richmond, Patrick Henry condemns arbitrary British rule and closes with "Give me liberty or give me death."

1776

Jan. Thomas Paine publishes *Common Sense,* a pamphlet urging colonial separation from Great Britain.

4 July The Declaration of Independence is signed by the Second Continental Congress.

1777

• William Cushing becomes chief justice of the superior court in Massachusetts after John Adams resigns from that post.

15 Nov. The Continental Congress adopts the Articles of Confederation, but the states do not complete ratifying them for four more years.

1778

6 Feb. France recognizes American independence and signs a treaty of alliance and commerce with the United States.

4 May Congress ratifies the treaty with France.

June Congress rejects British peace offers.

1779

21 June Spain declares war on Britain, but as an ally of France, not the United States.

1780

• Massachusetts adopts a constitution and a bill of rights.

1781

1 Mar.   Pennsylvania becomes the first state to gradually abolish slavery by declaring that any black child born after 1780 is free once he or she reaches the age of twenty-eight.

1 Mar.   Maryland is the last state to ratify the Articles of Confederation.

1782

• At the urging of Thomas Jefferson, the Virginia legislature passes an emancipation bill, making it lawful for any man "by last will and testament or other instrument in writing sealed and witnessed, to emancipate and set free his slaves."

1783

• The Massachusetts supreme court finds that the state constitution of 1780 legally nullified slavery by declaring all men "born free and equal."

• The slave trade is outlawed in Maryland.

A drawing by Richard Brunton of the infamous American prisoner of war camp
(Connecticut Historical Society, Hartford)

OVERVIEW

Taxing the Colonies. The regulation of trade and duties on imports were interlocking elements of British imperial structure. Trade between colonial merchants and non-British ports, both in Europe and in the West Indies, had grown to scandalous levels during the French and Indian War. The colonists not only traded with Britain's enemies but also generally avoided the payment of import duties. While the end of the war eliminated one type of illegal behavior, ship owners and merchants had become accustomed to the evasion of the revenue laws. The period from 1759 to 1776 was marked by a series of efforts by Great Britain to tighten the enforcement of the trade laws and to increase the collection of revenue. Each of these efforts was met with resistance that soon became cloaked in terms such as "liberty" and "rights of English subjects." William Pitt's circular letter in 1760, urging the colonial governors to halt imports from the French West Indies; the expansion of the use of writs of assistance in 1761 to search for smuggled goods; and the Sugar Act of 1763 were all consistent with the mercantile theory that trade bound the empire together and that the revenue from this trade financed the empire's government and defense.

The Stamp Act. The passage of the Stamp Act in 1765 and the colonial reaction to that act marked the turning point in Parliament's approach to taxation and in the colonists' relationship to the mother country. Prior to the Stamp tax the colonial assemblies levied taxes for the support of the colonial governments. The British government raised revenue only indirectly, from duties on imports and exports paid by merchants to the customs collector and then passed along to the ultimate consumer in the prices of the goods subjected to these duties. The Stamp duty was Parliament's first attempt to levy a direct tax on the colonists. Parliament, in debating the passage of the Stamp tax, focused on the need to raise revenue to help pay for the recent war against France and did not appreciate the importance that the colonists placed on this difference between direct and indirect taxes. The colonists saw the tax as extremely significant—not so much for the revenue it would produce but for the precedent it would establish—as Parliament's first exercise of the power of taxation in the colonies.

Fallout. The colonial assemblies immediately drafted resolutions and petitions asking for the repeal of the Stamp Act; the petitions were ignored. Efforts to boycott British goods began to develop, and resistance soon became more forceful. In August the first riots occurred as tax collectors were threatened and, in some cases, forced to resign. The Stamp Act Congress met in New York in October, and the delegates drafted another petition to the King. It was the breadth of the violent resistance to the Act, however, and not the petitions, that persuaded Parliament to repeal the tax. The repeal of the Stamp Act increased the colonists' confidence in their own power. Parliament had a different view—at the same time it repealed the Stamp Act, Parliament passed the Declaratory Act, asserting its authority to levy taxes on the colonists.

The Townshend Duties. Parliament returned to the approach of the indirect tax as a means to raise revenue from the colonies. The Townshend duties were heavier than earlier duties and covered a wide range of goods. The revenue provisions were accompanied by an increased level of administrative structure and additional courts in which trade-related disputes could be resolved. The colonists reacted with renewed boycotts of British goods. Merchants in nearly all the colonies agreed not to import British goods. The boycotts were fairly effective and resulted in enormous decreases in British exports to the colonies. Parliament reacted to pressure from British merchants and in 1770 repealed all the Townshend duties except the one on tea.

The Boston Massacre. Occasional outbursts of violence in Boston, sometimes related to mob efforts to enforce the boycotts of imports, led the colonial governor to ask that British troops be sent to preserve the peace. The troops arrived in 1768 and were as much a source of irritation as they were keepers of the peace. A confrontation with an unruly crowd provoked the Boston Massacre in 1770.

Communication. Each effort by Great Britain to exercise more control over the colonies or to raise more revenue was met by resistance. Not only was there resistance in each colony, but there was also a developing pattern of communication among the colonies to coordinate their efforts. The Stamp Act Congress, John Dickinson's "Letters from a Pennsylvania Farmer," the circular letter from Samuel Adams in 1768, the missives among the colonial merchants leading to the nonimportation agreements, the formation of committees of correspondence, and the two continental congresses reflected a natural progression of communication and cooperation that led the colonies to see the need for uniting.

Legal Profession. The enormous growth of commerce during this period fueled the development of the cities and towns as well as the westward expansion of the frontier. Society was becoming more complex, creating the need for competent lawyers. Leaders of the profession urged that the study of law become more formalized. Some prospective lawyers served as apprentices to established lawyers; some studied at the Inns of Court in London; and a few read law on their own. Whether any of these routes led to a better education than another was the subject of ongoing debate. Many prominent lawyers also urged that the requirements for admission to the bar become more rigorous. In several colonies the courts be-

gan to require some type of examination, usually in the form of interviews with lawyers already admitted to practice, before a new lawyer could appear in that court.

Revisions. Prior to the Revolution each of the provincial governments derived their powers from royal charters. In theory these governments continued in existence until, at the earliest, the formal declaration of independence in July 1776. However, many provincial governments were in disarray or totally non-functioning even before that date. Recognizing the deterioration of the governmental structure and preparing for inevitable independence, the Second Continental Congress passed a resolution on 15 May 1776 to recommend "to the respective assemblies and conventions of the United Colonies, where no government sufficient to the exigencies of their affairs have been hitherto established," that they adopt new governments. Some colonies simply carried forward their provincial charters, changing as little as they needed in order to reflect the break with Britain. Other colonies formed conventions to draft new constitutions. Some, such as Virginia, embarked on comprehensive reviews and revisions of their entire bodies of laws.

TOPICS IN THE NEWS

THE BOSTON MASSACRE TRIALS

Civil Disorder. Law and order deteriorated in Boston in the late 1760s as resistance to British rule developed into mob rule. In 1765, as part of the protest against the Stamp tax, a mob attacked the newly appointed tax collector, Andrew Oliver, brother of superior court justice Peter Oliver, and invaded and ransacked his house. He resigned his office the next day. Merchants' groups in several colonies agreed that boycotting British goods might be an effective form of protest, and they resolved not to import or sell British goods. In Boston, mob action enforced these promises of nonimportation and also thwarted efforts by the customs authorities to enforce the customs laws. Gov. Francis Bernard petitioned for British troops to help maintain a civil order. His pleas were answered in September 1768 when six hundred British troops landed in Boston.

Wintery Night. The presence of the troops seemed to have no effect in reducing the mob rule and the attacks upon the tax collectors, but their presence increased tensions between citizens and government. On

5 March 1770 a crowd confronted a squad of eight British soldiers. The soldiers were taunted by schoolboys throwing snowballs and felt threatened by a mob of men carrying clubs. Finally the eight soldiers loaded their muskets and formed a single line facing the crowd. Their commander, Capt. Thomas Preston, stood in front of his soldiers, urging the crowd to disperse, but to no avail. Someone yelled "Fire!" and shots rang out. The soldiers and the mob battled briefly, and when the fighting ceased, five civilians were dead. Captain Preston and the eight soldiers were arrested that night.

Getting Ready. Preparations for the trial began almost immediately. Witnesses were summoned to appear before justices of the peace to give depositions, and the military collected statements from more than ninety witnesses as well. The Sons of Liberty raised funds to help prosecute the soldiers and urged the hiring of a strong prosecutor to press the criminal case. They also tried to ensure that the defense be well represented too, so no one would suggest (after the expected convictions) that the proceedings had not been fair. John Adams was asked to represent Preston. Ad-

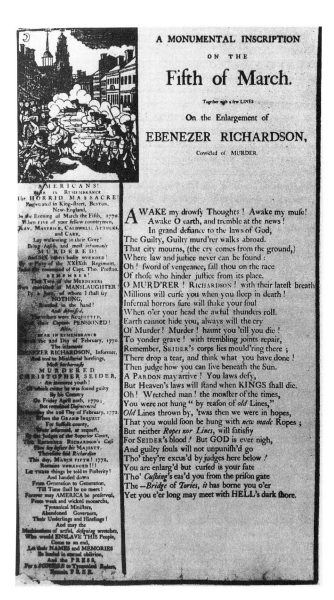

A broadside on the Boston Massacre (Massachusetts Historical Society, Boston)

ams took the captain's case because he believed the defendant was entitled to counsel and it was his obligation as a member of the bar to provide that service. He also agreed to defend the soldiers.

Defense Counsel. Adams, in preparing for the trials (the captain would be tried separately from the soldiers) faced a problem of tactics, which today would be considered one of professional ethics. Captain Preston had not actually killed anyone. He was accused of ordering his men to fire without sufficient provocation. The best defense for him was to deny that he had given the order to fire. The men, on the other hand, would have to argue that they fired because the captain had ordered them to do so, and had they disobeyed they would have been subject to a military punishment. This conflict between the interests of the two sets of defendants would in present-day courts prevent Adams from representing both the captain and the sol-

diers. However, the rules were not as strict at that time, and Adams did not step down.

Preston. Captain Preston's trial took five days, an unusually long time for a criminal trial in that era. The prosecution called more than twenty witnesses, who described the scene leading up to the shooting. Little by little they painted a picture of noise, confusion, and threats, and there were conflicting stories about whether Preston had ordered the men to fire. Some witnesses said they had heard him yell "Fire!" Others testified that church bells were ringing and some of his words, such as "Hold your . . ." might have been drowned out. Other witnesses said that someone in the crowd had yelled "Fire!" The cross-examination of these witnesses and the testimony of the twenty-two defense witnesses merely added to the uncertainty. The jury took only three hours to reach a verdict of not guilty.

The Soldiers. The eight redcoats went to trial a month later. No one contested the fact that five civilians were dead. The prosecution needed to prove that the eight soldiers were present at the massacre and that each had fired his musket. Then the burden would shift to the defense to prove that the firings were provoked, so that the deaths would be justifiable as self-defense. The testimony of the witnesses was similar to that in Preston's trial. The focus, however, was on the commotion, the taunting, and the apparent threats. Witnesses testified about iceballs and pieces of firewood being thrown at the

DEDICATED PROFESSIONAL

John Adams described how he became the lawyer for the British captain and his soldiers. In his *Autobiography* (1850–1851) he described the street scene immediately after the shooting and his reaction to it and then went on:

The next morning...Mr. Forrest [a Loyalist Boston merchant] came in. . . . With tears streaming from his eyes, he said Captain Preston [is] in prison. He wishes for counsel and can get none. I have waited on Mr. [Josiah] Quincy, who says he will engage if you will give him your assistance: without it positively he will not. . . . I had no hesitation in answering that counsel ought to be the very last thing that an accused person should want in a free country. That the bar ought in my opinion to be independent and impartial at all times and in every circumstance. And that persons whose lives were at stake ought to have the counsel they preferred. . . . [E]very lawyer must hold himself responsible not only to his country, but to the highest and most infallible of all tribunals. . . . He must therefore expect from me no art or address, no sophistry or prevarication in such a cause; nor anything more than fact, evidence and law would justify. . . . [Forrest said he thought Preston was innocent.] I replied that must be ascertained by his trial, and if he thinks he cannot have a fair trial without my assistance, without hesitation he shall have it.

troops. Several witnesses were sure that two of the soldiers had fired their muskets, but there was no testimony from any witness about the other six. The jury obviously thought that the soldiers had been provoked but perhaps should have waited longer before firing. They found the two who had fired guilty of manslaughter instead of murder and the other six not guilty of all charges.

The Sentences. The two soldiers, when they appeared in court for sentencing, claimed "benefit of clergy." This practice dates back to medieval times when a rivalry existed between the royal courts and church courts. A clergyman could not be tried in a civil court for most crimes. To prove his status as clergy, at a time when only clergy were literate, the clergyman had merely to read a passage from the Bible. This entitled him to the benefit of clergy, thereby escaping punishment. In time this practice was extended to all literate defendants and then to anyone who was a first offender. To prevent an offender from claiming the benefit a second time, he was subjected to branding on his thumb, and these two soldiers were so marked.

Public Reaction. The townspeople reacted rather calmly to the not-guilty verdicts. A debate in the newspapers followed, just as today, when litigants and lawyers retry their cases in the press. Adams later wrote that he heard his name "execrated in the most opprobrious terms" whenever he appeared in Boston thereafter. Perhaps it is significant that after a period of five years in which law and order had been displaced by mob rule, there was no violent reaction to the acquittals. The two juries performed their duties and reached unpopular verdicts, but many seemed to recognize that they had, given the evidence, followed their consciences.

Source:
Hiller B. Zobel, *The Boston Massacre* (New York: Norton, 1970).

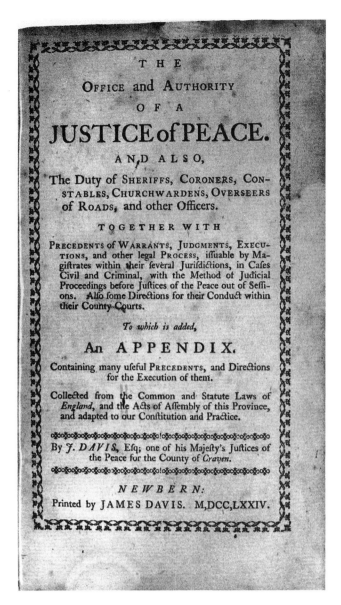

Title page for a popular handbook written in 1774

HOW PEOPLE BECAME LAWYERS

Growth of the Profession. As colonial society developed and commercial activity grew, so too did the need for competent legal counsel. The earliest colonists had brought with them the long-standing English sentiment against lawyers and had tried to do without them. Massachusetts (1641), Virginia (1658), and the Carolinas (1669) enacted statutes that prohibited pleading in court for hire. Gradually, at first, and with increasing momentum by the 1750s, lawyers became seen as a necessary evil. However, untrained or unprincipled practitioners created problems. In North Carolina lawyers were described as "cursed hungry caterpillars [whose fees] eat out the very bowels of our commonwealth." In 1771 John Adams described a tavern keeper who kept two books on a shelf in his tavern so that he could be "a sort of lawyer among [his customers]." In each colony the courts or the legislatures set rules limiting the ability of a lawyer to appear in court unless he had been admitted to practice. The requirements varied from court to court and colony to colony, but each required some form of training followed by an examination or interview administered by members already admitted.

Inns of Court. There were no law schools, so prospective lawyers prepared for the exam in several ways. The Inns of Court were not law schools. They are best described as eating and living clubs clustered around the courthouses in London. Lawyers lived there, and students would read law books, observe courtroom activities, and simply soak up the atmosphere of the British legal system. Since there was no formal aspect to the educational process, the degree of training varied enormously. Some who studied at the Inns of Court obviously benefited from their experience. John Dickinson of Pennsylvania developed an appreciation for the traditions and the orderly processes of the English legal system, evident years later when he wrote the "Letters from a Farmer in Pennsylvania." On the other hand Charles

Carroll of Maryland, who later signed the Declaration of Independence, wrote in 1762 that he found it difficult to study because of "loose and dissolute companions."

Apprenticeship. A clerkship, or apprenticeship, was the most frequently used avenue to the bar and yet was also the means most often criticized. The apprentice paid a fee to an established attorney in exchange for which the attorney trained the apprentice. In theory the apprentice was to study law in the office of a lawyer, observe court sessions, and perform routine tasks that were part of this training. In many cases these tasks were nothing more than endless copying of legal documents for two or three years. Carroll, after completing his studies in London, became an advocate for the apprenticeship system, pointing out that at least in this manner one might learn the practical side of the law. The more widely held view, however, was that the system did not work well. Adams served as an apprentice to a Massachusetts lawyer and described the study of law to be "a dreary ramble." William Livingstone, who apprenticed in New York, complained that a law clerk "trifled away the bloom of his age . . . in a servile drudgery nothing to the purpose, and fit only for a slave." Thomas Jefferson spent two years as a clerk for George Wythe, who later, in 1779, became the first professor of law at an American college. Though Jefferson admired Wythe and spent these years in intense and fruitful study, he later wrote that an apprentice was generally obligated to provide much more service to his teacher than the education was worth.

Reading the Law. A third method of study was the self-directed reading of law. Patrick Henry read Sir Edward Coke's *Institutes* (1628–1644) and the Virginia statutes for six weeks before being examined for admission to the bar. From his argument in the Parson's Cause, it is clear that he had also read some of the writings about natural law and the concept of a conditional covenant between a sovereign and the people. Alexander Hamilton read law books on his own and recorded in his journal that he had read not only the usual books, including Sir William Blackstone's *Commentaries on the Laws of England* (1765–1769) but also works by John Locke and others on natural law. Although as a student he complained, "I do wish the devil had old Coke, for I am sure I never was so tired of an old dull scoundrel in my life," Years later Jefferson acknowledged that Coke's *Institutes* "was the universal elementary book of law students."

Protecting the Public. Limitations on admission to practice protected not only the public but also the practitioners. Protecting the public was not easy because in most colonies admission to the bar was required only to appear in a particular court; it was not required for someone to handle other legal matters. Anyone, wrote Adams in 1759, including "deputy sheriffs, pettifoggers and even constables who filled all the writs upon bonds, promissory notes, and accounts, received the fees set for lawyers, and stirred up many unnecessary suits." Gradu-

ally the colonies developed rules and requirements for admission to appear in court. The Virginia assembly passed a law in 1748 authorizing its court to control admission to the bar. As a way of protecting the public, a Virginia lawyer could charge no more than five pounds for arguing a case in court. New Jersey's supreme court in 1755 appointed twelve sergeants at law, a ranking higher than the ordinary counselors. The sergeants had the power and duty to conduct examinations for bar admission. Similar arrangements came into being in most of the other colonies in the mid 1700s.

Protecting the Profession. Protection of the profession seemed to be a more significant role of the bar-admission process. In Rhode Island the members of the bar agreed to a fee structure, including a three-pound minimum for filing the pleadings in a case in the superior court. They also agreed not to defend anyone who was being sued by his lawyer for his fee. In New York City the lawyers who had been admitted to practice in the city's courts agreed in 1756 to take on no clerks, other than their own sons, for the next fourteen years. Perhaps the efforts of the New York bar succeeded too well. Lt. Gov. Cadwallader Colden complained in 1765 that lawyers and judges were too powerful. Their domination was "carried on by the same wicked artifices that the domination of the priests formerly was in the times of ignorance."

Sources:

Laurence Friedman, *A History of American Law* (New York: Simon & Schuster, 1985);

Bernard Schwartz, *Thomas Jefferson and* Bolling v. Bolling: *Law and the Legal Profession in Pre-Revolutionary America* (San Marino, Cal.: Huntington Library 1997).

THE PARSON'S CAUSE

Privy Council. The power of the Privy Council to approve or disapprove colonial legislation was an accepted notion from the days of the first English settlement. Any law passed by a colonial legislature needed the assent of the royal governor and the approval of the Privy Council before it could take effect. However, as the colonists began to challenge England's role in the control of purely local matters, this constitutional concept was called into question. One 1763 case, which would otherwise have been merely an obscure lawsuit by a clergyman for back pay, highlighted this challenge and also launched Patrick Henry's public career.

The Twopenny Acts. In 1696 the Virginia assembly had set the salary of the clergy of the established church at sixteen thousand pounds of tobacco per year. Tobacco was a commodity of relatively stable value and was a medium of exchange in commerce. Virginia planters sold tobacco through agents in England and bought manufactured goods with prices cast in terms of pounds of tobacco. It was legal tender for both public and private debts. The practice of paying clergy in tobacco continued until 1753, when the failure of the crop in two Virginia

Tobacco air-curing in a barn

counties made such payment difficult. In that year and again in 1755 the assembly allowed all debts in those counties to be paid in paper money instead of in tobacco at the rate of two pence per pound of tobacco. In 1758 the same law was extended to the entire province.

Outcry. The clergy were troubled and appealed to the bishop of London, asking him to petition the Privy Council to disapprove the 1758 act. They pointed out that they were continually in debt because they collected their salaries only after the end of their year of work. They ordinarily purchased all their necessities of life on credit and paid up in tobacco once a year. Now they would not be able to tender tobacco but would have to pay in locally issued paper money, which was subject to an unfavorable exchange rate overseas and was depreciating in value. Even worse, they pointed out, in 1758 tobacco was selling at about six pence per pound, so by getting paid at the rate of two pence per pound the clergy suffered an immediate reduction in income of two-thirds. In August 1759 the Privy Council repealed the 1758 act and disallowed the 1753 and 1755 statutes.

Maury. In 1762 James Maury, pastor of Fredricksville Parish in Hanover County, filed suit for his back pay. The county court ruled that, based on the Privy Council's disallowance, the act that allowed his parish to pay him in money instead of in tobacco was void, beyond the competence of the assembly to enact. All that remained was for a jury to determine the damages to which he was entitled. Maury's lawyer presented two witnesses, tobacco dealers who testified that the price of tobacco in 1759, the year of the dispute, was six pence per pound as opposed to the two pence provided by statute. The lawyer who had represented the parish in the first part of the case had withdrawn from the case and was replaced by Patrick Henry, who was at the time an unknown country lawyer.

Henry's Argument. Henry argued to the jury about natural rights and said that there was a conditional covenant between the King and his subjects. He told the jury that the 1758 act was a good law, enacted by the provincial assembly for a valid purpose. The compact between the king and the people, providing protection in exchange for obedience, did not allow such a law to be annulled. In fact, Henry said that the King, by annulling such an act "from being the Father of his people degenerated into a Tyrant, and forfeits all right to his subjects' Obedience . . . ." Henry went on to attack the clergy in general and Maury in particular in an inflammatory appeal to anticlerical prejudice. Clergymen were "rapacious harpies who would snatch from the hearth of their honest parishioner his last hoe-cake, from the widow and her orphan children their last milch cow, the last blanket, nay, the last blanket from the lying-in woman." Then tying together the two threads of his argument, he urged the jurors to "make such an example of the plaintiff, as might hereafter be a warning . . . not to dispute the validity of such laws, authenticated by the only authority which . . . would give force to laws for the government of the colony." Henry spoke for more than an hour. The jury retired and returned almost immediately with a verdict for the plaintiff of one penny; at that moment Henry became a leader in the struggle that led to the Revolution.

Sources:

Richard R. Beeman, *Patrick Henry: A Biography* (New York: McGraw-Hill, 1974);

Lawrence Henry Gipson, *The Coming of the Revolution, 1763–1775* (New York: Harper, 1954).

SLAVERY

Before the Revolution. Patrick Henry in 1773 admitted that he was baffled that slavery and religion could co-exist since Christianity's "chief excellence consists in sof-

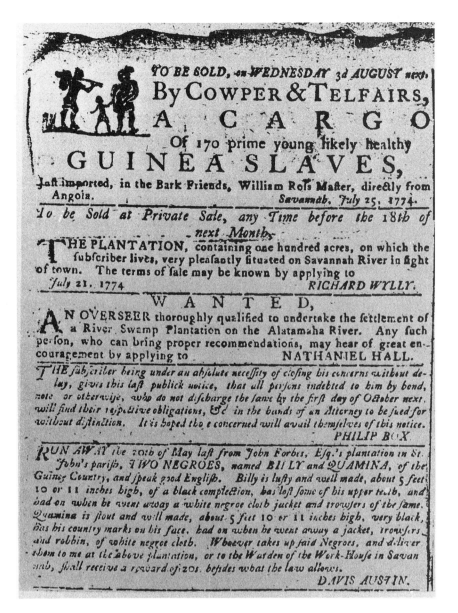

A Georgia handbill announcing the arrival of African slaves (Library of Congress)

tening the human heart, in cherishing and improving its finer feelings . . . ." He also wondered how in Virginia, "a country above all other fond of liberty," men could maintain an institution "as repugnant to humanity as it is inconsistent with the Bible and destructive to liberty." Yet he owned slaves, saying "I am drawn along by the general inconvenience of living without them, I will not, I cannot justify it." His proposed solution was simply the hope for some eventual emancipation. "Let us transmit to our descendants together with our slaves, a pity for their unhappy lot and an abhorrence for slavery."

Jefferson. Thomas Jefferson, also a slave owner, argued a case in a Virginia court in 1770 on behalf of a mulatto whose mother, at the time he was born, was bound in indentured service for a period of years. Jefferson argued that while the mother might still be subject to the indenture, the son should be free. "All men are born free

. . . with a right to his own person . . . . This is what is called personal liberty, and is given him by the author of nature . . . ." His argument failed in that slave-owning society, but his words were a preview of what he would write six years later in the Declaration of Independence.

Somersett's Case. A Virginia slave, James Somersett, was taken to England. When his owner tried to send him to Jamaica, Somersett took his case to court in 1772. Lord Chief Justice William Mansfield ruled that slavery could not exist without positive legislative enactments, and since Parliament had never created the institution, slavery did not exist in England. Hence, Somersett and any slave who set foot in England were free. While this was an important court decision, it seemed to be ignored in America.

Second Continental Congress. In the beginning of 1776 the Second Continental Congress began to discuss independence and urged the colonial assemblies to establish independent governments. As the assemblies and conventions prepared declarations of rights that might serve as the basis for new forms of government, they had difficult balancing acts to perform. They had to articulate a statement about freedom in a way that would stimulate revolutionary fervor yet not amount to abolition of slavery. The Virginia convention considered a resolution that "all men are born equally free and independent," to be too broad. They finally settled on "all men are by nature equally free and independent," and they enjoy their various rights "when they enter into a state of society." The delegates considered their slaves not part of society and thereby excluded from the declaration.

The New States. As the colonies declared independence they adopted constitutions and bills of rights. In many of the constitutional conventions, the delegates discussed the issue of slavery, but not one expressly abolished the institution in its constitution. (The 1777 constitution of Vermont had an abolition clause, but the region did not officially become a state until 1791.) Delaware's constitution prohibited the importation of slaves, and Virginia did the same by statute in 1778. Pennsylvania's assembly passed a statute in 1780 that provided for gradual abolition—any child born to a slave mother after 1780 would be free once he or she reached age twenty-eight. The Massachusetts House of Representatives in 1777 considered a bill that would abolish slavery, but decided not to act on it for fear of offending the Southern colonies. Three years later, however, Massachusetts adopted a bill of rights as part of its constitution that specified that "all men are born free and equal." In a 1783 superior court case involving a fugitive slave, Chief Justice William Cushing stated that this language had abolished slavery in Massachusetts. Jefferson drafted a plan (which was never formally submitted for legislative action) for the emancipation of all Virginia's slaves. He proposed removing them to some undetermined wilderness area, where they would be free and independent, and replacing them with white European immigrants.

Sources:

Willi Paul Adams, *The First American Constitutions* (Chapel Hill: University of North Carolina Press, 1980);

Dumas Malone, *Jefferson the Virginian* (Boston: Little, Brown, 1948);

Henry Mayer, *A Son of Thunder* (New York: Franklin Watts 1986).

TAX AND TARIFF LAWS AS CAUSES OF THE REVOLUTION

Mercantilism. The cry "No taxation without representation" is a shorthand expression that recalls a series of events. To understand the origins and significance of this slogan one has to examine the tax and tariff laws that were essential elements of Britain's mercantile economic theory at the time. Mercantilism was the philosophy which held that colonies existed for the benefit of the mother country. Colonies were sources of raw materials

An American medal bearing the image of William Pitt, considered a champion of colonial rights

for the home country's factories and markets for its manufactured goods. Commercial laws aimed to promote these objectives always. These statutes can be grouped as follows: laws that regulated the nationality of the owners and crew members of all ships entering colonial or home ports; laws governing the destinations of all products being shipped; tariffs, subsidies, and export taxes designed to promote certain industries; and prohibitions of competition in one area with protected industries of another area.

Molasses. Prior to 1733 the colonies had developed a thriving trade with the Caribbean, sending to the islands grain, vegetables, lumber, and fish in exchange for sugar and molasses. The New England colonies in particular were large distillers of rum that was consumed locally and was important as a medium of exchange in the fur and slave trades. Consistent with the mercantile theory, in order to protect the English colonies' sugar growers from competition with the other islands, the Molasses Act of 1733 imposed a six-pence-per-gallon tariff on molasses imported from French, Dutch, or Spanish islands and a one-penny tariff on molasses produced on Britain's sugar islands. A gallon of molasses delivered into the colonies cost about ten pence, including the cost of shipping, so this discriminatory duty on foreign molasses produced an enormous incentive for a distiller to avoid it.

Noncompliance. Parliament enacted the Molasses Act to protect the sugar planters, but they apparently did not realize the effect the tariff would have on the colonial purchasers. English planters supplied only about one-quarter of the molasses needed by the distillers. The high tariff on foreign molasses would have a stifling effect on

Portrait of Charles Townshend, chancellor of the exchequer (Scottish National Portrait Gallery, Edinburgh)

affected and the luxury nature of most of them tempered the resistance. Some colonial merchants and leaders pledged to boycott the products covered by the new duties. For the first time colonists argued that Parliament was depriving them of a fundamental constitutional right. A resolution of the Massachusetts House of Representatives maintained that the colonists had not consented to these taxes and all British subjects enjoyed the essential right to tax themselves.

Stamp Act. In March 1765 Parliament passed the Stamp Act, which imposed a tax on a wide variety of printed material such as newspapers, pamphlets, leases, legal documents, bills of lading and other shipping documents, licenses, and advertising leaflets. Buyers or issuers of taxed paper would pay the tax by buying revenue stamps, ranging from a halfpenny to twenty shillings, which were to be affixed to the paper. The Stamp Act was the first attempt by Parliament to impose an internal tax, as opposed to the previous duties that were all on goods imported into the colonies. In an effort to gain support for the new tax, the law provided that only Americans would be appointed as stamp-tax collecting agents. The wide variety of documents affected meant that the tax would affect all aspects of everyday life. (One writer suggested that coastwide shipping would be hard hit by the Stamp Act because he estimated that each time a ship cleared a port the cost of stamps for its documents would be about two pounds.) In addition, cases involving the enforcement of the act were to be tried in the admiralty courts. Although the new law was not to take effect until November 1765, the colonists' reaction was immediate and violent. In New York and Boston, mobs burned the stamps and ransacked the homes of both the lieutenant governor, Thomas Hutchinson, who supported the

the rum producers and would cause hardship in all the other industries that relied on rum as a medium of exchange. Even the local customs officers came to appreciate this burden because they allowed shippers to declare only a small fraction of their high-tariff cargoes. One can easily imagine the sort of connivance or corruption that was involved as both importers and customs officers shared a common objective of not paying the tariff. In fact the widespread evasion of the molasses tariff makes it clear why smuggling was thought of as a respectable activity.

Sugar Act. At the conclusion of the Seven Years' War, Britain found itself with an enormous national debt. In addition the territory taken from France required a military presence. Parliament determined that the colonies should contribute to the cost of the recent war and the future defense effort. The first step was the Revenue Act of 1764, generally referred to as the Sugar Act. This act reduced the tariff on foreign molasses from six pence per gallon to three pence (Parliament recognizing, at long last, that six pence was too high) but introduced new tariffs on sugar, wine, silk, and linen. Parliament also increased customs efforts to enforce the tariff. Colonial reaction was swift although the limited number of products

COMMON SENSE

First published in Philadelphia in January 1776, *Common Sense* was quickly reprinted and copies circulated throughout the colonies. Paine presented the arguments of natural law in a form that captured the attention of the general population. "Society in every state is a blessing, but Government, even in its best state, is but a necessary evil: in its worst, an intolerable one. Government, like dress, is a badge of lost innocence; the palaces of kings are built on the ruins of the bowers of paradise. . . . [Monarchy is an absurd form of government because one honest man is worth] all the crowned ruffians who ever lived." Paine referred to King George III as "the Royal Brute of Great Britain." He urged that separation from Britain was the only way for the colonies to avoid continued tyranny and commercial exploitation. "Oh, ye that love mankind! Ye that dare oppose not only the tyranny but the tyrant, stand forth."

John Dickinson wrote twelve "Letters from a Farmer in Pennsylvania to the Inhabitants of the British Colonies," which were published in the *Pennsylvania Chronicle,* a Philadelphia newspaper, at the rate of about one a week between December 1767 and February 1768. They were republished in other newspapers shortly after their appearance, and pamphlet versions soon circulated throughout the colonies. The content of each letter was as follows:

1.) 2 December 1767: The first letter opened with the statement: "I am a farmer, settled, after a variety of fortunes, near the banks of the river Delaware, in the province of Pennsylvania." The missive also described some of the author's personal qualities—his education, social status, interest in promoting the cause of liberty, and his view that men had to work to defeat new threats to their liberty.

2.) 7 December 1767: The second letter addressed the Townshend duties and focused on the difference between taxes designed to raise revenue and charges imposed for the regulation of trade. The author conceded that Parliament had the power to regulate trade since that benefited both the colonies and the mother country. If Parliament were to tax the colonists, however, they would be "taking money out of our pockets, without our consent. . . . Our boasted liberty is but a sound and nothing else."

3.) 14 December 1767: Dickinson urged resistance to the unconstitutional imposition of taxes. He argued against violence, however, because violence would lead to retaliation and eventually to separation, which he opposed. The missive described a series of possible, peaceful steps to be taken, such as petitions and nonimportation agreements.

4.) 21 December 1767: The fourth letter was a lengthy dissertation denying that there was any difference between internal taxes and external taxes. Both were unconstitutional according to Dickinson. The fact that the colonists had not previously protested against import duties in the past did not matter because the duties in the past had been regulatory charges, not taxes.

5 & 6.) 28 December 1767 and 4 January 1768: These two letters explained how one should determine whether a particular imposition was an allowable external imposition or an improper internal tax. The author suggested that Parliament's intent in enacting the measure was to be considered. If the intent was to raise revenue, the law was improper; if it was to regulate trade, the law was acceptable.

7.) 11 January 1768: The farmer asserted that the Townshend duties were an effort by a small faction in Parliament to undermine American freedom. Since the colonies were not represented in Parliament, the leadership was tempted to increase its popularity at home by imposing taxes on the colonies. The earlier effort, the stamp tax, had run into enormous opposition in the colonies. Now the leadership had decided to use indirect taxes, which were less understood.

8.) 18 January 1768: The farmer said Parliament's real purpose was described by Prime Minister George Grenville: to ensure "the dependence and obedience of the colonies." Parliament was seeking to have the colonies pay the cost of the recent war with France, yet the acquisition of Canada and Florida was of no benefit to the original colonies. Grenville had told the British public that the colonies were so "rolling in wealth, and...of so bold and republican a spirit that they are aiming at independence. . . . The only way to retain them in obedience is to...draw off part of their riches in taxes."

9.) 25 January 1768: In this letter the farmer argued that Parliament was trying to limit the colonial assemblies' power of taxation and appropriation. For example, the assemblies had no control over the judiciary or the colonial officials other than the ability to refuse to pay their salaries. The Townshend Acts, by providing that the Crown would pay these salaries, eliminated that important power. The statutes would limit the colonial assemblies to the making of laws "to yoke stray cattle."

10.) 31 January 1768: The farmer pointed to Ireland as an example of what would happen to the American colonies. In Ireland the royal government controlled the expenditure of all public money, and most of the civil offices were held by nonresidents.

11.) 8 February 1768: It was important that people appreciate the role of precedent and example with respect to government actions, the farmer argued, and immediate resistance to oppression was necessary. "When an act injurious to freedom has been done once, and the people bear it, the repetition of it is most likely to meet with submission."

12.) 15 February 1768: In conclusion the farmer appealed for unity among the colonies. He urged vigilance and resistance to oppression. If the colonies united and presented their grievances together, they would succeed.

tax policy, and the tax collector. In several cities mob action forced the newly appointed collectors to resign their offices. In Philadelphia a mob was unsuccessful in forcing that city's collector to resign, but he agreed not to sell any stamps until collectors in neighboring colonies did so.

Assemblies React. The colonial assemblies also reacted and debated resolutions to be sent to Parliament in protest. Patrick Henry argued in the Virginia House of Burgesses that the act was unconstitutional with his famous "Caesar had his Brutus" speech. The Massachusetts House of Representatives invited each of the colonies to send representatives to a meeting in New York to consider how the colonies, together, should respond to the act. This meeting, the Stamp Act Congress, was the first such congress initiated by the colonies. After two weeks of debate, the delegates agreed on moderately phrased petitions to Parliament and the king, in which they asked that the Stamp Act be repealed. Parliament reacted to the violence, to the complaints of English merchants about the boycotting of English goods, and to the petitions from the colonial assemblies and also recognized the obvious unenforceability of the Stamp Act. In March 1766 Parliament repealed the Stamp Act and at the same time enacted the Declaratory Act in which Parliament reaffirmed its right to tax the colonies.

Quartering or Mutiny Act. In May 1765 Parliament passed the Quartering or Mutiny Act, which required the colonists to provide barracks or other quarters for British troops stationed in the colonies. The act specified that, depending on the type of building provided, the colonists might also have to furnish the troops with "fire, candles, vinegar and salt, bedding, utensils for addressing their victuals and small beer or cider—or rum." The colonial assemblies were to appropriate money for these obligations in the same manner as they funded other local obligations. Nearly every colony resisted to some extent. Massachusetts refused to appropriate any money. New York appropriated the requested funds, except any money to buy salt, vinegar, cider, and rum. New York's refusal led Parliament to enact the Restraining Act, which would suspend the New York assembly unless that body complied with the Quartering Act provisions. (New York's assembly complied just in time to avoid the suspension.) Pennsylvania and Connecticut complied with the law in every respect, a fact that may have contributed to the change of heart in New York.

Townshend Acts. The 1766 repeal of the Stamp Act alleviated the constitutional crisis in the colonies, but it did nothing to help resolve Britain's financial problem. The continuing need for revenue led Parliament to try again. In June 1767 the chancellor of the exchequer Charles Townshend, who was responsible for financing the government, proposed a series of measures imposing duties, establishing a new customs board, and expanding the admiralty courts. The Townshend Acts imposed duties on a variety of English manufactured goods imported into the colonies—glass, paint, paper, and tea. Townshend said the distinction that American writers made between internal and external taxes was nonsense and that Parliament had the power to impose either type. However, since external taxes provoked less resistance, Parliament should impose these first. Money generated by these duties would pay the cost of colonial civil government, including the new customs administration. Colonial assemblies had traditionally paid for their own civil government and on several occasions withheld salaries of the governor or judges as a way to control these officials. The Townshend revenues were meant to provide a funding source that did not require appropriation by either colonial legislatures or Parliament—the king, through his customs agents, had control over this money.

Customs Commissioners. Another Townshend measure established a board of customs commissioners located in the colonies, replacing the power of the one in London. Since local customs officers were responsible to the board of customs commissioners, Parliament thought that a new body in the colonies would encourage more diligent and honest enforcement of the laws. Boston was selected as its location, and the residents immediately viewed it as another example of British oppression. The board became a focal point for resistance to Parliament's efforts as soon as the commissioners arrived in 1768. One famous incident was the seizure of John Hancock's ship, *Liberty*. However, the stronger enforcement of the customs laws and the abuses that arose from these efforts quickly contributed to the rising sentiment that the colonists' constitutional rights were being violated.

Sources:

O. M. Dickerson, *The Navigation Acts and the American Revolution* (Philadelphia: University of Pennsylvania Press, 1951);

Lawrence Henry Gipson, *The Coming of the Revolution, 1763–1775* (New York: Harper, 1954);

Hiller B. Zobel, *The Boston Massacre* (New York: Norton, 1970).

TAX LAW ENFORCEMENT

Types of Courts. The English legal system had several different sets of courts, each with its own rules of procedure and each dealing with a particular range of subjects. Most civil suits and criminal prosecutions were conducted in common-law courts, with trial by jury. These were familiar to many people in the colonies, as they sat in most places; other more-specialized courts with no juries were less well known. Admiralty courts handled controversies relating to maritime commerce, seamen's wages, and violations of the trade and navigation laws. Until the late 1760s there was only one admiralty court for the American colonies, and it sat in Halifax, Nova Scotia. It had little impact outside the area of international trade or shipboard controversies. However, this court became a focal point in the developing conflict between the colonies and Britain.

An engraving of John Malcolm, a customs official, being lowered by a rope from a window in his house before being tarred and feathered by a Boston mob in January 1774

Sugar Act. The Sugar Act of 1764 was designed to reorganize the colonial empire. The act set new customs procedures for intercolonial shipping, requiring shipping documents and other papers to be issued by customs officers. These documents had long been required in international trade, but for colonial merchants trading with the other colonies, the burdensome new paperwork served as an annoying imposition and, worse, threatened severe penalties for violations of these new laws. The Sugar Act extended the Halifax admiralty court's jurisdiction to any offense charged under the navigation, trade, customs, or revenue laws. This court would also have jurisdiction over all cases arising under the Stamp Act. Halifax was not a convenient location for a court to hear these cases. The Townshend Acts of 1767 added courts in three more cities: Boston, Philadelphia, and Charleston.

Penalties and Rewards. Penalties for violating customs regulations were severe, often including forfeiture of the vessel and the cargo. In admiralty court it was up to the owner of the ship or the property to prove his innocence rather than up to the prosecution to prove his guilt. Once a ship or its cargo (even if unloaded) were seized, the property belonged to the Crown unless the claimant could prove that he had not violated the law. The Sugar Act required the defendant to pay court costs, even if he was found innocent. Along with stiff penalties the Sugar Act offered significant rewards. The person who reported a violation would receive one-third of a seized ship's value; the governor of the colony where the

seizure was made received one-third; and the remaining one-third went to the imperial treasury. The informer's reward, coupled with the difficulty an owner faced in trying to reclaim seized property, amounted to a license for extortion. The 1768 prosecution of John Hancock shows the effect these new duties and trade rules, and the abuses they made possible, had on the colonists.

Liberty. Hancock was a prosperous Boston ship owner and merchant. However, his outspoken public stands against Parliamentary tax policies and the various trade and revenue enactments incurred the wrath of the Massachusetts royal governor. In June 1768 customs officials, responding to a tip that Hancock was violating the Sugar Act, searched his ship, *Liberty.* Charging Hancock with violating the customs laws, authorities seized the ship and sold its cargo, dividing the proceeds among themselves. A criminal prosecution against Hancock in admiralty court followed. He was arrested and required to post an excessive bail. Witnesses against Hancock gave written depositions and were not required to testify in court. One individual was even given a government job while the case was still pending. After the defense had rested its case, new prosecution witnesses testified in the judges' chambers. The case dragged on for five months and was extensively reported in the newspapers. Apparently officials in London were finally embarrassed by the abuse of the judicial process, and the criminal case was abruptly dismissed in March 1769. The impact of the case was that it demonstrated to the colonists the types of abuses that resulted when the customs policy was en-

The vice-admiralty court in Halifax, Nova Scotia

forced by self-interested officials and that maritime laws could be used to stifle political dissent.

Sources:

Laurence M. Friedman, *A History of American Law* (New York: Simon & Schuster, 1985);

Lawrence Henry Gipson, *The Coming of the Revolution, 1763–1775* (New York: Harper, 1954).

THOMAS JEFFERSON AND THE REVISION OF THE VIRGINIA LAWS

Background. The first actions by the Virginia House of Delegates after the Declaration of Independence were to prepare two significant pieces of legislation. One was a bill to eliminate fee tails, and the second was to appoint a committee of five to propose a general revision of the laws of the new commonwealth. Thomas Jefferson was assigned responsibility for the first, and he served on the committee of five, together with Edmund Pendleton, George Wythe, Thomas Lee, and George Mason. The five met to decide how they would approach this task and determined that they would "take up the whole body of statutes and Virginia laws, to leave out everything obsolete or improper, insert what was wanting, and reduce the whole within as moderate a compass as it would bear, and to the plain language of common sense, divested of the verbiage, the barbarous tautologies and redundancies which render the British statutes unintelligible." Mason resigned before the work started, and Lee died shortly thereafter. Jefferson was assigned the areas of crimes and punishments, descent, and religion.

Fee Tail. One provision of the English law of real estate, dating back to medieval times, was the fee tail, or the ability of a grantor (someone who sold real estate or left it to another by will) to provide that the grantee could not dispose of the property except to one or more of his heirs. This limitation, once attached to a piece of real estate, remained intact forever although a landowner could petition to end the restriction. This ability of a landowner to restrict the disposition of his property long after his death was fundamental to the maintenance of an aristocracy and was detested for just that reason. Jefferson introduced a bill that eliminated all existing tails and barred the creation of new ones. The bill was passed in a matter of days.

Law of Descent. Another key element of the law relating to real estate and inheritance was that of primogeniture, that the first-born son would inherit all of a father's real estate, regardless of the father's wishes. Entail allowed a landowner to will his estate to his family in perpetuity. Primogeniture and entail were vestiges of the feudal past and enabled the Old World–style aristocracy to continue in Virginia. With the elimination of primogeniture, a father could leave parts of his property to each of his children rather than being forced to favor one over all the others. Jefferson, by eliminating primogeniture and entail, saw himself as promoting social mobility and economic change.

Crimes and Punishments. Jefferson sought to relax the severity of the punishments meted out under the criminal laws. He believed that too many offenses were punishable by death and proposed that only murder and treason be capital offenses. Other crimes would be less severely punished, with a range of penalties that had a rational basis. In taking this approach Jefferson was reflecting the enlightened liberalism of the period. To demonstrate the development of the criminal code of the time, he traced many topics back to medieval period. In an impressive, scholarly fashion he compared laws of various eras by setting them forth in columns written in the languages in which the laws were originally adopted, including Latin and Old French. He suggested that public labor be a substitute for the death penalty. Prisoners would work on roads and canals, with the expectation that they would be reformed. The public was not yet ready for such an advanced notion, however, and his bill was defeated in the assembly.

Religious Freedom. Jefferson framed a bill for religious freedom as part of his work as a reviser. The Anglican Church, as the established church, was supported, and the clergy paid, by tax revenues. Every taxpayer contributed to the support of the established church even if he was a member of another sect. Jefferson believed that religion was a strictly private affair. While government should protect the public from possible injury, such a power did not extend to religion. "It does me no injury for my neighbor to say that there are twenty gods, or no god. It neither picks my pocket nor breaks my leg." Jefferson's view was that the state should neither support nor oppose any particular religion but should leave them alone. His notion of the separation of church and state eventually became the official American position.

Disestablishment. Jefferson's proposal extended beyond disestablishment of the Anglican Church and granted full religious liberty. However, public sentiment against the church had been building up. The *dissenters,* the term used to describe Presbyterians, Baptists, and Methodists, outnumbered the Anglicans. The Anglican clergy, "having been secured against rivalship by fixed salaries, did not give themselves the trouble of acquiring influence over the people," Jefferson noted in a letter to John Adams. The assembly in 1776 exempted dissenters from taxes for the church. Jefferson's bill provided that "no man shall be compelled to frequent or support any religious worship, place or ministry." While religious liberty was the subject of much discussion at the time, along with all the revolutionary notions about freedom, Jefferson's bill was so controversial that the bill was not introduced in the House of Delegates until 1779 and was not enacted until seven years later.

Sources:

Dumas Malone, *Jefferson the Virginian* (Boston: Little, Brown, 1948);

Bernard Schwartz, *Thomas Jefferson and* Bolling v. Bolling: *Law and the Legal Profession in Pre-Revolutionary America* (San Marino, Cal.: Huntington Library, 1997).

WRITS OF ASSISTANCE

Accepted Policy. In the eighteenth century Britain's trade and navigation laws reflected the mercantilist theory that a colony's main function was to be a source of raw materials for the mother country and a market for its manufactured goods. These advantages were meant to

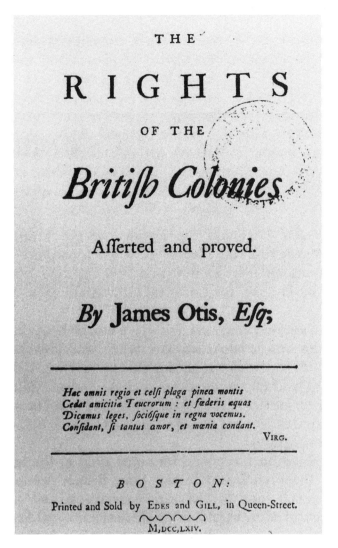

Title page for an influential statement on the constitutional position of the Thirteen Colonies

benefit the mother country and were denied to all foreign commercial rivals. Trade was conducted on British or colonial ships, and commerce between the colonies and non-British ports was limited to specific types of goods. Import duties were designed primarily to complement these trade objectives as well as to raise revenue.

Evasion. Smuggling of foreign products into the colonies, in order to get needed goods or to avoid having to pay the import taxes, had long been a common practice and was almost respectable. The laws had not been tightly enforced, and some colonists, John Hancock among them, had done quite well by evading the restrictions and the taxes. However, as overseas trade grew enormously during the 1750s and the commercial competition with France turned into war, Britain sought to enforce the restrictions against trading with the French and to raise revenue to pay for the war.

New Restrictions. In 1756 the Privy Council issued an order to all colonial governors that they stop all trade with the French. Four years later Prime Minister William Pitt issued a circular letter to all the colonial governors complaining of the lack of response to the repeated reports of trade with the French. He pointed out that this trade was sustaining the enemy's war effort, and he demanded that the governors take every legal step to stop the trade and punish the offenders. This would require customs officers in the colonies to search ships and warehouses to find and seize illegal goods.

Legality. Writs of assistance were court orders somewhat similar to search warrants in that they allowed government officials to search private property. They had first been authorized in England by an act of Parliament about one hundred years earlier, and their application was extended to the colonies by another act of Parliament in 1696. Since a customs officer, by his commission, was ordered to search for and seize smuggled goods, the writ was thought to be a means of protecting property owners from abuses by customs officials. The writ requested the court to direct a court officer to accompany the customs official to any place where he suspected smuggled goods might be stored and to assist the customs official in gaining entry. If the customs officer found goods that he suspected to be untaxed or from an illegal source, he could seize them. Seized goods would be sold by the customs officers, who kept a share of the proceeds for themselves and used a portion to pay their informers. The abuses were outrageous.

Controversy. A writ of assistance was a general authorization to search in that it did not have to describe the places to be searched or the goods to be sought, nor did it require the customs officer to convince a judge that he had probable cause that any suspect items might be present. A writ of assistance, once issued, stayed in effect for the life of the reigning monarch and for six months after his death. When George II died in October 1760, the chief British customs officer in the colonies applied for a new writ. Writs of assistance had been issued on several previous occasions by the court in Boston, but the climate in 1761 was ripe for a controversy. The chief justice of the superior court responded to the application by saying that he did not know whether it was proper for him to issue such a writ and asked for arguments to be presented in court in February 1761. The merchants of Boston were anxious to oppose the granting of new writs and hired James Otis to oppose their issuance.

Otis. The courtroom was crowded when the court met to hear the arguments. The lawyer for the Crown presented a quiet argument in favor of the issuance of the writ, based on the relevant points of law. When Otis rose to argue in opposition, he ignored the narrow points of law and embarked upon a four-hour oration, arguing that the writ was against the fundamental principles of English law and that such an act of Parliament was illegal. The obligation of the court in such instances, according to Otis, was to declare such laws to be void. Otis argued passionately that there was a body of fundamental law that was above Parliament: "Every man, merely natural, was an independent sovereign, subject to no law but the law written on his heart and revealed to him by his Maker . . . . His right to his life, his liberty, no created being could rightfully contest. Nor was his right to his property less contestable." As for a writ of assistance, Otis stated: "I will to my dying day oppose . . . all such instruments of slavery . . . and villainy. . . . And as it is in opposition to a kind of power . . . which in former periods of English history cost one King of England his head and another his throne, I have taken more pains in this cause than ever I will take again." The chief justice declared that he could see no foundation for granting the writ but deferred his decision until he could study the English practice on the subject. What he learned was that in England, writs were routinely issued. In November 1761 he finally issued the requested writ.

Significance. The political theories that Otis presented had been occasionally expressed in the writings of the time—the idea of fundamental law that Parliament could not violate and that if Parliament overstepped its authority, a court could check it by declaring such a law to be void. The real significance of the case was the impact Otis's argument had on his listeners because of the setting (the crowded courtroom in Boston) and his powerful delivery. Although Otis lost the case, as John Adams later described the event: "Otis was a flame of fire. . . . He hurried away all before him. . . . Every man of an immense crowded audience seemed to go away, as I did, ready to take up arms against Writs of Assistance. Then and there, was the first scene of the first act of opposition, to the arbitrary claims of Great Britain. Then and there, the child Independence was born."

Sources:

O. M. Dickerson, *The Navigation Acts and the American Revolution* (Philadelphia: University of Pennsylvania Press, 1951);

Lawrence Henry Gipson, *The Coming of the Revolution, 1763–1775* (New York: Harper, 1954);

Hiller B. Zobel, *The Boston Massacre* (New York: Norton, 1970).

HEADLINE MAKERS

JOHN ADAMS

1735-1826
LAWYER AND STATESMAN

Background. John Adams was born on 19 October 1735, the first of three sons of John and Susanna Boylston Adams. His father was a shoemaker and farmer in Braintree, Massachusetts. Adams graduated from Harvard in 1755, taught school for a year, and then, in order to avoid family pressure to study for the ministry apprenticed himself to James Putnam, a prominent Worcester lawyer. For two years he did routine clerical work in Putnam's office and bore "the disadvantage of Putnam's insociability, and neglect of me." However, Putnam had a good library, and Adams had enough free time for extensive reading of legal texts. At the end of his two-year apprenticeship, Adams sought admission to the Suffolk County bar.

Making the Grade. Admission to the bar in 1758 was not yet a formal procedure—an application to the bar simply had to be endorsed by several members. Adams asked James Gridley and James Otis (then two of the most prominent lawyers in Boston) for such endorsements. Each questioned him extensively on the classics of Roman law and were sufficiently impressed so that Adams was admitted in November. Adams sought to model himself after these elite members of the bar and to distance himself from the common colonial lawyers, the "pettifoggers and dirty dablers in the law," as he called them. In 1761, when he was invited to join a new bar association that intended to regulate the practice of law, he did so. The group proposed in 1763 to limit practice before the lower courts to "sworn attorneys," but the proposal was not adopted. When a more stringent set of rules was proposed in 1766, Adams was again an enthusiastic supporter.

Civil Cases. Several of the legal cases Adams handled reflected his classical scholarship. In 1766 he represented a whaling-ship captain in a dispute about the ownership of a whale. Adams's client had harpooned a whale, and shortly thereafter men aboard another ship also harpooned it. The custom in the whaling trade was that if the first harpoon's line was still attached to the boat when the second harpoon struck, the first boat was entitled to the whale. If the first boat's harpoon line was not still attached when the second ship hit the whale, the second boat was entitled to it. Adams prepared an argument in which he traced the development of the rules about property rights in wild animals, going back to Roman law. Seventy-four witnesses testified. Unfortunately no one seems to have recorded whether or not Adams won the case. Another civil case he handled was a divorce in which Adams was able to convince the court to apply English ecclesiastical law. The result was an unusually large alimony judgment for his client.

Criminal Cases. Three criminal cases that Adams handled between 1768 and 1770 gave him great visibility in the community and connected him with the resistance leaders. In 1768 Adams represented John Hancock in admiralty court for a lengthy dispute with customs authorities about his ship, *Liberty*. The issue in that case was whether Hancock might forfeit his ship for failure to pay some import duties. While Adams quoted extensively from the classical authorities about how the differences between the common law and the admiralty rules were being used to his client's detriment, he was not successful. Later that same year Adams defended a sailor who, in resisting being impressed into the Royal Navy, killed a British officer. Adams was able to convince an admiralty court that the common-law notion of justifiable homicide was applicable. Adams also represented the British Army captain and the eight soldiers accused of killing five townspeople in the Boston Massacre.

Public Official. Adams represented Massachusetts in both Continental Congresses. When independence was declared and Massachusetts established its new government, Adams was named chief justice. His activities in Congress, however, prevented him from taking the seat. He served as one of Congress's three commissioners to France at various times between 1777 and 1783. He also represented the colonies in Spain and Holland during these years, and in 1783 he negotiated the peace treaty that ended the Revolutionary War. Adams attended the Massachusetts constitutional convention and was the principal draftsman of the state's constitution (1780). In later years Adams served as ambassador to

Britain (1785–1789) and as vice president (1789–1796) and president of the United States (1796–1800).

Sources:

Daniel R. Coquilette, "Justinian in Braintree," in *Law in Colonial Massachusetts 1630–1800* (Boston: Colonial Society of Massachusetts, 1984);

Peter Shaw, *American Patriots and the Rituals of Revolution* (Cambridge, Mass.: Harvard University Press, 1981).

WILLIAM CUSHING

1732-1810
JURIST

Early Years. William Cushing was born in Scituate, Massachusetts, on 1 March 1732, the son of John and Mary Cushing. Both his father and grandfather were superior court judges and members of the governor's council. He attended a Latin school in Scituate and then Harvard College, graduating in 1751. He taught school for a year and considered preparing for the ministry, but in 1754 he began to study law as an apprentice in the office of Jeremiah Gridley. Admitted to practice in 1755, he practiced law in Scituate for five years and then moved to the district of Maine (still part of the province of Massachusetts Bay) as the lawyer for the Kennebec Proprietors, a land-development company. He was admitted as a barrister in 1762.

Provincial Judge. Cushing practiced law in Maine for eleven years, also sitting as a justice of the peace and a probate court judge. In 1772, when his father retired from the superior court, Cushing was named to fill the vacancy. As the political turmoil continued to develop in Massachusetts in the years leading up to the Revolution, Cushing was able to demonstrate political neutrality between the Whig and Tory factions. By the end of 1772 the British proposed to have the Crown, rather than the colonial assembly, pay the superior court judges. The objective was to free the judges of local political pressure, or to assure their loyalty to the Crown, depending on one's point of view. Cushing refused the Crown's salary, as did all but one of his colleagues, Chief Justice Peter Oliver. Cushing demonstrated his concern for the dignity of the judicial system, however, in a related matter. The public uproar against Oliver was so great that jurors refused to sit and be sworn when Oliver sat on the bench. Cushing, even though he differed with Oliver on the propriety of accepting the Crown's grant, had no trouble holding such jurors in contempt of court.

State Judge. As the provincial government fell into disarray in 1775, all of the superior court judges except Cushing stood by the Crown. Rebellious Massachusetts colonists developed a new government, led by a revolutionary council, composed of the legislators who favored

independence. This council reorganized the courts and named Cushing to the superior court of Massachusetts Bay. John Adams was named chief justice, but he was occupied in the Continental Congress. Cushing acted as chief justice at the first session of this new court in June 1776. He was elevated to the chief justice's seat when Adams resigned in 1777 and served for twelve more years in this capacity. Cushing was also a member of the 1779 state constitutional convention.

Slavery. The Massachusetts constitution, adopted in 1780, contained a bill of rights that stated that "all men are born free and equal." The constitution did not specifically mention slavery. In 1783 a white man was charged with assault when he tried to repossess an escaped slave. At the end of the trial, Cushing instructed the jury on the legal principles to be applied in deciding the charge. He said: "The right of Christians to hold Africans in perpetual servitude, and sell and treat them as we do our horses and cattle, that (it is true) has been heretofore countenanced by the Province Laws . . . . But whatever sentiments have formerly prevailed . . . a different idea has taken place with the people of America, more favorable to the natural rights of mankind . . . . Our Constitution . . . declaring that all men are born free and equal . . . is totally repugnant to the idea of being born slaves." This instruction effectively abolished slavery in Massachusetts.

After the War. Cushing was vice president of the state convention that ratified the United States Constitution in 1788, and he was the first associate justice named by George Washington to the U.S. Supreme Court in 1789, where he served for twenty-one years. He served as acting chief justice in 1793, in John Jay's absence, and administered the oath of office to Washington. Cushing and his wife, Hannah Phillips, whom he married in 1774, had no children. Cushing died on 13 September 1810.

Source:

David R. Warrington, "William Cushing," in *The Oxford Companion to the Supreme Court of the United States*, edited by Kermit L. Hall (New York & Oxford: Oxford University Press, 1992), pp. 213–214.

JOHN DICKINSON

1732-1808
LAWYER AND STATESMAN

Study Abroad. John Dickinson was born on 8 November 1732 into a wealthy, socially prominent Quaker family on the eastern shore of Maryland. Dickinson was schooled at home until 1750, when he went to Philadelphia to study law in the office of John Moland, a prominent attorney. Dickinson worked in Moland's office for three years, copying documents and studying in the company of other apprentices. In 1753 he went to London's Inns of Court to complete his legal education. The study of law in the Inns was an unstructured affair. Dickinson followed a daily regimen of reading law books, visiting law courts, and debating the fine points of law with fellow law students. He learned not only court procedure but also, from discussions with the other residents, how to organize and present his views on a variety of topics. This broad but rigorous legal training helped him develop an extensive knowledge of England's legal history and a keen insight into British politics. This close contact with politics taught him other, troubling lessons: he was distressed to learn that the members of the House of Lords were rather ordinary men, and he was even more disturbed to see corruption and incompetence among members of the House of Commons. He completed his training in London upon admission to the bar in 1757 and sailed home to Philadelphia.

Legislator. Dickinson began his legal practice as soon as he returned home. In Pennsylvania a long-running political feud was heating up at this time—the dispute between the supporters of the elected assembly and the supporters of the proprietorship. The assembly, deriving authority from the 1701 Charter of Liberties, had gradually increased its control of local financial affairs. The proprietary faction were the supporters of the heirs of William Penn. The proprietors, who owned one-tenth of all the land in the colony, also had some political powers—they appointed the governor and the judges. Dickinson did not get involved in this dispute at the outset of his political career, but when he was elected to the assembly in 1762, he was quickly forced to take sides.

Champion of the Status Quo. One of the leaders of the movement to replace the proprietary system with a royal charter form of government was Benjamin Franklin. He and his allies argued that the proprietors, as owners of one-tenth of all the land in the colony, had a conflict of interest on the issue of taxes, when, in their positions as governor's council members and judges, they needed to raise taxes and appropriate money for defense of western settlements. The antiproprietor faction urged a separation between the power of government and the ownership of property and sought to have the assembly petition the Crown for a change to a royal colony form of government.

Moderate Course. Dickinson pointed out that other colonies with royal charters chafed under many burdens and urged that Pennsylvania not change to a charter simply to spite the proprietors. More important, he argued, Pennsylvanians had benefits under their 1701 charter that they put at risk by asking for a change—complete religious freedom, with no oaths required for political participation, and the assembly was less subject to the will of the governor than were the legislatures of the royal colonies. Dickinson disliked the proprietary form of govern-

ment, but he saw too much to lose by changing to a royal charter. He advised bargaining with the royal authorities to solve the primary problem, the taxation dispute. Dickinson's arguments had only partial success in the assembly. The members voted to send Franklin to London to petition for a change of the charter, provided that he preserve Pennsylvania's civil and religious privileges. When Franklin arrived in London, in March 1765, as the Stamp Act controversy was gathering steam, Parliament's determination to tax the colonies made the antiproprietary petition a lost cause. Dickinson's analysis of the situation was clearly correct.

Stamp Act Congress. Pennsylvania sent Dickinson to the Stamp Act Congress in New York in September 1765. He gained widespread notice as the principal draftsman of the Congress's "Declarations of Rights and Privileges." The delegates acknowledged that the colonists were loyal to the British Crown and subject to the authority of Parliament. However, as Dickinson wrote: "It is inseparably essential to the freedom of a people, and the undoubted right of Englishmen, that no taxes be imposed on them, but with their own consent, given personally, or by their representatives." The Stamp Act Congress's resolutions and petition were sent to Parliament and helped convince Parliament to repeal the Stamp Act in 1766.

"Letters from a Pennsylvania Farmer." After the settlement of the Stamp Act controversy, Parliament passed three acts that rekindled the dispute: the Quartering Act required colonial legislatures to provide barrack necessities (candles, mattress straw, windowpanes, etc.) for British soldiers stationed in the colonies; the Restraining Act prohibited the New York assembly from meeting until it complied with the Quartering Act; and the Townshend Act imposed new duties on goods imported into the colonies from England. These three acts inspired Dickinson to write his most famous work: "Letters from a Pennsylvania Farmer." His first letter, published in a Philadelphia newspaper on 2 December 1767, described some personal qualities. He said he was a retired farmer, an educated gentleman interested in promoting the welfare of men, and one who believed that such welfare was best secured with liberty. At the rate of one letter every week for twelve weeks, the farmer wrote about these three acts. The letters were quickly republished in newspapers in other cities, and pamphlet versions soon appeared as well. The sober tone of the letters and their call for cautious opposition to the various tax acts awakened and unified people in all the colonies. The letters generated favorable comments in all the colonies and were discussed and praised in New England town meetings.

Continental Congress. In 1774 Dickinson was a delegate from Pennsylvania at the First Continental Congress. He played a prominent role outlining the grievances and drafting essays, resolutions, and petitions. He based his arguments on natural law and constitutional limitations of Parliament's power. He focused on two main grievances—Parliament's interference with the internal affairs of the colonies and its wrongful use of its power over trade. The Second Continental Congress convened in May 1775, after the battles at Lexington and Concord. Dickinson, working with John Duane of New York, proposed a plan for a reconciliation with Britain. He urged a three-staged approach: preparations for war, sending a petition to the king, and negotiating a permanent set of commercial regulations and a revenue settlement. Dickinson's insistence that Congress wait for a response to the Olive Branch Petition was the main controversy in the debate. The petition was sent in July, and support for Dickinson's position on reconciliation wasted away as months passed with no response from London. Finally, in November, Congress learned that the king would not respond. Dickinson's prestige in Congress waned rapidly.

Declaration of Independence. Dickinson labored under the conviction that reconciliation was still possible although he became increasingly doubtful. He simply was unable to make the same leap that so many others already had, that independence was inevitable. In Congress in June 1776 the delegates debated declaring independence. Dickinson urged that independence be deferred at least until the colonies could agree on how they would form a confederation and ascertain the likelihood of foreign help in the war. When the motion for independence was finally presented, Dickinson abstained and did not sign the Declaration of Independence. In the next several weeks he drafted the Articles of Confederation for a committee of the Continental Congress. On 20 July, Pennsylvania's provincial convention ousted him from the congressional delegation because he had not supported independence. Dickinson was not disappointed at his ouster, writing that "no youthful Lover ever stript off his cloathes to step into Bed to his blooming beautiful bride with more delight that I have cast off my Popularity."

Later Years. Dickinson spent the next several years out of the public spotlight. He moved to Delaware and resumed his law practice. In 1781, however, he was elected to Delaware's legislature. Later that year, under the then-current form of government, the legislature elected him president of the state for a three-year term. Dickinson's main interests were in Philadelphia, though, and in late 1782 he returned there, where he was promptly elected to the Pennsylvania legislature. Shortly thereafter the legislature elected him president of Pennsylvania. Dickinson was president of both states at the same time but resigned the Delaware office after three months. In 1783, believing there was a need for a college in the western part of Pennsylvania, he founded Dickinson College. He endowed the new school with two farms, totaling five hundred acres, and a library of 1,500 volumes. Dickinson represented Delaware at the Annapolis Convention in 1786 and at the Constitutional Convention in 1787. During the debate on ratification, Dickinson's "Letters from a Pennsylvania Farmer" were often cited by opponents of ratification. Dickinson wrote a series of essays signed "Fabius" in support of ratification. He helped write the Delaware constitution in 1792 and wrote occasionally on political matters for the next ten years. He died on 19 February 1808.

Sources:

Lawrence Henry Gipson, *The Coming of the Revolution, 1763–1775* (New York: Harper, 1954);

David L. Jacobson, *John Dickinson and the Revolution in Pennsylvania, 1764–1776* (Berkeley: University of California Press, 1965);

Charles J. Stille, *The Life and Times of John Dickinson* (Philadelphia: Historical Society of Pennsylvania, 1891).

JEREMIAH GRIDLEY

1701-1767
LAWYER

Youth. Jeremiah Gridley was born on 10 March 1701 in Boston, the second of three sons of Captain Richard and Rebecca Gridley. His father, a leather tanner, died in 1710 and left the family business in the hands of his eldest son, John. Jeremiah attended Harvard, graduating in 1725, after which he taught school, started and edited a literary magazine, and read theology and law. He married Abigail Lewis in 1730. Since, at the time, there were no formal educational requirements to be met, his independent study was sufficient to gain him admission to the bar. Gridley started to practice law in the mid 1730s.

Leader of the Profession. Gridley's education and intellect helped establish him quickly, and he was soon recognized as one of the most learned lawyers in Boston. Many students apprenticed themselves to him for their own study; among them were Oxenbridge Thacher, James Otis Jr., William Cushing (later a justice of the U.S. Supreme Court), and Benjamin Prat (later chief justice of the New York Supreme Court). John Adams studied informally with him. Gridley founded a marine insurance society, served as an overseer of the public schools, and was grand master of the Masons of North America. In 1755, after his wife's death, Gridley moved to Brookline, where he served as a moderator of the town meeting, representative to the legislature, and colonel in the militia.

Writs of Assistance. Gridley's most famous court appearance was on behalf of the Crown in the writs of assistance case. Writs of assistance were general search warrants that courts occasionally issued, in accordance with an act of Parliament many years earlier. A writ of assistance authorized customs inspectors to search for and seize any goods imported illegally, either because they were the result of trade with the enemy or because duties had not been paid. In 1761, when the question of the legality of these writs was to be argued in the superior court in Boston, Gridley was hired to argue in favor of the issue. Gridley presented a clear legal argument: Parliament had authorized exchequer courts in England to issue these writs to customs officers there, and the powers of the provincial superior courts and colonial customs officers were analogous to those of the exchequer courts and the English customs officers. Gridley conceded that abuses might occur, but that possibility did not outweigh the need to protect the revenue. Two of his former students, Thacher and Otis, argued in opposition, Otis making a fiery speech about natural law and the rights of Englishmen. Gridley's position was upheld by the court.

Stamp Act. Gridley was respected as a patriarch of the Boston bar. When the Stamp Act protests made it clear that no one would use stamped papers in court, effectively closing the courts, the town meeting in Boston asked Gridley to serve on a committee (along with Otis and John Adams) to petition the governor to open the courts in defiance of the Stamp Act. On 25 March 1767 he was appointed attorney general but died within the year on 10 September.

Source:

Charles R. McKirdy, *Massachusetts Lawyers on the Eve of the American Revolution* (Boston: Colonial Society of Massachusetts, 1984).

PATRICK HENRY

1736-1799
LAWYER AND ORATOR

Family. Patrick Henry, probably the most eloquent orator of the Revolution, was born on 29 May 1736, the second son of John and Sarah Henry. John had emigrated from Scotland in 1727 and befriended a countryman who had become a successful farmer and gentleman. Upon the friend's death John married his widow. Patrick and his brother were schooled at home, and when they came of age their father set them up as shopkeepers, but they quickly failed.

Alternate Vocation. When he was eighteen Henry married Sarah Shelton, and together they had six children. He tried unsuccessfully to farm the three hundred acres that were his wife's dowry. He opened another shop and then an inn and tavern. His establishments were located near the courthouse, and Henry decided to become a lawyer. He had to pass oral examinations given by two lawyers who had been appointed by the colony's Privy Court. Henry spent about six weeks immersed in the study of the laws of Virginia and Sir Edward Coke's *A Commentary upon Littleton* (1628–1644), an enormous treatise on the common law. (Most prospective lawyers spent a year or more mastering this material.) In April 1760 Henry passed several hours of rigorous oral examination and was admitted to the bar. For the next three years Henry rode the circuit, from county seat to county seat, handling the small cases that came the way of a country lawyer—enough to keep him busy and to support his family, but no more.

The Parsons' Cause. Henry won fame in 1761 for his argument on behalf of a church treasurer sued by a clergyman. Colonial law had set clergy salaries at sixteen thousand pounds of tobacco per year. When the tobacco crop failed in 1758, Virginia's assembly passed the Twopenny Act providing that debts payable in tobacco could be paid in paper currency at the rate of two pence per pound of tobacco. Since tobacco sold for six pence per pound at the time, creditors such as clergymen objected. Britain's Privy Council declared the law void. Several clergymen sued their churches for the difference due them. Henry, representing one church treasurer, held the jurors and the courtroom audience spellbound for an hour. The real issue, he argued, was the power of the colonial assembly to pass laws for the benefit of the people of the colony. The British constitution put limits on the King's power, and Henry questioned the power of the Privy Council to nullify a law passed by the colonial legislature. He described the compact that existed between a king and his subjects and suggested that the king could not violate that compact by nullifying an act by the people's assembly. Henry also argued that the clergy were not concerned with the welfare of all the people of Virginia, who would benefit from the Twopenny Act, but were concerned only with their own salaries. He denounced as "rapacious harpies" those clergy who were enemies of the people they were supposed to serve. Henry acknowledged that the jury had to find for the clergyman in this case because the Privy Council had nullified the Twopenny Act. However, he urged the jurors to teach the clergy a lesson for opposing an act of the colonial assembly. As soon as Henry finished his argument, the jurors returned a verdict. They upheld the clergyman and awarded him only one penny. Henry immediately became famous and was shortly afterward elected to the House of Burgesses.

"Treason!" Henry became a member of the House of Burgesses, the lower house of the Virginia assembly, in the spring of 1765, just as it was reacting to Parliament's passage of the Stamp Act. In 1764, when the Stamp Act was first proposed, the House of Burgesses petitioned Parliament, begging that the tax not be imposed. Henry joined a small group of members who urged the House to file a briefer, more forceful statement that would stir popular opinion against the Stamp Act. Henry proposed a resolution specifically denying Parliament's power to tax the colonies. More-cautious members argued against including such bold assertions in the resolution, as they thought it bordered on treason. Henry reportedly warned: "Caesar had his Brutus, Charles I his Cromwell, and George III. . . . ," at which point the Speaker, horrified, shouted "Treason!" Henry paused, then finished his sentence: " . . . may profit by their example. If this be treason, make the most of it." Parliament rescinded the Stamp Act, but as the issue of Parliament's power over the colonies recurred during the next nine years, Henry became increasingly bold. He was among the first members of the House of Burgesses to talk about separation from, instead of reconciliation with, England. His political fame boosted his law practice. He was one of the colony's leading political voices and one of its most successful trial attorneys.

Virginia Convention. In March 1775 Virginians convened to choose and instruct their delegates to the Second Continental Congress, to be held in August. Henry urged the formation, equipping, and training of a local militia for the purpose of defending the colony if needed. In his view the convention was now acting as the governing body and was preparing for war. Some delegates suggested reconciliation with Britain was still possible, but others argued that separation was inevitable. It was in the course of this debate, on the subject of forming a militia, that Henry made one of his most famous speeches. He reviewed the developing dispute with Britain, especially Parliament's tightening of restrictions as it sought to exert its control. This showed, Henry said:

> There is no longer any room for hope. . . . If we wish to be free we must fight. . . . An appeal to arms...is all that is left. . . . Gentlemen may cry "peace, peace" but there is no peace. [If war is coming, he said] let it come! Let it come!... Is life so dear, or peace so sweet, as to be purchased at the price of chains and slavery? Forbid it Almighty God. I know not what course others may take, but as for me—give me liberty or give me death.

Governorship. In May 1776, at the next colonial convention, Henry proposed a resolution that Virginia's delegates to the next session of the Second Continental Congress move for independence. His resolution also called for Virginia to draft a declaration of rights and to prepare a plan for its own government. In June he drafted a constitution for the new Commonwealth of Virginia, and by the end of that month the convention adopted a constitution and elected Henry the Commonwealth's first governor. He served for three years, creating an administrative and judicial system while simultaneously supporting the war effort. In 1777, two years after his first wife's death, Henry married Dorothea Dandridge, and he fathered eleven more children. By 1779 he was ready to retire from public life. After only one year he returned to the assembly, where he served for four years. In 1784 he was elected governor again and served three more years. During this period Henry helped pass a religious freedom law in Virginia. When the Constitution was presented to the states for ratification, Henry opposed it because of the lack of a bill of rights. He devoted his final years to his law practice and to western land speculations until his death in 1799.

Sources:

Lawrence Henry Gipson, *The Coming of the Revolution, 1763–1775* (New York: Harper, 1954);

Henry Mayer, *A Son of Thunder* (New York: Franklin Watts, 1986).

THOMAS JEFFERSON

1743-1826
LAWYER AND STATESMAN

Background. Thomas Jefferson was born on 13 April 1743 in Albemarle County, Virginia, the third child (and first son) of Peter and Jane Jefferson. His father was a successful planter, surveyor, and militia colonel and served two terms in the House of Burgesses. Jefferson attended a Latin school from the age of nine and when he was fourteen began attending a school run by the Reverend James Maury. He was in Maury's school when the Twopenny Act was passed but had left by the time Maury was the plaintiff in the Parson's Cause, the case that made Patrick Henry famous. Jefferson attended the College of William and Mary from 1760 until 1762 and spent the next five years studying law in the office of George Wythe, a prominent Williamsburg lawyer (who later became the first professor of law at an American college).

County Circuit. Jefferson was admitted to the bar in 1767 and began his practice as a country lawyer. He maintained a daily journal of his law practice, in which he noted the client's name, the subject of the case, the outcome, and the fee. Over the next seven years he recorded this type of information with respect to nearly one thousand cases. Most of these were small cases in the county courts, involving debt collection, land ownership, recovery of slaves, slander, and assault and battery. Jefferson rode the circuit, traveling from town to town, arriving in each county seat as the court began its session.

Williamsburg. He had a few cases in the General Court, which met in Williamsburg and involved more-significant matters. He recorded his arguments in two of these cases. In a 1770 case he represented a child who had been born to an indentured mulatto and was seeking his freedom. Jefferson argued that his client should be free because the indenture bound only the mother. He said that the statute "subjected to servitude the first mulatto only. . . . It did not, under the law of nature, affect the liberty of the children, because, under that law we are all born free." This view, which he would later include in the Declaration of Independence, fell on deaf ears. In the other General Court case in 1771, Jefferson represented church vestrymen who were trying to oust their minister. The defendant challenged the jurisdiction of the civil court to act in a church matter. Jefferson presented a scholarly argument showing how the court represented the King, and that the King certainly had the power to intervene in church matters. Edmund Randolph had observed other cases, in which Jefferson faced Henry, and he said: "Mr. Jefferson drew copiously from the depths of the law, Mr. Henry from the recesses of the human heart."

House of Burgesses. Jefferson was elected to the House of Burgesses in 1769. In his first term the House addressed the circular letter from Massachusetts, which objected to the Townshend duties. The royal governor, seeking to stifle dissent, abruptly dissolved the session. The members regrouped in a local tavern, called themselves an "Association," and adopted a nonimportation agreement. This Association was the forerunner of the conventions that later became substitutes for the provincial assemblies. When the members met as an association, they were able to meet when they decided to meet, to discuss the issues of the day. Since the Association was not the official assembly, the members were not dependent upon the royal governor to call them into session, nor could their debate be cut short by the governor's dissolving the meeting. Jefferson's ability as a writer and his views on freedom made him a leader in the House, in the associations and conventions that met when the House was not in session, and at the Continental Congresses.

Later Career. During this time Jefferson practiced law, served as a burgess, and began to build his mansion at Monticello. In 1772 he married Martha Wayles Skelton. He decided to devote his energies to his house and plantation and retired from the practice of law in 1774. He continued in public service, however, and served in the Continental Congress in 1775 and 1776, where he wrote the Declaration of Independence. After the declaration was voted he returned to Virginia, where he served in the House of Delegates (1776–1779) and then as governor (1779–1782) and drafted a constitution for the state in 1783. Jefferson later served as secretary of state in the Washington administration and was elected the nation's third president in 1800.

Sources:

Dumas Malone, *Jefferson the Virginian* (Boston: Little, Brown, 1948);

Samuel Eliot Morison and others, *The Growth of the American Republic* (New York: Oxford University Press, 1969).

PETER OLIVER

1713-1791

ENTREPRENEUR AND JURIST

Wealth. Peter Oliver was born in Boston on 26 March 1713, the second son of Daniel and Elizabeth Oliver, a prominent Boston couple. He graduated from Harvard College in 1730, married Mary Clark in 1733, and had six children. Oliver and his brother Andrew operated a Boston importing business for several years though his interests were not in trade but in science and literature. In 1744 Oliver bought an iron works in Middleborough, a small town about thirty miles from Boston. The mill made cast-iron household products and cannonballs. It proved so successful that Oliver was able to build Oliver Hall, one of New England's finest mansions, with woodwork and artwork imported from England, and elaborate gardens.

Judge and Councilman. Even though Oliver had no legal education, in 1744 he was appointed a justice of the peace. In 1747 he was named to the court of common pleas, where he supervised the building of a new courthouse and served as a guardian for a local tribe of Indians. In 1756 he was named a justice of the superior court. He also served in the assembly and in 1759 was elected to the council, the legislature's upper house. He supported Parliamentary efforts to pay for the war with France by taxing commerce and cracking down on smuggling. Oliver traced opposition to the Crown's policies to merchants whose fortunes had come from smuggling, which was considered dishonorable in England, yet "it is in New England so far from being reproachful that some of the greatest fortunes there were acquired in this disgraceful trade, and the proprietors of them boast of their method of acquisition." Smuggling bred corruption and immorality, he charged, and the merchants who benefited used their influence on the common people who were, he wrote, "like the mobility of all countries, perfect machines, wound up by any hand who might first take the winch." Judge Oliver distrusted both the merchants of Boston and their followers.

Outcast. Beginning in 1765 the Sons of Liberty, whom Oliver and others referred to as the Sons of Anarchy, were using mob action in Boston as a political weapon against the British. During the Stamp Act riots in the summer of 1765, mob violence was directed against colonial officials. Oliver's brother Andrew had been appointed a stamp distributor, and the mob reacted by burning him in effigy and then destroyed his house and office. Later that fall Peter Oliver refused to sit in court because of the threats of mob violence. He supported the stamp tax to the point that, even after being assured of his personal safety, he said he would not hold court without properly stamped legal papers. When the governor prevailed on Oliver to open court anyway, he said he would do so but that he was acting under duress. As a declared supporter of the Stamp Act, Oliver was not reelected to the council in 1766. Harassment of Crown officials by the Sons of Liberty took many forms—they even pressed Oliver's creditors not to finance his iron-works trade, so Oliver was forced to mortgage all his property. He welcomed the arrival of British troops in Boston in 1768, expecting that he would then be able to walk the streets of Boston safely.

Boston Massacre Trial. In March 1770 a confrontation between eight British soldiers and a taunting mob resulted in the Boston Massacre. Capt. Thomas Preston and later, in a second trial, the eight soldiers were tried in superior court for murder. Oliver was one of the three judges on the bench for these trials. (John Adams was one of the lawyers for the defense in both trials.) Oliver's conduct in the trials was generally recognized as fair. In his instructions to the jury at the end of the trial, Oliver summarized the evidence in a way that made clear the mob's provocation of the soldiers. The captain and the soldiers were acquitted of the charge of murder although two of the soldiers were found guilty of manslaughter. Lt. Gov. Thomas Hutchinson was so pleased with Oliver's conduct of the trial and its outcome that he urged the army to buy several tons of cannonballs from Oliver's iron works. In January 1772 Oliver was named chief justice of the superior court.

Impeachment. Oliver had frequently complained about the low salary he received as a judge (£120 per year as associate justice and £150 as chief justice) and often threatened to resign from the bench. In 1772, as civil disorders became more frequent, the British devised a plan that they thought would maintain some loyalty among judges. Superior court judges would all receive a £200 raise, paid by the Crown, in addition to their salaries already paid by the provincial government. Public reaction to this plan was immediate outrage because the judges would become dependent on the Crown rather than be loyal to the provincial laws. All of the judges except Oliver quickly renounced the grants. The House of Representatives urged that Oliver be removed from office and began impeachment proceedings. Lieutenant Governor Hutchinson attempted to block these proceedings, but public opinion was so inflamed against Oliver that jurors refused to serve while he was on the bench.

Besieged and Exiled. By August 1774 Oliver was effectively forced from the bench, and he left Oliver Hall to live under the protection of the British troops in Boston. His wife died in March 1775. Oliver remained active in Loyalist political circles until March 1776, when the British evacuated their troops and Loyalists from Boston. He sailed to Halifax and later to London, where he was received by the King. He lived in England until his death on 12 October 1791.

Source:
Lawrence Henry Gipson, *The Coming of the Revolution, 1763–1775* (New York: Harper, 1954).

JAMES OTIS JR.

1725-1783
LAWYER, STATESMAN, AND WRITER

Assessment. James Otis Jr., a Massachusetts lawyer, legislator, and writer, took an active role in opposing the king and the provincial governor on a continuing basis from 1760 until the beginning of the Revolution. A powerful orator and a prolific writer, he was a prominent spokesman for the revolutionary cause. (His sister, Mercy Otis Warren, wrote several famous propaganda plays in the 1770s.) Whether his motive at any one instant was patriotic, a mere personal vendetta, or a manifestation of mental illness is still the matter of debate.

Early Years. Otis was born on 5 February 1725 in Barnstable, Massachusetts, the first of thirteen children of James and Mary Otis. Otis's father, James, a politically active businessman, became a lawyer and county court judge in Barnstable. He gained the rank of colonel in the militia and wore the title proudly until his death in 1778. James Jr. attended Harvard College from 1739 to 1743, then spent a year studying literature and philosophy. He apprenticed himself to Jeremiah Gridley, a prominent Boston lawyer. In 1748 he began practicing law in Plymouth but was not able to develop his practice; he moved to Boston in 1750 and was more successful. He married Ruth Cunningham, the daughter of a wealthy Boston merchant, in 1755.

Family Feud. In 1749 Thomas Hutchinson (then a member of the governor's council) introduced a paper-money bill in the legislature. The bill was passed, in large part thanks to the efforts of Otis's father (then the Speaker of the House). The senior Otis expected a significant political favor in exchange for his support, and he understood that he would get a seat on the superior court when one became available. In 1760 Chief Justice Stephen Sewall of the superior court died, and Colonel Otis thought he would finally get his seat on that court. James Jr. lobbied Hutchinson, who was then lieutenant governor, on his father's behalf. However, Francis Bernard, the new royal governor, felt pressure from London to name someone who would be sure to carry out the new, tighter trade rules. He named Hutchinson (who kept his positions as lieutenant governor, governor's councilor, and probate judge). The Otises thought that Hutchinson had betrayed them, a personal grievance that would have profound political consequences.

Writs of Assistance. In 1760 the customs commissioner applied to the superior court for a new writ of assistance. A writ of assistance was a court order similar to a modern search warrant although it was one of general and ongoing application—it did not require a customs officer to assert any probable cause before he searched a property or seized any suspected goods. A writ of assistance, once issued, was valid for as long as the reigning king lived, plus six months. King George II had died in October 1760, so a new writ was needed. Otis agreed to represent a group of Boston merchants to argue against the issuance of any new writs. Otis presented a strong political and philosophical argument but also referred to Hutchinson's accumulation of offices. His ringing oratory, in which he denounced the writs as violations of fundamental law and therefore unconstitutional, brought him immediate fame and led to his election to the assembly a few months later.

Legislature. Almost immediately upon election Otis joined his father (still Speaker of the House) in opposing the governor's proposal on a coinage bill. His opposition was both on the subject matter and also as a personal attack on Hutchinson. The irony of the situation was that twelve years earlier Colonel Otis had supported a similar bill proposed by Hutchinson. The younger Otis, in arguing against the proposal, avoided any reference to his father's change of position or to the political feud that flowed from that bill and the colonel's claim to the superior court seat. For the next ten years Otis alternated between leading the opposition to the administration's programs (always intertwined with the personal attack on Hutchinson) and, on occasion, providing key support. Judge Peter Oliver, a friend of Hutchinson's, once wrote about Otis: "He will one time say of the Lieutenant Governor, that he had rather have him than any man he knows, in any one office, and the next hour will represent him as the greatest tyrant, and most despicable creature living."

Writings. In 1762 the governor asked the legislature to approve a small military expenditure that he had authorized while the assembly had been in recess. Otis voiced a vigorous protest, defending the legislature's prerogatives over money matters. He compared the governor's action to one that, if done by the king when Parliament was not in session, would be the act of a tyrant. He wrote an essay, "A Vindication of the Conduct of the House of Representatives," to explain his opposition and to defend himself from charges that his remarks had amounted to treason. In 1764 and 1765 he wrote several long essays about the Stamp Act, first denying Parliament's power to tax the colonies but later acknowledging that power.

Insanity. His behavior in the legislature was erratic. He frequently took a strong stand on one side of an issue and then abruptly, for no apparent reason, reversed his position. The question of whether Parliament had the power to enact the Stamp Act was the most noteworthy example of this change. Similarly he maintained an ongoing personal vendetta against Hutchinson though, at least once a year, reached a reconciliation with him. This unpredictable behavior hinted of insanity. Several times in the late 1760s he made speeches in the House that were described as the rantings of a madman. In September 1769 he accosted the customs commissioner John Robinson in the British Coffee House. In the ensuing brawl Otis received a severe gash on his head. After that point many people, including John Adams, said that Otis was "not in his perfect mind." He apparently cracked in 1770 and in a mad rage broke several windows in Boston's town hall. His family took him to the countryside for a month. Thereafter, Otis faded in and out of sanity. Nevertheless he continued in the legislature, alternating between support for and opposition to the Crown. He opposed independence at first and later supported it. Otis was struck by lightning and died on 23 May 1783.

Sources:

John R. Galvin, *Three Men of Boston* (New York: Thomas Y. Crowell, 1976);

Peter Shaw, *American Patriots and the Rituals of Revolution* (Cambridge, Mass.: Harvard University Press, 1981).

PUBLICATIONS

John Adams, *A Dissertation on the Canon and Feudal Law* (London, 1765)—four articles originally published in a Boston newspaper in which Adams developed his view of the constitutional relationship between the colonists and the Crown. He started with the history of feudal law and traced the development of individual liberty since the Age of Enlightenment;

Adams, *Novanglus, and Massachusettensis; or, Political Essays* (Boston: Printed & published by Hews & Goss, 1819)—a series of twelve letters (published in a Boston newspaper between 23 January and 17 April 1775) in which Adams tried to propose a commonwealth status for the colonies, under the British Crown. He explored English constitutional history and principles of natural law to describe a possible framework for resolving the imperial crisis. A thirteenth letter in the series was never printed because the battles at Lexington and Concord on 19 April suspended most publishing in Boston;

John Almon, ed., *A Collection of Tracts, on the Subject of Taxing the British Colonies in America*, 4 volumes (London: John Almon, 1773);

Edmund Burke, *Speech on Conciliation with the Colonies* (New York: James Rivington, 1775)—the text of

Prime Minister Burke's speech in Parliament on 22 March 1775 was published immediately in London and later in New York;

John Dickinson, *An Essay on the Constitutional Power of Great-Britain over the Colonies in America...* (Philadelphia: Printed and sold by William and Thomas Bradford, 1774)—written for the benefit of the delegates to Pennsylvania's 1774 convention to help justify resistance to parliamentary authority;

Dickinson, *Letters from a Farmer in Pennsylvania to the Inhabitants of the British Colonies* (Philadelphia: Printed by David Hall and William Sellers, 1768; London: Printed by J. Almon, 1768)—twelve letters published in a Philadelphia newspaper attacking the Townshend duties as illegal because Parliament had no right to levy internal taxes on the colonies;

Alexander Hamilton, *The Farmer Refuted: or, A More Impartial and Comprehensive View of the Dispute between Great-Britain and the Colonies...* (New York: Printed by James Rivington, 1775)—Hamilton's first national exposure resulted from this pamphlet. He argued that the conflict between England and the colonies could be resolved if England's regulation of trade did not include an effort to raise revenue;

Francis Hargrave, *An Argument in the Case of James Sommerset* (Boston: E. Russell, 1774)—Sommerset was a slave from Virginia who, while in England with his master, escaped. When he was recaptured he petitioned for his freedom. The pamphlet summarizes the argument in which Hargrave, one of Sommerset's lawyers, described why slavery was not lawful in England;

John Hodgson, *The Trial of William Wemms, et al.* (Boston: J. Fleming, 1770)—notes taken in shorthand at the trial of the eight soldiers involved in the Boston Massacre;

Thomas Jefferson, *A Summary View of the Rights of British America...* (Williamsburg: Printed for Clementina Rind, 1774; London: Printed for G. Kearsly, 1774)—instructions written by Jefferson for the Virginia Convention in August 1774 and published in pamphlet form and circulated by Patrick Henry at the First Continental Congress in Philadelphia;

James Otis Jr., *The Rights of the British Colonies Asserted and Proved* (Boston: Printed and sold by Edes & Gill, 1764; London: Printed for J. Almon, 1765)—written while the Stamp Act was being debated in Parliament but before the statute was passed, this pamphlet denies Parliament's right to tax the colonies;

Otis, *Vindication of the British Colonies, Against the Aspersions of the Halifax Gentleman, in his Letter to a Rhode-Island Friend...* (Boston: Printed and sold by Edes & Gill, 1765; London: Printed by J. Almon, 1769)—reflects a reversal of Otis's view of a limit on the power of Parliament to tax the colonies;

Otis, *A Vindication of the Conduct of the House of Representatives of the Province of the Massachusetts-Bay* (Boston: Printed by Edes & Gill, 1762)—one of the earliest statements of the principles that led to the Revolution. Begun as a protest against the royal governor's incursion into the colonial assembly's power to spend tax revenue, the pamphlet goes on to argue in favor of constitutional limits on the Crown;

Thomas Paine, *Common Sense* (Philadelphia: Printed and sold by R. Bell, 1776)—probably the single most influential publication of the era. Paine presented, in popular form, an exposition of his views on natural rights.

LIFESTYLES, SOCIAL TRENDS, AND FASHION

by PAUL FOOS

CONTENTS

Sidebars and tables are listed in italics.

1754

- John Woolman writes *Some Considerations on the Keeping of Negroes Recommended to the Professors of Christianity of Every Denomination.* It is published and distributed by the Philadelphia Society of Friends.

- Benjamin Franklin makes an overland trip from Philadelphia to Portsmouth, New Hampshire, in eighteen days.

1755

- British authorities remove about six thousand French Acadians from Nova Scotia and transport them to the thirteen colonies.

18 Nov. New England is shaken by an earthquake.

1756

26 July The *Boston Evening Post* has an advertisement for Boston bottles, the forerunner of the modern corsage. These small, ribboned glasses filled with water contain flowers and are worn on dresses.

1757

- Benjamin Franklin designs whale-oil street lamps for use in Philadelphia.

- The first exhibition of colonial paintings is held in New York.

- William Smith's *History of New York* is published in London.

Oct. *The American Magazine,* an early literary magazine, begins publication in Philadelphia.

1758

- *The Way to Wealth,* by Benjamin Franklin, is published.

1759

- Francis Hopkinson writes "My Days Have Been So Wondrous Free," America's earliest secular musical composition.

- Halley's Comet reappears as predicted.

- The Reverend Andrew Burnaby begins a one-year tour of the colonies, and his account is published in 1775 as *Travels through the Middle Settlements in North America.*

1760

- The population of the thirteen colonies is estimated at 1,593,625.

- Benjamin West of Pennsylvania arrives in Italy and becomes the first American to study art in Europe.

20 Mar. Boston is swept by a disastrous fire.

26 Oct. George III ascends the British throne.

1761

- John Winthrop leads an expedition to Newfoundland to observe the transit of Venus across the Sun.

15 Dec. The slave Jupiter Hammon publishes the first known work of poetry by an African American, *Salvation by Christ with Penitential Cries.*

1762

- John Woolman publishes *Considerations on the Keeping of Negroes: Part Second,* stirring up strong antislavery activity among Quakers.

1764

- An employers' association is organized in New York.

1765

- A chocolate factory that uses cacao beans imported from the West Indies is established in Massachusetts.
- Acadian refugees begin to arrive in Louisiana.
- The New Jersey assembly appropriates £200 for unemployment relief.

1766

- Slaves revolt in South Carolina.
- Tenant farmers in the Hudson River Valley of New York fight sheriffs and British troops in protest against seizures of farms for debt.

1767

24 Apr. The *Prince of Parthia,* a play by Thomas Godfrey, opens at the Southwark Theater in Philadelphia, the first permanent theater in the colonies.

1768

- The last execution for witchcraft takes place in Connecticut.
- Regulators begin a three-year revolt in western North Carolina. Frontier farmers fight the colonial government and tidewater elites in protest over unfair taxation and bonds of debt.

18 July John Dickinson's "Song for American Freedom," a patriotic ballad, is published in the *Boston Gazette;* it is later reprinted as "The Liberty Song."

1769

- The Old Colony Club is formed at Plymouth, Massachusetts, to commemorate the landing of the Pilgrims in 1620.

1770

- The only known interior water closet in colonial America is installed at Whitehall, a late Georgian mansion in Anne Arundel County, Maryland.

- The population of the thirteen colonies is estimated at 2,148,076.

1772

- *The Progress of Dulness,* a satire on education and the clergy by John Trumbull, is published.

1773

- *Poems on Various Subjects* by Phillis Wheatley, a young slave girl in Boston, is published.

- President Ezra Stiles of Yale College and Dr. Samuel Hopkins advocate the colonization of West Africa by free blacks.

Mar.   The colonial legislature of New York outlaws the discharging of firearms and explosives on New Year's Day, in response to the rioting which occurred the previous January.

25 June Several slaves of Massachusetts present a petition before the colony's House of Representatives calling for emancipation and the settlement of freedmen on a grant of land.

1774

- A slave revolt occurs in St. Andrew's Parish, Georgia. Twelve slaves kill four whites but are captured, and two leaders of the revolt are burned alive.

- Rhode Island and Connecticut prohibit the importation of slaves.

20 Oct. The Continental Congress orders that the colonies "discountenance and discourage all horse racing and all kinds of gaming, cock fighting, exhibitions of shows, plays and other expensive diversions and entertainments."

1775

- The United Company of Philadelphia for Promoting American Manufactures is organized.

- The words of the song "Yankee Doodle" are written by Edward Barnes and set to an old English tune.

6 Mar.   Prince Hall and fourteen other free blacks become members of a British army lodge of Freemasons. After the British evacuate Boston, American authorities give Hall and his associates permission to form what becomes known as African Lodge Number One of Freemasons.

14 Apr. The first abolition society in America is organized in Pennsylvania.

7 Nov.	John Murray, Earl of Dunmore, British governor of Virginia, issues a proclamation freeing all servants and slaves willing to join the British army in fighting the Rebels.
31 Dec.	George Washington reverses an earlier decision and allows free blacks to be recruited into the American army.

1776

- The Philadelphia Friends' Meeting dismisses those members holding slaves.
- Devereux Jarratt writes *A Brief Narrative of the Revival of Religion in Virginia,* an account of the Great Awakening.

1777

13 Jan.	Eight blacks in Boston petition the General Court of Massachusetts, calling for the abolition of slavery.
2 July	The Vermont state constitution abolishes slavery and adopts universal male suffrage without regard to property. Vermont had declared itself an independent state six months earlier, and it does not officially join the Union until 1791.
27 Nov.	The confiscation of Loyalist property is approved by Congress.

1778

- Virginia abolishes the slave trade.

1779

- The play *The Motley Assembly,* a political satire lampooning unpatriotic Boston aristocrats and supposedly written by Mercy Otis Warren, debuts.

30 June	Gen. Henry Clinton issues a second appeal to slaves to join the Loyalist cause. His proclamation promises freedom for any slave who deserts an enemy master and enters the British lines. However, the decree allows for the sale of black soldiers captured in the service of the enemy.

1780

- The population of the thirteen colonies is estimated at 2,780,361.

1 Mar.	The Pennsylvania legislature provides for gradual emancipation of slaves.
7 June	The Massachusetts state constitution, the first to be adopted by a convention specifically called for that purpose, is ratified by popular vote. Its bill of rights, containing the phrase "all men are born free and equal," is understood by some to apply to slavery.
10 June	*Sentiments of An American Woman,* by Esther DeBerdt Reed, calls on women to sacrifice all luxuries and contribute money to the American army.

1781

2 Jan.   Pennsylvania troops in Morristown, New Jersey, break camp and demand back pay; Congress subsequently yields to their demands.

Spring   Continental money ceases to have value and "Not worth a Continental" becomes a popular phrase.

1782

•   *Letters from an American Farmer,* by Michel-Guillaume-Jean de Crèvecoeur, is published.

1783

•   A postwar depression begins.

•   Quaco, a slave, is declared free by the Massachusetts courts under the new state bill of rights.

•   Meanwhile the Massachusetts state supreme court abolishes slavery.

13 May   The Society of Cincinnati is formed by former officers of the Continental Army.

June 30   Congress meets in Princeton, New Jersey, following a mutiny of unpaid soldiers in Philadelphia.

3 Nov.   The Continental Army disbands by congressional order.

A tavern sign painted by a limner
or itinerant artist (Connecticut
Historical Society, Hartford)

OVERVIEW

An Era of Contrasts. The revolutionary era was bracketed by two long wars in which much blood and money were spent. Yet, paradoxically, in this age the population of British North America surged upward, and colonial merchants and planters became lavishly wealthy. The French and Indian War brought unprecedented levels of British government spending to the colonies, and many a colonial merchant made his fortune outfitting British soldiers and ships. New England and New York merchants, Pennsylvania farmers, and Southern planters profited from wartime spending and increasing intercolonial trade. In the backcountry European settlers engaged in a bloody war of attrition with Native Americans, steadily pushing them off valuable land. Tens of thousands of people poured into the colonies from Europe and Africa, feeding a seemingly inexhaustible demand for labor in fields and workshops.

Colonial Culture: New Fortunes. The rising wealth of upper- and middle-class colonists was largely spent in imitation of European habits and tastes. The styles of the French court predominated in the 1760s and early 1770s, with the emphasis on mannered attire and etiquette. Men in powdered wigs and women in French corsets set the tone among the colonial elite. Although they could not attain the levels of style and grandeur of European royalty, American elites put on an elaborate display of elegance and courtly manners. Even at the lowest levels of colonial society the material standards of life were improving from the primitive conditions of the early 1700s. Colonists expected and got a certain level of comfort, if not luxury. Bedsteads, tableware, and tea sets, mostly imported from Europe, took their place in the humblest of homes.

Population Growth. The period from 1700 to 1775 was one of the most extraordinary periods of population growth North America has ever experienced. Immigration and natural growth contributed to a tenfold increase in population. At the outbreak of the Revolution nearly one-half of the residents of the thirteen colonies were immigrants or the children of immigrants. Germans, Scots, Irish, Welsh, and English flooded into the colonies, particularly after 1730, and a booming Atlantic slave trade ensured that a large segment of this new population was African. Many Europeans arrived as indentured servants and virtually all African migrants were slaves. The Revolution disrupted transatlantic migration, but by that time America was already a rich landscape of various languages, dialects, and races.

The Laboring Poor. Along with new wealth came new classes of laboring poor and indigent paupers in the colonies. Immigrants and the rural poor tramped in and out of the colonial cities in an unending search for employment. America was a land of vast natural resources; food and drink were abundant in this landscape but not always distributed equitably among the population. Urban workers dug oysters from tidal basins during times of unemployment; slaves and servants on plantations lived on cornbread and salt pork as they labored to produce valuable export crops. Work was often sporadic, dependent on the seasons and fluctuations in trade. Refugees from colonial wars sought shelter in the bustling cities along the coast, further adding to the problems of municipal governments as they tried to manage and contain the problems of poverty. Quaker and Puritan moralism governed most experiments in poor relief, but attacking laziness and immorality did little to solve the serious problems of colonial society.

Unification. The escalating conflict with Britain unified this diverse and changing society in a surprisingly short period of time. Although colonists came from many different backgrounds, most, if not all, deeply resented military coercion and restrictions on their lifeline, international trade. The nonimportation and home-manufacture drives of the 1760s and 1770s were largely symbolic, but they touched nearly every level of society and permanently changed the self-image of the colonists. Everyday items such as tea or linen were suddenly loaded with political meaning, a meaning that soon permeated society as colonists took sides over resistance to England. Patriot organizations crossed class and ethnic boundaries and brought enormous social pressure to bear on those who trafficked in boycotted goods.

A Message of Equality. As American women took to their spinning wheels and American men wore home-spun clothing, they had little impact on the vast British export trade, but the virtue and simplicity of these demonstrations were a powerful affront to British aristocracy and power. The revolutionary movement contained a message of equal rights that had a powerful appeal to colonists who had known nearly every degree of servitude and dependence.

Wartime Life. From 1775 to 1783 armies marched across the colonial landscape; ports were blockaded; and thousands were made refugees. People under military attack or occupation still had to contend with the daily struggle of feeding their families and maintaining their way of life and communities. Soldiers enlisted for a few months of fighting and returned to tend to their farms. But many fell prey to death and disease or found that the enemy had occupied their homes. As men went to war, women often took over traditional male roles of running farms and businesses. Women alone had to deal with the horrors of occupation or face the uncertainties of refugee status. American women, for the most part, stood up well to this challenge and took on public political roles, supporting the Revolution with household production and fund-raising drives. In a society that held women to be inferior, women could issue a bold challenge to men by being resourceful and courageous in the face of hardship and danger. The equality preached by the revolutionaries was never fully extended to women, but it was not expressly denied to them either, and it seemed to infect them with a spirit of independence.

Slavery and Equal Rights. The promises of equality also excluded African Americans, whose labor was crucial to the colonial economy. Nonetheless free blacks and slaves seized the rhetoric of freedom or the divisions among Europeans to create opportunities for freedom. A growing number of whites and blacks in the North attacked the hypocrisy of slavery, and by the 1780s slavery was dying north of Maryland. This by no means happened without a struggle. The determined efforts of antislavery activists pressing their cases in legislatures and courts brought this result. Slave labor was valuable even in the North, and doctrines of white supremacy remained stubbornly enshrined in law and social practice. In the South, on the other hand, Patriots became hardened in their commitment to slavery as the British enlisted slaves in their army or liberated them from their former masters. Some eighty thousand to one hundred thousand slaves took advantage of wartime conditions to escape their bondage although the retreat of the British armies meant that many would be reenslaved.

Contested Frontiers. The Revolution was fiercely contested on the western frontiers of British North America. This contest had less to do with imported tea and British taxes than with the land hunger of white settlers and the desperate defense of Native Americans trying to hold onto land and sovereignty. The trans-Appalachian frontier was a zone of warfare and personal violence between Indian and settler, but it was also the site of an amazing amount of cultural sharing and cooperation. Europeans had been trading in this region for more than 150 years. Close trading and political and personal alliances had formed between Indians and Europeans. The fur trade transformed Indian society, bringing great dependence on trade goods and the few Europeans who carried out that trade. Unrestricted immigration to the frontier threatened trade and British sovereignty. The British tried, but failed, to stop this migration, and to many Indians the British seemed to be their natural allies against settler encroachment. Indian tribes that allied themselves with the revolutionaries earned little gratitude from the new nation and soon found themselves dispossessed of their lands.

TOPICS IN THE NEWS

ATLANTIC MIGRATIONS

Population. In 1700 about 250,000 inhabitants, white and black, lived along the seaboard and in the foothills of the Appalachians. Most of the whites were of English descent. Hundreds of thousands of Indians inhabited the backcountry. By 1776 the population of the colonies was about 2.5 million; immigration and a high birthrate were responsible for this tremendous growth. About one-half of the population in 1776 had migrated from the Old World—Europe or Africa—or were the children of immigrant parents. Traveling across the colonial landscape in the 1750s and 1760s, one would have heard a staggering variety of languages and dialects.

Germans. About 10 percent of the population in the mid 1700s was German-speaking. Approximately five hundred thousand people emigrated from southwestern Germany and Switzerland in the eighteenth century: not all went to the New World. Many went north to Prussia;

others went east to the Danube; and about two-fifths went to Pennsylvania. Germans dispersed through the Middle and Southern colonies and were known as hardworking and thrifty farmers.

Scots. From Scotland came thousands driven from the land by greedy landlords and the sinking fortunes of workers in the woolen industry. Landlords enclosed their estates—that is, they ejected tenant farmers and raised livestock with hired labor. Traditional handloom weavers were being rapidly displaced by the growing wool industry in England. These conditions drove many Scots to England and America. In the latter place they settled heavily in the backcountry of North Carolina and along the Hudson River valley of New York.

Scots-Irish. The Northern Irish, sometimes called Scots-Irish, also arrived by the tens of thousands in the 1750s and 1760s. This group was making a second overseas immigration; during the seventeenth century the English settled these Scots in northern Ireland to help colonize and dominate the Catholic Irish. But economic conditions were deteriorating in Ireland too, and overall some 250,000 people emigrated from northern Ireland. They settled across the backcountry from South Carolina to Maine. Independent-minded and hardy, they pushed westward, trying to stay out of the reach of colonial governments and land speculators.

Africans. Throughout the first three-quarters of the eighteenth century, Africans constituted more than one-half the immigrants to the thirteen colonies. This forced migration was driven by the lucrative trade in tobacco, rice, and other plantation crops. British and American traders dominated the North Atlantic slave trade, shipping thousands of captives a year under brutal conditions. Slaves were packed in dark holds and treated

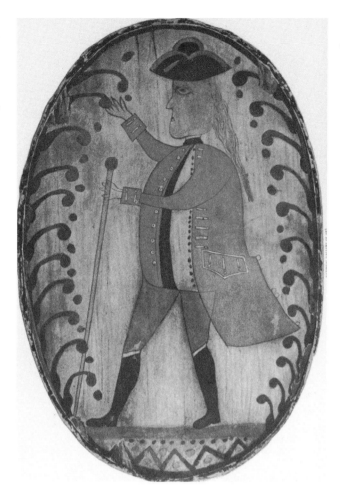

A folk-art painting of a Pennsylvania farmer, circa 1770 (National Gallery of Art)

as cargo: valuable, but with a certain amount of "damaged" and "lost cargo" to be expected. Slaves constituted

IMMIGRATION TO THE THIRTEEN COLONIES

The population of the thirteen colonies grew tenfold from 1700 to 1776. The Revolution and the Napoleonic Wars in Europe caused a disruption of immigration and depressed the slave trade. Immigration did not pick up again until after 1815.

Decade	Africans	Germans	N. Irish	S. Irish	Scots	English	Welsh	Other	Total
1700–1709	9,000	100	600	800	200	400	300	100	11,500
1710–1719	10,800	3,700	1,200	1,700	500	1,300	900	200	20,300
1720–1729	9,900	2,300	2,100	3,000	800	2,200	1,500	200	22,000
1730–1739	40,500	13,000	4,400	7,400	2,000	4,900	3,200	800	76,200
1740–1749	58,500	16,600	9,200	9,100	3,100	7,500	4,900	1,100	110,000
1750–1759	49,600	29,100	14,200	8,100	3,700	8,800	5,800	1,200	120,500
1760–1769	82,300	14,500	21,200	8,500	10,000	11,900	7,800	1,600	157,800
1770–1775	17,800	5,200	13,200	3,900	15,000	7,100	4,600	700	67,500
TOTAL	278,400	84,500	66,100	42,500	35,300	44,100	29,000	5,900	585,800

All figures are approximate.

Source: Aaron S. Fogleman, *Hopeful Journeys: German Immigration, Settlement, and Political Culture in Colonial America, 1717–1775* (Philadelphia: University of Pennsylvania, 1996).

A painting of wealthy colonials enjoying musical entertainment (Colonial Williamsburg Foundation, Virginia)

nearly one-half the population of the Chesapeake colonies.

Decline in Immigration. From 1775 to the mid 1780s immigration to the colonies suffered a drastic decline. England's naval blockade all but stopped regular immigrant traffic. European immigration was slow to revive in the years after the Revolution although the slave trade revived quickly. The slave population increased by about 40 percent from 1780 to 1790, well ahead of the general increase in population.

Sources:

Bernard Bailyn, *The Peopling of British North America: An Introduction* (New York: Knopf, 1986);

Aaron S. Fogleman, *Hopeful Journeys: German Immigration, Settlement, and Political Culture in Colonial America, 1717–1775* (Philadelphia: University of Pennsylvania, 1996);

David W. Galenson, *White Servitude in Colonial America: An Economic Analysis* (Cambridge: Cambridge University Press, 1981).

EIGHTEENTH-CENTURY STYLE AND CULTURE

New Fortunes, New Tastes. In Europe a rigid code governed dress and manners. Members of each social class or profession dressed a certain way, clearly identifying individuals as belonging to a particular category. People found no compelling need to change these social markers. But in the eighteenth century a revolution in the production of textiles brought easily made clothing and other consumer accessories. The notion of fashion and changing styles emerged. Wealthy and middling folk could vary their dress to suit fashion and individual taste, and it became more difficult to guess a person's position just by his clothing.

Luxury. By the mid eighteenth century, prosperity among the merchant and planter classes of British North America brought an increasing display of luxury goods. Wealthy colonials bought the latest clothing, carriages, and fine houses furnished in mahogany. They employed liveried servants to drive their coaches and wait at tables set with fine china. In the 1750s and 1760s increases in British government spending in the colonies, particularly on the military, brought surging wealth to North American merchants. Trade with Great Britain and among the colonies was booming. Colonial cities became arenas for competitive displays of wealth. In Philadelphia the tax rolls between 1756 and 1772 record a tripling of the number of taxpayers claiming "gentleman" status.

Conspicuous Consumption. While the boycotts of the pre-Revolutionary period and the turmoil of the Revolution disrupted consuming habits, the interruption was brief. By the early 1780s, as the war had moved to the Southern colonies, foreign visitors noted that the wealthy of New York continued to build lavish houses and ride in fine carriages. Even struggling farmers of the backcountry and laborers in the cities developed a taste for consumer goods in this period. Inventories of estates in the mid to late eighteenth century show that humble farmers owned earthenware dishes and bowls, forks, pewter teapots, blankets, and bedsteads whereas earlier in the century they had made do with wooden bowls and rough homemade furniture. Tea drinking was the great leveler of social habits. People of every class in the colonies drank tea, and most had the appurtenances that went with the tea habit: cups, sugar bowls, and kettles. Even the inmates of the Philadelphia almshouse demanded tea, and they wanted imported bohea tea, not some inferior substitute.

Given below are estimates of personal wealth and prices of various consumer goods in the last year of prosperity before the disruptions of warfare and blockade. The first table gives samples of net worth of colonists throughout the income range, measured in total assets, including houses, possessions, land, servants, and slaves:

Net Wealth of Residents of the Thirteen Colonies

Income Group	Total Net Wealth for Least Wealthy Member of Each Income Group (in Pounds Sterling):
Richest One Percent	£2,271.6
Next Richest One Percent	1,763.3
Richest Ten Percent	591.2
Ninth Decile	335.5
Eighth Decile	209.6
Seventh Decile	146.7
Sixth Decile	84.6
Fifth Decile	45.9
Fourth Decile	25.8
Third Decile	11.3
Second Decile	4.3
Poorest Ten Percent	-199.8

The second table gives some prices for various goods found in the estates of deceased American colonists in the year 1774. It shows the range of goods—and human property—that colonists owned and what each income group might have been able to afford:

Items in the Estates of Colonial Americans

Item	Appraised Value in Pounds Sterling
Cow	£3.53
Barrel of pork	0.15
Small washing tub	0.15
Loom	0.96
2 Tea pots, bowl, cream jug	0.03
Bed, etc.	1.77
10 bushels of oats	0.56
Year-old colt	2.25
3 Pounds coffee	0.11
Gun	0.45
Brass kettle	0.45
6 Silver teaspoons	0.30
Watch	2.48
Fine shirt	0.23
Woolen shirt	0.08
Mahogany stand and tea urn	2.86
12 Mahogany chairs, hair bottoms	7.15
Large family Bible	0.86
Scotch carpet	2.15
Diamond ring	10.01
Negro man	60.06
Negro "wench"	46.48
Negro boy	35.75
Negro girl	28.60
Young mulatto male child	7.15

Source: Alice Hanson Jones, *Wealth of a Nation to Be: The American Colonies on the Eve of the Revolution* (New York: Columbia University Press, 1980).

Elite Style. Men were the peacocks of the mid eighteenth century, perhaps because they had a stronger public presence, while women were relegated to the household much of the time. The fashions of the French court reigned over the English-speaking world during most of the 1700s, and for men this meant closely fitting coats and knee breeches made from rich, brightly colored silks and velvets, lace trim on collars and cuffs, and white silk stockings. The essential mark of a gentleman, though, was a wig, preferably made from women's hair and powdered white. These fashions were difficult to maintain, and even the richest colonials struggled to maintain the standards of the fabulously wealthy English gentry and royalty. The richest planters and merchants eagerly awaited ships bearing European goods and would buy only the latest fashionable items. Middle-class lawyers, doctors, and shopkeepers copied the styles of the colonial gentry as best they could though their coats were cut more simply and their wigs of wool were horse or goat hair.

Wigs. The full regalia of a gentleman required a complete team of servants, valets, and butlers, not to mention personal tailors, seamstresses, cordwainers (shoemakers), wig makers, and dressers. The wig was a particularly troublesome article, uncomfortable and difficult to maintain. Wealthy men kept their heads shaved and wore nightcaps or turbans in private. Going into public in the powdered wig of a gentleman meant that the hair of the wig first had to be smeared with a grease made from animal fat, curled with a hot iron, and rolled in papers. It was then placed on the head of the wearer and dusted with plaster of paris or flour. If the wig was too tight, the wearer suffered from itching and heat, if too loose he risked it going askew or falling off altogether. Wigs were so heavy and precarious that gentlemen required special lessons on how to walk while wearing them. Abrupt motions could cause a shower of white powder to fall on one's shoulders.

Wigs and Social Distinctions. Subtle differences in class and profession were discernible to some by the style of wig a man wore. Doctors sported a "physick's" wig that was teased in a fashion known as a "natty bob." Ministers wore the parson's wig with rows of neat curls. Certain crafts were exempted from the burdens of wig wearing; artists and wealthy artisans—men who had to work with their hands—were permitted the liberty of appearing in their own hair. The silversmith Paul Revere and painter Benjamin West are shown in portraits sporting natural heads of hair.

Women's Hair. Women in the eighteenth century generally kept their hair covered with hoods or caps. However, in the 1770s the style changed, and fashionable women wore huge, elaborate, powdered hairdos. American women generally did not wear wigs but favored "rats," or hairpieces, which they added to their hair for more stunning height and fullness. These pieces were literally glued on and were so difficult to arrange that women had their hair done only once every month. In the meantime they slept with their necks resting on wooden blocks instead of pillows to prevent their hair from falling into disarray. Women also tried to dress in the fashions of the French court and thus wore tightly laced corsets and low-cut gowns.

Etiquette. While any upstart who acquired wealth could purchase fashionable clothes, moving among the colonial elite required breeding and manners that could take years or a lifetime to acquire. The mark of a gentleman was to be perfectly at ease in society, confident in the manners he had learned from birth. However, colonial gentry still felt inferior to Europeans and strove to keep up. Books of etiquette were quite popular. Less-wealthy Americans in particular resorted to these guides so as not to appear gauche among the gentry. Colonials looking to fit into high society went to tutors to rid themselves of regional accents and to learn a smattering of literature, painting, and sculpture. They acquired some training in music, fencing, and above all, dancing.

Dancing. The essential skill of a gentleperson was dancing. Around it revolved all social rituals, socializing, business, and courtship. Among the Chesapeake gentry, balls were the center of social life. Those who could not perform gracefully on the dance floor were subject to ridicule and ostracism. French minuets were popular, as were dances derived from English country reels. Southerners were also handy at rollicking jigs derived, at least in part, from African American dancing. Philip Fithian, a Northerner, lived as a tutor on a Virginia plantation in 1773–1774 and wrote of his intense embarrassment at not being an accomplished dancer. He abstained from dancing rather than cutting an awkward figure on the dance floor. Fithian recorded in his diary that dancing was "a necessary qualification for a person to appear even decent in Company!" While the social life of the upper classes had its intensely ritualized and formal aspects, the gentry, in fact, engaged in many of the same activities as Americans of all classes. Drinking, horse racing, bear-baiting, cock fights, card playing, and dancing formed the central repertoire of social activities among both rich and poor.

Sources:

Cary Carson and others, eds., *Of Consuming Interest: The Style of Life in the Eighteenth Century* (Charlottesville: University Press of Virginia, 1994);

Ronald Hoffman, ed., *Economy of Early America: The Revolutionary Period, 1763–1790* (Charlottesville: University Press of Virginia, 1988);

Alice Hanson Jones, *Wealth of a Nation to Be: The American Colonies on the Eve of the Revolution* (New York: Columbia University Press, 1980);

J. A. Leo LeMay, *Robert Bolling Woos Anne Miller: Love and Courtship in Colonial Virginia, 1760* (Charlottesville: University Press of Virginia, 1990);

Stephanie G. Wolf, *As Various as Their Land: The Everyday Lives of Eighteenth-Century Americans* (New York: HarperCollins, 1993).

EXPANSION AND WAR ON THE FRONTIER

Threats to Indian Survival. From 1754 to 1763 fighting raged along the western and northern expanses of British North America as American colonials and British soldiers warred against the French. On both sides Indian allies did much of the fighting; Indians had a vital interest in trading furs and deerskins with Europeans and had become dependent on manufactured goods and food they obtained in this trade. They willingly went to war for their white trading partners, killing both European settlers and other Native Americans. Ironically, in helping to win the war on the frontier, British-allied Indians created more-favorable conditions for whites to settle on their lands.

The Proclamation of 1763. The British government tried to reward their Indian allies with the Proclamation of 1763, forbidding white settlers from crossing the Appalachian Mountains. The Crown wanted nothing to disturb their partners in the fur trade and knew independent-minded settlers threatened lucrative trading alliances. However, the British were unable to close the floodgates that opened in the mid 1700s. Thousands of settlers were already living beyond the mountains, enough that four thousand of them died, either in battle or from Indian raids, in the French and Indian War. Great Britain's victory in 1763 only made the frontier more attractive, removing the French threat and cutting off arms and food supplies to French Indian allies.

Pontiac's Rebellion. Pontiac was an Ottawa chief who in 1763 led a confederation of several tribes of the Mississippi River valley and lower Great Lakes region. No longer able to play the French against the English, Pontiac's alliance sought to drive the English from the territory west of the Allegheny Mountains. They were forced to accept a peace in 1766 after killing thousands of whites and taking eleven western forts. Settlers from the English colonies continued to pour over the mountains. These settlers were determined to drive all Indians away from white settlements despite the Indians' allegiance to the British. Land speculators also encouraged the settlers to acts of hostility against Indians, hoping to open up more land and increase the value of their holdings. This combination of circumstances prompted the Paxton Boys's massacres of peaceful Christianized Indians.

Source:

Francis Jennings, *Empire of Fortune: Crowns, Colonies, and Tribes in the Seven Years' War in America* (New York: Norton, 1988).

FOOD AND SOCIAL DIVERSITY

Diet. Americans of the revolutionary era relied heavily on salted meat, root vegetables, milk, and porridge. The frontier experience, a foundation of colonial society, had eliminated all but the hardiest of vegetables from the diet. Beans, turnips, potatoes, and sweet potatoes were easy to grow and could be stored for long periods of time. Regional variations in diet among the colonies were significant, determined by what foods were at hand and on the origins of the people who settled there.

The Breadbasket. New York, New Jersey, and particularly Pennsylvania made up the breadbasket of the British colonies; the farmers of eastern Pennsylvania produced most of the wheat consumed in Canada and the West Indies. Consequently the diet in this region was more varied than in other colonies. The Germans and the Dutch introduced many foods to the bland English diet, including cheeses, wheat bread, salads, apples, and vegetables. Cabbage, eaten as a salad or as sauerkraut, was a popular vegetable. Dr. Benjamin Rush, a prominent Philadelphia physician, believed that German immigrants had introduced green vegetables to that city, and he applauded this addition to the diet of city dwellers. Other observers claimed that the Hessian troops, whom the British hired to fight in the colonies, introduced kohlrabi, broccoli, and black radishes during the Revolution.

The Backcountry. The Scots-Irish of the Pennsylvania and Southern backcountry depended on hunting, fishing, and wild fruits and greens. Their diet included bear, venison, rabbit, squirrel, woodchuck, and turkey. This group rarely stayed in one place long enough to establish regular crops, but even a small patch of cleared land yielded sweet potatoes and turnips. Cows were prized on the frontier since their milk could be made into corn and rye mush. Without milk the frontiersmen made their mush from molasses, honey, or meat gravy. Life on the frontier often meant adopting Indian foodways; frontiersmen hunted and prepared their food using techniques learned from Native Americans. They grew corn, beans, and squash in the same field in imitation of the natives.

New England. In New England the easily grown pumpkin was eaten roasted, boiled, and mashed and was made into bread, cakes, and pies. Traditional English fare, milk porridge and white bread formed a dietary staple. Pigs could be raised nearly anywhere and left to forage in woodlands or even among the refuse in city streets. City authorities paid a functionary known as a "hog-reeve," or herder, to keep these surly and often dangerous foraging swine under control. The abundance of pigs meant that pork was ever present in the American diet, usually dried and preserved in salt. A British officer observed that fresh meat was eaten only when a fox got hold of a chicken and could be frightened into surrendering it.

Seafood. Most residents of the thirteen colonies lived within miles of the ocean or tidal rivers; thus seafood was an inevitable part of their diet. Shellfish were plentiful and cheap and formed the mainstay of the diet of the poor. Lobsters were not considered a delicacy and were common fare for humble New Englanders. In the streets of New York oyster venders pushed barrows laden with

DINING-HALL DELIGHTS

A menu from the College of Rhode Island, now Brown University, gives a glimpse of the bland fare that seems to have been the lot of college students in the 1780s. At the end of the Revolutionary War the teenage, male, mostly ministerial students of the college took their dinners—that is, their midday meal—in a common dining hall, as given in a typical weekly menu:

Two meals of salt beef and pork, with peas, beans, greens, roots, etc., and puddings. For drink, good small beer and cider.

Two meals of fresh meat, roasted, baked, broiled, or fried, with proper sauce or vegetables.

One meal of soup and fragments.

One meal of boiled fresh meat with proper sauce and broth.

One meal of salt or fresh fish, with brown bread.

Suppers were of hasty pudding, rice, corn mush, white bread, or milk porridge with tea, coffee, or chocolate. Meals, especially dinner, would vary during the week by the addition of puddings, apple pies, dumplings, or cheese as often "as may be convenient and suitable."

Breakfasts were also probably quite plain, as attested to by John Adams; he said that when he attended Harvard College, he received bread, biscuit, and milk in the morning.

The ageless complaints of students about dining-hall fare resonate in the outcries of classmates of Thomas Jefferson at the College of William and Mary. In 1760 students demanded both salt and fresh meat at dinner and puddings and pies on Sunday and two times a week.

Sources: Richard J. Hooker, *Food and Drink in America: A History* (Indianapolis & New York: Bobbs-Merrill, 1981);

Robert B. St. George, ed., *Material Life in America, 1600–1860* (Boston: Northeastern University Press, 1988).

Fragmentary existing records give us a glimpse of the diets of soldiers, prisoners, and slaves, who ate well or badly, depending on availability of food and the relative largesse or stinginess of those who provided their daily fare. Modern nutritionists consider an adequate daily diet for a man of average physical activity to be between 3,000 and 3,200 calories. Men who perform heavy labor require about 4,550 calories. Men of the revolutionary era may have needed fewer calories because of their slightly smaller stature. However, their work may have been a good deal more strenuous without modern machinery. Total calories, also, do not reflect good nutrition, something that is apparently lacking from most of the diets below.

Basic Weekly Diets of Selected Groups, 1755–1790

(all amounts in pounds or gallons unless otherwise specified)

Year and Population	Cals per day	Bread	Flour	Oatmeal	Peas	Rice	Cornmeal	Fish	Beef	Pork	Cheese	Butter	Beer	Molasses
About 1790, slaves on George Washington's plantation	2,800						11.3	2.4						
1780, French prisoners returned to France and English repatriates	3,100	7							7				3 1/2	
1780, Continental Army Ration	2,600–4000	7 or	7				1 3/4		7 or	6 1/2				
1776, Tory Prisoners in Maryland	3,600–4200	7 or	7		3 pts.		1 qt.		7 or	5 1/4				7 gills
1775, Continental Army Ration	3,000–5,400	7 or	7		3 pts.		1 pt.	7 or	7 or	5 1/4			1 3/4 or 2/3	
About 1770, Convicts sent to Va., Md., and the Carolinas from England	2,000	4 2/3		1 2/3	1				2/3	1/2	2/3			
1761, British Army in Canada	3,300–3,800	7			3 pts.	1/2			7 or	4		3/8		1 1/4
1757, Virginia Militia in the field	2,900	7						7 or	7 or	7				
1755, Acadians sent to Maryland	1,400	5								1				

Sources: *Historical Statistics of the United States, Colonial Times to 1970* (Washington, D.C.: Department of Commerce, Bureau of the Census, 1975);

Billy G. Smith, "The Material Lives of Laboring Philadelphians, 1750–1800," in *Material Life in America, 1600–1860*, edited by Robert B. St. George (Boston: Northeastern University Press, 1988).

shellfish and cried their wares as they went; these were usually poor women looking to make a few pence. A French refugee, Moreau de Saint Méry, wrote "Americans have almost a passion for oysters, which they eat at all hours, even in the streets."

Southern Plenty and Paucity. Milk, particularly served in corn or wheat porridge, was a staple in New England and the Middle colonies, but in the warmer Southern colonies it was hard to keep milk fresh and was thus rare. An itinerant minister, Charles Woodmason visited the South Carolina backcountry in 1767 and found "no Eggs, Butter, Flour, Milk, or anything but fat rusty Bacon, and fir Water, with Indian Corn Bread." In other locales he found bacon and eggs, but only rarely milk or fresh meat. A poor woman in South Carolina described her diet as consisting mainly of corn mush, salt beef, and water. But with the proper means even the Southern diet could encompass a range of delicacies. Harriot Horry, daughter of a South Carolina planter, compiled a cookbook in 1770 that included beef, veal, and seafood dishes along with Shrewsbury cakes and cheesecakes, marmalades, gingerbread, almond cream, and strawberry jellies.

Food Shortages. British and American soldiers and Patriot and Loyalist partisans destroyed the farms, crops, and livestock of their enemies during the Revolutionary War. Food shortages became common in both the armies and the cities of the thirteen colonies. The Continental Army lacked bread and survived on a half ration of rice in 1779. During 1780 and 1781 the army at times lacked both meat and flour; at one point each man subsisted on four ears of corn per day. With the severe devaluation of Continental paper money, food prices rose; hoarding and profiteering were common in the cities. Potatoes became a staple food in the North for both armies and civilians. John Adams wrote to his wife, Abigail, that if necessary they would subsist on potatoes rather than submit to the British. At the time, however, the Adamses were living comfortably, lacking only coffee, sugar, and pepper.

Price Controls. In Philadelphia the radicals who had been the mainstay of the revolutionary movement issued loud complaints against speculators in food and other necessities. In 1779, as paper currency became nearly worthless and as food prices soared, artisans on the Committee of Observation and Inspection exerted informal but firm control over the prices of essential commodities. Daniel Roberdeau, committee chairman and militia general, drew up a list of prices for food and threatened to punish merchants who did not hold to it. In other cities and towns groups of citizens seized food from merchants they thought were squeezing excessive profits from a desperate situation. Merchants, local leaders, and the common people had traditionally agreed on a notion of a "just price" for basic foodstuffs. Farmers and laboring people at times exerted pressure to see that these standards were observed.

Free Trade. Revolutionary-era merchants were engaged in a thriving world trade; notions of free competition prevailed, and following the writings of the economist Adam Smith, many merchants believed that over time the "invisible hand" of the market would intervene to regulate prices and supplies. However, theoretical nostrums did little to alleviate the real pain caused to the people when merchants withdrew scarce food from the market in hopes of obtaining a better price at a later date. The Committee of Observation and Inspection and angry citizens went beyond the law, confronting merchants and forcing the price of food into line. After the war such extreme measures were ruled illegal, and the traditional notions of price controls were swept away in favor of the emerging free market. As the war moved southward around 1780, most of the North began to return to its normal condition of food surpluses.

Sources:

Eric Foner, *Tom Paine and Revolutionary America* (Oxford & New York: Oxford University Press, 1978);

Richard J. Hooker, *Food and Drink in America: A History* (Indianapolis & New York: Bobbs-Merrill, 1981);

Reay Tannahill, *Food in History* (New York: Stein & Day, 1973).

THE FREE BLACK COMMUNITY

Work and Community. Free blacks gravitated to the Northern cities looking for work and a community. In 1790 the North was home to only 5.7 percent of the total black population of the colonies but harbored nearly one-half of the free black population. In New York and other cities a large slave and free-black population existed side by side and mingled in the streets on a daily basis, along with white servants and workers. Free blacks found sporadic employment as laborers and tradesmen: wagon drivers, construction workers, tailors, shoemakers, and sailors.

Churches. Though few free blacks prospered in the Northern cities, they did find some degree of freedom, and they deeply treasured the community life they built there. Churches were an important gathering place, and in the mid 1700s blacks often worshiped with white congregations; African Americans did not establish their own congregations with their own ministers until the 1790s. However, they were making considerable progress toward these goals in the 1770s and 1780s. Philadelphia in particular was a center of black Christianity: many free blacks who obtained their freedom in the Chesapeake region came to Philadelphia and became members of Methodist and Baptist congregations. In the South during the great religious revivals of the mid 1700s blacks and whites worshiped together on surprisingly friendly and equal terms. In the North urban churches had many wealthy patrons who objected to the presence of blacks; they often relegated them to balconies or the back of the church even though African societies within the churches raised funds for maintenance and ministers' salaries.

Absalom Jones. Absalom Jones was one of the first black Methodist preachers in this era before black churches. Born a slave in Delaware, he was brought by his master to Philadelphia in the 1760s to work in a store. A clerk taught him how to write, and he studied at Quaker Anthony Benezet's school for blacks. Purchasing his freedom in 1768, he became a lay preacher in the Methodist Church. Along with Richard Allen, another early black preacher, Jones established an informal but tightly knit black community within the white church. From such humble beginnings Philadelphia became a center of black religious and social life and was a beacon to Southern slaves until the abolition of slavery, nearly one hundred years later.

"Negro Election Days." By no means were all African Americans Christians, and since many were not even American born, the social life in black communities incorporated elements of Christianity, secular customs, and African religion and ritual. The growing direct importation of African-born slaves around mid century infused black life with renewed African traditions. Blacks had their own holidays and celebrations that paralleled those of whites but incorporated features unique to black life. So-called Negro Election Days were common in Northern locales, particularly where many in the black population were African born. Beginning as early as 1741 blacks in several towns in the North, particularly in New England, began to hold elaborate election-day ceremonies, usually in May or June, following the wake of the General Election Day of New England whites. In a series of parades, games, dinners, dances, and other celebrations the black community elected governors, kings, and other officials. In the Newport election parade "all the various languages of Africa, mixed with broken . . . English, filled the air accompanied with music of the fiddle, tambourine, the banjo, drum, etc." The actual election procedures varied, sometimes taking the form of a voice vote or caucus, but at other times depending on footraces or tests of strength between candidates. The actual authority of these officials was unclear, and was, in any case, largely ignored by whites. But the kings and governors often took on the role of informal spokesman among blacks, free and slave. Whites tolerated the festivities as a means for the blacks to let off steam, and while they may have been concerned that blacks organizing politically might pose a threat, often the black officials used their positions to complement white politics. During the Revolution several governors served with the Patriot army, and one of them, Guy Watson of Rhode Island, was a leading figure in the capture of British general Richard Prescott in Newport in 1777. In other cases the elected officials were figures of fun and self-parody: members of the community elected the king and then were free to verbally abuse and ridicule him in any manner they wished. These rituals had strong echoes of West African ceremonies, particularly the *Apo* ceremony of the Ashanti tribe of Ghana. The Election Days also encompassed some of the same sorts of revelry and parades as white election-day celebrations, and they evolved at about the same time in American history. Negro Election Day survived well into the mid nineteenth century until the time when African Americans had political rights recognized by the larger society.

Sources:

Philip S. Foner, *History of Black Americans: Volume I, From Africa to the Emergence of the Cotton Kingdom* (Westport, Conn.: Greenwood Press, 1975);

Sidney Kaplan, *The Black Presence in the Era of the American Revolution, 1770–1800* (New York: New York Graphic Society, 1973);

Gary Nash, *Forging Freedom: The Formation of Philadelphia's Black Community, 1720–1840* (Cambridge, Mass.: Harvard University Press, 1988);

Joseph P. Reidy, "Negro Election Day and Black Community Life in New England, 1750–1860," *Marxist Perspectives*, 1 (Fall 1978): 102–117;

Jessie C. Smith and Carrell P. Horton, eds., *Historical Statistics of Black America* (Detroit: Gale Research, 1995);

Melvin Wade, "Shining in Borrowed Plumage: Affirmation of Community in the Black Coronation Festivals of New England, ca. 1750–1850," *Western Folklore*, 40 (July 1981): 171–182.

THE FREEDOM TO IMBIBE

Rum. Alcohol was a feature of the American table and, in some form, appeared at every meal. Americans imbibed freely of beer, cider, wine, whiskey, and rum. The greatest change in American drinking habits in the 1750s through the 1770s was the increased consumption of New England rum. Rum declined in price because of the booming trade in its basic ingredient—West Indies molasses. The merchants of New England bought molasses in the Indies, shipped it home, and manufactured it into rum in more than 150 distilleries. They hauled their rum casks to Africa, where they exchanged them for slaves, who were in turn shipped to the West Indies. New England produced enough rum for export and for home consumption, and it became the favorite drink of poor men. The Sugar Act of 1764 threatened the New England trade in molasses and rum, and some observers claimed that it was the endangering of this trade, far more than trade in tea, that aroused American ire toward Great Britain.

Temperance. A few voices in favor of temperance began to be raised in the 1770s; Anthony Benezet, a Quaker and antislavery activist, compared slavery to America's dependency on Great Britain and asserted that both forms of bondage were akin to the tyranny of the rum shop. Benezet and other reforming Quakers made great headway in getting the Society of Friends to reject the use of distilled beverages. Dr. Benjamin Rush noted the potentially harmful physical effects of strong drink in his 1772 pamphlet *Sermons to Gentlemen upon Temperance and Exercise*. Rush proposed the novel ideas of moderate drinking, eating, and exercise.

Rum and Lead Poisoning. In the 1740s doctors identified a crippling illness they called the West Indies Dry Gripes. This debilitating disease was a form of lead poi-

An engraving of men enjoying food and drink at a tavern, circa 1750 (Ardents Collection, New York Public Library)

soning caused by drinking rum made in lead stills. It caused intense stomach pain and could leave a victim paralyzed. It was not until 1768 that Massachusetts passed a law forbidding the use of lead still heads.

Tavern Regulation. Wealthy and influential Americans raised objections to the social consequences of drinking in the 1750s and 1760s, if not to drinking itself. Public houses, or taverns, were a nuisance in colonial cities, catering to a rough mixture of patrons and often became the scenes of fights and riots. Benjamin Franklin in 1764 called taverns "a Pest to Society." English common law recognized the right of citizens to sell drink from their houses; anyone could set up a barrel of rum in his house and call himself a tavern keeper. John Adams tried to pass laws regulating taverns in Braintree, Massachusetts, but found little enthusiasm for his cause. Sales of liquor on Sundays, gambling in taverns, sales to slaves, drinking off premises, and other abuses continued despite efforts at regulation. Alcohol remained at the center of social life in homes and taverns. When George Washington ran for the Virginia legislature in 1758, he had his agent dole out three and three-quarters gallons of beer, wine, cider, or rum to every voter. Washington had second thoughts about this tactic, worrying that he had not been generous enough.

Drink and the Revolution. Public houses became increasingly important with the approach of the Revolu-

tion as meeting halls for Patriot committees and as places where all social classes could gather to discuss the issues of the day. Coffeehouses were patronized mainly by wealthy merchants, many of whom had loyalist sympathies. Militia commanders used taverns as headquarters for recruiting, mustering, and paying soldiers. Patriots constructed liberty poles in front of taverns in celebration of the Declaration of Independence and the repeal of the Stamp Act. British authorities called taverns "nests of sedition" but could do little to eradicate them. The success of the Revolution increased the prestige of the taverns in which committees and militiamen met, and Americans came to associate their political freedom with the freedom to imbibe as they wished. With the development of political life after the Revolution taverns became centers of electoral politics, and dispensing liquor to voters was an enduring tradition.

Sources:

C. C. Pearson, *Liquor and Anti-Liquor in Virginia, 1619–1919* (Durham, N.C.: Duke University Press, 1967);

W. J. Rorabaugh, *The Alcoholic Republic: An American Tradition* (Oxford & New York: Oxford University Press, 1979);

Reay Tannahill, *Food in History* (New York: Stein & Day, 1973).

FRONTIER LIFE: BLENDING CULTURES

Social and Cultural Accommodation. In 1754 many Native American people living in the trans-Appalachian region had been in close contact with white colonists for

A rural cornhusking bee, circa 1770

at least one hundred years, and their way of life combined Indian and European ways. Indians relied on a range of manufactured tools, weapons, pots, and decorative items. In fact the consumer revolution among the Indians was well underway in the late 1600s and early 1700s, well ahead of the trend in the white-settled areas of British America. Many influential figures among Indians and whites crossed over from one cultural sphere to another, speaking various European and Indian languages and intermarrying, and forming political alliances between the two rapidly merging worlds. In New England some Indians still lived in traditional wigwams, but they filled them with European-manufactured furniture and decorative items. Some members of the Oneida tribe of the Iroquois confederacy practiced Presbyterianism, although simultaneously retaining traditional beliefs and rituals. Some Indians adopted European dress but retained the loincloths and nose rings of their own cultures.

Alcohol. While Indians successfully adapted some European ways and artifacts, the widespread introduction of alcohol proved disastrous for their societies. Drinking fed the violence and social dislocation that came with European contact; it also increased susceptibility to European diseases, which took a frightful toll. Europeans were aware of the ill effects liquor had on Indians and often promoted its distribution to increase those effects.

White Settlers, Indian Ways. Europeans on the frontier adopted Indian ways in the form of clothing, canoes, and native foods. They grew Indian corn and hunted just as Native Americans did. Frontiersmen routinely wore breechcloths and leggings and were quite proud of their ability to hunt and live off the land like Indians. Some settlers even lived in Indian communities and married Indian women.

This proximity and intermarriage into Indian clans facilitated trade and provided mutual protection against enemies. In the mid 1770s twenty whites lived in the Shawneee town of Chillicothe in what is now Ohio. Three hundred English and Scots lived among the Creeks in present-day Alabama.

Conflicts. Despite the exchanges and mixing of culture the legacy of the frontier was conflict rather than cooperation. Indian population was declining, mainly due to disease. White population was skyrocketing from immigration and natural increase. Whites on the frontier resented restrictions on their movements and taxation imposed by British officials. They complained that the colonial government favored Indians over whites and complained of their lack of representation in colonial legislatures. Frontier settlers were buffeted about by land speculators who bought up vast regions of the backcountry and charged high prices for land that the settlers themselves had cleared, cultivated, and made valuable. In a hostile world settlers took out their frustrations upon those least able to defend themselves, usually Native Americans. In the early 1770s the backcountry was ready to explode, with resentment of British Indian policy breaking out in random massacres of Indian settlements.

Source:
Colin G. Calloway, *The American Revolution in Indian Country: Crisis and Diversity in Native American Communities* (Cambridge & New York: Cambridge University Press, 1995).

INDENTURED SERVITUDE

Servitude. Many Europeans came to North America under the condition that they perform several years of involuntary labor to pay for their transportation to the New

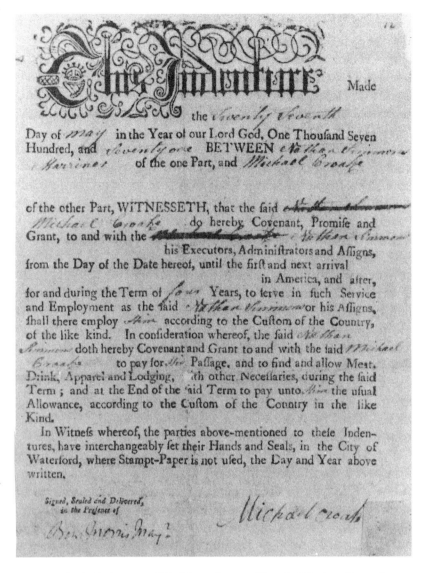

A colonial indenture, 1771 (Massachusetts Historical Society, Boston)

World. These men and women were known as indentured servants, or in the case of the Germans, redemptioners. In the major port cities of Great Britain many jobless individuals signed contracts to work for a term of years, at the end of which time they might be paid a freedom wage—a small amount of money, some tools, or simply the clothes on their back. Conditions of servitude varied widely; some servants were able to become independent farmers or artisans at the end of their terms. Others, unable to improve their fortunes, simply signed on for another term. Indentures had been quite common in the 1600s, and servants formed the backbone of the labor force in the Chesapeake region. But as slave prices declined in the late 1600s and early 1700s, white servants were gradually displaced as the main source of plantation labor. Even so, many artisans, displaced farmers, and young people without prospects signed on for terms of four to seven years. The port cities served as great clearinghouses for these servants. They waited by the docks or in boardinghouses to be taken to interior farms, where they were put to work.

German Redemptioners. More than seventy thousand German redemptioners arrived in Philadelphia before U.S. independence. They swarmed around the wharf area and as they were taken away to work on farms were quickly replaced on the docks by newer arrivals. German servants were called redemptioners because the captain of the ship that brought them over had to personally sell their labor contracts, thereby "redeeming" the cost of their passage. In 1775 hundreds of desperate redemptioners were packed into dockside boardinghouses run by German widows, waiting for someone to purchase their labor. Warehoused under these conditions for months, they suffered greatly, and many died of malnutrition and diseases. They also passed diseases to the natives and increased the death rate in the city.

Decline of White Indentures. Only the dynamic birthrate among the youthful population of the colonies offset these horrendous losses. As Patriots began to demand an end to their "slavery" to the British Crown, many North Americans, black and white, were working in conditions

A story of a typical immigrant of the 1770s reflects the circumstances of a man leaving his isolated rural home in search of work, with no intention of going to America, and with every intention of returning to his native place after finding work away from home. The North American colonies became another stop on the ever-widening circuit of the unemployed of Europe. John Harrower, a Scot, found work on the New World periphery but did not live to return home.

Harrower was a shopkeeper and tradesman from the town of Lerwick in the Shetland Islands. He left home "in search of business" carrying eight and one-half pence in cash and three pounds worth of wool stockings he hoped to sell along the way. He hoped to find work in the cities of Great Britain or Holland, earn some money, and return home. He tramped unsuccessfully around Scotland, finding nothing, then made his way south, walking eighty miles from Portsmouth to London.

The English capital was overflowing with skilled but unemployed workers like himself, many of them reduced to beggary. Having exhausted his meager funds, Harrower sold himself into four years of indentured servitude on a Virginia plantation.

After a month at sea on the ship *Planter* Harrower was handed over to a merchant who dealt in indentured servants. The tobacco planter Col. William Daingerfield, needing a tutor for his children, bought Harrower's four years. Harrower was relatively fortunate; he was treated with kindness and respect. Harrower apparently liked the New World, for he put aside some money and planned to bring his wife and children over to Virginia. But his plans came to naught, and he was still a servant when he died in 1777.

Source: Bernard Bailyn, *The Peopling of British North America: An Introduction* (New York: Knopf, 1986).

---

of servitude. Indentured servitude came to an end only gradually in the nineteenth century as the fares for the transatlantic crossing decreased. Immigrants could then save enough money to travel to America without a price on their heads.

Sources:

Bernard Bailyn, *The Peopling of British North America: An Introduction* (New York: Knopf, 1986);

Aaron S. Fogleman, *Hopeful Journeys: German Immigration, Settlement, and Political Culture in Colonial America, 1717–1775* (Philadelphia: University of Pennsylvania, 1996);

David W. Galenson, *White Servitude in Colonial America: An Economic Analysis* (Cambridge: Cambridge University Press, 1981).

THE MOVEMENT FOR EMANCIPATION

New England. As the rhetoric of freedom rang out across the colonies in the early 1770s, blacks in the North raised their voices against the injustices of slavery and legal discrimination against freedmen. In 1773 and 1774 slaves in Massachusetts sent a series of petitions to the colony's legislature asking for emancipation and requesting that they either be settled on a grant of land in the colony or given passage to Africa. These slaves described themselves as a "Grate Number of Blacks of this Province who are held in a State of Slavery within the bowels of a free and christian country" who claimed in "comon with all other men a natural right to our freedom without Being depriv'd of them by our fellow men. . . ." The petitioners failed to gain the support of the legislature.

Hall and Cuffe. Nevertheless agitation continued in Massachusetts. Prominent free blacks, including Freemason and businessman Prince Hall and shipping merchant Paul Cuffe, petitioned the legislature again in 1777. They spoke out on behalf of abolition as Massachusetts delegates met to write a constitution for the state in 1778. At first things went badly as delegates explicitly banned black citizenship. However, the determined efforts of the Reverend William Gordon to eliminate this constitutional provision were successful. The constitution of 1780 did not explicitly ban blacks from citizenship though it did prohibit them from voting. The declarations of universal equality in the constitution, however, opened the door for the courts to rule that slavery was unconstitutional; a state supreme court justice did precisely that in 1783.

Vermont. The first legal abolition of slavery in the colonies took place in Vermont. Declaring itself an independent state on 16 January 1777, Vermont adopted a constitution the following July that explicitly banned servitude. The area had a mere handful of slaves and only fifty black residents in 1780.

Pennsylvania. In Philadelphia Dr. Benjamin Rush wrote and spoke out against slavery and the slave trade. He advocated gradual emancipation and called on the colonies to write it into law. The hypocrisy of slavery was troubling to many advocates of independence. Thomas Paine called for the abolition of slavery more than a year before he published *Common Sense* (1776), the pamphlet that rallied Americans to the cause of independence. Quakers in Pennsylvania agitated for a law abolishing slavery but met with strong resistance, particularly from Scots-Irish Patriots of the backcountry. The best that Pennsylvania could manage was a gradual emancipation law that passed the legislature in 1780. Despite this legal failure, slavery was crumbling in Pennsylvania as else-

Leg and neck irons used to restrain slaves (private collection)

where in the North. There were only 239 slaves in the state at the census of 1790.

Military Emancipation. As the Continental Army took shape in 1775, George Washington restricted the enlistment of blacks to those who had already served in local militias. Southern delegates to the Continental Congress tried to remove all blacks from Patriot service. But in November 1775 John Murray, Lord Dunmore, the British governor of Virginia, changed the racial character of the war by issuing a proclamation of emancipation to all blacks who would desert the Patriot cause and join the Loyalists. Only three hundred slaves initially responded to Dunmore's call for an Ethiopian Regiment, but it was enough to throw the Patriots into a panic. An alarmed Washington wrote "If that man, Dunmore, is not crushed before Spring he will become the most dangerous man in America. . . . Success will depend on which side can arm the Negroes the faster." Washington ordered his officers to enlist a limited number of free blacks but arbitrarily excluded many free blacks and all slaves. The hardest fighting of the Revolution took place in the South, and Washington realized that the Patriots had to offer some incentive to blacks to prevent large-scale revolts. The revolutionaries began to offer freedom to slaves of Loyalists who were willing to serve in the militia or the Continental Army.

Occupation Brings Freedom. From 1775 through 1783 the British at various times occupied Boston, Philadelphia, and New York. British offers of freedom riveted the attention of slaves. Many whose masters had not evacuated them to unoccupied areas gained at least temporary freedom by joining forces with the British, serving in the army or navy. When the British evacuated Philadelphia in 1778, many of the freed slaves left with the British army. Five years later, with the rebel victory, the British evacuated their last stronghold in the North, New York City. They took with them three thousand former slaves, whom they shipped to Nova Scotia. Many others had died in military service or remained behind, hoping to evade reenslavement by former masters.

Military Strategy. In 1779, as the battles of the Revolution moved to the Southern colonies, British general Henry Clinton issued another freedom proclamation while occupying large areas of South Carolina. However, the British army could not handle the thousands of slaves who arrived at their encampments. Putting many of them to work or under arms, they sent most back to their plantations and established military police to keep order on the plantations. The British saw a chance to do great harm to the Patriot cause by undermining their valuable agricultural production and setting the slaves in revolt. Patriot militias in South Carolina and Georgia spent much of their time guarding slaves rather than fighting the British, so dependent were they on continued production of tobacco, rice, indigo, and cotton. Even so, the Revolution provided blacks with increased opportunities to escape, either to the wilderness or to the British lines. Slaves could also negotiate better terms of work on the plantation, with their masters short of manpower. The drivers or supervisors of labor gangs on plantations had been white. Planters during the Revolution were forced to trust black drivers, and in return these drivers kept order and kept their fellow slaves loyal to the Patriot cause. Eventually about five thousand blacks would serve the Patriot cause while eighty thousand to one hundred thousand blacks would either fight for the British or es-

Henry Dawkins's 1764 engraving of Philadelphians preparing to repel the Paxton Boys
(Library Company of Philadelphia, Pennsylvania)

cape to the protection of the royal army. At the end of the Revolution the British evacuated twenty thousand blacks to various overseas destinations, including Sierra Leone in West Africa, Jamaica, and Great Britain.

Sources:

Ira Berlin and Ronald Hoffman, eds., *Slavery and Freedom in the Age of the American Revolution* (Charlottesville: University Press of Virginia, 1983);

Philip S. Foner, *History of Black Americans: Volume I, From Africa to the Emergence of the Cotton Kingdom* (Westport, Conn.: Greenwood Press, 1975);

Sidney Kaplan, *The Black Presence in the Era of the American Revolution, 1770–1800* (New York: New York Graphic Society, 1973);

Jessie C. Smith and Carrell P. Horton, eds., *Historical Statistics of Black America* (Detroit: Gale Research, 1995).

THE PAXTON BOYS'S MASSACRE

Frontier Rage. The bitterness of whites in the back-country of Pennsylvania was substantial after years of bloody guerrilla warfare with various Indian tribes. In late 1763 settler rage led to vindictive bloodletting against the Indians and open confrontation with a colonial government they felt had failed to protect them. A band of frontier ruffians, self-styled the Paxton Boys (after one of the towns on the Susquehanna River from which they came), lashed out against the so-called civilized Indians in the praying or mission towns of southeastern Pennsylvania.

Conestoga Manor. On 15 December 1763 this small band of fifty-seven men descended on the village called Conestoga Manor, a government-protected settlement where some twenty Conestoga Indians lived peacefully, cultivating the soil and practicing Christianity under the direction of Moravian missionaries. The settlement was hundreds of miles from territory threatened by warlike tribes and was surrounded by white-settled areas. Finding only six Indians at home—three men, two women, and one boy—they killed and scalped these hapless victims. They then set the village on fire, celebrated their "victory," and rode off in search of the other Conestogas. Officials in the town of Lancaster heard of the massacre and, wishing to protect the remaining residents of Conestoga Manor, gathered them in the county workhouse.

BENJAMIN FRANKLIN SPEAKS OUT AGAINST THE PAXTON BOYS

As a Quaker and a prominent member of the Pennsylvania legislature, Benjamin Franklin had strong moral and political objections to the massacres of Conestoga Indians. Franklin denounced the attackers in a pamphlet published in early 1764, finding them markedly inferior to "Heathens, Turks, Saracens, Moors, Negroes, and Indians, in the Knowledge and Practice of what is right." Franklin described the brutal killing of fourteen defenseless Indians at the Lancaster workhouse and remarked on the casual departure of the perpetrators:

The barbarous Men who committed the atrocious Fact, in Defiance of Government, of all Laws human and divine, and to the eternal Disgrace of their Counry and Coulour, then mounted their Horses, Huzza'd in Triumph, as if they had gained a Victory, and rode off—*unmolested!*

The Bodies of the Murdered were then brought out and exposed in the Street, till a Hole could be made in the Earth, to receive and cover them.

But the Wickedness cannot be covered, the Guilt will lie on the whole Land, till Justice is done on the Murderers. THE BLOOD OF THE INNOCENT WILL CRY TO HEAVEN FOR VENGEANCE.

Source: Benjamin Franklin, "A Narrative of the Late Massacres" in *The Papers of Benjamin Franklin,* volume 2 (New Haven & London: Yale University Press, 1967).

A painting of King Street (now State Street) in Boston, circa 1770 (Massachusetts Historical Society, Boston)

Lancaster. However, the frontiersmen had little respect for, or fear of, the authorities, so great was the sympathy for their cause (if not necessarily their tactics) among the population. On 27 December they gathered at the workhouse and massacred the rest of the Conestogas. The sixteen unarmed Indians divided into family groups, fell to their knees, and declared their love of the English. They were murdered while in the posture of prayer, and the Paxton Boys mounted their horses and rode off in celebration. It is not clear whether the local authorities at Lancaster had offered some show of resistance or if they stood by passively. No witnesses could ever be found to testify against the members of this mob, and they went unprosecuted.

The Government Retreats. The colonial authorities in Pennsylvania demanded justice against the killers, and frontiersmen rallied in their defense. Instead of there being a trial, Philadelphia was forced to raise a militia to defend itself against a ragtag army of six hundred frontiersmen who marched on the capital demanding military protection for the backcountry, relief from taxation, and greater representation in government. The colonial government forestalled any violence by accepting a formal petition from the protesters. This lack of vigorous action in the face of open defiance of colonial authority reflected the sharp division in public opinion, and not just on the frontier. The Quakers who dominated the legislature (including Benjamin Franklin) expressed their outrage, but they realized they faced a formidable mass of poor and middling folk in the West and in the suburbs of Philadelphia who sympathized with the Paxton Boys's basic motivations. These less wealthy and politically disfranchised folk tended to be Lutherans and Presbyterians, and they were contemptuous of Quaker and Moravian missionary efforts among Indians. The colonial government worried that widespread lawlessness might even extend to a massacre of the Indians sheltered on Providence Island in Philadelphia.

Sources:

Francis Jennings, *Empire of Fortune: Crowns, Colonies, and Tribes in the Seven Years' War in America* (New York: Norton, 1988);

Matthew Smith, *A Declaration and Remonstrance of the Distressed and Bleeding Frontier Inhabitants of the Province of Pennsylvania* (Philadelphia: Printed by W. Bradford, 1764).

POOR RELIEF IN REVOLUTIONARY BOSTON

Boston's Poor. Decades of war with France in the mid eighteenth century left Boston with a large population of widows and refugees and a permanent class of poor residents. Children of the indigent were "bound out" as apprentices. This was thought to be a good way of removing poor children from the relief rolls and reintegrating them into society. The city fathers of Boston were also troubled by the armies of transient poor that tramped from town to town seeking relief at the almshouses. Boston authorities established a practice of "warning out" transients—that is, publicly declaring them ineligible for poor relief. The city rejected thousands in the 1750s during the French and Indian War, when refugees from war zones swelled the ranks of the transient poor. In addition job seekers from Massachusetts villages and towns appeared in increasing numbers in Boston. Warned out of one town, these mostly young and single transients would move on to the next, either to find relief at an almshouse or seasonal farmwork. Some found work as servants, but most were fleeing from servitude or at the end of their terms of indenture had taken to the highway in search of work.

The Manufactory House. In Puritan Boston the religious and governing classes had a hard time accepting that poverty could be the result of anything but individual laziness. But by mid century it was apparent that many were chronically without work due to the severe dislocations of war and economic fluctuations. A typically Puritan solution was tried: establishment of workhouses or manufactories where the poor, particularly women, could produce goods to defray the cost of their upkeep. A few schemes tried around mid century attempted to establish manufactories of cloth. In 1753 a Linen Manufactory House opened, supported by private subscriptions, with three hundred spinsters tending the looms. Boston's ministers supported the operation in sermons and appealed for donations. But the manufactory was never self-supporting, and in 1758 it was forced to close due to lack of funds. The idea was not a bad one, but cheap British imports easily undercut home manufactures in price. There was also the factor of resentment among the poor women of Boston. Working in a manufactory took them away from their families and homes, which proved a great hardship. Women were more willing to spin cloth at home, and the poor in fact often resorted to this sort of labor, working for local merchants at low piece rates. They deserted the manufactories despite the exhortations of ministers and the threats of city officials to cut off relief for the poor.

Home Manufactures and Work Relief. Bostonians once again sought to put the poor to work spinning cloth in the 1760s during the boycotts of British imports. Wealthy Tories pointed to previous failures at cloth manufacture and disparaged the efforts of the Patriots. A prominent Boston radical and entrepreneur, William Molineux, organized a plan under which poor women could manufacture cloth in their homes. He hired school mistresses to teach poor women to spin. Molineux gained a great deal of goodwill among the poor for allowing them to work at home. He combined defiance of the royal governor with attempts at bettering the social welfare of the city. This effort met with only mixed success, but poor women were heartened, knowing that the wives of wealthy Patriots were also spinning cloth in their homes.

Source:

Gary B. Nash, *The Urban Crucible: Social Change, Political Consciousness, and the Origins of the American Revolution* (Cambridge, Mass.: Harvard University Press, 1979).

POVERTY AND SOCIAL REFORM: NEW YORK AND PHILADELPHIA

New York. By the 1760s immigrants were entering New York in large numbers, overloading the almshouse, and bankrupting the city treasury. In 1776 the Patriot government attempted to employ the poor in industrious pursuits, but when the British threatened to invade the city, Washington had the poor removed to the surrounding countryside so as not to distract the troops with their "shrieks and cries." They were replaced by a flood of Loyalist refugees whom the British occupiers quartered in the almshouse.

Philadelphia's Poor. Philadelphia, a major clearinghouse for immigrants and refugees, also developed a permanent underclass in the second half of the eighteenth century. Laborers, merchant seamen, and tailors composed the lowest ranks of the working population. Below these groups were widows, the disabled, and the elderly who remained in the grasp of public and private relief. In the bad times that regularly disrupted the city's trade, members of these groups would end up on the relief rolls. A particularly cold winter could cause the Delaware River to freeze, throwing sailors and dockworkers onto the public charity. In 1776 the Overseers of the Poor observed that most of those admitted to the almshouse were "naked, helpless and emaciated with Poverty and Disease to such a Degree that some have died in a few days after their admission." More than one-half of the inmates of the almshouse suffered from some form of ailment though some may have only feigned an illness, such as "sore legs," which reached epidemic proportions among aid recipients.

A Permanent Underclass. The development of a permanent underclass is suggested by the steady increases of robberies in Philadelphia, which accounted for about 80 percent of all crimes and were committed, it was said, mainly by Irish and African Americans. In the later years of the eighteenth century the poor were a more or less fixed group, consisting of one-fourth of the city's sailors, one-sixth of cordwainers, and one-eighth of the tailors, weavers, and breechmakers.

The Bettering House. As in Boston, Philadelphia tried employment schemes for its swelling underclass: a linen manufactory failed as resoundingly as its Boston counterpart. The prominent Philadelphian Benjamin Franklin expressed the opinion in 1753 that nothing was more responsible for creating poverty than the availability of public relief for the poor. In 1766, with 220 paupers subsisting in an overcrowded almshouse, a group of Quaker merchants embarked on a privately funded scheme to build the Bettering House, a combined almshouse for the elderly and disabled and workhouse for the able-bodied poor. The poor were set to picking oakum (hemp fibers coated with tar and used for caulking seams) and other menial tasks, which the house managers contracted out to local manufacturers. This new program differed from other workhouse programs in that it was administered by a private group, to whom the city had granted the authority to compel the poor to cooperate—or face a complete cutoff of relief. Franklin had a hand in the new venture, asserting that "Frugality and Industry will go a great way towards indemnifying us." The Bettering House was a total privatization of public relief and an attempt to turn it into a profit-making, or at least a break-even, venture. The managers of the Bettering House worked hard to eliminate disbursements of charity to those residing in private homes, so-called outdoor relief. They instead tried to force those in need of relief into the Bettering House, where their labor would repay the system. The poor resisted these changes, as did the overseers of the poor—who were mainly from the artisan class. The poor evaded service in the house, and the overseers neglected to enforce confinement and also were lax in collecting poor taxes for the support of the Bettering House.

Revolutionary Poor Relief. Artisans and merchants had their own plans for making useful citizens of paupers. They too supported spinning and weaving programs for the poor, but they turned a more sensitive ear to the needs of the poor themselves. Also, they avoided the moralistic tone of the Bettering House managers and treated the poor as citizens with a vital role to play in the fight against British imports. Their efforts met with only limited success but with a great deal of popularity for a few years during the nonimportation drives of the 1760s. In New York the Society for Promoting Arts, Agriculture and Economy capitalized on popular support for home manufactures and brought "above three hundred poor and necessitous persons" into their cloth-manufacturing operation in 1768.

The United Company of Philadelphia. In Philadelphia radical artisans led by Daniel Roberdeau set up the United Company of Philadelphia for Promoting American Manufactures. They operated under the same principles as William Molineux in Boston, allowing the poor to work at home, and achieved the greatest success of any of the prewar manufacturing schemes. The United Company prospered while the Bettering House floundered, with its rigid discipline and Quaker moralism.

Sources:

John K. Alexander, *Render Them Submissive: Responses to Poverty in Philadelphia, 1760–1800* (Amherst: University of Massachusetts Press, 1980);

Robert E. Cray, *Paupers and Poor Relief in New York City and Its Rural Environs, 1700–1830* (Philadelphia: Temple University Press, 1988);

Gary B. Nash, *The Urban Crucible: Social Change, Political Consciousness, and the Origins of the American Revolution* (Cambridge, Mass.: Harvard University Press, 1979);

Billy G. Smith, *The "Lower Sort": Philadelphia's Laboring People, 1750–1800* (Ithaca, N.Y. & London: Cornell University Press, 1990).

THE REVOLUTION BRINGS CULTURAL CHANGE

Revolutionary Style. Among the Puritan elites of Boston and the Quaker merchants of Philadelphia the

---

A BRITISH SUBJECT'S VIEWS ON THE REVOLUTION

Nicholas Cresswell was a wealthy English landowner who traveled through the North American colonies from 1774 to 1777 looking for a suitable place to establish a plantation. Caught up in the maelstrom of Revolution, with diminishing hopes of a quick British victory, he returned to England, having rid himself of any notions of becoming a colonist. While staying in Virginia he received news of the American victory at Trenton; his diary captures his surprise and displeasure:

Wednesday, January 1, 1777: Spent the day very happily at Mr. Gibbs with a few of his friends, dancing and making ourselves as merry as Whiskey, Toddy and good company will afford. . . .

Monday, Jan. 6th, 1777: News that Washington had taken 760 Hessian prisoners at Trenton in the Jerseys. This afternoon hear he has likewise taken six pieces of Brass Cannon.

Tuesday, Jan. 7th, 1777: The minds of the people are much altered. A few days ago they had given up the cause for lost. Their late successes have turned the scale and now they are all liberty mad again. Their Recruiting parties could not get a man (except he bought him from his master) no longer since than last week, and now the men are coming in by companies. . . . Volunteer Companies are collecting in every County on the Continent and in a few months the rascals will be stronger than ever. Even the parsons, some of them, have turned out as Volunteers . . . summoning all to arms in this cursed babble. D___ to them all.

Source: *Journal of Nicholas Cresswell, 1774–1777* (Port Washington, N.Y.: Kennikat Press, 1968).

---

growing taste for high style and conspicuous consumption did not go unheeded. They built palatial homes and wore imported fabrics. To avoid ostentation that might clash with their religious doctrines, however, they adopted the neoclassical styles in homes and decor that were becoming popular during the revolutionary era. As republican ideas became popular in Europe and America, excessive ornamentation and showy wealth came to be considered gauche. The clean lines of classic Greek and Roman architecture and furniture design (although using the best materials and finishes) came to symbolize not only good taste but also a certain political orientation. Some commentators, however, believed that high living, replete with servants, footmen, and carriages, mocked the republican simplicity of neoclassical styles.

Funerals and Simplicity. Expressions of solidarity with the Patriot movement changed nearly every aspect of colonial life. Funerals, previous to the nonimportation movement, had been an occasion for great displays of wealth, with fine carriages and mourners dressed in the finest clothes they could afford. Families often went deeply into debt to finance these affairs. In the late 1760s mourners adopted simple garb for funerals, often just a black ribbon for the arm or the hat. This constituted a highly public political statement, one that infuriated rich Tories as they witnessed these austere processions.

Freedom of Movement. Clothing tastes changed around the time of the Revolution, and many of the most bizarre styles began to go out of vogue. The influence of revolutionary ideas in America and Great Britain swung the pendulum back toward a republican simplicity. Men began to wear English "country clothes, loose trousers and jackets and high boots." It became acceptable to wear one's own hair again. Women adopted high-waisted, looser dresses. These fashions, which allowed greater freedom of movement and were more adaptable to the homespun fabrics, were the visible embodiment of revolutionary politics in the colonies. This new freedom of dress extended to children, who for decades had been corseted under layers of petticoats and stiff bodices. Boys and girls, it was thought, needed·to be restricted in their movements to develop proper comportment and behavior. By the 1770s parents discovered John Locke's writings on child rearing. Nearly a century earlier Locke had urged parents to allow children freedom of movement, asserting that play was a natural part of human development. Boys in the eighteenth century had remained in petticoats until age six or seven but around the time of the Revolution began to adopt trousers by age three or four, allowing for greater freedom of movement.

"Buy American." The growing rift with Great Britain in the 1760s produced a new sense of independence in the colonies; the boycotts of British products and "buy American" campaigns encouraged colonists to look for unique ways to express their American identity. The British Crown imposed tariffs, taxes, and restraints on trade in the 1760s and 1770s, and colonists responded by boycotting British imports. One of the most important British imports was textiles, and Patriots organized drives to produce American-made textiles. Women came together to spin thread and weave cloth for the cause of independence. Their output was relatively small, but they were making a political statement that electrified the colonies and caused great concern to the Crown and British merchants.

Homespun. In New England "spinning crazes" had cropped up from time to time since the 1720s, organized to encourage industry among young women and as an expression of rural values of self-sufficiency. The political sewing circles of the 1760s and 1770s surpassed all previous efforts. It became acceptable at all levels of society, at least among the patriotically inclined, to turn one's hand to the spinning wheel. It also became fashionable and patriotic to wear clothing made from homespun. Colonial merchants pioneered this new fashion trend, putting away for the moment their lavish imported garb. The students of Harvard College, Yale College, and the College of Rhode Island (now Brown University) appeared at commencement during the late 1760s wearing homespun suits. Such displays irritated royal officials and transmitted a consciousness of the boycott to other young people.

Enforcing Boycotts. The boycotts and home-manufactures drives ebbed after the repeal of the Stamp Act in 1766 but picked up again with a vengeance from 1767 to 1770 under the hated duties imposed by the Townshend Acts. Imports surged to new highs in 1772–1773, but with the crisis of the prerevolutionary years, what one wore, ate, and drank came to have serious implications indeed. In 1774 Congress established the Continental Association to enforce the boycotts. The association formed local committees that used community pressure against consumers and merchants who used or traded in boycotted goods. The committees distributed petitions that allowed citizens to record their compliance with the boycott and their protest against Crown policies. Porters and washerwomen signed the petitions even though most of the boycotted items were beyond the reach of their purchasing power. Almshouse residents collected rags to make "patriotic paper." Continental Association committees along with local Sons of Liberty did not stop short of violence as they seized and burned proscribed goods and tarred and feathered noncompliant merchants and customs informers.

Symbolic Acts. Community pressure and individuals' desires to make a statement brought about acts that had a symbolic impact, if little effect, on Britain. Tea became a prime symbol of either resistance or loyalty. The Tea Act of 1773 made this most civilized and social drink a weapon in the trade wars. People in small towns gathered tea and other proscribed items from their humble pantries and burned them in the town square in a quieter version of the dumpings of tea in Boston and other cities. The beginnings of military confrontation in 1775 brought a naval blockade of the colonies, and this further disrupted imports, making home manufactures a necessity rather than a political choice.

Sources:

Cary Carson and others, eds., *Of Consuming Interest: The Style of Life in the Eighteenth Century* (Charlottesville: University Press of Virginia, 1994);

Mary Beth Norton, *Liberty's Daughters: The Revolutionary Experience of American Women, 1750–1800* (Boston & Toronto: Little, Brown, 1980).

THE REVOLUTION ON THE FRONTIER

Difficult Choices. With the outbreak of war between the colonists and the British, Indians once again had to choose sides or maintain a precarious neutrality. Many Indians took the British side in the Revolution, hoping to curtail rapacious settlers. A few tribes, living in close daily contact with frontier whites, cast their lot with the Patriot cause. But despite their affiliation in the Revolution, most Indian tribes retained a strong sense of physical and political boundaries and jealously guarded their independence. Indians and colonists burned each others' villages in a war of attrition, and with the Patriot victory pro-British tribes were driven out of their villages into defensive settlements under the protection of the Crown. The American victory brought further encroachments on Indian sovereignty. Indians could no longer play warring whites against one another to obtain concessions. They also could not restrain the western advance of colonists although the British retained their forts in the West. In the South the Creeks and Cherokees, after having fought long and hard for the British, were left surrounded by settlers of the new United States. The Iroquois, who had for the most part fought with the British, were driven to a defensive position at Fort Niagara, New York. At war's end some returned to their villages and resumed trading activities with whites. Many, however, went into exile in Canada, along with tribal leaders such as Joseph and Molly Brant.

Stockbridge. The Stockbridge Indians of western Massachusetts were a mixed tribal group made up of Mahicans (Mohicans), Housatonics, and others. In 1740 Protestant missionaries gathered this mixed group on the Stockbridge grant, hoping that by adopting Christianity the Indians would become valuable allies against the Iroquois to the west. Their settlement was one of the praying towns, where displaced Native Americans tried to live and worship according to European customs. Dozens of young Stockbridge warriors served in the American army, some of them joining as minutemen even before the war began. They distinguished themselves at the Battle of White Plains (1776) and in campaigns against the Iroquois. They acted as negotiators with tribes such as the Oneidas, keeping them on the Patriot side when they wavered. But back home their townsmen were sinking into debt and alcoholism, selling off bit by bit their original landholdings. The town of Stockbridge, which had been but part of a large grant of Indian land, gradually fell entirely into white hands: the last Indian plot was sold in 1783. Indians remained in the town as laborers and derelicts or moved off to other settlements.

Sources:

Colin G. Calloway, *The American Revolution in Indian Country: Crisis and Diversity in Native American Communities* (Cambridge & New York: Cambridge University Press, 1995);

Journal of Nicholas Cresswell, 1774–1777 (Port Washington, N.Y.: Kennikat Press, 1968);

Thomas P. Slaughter, *The Whiskey Rebellion: Frontier Epilogue to the American Revolution* (Oxford & New York: Oxford University Press, 1986).

SLAVERY IN THE NORTHERN COLONIES

North and South. During the age of the Revolution enslaved African Americans seized opportunities to obtain freedom. However, these opportunities did not come mostly from the Patriot side. The British on two occasions proclaimed freedom to slaves who joined the Loyalist cause. The Revolution produced two distinct outcomes for African Americans. In the North the ideas

---

SLAVE AND FREE AFRICAN AMERICANS

The census of 1790 reflects the decline, but not disappearance, of slavery in the North and its persistence and growth in the South. The manumissions of the revolutionary years left many free blacks in the North and the Chesapeake region, but the majority of African Americans were still in slavery.

Slave and Free Blacks: Distribution, by States, 1790

State	Free Black Population	Slave Population
Maine	536	—
New Hampshire	630	157
Vermont	269	—
Massachusetts	5,369	—
Rhode Island	3,484	958
Connecticut	2,771	2,648
New York	4,682	21,193
New Jersey	2,762	11,423
Pennsylvania	6,531	3,707
Delaware	3,899	8,887
Maryland	8,043	103,036
Virginia	12,866	292,627
North Carolina	5,041	100,783
South Carolina	1,801	107,094
Georgia	398	29,264
Kentucky	114	12,430
Tennessee	361	361
United States	**59,557**	**697,624**

Source: Jessie C. Smith and Currell P. Horton, eds., *Historical Statistics of Black America* (Detroit: Gale Research, 1995).

---

of the Revolution and the economic irrelevance of slavery produced gradual emancipation. Free blacks gravitated toward the cities, to live mainly in impoverished circumstances. In the South the British challenge to slavery reinforced the determination of Patriot farmers and planters to defend their slave system. A mere twenty thousand out of some six hundred thousand slaves left the colonies along with the retreating British army.

A Diverse Labor Force. Slaves and free blacks formed a vital part of the Northern workforce. By 1750 Great Britain had consolidated control of the slave trade, taking much of the transatlantic traffic away from the Spanish and Portugese. Large cargoes of slaves arrived in Northern ports for sale and distribution throughout the colonies. Prior to mid century, slaves were expensive and less than abundant in North American slave markets. Most imported slaves were the surplus from West Indian plantations. But with direct large-scale importations from Africa slaves could be employed in a variety of roles in the North. In the 1760s blacks made up more than three-quarters of Philadelphia's servant population.

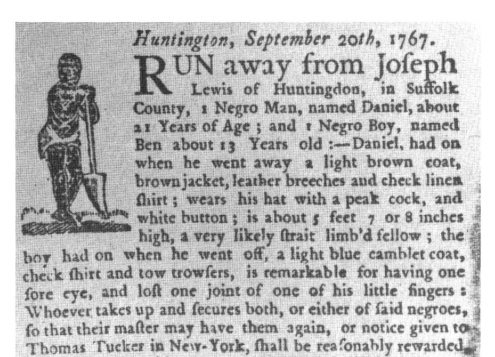

A New York newspaper announcement about fugitive slaves (Library Company of Philadelphia, Pennsylvania)

Slaves worked in distilleries, shipyards, manufactories, farms, lumber camps, and ropewalks. Slaves in the cities were often apprentices and helpers in artisan shops. Most lived singly or in groups of two or three in a home or workshop. New York had an unusually high proportion of skilled slaves who learned valuable trades working alongside artisan masters. They were masons, shipwrights, goldsmiths, and glaziers, among others. Despite the wave of sentiment for emancipation that swept the North in the Revolutionary era, New York did not free all its slaves until 1827. New Jersey's gradual abolition law meant that there were still a handful of slaves in the state in 1860 on the eve of the Civil War.

Runaways. Small free-black communities provided a refuge for escaped slaves, but since slavery was the law in every colony, fugitives had to keep on the move. Even the largest of colonial cities were really only small towns, by today's standards, and strangers soon attracted attention. Owners of runaway slaves posted advertisements in colonial newspapers offering rewards for their capture. Some escapees were able to remain at large for long periods by signing on as sailors on trading and whaling vessels.

Decline. In the colonies north of Maryland slavery would eventually lose ground to free labor. The number of slaves in the North fell rapidly in the 1760s and 1770s. Philadelphia had about fourteen hundred slaves in 1767; in 1775 it was home to just seven hundred slaves. The city was a center of antislavery agitation: Quakers and revolutionary pamphleteers denounced slavery in pamphlets distributed to blacks and whites. The influence of antislavery groups contributed to an increase in manu-

missions—outright grants of freedom to slaves by their owners. In addition the ideals of freedom associated with the Revolution and changes in the economy made slavery less viable in the North.

Sources:

Ira Berlin, "Time, Space and the Evolution of Afro-American Society on British Mainland North America," *American Historical Review*, 85 (1980): 44–78;

Philip S. Foner, *History of Black Americans: Volume I, From Africa to the Emergence of the Cotton Kingdom* (Westport, Conn.: Greenwood Press, 1975);

Sidney Kaplan, *The Black Presence in the Era of the American Revolution, 1770–1800* (New York: New York Graphic Society, 1973);

Gary Nash, *Forging Freedom: The Formation of Philadelphia's Black Community, 1720–1840* (Cambridge, Mass.: Harvard University Press, 1988);

Jessie C. Smith and Carrell P. Horton, eds., *Historical Statistics of Black America* (Detroit: Gale Research, 1995).

SOUTHERN SLAVERY

New Arrivals. The South encompassed distinct regions determined by the climate, soil, and types of crop that could be grown and exported. Heightening these differences in the Revolutionary era was the huge influx of African-born slaves after mid century. In many regions these new arrivals were received in various ways by both whites and native-born blacks, or Creoles.

The Chesapeake. In the mid 1700s the largest slaveholding region was the Chesapeake, the colonies of Virginia and Maryland, where tobacco was a valuable cash crop. Slaves worked in gangs on tobacco plantations under white overseers. In many counties of Virginia, blacks outnumbered whites and statewide were only slightly in the minority. In 1776 more than one-half of the blacks in America lived in Maryland and Virginia. The slave population in the Chesapeake grew rapidly in the 1760s and 1770s, fueled by imports, but more important, by natural increase. American-born slaves had established their own mode of accommodation to the planters and to colonial culture. Slaves generally had their own garden plots on the plantations and had informal arrangements whereby members of slave families were kept together or at least in close proximity. New arrivals from Africa were a minority in this region and tended to assimilate into creole cultural and social life. The great increase in the slave population, however, had a negative impact on free blacks in the Chesapeake region. They became increasingly a minority of the black population, and changes in the law tended to treat all blacks as slaves. Many moved to Northern cities for work and community life.

Revolutionary Upheaval. The Revolution brought great changes to the Chesapeake, especially in Virginia, where the British invasion of the coastal, or Tidewater, region caused planters to move large numbers of slaves inland to the Piedmont, or hill country. The disarray caused by Gen. Charles Cornwallis's invasion allowed many Tidewater slaves to escape, either fleeing north or serving in the Patriot army or in Lord John Dunmore's Ethiopian Regiment. In the seaport towns of Virginia and Maryland slaves heard of the movement for abolition that was taking place in the North and were inspired to take action on behalf of their own freedom.

Tobacco. The British blockade stopped the tobacco trade for several years. It had something of a revival in the 1780s, but tobacco was never as lucrative as it was in the prewar years. In the nineteenth century slaves would be moved south and west, and cotton would become "king" of the export trade.

The Coastal Lowlands. Along the coast from North Carolina to Georgia planters took up the cultivation of rice, indigo, and cotton. As early as 1720 blacks outnumbered whites two to one in South Carolina. The surge of the African slave trade in the 1750s produced great changes in the slave population of the coastal lowlands. The new arrivals were shipped in disproportionately high numbers to this region and on the rice plantations made up the vast majority of the workforce. The imported slaves were primarily male and had appallingly high death rates, being unaccustomed to the brutal conditions of plantation slavery and having no resistance to New World diseases.

Rice Slaves. As harsh as the conditions were on the Carolina and Georgia plantations, the phenomenon of absentee planters and the task system of labor allowed for some degree of independent labor and society among low-country slaves. While tobacco and cotton cultivation was carried out under gang-labor conditions with white drivers, rice agriculture in South Carolina and Georgia often involved only loose supervision of slaves due to the distaste of whites for the steamy climate of the coast and the slaves' skill at producing this crop on their own. Many of the slaves imported for rice cultivation came from the southwestern coast of Africa, what is today Angola, and had raised this crop prior to being enslaved. Many of their religious and social customs survived and blended with American customs. They retained some of their own language and spoke a dialect called Gullah. The cohesiveness of slave society in South Carolina left that region vulnerable to periodic slave revolts, the largest and most famous of which occurred in 1739, in which thirty whites were killed. Another revolt in 1775 left four whites dead. The proximity of slaves in South Carolina and Georgia to regions unsettled by whites allowed for the possibility of escape either to Indian communities or to form their own rebel or "maroon" groups that remained at large in the swamps and forests, raiding plantations and farms for food.

Creoles. Creole, or American-born, slaves in this period gravitated away from the plantations toward the cities, where they were in demand as servants, laborers, and artisans. Their facility with the English language and colonial society brought them closer to their white masters and created a class division between Creoles and lowland plantation slaves. A small group of Creoles of Savannah, Charleston, and other low-country cities attained freedom and wealth, their unusual intimacy with the planter class having produced mulatto offspring, who were accorded special rights and privileges. Occasional racial intermixing in the low-country cities contributed to the Creoles' separation from plantation slaves through the general "lightening" of the Creole's complexion.

Living Conditions. Throughout the South slaves were often poorly fed, housed, and clothed. They were valuable enough as property that whites did not want to jeopardize their survival but nonetheless allowed them only a minimum level of subsistence. Slave food consisted of an unending diet of corn bread, corn mush, sweet potatoes, and root vegetables. Minimal quantities of meat, nearly always fat bacon, were allowed, usually during harvest time. Slaves were often allowed to cultivate their own vegetable gardens, but this was considered a privilege rather than a right, and slaves had to negotiate for plots of land and time off, usually on Saturdays, to work this land. The Revolution provided an excellent opportunity for obtaining private gardens, for which the slaves promised not to desert to the British cause (or to the Patriots if their masters were Loyalists).

Sources:

Ira Berlin, "Time, Space and the Evolution of Afro-American Society on British Mainland North America," *American Historical Review,* 85 (1980): 44–78;

Philip S. Foner, *History of Black Americans: Volume I, From Africa to the Emergence of the Cotton Kingdom* (Westport, Conn.: Greenwood Press, 1975);

Sidney Kaplan, *The Black Presence in the Era of the American Revolution, 1770–1800* (New York: New York Graphic Society, 1973);

Jessie C. Smith and Carrell P. Horton, eds., *Historical Statistics of Black America* (Detroit: Gale Research, 1995).

WOMEN IN THE REVOLUTIONARY ERA: DOMESTICITY AND PUBLIC PROTEST

The Revolution. Women were barred from most public roles in the eighteenth century; their lot was to maintain the household and raise children. Yet the revolutionary crisis brought political meaning to the everyday activities of women, and these activities became potent public demonstrations of solidarity with the Revolution. Women became crucial to the home manufactures movement, spinning and weaving cloth and observing boycotts of British goods. Although little progress was made in replacing the massive quantities of imports, women played an important symbolic role, stepping forward from their customary reticence and providing a rebuke to men who hung back from taking a more active role in the Revolution. The real trial for many women came during the years of the war, when men were absent as soldiers or refugees, and women adopted male roles such as managing farms and businesses. Women had to stand up in the face of food shortages and the depredations of occupying soldiers.

Spinning. Colonists launched various schemes to manufacture homespun cloth, and these were a vital part of resistance to British rule. The spinning crazes of the eighteenth century were unusual only in that they focused attention on an activity that occupied a great deal of women's time and that normally was taken for granted as a common domestic activity. Girls were taught to spin from early childhood; toddlers at play on a Virginia plan-

A 1779 woodcut of a female Patriot with a musket and powder horn (New-York Historical Society)

tation would tie a string to a chair "and run buzzing back [and forth] to imitate the Girls spinning." Teenage girls and young women spent days of drudgery at the spinning wheel turning out skeins of cotton and wool thread. Women took the cotton and wool thread they spun and wove it into cloth on hand looms. One teenage girl recorded in her diary that she had woven 176 yards of cloth in a three-month period. Having completed this task, she wrote "welcome sweet Liberty, once more to me." Women sometimes turned this mundane activity into a social occasion; spinning frolics and quilting bees could last several days and end with dancing.

Married Women and Spinsters. Women also contributed valuable cash income to the household by selling the thread and cloth they produced or by sewing and mending. The centrality of spinning and weaving to women's lives is indicated in the term *spinster*, an unmarried woman. Married women, as their daughters grew up and became skillful at manufacturing cloth, could delegate these chores and spend their time in the hundreds of other tasks that went into managing a household.

Urban Women. Wealthier women and those living in or near cities were not so much occupied with making cloth; they could buy mass-produced cloth from Great Britain cheaper than they could make it themselves.

"A LADY'S ADIEU TO HER TEA-TABLE"

In the months before the outbreak of the Revolution a short poem began to appear in colonial newspapers supporting the boycott of imported tea. The poem took the form of a tongue-in-cheek lament of a lady who preferred liberty to luxury. The poem portrays the tea table as the center of a social world.

FAREWELL the Tea-board with your gaudy attire,
Ye cups and ye saucers that I did admire;
To my cream pot and tongs I now bid adieu;
That pleasure's all fled that I once found in you.
Farewell pretty chest that so lately did shine,
With hyson and congo and best double fine;
Many a sweet moment by you I have sat,
Hearing girls and old maids to tattle and chat;
And the spruce coxcomb laugh at nothing at all,
Only some silly work that might happen to fall.
No more shall my teapot so generous be
In filling the cups with this pernicious tea,
For I'll fill it with water and drink out the same,
Before I'll lose LIBERTY that dearest name.

Source: Rodris Roth, "Tea Drinking in Eighteenth-Century America: Its Etiquette and Equipage," in *Material Life in America, 1600–1860*, edited by Robert B. St. George (Boston: Northeastern University Press, 1988).

Housewives in the cities did not by any means live lives of leisure. They still faced endless chores of sewing, baking, cooking, preserving, butchering and salting meat, child rearing, and cleaning. City households were held to much higher standards of cleanliness than those of farmers. But in 1765 many of these women took to the distaff, in solidarity with the boycott movement, and returned again to spinning in the early 1770s with the renewal of conflict with Great Britain.

Wartime Disorder. The war brought added hardship to women who were left alone while their husbands were in the military or refugees. Other women became refugees, fleeing before the approaching armies. The soldiers and the disorder they wrought brought on epidemics of dysentery and smallpox, which added greatly to the misery of wartime. Women in occupied areas also faced the threat of rape; many female residents of Connecticut were assaulted by English and Hessian troops who passed through the area in 1779. British soldiers brutally and repeatedly raped women in New Jersey and Staten Island during several months of occupation in 1776.

Managing Farms. Women left in charge of households took on the business and legal affairs of their husbands, who often had little confidence that their wives could handle such matters. But most women rose to the occasion, selling crops and livestock and overseeing hired men and the harvests. Elizabeth Murray Smith Inman had to take over the management of her Cambridge farm when her husband Ralph was trapped in Boston during the American siege (1775–1776). Ralph was so frightened by the situation in Boston that he planned to immigrate to London. Elizabeth beseeched him to stay or to give her power of attorney so that she could sell the crop she had just harvested. Elizabeth Inman managed the farm during her husband's absence and eventually convinced him not to flee the country.

Quartering Troops. Those women left alone to manage households often had the additional burden of quartering troops, American and British. Lydia Post, a Long Island farm wife with Patriot sympathies, was forced to quarter Hessian troops in her house. These soldiers lived in the kitchen, which was barred off from the rest of the house. They drank, gambled, and fought, dancing and playing music late into the night. The Hessians cut up fences for firewood, allowing cattle to stray into the woods. Post was most concerned for her children, of whom the soldiers, however, seemed fond. The Hessians made them baskets and taught her son German. She worried lest her children "should contract evil."

Social Opportunities. Military occupation, even by friendly troops, was a trying circumstance, productive of many evils. However, some young women were delighted by the presence of soldiers and officers, whose presence provided opportunities for dances, parties, and socializing. Newport socialites gloried in the presence of "the

---

THE PATRIOTISM OF AMERICAN WOMEN

The French general François Jean, Marquis de Chastellux, commented on life among Philadelphia's elite during wartime.

December 1, 1780. The 1st of December commenced, like every other day in America, by a large breakfast. . . . A few loins of veal, some legs of mutton, and other trifles of that kind always slip in among the teacups and coffee cups at breakfast and are sure of meeting a hearty welcome. After this slight repast, which lasted only an hour and a half, we went to visit the ladies, according to the Philadelphia custom, where the morning is the most proper hour for paying calls. We began with Mrs. Bache. . . . She conducted us into a room filled with needlework, recently finished by the ladies of Philadelphia. This work consisted neither of embroidered tambour waistcoats, . . . nor of gold and silver brocade—but of shirts for the soldiers of Pennsylvania. The ladies had bought the linen from their own private purses, and had gladly cut out and stitched the shirts themselves. On each shirt was the name of the married or unmarried lady who made it, and there were 2200 shirts in all.

Source: Howard C. Rice Jr., ed., *Travels in North America in the Years 1780, 1781 and 1782 by the Marquis de Chastellux*, 2 volumes (Chapel Hill: University of North Carolina Press, 1963

---

flower of the French army, some very elegant young men," whom they actively courted.

Loyalist Women. Loyalist women were in a particularly difficult position during wartime, faced with large and vigorous Patriot contingents within their communities. Unless they were protected by British military occupation, their situation was precarious. Former friends and neighbors shunned them and often seized their homes and property. A Virginia Loyalist, exiled to Canada, pined for her home: "Poverty there would have been much more tolarable [*sic*] to us, we sincerely wish we had never left that Country." It was the lack of support that made the war particularly hard for Loyalists; Patriots under similar circumstances could turn to a much larger and more sympathetic community. Friendless and alone, Loyalists were forced to take refuge with the British army and eventually to immigrate to Canada, the Caribbean, or England.

The Ladies' Associations. Other women were in a position to take an active role in the war, not by fighting but by forming organizations to raise funds for the troops. As the fighting dragged into its fifth year, the Continental Army was living under deplorable conditions, badly fed and clothed and subject to disease. Esther DeBerdt Reed of Philadelphia exhorted local women to give up "vain ornaments," fashionable clothing, and other unnecessary expenses and raise money to contribute to the troops. Reed published her broadside, *Sentiments of an American Woman,* in June 1780, and it met with an immediate response; influential women of Philadelphia organized with the aim of personally raising money for the troops. These women solicited contributions door to door, violating conventional norms of female reticence. They went among immigrants, the poor, and servants to collect even the smallest donations.

Reed and Washington. The Philadelphia organization collected more than three hundred thousand Continental dollars, which because of inflation amounted to about $7,500 in specie. News of their effort spread throughout the colonies. The press reported their accomplishment with a mixture of condescension and admiration. Ladies' Associations formed in New Jersey, Maryland, and Virginia and collected substantial sums of money. In July 1780 Esther DeBerdt Reed presented her impressive contribution to Gen. George Washington. She then was so bold as to suggest how he should use it. She favored distributing the money among the men while Washington preferred to purchase shirts for the

soldiers. Washington, of course, got his way, explaining that money in the soldiers' pockets would quickly be converted into rum and discipline would suffer.

Vital Effort. Despite a great deal of male condescension toward the efforts of the Ladies' Associations, the women involved were quite proud of their accomplishments and circulated *Sentiments of an American Woman* among friends and acquaintances. Women understood the vital part they played in the Revolution even if few men would acknowledge it.

Sources:

Ronald Hoffman and Peter J. Albert, eds., *Women in the Age of the American Revolution* (Charlottesville: University Press of Virginia, 1989);

Mary Beth Norton, *Liberty's Daughters: The Revolutionary Experience of American Women, 1750–1800* (Boston & Toronto: Little, Brown, 1980);

Stephanie G. Wolf, *As Various as Their Land: The Everyday Lives of Eighteenth-Century Americans* (New York: HarperCollins, 1993).

HEADLINE MAKERS

MARY (MOLLY) BRANT

1736-1796
MOHAWK POLITICAL LEADER

Influence. Elder sister of the Mohawk leader Joseph Brant (Thayendanegea), Mary, called Molly, was the common-law wife of the most powerful British official west of the Allegheny Mountains. She was also the most influential Mohawk leader during the French and Indian War and the Revolution. Molly Brant looked after the interests of her people and spared them the devastation visited upon other Iroquois tribes.

Marriage. Molly's station in life improved markedly when she was seventeen: her mother, Margaret, married the sachem Brant, a military leader and trader. At the age of twenty-one Brant was already a mature woman by Iroquois standards. She had become an important political figure around the council fire at Canajoharie. She was adept as a healer, apparently having some command of herbal medicines. Brant took another step up in the world in 1759, when she entered the household of the British superintendent of Indian affairs, Sir William Johnson. Johnson's wife had recently died, and Brant came to him

first as housekeeper and then as mistress. The Mohawks of Canajoharie legitimized the alliance in frontier terms by presenting Sir William with a tract of land and addressing him as "Affectionate Brother and Friend." As Johnson's wife, Brant cemented an alliance between the Mohawks and the representatives of the British Crown that would last for decades. Straddling two cultural worlds, her power in the Iroquois tradition was rooted in the matrilineal tradition of that society, in which women's descent determined kinship ties and clan boundaries. Women were political leaders of the community while men were war chiefs. Her influence and that of other Mohawk leaders kept the tribe out of Pontiac's Rebellion of 1763, in which their Iroquois brethren the Senecas were engulfed. Sir Johnson, though angered at Seneca massacres of whites, made peace with that tribe.

Mistress of Johnson Hall. At Johnson Hall, a few miles from Schenectedy, Brant reigned over tributary whites and Mohawks, dispensing favors of clothing, blankets, and alcohol to Indians and controlling precious land grants to whites. She outlived her influential parents and accumulated more power in her own right than even her father. She controlled a great deal of trade, more in fact than did Johnson himself, and her influence extended up and down the Mohawk Valley, reaching even into Albany. Brant and Sir Johnson encouraged the trade in furs and European consumer goods that brought traders and land speculators to the Mohawk Valley, which they usurped from its original inhabitants. Brant facilitated this transition but alleviated the plight of her people whenever possible. She also remained defiantly Mohawk, refusing to learn English or adopt European customs or dress.

The Revolution. With Johnson's death in 1774, Brant remained a wealthy and influential Mohawk leader. She orchestrated the tribe's Loyalist strategy, and, utilizing her spies, she gave important information to the British, resulting in the ambush of Gen. Nicholas Herkimer's forces at Oriskany in 1777. Brant retreated with her family and tribe to Fort Niagara and later went to Montreal, retaining control over trade and Indian politics. After the war the British settled her with a pension and a home in Kingston, Ontario, where she remained active in Iroquois politics, supporting her people in disputes with both British and Americans.

Sources:

Colin G. Calloway, *The American Revolution in Indian Country: Crisis and Diversity in Native American Communities* (Cambridge & New York: Cambridge University Press, 1995);

James T. Flexner, *Mohawk Baronet: Sir William Johnson of New York* (New York: Harper, 1959);

Isabel T. Kelsay, *Joseph Brant, 1743–1807: Man of Two Worlds* (Syracuse, N.Y.: Syracuse University Press, 1984).

DEBORAH SAMPSON GANNETT

1760-1827
CONTINENTAL SOLDIER

Fame and Obscurity. Deborah Sampson Gannett was a controversial figure in her own time. Born into poverty, she achieved fame and a certain notoriety only to sink into obscurity again. Assuming male dress and the name Robert Shurtlieff, Deborah enlisted as a soldier in the Continental Army, saw action, and was wounded. She was discovered, and as her story was retold and exaggerated, she became something of a celebrity in the years after the war.

Early Life. Deborah Sampson was one of seven children born into a Plympton, Massachusetts, family. When her father abandoned the family, Deborah became an indentured servant and was adept at the innumerable chores of farm life. She also learned to read and write, and when she was eighteen, she taught school in the town of Middleborough. Tall (probably 5'7"), strong, and agile with brown hair and brown eyes, Deborah was considered plain by the standards of her day, but she could converse intelligently about politics, theology, and the war that engulfed the country during those years.

Army Service. Sometime in 1781 or 1782 Sampson assumed her male guise and visited army recruiting centers in nearby Massachusetts towns. She tried to enlist in the army at Middleborough but was detected; she went to New Bedford to sign on to a privateer but met with difficulties there too. Finally, in Bellingham she enlisted in the Continental Army and received a signing bounty of sixty pounds. With fifty other recruits she marched to West Point, New York, and received a uniform and military equipment. Women were not unknown in army camps; they were a common presence as servants and prostitutes. But Sampson's masquerade was unique though there was nothing remarkable about Sampson/Shurtlieff's military career except for her gender. She probably enlisted after the siege of Yorktown but saw action in New York against Loyalists and Indians. While fighting Loyalist cavalry near Tarrytown in 1782, Sampson was wounded, but she managed to escape being found out as a woman. She and her company were called to Philadelphia in the summer of 1783 to suppress a threatened mutiny of soldiers demanding their wages. Sampson contracted a fever in Philadelphia, and the attending doctor, Barnabas Binney, recognized her as a woman. Binney did not denounce her to the military authorities. She received an honorable discharge in October 1783 and headed home to Massachusetts, where she was expelled from her Baptist congregation for "Dressing in mans Clothes and inlisting as a soldier." A few newspaper accounts concerning her exploits appeared in New York and Massachusetts. But she settled down to a rather mundane life, marrying Benjamin Gannett in 1785 and bearing three children.

Fame and Last Years. In 1797 Herman Mann, a newspaper publisher, wrote an account of Sampson Gannet's military career, *Female Review: or, Memoirs of an American Young Lady.* This heavily fictionalized account brought renewed interest in Sampson Gannet just as Americans were looking back on the Revolution with nostalgia and pride. At the same time Sampson Gannett's application for a soldier's pension was stalled in Congress. The talented and famous poet Philip Freneau took up her case in an epic poem: "A Soldier should be made of Sterner Stuff—On Deborah Gannett." He invoked shame on "Ye congress men and men of weight, Who fill the public chairs" for their inaction on behalf of "her who handled sword and spear" and "Despis'd the Briton's rage."

Speaking Tour. Five years later, in 1802, Sampson Gannett, the only known female veteran of the Revolutionary War, embarked on a speaking tour through the Northeast, appearing in uniform at theaters, giving a speech ghostwritten for her by Mann. Taking advantage of popular curiosity, Sampson Gannett capitalized on her fame. Her diary from this period shows her to have had a practical turn of mind; she arranged her own bookings and took care of details of costume and printing handbills.

Widower and Heirs. After her brief turn in the public spotlight Sampson Gannet returned to her family. In 1837, ten years after her death, Sampson Gannet's husband, Benjamin, applied for a widower's pension. Benjamin died before Congress could act on the request, but eventually eighty dollars per year was allocated "for the relief of the heirs of Deborah Sampson Gannett," the heirs being her two daughters. Deborah Sampson Gannett was an ordinary person of extraordinary character and ambition—a soldier during turbulent times and a self-promoter during a time of Patriotic enthusiasm. Remarkably, she defied the sexual conventions of her time and not only got away with it but also capitalized on her transgression, becoming a hero of the Revolution.

Sources:

Vera O. Laska, *"Remember the Ladies": Outstanding Women of the American Revolution* (Boston: Commonwealth of Massachusetts Bicentennial Commission, 1976);

Fred L. Pattee, ed., *The Poems of Philip Freneau: Poet of the American Revolution* (New York: Russell & Russell, 1963).

GEORGE ROBERT TWELVES HEWES

1742-1840
SHOEMAKER

Origins. George Robert Twelves Hewes was the sixth of nine children, being the fourth of seven sons. His father, also named George, was a Massachusetts tanner who ended up in debtors' prison at least twice. Hewes's father died young, and George was sent into apprenticeship as a shoemaker. Shoemaking was a poor man's trade and not a desirable way to start out in life, but Hewes had little choice. He was bound to a harsh master, ill fed and clothed and possessed a streak of lively mischief that earned him the occasional whipping.

Boston Youth. He and his fellow apprentices scavenged about the town of Boston, looking to beg or steal anything they could get to eat. Hewes played pranks on his master and drank and frolicked in the streets during public celebrations, along with the hundreds of servants, apprentices, laborers, and artisans of Boston. During the 1750s and 1760s, Pope's Day (5 November) was a particularly boisterous holiday. Young people formed into companies and paraded with effigies of the Pope, the Devil, and other hated figures, exacting treats and money from the wealthy of the town and brawling with rival groups. Hewes finished his apprenticeship in 1763; standing only 5'1", he was too small to join the British army though he tried. He struggled as a shoemaker, built a shop, and married at age twenty-six. His wife was the daughter of a poor church sexton and brought him no dowry. Hewes tried his hand at fishing, and like his father, found himself frequently in trouble for debts. He was imprisoned when he could not pay for the suit in which he wooed his future wife.

Revolutionary Activity. Despite his insignificant stature and prospects, Hewes became an active participant in the events that rocked Boston and led to revolution. In 1770 four thousand British soldiers were stationed in a town of fewer than sixteen thousand inhabitants. The common people of the town clashed with the soldiers, who competed for jobs and housing. A series of violent incidents, including the murder of an eleven-year-old boy by a customs informer, led to boiling tensions. Hewes was among the crowd outside the British barracks on King Street on the night of 5 March 1770 and was a participant in the deadly affray known as the Boston Massacre. A sentry struck the unarmed Hewes on the shoulder with his musket, and he stood among the crowd as British troops shot and killed five citizens.

Sons of Liberty. In the angry days after the massacre Hewes gave a deposition for the prosecution of the British soldiers who fired on the crowd. Hewes's courage and outspokenness came to the notice of prominent revolutionaries in the town. His street savvy was useful to the Sons of Liberty, the Patriot group that organized demonstrations against British taxation and oppression. Among his other resources, Hewes had a knack for whistling; he could issue a shrill and piercing signal during an important moment of a demonstration, calling the crowds to order for instructions or maneuvers. On the night of 16 December 1773 Hewes's talents for civil unrest reached their historic pinnacle as he was among the small group of disguised men that boarded three merchant ships and dumped tea into Boston Harbor. Hewes, dressed as an Indian, his face and hands daubed with coal dust, was an officer in the raid: one participant recollected serving under "Captain Hewes." The Boston Tea Party was not by any means an uprising of the rabble: wealthy merchants and lawyers such as John Hancock and Samuel Adams coordinated the event. Tea dumpings took place from Nova Scotia to South Carolina. But young and obscure men led the raid so as to deflect attention from the more prominent Patriots.

War Activities. Hewes continued as an important figure in the streets of Boston, but by 1775 the number of British troops grew to a staggering 13,500. Soldiers broke up Hewes's shoe-repair shop and used it for firewood. The day after the Battle of Bunker Hill he saw the corpses of British soldiers dumped into an open pit on the common. Hewes escaped the British quarantine of the city and compiled an impressive war record with several stints as a militiaman and a privateer. Like many revolutionary soldiers, he enlisted for one- to three-month periods, returning home to work and take care of his family. Privateering was government-sanctioned piracy. The Continental Congress authorized voyages to raid British shipping, the spoils to be divided among the crew. Hewes made little profit on these voyages; he continued to live from hand to mouth, supporting his wife and four children. Hewes put in a total of twenty months service in the Patriot cause, well above the average, and then returned to his workaday world, where he struggled to support his family until the 1830s, when he became a fixture at parades as one of the oldest known surviving revolutionary veterans. He applied for a pension and produced the required documentation to prove his service. Still lively and quick-witted in his nineties, he attracted the attention of journalists and biographers. Two books were written in these years based on his recollections of his experiences.

Source:
Alfred F. Young, "George Robert Twelves Hewes (1742–1840): A Boston Shoemaker and the Memory of the American Revolution," *William and Mary Quarterly*, 38 (1981): 561–623.

JOHN WOOLMAN

1720-1772
ANTISLAVERY PIONEER

Quaker Youth. John Woolman was a devout Quaker who by his personal example and eloquent testimony became one of the revolutionary era's strongest advocates of the abolition of slavery. Woolman was born in Burlington County, New Jersey, and grew up in the tightly knit religious community the Society of Friends, also known as the Quakers. Woolman was the fourth of thirteen children. His father was a farmer, and the family was of middling status. The Quakers believed in simple living, fellowship, and personal devotion to God. The Bible and other religious books were read aloud on Sundays in Quaker households, and the Woolman house was no exception. John received about ten years of schooling and for the rest of his life voraciously read and pursued his own education. At age twenty-one he moved to Mount Holly, New Jersey, where he set up his own successful store. He also worked as a teacher and did legal work, drawing up wills and contracts. Despite his success in business, Woolman taught himself to be a tailor, believing that his religion valued simplicity over worldly success. At age thirty-six he withdrew from business altogether, devoting his energies to religious work.

A Personal Crusade. The Society of Friends had no regular clergy. Church members with a special gift for speaking could do so at weekly meetings. They could also go on missionary travels with the recommendation (but without the pay) of their home congregation. From age twenty-three to his death Woolman went on approximately thirty such missionary journeys, from New England to the Carolinas. Wherever he went he urged Quakers to live simply and to harm no one. He called upon the Society of Friends to abstain from paying war taxes to support the British government's wars against the French and the Indians. But increasingly slavery preoccupied Woolman in his thoughts and preaching.

Slavery and Sin. Woolman grew steadily in his conviction that owning slaves was a sin in the eyes of God. His first concern was to absolutely purify himself of any personal connection with slavery or its fruits. Woolman made himself conspicuous by wearing undyed clothes: dyes were made by slave labor. He also abstained from using slave-produced items such as sugar and silver tableware. Many Quakers, North and South, owned slaves, and he sought to cleanse his church of this wrong-doing. Visiting the homes of slave owners, he calmly argued the wrongs of the slave system. Wishing not to be personally implicated by slavery, he paid either his host or the host's slaves for food received in the slave owners' houses.

Early Quaker Antislavery. There had been antislavery stirrings in the church in earlier years: in the 1730s a sincere but eccentric Quaker, Benjamin Lay, harangued the Society of Friends meetings on the evils of slavery. He kidnapped a Quaker child to demonstrate the grief slaves felt when family members were sold. In 1738, at the annual meeting in Burlington, New Jersey, Lay threw a substance that appeared to be blood on the assembled the Society of Friends, who ignored his message and ejected him from the church.

Message. Woolman, however, found a more receptive audience among Quakers in the 1750s, delivering his message of antislavery more soberly and plausibly than Lay. He communicated his own turmoil and guilt over slavery in such a convincing manner that he touched the consciences of thousands of people to whom he spoke or addressed his writings. In 1754 the Yearly Meeting of the Society of Friends at Philadelphia endorsed Woolman's antislavery pamphlet, *Some Considerations on the Keeping of Negroes*, publishing it and sending it out to other Quaker congregations. His personal mission was now disseminated in print, and others began to take up the cause, including Anthony Benezet, who quoted Woolman in an antislavery publication that gained much attention in 1759. In 1762 Woolman published his *Considerations on Keeping Negroes: Part Second*, which had an even stronger effect on Quakers. The antislavery movement grew within and outside the church, and manumissions of slaves became common in Pennsylvania.

Legacy. In 1776 the Philadelphia Yearly Meeting officially prohibited the Society of Friends from owning slaves. Woolman had died two years earlier, but others carried on his work. Benezet tirelessly distributed anti-slavery writings in England and America. Benjamin Lundy, a follower of Woolman, continued antislavery missionary work in the early 1800s and in turn inspired William Lloyd Garrison and other leading American abolitionists. Woolman's *Journal* was published in 1776 and became an inspiration to advocates of peace and the abolition of slavery. Eighty years after Woolman's death the governor of the slave state Missouri blamed Woolman's *Journal* for the "evils" of the abolitionist movement.

Sources:
William A. Beardslee, ed., *The Works of John Woolman* (New York: Garrett Press, 1970);

Phillips P. Moulton, ed., *The Journal and Major Essays of John Woolman* (Oxford & New York: Oxford University Press, 1971);

Jean R. Soderlund, *Quakers and Slavery: A Divided Spirit* (Princeton, N.J.: Princeton University Press, 1985).

PUBLICATIONS

Anthony Benezet, *Observations on the Inslaving, Importing and Purchasing of Negroes* (Germantown, Pa.: C. Sower, 1760)—In *Observations* he stated: "I am bold to assert, that the notion entertained by some, that the blacks are inferior to the Whites in their capacities, is a vulgar prejudice, founded on the Pride or Ignorance of their lordly Masters, who have kept their Slaves at such a distance, as to be unable to form a right judgment of them";

Benezet, *The Perfect Enemies of America Laid Open: Being Some Account of the Baneful Effects Attending the Use of Distilled Spirituous Liquors, and the Slavery of the Negroes* (Philadelphia: Printed by J. James, 1774)—Benezet was a Philadelphia Quaker and a schoolteacher who worked tirelessly for social justice in the mid eighteenth century. He founded a night school for blacks in 1759 and wrote books denouncing war and slavery and advocating the rights of Native Americans;

Reverend Andrew Burnaby, *Travels through the Middle Settlements in North America in the Years 1759 and 1760, with Observations upon the State of the Colonies* (London: T. Payne, 1775)—a detailed travel account that, contrary to its title, describes conditions from Massachusetts to Virginia. Burnaby is best at describing natural phenomena and takes a condescending, Tory view of American government and institutions;

Michel Guillaume Jean (J. Hector St. John) de Crèvecoeur, *Letters from an American Farmer: Describing Certain Provincial Situations, Manners and Customs, Not Generally Known, and Conveying some Idea of the Late and Present Interior Circumstances of the British Colonies in North America* (London: Printed for Davies & Davis, 1782)—De Crèvecoeur was a French officer in the French and Indian War who settled in New York after the British victory in Canada, taking up the life of a farmer, as he describes himself in the title of his book. He traveled widely in diverse parts of North America observing manners, customs, and frontier life in the colonies. His book was extremely popular in France and England and gave Europeans their first views of American life;

Encyclopédie Perruquière (Paris, 1762)—The Encyclopedia of Wigs was a guidebook for men of fashion describing and illustrating more than 115 styles of hairpieces. For prominent and wealthy colonists, keeping abreast of European fashions was a must, and books on clothing and etiquette were popular in America. The wig was a particularly important item of fashion, and it was essential to wear precisely the style appropriate to one's profession or station in life;

Benjamin Rush, *Sermons to Gentlemen upon Temperance and Exercise* (Philadelphia: John Dunlap, 1772)—Published anonymously, this was among the first American works on hygiene and a pioneering work devoted to moderation in drink and physical health. Rush exhibits staggering common sense for this time period, when alcohol was consumed at nearly every meal and was thought to be a tonic for a thousand ills;

Samuel Stearns, *North American Almanack for 1776* (Worcester, Mass., 1776)—Stearns's almanac was one of the best of a genre that was vastly popular in the 1760s and 1770s. It was published yearly throughout the period and like others of its ilk, published information about astronomical and astrological phenomena, sunsets, tides, and weather predictions. It also contains verse, recipes, lists of public officials, tables of distances, and other items of interest. Most important, almanacs contain commentary on current events and politics, which helped keep Americans informed on the significant events of the Revolutionary period. Stearns's 1776 issue contains a graphic description of the Battle of Lexington;

John Trumbull, *M'Fingal* (Philadelphia: Printed & sold by William & Thomas Bradford, 1776; Hartford, Conn.: Hudson & Goodwin, 1782)—a poem in four parts, two of which were published in 1776 and the final two published six years later. This epic work satirizes the cause of Loyalists and was a political argument for independence. It was widely popular in the colonies;

Noah Webster, *A Grammatical Institute, of the English Language, part I* (Hartford, Conn.: Printed by Hudson & Goodwin for the author, 1783)—the famous blue-backed speller that taught schoolchildren in the American vernacular for generations. It has never gone out of print and is estimated to have sold one hundred million or more copies.

MILITARY

by JOSEPH M. MCCARTHY

CONTENTS

Sidebars and tables are listed in italics.

1754

•	The French and Indian War, the North American theater of the Seven Years' War in Europe, begins.
Jan.	Gov. Robert Dinwiddie of Virginia, fearing French encroachment in western Virginia, sends Capt. William Trent to build a fort at the junction of the Allegheny and Monongahela Rivers (site of modern Pittsburgh, Pennsylvania).
17 Apr.	French troops drive away Trent and erect Fort Duquesne.
May	Governor Dinwiddie gives George Washington charge of a militia unit with the mission of seizing Fort Duquesne.
28 May	Washington defeats the French near Great Meadows (present-day Uniontown, Pennsylvania).
June	Lacking sufficient force to attack Fort Duquesne, Washington builds Fort Necessity at Great Meadows.
3 July	French troops force the surrender of Fort Necessity, allowing Washington and his men to march out with the honors of war.

1755

20 Feb.	Maj. Gen. Edward Braddock arrives at Hampton Roads, Virginia, with two British regiments to assume responsibility as British commander in chief in North America.
14 Apr.	Braddock and the colonial governors plan attacks on the French at Fort Duquesne, Crown Point, Fort Niagara and in Nova Scotia.
June	Braddock advances on Fort Duquesne with 1,400 British troops and 450 colonial militia.
16 June	Fort Beauséjour, guarding the top of the Bay of Fundy, surrenders to a British and colonial force under Colonels Robert Monckton and John Winslow.
9 July	Braddock's force is destroyed, and he is mortally wounded in the Battle of Monongahela, seven miles from Fort Duquesne.
Aug.	Massachusetts governor William Shirley, Braddock's successor as commander in chief, leads an expedition up the Mohawk River in New York to attack the French at Fort Niagara.
8 Sept.	Sir William Johnson defeats Baron Ludwig August Dieskau in the Battle of Lake George. Frustrated by the unreliability of his militia, Johnson abandons the attack on Crown Point and builds Fort William Henry at the head of Lake George.
8 Oct.	Six thousand Acadians of French ancestry, though neutral in the wars between France and England, are deported from what is now Prince Edward Island, New Brunswick, and Nova Scotia.
24 Oct.	Governor Shirley abandons the attack on Fort Niagara, leaving a small garrison at Oswego to menace French lines of communication.

1756

11 May	Gen. Louis-Joseph de Montcalm-Gozon, Marquis de Montcalm de Saint Véran, arrives to take command of French regular troops in Canada, with Gov. Pierre de Rigaud Vaudreuil continuing to command the militia.
18 May	Great Britain officially declares war on France.
23 July	Gen. John Campbell, Earl of Loudon, arrives to take command in British North America.
14 Aug.	Montcalm overwhelms the garrison at Oswego and destroys the fort there.

1757

•	Prime Minister William Pitt assumes direction of the war against France.
30 June	Loudon arrives in Halifax to mount an attack on Fort Louisbourg.
9 Aug.	Montcalm captures Fort William Henry. While the British and colonials who had surrendered are marching out with the honors of war, the Indian allies of the French attack them.
24 Sept.	The Louisbourg expedition is abandoned after the British fleet blockading the port is scattered by a storm.
30 Dec.	Gen. James Abercrombie replaces Loudon as British commander in chief.

1758

9 Feb.	Gen. Jeffrey Amherst arrives in North America with troops earmarked to attack Louisbourg.
30 May	Amherst and Gen. James Wolfe arrive at Louisbourg with nine thousand British regulars and five hundred militia.
2 June	The siege of Fort Louisbourg begins.
July	Gen. John Forbes begins an advance on Fort Pitt over the route used by Braddock. Col. George Washington commands a Virginia regiment.
8 July	Montcalm with three thousand men defeats Abercrombie's army of fifeeen thousand in the Battle of Ticonderoga.
27 July	Fort Louisbourg falls.
27 Aug.	Col. John Bradstreet seizes Fort Frontenac in Ontario (now Kingston).
24 Nov.	To prevent its capture, the French blow up Fort Duquesne and retreat; Forbes rebuilds it and names it Fort Pitt.

1759

•	William Pitt plans a three-pronged attack on the French in North America: Fort Niagara is to be seized to prevent French attacks on western settlements from the St. Lawrence River; Montreal and Quebec are to be threatened by an attack up the Champlain Valley; and Quebec is to be attacked by an expedition down the St. Lawrence River.

	June	Brig. Gen. John Prideaux begins the siege of Fort Niagara and is accidentally killed during the bombardment of the post.
	26 June	Gen. James Wolfe begins the siege of Quebec with nine thousand troops facing the Marquis de Montcalm's fourteen thousand soldiers.
	25 July	Sir William Johnson captures Fort Niagara.
	26 July	General Amherst drives the French out of Ticonderoga.
	31 July	British and colonial troops capture Crown Point.
	12 Sept.	Having found a footpath up seemingly impassable cliffs, British troops ascend by night to attack Quebec.
	13 Sept.	Wolfe defeats Montcalm in battle on the Plains of Abraham outside Quebec; both generals are killed.
	17 Sept.	Quebec surrenders.
1760	28 Apr.	French forces under Gen. François de Lévis defeat the British in another battle on the Plains of Abraham.
	16 May	British reinforcements lift the French siege of Quebec.
	Sept.	British and colonial troops from Oswego, Crown Point, and Quebec converge on Montreal.
	8 Sept.	General Amherst captures Montreal.
1761	•	Maj. Robert Rogers occupies Detroit and other former French posts on the Great Lakes.
1762	Feb.	The Caribbean island of Martinique is captured by Adm. George Rodney.
	20 June–10 Aug.	The British beseige Havana, Cuba, and capture it from Spain.
	5 Oct.	The British capture Manila, the Philippines, from Spain.
	3 Nov.	The preliminary peace treaty between the British and French is signed at Fontainebleau.
1763	10 Feb.	The Treaty of Paris ends the Seven Years' War.
	7 May	The Ottawas and allied tribes under Pontiac besiege Detroit to prevent British settlement of western territories.
	May–June	Indians destroy all forts west of Niagara except Fort Pitt and Detroit; more settlers are slaughtered than at the height of the French and Indian War.

4–6 Aug.   A column of British and colonial troops advancing to relieve Fort Pitt is ambushed but routs its attackers in the Battle of Bushy Run.

7 Oct.   King George III signs a proclamation forbidding settlements west of the Appalachian Mountains and ordering settlers in western Ohio out of Indian lands.

12 Oct.   Western Indians (with the exception of Pontiac) make peace with the British.

30 Oct.   Pontiac lifts the siege of Fort Detroit.

1770

16–18 Jan.   A skirmish occurs at Golden Hill, New York, between British regulars and the Sons of Liberty.

5 Mar.   British regulars in Boston fire on a mob, killing or mortally wounding five people.

1771

16 May   At the Battle of Alamance Creek, North Carolina, militiamen suppress a rebellion by frontiersmen.

1774

10 Oct.   Virginia militia sent by Gov. John Murray, Earl of Dunmore, suppress a Shawnee Indian uprising in the Battle of Point Pleasant, at the mouth of the Kahahwa River.

1775

19 Apr.   Seven hundred redcoats sent by the governor of Massachusetts to seize arms held by colonists at Concord fire on 70 colonists at Lexington Green, killing 8 and wounding 10. On the way back to Boston the British suffer 73 killed, 174 wounded, and 26 missing.

Apr.   The American siege of Boston begins.

10–12 May   Col. Ethan Allen of Vermont and his Green Mountain Boys capture Fort Ticonderoga and Crown Point.

12 June   Lumbermen in Machias, Maine, seize the British cutter *Margaretta*.

15 June   George Washington is named to command the Continental Army besieging Boston.

17 June   The British sustain heavy losses in overcoming colonial positions at the Battle of Bunker Hill.

3 July   Washington takes command at Cambridge.

2 Nov.   Gen. Richard Montgomery captures the Canadian town of St. John's.

13 Nov.   Montgomery occupies Montreal.

| 31 Dec. | The Americans are repulsed in an attack on Quebec, with Montgomery and one hundred others killed; among the three hundred wounded is Benedict Arnold. |

1776

Jan.–May	Arnold besieges Quebec.
27 Feb.	North Carolina Rebels defeat an army of Tories in the Battle of Moore's Creek Bridge.
17 Mar.	The British abandon Boston, sailing to Halifax, Nova Scotia.
23 Mar.	Congress authorizes privateers to capture British ships.
6 May	British reinforcements arrive at Quebec, and Americans retreat to Montreal.
May–June	Washington moves the Continental army to New York.
4 June	Gen. Sir Henry Clinton besieges Charleston, South Carolina.
8 June	Gen. John Burgoyne with eight thousand troops routs an American army of two thousand at Trois Rivières.
June–July	The Americans retire to Fort Ticonderoga as Canadian governor Guy Carleton prepares an invasion of New York.
28 June	After the British fleet is severely damaged by American artillery, Clinton lifts the siege of Charleston.
27 Aug.	Lord William Howe wins the Battle of Long Island, compelling Washington to evacuate his troops to Manhattan.
6–7 Sept.	David Bushnell's *American Turtle,* a one-man submersible craft, attacks a British warship off Staten Island, the first submarine attack in the history of warfare.
12 Sept.	Washington retreats from New York.
16 Sept.	In the Battle of Harlem Heights, Washington's army briefly checks the British pursuit.
28 Oct.	Washington is defeated at White Plains.
28 Oct.	An American flotilla on Lake Champlain is defeated in the Battle of Valcour Island, but the British withdraw to Canada for the winter.
20 Nov.	Forts Washington and Lee fall, forcing the Continental Army to retreat through New Jersey.
26 Dec.	Crossing the Delaware River by night, Washington surprises and routs the Hessian garrison of Trenton.

1777

5 July	British and Canadian troops under Gen. John Burgoyne capture Fort Ticonderoga, hoping to link with forces moving northward from New York City to isolate the New England colonies.
25 July	Col. Barry St. Leger besieges Fort Stanwix at Rome, New York, with a force of British, Hessians, Loyalists, and Indians.
8 Aug.	Hurrying to the aid of Fort Stanwix, Gen. Nicholas Herkimer's militia is defeated in the Battle of Oriskany.

16 Aug.	German troops sent into Vermont by Burgoyne to seize arms are defeated by Col. John Stark at the Battle of Bennington.
23 Aug.	St. Leger abandons the siege of Fort Stanwix.
11 Sept.	Having brought troops up Chesapeake Bay, Lord William Howe defeats George Washington at the Battle of Brandywine, forcing him back to Philadelphia.
19 Sept.	Finding Americans under Gen. Horatio Gates entrenched on Bemis Heights, eight miles from Saratoga, New York, Burgoyne attacks their left flank at Freeman's Farm but meets with defeat.
26 Sept.	Howe seizes Philadelphia.
4 Oct.	Washington is defeated at Germantown.
7 Oct.	In the Battle of Bemis Heights, Burgoyne fails to turn the Americans' left flank and has to retreat.
17 Oct.	Surrounded by a superior American force, Burgoyne surrenders his army.

1778

•	The Continental Army, starving and freezing in winter quarters at Valley Forge, Pennsylvania, continues to drill and train, learning new skills from Baron Friedrich Wilhelm Ludolf Gerhard Augustin von Steuben.
23 Apr.	Capt. John Paul Jones raids ashore in the British Isles.
17 June	France declares war on Britain.
18 June	Sir Henry Clinton, Lord William Howe's successor, evacuates Philadelphia and marches toward New York.
28 June	Washington's troops attack Clinton's army at Monmouth Courthouse, New Jersey.
3 July	Indian allies of the British massacre settlers in the Wyoming Valley in Pennsylvania.
23 Sept.	John Paul Jones, commanding the USS *Bonhomme Richard,* captures the HMS *Serapis.*
11 Nov.	Indians massacre settlers at Cherry Valley, New York.
29 Dec.	British troops under Lt. Col. Archibald Campbell capture Savannah, Georgia.

1779

29 Jan.	Campbell seizes Augusta, Georgia.
25 Feb.	George Rogers Clark, commanding a small force of American militia, captures Vincennes, Indiana.
31 May	The British capture Stony Point, New York.
16 June	Spain declares war on England.
16 July	American general Anthony Wayne recaptures Stony Point.

3 Sept.	French troops under Adm. Jean-Baptiste-Charles-Henri-Hector d'Estaing and Americans under Gen. Benjamin Lincoln besiege Savannah.
9 Oct.	The French and Americans are defeated in an assault on Savannah.
28 Oct.	The siege of Savannah is lifted.
26 Dec.	Clinton sails from New York to attack Charleston, South Carolina.

1780

14 Mar.	Spanish forces capture Mobile from the British.
11 Apr.	The siege of Charleston begins.
12 May	Charleston surrenders. Clinton returns to New York, leaving Gen. Charles Cornwallis to complete the conquest of the Carolinas.
11 July	A French army of five thousand under Gen. Jean-Baptiste-Donatien de Vimeur, Comte de Rochambeau, lands at Newport, Rhode Island, to cooperate with the Americans in a proposed assault on New York.
16 Aug.	General Gates's militia is defeated in the Battle of Camden, leaving only guerrilla forces to contend with the British in the Carolinas.
23 Sept.	Benedict Arnold's treacherous attempt to surrender West Point to the British is discovered. He flees to the British and is commissioned a brigadier in their army.
7 Oct.	Carolina and Virginia frontiersmen destroy a force of more than one thousand Tory militia men in the Battle of King's Mountain, leading General Cornwallis to abandon plans to invade North Carolina.
2 Dec.	Gen. Nathanael Greene takes command of the American forces in the Carolinas.
20 Dec.	Greene sends Gen. Daniel Morgan on a march through the western Carolinas.
20 Dec.	Britain declares war on the Netherlands, which has been supplying the rebellious colonists.

1781

5 Jan.	Benedict Arnold, now in British uniform, captures Richmond, Virginia.
17 Jan.	British cavalry leader Banastre Tarleton catches Morgan's force, but he is defeated at the Battle of Cowpens.
Jan.-Mar.	Cornwallis pursues Greene's army.
15 Mar.	Cornwallis wins a costly victory at Guilford Court House, North Carolina. Realizing he cannot maintain control of the Carolinas, he moves into Virginia.
19 Apr.	Greene's army moves toward Camden but is checked at the Battle of Hobkirk's Hill.
May–July	Gen. Marie-Joseph-Paul-Yves-Roch-Gilbert du Motier de Lafayette, commanding American forces in Virginia, conducts a war of maneuver, refusing to let Cornwallis bring him to battle.

9 May	The British surrender Pensacola to Spanish forces.
19 June	Greene's siege of Fort Ninety-Six in southwestern South Carolina results in a British withdrawal toward Charleston.
4 Aug.	Under orders from Clinton, Cornwallis occupies Yorktown, Virginia.
13 Aug.	A French fleet under Adm. De Grasse sails for the Chesapeake Bay.
21 Aug.	Realizing that Cornwallis could be trapped, Washington leads his army south from New York.
30 Aug.	De Grasse arrives off Yorktown and reinforces Lafayette with infantry.
5–9 Sept.	Naval fighting off Yorktown results in a French victory.
8 Sept.	Checked at the Battle of Eutaw Springs, Greene nevertheless compels the retreat of the British army to Charleston.
14 Sept.	Washington's troops begin arriving at Williamsburg to reinforce Lafayette.
28 Sept.	Seventeen thousand French and American troops begin the siege of the eight thousand British troops in Yorktown.
19 Oct.	Cornwallis surrenders.
24 Oct.	Clinton arrives too late to save Cornwallis and sails back to New York.
Nov.	Washington marches back to New York.

1782

•	Greene besieges Charleston while Washington blockades New York.
30 Nov.	The Treaty of Paris is signed.

1783

15 Mar.	At army headquarters in Newburgh, New York, Washington denounces a threat by officers to rebel against Congress.
15 Apr.	The Continental Congress ratifies the Treaty of Paris.
21 June	Mutinous Pennsylvania troops surround Congress's meeting place to demand their pay; Congress leaves Philadelphia for New Jersey.
25 Nov.	The British evacuate New York.
23 Dec.	Addressing Congress in Annapolis, Maryland, Washington resigns his commission as commander in chief of the Continental Army.

OVERVIEW

Background. By 1755 the ninety thousand French colonists along the St. Lawrence River in North America had fought several wars with the 1.5 million English colonists on the eastern seaboard. Most of these wars were the result of conflicts fought mainly in Europe, and a few were strictly local struggles. None of them settled the issues at stake in North America. The French wanted an empire extending from the Atlantic Ocean to the Gulf of Mexico, and to secure it they claimed all lands watered by streams flowing into the St. Lawrence River the Great Lakes, and the Mississippi River. Meanwhile the English claimed all lands occupied by their allies, the Iroquois Indians, including the southern banks of the Great Lakes and the St. Lawrence River, as well as the northern part of the Mississippi River. Both sides resorted to arms in what became known in North America as the French and Indian War and spread worldwide as the Seven Years' War. British and French armies, their colonial militias, and the Indian allies fought a wilderness war in which the methods of fighting were largely imported from Europe. The decisive victory of the English removed French Canada as a threat to the English colonists. Without that threat colonists could see no reason why they should pay taxes to support English armies in North America. Outrage at such taxes was one of the sparks that lit the American Revolution, and the military skills colonists had learned fighting the French were a major factor in their winning their freedom from England.

Infantry. The foot soldier was the core of any European army. A professional enlisted for a long period of time, and he was taught his trade by brutal discipline and constant drill. The main focus of the drill was loading and firing his musket. This weapon was heavy and awkward to use. It had to be stood on end, powder poured down its barrel, wadding and shot tamped in, then brought to the shoulder and fired, all while its user was under hostile fire. Pulling the trigger created a spark that ignited the pan of powder and fired the musket. Under ideal conditions a well-trained soldier could get off three shots per minute, but on the battlefield one shot was more realistic. The lead musket ball was three-quarters of an inch in diameter, large and heavy enough to knock a man flat even when it didn't hit him in a vital spot. The musket was accurate up to 120 yards. In battle the infantry was drawn up in long parallel lines, shoulder to shoulder, and marched in lockstep toward the waiting enemy. Within musket range the lines halted, and the front line discharged their muskets at the enemy at an officer's signal and then stepped to the rear to reload while the next rank stepped up to fire. Of course, the enemy was also firing. A bayonet or cavalry charge on a weakened enemy would decide the outcome. Rifles were far more accurate than muskets, but they took longer to load and so could be used only by snipers on the periphery of engagements. (The rifle was also more fragile and expensive than the musket). The colonials did not have long-service professional armies since those were ill suited for campaigns against Indians. Instead, the various colonies required that able-bodied men present themselves periodically, with their own weapons and provisions, for training as a militia. Though they practiced some European drills, the North American colonists were able to draw upon 150 years of campaigns against Indians in which they developed small-unit tactics emphasizing ambushes, raids, and careful use of cover.

Field Artillery. The artillery pieces that accompanied infantry were made of bronze and sometimes iron, weighed about a ton, were mounted on wooden carriages with iron wheels, and were pulled by a team of four or more horses. Aiming them was an art rather than a science, and since the force of their blast rolled them backward when they were fired, they had to be wrestled into position for every shot by a crew of five or more men. To fire the gun a noncommissioned officer first aimed it, and then a loader rammed in a bag of powder and a ball. Then the firer applied a slow match to the touchhole while the rest of the crew got out of the way of the recoil. A practiced crew could get off two shots a minute, but their efficiency could be decreased by fatigue and enemy fire. The size of a cannon was known by the size of its shot: for example, a three-pounder fired a three-pound cannonball. Larger guns were usually reserved for sieges.

Cavalry. Despite popular notions of gallant warfare, horsemen were not used for shock attacks in set-piece battles since horses would shy before massed and determined infantry. In formal battles cavalry was used to harass the enemy's flanks and disrupt his lines of communication to the rear or was saved for when infantry that had been weakened and demoralized by artillery and musketry could be panicked by a cavalry charge. Most of the time cavalry was used to disrupt infantry columns, to scout, and to raid. The nature of the North American terrain greatly favored light cavalry. Light cavalry could move about easily and quickly and live off the land rather than depend on supply trains.

Fortifications. Fortress-building reached its apogee in the eighteenth century. Building a fort was a masterwork of engineering. The fort had to be sited in the best possible position, designed so that it took maximum advantage of the terrain. The best forts were star shaped so that one part of the fort could give covering fire to other parts. They were protected by moats and outerworks sculpted so as to put the enemy at the greatest disadvantage. To attack one of these forts required ingenuity and engineering skill. Usually it was a matter of digging parallel trenches closer and closer so as to get artillery into the best possible position to bombard the fort. North America had fortresses constructed on the European model, such as Louisbourg on Cape Breton Island, and adaptations of that style to suit indigenous habits, such as Ticonderoga in upstate New York.

Terrain. Unlike western Europe, where the British and French armies were accustomed to campaigning in areas that had long been cleared for agricultural purposes and had many towns and roads, North America presented forbidding problems for transporting armies, weaponry, and supplies. If armies in Europe could count on "living off the land"—that is, foraging for foodstuffs from the local population—in North America the farms were much fewer and more scattered. They had to carry most of their own food, putting a heavy burden on their maneuverability. The road network in colonial America was also limited. As a result armies had to choose between struggling through large tracts of almost impenetrable wilderness or transporting men and supplies by a few strategically important waterways. Thus upstate New York, especially the region around the Mohawk and Hudson River valleys and Lake Champlain, was frequently the site of military activity. In the winter, when lakes and streams froze and roads were snow-covered or muddy, armies had to go into winter quarters and wait for the next campaigning season.

Colonial Victory. In the Seven Years' War, Prime Minister William Pitt's genius and the worldwide commitment of British resources brought an end to the French empire in North America. The experience was a military education for the English colonists. Prior to the war only the New Englanders had a tradition of military activity and training, due to their proximity to the French and the frequent hostilities between them. By the end of the war colonists of the Middle and Southern colonies had been exposed to systematic training, and their officers had gained command experience. The English colonists now knew how to fight in the European fashion as well as how to fight irregular actions. When the Revolutionary War came, their military performance was effective enough to encourage the French to settle old scores by joining the war on the side of the colonists. Putting down so extensive and persistent an insurrection was beyond the will and resources of the British empire.

TOPICS IN THE NEWS

FRENCH AND INDIAN WAR: BRADDOCK'S DEFEAT

Forks of the Ohio. Of all the leaders of the English colonies, Gov. Robert Dinwiddie of Virginia was the most concerned about the way the French and their Indian allies were behaving in the Ohio River valley. He and other Virginians had invested in companies that intended to acquire land in the Ohio valley and were desperate to forestall any French control of the area. Virginia legislators were reluctant to raise and pay for troops, so when he learned that the French were building forts on the Allegheny and Ohio Rivers, the best he could do was commission the twenty-two-year-old George Washington as lieutenant colonel in charge of about 150 militiamen and send him in the spring 1754 to build a fort where the Monongahela, Allegheny, and Ohio Rivers met. The move was too late. The French had already arrived at the Forks of the Ohio and built Fort Duquesne. Washington built his own fort some miles away at Great Meadows. His inexperience showed in the faulty design of his fort, and the French easily captured it.

A painting of the French and Indian ambush in July 1755 of Maj. Gen. Edward Braddock's column near Fort Duquesne in present-day Pennsylvania (Wisconsin State Historical Society, Madison)

Enter Braddock. In April of the following year Maj. Gen. Edward Braddock arrived in Virginia as commander in chief of British forces in North America. He brought with him two regiments of British soldiers to form the core of an expedition against the French. Meeting with Dinwiddie, Massachusetts governor William Shirley, and other colonial officials, he elaborated a grand strategy for dealing with the French: the capture of the four French forts that hemmed in the English colonists. These were Fort Beauséjour on the Bay of Fundy in Canada; Crown Point on Lake Champlain in upstate New York; Fort Niagara at Niagara Falls, New York; and Fort Duquesne. With George Washington as one of his aides, Braddock would attack Fort Duquesne. A blunt and short-tempered soldier, Braddock was infuriated by the colonial politicians. The regiments he had were understrength and would have to be reinforced with colonial troops. Pennsylvania refused to contribute troops despite the French threat to its western settlements. North Carolina and Maryland sent two companies, and Virginia dispatched nine. If this situation were not bad enough, Braddock was faced with a long march from the Virginia coast to Fort Duquesne through rough lands and dense forests, which would not have been the case had he started from Philadelphia. Despite the difficulty of the task, he was contemptuous of advice from colonials and insisted on assembling a huge train of wagons to carry his supplies. Local contractors cheated him on supplies, and wagons were found only with difficulty.

The March. To cut a usable track through the almost impassable forest, Braddock had three hundred axemen cut a swath twelve-feet wide. The army was four miles long as it toiled along the path; artillery was manhandled along; wagons broke down; and the troops were miserable in the summer heat. In ten days the column had covered only twenty-two miles. Following Washington's advice, Braddock culled out a smaller force to press forward with lighter loads, leaving the supply train to advance as best it could. This column covered four miles a day and in thirty days was about eight miles from Fort Duquesne.

Disaster. On the morning of 9 July, Braddock's army forded the Monongahela River in fine order, its band playing. Fort Duquesne was almost within sight, and the French had not been heard. In fact, all was confusion at the fort. Indian scouts had reported the arrival of Braddock's army, and the French commander realized immediately that he could not hope to win an open battle or withstand a siege. He had only a handful of Canadian troops and about eight hundred Indians. His only hope was to ambush the column in the woods. Captain Daniel Beaujeu led the Canadians and Indians on a dash from the fort. As soon as they contacted Braddock's army, the British troops formed line and routed the Canadians with a few volleys. Beaujeu was immediately killed, but his subordinate rallied the Indians in an attack on the British flanks. Soon the British were galled by bullets from an unseen enemy and from unexpected directions. The British lines began to collapse, and knots of men, ten or twelve strong, were firing blindly at the woods, often hitting their own comrades. Braddock was infuriated and tried to force his troops back into line. He was especially angry at the Virginians, who had broken ranks to fight from cover. He had four horses killed under him before he himself was wounded through the lungs. Sixty-three of his eighty-six British officers were killed or wounded, and Washington was the only one of his aides to be unharmed. What was left of his army was a routed mob, fleeing its way back across the river to safety. Of the 1,459 men in the army, 977 had been killed or wounded. Braddock died four days later, and wagons were driven over his grave so that the Indians would not find it and desecrate the corpse. Washington helped lead the remains of his army home. Afterward there was much criticism of Braddock for not having listened to the colonials, and many expressed the opinion that European tactics were unsuited to fight in America.

Source:
Paul E. Kopperman, *Braddock at the Monongahela* (Pittsburgh, Pa.: University of Pittsburgh Press, 1976).

FRENCH AND INDIAN WAR: FAILURE OF A STRATEGY

Fort Beauséjour. Less than a month before Maj. Gen. Edward Braddock's disaster, the colonials had experienced success in implementing another part of the four-pronged strategy to deal with the French. An expedition of colonials, stiffened by a few British regulars, had landed at the top of the Bay of Fundy to deal with Fort Beauséjour. This fortress protected the lines of communication between Canada and the great fort at Louisbourg. A small British stronghold, Fort Lawrence, within sight of Beauséjour, was the only bar to any French attack on Nova Scotia. In May 1755 two thousand colonials landed near Fort Lawrence and set about capturing Beauséjour. Forcing their way across a river and pushing aside French defenders, the colonials occupied the hills behind the fort. With two small mortars, they began a harassing fire while waiting for the cannon to be brought up. Three days later, one of the mortar bombs burst in what the French defenders had thought was a bombproof shelter, killing six French officers and a captive. The commander of the fort, not a soldier but a corrupt profiteer, quickly surrendered the fort. The big guns brought for the siege, the kind the fort had been built to withstand, were not even in position.

Shirley's Failure. The third part of the plan was undertaken by Gov. William Shirley of Massachusetts. When Braddock's army was destroyed, Shirley was leading 1,500 men up the Mohawk River to capture the French fort at Niagara. As enthusiastic as he was, Shirley was baffled by the logistical problems of moving an army. By the beginning of September, he had made it only as far as Oswego. There he got unwelcome news. The French had not only reinforced Fort Niagara but had gathered a force at Fort Frontenac across Lake Ontario, intending to capture Oswego. If Shirley went forward, he'd be caught between the French at Niagara and the French at Frontenac. The French saw an opportunity and diverted Baron Ludwig Dieskau from marching to Niagara and sent him down Lake Champlain to attack Albany and New York City. Abandoning his plan, Shirley left two regiments to hold Oswego and returned to New England.

DEATH IN THE FOREST

Nine days after Maj. Gen. Edward Braddock's army was cut to pieces near Fort Duquesne, Col. George Washington wrote his account of the battle in a letter to his mother:

Honored Madam:

As I doubt not but you have heard of our defeat, and perhaps have it represented in a worse light (if possible) than it deserves. I have taken this earliest opportunity to give you some account of the engagement as it happened, within seven miles of the French fort, on Wednesday, the 9th inst.

We marched on to that place without any considerable loss, having only now and then a straggler picked up by the Indian scouts of the French. When we came there, we were attacked by a body of French and Indians, whose number (I am certain) did not exceed 300 men. Ours consisted of about 1,300 well-armed troops, chiefly of the English soldiers, who were struck with such a panic that they behaved with more cowardice than it is possible to conceive. The officers behaved gallantly in order to encourage their men, for which they suffered greatly, there being near 60 killed and wounded—a large proportion out of the number we had!

The Virginia troops showed a good deal of bravery, and were near all killed; for I believe out of three companies that were there, there are scarce 30 men left alive. Captain Peyrouny and all his officers, down to a corporal, were killed; Captain Polson shared near as hard a fate, for only one of his was left. In short, the dastardly behavior of those they call regulars exposed all others to almost certain death; and, at last, in despite of all the efforts of the officers to the contrary, they broke and ran as sheep pursued by dogs; and it was impossible to rally them.

The general was wounded; of which he died three days after. Sir Peter Halket was killed in the field, where died many other brave officers. I luckily escaped without a wound, though I had four bullets through my coat, and two horses shot under me. Captains Orme and Morris, two of the general's aides de camp, were wounded early in the engagement, which rendered the duty hard upon me, as I was the only person then left to distribute the general's orders; which I was scarcely able to do as I was not half recovered from a violent illness that confined me to my bed and a wagon for above ten days.

I am still in a weak and feeble condition; which induces me to halt here two or three days in hope of recovering a little strength to enable me to proceed homeward. . . .

P.S. We had about 300 men killed and as many, and more, wounded.

Source: John C. Fitzpatrick, ed., *The Writings of George Washington from the Original Manuscript Sources, 1745–1799*, 39 volumes (Washington: U.S. Government Printing Office, 1931–1944), volume 1, pp. 150–152.

A Missed Opportunity. The last prong of the strategy developed by Braddock and the provincial governors was the reduction of Crown Point on Lake Champlain. In August an army made up of thirty-five hundred troops from five different colonies and about three hundred allied Indians started toward Crown Point from Albany under the command of Sir William Johnson. A man of great political power who was known as a friend of the Indians, Johnson had no military background. On the way north he built Fort Edward on the Hudson River; he then moved further north with two thousand of his men and built Fort William Henry on Lake George. At the same time Dieskau was marching from Canada with four thousand men. After reinforcing the garrison at Crown Point, Dieskau built Fort Ticonderoga at a strategic spot fifteen miles down Lake Champlain. He was heading for the Hudson River with nine hundred French troops and six hundred Indians when he blundered into Johnson on 8 September. In the ensuing battle the French troops met a fate similar to Braddock's while Dieskau was wounded and captured. With reinforcements coming in, Johnson was well poised to push on and reduce Ticonderoga and Crown Point, but he feared that his militia were not up to the task and settled down to hold Fort William Henry. The grand design for depriving the French of their forts had failed miserably, and the English settlers of the Ohio valley and western Pennsylvania were paying the price, being slaughtered by the Indian allies of the French.

Source:
Howard H. Peckham, *The Colonial Wars, 1689–1762* (Chicago: University of Chicago Press, 1964).

FRENCH AND INDIAN WAR: FORT WILLIAM HENRY

Montcalm. In May 1756, as the hostilities in America were about to flare into a European war, Louis-Joseph de Montcalm-Gozon, Marquis de Montcalm de Saint Véran, arrived in Canada with reinforcements from France. He found a difficult situation. The governor, Pierre de Rigaud, Marquis de Vaudreuil, was the commander of fourteen thousand Canadian militia men and of the fifteen hundred marines in the colony. Montcalm directly commanded only six regiments of regulars, a total of about four thousand men. In this situation of divided military command, the two men found it increasingly difficult to deal with one another. Vaudreuil was jealous of Montcalm's power, and Montcalm was contemptuous of the corruption of the government of New France. Nevertheless, they managed to agree on an offensive against Oswego. As a trading post Oswego had cut into what the French regarded as their monopoly of the fur trade. As a fort it threatened the security of French travel from the St. Lawrence River to the Mississippi River by way of the Great Lakes. Montcalm first went to Fort Ticonderoga to convince the English that an offensive would be directed toward Fort William Henry. He then hurried to Fort Frontenac and by 10 August was at Oswego with three thousand Frenchmen, Canadians, and Indians. After a brief bombardment the discouraged garrison, many of them ill, surrendered. For a price of thirty killed and wounded Montcalm had captured six hundred men with all of their provisions, more than one hundred cannon, and six armed sloops. More important, perhaps, he had so impressed the Indians that they joined the French cause in droves, with more than two thousand of them meeting Montcalm in Montreal to pledge their allegiance.

Failure at Louisbourg. On Cape Breton Island, north of Nova Scotia, stood one of the most formidable forts in the world. Named Louisbourg after the French king, its construction had cost so much that the king was fond of joking that any day he expected to look out the window of his palace in France and see it looming on the horizon. This fort guarded warships that could protect French fishing boats off the Grand Banks, bar an enemy sailing into the mouth of the St. Lawrence River, or trap an enemy fleet that managed to reach the river. If Quebec was to be attacked from the sea, Louisbourg would have to be seized. It had, in fact, been captured by New Englanders in 1745 during King George's War (1740–1748). To the outrage of the colonists, it had been returned to France in the peace treaty. In the spring of 1756 Gen. John Campbell, Earl of Loudon, the new British commander in North America, assembled fifteen thousand troops to bring them to Halifax, Nova Scotia, to attack Louisbourg. The expedition went slowly. Loudon had difficulty rounding up enough sailors to transport his troops from New York and then had to wait until a fleet arrived from England. While the troops drilled in Halifax, news came that eighteen French battleships had arrived at Louisbourg. The British admiral could not tempt them to sail out to fight him, and their guns, combined with those of the fortress, made an attack on Louisbourg suicidal. On 24 September the expedition was abandoned after a storm scattered the British fleet.

Montcalm Loses Control. To mount the Louisbourg attack British troops had been taken from Forts Edward and William Henry, leaving only twenty-three hundred regulars and fifty-five hundred colonials to defend them. Col. Daniel Webb kept most of these troops with him at Fort Edward, allowing only seven hundred and fifty regulars and twelve hundred New Englanders to defend Fort William Henry. On 3 August 1757 Montcalm appeared before Fort William Henry with four thousand French troops and one thousand Indians. After a four-day artillery duel all of the fort's guns were disabled, and the militiamen were near mutiny. Lt. Col. George Monro surrendered the fort on terms that allowed his men to march out with the honors of war, providing they promise not to do any further fighting for eighteen months. On 9 August, as the unarmed garrison prepared to march to Fort Edward, the Indian allies of the French attacked them. Though Montcalm threw himself into the midst of the Indians to try to restrain them, the Indians massacred more than two hundred of the soldiers and about one hundred of their wives and children. Colonel Webb at Fort Edward had not sent aid during the battle and now decided that a counterattack was not possible. He was so demoralized that Montcalm could easily have destroyed Fort Edward and menaced Albany, but he had no supplies of food and had to fall back to Fort Ticonderoga.

Source:

Ian K. Steele, *Betrayals: Fort William Henry and the Massacre* (New York: Oxford University Press, 1990).

FRENCH AND INDIAN WAR: LOUISBOURG

Capture. After the disasters of 1755, 1756, and 1757 came the glory days for Britain. In 1757 the energetic and farsighted William Pitt became prime minister. His visionary eye saw opportunity in America. Subsidizing the Prussian king's army to keep the French busy in Europe, Pitt began pouring reinforcements into North America and choosing talented officers to command them. The first fruit of his efforts was the capture of Louisbourg. In the summer of 1758 he sent Gen. Jeffrey Amherst with nine thousand British regulars and five hundred colonials to Nova Scotia. More than six thousand French soldiers and sailors, twelve ships, and nearly eight hundred guns waited at Louisbourg. While Adm. Edward Boscawen kept the French fleet from intervening, Gen. James Wolfe, a young officer whose performance in Europe had caught Pitt's eye, led assault troops in whaleboats toward the shore in the face of heavy artillery and musket fire from the dunes. He had already decided that the attack could not succeed when some boatloads of soldiers found a safe landing spot by accident. They drove the French back into the fort, and General Amherst began the siege. Days of bombardment by heavy artillery slowly destroyed the living quarters of both troops and civilians inside the fort. The French ships in the harbor were destroyed by raids from the British fleet, removing any hope of escape. At last the French civilians implored the commander to surrender before the walls were breached and they found themselves in the middle of a firefight inside the fort. On 27 July the French flag was lowered. This time the fort would not be returned to the French. After the war it was destroyed and the stone hauled away for building projects.

Setback at Ticonderoga. While the siege of Louisbourg was under way, Gen. James Abercrombie was at Fort Ticonderoga. Commanding a force of twelve thousand (half of them regulars) to the Marquis de Montcalm's three thousand defenders, he failed to surround the fort to cut off the possibility of resupply or retreat or to find high ground from which to bombard the fort. Instead, on 8 July he launched a full frontal assault by wave after wave of infantry, who were slaughtered while advancing slowly over trees the French had felled to create clear lines of fire. When Abercrombie finally called off the attack, there were more than a thousand corpses piled

up for the French Indians to scalp. Two months later he was replaced by Amherst.

A Fort for Pitt. West of Ticonderoga, Lt. Col. John Bradstreet led an amphibious expedition up the Mohawk River to Lake Ontario to deal with Fort Frontenac. Avenging the loss of Fort Oswego, he blew up Frontenac on 27 August, seized the boats with which the French had patrolled Lake Ontario, and confiscated the year's profits from the fur trade. Most important of all, he denied the French easy access by boat to the western territories. Meanwhile Brig. John Forbes was leading a mixed force of British regulars and colonial militia in another attack on Fort Duquesne, his campaign planned in part by George Washington, who was returning to the scene of his earlier humiliations in command of a Virginia regiment. Though the way Forbes chose was easier than Braddock's wilderness route, it was a long march for the troops. Forbes was sick much of the time and devoted what energy he had to fortifying a line of escape in case of failure. The army was bogged down in mud early in November when word reached it that the French were abandoning the fort. Deprived of supplies by the fall of Frontenac, the French commander had decided he could not hold, so he destroyed the fort on 24 November and carried off all his guns and supplies. The triumphant Forbes wrote to William Pitt, christening the place "Pittsburgh" as his tribute to the man whose vision and determination had made victory against the French possible. The last casualty of the campaign was Forbes, who died in March of the following year of illnesses he had contracted on the march.

Sources:

Francis Jennings, *Empire of Fortune: Crowns, Colonies, and Tribes in the Seven Years War in America* (New York: Norton, 1988);

Francis Parkman, *Montcalm and Wolfe*, 2 volumes (Boston: Little, Brown, 1884).

FRENCH AND INDIAN WAR: QUEBEC

The Advance by Land. For the new year of 1759 William Pitt envisioned a three-pronged attack on French Canada: one force would take Fort Niagara and move down the St. Lawrence River to menace Montreal; another force would capture Fort Ticonderoga and Crown Point and advance up the Champlain valley on Montreal and Quebec; and an amphibious force would attack Quebec up the St. Lawrence River. The first two parts were complete by the end of July. Advancing up the Mohawk River valley, Brig. John Prideaux recaptured Oswego and sailed down Lake Ontario to besiege Fort Niagara. Before it capitulated on 25 July, Prideaux was killed in action. On the next day Gen. Jeffrey Amherst led an army of more than ten thousand in the capture of the weakened garrison of Fort Ticonderoga. The following week he took Crown Point, but he advanced no farther.

The Amphibious Assault. Gen. James Wolfe was put in charge of the most promising and most difficult task, the assault on the fortress of Quebec by combined opera-

The ruins of Notre Dame des Victoires in Quebec following the British siege of 1759

tions of the navy and the army. Departing England in February, he used the transatlantic crossing to cement a sound working relationship with Vice Adm. Sir Charles Saunders, who would command the nearly two hundred ships in the expedition. At Louisbourg they loaded supplies and the four thousand infantry in Wolfe's command, almost all of them regulars, and sailed into the mouth of the St. Lawrence River. When Wolfe's troops disembarked on Orleans Island below Quebec, they found the Marquis de Montcalm's fourteen thousand troops encamped on the opposite shore from the St. Charles River to the Montmorency River. Montcalm had geography on his side: the fortress of Quebec was high above the river, protected by cliffs to its west and his formidable defense force to its east. Many thought it was impregnable.

The Plains of Abraham. Montcalm had the upper hand but was tormented by the collapse of his relations with Gov. Pierre de Rigaud, Marquis de Vaudreuil. They hated one another, and Montcalm often thought he was menaced less by Wolfe than by Vaudreuil. Wolfe was in a precarious situation. He was plagued by illness and by the near insubordination of commanders who resented his lack of noble birth and thought themselves better qualified for command. As time passed and Montcalm groped about for a way to attack Quebec, sickness and discipline problems began to appear in his troops. Admiral Saunders began speculating about the latest date he would have to sail his ships out of the river to avoid having them iced in. Wolfe first landed troops on the north side of the river, across the Montmorency from Montcalm. Though Wolfe could not advance from this spot, with Montcalm's entire army and two rivers separating him from Quebec, he could bombard the town and freeze

Montcalm in place. He then sent Saunders upriver past Quebec to look for alternate landing sites and to confuse and exhaust the French troops to the west of the town. After weeks of seeking a landing site Wolfe's scouts spotted a narrow defile leading up the cliffs on the river's north bank to the Plains of Abraham. Faking a landing on Montcalm's left on the night of 12 September, Wolfe embarked infantry in boats above the town and floated them downriver to the bottom of the defile. Scouts scaled the path, killed the sentries, and led the first infantry to the top. At daybreak, forty-eight hundred British were on the grassy field near the weak west wall of Quebec. By ten o'clock Montcalm had rushed four thousand soldiers through the streets of the town and led them against the single British line. At forty yards the British fired twice and then lunged forward in a bayonet attack. Though losses were about equal, and both Montcalm and Wolfe were killed, the French position was lost, and Quebec surrendered five days later.

Collapse of Canada. Though Quebec was captured, Montreal was still unthreatened, and Gen. François-Gaston de Lévis was rallying the French and colonial troops to defend their country. In April 1760 he arrived at the doors of Quebec and besieged the British garrison of seven thousand with a force of nearly twice that size. Though he defeated the British in a second battle on the Plains of Abraham, he was forced to raise his siege when a British fleet arrived two weeks later. By September three British columns were converging on Montreal, one from Oswego, one from Crown Point, and one from Quebec. There was no recourse. On 8 September, Governor Vaudreuil surrendered Montreal and all of French Canada with it.

A painting of George Washington taking command of the Continental Army in Cambridge, Massachusetts (Bettmann Archive, New York)

Source:
C. P. Stacey, *Quebec, 1759: The Siege and the Battle* (Toronto: Macmillan, 1959).

REVOLUTIONARY WAR: NORTHERN THEATER

The Powder Keg. However intricate the political causes of the American Revolution, the military flashpoint was a simple matter. On the night of 18 April 1775 the governor of Massachusetts, Gen. Thomas Gage, sent a column of troops under Lt. Col. Francis Smith and Maj. John Pitcairn to seize weapons and gunpowder stored by the Massachusetts Provincial Congress at Concord, some sixteen miles west of Boston. Early in the morning of the nineteenth, Pitcairn, pushing ahead with six companies to secure the bridges over the Concord River, encountered on the town green at Lexington a local company of militia captained by John Parker. Pitcairn ordered them to disperse. A single shot was fired, nobody knows by whom, and the British troops fired several volleys into the colonials, killing eight of them and wounding ten. The colonials scattered; Smith came up with the rest of the troops; and the British moved off toward Concord. There Smith destroyed what stores the colonials had not spirited away and turned back for Boston. Word of the massacre had spread and militiamen swarmed to the attacked, sniping at the column of redcoats from behind trees and stone walls along the route. At Lexington, Smith found Lord Hugh Percy and 900 men come to reinforce him. These troops provided even more targets for the angry colonists, who harassed their march all the way back to Boston. The British commanders did what they could, detaching small parties to chase snipers and burn houses that had sheltered them, but at the end of the day the British casualties amounted to 73 killed, 174 wounded and 26 missing while only 93 patriots were killed or wounded.

The Siege of Boston. Soon the Massachusetts Provincial Congress decided to raise a force of 13,600 militia under Gen. Artemas Ward to be sent to surrounding colonies for assistance. Within days a force of nearly 17,000 colonists was camped in an arc around Boston, besieging the British garrison of about 3,500. Soon generals William Howe, John Burgoyne, and Henry Clinton arrived in Boston with reinforcements. Realizing that the peninsula on which Boston stood could be bombarded by artillery placed on the heights of either Dorchester to the south or Charlestown to the north, they planned to seize both those places. On 17 June they woke to find that 1,200 colonists had fortified Breed's Hill on Charlestown. By midafternoon, British troops had been ferried across the harbor and drawn up in lines to attack the patriot redoubt. As they advanced up the hill, Loyalists on Boston's rooftops and in the rigging of ships set up a cheer. Patriot fire discipline was excellent. Col. William Prescott had told them, "Don't fire until you see the whites of their eyes," so that the British were within fifty yards of the fortifications when the first Patriot volley tore into them. The British renewed the attack with similar results. They began ferrying reinforcements across the harbor, aghast at the sight of veteran regiments fleeing in panic. General Howe lost every

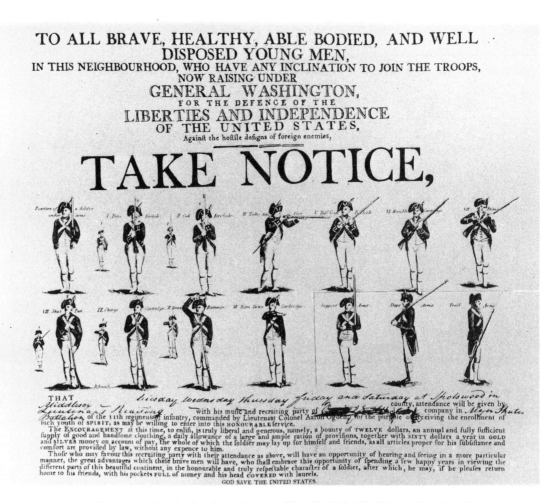

A recruiting poster for the Continental Army (New York Public Library, New York)

man on his staff. At length, the colonists ran out of ammunition and the British swept the position. The Americans had paid a steep price in this erroneously named Battle of Bunker Hill, with 140 killed, 271 wounded, and 30 captured, but the British had 226 dead and 828 wounded, an appalling casualty rate. Now the whole world knew that colonial militia could stand up to British regulars in battle. By July, George Washington had arrived in Cambridge as the new American commander in chief. On 4 March 1776 he made the move the British had feared, placing cannon atop Dorchester Heights and beginning to bombard the city and the British fleet. On 17 March the British evacuated Boston.

Attacks on Canada. As soon as hostilities began, colonials in the New England area began operations against Canada. They had suffered attacks from that direction over more than a century and they felt sure that Canada would serve as a staging area for the British army. On 10 May, less than a month after the battles of Lexington and Concord, Col. Ethan Allen and his Green Mountain Boys, a Vermont militia regiment, surprised and captured Fort Ticonderoga on Lake George in upstate New York. Two days later they seized nearby Crown Point on Lake Champlain. By August an American force was heading into Canada from Ticonderoga, capturing the town of St. John's on the

Richelieu River on 2 November and marching into Montreal eleven days later. Joining up with a force that Col. Benedict Arnold had marched up from Boston through Maine, the colonials attacked Quebec on 31 December 1775 but were repulsed with heavy losses. Arnold besieged the city until May and retreated to Montreal. Another attempt on Quebec met defeat at Trois Rivières in June 1776 and the Americans had to retreat from Canada. These rash actions had forestalled any invasion from Canada in 1776, and the guns of Fort Ticonderoga, manhandled across New York and Massachusetts by troops under Col. Henry Knox, had been used in the siege of Boston.

New York City. As soon as the British were out of Boston, Washington guessed that they would move against New York as a means of cutting off New England from the rest of the colonies, and he hurried south to fortify it. By the time that General Howe arrived at Staten Island on 2 July 1776 with thirty-two thousand troops, Washington had constructed fortifications on Brooklyn Heights, Governor's Island, and lower Manhattan. His army numbered only about eighteen thousand men, one-half of them in Brooklyn, the other in Manhattan. When Howe ferried twenty thousand men to Long Island, Washington fought them European-style on open ground. Many of his officers

After the evacuation of Boston by British troops and Tory civilians on 17 March 1776, this bleak portrait of the aftermath of the event was noted in a letter written on board a British ship lying just outside Boston Harbor, and printed in the *Morning Chronicle* and *London Advertiser* on 6 May:

One hundred and forty vessels, great and small, are arrived in this road from Boston, in the most distressed condition that can possibly be described, with General Howe, his army, and about 1500 inhabitants (friends to the government) of that place. Where they are bound to, we are at a loss to know. Certain it is, however, they are all drove from Boston by General Washington's army, after a cannonading of fourteen days, whereby one third of the town was destroyed, and a number of the King's troops killed, and a great many much wounded, owing chiefly to the quantity of shells the Provincials kept continually pouring into the town. The English troops, and the Tories, embarked on board the above vessels in the greatest disorder and confusion pen cannot describe, leaving behind two month's provisions, a large quantity of cloathing belonging to the regulars, a number of puncheons of rum, together with the artillery, cannon, and the greatest part of the ammunition. General Howe left seven men of war at Boston, one of which, by some accident, ran on shore, and it is feared the crew are made prisoners, and the vessel, with all her cannon and stores, fallen into the possession of the Provincials.

Source: Margaret Wheeler Willard, ed., *Letters on the American Revolution, 1774–1776* (Port Washington, N.Y.: Kennikat Press, 1968), pp. 291–292.

were unused to command, and some of the militia panicked. The Battle of Long Island went down as a British victory, with the colonials losing more than one thousand men. The fortifications on Brooklyn Heights were now untenable, and Washington had to evacuate Long Island. In thirteen hours he managed to bring nine thousand men with their artillery and supplies across the East River to Manhattan Island, a brilliant feat. Washington himself was the last American to embark. Unable to defend New York effectively, Washington soon withdrew northward to Harlem Heights and was gradually pushed farther north by Howe. By November he was retreating southward through New Jersey and Howe was settling into winter quarters in New York. On the day after Christmas, Washington surprised the Hessians at Trenton, winning a great victory, but the British were safely in control of New York and able to make it their headquarters for the rest of the Revolution.

Source:
Christopher Ward, *War of the Revolution,* 2 volumes (New York: Macmillan, 1952).

REVOLUTIONARY WAR: SARATOGA

British Strategy. In the beginning of 1777 Gen. John Burgoyne decided to do what the colonists' early attacks on Canada had prevented: split the New England colonies from the rest of the colonies by establishing control of the Lake Champlain and Hudson River valleys in upstate New York. He would march down Lake Champlain from Montreal while Col. Barry St. Leger would move down the Mohawk River valley from Lake Ontario. Meanwhile, Gen. William Howe would be striking north from New York City up the Hudson River. These three expeditions would come together in Albany. Though the idea was Bur-

The Grand Union flag raised by the Continental Army on 1 January 1776
(Mastai Collection, New York)

Front page of a Connecticut newspaper announcing the surrender terms of British general John Burgoyne's army at Saratoga, New York

goyne's, the planning was done in London and was fatally flawed. General Howe was encouraged rather than ordered to march to Albany. This error doomed the entire plan.

Burgoyne Alone. On 1 July, Burgoyne with more than seven thousand regulars and one thousand Indians arrived at Fort Ticonderoga, garrisoned by twenty-five hundred colonials who lacked artillery. They evacuated the fort on 5 July. Through July and August, Burgoyne toiled down bad forest roads in pursuit of the Americans. While he was doing so, American reinforcements were arriving in the area, though they could not prevent his seizing Fort Edward. On 3 August, Burgoyne realized that the plan had gone awry, that Howe was not moving up from New York. He had the choice of returning to Canada, staying and holding forts Edward and Ticonderoga, or proceeding forward. Decid-

ing that he would have a clearer view of the situation when his force and Leger's linked up, he continued toward Albany. But all was not well with St. Leger. By the end of July he had passed Oswego and was besieging Fort Stanwix on the Mohawk River. That was as far as he got. He defeated one American relief column at Oriskany, but with another one under Benedict Arnold approaching, St. Leger's Indian allies deserted him, and he retreated to Oswego. Burgoyne was alone.

Victory. By now it was equally dangerous for Burgoyne to advance or retreat, because so many colonial troops had been drawn to the area. Hoping to profit more from advancing, he crossed the Hudson River on 13 September and confronted Gen. Horatio Gates, who had fortified Bemis Heights, about eight miles from Saratoga. Gates's right flank was anchored on the Hudson, so on the nineteenth

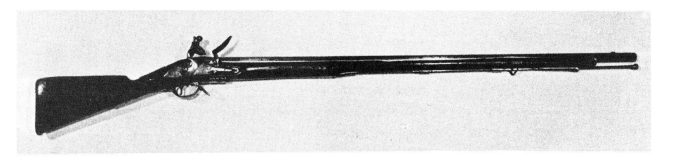

A Brown Bess musket, the standard British infantry weapon in the eighteenth century

Burgoyne attacked his left at Freeman's Farm. The hero of the day was Benedict Arnold, who was still smarting from not having been offered Gates's job. He plunged into the attack, driving his troops forward with a great deal of tactical skill. He could have beaten Burgoyne even more badly, but Gates refused him reinforcements. After the battle the jealous Gates removed Arnold from his command. Burgoyne dug fortifications, hoping for help from New York. There was, in fact, an expedition sent a few miles up the Hudson River, but it was intended as no more than a diversion. Burgoyne had no choice but to return to the attack on 7 October. A rifle regiment under Col. Daniel Morgan stalled the British attack by picking off the bravest and best of the British officers. Arnold disobeyed Gates and hurried into action at the head of the New England regiments and routed the confused British. When Burgoyne surrendered his army on 17 October, not only was the splitting of the colonies a dead letter, but New York and New England were largely cleared of British troops for the remainder of the conflict (although there were still some local attacks by Tories and their Indian allies). More important, the skill and valor of the Americans had so impressed the French that by the following February they had signed an alliance with the Americans, and they joined the war against the British in June 1778.

Sources:

Richard M. Ketchum, *Saratoga: Turning Point of America's Revolutionary War* (New York: Henry Holt, 1997);

Max M. Mintz, *The Generals of Saratoga: John Burgoyne and Horatio Gates* (New Haven, Conn.: Yale University Press, 1990).

REVOLUTIONARY WAR: THE SERAPIS

War at Sea. From the beginning of the war the sea was a vital theater, giving the British navy an avenue for moving troops quickly and easily from the mother country to North America or from one colony to another. This meant that a great deal of the military action would occur around the great colonial ports: Boston, Newport, New York, Philadelphia, Norfolk, and Charleston. Disrupting British control of the sea was a constant concern for the colonists, one expressed as early as 12 June 1775, when a party of lumbermen in Machias, Maine, boarded and confiscated the *Margaretta*, a British armed cutter. Soon seaside towns were seizing British vessels in port, sending boats out to harass shipping near the shore, and smuggling weapons. On 18 October Adm. Thomas Graves attacked what is now Portland, Maine, burned most of the town and captured or destroyed the ships in the harbor. No coastal community was safe from British sea power. Congress purchased eleven vessels to refit for the Continental Navy, but the effectiveness of the British blockade made many wonder if they would ever be able to put to sea. Therefore, Congress licensed privateers, private ships authorized by formal letters of marque and reprisal, to raid commerce.

A Heroic Career. On 6 August 1776 Lt. John Paul Jones was ordered to sea in his first independent command. His determination and audacity made him the greatest American naval hero of the war. Commanding the sloop of war *Ranger,* he took the fighting to the British Isles. When he sailed into the Irish Sea in the spring 1778, he was doing no more than Capt. Lambert Wickes in *Reprisal* and Capt. Henry Johnson in *Lexington* had done in 1777. Instead of merely raiding commerce, however, Jones raided ashore in Whitehaven Harbor (from which he had sailed for Virginia at age seventeen), spiking the artillery that defended the port, setting ships afire and hoisting a few glasses in the local pub. He followed on 23 April by landing on St. Mary's Isle in Kirkcudbright Bay to take the Earl of Selkirk as a

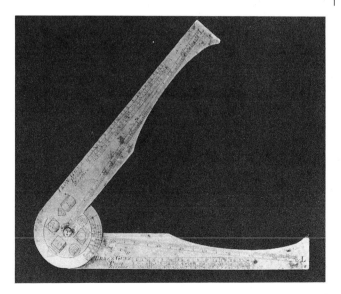

An artilleryman's calipers, circa 1750 (Harold L. Peterson Collection)

John Trumbull's circa 1780 drawing of Americans aboard the British prison ship *Jersey*
(Fordham University, New York)

hostage. Fortunately for the earl, he was not at home, and his wife refreshed the raiding party with a cup of wine. Insignificant raids though these were, they were an invasion of the British Isles and a great propaganda victory for Jones and the American cause. His finest moment came on 23 September 1779. Commanding *Bonhomme Richard,* a converted merchant ship with 42 guns, Jones did battle with the British 44-gun frigate, *Serapis,* commanded by Capt. Richard Pearson. Early in the battle, Pearson ran his bow into Jones' stern and asked if the American was surrendering. Jones replied, "I have not yet begun to fight," nor had he. For two hours the ships grappled together bow to stern, muzzle to muzzle, so close *Serapis* could not open her gun ports and had to blow them off from inside. Although the *Bonhomme Richard* was sinking, the British captain lost his nerve and surrendered. Having nailed his flag to the mast, he now had to tear it down with his own hands. Jones had achieved undying fame.

The French Fleet. When the French joined the war on Britain, they brought troops and military expertise, but, perhaps more important, they brought their fleet. From 11 July 1778, when Adm. Jean-Baptiste-Charles-Henri-Hector, comte d'Estaing, briefly blockaded the British in New York, the operations of the French fleet in North American and Caribbean waters altered the calculus of power. The Americans were assured of supply lifelines to the rest of the world; the delivery by the French of much-needed arms and ammunition; and a slackening of British ability to use the sea freely for military purposes. It was the French fleet sailing from the Caribbean under Adm. François-Joseph-Paul de Grasse that provided a copybook exercise in combined operations by landing troops to strengthen the siege of Yorktown, preventing the British fleet from interfering, ferrying American troops to the scene of battle, and doing all of these while maintaining constant, clear, and effective communication with the American land-based forces. Though fought largely on land, the Revolutionary War could not have been won without sea power.

Sources:

Alfred Thayer Mahan, *The Major Operations of the Navies in the War of American Independence* (London: Sampson, Low, Marston, 1913);

Samuel Eliot Morison, *John Paul Jones: A Sailor's Biography* (Boston: Little, Brown, 1959).

REVOLUTIONARY WAR: SOUTHERN THEATER

The Central Campaign. While Gen. John Burgoyne's plan was being made and coming to grief, Gen. William Howe was trying to bring George Washington to battle in New Jersey and was being frustrated in the attempt. In July 1777 he sailed from New York and landed at the head of Chesapeake Bay. At the time he should have been moving up the Hudson River to relieve Burgoyne, he was brushing Washington aside at Brandywine and moving into Philadelphia. In the winter of 1777–1778 the American army endured freezing cold and starvation rations at Valley Forge while Howe was warm and well fed only thirty miles away. But the army that marched out of Valley Forge in the spring was tougher, more disciplined and more skilled due to the training efforts of the German officer Baron Friedrich Wilhelm Ludolf Gerhard Augustin von Steuben. On 18 June, the day after France declared war on Britain, Sir Henry Clinton, Howe's replacement as British commander in chief, began the move from Philadelphia back to New York. At Monmouth Courthouse, the Americans attacked the British column's rear guard, and fought the enemy to a standstill. After Clinton returned to New York City, he was blockaded there by Washington for the rest of the war. In effect, Clinton had ended the attempt to control the Middle colonies.

A New British Strategy. From New York, Clinton attempted to wage a more vigorous war, using the power and

A caltrop, used as a hazard to the hoofs of horses (Harold L. Peterson Collection)

support began a siege of Charleston in early 1780. The garrison surrendered on 12 May and Clinton embarked for New York, leaving Cornwallis to his task. Within three months Cornwallis overran South Carolina. His most effective weapon was Lt. Col. Banastre Tarleton, a tactically gifted and ruthless cavalryman. But Tarleton's zeal was a two-edged sword. After his men bayoneted some Americans trying to surrender at the Waxhaws settlement along the North Carolina–South Carolina border, Patriot guerrillas were energized by vivid and sometimes fanciful tales of the atrocity. Nonetheless, Cornwallis piled success on success. When Gen. Horatio Gates marched into South Carolina, Cornwallis met him at Camden on 16 August 1780. With his best troops advancing on American militiamen weakened by dysentery, Cornwallis destroyed the American force and sent General Gates fleeing in panic. This was the lowest ebb of Patriot fortunes in the Carolinas.

The Road to Cowpens. The way now stood open for Cornwallis to invade North Carolina. Brushing aside hastily assembled militia units, he advanced toward Charlotte, with a force of Tory militia under Maj. Patrick Ferguson marching on a parallel line to the west. Ferguson was foolish enough to announce his intention to destroy the Watauga frontier settlements and hang its leaders for their support of the South Carolina Patriots. This threat, along with the bloodthirsty reputation that was attached to Tarleton, brought the frontiersmen out in a fury. Meeting Ferguson at King's Mountain on 7 October, they slaughtered him and his force. Cornwallis had to retreat to South Carolina, while Tarleton spent the autumn trying to deal with guerrilla forces led by Francis Marion. Soon Continental troops and militia under the new commander of the Southern Department, Gen. Nathanael Greene, arrived to deal with the situation. Greene took half his force and menaced Charleston, sending the other half under Gen. Daniel Morgan to loop through the western Carolinas. Cornwallis then divided his forces into three: Gen. Alexander Leslie would cope with Greene; Tarleton

agility of the British navy. His first stroke was the capture of Savannah, Georgia, on 29 December 1778, by an amphibious attack of thirty-five hundred regulars from New York and one thousand local Tories under Col. Sir Archibald Campbell. This inflamed the Tories of the Southern region and soon their militiamen were attacking throughout Georgia and the Carolinas. By September, a four thouand-man French amphibious force under Adm. Jean-Baptiste-Charles-Henri-Hector d'Estaing was cooperating with militia and Continentals from Charleston in trying to retake Savannah. When this siege failed, Gen. Charles Cornwallis proposed to Sir Henry Clinton that if Charleston, South Carolina, were captured all of the Carolinas could easily be pacified. Clinton sailed from New York with eight thousand troops and with local Tory

A Revolutionary War powder horn with etchings (Harold L. Peterson Collection)

would stalk Morgan; and Cornwallis would follow behind Tarleton.

Double Envelopment. In the Second Punic War against Rome, the Carthaginian general Hannibal performed a remarkable feat at Cannae in 216 B.C., destroying an entire Roman army by passing both its flanks and surrounding it in the course of battle. Daniel Morgan accomplished the same feat at the Battle of Cowpens in northwestern South Carolina. As Tarleton's eleven hundred troops attacked up a hill, a line of American riflemen fired two volleys and then retreated to join a second line of militia. Again, two volleys were fired before they all retired around the left of a picked force of Continentals and militiamen just below the crest of the hill. As the Continentals grappled with Tarleton's soldiers, cavalry swept down the hill on the British right flank, and the re-formed militiamen swarmed to attack both flanks. Surrounded and facing a spirited bayonet charge by the Continentals, the British surrendered. Tarleton's courage and leadership could not save the day. He tendered his resignation to Cornwallis, who graciously declined to accept it. Tarleton was not so gracious writing his account of the battle years later: he blamed his defeat on Cornwallis for not coming forward quickly enough to rescue him.

Source:
Henry Lumpkin, *From Savannah to Yorktown: The American Revolution in the South* (Columbia: University of South Carolina Press, 1981);

John S. Pancake, *This Destructive War: The British Campaign in the Carolinas, 1780–1782* (Tuscaloosa: University of Alabama Press, 1985).

REVOLUTIONARY WAR: THE WORLD TURNED UPSIDE DOWN

Chasing an Elusive Foe. After Cowpens, Gen. Charles Cornwallis chased Daniel Morgan and Nathanael Greene into Virginia, then made his headquarters at Hillsboro, North Carolina. Almost immediately Greene marched back and awaited Cornwallis's attack at Guilford Courthouse. Cornwallis won the battle against superior numbers, but at an unacceptable price: while Greene was able to march off with most of his troops, Cornwallis had lost one-third of his soldiers. There was no option for Cornwallis but to leave the Carolinas and march into Virginia. As soon as he did so, Greene began pressing on to Charleston. It took months, and Greene lost engagements at Hobkirk's Hill, Fort Ninety-Six, and Eutaw Springs, but by September he had invested Charleston and had a free hand in the Carolinas and Georgia.

Yorktown Campaign. Arriving in Virginia, Cornwallis added to his command those troops who had been fighting there under Benedict Arnold, who was now wearing a British uniform. In command of eight thousand men, he spent from May to July trying to maneuver Gen. Marie-Joseph-Paul-Yves-Roch-Gilbert du Motier de Lafayette's American army of about thirty-five hundred into battle. He could not do so, and, acting under orders sent from New York by Sir Henry Clinton, moved his troops to Yorktown at the tip of the York peninsula to establish another naval base from

George Washington's leather campaign trunk (Mount Vernon Ladies' Association of the Union, Mount Vernon, Virginia)

which to conduct amphibious operations. Even as he did so, George Washington was in contact with the French fleet under Adm. François-Joseph-Paul de Grasse, hoping to arrange for the French fleet either to assist in an attack on New York or secure the Chesapeake Bay area. De Grasse sailed north from the West Indies on 13 August, at about the time Washington learned of Cornwallis' move to Yorktown. By 21 August, Washington had left a small force at New York to decoy the British and was marching his army south. By 31 August, De Grasse had landed troops at Yorktown to augment Lafayette's forces. After beating back a British fleet that sought to drive him from the area, De Grasse sent ships up Chesapeake Bay, made contact with Washington, and transported his army to Williamsburg. The perfect coordination of the French navy and the Continental Army had doomed Cornwallis.

"The World Turned Upside Down." Cornwallis was too much of a professional to misread the situation. His eight thousand troops faced over seventeen thousand American Continentals, Virginia militia, and French regulars. He held his position for a month, then negotiated a surrender. The British regiments laid down their arms and marched out to the sound of military bands playing a peculiarly appropriate song, "The World Turned Upside Down." The disaster at Yorktown deprived the British of the means and the will to carry on. Washington moved back to New York to renew the blockade of Clinton. The power of the British in the colonies reached only to the outskirts of New York. Peace negotiations began in April and the Treaty of Paris ending the war was signed on 30 November. The French troops had already returned home to France. The Patriots in the colonies were left to construct their own nation and restore order and prosperity. Those who were most discomfited were those colonials who had been loyal to the King. They now faced the wrath of their neighbors in a new nation, or exile.

Source:
Christopher Ward, *War of the Revolution*, 2 volumes (New York: Macmillan, 1952).

The Badge of Military Merit (the first Purple Heart) awarded to Sgt. Elijah Churchill, 1 May 1783 (New Windsor Cantonment, Connecticut)

Facsimile of a discharge of an African American soldier who served in a New England regiment (National Archives, Washington, D.C.)

HEADLINE MAKERS

BENEDICT ARNOLD

1741-1801
GENERAL

A Synonym for Treachery. In the first two years of the Revolution, Benedict Arnold made a reputation as a daring and skilled fighter, perhaps the best tactician who fought in the Revolution. His bold leadership was decisive in winning the pivotal battle of Saratoga. If the serious wound he sustained there had killed him, his military glory would be immortal. Yet few remember today his feats of arms in behalf of the Revolution, while any child knows that "a Benedict Arnold" is a traitor.

Background. Born in Norwich, Connecticut, Arnold was brought up in a strict religious household and attended boarding school for three years before being apprenticed to an apothecary in 1755. He joined the militia in the French and Indian War, deserted, returned to duty and deserted again. In 1762, when his parents died, he opened an apothecary shop in New Haven. Five years later, when he married into a prominent family, he was a successful businessman, trading and perhaps smuggling in the West Indies and Canada. He became captain of a Connecticut militia company in 1775 and participated in the Siege of Boston.

Years of Glory. Soon Arnold had wangled a colonelcy in the Massachusetts militia with the task of raising a regiment with which to capture Fort Ticonderoga. Ethan Allen had already set out on that mission, and Arnold joined him as a volunteer. His wife having died on 19 June, Arnold assuaged his grief by leading an expedition through the Maine woods to link up with Gen. Richard Montgomery in an attack on Quebec. The attack, launched on the last day of 1775, was unsuccessful; Montgomery was killed and Arnold wounded. Holding his position and continuing to threaten Quebec, Arnold was promoted to brigadier

general. In May he had to retreat to Montreal in the face of British reinforcements. By July all American forces had been driven out of Canada and were trying to forestall a British offensive down the Lake Champlain and Hudson River valleys to New York. Arnold patched together a makeshift flotilla of gunboats on Lake Champlain and led them into battle at Valcour Island. In two sharp fights on 11 and 13 October 1776, his boats were destroyed. Nonetheless, he had held up the advance, and it was now too late in the year for the British to march any farther. For this feat Arnold expected promotion to major general. When it was not forthcoming, he threatened to resign but was persuaded not to by George Washington. The promotion came after he repulsed a British landing at Danbury, Connecticut, in April 1777. His finest hour came at Saratoga. Under the command of Horatio Gates in the Battle of Freeman's Farm on 19 September, Arnold's troops hurled back Gen. John Burgoyne's attack on the colonial left and might have destroyed the British if Gates had released troops for a counterattack. When he protested to Gates after the battle, he was relieved of his duties. The British attacked again on 7 October. Without a command, Arnold raced to the battlefield and led an attack that broke the British, sustaining a crippling wound in the process. Saratoga was the turning point of the war, and Arnold was the turning point of Saratoga.

Years of Shame. When he was able to walk again, Arnold was assigned to the command of Philadelphia. Soon he was accused of corruption and subjected to an investigation. Though he married Peggy Shippen, daughter of a prominent Loyalist Philadelphia family, he was blackballed socially. Enraged by this treatment, in May 1779 he opened a treasonous correspondence with Sir Henry Clinton, the British commander in chief. Although he received only a mild reprimand as punishment for his activities in Philadelphia, Arnold, now commanding the American stronghold at West Point on the Hudson River, determined to revenge himself by giving up the fortress to the British. After his British contact, Maj. John André, was caught, Arnold defected to the British on 25 September 1780. He was commissioned as a brigadier general of provincial troops and commanded a force that burned Richmond,

Virginia, early in 1781. His last command was in his home state of Connecticut, where he burned New London. In December 1781 he sailed for London.

The Wages of Sin. As a traitor, Arnold was valuable to the British but not particularly well liked. His fellow officers disdained him, and the British government rewarded him with a small pension. In 1787 he moved to St. John, New Brunswick, and tried to emulate his former success in trading between Canada and the West Indies. His reputation for treachery was an immense obstacle to any business success. His explanation that he had acted to hasten the demise of a revolution that was politically rotten and doomed to failure was too self-serving to be convincing. It was all too evident that whatever problems Arnold had with the Congress in being slighted for promotion and being court-martialed were the fault of his own towering ambition and greed. Moving back to London in 1792, he lost heavily on privateering ventures during the 1793–1800 hostilities against the French. He even tried to obtain a command in the British Army but found himself an object of loathing in military circles. He died of dropsy in 1801.

Sources:

Brian Richard Boylan, *Benedict Arnold: The Dark Eagle* (New York: Norton, 1973);

James Kirby Martin, *Benedict Arnold, Revolutionary Hero: An American Warrior Reconsidered* (New York: New York University Press, 1977);

Randall W. Stern, *Benedict Arnold: Patriot or Traitor* (New York: Morrow, 1990).

MARIE-JOSEPH-PAUL-YVES-ROCH-GILBERT DU MOTIER, MARQUIS DE LAFAYETTE

1757-1834

FRENCH OFFICER

Hands Across the Sea. More than anyone else, Marie-Joseph-Paul-Yves-Roch-Gilbert de Motier, Marquis de Lafayette symbolizes the assistance Americans received from Europeans in their struggle for independence. Baron Friedrich Wilhelm Ludolf Gerhard Augustin von Steuben wrote the tactical manual for the American army and drilled it in European methods; Jean-Baptiste-Donatien de Vimeur comte de Rochambeau commanded an army at Newport and Yorktown; Adm. François-Joseph-Paul de Grasse was crucial to the victory at Yorktown; Baron Johann de Kalb commanded a division and was wounded at Camden; Thaddeus Kosciusko designed the defenses at Saratoga and West Point; and Count

Casimir Pulaski was mortally wounded at the head of his cavalry unit at the siege of Savannah. But no foreign officer was so revered in his lifetime and afterward as the Marquis de Lafayette.

Background. Born in the Auvergne, Lafayette was orphaned before his second birthday when his father was killed at the Battle of Minden. His mother died in 1770, while he was studying at the Collège du Plessis of the University of Paris. He joined the King's Musketeers in 1771 and purchased a commission as captain in the dragoons in 1774, after marrying into the powerful Noailles family. Wealth and an entrée at the French court were not enough to satisfy him. In 1776 he offered his services to the Continental Army and was commissioned a major general.

War and Diplomacy. Serving as an unpaid volunteer without a command, Lafayette distinguished himself at once, fighting gallantly and sustaining a leg wound at Brandywine on 11 September 1777. When he returned to duty in December, it was as aide-de-camp to Gen. George Washington. His support was invaluable to Washington in the bleak days of Valley Forge. By the time he fought in the Battle of Monmouth in June 1778, he had an excellent reputation and a close relationship with Washington, who appointed him liaison officer when Admiral d'Estaing's fleet arrived. In 1779 he returned to France bearing messages from the Continental Congress and helping arrange for a French expeditionary force. He was promoted to colonel in the French army for his efforts. Returning to the colonies, he was given command of the Virginia light infantry, refusing to let the numerically superior British close with his smaller force until Gen. Charles Cornwallis moved into Yorktown. Here once again his skills in liaison between French and American forces were of inestimable value in arranging the amphibious siege of Yorktown. When he returned to France in 1782, it was as a major general in the French army.

An Eventful Life. Having accomplished more than most people do in a long life, Lafayette was only twenty-five and his rendezvous with destiny not yet complete. Upon the fall of the Bastille in 1789, he took command of the Paris National Guard to secure the city and promote reform. His moderation satisfied neither the reactionaries nor the radicals. After briefly commanding the French army in the war with Austria, he was charged with counterrevolutionary treason, fled to Austria, and was imprisoned there for five years as a revolutionary. During Napoleon Bonaparte's reign he remained politically inactive but after 1815 served in the Chamber of Deputies and took part in many French and European political movements advancing democracy and the rights of man. When he toured America from 1824 to 1825 as part of the celebrations of the American Revolution, he was received with wild enthusiasm. In the French

Revolution of 1830 he once again commanded the National Guard, then resigned to protest the stalling of reforms. When he died in 1834, he was buried in American soil brought to Paris for his grave.

Icon of Democracy. Though Lafayette was a skilled commander, it was his role as a symbol that immortalized him. Initially this role cast him as a symbol to the Americans of the support of the outside world for their cause, then as a symbol to the French of the worthiness of that cause. By the end of his life, he had come to symbolize the worldwide aspiration for democracy and the rights of man, and he was looked to by Belgians, Irish, Greeks, and South Americans as inspiration for their freedom struggles; but no one lionized him quite as much as the Americans, and when an American army landed in France in 1917 to fight alongside the French in World War I, it was an American general who said, "Lafayette, we are here!"

Sources:

Peter Buckman, *Lafayette: A Biography* (New York: Paddington Press, 1977);

Marie-Joseph-Paul-Yves-Roch-Gilbert du Motier Marquis de Lafayette, *Lafayette in the Age of the American Revolution: Selected Letters and Papers, 1776–1790* (Ithaca, N.Y.: Cornell University Press, 1977);

Constance Wright, *A Chance for Glory* (New York: Holt, 1957).

ROBERT ROGERS

1731-1795
FRONTIER SOLDIER

Background. The strange career of Robert Rogers is ample proof that some skills and attitudes that produce success in war, such as aggressive ambition, great daring, trickery, and contempt for rules, may be just the reverse of what is needed for success in peacetime. Born in Methuen, Massachusetts, Rogers grew up on the New Hampshire frontier, hunting, trapping, trading, and occasionally smuggling. In the summer of 1755 he joined the New Hampshire militia to escape trial as a counterfeiter. In August and September of that year he distinguished himself in the failed attempt by William Johnson to capture the French fort at Crown Point.

Ranger Leader. In March 1756 Gov. William Shirley of Massachusetts made Rogers a captain commanding a company of men charged with the task of raiding deep into French territory to attack outposts, disrupt communications, ambush supply trains, spread terror among the Indian tribes allied with the French and bring back information on French movements and plans. Operating from Fort William Henry in upstate New York, Rogers made himself thoroughly familiar with all the terrain around Crown Point and Fort Ticonderoga, coming close enough to draw plans of the fortifications and, in one instance, carry off a sentry who had challenged him. He was a natural leader, one whose woodcraft and smuggling experience were useful to his mission. Moving quickly, burdened by only the minimum of food and arms, using waterways by night and resting by day, his rangers were soon enough of a problem for the French to offer a reward to anyone who could kill or capture Rogers. In January 1757 his force of 68 rangers was ambushed near Fort Ticonderoga by nearly 200 French. Rogers was wounded and lost 20 men, but in return killed and wounded more than 37 French. Promoted to a major in 1758, Rogers commanded nine companies of rangers, and British officers were often sent to him to learn the art of wilderness warfare. In addition to leading raids deep into French territory, Rogers and his rangers scouted for several British regular armies, notably at the assault on Fort Ticonderoga in 1758, the advance on Crown Point in 1759, and the attack on Montreal in 1760. In September 1759 he raided into Canada to destroy the Abenaki stronghold at St. Francis, and he and his rangers suffered extraordinary hardships in escaping from large bodies of pursuers.

Disgrace and Obscurity. In 1761 Rogers married a clergyman's daughter, Elizabeth Browne of Portsmouth, New Hampshire, but found he had no taste for everyday life in a peaceful, well-established community. Instead, he went south to command a military unit fighting against Cherokees in South Carolina, then commanded a company of New Yorkers in Pontiac's rebellion. After a visit to England, where he published his journals and was acclaimed as a hero, he returned to North America to a command at the fur trading post at Fort Michilimackinac on Lake Michigan. His sloppy business practices and involvement in smuggling and other shady schemes led to his arrest and trial for treasonous dealings with the French. Though acquitted, he found it difficult to secure another post and returned to England where he wangled a commission as colonel of a British regiment but soon found himself imprisoned for debt. After his brother paid his creditors, he got out of prison and came back to North America, where he tried to sell his services to both the colonials and the British in 1775. George Washington had him arrested as a spy in 1776, but he escaped and raised a Loyalist regiment of rangers for the British. He lost his command to his brother because of his drunkenness and dishonesty. After his wife divorced him, he returned to London in 1780 and lived fifteen more years in poverty, dying in a boardinghouse.

Sources:

John R. Cuneo, *Robert Rogers of the Rangers* (New York: Oxford University Press, 1959);

Robert Rogers, *The Journals of Major Robert Rogers* (New York: Corinth Books, 1961).

GEORGE WASHINGTON

1732-1799
AMERICAN COMMANDER IN CHIEF

A Hero Larger Than Life. George Washington's role as military commander of the Revolution and first president of the United States seems to have elevated him so far beyond most mortals that he appears not to have inhabited human flesh but marble or bronze. Too heroic, too venerated, he also seems too remote. He would not have recognized himself. Ambitious though he was, it was the constant recognition of his own limitations and the constant struggle against them that made him successful and worthy of imitation.

Background. Born in Virginia, educated only intermittently, he developed such skill in surveying that at age sixteen he was commissioned to survey the Shenandoah Valley. In 1752 he inherited his family estate at Mount Vernon and was made major in the militia. Gov. Robert Dinwiddie sent him late in 1753 to warn off the French who were fortifying the Ohio River valley, and in the next year it was an expedition led by Washington that fired the first shots of the French and Indian War. He was an aide to Maj. Gen. Edward Braddock at the disastrous Battle of the Monongahela and led the survivors back to Virginia. In 1758 he commanded Virginia troops in an expedition that avenged Braddock's defeat. The following year he married Martha Custis and settled down to the life of a well-to-do planter. Elected to the Virginia House of Burgesses, he took a leadership role in protesting the ban on western settlement, opposing the Stamp Act and advocating resolutions against English imports. When the Continental Congress met, Washington was a delegate from Virginia. John Adams convinced the Congress that Washington's military experience was too valuable to waste and secured him appointment as commander in chief on 17 June 1775.

The Burden of Leadership. When Washington arrived to assume command of the siege of Boston, he found an untrained army that has been aptly called "a rabble in arms" and that was rapidly disintegrating because militia troops had been enlisted only for short terms and were already leaving. His rebuilding the army was crowned by the capture of Boston, but its shortcomings became only too clear in his defense of New York. Though Brooklyn Heights was fortified, he met the enemy in the open field and was soundly defeated, a setback lessened by his skill in evacuating his troops. Local successes against British attacks in Manhattan were nullified by the British skill in outflanking Washington, and he was forced to abandon New York and retreat through New Jersey. Defeated, his army exhausted, he had to retrieve the situation. At dawn on 26 December 1776 he surprised and captured the entire garrison of Trenton with all its supplies. This brought Lord Charles Cornwallis with a superior force to trap him. Evading the trap, Washington attacked reinforcements coming to Cornwallis and captured their supplies. With the colonials emboldened, resupplied, and threatening their lines of communication, the British evacuated New Jersey. Washington had saved the Revolution, and his army survived to fight another day, but 1777 brought mostly disappointment. He could not defend Philadelphia and had to winter in Valley Forge in 1777–1778, his army enduring physical and psychological discomforts from the weather and inadequacy of food and supplies. Washington was enduring the torments of interfering politicans, unreliable subordinates, and uncooperative state militias. He often had to struggle for self-control against a sharp temper. Only by maintaining his self-control could he maintain control of the difficult situation with which he was faced.

The Glory of Leadership. During the winter at Valley Forge, a German general, Baron Friedrich Wilhelm Ludolf Gerhard Augustin von Steuben, taught European drill and tactics to the troops, keeping them too busy to succumb to hunger, cold, and boredom. A more skilled Continental Army met the British in the campaigns of 1778, at the end of which Philadelphia was back in American hands and Washington was blockading the British army in New York. The war moved to other theaters, and Washington had to command from a distance while menacing New York. When the evolution of the campaign in the South brought Cornwallis to Yorktown with his army, Washington was clear-sighted and bold in his response. Maintaining a perfect coordination with the French fleet, fooling Sir Henry Clinton into believing that he had not left, Washington marched his army southward and received Cornwallis' surrender. It was only fitting that the man whose will and hard work had carried the American cause so far and whose strategic brilliance had designed victory should be the winner of the battle that eliminated the British grip on the colonies.

Onward and Upward. In 1783 Washington resigned his commission and returned to Virginia. Like Cincinnatus, the Roman general he so admired, Washington desired to return to farming after his heroic performance, but he was the indispensable man. Reluctant as he was to leave his estate, when the Constitutional Convention met in Philadelphia in 1787, he was present and elected chair. On 6 April 1789 the electors unanimously chose him to be first president of the United States, a post he held for eight years. His sense of duty and his calmness were enormously valuable to the political functioning of the new country. His Farewell Address in 1797 urged Americans to submerge the interests of parties and factions for the sake of national unity. He died in 1799, not only having made the existence of his country possible but, by his modesty in office, decisively shaping the democratic tradition of the presidency.

Sources:

James Thomas Flexner, *George Washington*, 4 volumes (Boston: Little, Brown, 1965–1972);

Douglas Southall Freeman, *George Washington: A Biography*, 7 volumes (New York: Scribners, 1948–1957).

PUBLICATIONS

An Authentic Register of the British Successes: being a Collection of all the Extraordinary and some of the Ordinary Gazettes from the Taking of Louisbourgh, July 26, 1758, by the Honourable Admiral Boscawen and Gen. Amherst, to the Defeat of the French Fleet under M. Conflans, Nov. 21, 1759, By Sir Edward Hawke. To which is added, A Particular Account of M. Thurot's Defeat, By Captain John Elliott (London, 1760);

Lt. Gen. John Burgoyne, *A State of the Expedition from Canada as Laid before the House of Commons with a Collection of Authentic Documents* (London: Printed for J. Almon, 1780);

John Campbell, Earl of Loudon, *The Conduct of a Noble Commander in America Impartially Reviewed with The genuine Causes of the Discontents at New York and Hallifax and The True Occasion of the Delays in that Important Expedition* (London, 1758);

John C. Clarke, *An Impartial and Authentic Narrative of the Battle Fought on the 17th of June, 1775 Between His Brittanic Majesty' Troops and the American Provincial Army, on Bunker's Hill, Near Charles-Town, in New England* (London, 1775);

John Entick, *The General History of the Late War: Containing it's Rise, Progress, and Event, in Europe, Asia, Africa, and America*, 5 volumes (London: E. Dilly, 1763–1764);

Executive Council of the State of Pennsylvania, *Resolutions relating to the oppressive conduct of Major General Benedict Arnold during his command in Pennsylvania* (Philadelphia, 1779);

Joseph Galloway, *Historical and Political Reflections on the Rise and Progress of the American Rebellion* (London: Printed for G. Wilkie, 1780);

Galloway, *Letters to a Nobleman on the Conduct of the War in the Middle Colonies* (London: J. Wilkie, 1779);

The History of the Civil War in America . . . 1775, 1776, and 1777. By an Officer of the Army (London, 1780);

Lt. Gen. Sir William Howe, *The Narrative of Lieut Gen Sir William Howe in a Committee of the Whole House of Commons on the 29th of April, 1779 Relative to His Conduct during His Late Command of the King's Troops in North America* (London: Printed by H. Baldwin, 1780);

An Impartial History of the Late Glorious War, from it's Commencement to it's Conclusion; Containing an Exact Account of the Battles and Sea Engagements, Together with Other Remarkable Transactions, in Europe, Asia, Africa, and America (London, 1769);

John Knox, *Historical Account of the Campaigns in North-America*, 2 volumes (London: Printed for the author, and sold by W. Johnston, 1769);

Thomas Mante, *The History of the Late War in North-America, and the Islands of the West Indies, including the Campaigns of MDCCLXIII and MDCCLXIV Against His Majesty's Indian Enemies* (London: W. Strahan & T. Cadell, 1772);

Israel Maudit, *Three Letters to Lord Viscount Howe, with Remarks on the Attack at Bunker Hill* (London, 1781);

Pierre Pouchot, *Mémoires sur la dernière guerre de l'Amérique septentrionale, entre la France et l'Angleterre*, 3 volumes (Yverdon, Switzerland, 1781);

Proposals for Uniting the English Colonies on the Continent of America so as to enable them to act with Force and Vigour against their Enemies (London, 1757);

Robert Rogers, *Journals* (London: J. Millan, 1765).

RELIGION

by JOHN T. O'KEEFE

CONTENTS

Sidebars and tables are listed in italics.

1754

- The Philadelphia Yearly Meeting of the Society of Friends issues an epistle condemning slave trading and slaveholding, making the Quakers the first American religious body to take a unified stand against slavery.

18 Dec. Congregational minister Eleazar Wheelock accepts two Delaware Indians into his home in Lebanon, Connecticut, for religious training, the first step in establishing a school that would train Native Americans for missionary work among their own people.

1755

- The Quakers withdraw from the Pennsylvania assembly in response to a debate over public funding of defense measures on the Pennsylvania frontier, something that violated Quaker pacifist principles.

16 May Elizabeth Ashbridge, female Quaker minister, dies.

1756

2 Jan. Congregational minister Isaac Backus forms his first Baptist congregation by separating with some followers from the Congregational Church of Marlborough, Massachusetts. Backus will serve for more than fifty years, becoming a leader of the American Baptists and a spokesman for the principle of the separation of church and state.

Nov. Six thousand Catholic French Canadians are expelled from Acadia; more than four hundred are sent to Philadelphia, where Anthony Benezet leads Quaker efforts for their relief and they prompt an outburst of anti-Catholic fears in the British colonies.

1758

- The Presbyterian Synods of New York and Philadelphia merge, as both groups acknowledge the importance of direct personal experience of grace as part of their religion and so end the schism that has divided Presbyterians in the Middle colonies over revivalism since 1741.

22 Mar. Jonathan Edwards, president of the College of New Jersey (later Princeton University) dies; earlier he led the revivals of the Great Awakening from his post in Northampton, Massachusetts, and was the most significant theologian in colonial America.

29 Nov. Experience Mayhew, liberal Congregational missionary to the Native Americans of Martha's Vineyard, Massachusetts, and father of Jonathan Mayhew, who followed and expanded his father's liberal and rationalist teachings, dies.

1759

22 Apr. James Freeman, later a leader in the movement for rational religion and pastor of King's Chapel, Boston, America's first Unitarian church, is born.

1760

- Count Nicholaus Ludwig Zinzendorf, leader of the Moravians, the most influential of many German pietistic sects located in the Pennsylvania backcountry, dies.

14 Feb. Richard Allen is born; he later establishes the African Methodist Episcopal Church, the first African-American denomination.

1761

4 Feb. Samuel Davies dies; he led the Presbyterian revivalist of Virginia and was president of the College of New Jersey (later Princeton University), the intellectual center of American revivalistic Protestantism.

1763

- The Touro Synagogue in Newport, Rhode Island, home of colonial America's most prominent Jewish congregation, is dedicated.

- In Virginia a court ruling vindicates the right of Anglican ministers to their back pay, but at the cost of defense attorney Patrick Henry's stirring accusation that they are disloyal to the colonies and agents of disorder.

29 Aug. Devereux Jarratt begins his career as an Anglican evangelical by becoming the rector for three churches in Bath, Dinwiddie County, Virginia, a post he will hold until his death in 1801.

1764

Mar. Baptists in Providence acquire a charter for the College of Rhode Island (later Brown University), the first Baptist college in America and notable for the ecumenical nature of its governing board, which includes Congregationalists, Quakers, and Episcopalians in addition to Baptists.

23 July Gilbert Tennent, Presbyterian revivalist and leader of the Great Awakening in the Middle colonies, dies.

1765

- Indian missionary Samson Occom and Reverend Nathaniel Whitaker leave for England to raise funds for Eleazar Wheelock's Indian Charity School; their two-year trip will secure more than £12,000 in contributions.

1766

9 July Jonathan Mayhew dies; as a leading rationalist minister he provided a theological rationale for America's resistance to the abuses of British rule during the Stamp Act crisis.

1767

8 Sept. Baptists from four New England churches bond together in the Warren Association, a loose alliance that is designed to provide a forum for theological discussions and for settling disputes, as well as for organizing joint efforts, such as missionary work; by 1780 it has thirty-eight members and has become a significant sponsor of Baptist efforts throughout New England.

1768

• Conrad Beissel, a convert to the German pietistic sect called the Church of the Brethren (or Dunkers) and founder of the Ephrata Community, an early religious utopian community in Pennsylvania and a model for later communitarian efforts, dies.

1769

16 July The Roman Catholic mission at San Diego, California, is founded by Fray Junipero Serra, the Franciscan monk who led Spanish missionary efforts in the American Southwest from 1767 to his death in 1784; Serra founded twenty-one missions to Christianize the Native American population.

13 Dec. New Light Congregationalist Eleazar Wheelock founds Dartmouth College in Hanover, New Hampshire, to pursue his mission to the Indians.

1770

21 July John Murray, a leader of the Universalist movement, arrives in New Jersey from England and soon takes up a career as an itinerant preacher of radical evangelical Protestantism.

30 Sept. George Whitefield, Anglican missionary and itinerant leader of the revivals of the Great Awakening, in Newburyport, Massachusetts, dies.

1771

27 Oct. Francis Asbury, Methodist itinerant missionary and later first bishop of the American Methodist Episcopal Church, arrives in Pennsylvania.

1772

8 Oct. John Woolman dies; a Quaker journalist and reformer, he led the antislavery movement that developed among the Quakers in the 1750s.

1773

• Indian missionary Samson Occom obtains a land grant from the Oneida tribe in New York; he plans to move there and found an Indian community that could be free of interference from whites, a scheme that would lead to the founding of Brothertown in 1785.

Feb. Charles Carroll of Carrollton, a Roman Catholic, publishes his "First Citizen" letters in the *Maryland Gazette,* attacking the royal governor and defending the ability of Catholics to be true patriots despite religious ties to Rome.

July — The first annual conference of Methodist clergy in America occurs and is led by Reverend Thomas Rankin.

1774

• Philadelphia Quakers vote to formally disown their members who refuse to free their slaves.

6 Aug. — Shaker leader Ann Lee and a small band of followers arrive in New York from England and soon move to a small town outside Albany.

Sept. — Baptist minister Isaac Backus presents a request to the First Continental Congress asking for a declaration of full religious liberty for Americans.

17 Sept. — The First Continental Congress adopts the Suffolk Resolves in response to the Coercive Acts; they include an attack on the guarantee of religious freedom to French Canadian Roman Catholics.

1775

• The Baptist Warren Association declares its support of the revolutionary movement but continues to agitate for a promise of liberty of conscience under the new regime, setting the tone for evangelical engagement with the independence movement.

1776

• Devereux Jarratt, Anglican evangelical, prompts the largest revival of his career in Brunswick and Sussex counties in Virginia.

• Virginia ceases to pay Anglican clerical salaries from tax revenues, the first step in the disestablishment of the Anglican Church, a process completed in 1786 with the passage of Jefferson's Act for Establishing Religious Freedom in Virginia.

• Virginia Anglicans meet to begin to reorganize their denomination as an American body and vote to omit prayers for the king from their liturgy.

1778

8 July — Ezra Stiles is installed as president of Yale College, marking the college's move away from the enthusiasm of the revivals of the Great Awakening and its embrace of the Enlightenment emphasis on rationalism and more-liberal thinking.

1779

4 June — The Virginia legislature first considers Thomas Jefferson's proposed Act for Establishing Religious Freedom in Virginia, a law guaranteeing freedom for religious thought and practice, that will pass in 1786.

1780

Mar.–June After attending the Massachusetts state constitutional convention, Baptist minister Isaac Backus leads the public debate over protections for individual congregational autonomy to be included in the state's new constitution, a step in the legal protection of religious freedom.

19 May Darkness covers the northern part of the country for much of the day, apparently due to smoke from fires for land clearing on the frontier, but this "Dark Day" heightens the expectations of many people that the end of the world is at hand, an expectation also fueled by the disruptions of wartime and the emotions of the revivals occurring in New England.

12 June Vermont Baptists found the Shaftesbury Association, a congress of churches established during the wartime revivals on the New England frontier, indicating the tremendous growth of the Baptists during this period and the increasingly settled nature of religious life in the interior parts of the new nation.

1781

• A group of Philadelphia Quakers who had been disowned for their support of the Revolutionary War in violation of pacifism form the Society of Free Quakers, also known as the Fighting Quakers.

May Shaker founder Ann Lee begins a preaching tour of New England and upstate New York that will last until September 1783.

1782

8 Sept. The congregation of King's Chapel, Boston's Anglican Church, invites rationalist James Freeman to serve as its "reader," or lay minister, the first step toward the emergence of this church as America's first Unitarian congregation.

1783

25 Mar. Ten Episcopalian ministers meeting in Woodbury, Connecticut, choose their colleague Samuel Seabury to be their first bishop, and they send him to England for consecration.

OVERVIEW

Changing Hearts. Looking back on America's War for Independence from the perspective of 1818, former president John Adams commented that the "Revolution was in the Minds and Hearts of the People." Adams's idea was that establishing the United States was more than just a matter of military victories or even establishing new political institutions. Rather, the experience of revolution went much deeper, and this era involved significant changes in how the American people looked at their world. This was as true for religion in the revolutionary era as for politics or society. As Adams added, the colonists' revolution included a "Change in their Religious Sentiments of their Duties and Obligations." In religion as in politics and society, Americans in this period struggled to balance new ideas and new institutions against the ways that had served them at least since the beginning of European settlement more than 150 years earlier. People changed their minds, as they experimented with new religious ideas, and also changed their hearts, as the emotional experience of God's grace became the center of what religion meant to more and more Americans.

Variety. The revolution in religious culture was not easy, however. The hearts and minds of the people changed slowly and unevenly. At the beginning as well as the end of the period, Americans held a wide range of religious beliefs and engaged in an equally wide range of religious practices. The weakness of colonial religious and political institutions made this possible, as did the vastness of the land that early Americans populated. Religious variety also grew with immigration, which increased quickly after 1750 and made America one of the world's most ethnically and religiously diverse places. Philadelphia was a major entry port, and the city and its surrounding countryside filled as the settled Quakers mixed with emotionally pious Germans of many sects. A large migration of Scots-Irish arriving in the 1760s and 1770s was especially important. They brought with them a set of traditions similar to those brought over by the Puritans of the seventeenth century. Their arrival helped revitalize that tradition, especially as they participated in revivals promoted by the Presbyterians on the western frontier of the Middle colonies. Those revivals had their beginnings in the 1730s and continued sporadically through-out the revolutionary period, spreading from group to group. Soon, Baptists and Methodists challenged Presbyterian power, especially as the revivals moved to the Southern colonies. There were also small, independent groups started by individuals who had intense religious experiences and tried to bring others to their views. Even New England, with its well-established Congregationalism, experienced increasing variety in religious life, as liberal and revivalistic wings of Congregationalism competed for converts, and Baptists and independents made significant inroads. In the cities small groups of Jews and Roman Catholics began to make their presence felt. Finally the forced migration of Africans brought still other forms of religious beliefs to the new nation even though their practices were often severely restricted as efforts were made to make slaves conform to Christianity.

Religious Disaffection. Despite the forces tending to make variety the hallmark of American religion in the revolutionary period, a number of general characteristics were part of the experience of nearly all religious Americans in this time. One was that relatively few Americans actively practiced religion in a formal sense during these years. Rates of church membership and attendance in these years were probably lower than at any other point in American history. One obvious reason is the disruption in all aspects of life that the Revolutionary War caused. In those uncertain days numerous pulpits were empty for at least a part of the time. Many important ministers were directly affected by the war. Timothy Dwight became a chaplain for the Continental Army while Samuel Seabury ministered to British soldiers. Some were even soldiers themselves. Henry Muhlenberg, credited by many as a founder of the Lutheran denomination in America, became a general and led a brigade against Lord Charles Cornwallis at the Battle of Brandywine, Pennsylvania. Aside from the loss of their pastors' attentions, many congregations were further weakened with the death or departure of lay members. The Anglican Church suffered particularly, since so many of its members were Loyalists and left for Canada or England as the war ended. Other groups struggled with dissension over the conflicting political goals of their members. The decline in religious affiliation was all the more striking given the religious revivals that characterized the early years of the revolutionary era. Ironically, the religious fervor of the early years may have contributed to the fallow years of the war, as people were unable to sustain the intensity of the revivals. The period as a whole was a paradoxical time of both growth and loss of vitality.

Challenge of Reason. More fundamentally, the new republican ideals that became prominent in this period challenged the existing religious order and drew many away from their old churches. Some people were too preoccupied with the pressing political and social concerns of a new nation to spend much time on religious matters. Others were engaged with religion but found themselves interested in new ideas. Rationalist, liberal groups emerged in New England Congregationalism especially, stressing the large scope of human reason, the freedom of human will, and the importance of human moral reasoning as the centers of their religious lives. These liberals saw themselves as continuing the development of the Puritanism that English settlers brought with them, but their opponents saw them as dangerously unorthodox. Others left religion for deism, a religious rationalism related to the ideals of the European Enlightenment that were so important in the development of American republicanism. Others simply turned away from organized religion to more-private forms of worship and belief, translating the emerging democratic confidence in the dignity and authority of each individual into the realm of religion. Whatever the reason, the traditional churches found themselves pressured to adapt to new conditions, which some groups did more successfully than others.

Church-State Relations. One of the most significant of these new conditions was the formal relationship between the churches and the state. Going into the Revolutionary War, most colonies had an established church, an official church that received support from the government although in no colony was membership in that church required. The war and the ideas linked to it made people reevaluate these connections. As Americans began drafting their state constitutions after 1776, many included in them a list of fundamental, protected human rights, and nearly all included some notion of freedom of religion. No American in 1776 contemplated a nation with the religious pluralism that the United States has today. But nearly all early Americans valued the right of individuals to practice their sincerely held religious beliefs without interference from the state. The exact form that religious tolerance should take was hotly debated in the revolutionary era. American churches were divided on this topic, and the conflicts over this issue, as well as the new religious choices that came with increased explicit protection for religion, challenged the older, established religions to keep pace.

Voluntary Denominations. Probably the most successful response to the combination of religious diversity, religious apathy, and religious freedom was the gradual emergence of the idea of religious denominations that would exist side by side in the new nation. By the end of the Revolution most Americans had abandoned any idea that all citizens needed to be included in any one church, as was still the rule in much of Europe. Instead the governments established in the states during the Revolution and the federal government established in the 1780s created an equality among the various religions, or at least among the forms of Protestantism. Instead of relying on the state for support, the denominations slowly embraced the idea that a stronger church comes from the voluntary support of individuals. This was truer to the ideals of biblical Christianity and more practical in the context of early American society. It also corresponded to the emphasis placed by many revivalistic groups on intensely individual conversion experiences. This system took a long time to develop fully. Massachusetts was the last state to end its support for an established religion, in 1833. Yet the pattern of free access to all religions and of general respect for them all was established in the revolutionary period and persists as the most distinctive feature of American religion to this day.

A Religious Nation. Despite the formal separation of church and government, the Revolution forged close links between religion and the nation. The patriotism of many Americans for the independence movement corresponded to the enthusiasm many had for Christ as well. Many took their surprising success against the far-more powerful British forces as a sign of God's special favor. They remembered that some of their ancestors had come to America at least partly on God's mission, whether to secure religious freedom for themselves or to bring Christianity to America. They saw the Revolution as a continuation of that sacred task and the new nation as a sign of purity in a fallen world. Some groups were fascinated with the idea of the end of the world and the second coming of Christ and thought winning the war was a sign of the imminence of those events. The union of states became a kind of religious object. In the first stirrings of what we now call America's "civil religion," religious imagery and nationalist imagery merged in speeches and sermons throughout the era. Congregationalist Ezra Stiles spoke for many when, in a sermon preached in 1783, he painted a rosy picture of the future strength and prosperity of the United States, based on the liberty that Americans enjoyed as the main blessing of God.

A Religious Culture. In the end it is too simple to say that religion caused the American Revolution or that revolutionary feelings caused the changes in America's religious landscape in these years. The relations are more complex and indirect. Religion was important in the American Revolution, however, because America's distinctive culture in the period was fundamentally religious. Despite low rates of formal church membership, religious themes and conflicts were at the center of most Americans' lives. As the Revolution progressed, the kind of religion most Americans experienced, in whatever different ways, was beginning to be more closely related to the political and social changes taking place at the same time. The religion of the American Revolution took various forms, but by 1783 there were several unifying elements that connected it to the goals of the new nation. Lay people were important, and the status of the clergy was declining. The power located in church pews rather than in pulpits was a tribute to the dignity of individual believers. The religion of most Americans of the 1780s attached great significance to individuals' ability to read and interpret the Bible for themselves even though that offered the chance that unusual or disruptive ideas might come forward. Individual behavior was important too, and more and more Americans were stressing religion as

an ethical system of justice and brotherhood rather than focusing on obscure theological controversies. Religion was also on the move, just as the American population was. Revivals and itinerant ministers accompanied settlers to the frontiers and helped to establish culture and morality in those areas. All these features corresponded to the political ideas at the Revolution's heart. Distrust of executive powers, decentralized political authority, and republican moral order were analogues to experiences many Americans had in their churches and private spiritual lives. Religious Americans of all kinds were revolutionary Americans as well.

TOPICS IN THE NEWS

ANGLICANISM AND REVOLUTION

Anglicans and Empire. One of the closest connections between religion and the American Revolution involved the Anglicans. These people belonged to the official Church of England, which enjoyed the protection of the state and was supported by tax money. In five of the thirteen colonies the Anglican Church was the legally established religion in the 1750s and 1760s. Anglicanism was a version of Protestantism, distinguished by the fact that the king of England was the official religious leader as well as the head of state. Theologically it was closely related to the Calvinist reformed tradition, the religion of the Puritans who settled New England, but Anglicans were more moderate in tone and placed greater importance on more-elaborate rituals. As a belief and a practice, then, it fit comfortably among the varieties of Christian religions practiced by most early Americans. The feature that most set Anglicans apart from other American Protestants was the presence of bishops as religious leaders. Most reformed Protestant denominations were congregational, giving authority to individual churches to govern their own affairs, without interference from any central authority, such as the Pope exercised in Roman Catholicism. Anglicans rejected the authority of the Pope but did not abolish the bishops' role in church government. Anglicanism was among the most hierarchical of early American religious groups, with individual congregations or parishes run by a priest, who was answerable to a bishop. It also was intimately connected to Britain's effort to shape an empire out of

the individualistic American colonies. Most people considered church and state to be mutually supportive and believed that one could not exist for long without the other. This idea was fundamentally challenged by the American Revolution, which ended with the separation of church and state. In the 1750s, however, the British tried to strengthen their political control over the colonies through religious means that involved the Anglican Church.

Missions. The Anglicans pursued their efforts through a series of missionary ventures run by the Society for the Propagation of the Gospel (SPG), based in London. The SPG recruited young Englishmen to become Anglican priests in the American colonies, educating them and supporting them in their initial work. It raised money tirelessly in England to support these efforts and sent books and other supplies, as well as ministers, to all the American colonies. It sponsored more than three hundred ministers from its founding in 1701 until the coming of the Revolution. In its efforts to reach as large a proportion of the American population as possible, including Indians and slaves, and to do this in a organized way, the SPG was one of the most important ties between Britain and America during the late colonial period. This was true despite the failure of these missions as religious ventures. Relatively few Americans were drawn to Anglicanism, and some, especially in the Puritan Northern colonies, were hostile to the practices of Anglicanism, which labored under various legal restrictions in these areas. Nevertheless, by the revolutionary

Interior view of Aquia Anglican Church, Stafford County, Virginia, built in 1757

period the Anglican Church had a presence in every colony. In some cases that presence was substantial even though Anglican numbers might be small. In New York and Pennsylvania, for example, Anglicans were instrumental in founding King's College (later Columbia University) in 1754 and the Philadelphia College and Academy (later the University of Pennsylvania), which granted its first bachelors degrees in 1757.

Weakness. The Anglican Church was strongest in the Southern colonies, where it was the established religion. Even there, however, it was a weak presence. Churches were few and far between, and priests to serve them were even rarer. Because of the weakness of the ministry, lay people, called vestrymen, were the main powers within the church. These men, the elders of the church and usually also the local planter gentry, controlled the church's finances and were in charge of choosing and supporting the minister. Ministers beholden to the gentry for support tended to emulate their manners and echo their values. This limited the church's appeal to the lower orders, who understandably had less interest in maintaining a strongly hierarchical social order, especially with the arrival of revolutionary republican values. Many Anglican ministers put their material interest before the spiritual needs of their parishes, further limiting their influence. Finally, recruiting better clergymen was made harder because every Anglican priest had to be ordained by a bishop

in England. The long and expensive journey to London was possible for only a relatively few men.

Evangelicalism. In response to the church's weakness, as well as to the Great Awakening and its aftermath, a small evangelical movement developed in Virginia Anglicanism. Devereux Jarratt and a few other Anglican priests had come to a more lively appreciation of their faith through the preaching of Presbyterians in the Virginia backcountry. They tried to bring that spirit into their own pastoral work within the Anglican Church. Jarrett worked in rural Dinwiddie County from 1763 until his death in 1801, sparking a revival that smoldered for many years. Jarrett and his associates preached throughout the parishes of southern Virginia and northern North Carolina. He reached many people who were normally disenchanted with the elaborate ways of gentry Anglicanism. His work indicates how flexible revivalism was in meeting the needs of various Protestant groups. Jarrett's movement was small, however. Evangelical Anglicanism was undermined by the emergence of Methodism, by conflict with other revivalistic groups in the South, and by the opposition of many Anglicans to the independence movement.

Methodism. In 1772 the first Methodist preachers began to arrive in Virginia. Jarrett supported their work at first but later realized how different their beliefs were from orthodox Anglicanism. Methodism began as an evangelical reform movement within the Church of England, just as Jarrett had tried to bring revivalism to colonial Anglicanism. The English leaders John Wesley and his brother Charles had both been in America in the 1730s as associates of George Whitefield, the most prominent itinerant of the American Great Awakening. The Wesleys developed a different set of beliefs than Whitefield, however, who never formally broke with the Church of England. In addition to promoting revivals as the means to an awakening to sin and redemption, the Wesleys stressed the discipline of the godly life as a way of coming to that awakening. They preached that a perfect adherence to Christian principles was possible. This perfectionism was a way of offering hope to their listeners that a better life in this world would be the result of better relations with God, thus motivating them to greater spiritual efforts. The disciplined life of the individual was mirrored in the disciplined life of the church, and Methodists developed a highly centralized organization that left them well positioned to promote their beliefs at every opportunity. They drew on the tradition of Anglican missionary work to send their own preachers to America. These men brought more than four thousand people into their fold between 1768 and 1776. One of the greatest of these was Francis Asbury, a lay preacher when he arrived in Pennsylvania in 1771. Asbury and his colleagues developed a number of techniques that became key features of American evangelicalism. One was circuit riding, the organized itinerancy of ministers who traveled from town to town on the frontier, serving small groups in sequence over the course of a few months and then starting the circuit over again. In Virginia, Jarrett and like-minded Anglicans welcomed the first Methodists but later broke with them over their different beliefs. By 1776, with the coming of war, both Anglicans and Methodists experienced severe strains, as they were identified with the Loyalist side. Methodists were better posed to recover from the period of disruption, given their closer connections to the common people of the South who had supported the independence movement and who fueled the western expansion that resumed after the war. In 1784 Asbury led the Methodists in forming their own separate church. By this time Jarrett still continued his effort to end the "carnal repose" of his fellow churchmen, but with increasingly limited results.

Bishops. One key problem for American Anglicans was that there was no American bishop. This fact greatly impeded the growth of the religion. In order to become priests men had to be ordained by a bishop in a ceremony called the laying on of hands. The ritual symbolized the connection of all priests, through their bishops, with the entire line of priests and bishops stretching in an unbroken chain back to Christ and his apostles, thought by Anglicans to be the first bishops of the church. Since there were no bishops in America, men who wanted to become priests had to travel to England for training and ordination. While this meant that Anglican priests could be well educated and worldly, something that often appealed to the parishioners they eventually served, it also meant that relatively few priests were ordained. The cost of ordination, in time and money, was simply too high. From time to time since the late 1600s, some men had advocated the appointment of a bishop who would reside in America and care for the church there. These arguments went nowhere before the revolutionary period, when they began to be advanced more seriously. In 1758 Thomas Secker became the archbishop of Canterbury, the highest ranking cleric in the Anglican Church. Secker was deeply interested in the colonial church and wanted to strengthen it by appointing its own bishop. He supported other actions designed to improve the church's situation, such as the establishment of yearly meetings of priests in each colony, starting with New Jersey in 1758. These conventions began to agitate for an American bishop. This combined with a renewed missionary push into New England to ignite the suspicions of non-Anglicans about the purpose of a bishop. Many Congregationalists resented the notion that they needed missionaries. They thought the elegant lifestyle of the Reverend East Apthorp, the missionary who arrived to serve Cambridge, Massachusetts, in 1760, was a sign of the decadent society that Anglicanism would produce. They also feared that Anglicans sought political as well as religious power, and their suspicions soon became part of the wider apprehension about British imperialism and oppression.

RELIGIOUS DIVERSITY IN EARLY AMERICA

Philadelphia was America's largest city during the revolutionary period and its most diverse. It offered its visitors a wide range of experiences including religious experiences. John Adams represented Massachusetts during the First Continental Congress held in Philadelphia in 1774, and he savored the new opportunities he found there. On Sundays he often visited various churches, recording his impressions in his diary, as in these excerpts.

11 September 1774. Mr. Reed was so kind as to wait on us to Mr. Sprouts Meeting, where we heard Mr. Spencer. These Ministers all preach without Notes. We had an Opportunity of seeing the Custom of the Presbyterians in administering the Sacrament. The Communicants all came to a row of Seats, placed on each Side of a narrow Table spread in the Middle of the alley reaching from the Deacons Seat to the front of the House. Three setts of Persons of both sexes, came in Succession. Each new sett had the Bread and the Cup given to them by a new Minister.... Each Communicant has a token, which he delivers to the Deacons or Elders, I dont know which they call em.

9 October 1774. Went to hear Dr. Allison, an Aged Gentleman. It was Sacrament Day and he gave us a sacramental Discourse. This Dr. Allison is a Man of Abilities and Worth, but I hear no Preachers here like ours in Boston, excepting Mr. Duche. Coombs indeed is a good Speaker, but not an original, but a Copy of Duche. . . . Went in the Afternoon to the Romish Chappell and heard a good discourse upon the Duty of Parents to their Children, founded in Justice and Charity. The Scenery and the Musick is so callculated to take in Mankind that I wonder, the Reformation ever succeeded. The Paintings, the Bells, the Candles, the Gold and Silver. Our Saviour on the Cross, over the Altar, at full Length, and all his Wounds a bleeding. The Chanting is exquisitely soft and sweet.

23 October 1774. In the Afternoon I went to the Baptist Church and heard a trans Alleganian—a Preacher, from the back Parts of Virginia, behind the Allegany Mountains. He preached an hour and an half. No Learning—No Grace of Action or Utterance—but an honest Zeal. . . . In the Evening I went to the Methodist Meeting and heard Mr. Webb, the old soldier, who first came to America, in the Character of Quarter Master under Gen. Braddock. He is one of the most fluent, eloquent Men I ever heard. He reaches the Imagination and touches the Passions, very well, and expresses himself with great Propriety. The Singing here is very sweet and soft indeed. The first Musick I have heard in any Society, except the Moravians, and once at Church with the organ.

Source: L. H. Butterfield, ed., *The Diary and Autobiography of John Adams, 1771–1781*, volume 2 (Cambridge, Mass.: Harvard University Press, 1961), pp. 131–132, 149–150, 156.

Debate. The end of the Seven Years' War only increased these fears. The acquisition of Canada from France as part of the peace settlement along with the cost of the war led Britain to reassess the organization and management of its colonies. Secker took the opportunity to petition for a bishop. At the same time, in 1763, Jonathan Mayhew, one of the leading Congregational ministers of Boston, published an attack on the Anglican missionary effort that provoked a lengthy debate in the colonial newspapers about Anglicans and their motives. The debate was quite inflammatory. John Adams, for one,

---

CHURCH MEMBERSHIP IN REVOLUTIONARY AMERICA

The distractions and disruptions of the American Revolution combined to mark this period with some of the lowest rates of church membership in our history. The year 1780 is often considered the low point, with probably only about 10 percent of Americans formally claiming church membership, although many more attended church regularly. Membership rates declined when measured against the growth in population, yet all the major denominations grew during the revolutionary era, as the following chart of the number of congregations shows:

Denomination	1740	1780
Anglican	246	406
Baptist	96	457
Congregational	423	749
Lutheran	95	240
Methodist	0	65
Presbyterian	160	495
Roman Catholic	27	56

The ongoing influence of the revivals can be seen especially in the growth of the evangelical Baptists and Methodists. About 125 new Baptist churches were founded in New England during the revolutionary era, but their most dramatic growth came in the Southern states and on the frontier. Baptists formed 67 new churches in Virginia between 1770 and 1780. The Methodists had fewer than 1,000 members in 1771, but around 4,000 in 1775 and 15,000 by 1784, when they formed an independent church. Most of these were in the South. The membership of both of these groups would grow explosively in the nation's first few decades.

Sources: Roger Finke and Rodney Stark, *The Churching of America* (New Brunswick, N.J.: Rutgers University Press, 1992), pp. 24–30;

Edwin S. Gaustad, *Historical Atlas of Religion in America,* revised edition (New York: Harper & Row, 1976), p. 4.

---

thought the fear of bishops was widespread and significant for the coming of revolution. He wrote that "the apprehension of Episcopacy contributed . . . as much as any other cause, to arouse the attention not only of the inquiring mind, but of the common people, and urge them to close thinking on the constitutional authority of parliament over the colonies." Antiepiscopal feeling soon merged with even older and deeper antipapist prejudice, as rumors spread in the late 1760s over the religious plans for Catholic Quebec. As a Roman Catholic bishop arrived there, and later Britain guaranteed Catholic freedom of worship in the 1774 Quebec Act, non-Anglicans throughout the thirteen colonies came to fear for their own religious liberty. As political events developed at the same time, freedom from a central religious authority came to be one of the principal values of the independence movement. The more Americans committed themselves to the cause of religious freedom, the fewer were interested in Anglicanism's royalist politics or episcopal hierarchy.

Decline. The long decline of Anglicanism can be seen in the series of events that ended in the 1786 disestablishment of the church in Virginia, its stronghold. At the center of the process was a cultural revolution as profound as the political one occurring at the same time. The revivals in the Virginia backcountry had swelled the numbers of Presbyterians, Methodists, and especially Baptists in Virginia in the 1750s and 1760s. While Anglican numbers probably grew as well in these years, they hardly kept pace with the explosive growth of the other groups. Revivalism's growth presented a fundamental challenge to the social order of the colony. Virginia society rested on a close connection between genteel planters and the church. This order broke down as individuals left the established parishes and formed their own churches led by lay preachers. Revivalistic enthusiasm became a model for acceptable behavior, however impolite it appeared to the gentry. The itinerant minister became the chief moral spokesman, replacing a weak, often nonexistent Anglican priest. Baptist ministers gained adherents from people, mainly on the frontier, who were also challenging the political arrangements that concentrated power in the hands of Tidewater plantation owners. The political conflict between these groups paralleled the religious developments of the same time. As their influence spread through the 1770s, the Baptists came to offer an alternative social order, based on egalitarian fellowship rather than hierarchy and having love rather than deference as its core value. As the American Revolution developed, the Baptist alternative was poised to become the dominant pattern for the new nation.

The Parsons' Cause. The shift in religious power is symbolized in the Parsons' Cause, a legal case involving the payment of clerical salaries. Traditionally, Virginia ministers were paid in set pounds of tobacco. In 1758 the Virginia assembly passed the Twopenny Act, which allowed the salaries to be paid in money at the rate of two

cents per pound of tobacco. At the time, the price of tobacco was rising, and the effect of the act was to let the
vestrymen, rather than the ministers, benefit from the
price increases. The church objected and managed to
have the law disallowed by the king, who considered it an
attack on his religious representatives and so on the royal
prerogative. Reverend James Maury of Hanover County
then sued to collect the back pay owed to him. Other
parsons filed similar cases and made a stand for the dignity, independence, and power of the clergy. Maury prevailed in his 1763 case, but his victory backfired in the
long run. The defendants secured Patrick Henry as their
lawyer, and Henry made a name for himself in this case
as he rose to the defense of colonial liberties. Henry argued strongly that the colony had a right to pass laws in
its own defense even if they weakened the king. He cast
the Anglican clergy as enemies of the peaceful order of
colonial life, an image they were never able to shake.
From this point on, Anglicans were identified with excessive royal power and with oppressive British imperial
designs. They were marked as unpatriotic foes of American freedom.

Disestablishment. Support for Anglicans waned until
1779, when the state stopped paying clerical salaries
through tax revenues. The final disestablishment of the
church came only after the war, in 1786, as Virginia
passed an Act for Religious Freedom that set the pace for
the separation of church and state later embodied in the
First Amendment to the United States Constitution.
These years were the low point for American Anglicans,
who were deeply divided politically and religiously.
Many were joining the Methodists, as that group began
to take independent shape, starting with a series of annual clerical conferences that began in 1773. They would
form a national organization in 1784, successfully combining the organizational strengths of the Anglican
Church with the emotions of the revival. The remaining
Anglicans struggled to find a new identity. Now called
Episcopalians, those from the Southern and Middle
states began a series of meetings in the early 1780s. They
endorsed measures to make their group more democratic, including greater lay participation. This effort
alarmed a group of Connecticut Episcopalians. Meeting
in 1783, this group selected one of their own, Samuel Seabury, to be their bishop and sent him to England to secure consecration in that office. Seabury was eventually
successful, but this struggle further weakened the national body. It was not until 1789 that the Protestant
Episcopal Church was firmly established.

Sources:
Carl Bridenbaugh, *Mitre and Sceptre* (New York: Oxford University
   Press, 1962);

Rhys Isaac, *The Transformation of Virginia, 1740–1790* (Chapel Hill:
   University of North Carolina Press, 1982);

John Woolverton, *Colonial Anglicanism in North America* (Detroit:
   Wayne State University Press, 1984).

BAPTISTS

Growth. Although the revolutionary period as a
whole was a time of religious disaffection, two groups in
particular resisted that tendency. Along with the Methodists, the Baptists laid the groundwork in these years
for the spectacular growth that they experienced in the
early national period. In 1740 there were only thirty-
three Baptist churches in the New England colonies and
few elsewhere. Most of these predated the Great Awakening, and they did not adhere to the revivalistic principles that soon became popular. Many were so-called
General Baptists, who were much less rigid in their
thinking about salvation than most of their Calvinist
neighbors. By 1784 there were more than 150 Baptist
congregations in New England alone, with more than
8,000 communicants, and by 1790 Virginia had more
than 200 churches. Most of these were of a different
character than the General Baptists. These were the
Separate Baptists, named this because many emerged
during the revivals as believers separated from their old
churches and formed new congregations on strict Calvinist principles. The experiences of these groups were so
fundamental to the patterns of religious development in
America that they deserve to be examined in detail.

Baptist Beliefs. Baptists were distinguished from
other Protestants by the way they baptized converts. Instead of sprinkling the head of newborn children with
water as a sign of welcome into God's community, Baptists believed in immersing converts completely in water,
following the biblical example. They also rejected the
idea of baptizing children since they thought that baptism should mark a person's free acceptance of God's
presence in their life, something only an adult was capable of doing. By having only full believers as members,
Baptists hoped to purify the church even further than
their Puritan ancestors had been able to do. This was a
controversial position since many people were eager to
have the church's symbolic protection extended to their
children. To many, leaving their children outside the
church was tempting fate even if they agreed that people
should eventually come to their own acknowledgment of
sin and acceptance of God's forgiveness. The difficulty of
accepting these beliefs kept the numbers of Baptists
small in the American colonies before 1750. The Baptists also highly valued the independence of their individual congregations. They disliked the efforts of Congregationalists to place some general authority in groups
of neighboring ministers joined in regional consocia-
tions, or the similar practice of Presbyterians who organized churches under regional governing bodies called
synods. For Baptists each congregation stood apart from
all others and could follow its own way. They also rejected the need for an educated clergy, opening the way
for greater lay authority over religious matters.

New England. Baptists grew dramatically in the years
after the Great Awakening of the 1740s. Many of the
people touched by the intense religious feelings of that

period continued their spiritual journeys after the mass experiences of the revivals faded away. They were encouraged by the revivals' emphasis on personal religious experiences of conversion, which they called the New Birth. These people, called New Lights, found themselves increasingly unable to share worship with their Old Light neighbors who remained untouched by the experience of rebirth in the spirit that was the key feature of a successful revival. Many decided to separate. In town after town in New England and in the Middle colonies, the church broke into two groups, often after intense disagreements over theology and church property. Many of these Separate Congregationalists eventually embraced Baptist principles, and they continued to search for the purest church possible. Across the colonies at least 130 new Baptist congregations formed in this way. They were helped in this process by Baptists sent after 1762 from the Middle colonies, including James Manning, Hezekiah Smith, and Samuel Stillman. These men were college-educated ministers and brought with them organizational experience that New England Baptists lacked. They were instrumental in establishing Rhode Island College (later Brown University) in Providence in 1764, an important step in providing a more-able ministry for the spread of Baptists during the early national period. They also helped form the Warren Association in 1767, a loose association of Baptist congregations. Despite the independence of those congregations, they needed a forum for the discussion of theology and disputes and the coordination of various religious efforts, including the campaign for greater religious liberty. The Warren Association was the first such body in New England. By 1780 it had thirty-eight members, and there were four other such groups in New England.

Isaac Backus. The best illustration of the growth of Northern Baptists in the years following the Great Awakening and during the Revolution is the career of Isaac Backus. Backus had experienced conversion during the revivals of the Great Awakening and became a New Light Congregational minister in the small town of Middleborough, Massachusetts, in 1748. He gradually became a Baptist, following the logic of his reading of the Bible, but for a time he refused to impose this belief on his congregants. Although he tried to foster tolerance in his church, dissension followed, and in 1756 he and some of his congregation formed a separate Baptist church. Backus served that church for fifty years. In keeping with his separatist and Baptist origins, the great theme of his life's work was promoting the sanctity of an individual's conscience. He worked to bring his congregants to an interior awareness of God's power that would lead them to baptism and struggled against many obstacles in the path of his vision of true religion.

Church and State. Those obstacles included the colonial and, later, state laws that tried to ensure religious conformity. During these years Congregationalism was the established religion in New England, except in

Rhode Island. It was supported by taxes that paid ministers' salaries, and there was only limited toleration for dissenting groups. Baptists were exempted from the taxes, although they had to petition for the privilege of not paying them, a time-consuming process that often went against them despite the letter of the law. Backus fought those restrictions and in the process became an important early spokesman for American religious freedom. In 1769 a long series of disagreements over the tax involving the Baptists of Ashfield, Massachusetts, provoked the Warren Association to form a committee to attack the problem in an organized way and petition the government for redress. The matter eventually reached the king, who decided in favor of the Baptists in 1771. This case was only one of many, however, and by 1773 Backus led the Baptists in endorsing broader opposition to the system of limited toleration. Backus began to argue that governments should never be allowed to interfere with church matters and to consider religious liberty as a natural right, not a privilege granted selectively by the state. Backus's tract, *An Appeal to the Public for Religious Liberty* (1773), made the case for the separation of church and state. Backus's vision for the new order was not a secular one, however. He considered the separation necessary in order to promote true religion, which in his experience was being held back by the state. Instead he offered a picture of a voluntary religion, where true believers would come to embrace their faith in the absence of any influence other than God's spirit. At this point the cause seemed stalemated since the legislature would not change the rules and the Baptists were reluctant to appeal to the king, given how unpatriotic that would seem. The same year, though, saw the Boston Tea Party, and in 1774 the First Continental Congress met to deal with the growing crisis. Backus made the Baptists' appeal to Congress. Congress was not able to respond immediately, but Backus's efforts helped put religious liberty at the center of the goals of the Revolution. The Baptists supported the Revolution as it advanced, and Backus had greater success when it came time to form the new state governments. Backus worked hard behind the scenes of the Massachusetts constitutional convention in 1779 to insure the protection of religious liberty. The final version did protect individuals' right to their own beliefs but still allowed for religious taxation, and so the fight continued. It lasted beyond Backus's death in 1806, and the final dismantling of this system came only in 1833. Despite this delay, Backus's defense of religious freedom and the separation of church and state was crucial during the formation of the new nation. Only Thomas Jefferson had a comparable influence on this issue.

Baptists during War. The Baptists were the main beneficiaries of the revivals that took place during the war years in New England. From 1778 to 1782 a revival called the New Light Stir replayed the emotions of the Great Awakening across the mountainous terrain of the Northern frontier areas. It was fueled by the uncertainty

Roman Catholics accounted for fewer than thirty-five thousand of the roughly four million people living in the former colonies at the end of the War for Independence. It was not until 1790 that an American bishop was appointed and the church began a period of growth that would make it the largest single religious group in the United States by the time of the Civil War. Despite their small numbers, Catholics had a large role to play in the emerging American culture, even if that role was not exactly welcome. Prejudice against Catholics was strong in colonial America. In part this was because of the old rivalry between all Protestants and the Roman church they broke away from. Many American Protestants, especially those in New England, were descendants of Puritan settlers who had a special animosity toward Catholics. To the Puritans the Catholics stood for the elaborate religious ceremonies and the hierarchy of bishops that had been at the heart of their original quarrel with other English Protestants and had motivated their move to America. Sermons denouncing the Pope were a staple of Puritan literature despite the lack of any real threat to American Protestantism from Catholicism in this period. Nevertheless fears about Catholics came to the forefront several times in the revolutionary era.

In 1756, during the Seven Years' War, 454 French Canadian Catholics arrived in Philadelphia. They were part of a group of 6,000 Catholics who had been forced to move from their homes in eastern Canada by the British, who were trying to break up potential French allies. Their arrival caused an uproar in Pennsylvania, still reeling from France's devastating victory over General Braddock at Fort Duquesne, near present-day Pittsburgh, a few months earlier. The colony quickly filled with rumors of "popish plots" to seize power. A special census of Catholics in the colony revealed only around 1,300 potential enemies, but it did not alleviate fears. Only the Quaker dominance of the legislature kept restrictions on Catholic religious practices from being enacted. Tensions flared again in 1774, when Parliament passed the Quebec Act that guaranteed religious freedom for Catholics in Canada. The Continental Congress quickly condemned this act in the Suffolk Resolves of September 1774. Anti-Catholicism was in the press as well. Charles Carroll of Carrollton, later the only Catholic to sign the Declaration of Independence, used letters in the *Maryland Gazette* in 1773 to mount a defense of Catholics' ability to be true patriots, against attacks by Daniel Dulany, an ally of the unpopular royal governor. There were bad feelings in the army too. George Washington intervened in 1775 to stop the troops from burning the Pope in effigy as part of a traditional Guy Fawkes Day celebration. Still hoping that the Canadians would join the American fight, he said, "To be insulting their Religion, is so monstrous, as not to be suffered or excused."

Source: John Tracy Ellis, *American Catholicism*, second edition (Chicago: University of Chicago Press, 1969), pp. 28–40.

and social disruption of the war. People in the area were finding it difficult to cope with these problems without the help of religion, and churches were only poorly supported in this sparsely settled land. Baptists tried to fill the gap. The Warren Association sent four missionaries north in 1778 in response to a request from Baptist elder Caleb Blood of New Hampshire. Their success prompted four more to arrive in 1779, and by 1780 the Baptists had six new churches along the northern reaches of the Connecticut River and informal meetings in at least a dozen other towns. Even further north Baptist itinerant minister Samuel Shepard reported that "some hundreds of souls are hopefully converted." The years 1780 and 1781 saw record numbers of baptisms in the churches joined in the Warren Association, which nearly doubled its membership in these two years, as it forged one of the most successful domestic missionary efforts ever pursued. As early as June 1780 a new association formed in Shaftesbury, Vermont, to provide structure and moral guidance to the new frontier churches. Before 1778 New England Baptists had founded a total of fifty-three churches; thirty-six more emerged from 1778 to 1782, indicating the power of this revival movement, and the appeal of Baptist thought and practice, especially on the frontier.

Southern Baptists. Baptists grew even more dramatically in the Southern colonies in the revolutionary period. Preachers from New England helped spread the Baptist principles they had just embraced as they traveled through the Chesapeake Bay colonies during and after the Great Awakening. Shubael Stearns was one such person, heading south from Connecticut in 1754 and founding six churches in northern North Carolina. In 1758 they associated together in the Sandy Creek Association. Stearns and his fellow itinerants aggressively promoted their beliefs along the coast and into the backcountry. In newly settled areas, with immigrant populations, they offered discipline and a sense of belonging through conversion and baptism. That sense of orderliness was comforting to many, especially since it was attuned to life in these areas. Baptists did not value the trappings of more-formal religion, and they had egalitarian principles, such as allowing lay preaching, that appealed to men and women trying to make new lives for themselves far from established towns. Baptists also innovated to maintain this appeal. They developed new rituals, such as laying hands on the sick and washing each other's feet, that were based in the Bible and also emphasized the interdependence of their members. Baptists grew steadily, as small groups of neighboring families were converted by itinerants. The first Virginia church came in 1760, and they moved north of the James River into more-settled parts of the Tidewater area in 1767. Between then and 1774 fifty new churches formed, as Baptists took the lead from Presbyterians as the religion of the evangelical South.

Conflict with Anglicans. Baptist growth in the South was also encouraged by the weakness of the Anglican Church there. It was much less able than New England Congregationalism to resist the challenge presented by the Baptists. Given the few Anglican ministers available, for example, the Baptist practice of lay preaching was much easier to promote. Baptists offered an alternative to an establishment that was often absent, and in many places were the first religious authorities on the scene. They were not afraid to explicitly reject the restrictions the colonies tried to place on them. They failed to apply for preaching licenses, and they freely attacked the Anglican ministry as immoral and ineffective. They were often jailed for disturbing the peace in these ways, although this hardly affected their popularity. Aside from the formal challenges Baptists presented to Southern laws on religion, they offered a broader cultural challenge as well. The statutes were also fiercely resisted by Anglicans and their gentry allies. As Baptists gained strength during the 1760s, they began to be more critical of the gentry lifestyle. They considered the dancing, gambling, and horse racing that was the basis of polite Southern society to be immoral. These activities, once the signs of social order, came to be seen as disorderly. Baptist preaching focused on a new kind of order, one based on the moral rules contained in the Bible. Many people came to prefer this kind of order, especially as the political challenges of the Revolution began to emerge. Then, Anglican gentry were associated with the immorality of British imperial rule while the Baptists seemed to stand for the republican virtue that was the basis of the new nation's existence. The end result was that the Baptist challenge to Anglican religious authority came to be part of a larger effort to establish a more open society, with more opportunities for people from lower social levels to have important public roles to play. Just as the uneducated preacher was a valued member of the Baptist order despite his lack of a college degree or training in genteel manners, so could every farmer be a valued republican citizen. The logic behind Baptist beliefs ultimately would find its parallel in the democratic society that developed in the early nineteenth century and in the antislavery movement that led up to the Civil War.

Methodist Rivals. Baptists prevailed against an established church that was further weakened by a revival movement that emerged from within. This was the Methodist movement, and by the 1770s Methodists were rivals of the Baptists as well. Although both groups shared an emphasis on conversion through emotional preaching and ecstatic experience, there were important differences between them that over time let them appeal to somewhat different groups. The Baptists never left the path of strict Calvinism, and always adhered to the doctrine of God's election of the saints and the inability to earn one's salvation. The Methodists placed more stress on behavior and free will. They emphasized the discipline of a godly life, a factor appealing to the slowly emerging middle class, with their need for thrift and industriousness. Even more important, Methodists were centrally organized. While Baptists expanded through individual missionary efforts sponsored by one or a few churches, the Methodists arranged for itinerant ministers to cover the backcountry in an orderly way. This systematic recruiting effort brought thousands into their meetings, and laid the basis for the huge revival meetings on the frontier in the 1790s and early 1800s. Baptists did not lose their appeal by not following these methods. They always remained true to the ideal of the independent congregation. After the end of the Revolution, with egalitarianism sweeping the country and the beginnings of a more democratic society, this form of organization had tremendous appeal to many people. As the new nation moved west, Baptists and Methodists together led the way to founding a godly nation.

Sources:

Rhys Isaac, *The Transformation of Virginia, 1740–1790* (Chapel Hill: University of North Carolina Press, 1982);

Donald Mathews, *Religion in the Old South* (Chicago: University of Chicago Press, 1977);

William G. McLoughlin, *Isaac Backus and the American Pietistic Tradition* (Boston: Little, Brown, 1967).

QUAKERS

Radical Roots. The Society of Friends, or Quakers as they are better known, have always stood apart from the mainstream of American religion. Because of this, they offer some important lessons about the range of religious beliefs and practices in early America. During the revolutionary era Quakers dominated Philadelphia, at the time the largest city in America and a center of support for independence. They struggled in special ways with the relations between religion and the American Revolution. Their struggles were rooted in their particular beliefs. Quakers believed in the inner light. This was the notion that God was a spiritual presence within each individual and could speak to all humans through the words and actions of anyone. Their spiritualism led them to reject worldliness more than most Protestants, and they became easy to recognize by their use of the informal pronouns *thee* and *thou* and their refusal to doff their hats to their social superiors since they tried at all times to promote a spiritual equality. Quakers also refused to take oaths. Quaker worship also emphasized equality by letting all persons participate on the same basis. Quakers had no ordained ministers, and at services there was no public Bible reading or sermon, just silence, until the spirit moved someone to speak about a religious story or some personal experience. Women could speak as well as men, although over time, men and women came to meet for worship separately. Quakers read the Bible, but because of their highly individualized and spiritual attitudes, the story of Jesus's death and resurrection did not have the same importance for them as for most early Americans. Most orthodox Americans considered Quaker beliefs to be radical and threatening to the social and religious order based on biblical authority. They were outcasts in many parts of America and tended to live together in separate communities, although by 1770 these communities were found all along the Atlantic seaboard.

Social Prominence. The largest Quaker communities were in the parts of Pennsylvania and New Jersey centered around Philadelphia. The English Quaker William Penn founded the city in 1682 as a refuge for his coreligionists and guaranteed religious toleration and freedom of conscience in the colony's frame of government. By the 1750s, Philadelphia was a large city, remarkable for its ethnic and religious diversity. Quakers mingled on the streets with Scots-Irish Presbyterians, English Congregationalists, Swedish Lutherans, Dutch Reformed Protestants, German Moravians, Anglicans, and even Roman Catholics. If Quakers were religiously just one group among many tolerated equals, socially and politically they were Pennsylvania's first citizens. The colonial government concentrated political power in Quaker hands. The city's commerce was similarly focused on the tight networks of Quaker families on both sides of the Atlantic that controlled shipping and trade and made the Quakers' countinghouses at least as important as their meetinghouses. Many Quakers felt they had declined from the intense spirituality of the group's early days. The coming of the Seven Years' War changed this, however.

Challenge. As war began in 1754, Quaker leaders found it more and more difficult to reconcile their social position with their religious beliefs. One of those beliefs was pacifism. Most Quakers obeyed the biblical order to submit to the legitimate civil authority even though it meant agreeing to requests from the government for money that would be used for war as well as for peaceful purposes. In 1755, however, Gen. Edward Braddock was ambushed by French and Indian forces at Fort Duquesne in western Pennsylvania. This stunning defeat prompted the Pennsylvania assembly to take the military initiative

for the first time and vote for funds to raise a militia and defend the frontier. Many Philadelphia Quakers, some of whom saw Braddock's defeat as a sign of God's judgment on their worldly ways, developed a crisis of conscience. In 1755 several prominent Quakers issued a statement supporting tax resistance on religious grounds, one of the first signs of a deeper reform movement within American Quakerism. The reformers challenged those Quakers in the assembly to withdraw from public affairs in order to limit their involvement with the war and to avoid contradicting their religious beliefs. Ten members obeyed the call by resigning or refusing to run for reelection. Some would later reenter the assembly, but after 1756 the Quakers would never have a majority in the legislature again. The Quakers' withdrawal was not only an important step in religious reform but also marked significant political changes. Until the Revolution, the political initiative in Pennsylvania would be taken by the colony's governor, or proprietor, who lived in England, because there was no longer a powerful enough group on the scene in Philadelphia to control the political process. The principles the Quakers in the assembly had supported continued to be important, but they were now articulated by Benjamin Franklin and his party of supporters rather than by devout Quakers, who mainly removed themselves from politics to concentrate on business and religion.

Revolution. The growing conflict with Britain after the end of the Seven Years' War brought new problems to Quakers. One of the basic beliefs of the Society of Friends was pacifism. The duty to testify to peace at every opportunity was taken seriously by most Quakers and had been at the root of the 1755 withdrawal from colonial government. As the Stamp Act crisis began to move Americans toward independence, Quakers were caught in the middle. At first Americans pursued economic measures, such as nonimportation, which at least some Quakers were willing to support as nonviolent. Others objected to any form of resistance to the acknowledged government, including boycotts. The coming of actual war in 1775 made it even harder for Quakers to participate in the patriots' efforts even if they disagreed with Britain's actions. Most Quakers refused to participate in the framing of the new state governments forming after 1776 or to serve in the Continental Army or in the state militias. They were criticized by their neighbors for their principled stand against war and were fined and punished by the American governments. Quakers endured their sufferings and sought other ways than fighting to share in the burden of war. In Boston and other battle areas, for example, they offered medical help to the wounded on both sides. The American Revolution was a civil war in part, and it divided Quakers just as it divided other American groups. A significant minority of the Society of Friends supported the American cause and paid war taxes and even did military service. For this, many were disowned by the Quaker communities. In 1781 a few of these people, led by Samuel Wetherill Jr. and including seamstress Betsy Ross, broke away and formed the Society of Free Quakers in Philadelphia. This small group was a refuge for the Society of Friends, who actively supported American independence as well as the principles of Quakerism. Most Quakers desperately tried to remain neutral during the war, but their witness for peace was taken as support for the British by

---

RELIGIOUS HYMNS

Religious singing in the revolutionary period was much less common and much simpler than it is today. Few people had the time to devote themselves to music, and few congregations had the wealth to pay for organs or choirs. Some groups, such as the most traditional Congregationalists, frowned on all singing other than the chanting of psalms and refused to allow musical instruments into the service. By far the most important musical figure was the English Dissenting minister Isaac Watts. Watts wrote numerous hymns based on the psalms, that were more elaborate than the plain chants of the earlier colonial period. Editions of Watts's hymns were among the best-selling books in eighteenth-century America.

Americans started writing their own hymns during the mid 1700s, spurred on in part by the intense religious feelings associated with the revivals. As the revolution developed, some of these hymns became as much about patriotism as religion. William Billings, one of America's first professional church musicians, wrote the following hymn, "Chester," in 1778. It demonstrates how close the connection between religion and politics could be for many Americans. As soldiers sang it over and over, "Chester" became an unofficial anthem of the American Revolution.

Let tyrants shake their iron rod,
And slavery clank her galling chains.
We fear them not; we trust in God;
New England's God forever reigns.
When God inspired us for the fight
Their ranks were broke, their lines were forced;
Their ships were shattered in our sight
Or swiftly driven from our coast.
The foe comes on with haughty stride;
Our troops advance with martial noise.
Their veterans flee before our youth,
and generals yield to beardless boys.
What grateful offerings shall we bring?
What shall we render to the Lord?
Loud Halleluiahs let us sing,
And praise his name on every chord.

Source: Albert Christ-Janer and others, *American Hymns, Old and New* (New York: Columbia University Press, 1980), p. 143.

---

most of their neighbors. Pacificism further isolated the Society of Friends from the mainstream of American society.

John Woolman. One of the supporters of the 1755 tax-resistance movement was a man named John Woolman. Woolman wrote a detailed spiritual diary that was published a year after his 1772 death. The *Journal* made Woolman a well-known model of the Quaker spirituality that reasserted itself after the 1750s. In the *Journal* the daily events of Woolman's life are much less prominent than his thoughts on religious matters and moral action. Everyday life is important only as it leads to spiritual growth. Woolman was a shopkeeper for a while, but his work eventually brought Woolman to an appreciation of the destructive power of the desire for luxury goods. Because of this, he became a traveling minister and schoolteacher. Over the years his typically Quaker openness to finding spiritual possibilities everywhere led him to understand religion as the center of his life and as something that incorporated many elements. The *Journal* records these. It has elements of revivalistic Christianity, as when Woolman describes his spiritual awakening as a feeling of God "in my soul, like a consuming fire." He considered Jesus an important religious personality, but was less moved by the specific doctrines most Christians found in the Bible. Instead he preferred to chart the movement of the spirit within himself, and to describe this he took up the Quaker language of "singleness of heart," "clearness" and "purity." He described visions where he was able to communicate directly with the light, the preeminent Quaker symbol of the presence of God. Finally he was drawn to nature as a source of guidance about spiritual truth and good behavior. It led him to think of harmonious relations between humans and nature as part of the moderation in all things that Woolman held out as the ideal that the Society of Friends should pursue. Again, Woolman's central complaint was about worldliness. He wrote that "the least degree of luxury . . . hath some connection with evil, hath some connection with unnecessary labor."

Reform. Woolman's personal journey toward a more saintly life was mirrored in a broader reform movement that preoccupied American Quakers throughout the revolutionary era. Giving up political offices was one thing, but giving up the genteel lifestyle pursued by elite Quakers in Philadelphia and elsewhere was another. From the 1750s on, reforming Quakers reminded their neighbors of the traditions of the Society of Friends, which historically had promoted a simpler existence oriented toward spiritual growth rather than accumulating wealth and material goods. They thought the evangelical Protestants around them, still in the throes of the emotionalism of the Great Awakening, rightly thirsted for a greater appreciation of the spirit even if they were doing it in a distastefully enthusiastic manner that did not accord with the quiet ways of Quakerism. The reformers, including John Churchman, Sophia Hume, Catherine

Phillips, and Israel and John Pemberton, took up the idea of Quaker discipline, stressing Quakerism as a complete form of life rather than a religion that could be separated from the rest of one's existence. These men and women traveled through America, visiting Quaker meetings and speaking tirelessly about the importance of bringing children up in the Quaker tradition and putting the beliefs of the Society of Friends into action at every opportunity. Visiting committees were formed in many areas to visit Quaker families in their homes and observe the ways Quaker principles were being practiced. By the 1770s there had been a marked increase in cases of discipline for neglect of these principles in Quaker communities throughout the colonies. The stricter Quakerism that was emerging focused on the Quaker family as the core of a purer, more religious society. It meant, in the end, greater separation between Quakers and the rest of American society. The reform movement corresponded with the political isolation of the Quakers during the Revolutionary War. The Society of Friends became more and more like a sect, removed from the general trend of American Protestantism toward greater denominational interaction and toleration. Quakers lost their direct influence over society, as they became increasingly tribal, but they became a prophetic voice, urging reforms that would only be realized well into the nineteenth century.

Abolition. The most significant of these was agitation against slavery. Woolman was also important in this movement, which had deep roots in the Quaker vision of the spiritual equality of all believers. Many American Quakers held slaves and engaged in the slave trade just like their non-Quaker neighbors. Slowly, over the first half of the eighteenth century, opposition to both of these practices grew. The Quaker belief in the ongoing presence and teaching of the spirit within the Quaker meeting gave them an opportunity to reflect on their behavior and develop new ideas in response to it over time. This is what happened with slavery, as gradually more and more Society of Friends members came to see slavery as incompatible with their religious culture. Various meetings, including the Philadelphia Yearly Meeting, the general governing body of the large Pennsylvania Quaker community, spoke out about the evil of the slave trade and later, of slaveholding. Woolman was one early convert to antislavery, and he wrote a treatise about slavery in 1746 that was finally published in 1754. That same year the Philadelphia Yearly Meeting issued an epistle, or letter to the community, that declared slaveholding as unrighteous. In 1758 the Yearly Meeting took the first step toward enforcing that judgment. A committee was formed to visit local meetings and individuals, to educate them about the policy, and to impose sanctions on those who continued to be involved with slavery. The committee included Woolman, and he added these duties to his other chores as a traveling Quaker minister.

Anthony Benezet. The most significant antislavery activist among the Quakers was Anthony Benezet, who took up the emerging antislavery feeling of the 1750s to the next level, linking it to a more general humanitarian movement. Benezet came from a French Protestant family and converted to Quakerism after his immigration to America in 1731. Like his friend Woolman, he became a teacher. In 1755 he opened the first advanced school for Quaker girls and later taught in the first Quaker school for blacks. Benezet read widely and wrote on many topics. His broad interests deeply informed his stand against slavery, which he attacked with arguments drawn from many disciplines. As part of his exploration of the effects of the slave trade, Benezet wrote the first English-language history of West Africa. As Americans began to complain about their enslavement by the British during the Stamp Act crisis, Benezet taught and wrote to remind them of the conditions of African American slaves. This writing was some of the first to make an appeal against slavery on humanitarian grounds, trying to establish an emotional bond between slaves and white readers that would move the readers against slavery. Benezet also argued that blacks were not naturally inferior to whites and that the differences between the races could be accounted for by the degrading experience of life in bondage. These powerful arguments slowly had an effect. He reached several readers in England and Europe and made an important contribution to the emerging abolition movement in Britain. In America, Benezet's work first had an effect in New England, where Quaker meetings in the 1770s began to urge their members to free their slaves. Philadelphia followed in 1774, when the meeting passed measures to disown members who refused to free slaves. In 1775 Benezet formed the first American antislavery society, designed to protect free blacks unlawfully held in bondage. Benezet was an important supporter of the decision of the Pennsylvania assembly in 1780 to end slavery gradually. The Philadelphia Quakers in 1783 rightly took credit for their efforts against slavery that led the new nation in an effort that would conclude only some eighty years later. To Benezet goes the credit for giving the antislavery movement its grounding in humanitarianism, something that would link it to the powerful reform movements of the nineteenth century and give it the broadest possible appeal.

Sources:

Hugh Barbour and J. William Frost, *The Quakers* (New York: Greenwood Press, 1988);

Thomas E. Drake, *Quakers and Slavery in America* (New Haven: Yale University Press, 1950);

Jack D. Marietta, *The Reformation of American Quakerism, 1748–1783* (Philadelphia: University of Pennsylvania Press, 1984).

Phillips P. Moulton, ed., *Journal and Major Essays of John Woolman,* (New York: Oxford University Press, 1971);

RATIONAL RELIGION

Cult of Reason. The eighteenth century is often called the Age of Enlightenment, alluding to the movement of thought that spread from France throughout Europe and to North America. The Enlightenment was

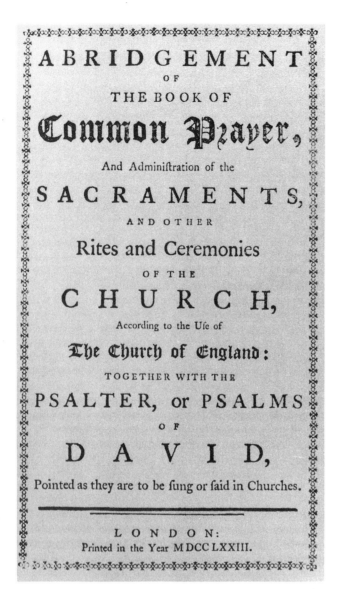

ABRIDGEMENT
OF
THE BOOK OF
Common Prayer,
And Adminiſtration of the
SACRAMENTS,
AND OTHER
Rites and Ceremonies
OF THE
CHURCH,
According to the Uſe of
The Church of England:
TOGETHER WITH THE
PSALTER, or PSALMS
OF
DAVID,
Pointed as they are to be ſung or ſaid in Churches.

LONDON:
Printed in the Year MDCCLXXIII.

Title page for a 1773 religious text by Benjamin Franklin and
Sir Francis Dashwood

primarily an intellectual phenomenon, one that broke with traditional ways of thinking about the world. French Enlightenment thinkers such as Voltaire, Denis Diderot, formed a loosely associated group that came to be known as the philosophes. They stressed the importance of reason as the key to knowledge. They rejected more-traditionally religious notions of revelation from God as the source of information about the world and pursued their own inquiries into truth, confident that human reason was the only tool they needed. They began investigating and cataloguing nature and rethinking the questions of the meaning of life, with a new emphasis on the importance of human actors and human thought. Although this cult of reason began in France and received its most extreme form there during France's own revolution of 1789, it took hold in America too. American political leaders were aware of the implications of the Enlightenment faith in human reason, as they came to reject what they considered arbitrary monarchical rule in favor of a republican government that reflected the voices of all citizens. Likewise, some Americans came to emphasize the role of reason in religion and the ability of each person to come through rational processes to an awareness and appreciation of God.

English Sources. The faith in reason had sources besides revolutionary French philosophers. One of the most important was the work of the great English scientist Isaac Newton. Newton was perhaps the thinker most responsible for bringing on the new confidence in rationalism. Newton uncovered and explored a series of laws of physics by which the natural world was governed. He and his followers came to conceive of the world as a piece of carefully calibrated machinery, set up in the beginning by God but running on its own unchangeable principles ever since. With enough time humans could use the scientific method of empirical investigation and inductive reasoning to understand fully the workings of the universe. Significantly, Newton was devoutly religious, and he pursued his work in a religious context. The ultimate goal for him was not merely understanding the mechanical workings of nature but also to have a glimpse of the mind of God embedded in natural processes. He spent much time trying to calculate the precise date of the end of the world, for example, using his investigation of nature to expand his religious knowledge. This aspect of Newton's life gradually was forgotten. As his work began to be known in America through teaching at the college level after 1700, many of his followers were much more moved by his embrace of reason than his interest in revelation.

Lockean Roots. The work of the English philosopher John Locke complemented Newton's efforts and was even more important for the introduction of rational principles into religious thought and practice. Locke is best known today for his studies of government, which had an important influence on American thinkers such as Thomas Jefferson and James Madison, and through them on the form of government established by the United States. However, Locke's earlier work was in the realm of human psychology and religion. His *Essay Concerning Human Understanding* (1690) was a basic college text in America throughout the eighteenth century. Here and in other works Locke shaped the understanding of how the mind worked and influenced prospective ministers in their grasp of how to appeal to the mind. Again rational principles were foremost. From Locke a large group of American religious figures came to believe that the purpose of life was happiness in this world and in the next, that reason could help people become happy, and that progress toward happiness was inevitable, given the power of reason. These views challenged the older Calvinist view of the world, brought to America by the Puritans. Rational religion eventually came into conflict with more-orthodox beliefs in the sovereignty of God and predestination to salvation, but these tensions developed only during the course of the revolutionary period.

Edwards and Reason. In New England, Jonathan Edwards was a significant figure who attempted to strike a balance between reason and traditional religion. Edwards was the pastor of the church in Northampton, Massachusetts, and was a leader of the Great Awakening, the evangelical revival that swept through many of the colonies beginning in the 1730s and 1740s. In a number of theological and pastoral publications of the 1750s, Edwards stressed the role of an emotional personal conversion to Christ in the development of true religious feeling. He did this in a rationalist framework, however, having been influenced by reading Locke's work while he was at Yale College. His *Treatise Concerning Religious Affections* (1746) was at once a defense of the revival experience as well as an effort to bring religious feeling into the framework of Locke's insights into the working of the mind and the relation between consciousness and the material world. In the revolutionary period Edwards followed up that work with *Freedom of the Will* (1754), which described the world as an orderly universe. Edwards also maintained that the order was set out by God, he avoided giving humans too much freedom at the expense of God's power, this belief kept his thinking firmly within the traditions of Calvinism. Later works on virtue and original sin continued, exploring the implications of the rationalist and progressive understanding of human nature. Edwards always found ways to use rationalist tools to affirm the traditional religion he and his revivalistic followers preached.

Conflicts. Not all accepted Edwards's view that reason and religion were in agreement. By the 1750s the role of reason and the related issue of the power of humans to affect their own fate were the most important points of contention between the revivalists and the liberals, the two main groups that emerged in American religion in the aftermath of the Great Awakening. Boston was the center of liberal religious thought in the revolutionary era. Its religious leaders took rational religion in several directions. Jonathan Mayhew of West Church stressed the theme of free will and connected religion to the revolutionary politics of the time. Charles Chauncy of neighboring First Church was less interested in politics and more engaged with the question of salvation, as he came to believe Christ's suffering had redeemed all humans, not just an elect few. One of the most representative figures of rational religion and strongest opponents of the emotions of revivalism was Ebenezer Gay. Gay was the minister of Hingham's First Church, just outside Boston, from 1718 until his death in 1787. During these sixty-nine years he shaped the thinking of many liberal rationalists, including Mayhew, who was his close friend. Gay himself was shaped by his reading at Harvard College, which included the European rationalists and the English religious writers they influenced. From these men Gay developed his own faith in a benevolent God who reasonably loved his creation rather than the more vengeful God of orthodox Calvinism. Gay

objected when that image of God became more popular during the revivals. Instead he wanted people to question their traditions and "Open their Eyes to the Light, and yield to the Evidence of Truth," as he said in a 1752 sermon. Gay hated disorder and emotion and worked hard to avoid controversy in his church and town. Nevertheless he became the center of the heated theological conflict dividing rationalist liberals from orthodox revivalists. In 1759 Gay published *Natural Religion as Distinguish'd from Revealed*, a major defense of liberal thinking against the attacks of evangelicals, especially against the writings of Edwards, including Edwards's 1758 defense of the traditional view of original sin. At the heart of Gay's answer was the argument that there was no contradiction between the revelations contained in Scripture and the work of reason in exploring and understanding nature. This defense of natural religion directly opposed the revivalists' belief that there was a fundamental difference between the human world and the realm of the divine, a chasm that could be crossed only by God. Gay's view opened up the possibility that what humans did on their own could make a difference in their ultimate fates, a revolutionary doctrine indeed.

Revolutionary Tendencies. Evangelicals may have been right to fear reason as the basis of religion since the revolutionary implications of rational religion were far reaching socially as well as theologically. Gay opposed the Revolution as another example of the disorderly emotionalism that he disliked about the revivals. Other rationalists took a different view. Mayhew and others led the way in developing the idea of freedom that was one of the central rationalist principles. As the political developments of the 1760s and 1770s got underway, this idea obviously echoed the new concepts of political freedom. In his preaching about the Stamp Act crisis of 1765, Mayhew stressed the need for government to behave morally and be accountable to its subjects. He argued that it was right for people to protest unjust leaders, a moral defense of the Revolution just beginning. In this, Mayhew followed Gay's principles even though Gay himself was uncomfortable about the end results. Gay and other rationalists believed in the power of reason to govern human life, and morality was a central theme of their preaching and writing. Part of reason was a moral sensibility, the power to judge right from wrong. All humans had this ability and so had the right to make these judgments for themselves. This too was a revolutionary idea in a world shaped by deferential social relations rather than democratic principles.

Unitarianism. The most advanced institutional form of this rational religion was Unitarianism, a denomination that arrived in America through the contacts between liberal Bostonian ministers and English Unitarians. The full emergence of this group would await the early nineteenth century, but the groundwork was laid in the revolutionary period. In March 1776 the British withdrew from Boston, taking with them the rector of

Just before his death in 1790 Benjamin Franklin responded to a question from Ezra Stiles, the president of Yale College, with a statement of his religious beliefs. Franklin's letter is a good example of the deist religious beliefs of some revolutionary leaders, of their interest in religion as a moral system, and of the way these ideas mixed with traditional Christianity. Franklin wrote:

Here is my Creed. I believe in one God, Creator of the Universe. That he governs it by his Providence. That he ought to be worshipped. That the most acceptable Service we render to him is doing good to his other Children. That the soul of Man is immortal, and will be treated with Justice in another Life respecting its Conduct in this. These I take to be the fundamental Principles of all sound religion, and I regard them as you do in whatever Sect I meet with them.

As to Jesus of Nazareth, my Opinion of whom you particularly desire, I think the System of Morals and his Religion, as he left them to us, the best the World ever saw or is likely to see; but I apprehend it has received various corrupting Changes, and I have, with most of the present Dissenters in England, some doubts as to his Divinity; tho' it is a question I do not dogmatize upon, having never studied it, and think it needless to busy myself with it now, when I expect soon an Opportunity of knowing the Truth with less Trouble.

Source: Benjamin Franklin, *Writings*, edited by J. A. Leo Lemay (New York: Library of America, 1987), p. 1,179.

King's Chapel, the local Anglican church. Many of the lay members left as well, but those who remained continued to meet together. In 1782 they asked John Freeman to be their lay reader. By 1787 the congregation renounced their ties to the Episcopalian Church then replacing Anglicanism, ordained Freeman as their minister, and declared themselves Unitarians. Other Congregational churches eventually followed. Unitarians, like other liberals, believed in the power of reason and the benevolence of God. They went further, though, in their critical examination of the Scriptures. They concluded that there was no evidence there for the doctrine of the divinity of Christ and argued that there was only one God, not a trinity. Their rethinking of God paralleled the earlier rethinking of human nature, taking it one step further. This idea was radical and Americans expressed it only cautiously in these years. Freeman was more extreme than most on this question, believing that Christ was only human, although he had a special mission from God. Most early Unitarians thought that Christ had some special status, less than God but more than humans. There were few early converts to Unitarianism in the revolutionary period, and even later its numbers were small, although its influence on nineteenth-century American culture was immense.

Deism. A few revolutionaries went even further than the Unitarians, rejecting traditional notions of God entirely. These were the deists, and they included several leaders of the independence movement and framers of the new nation. Deists took the notion of natural religion to an extreme, seeing nature itself as a sort of impersonal god, a rational organizing principle behind all life. They were not interested in the Bible and its traditional images of God and abandoned the idea of specific divine revelations. Deism flourished briefly after the end of the Revolutionary War, as traditions of all kinds were abandoned and the new nation took shape. In the revolutionary period there were few deists, but to many early Americans they presented a serious threat to the social order and indicated the limits of revolutionary fervor. The collapse of traditional religion seemed to undermine the entire society in the eyes of some. These people worried about how to give moral guidance to people in the absence of the tools of the Bible and the threat of divine punishment for sin. In 1759 Ezra Stiles, later the president of Yale College, worried that "Deism has got such a Head in this age of Licentious Liberty" that colleges should lead the way to "conquer and demolish" before disorder reigned. Similarly, Benjamin Franklin, despite his own radical religious ideas, warned a correspondent in the 1780s against publishing a deist tract. He said, "If men are so wicked as we now see them *with religion,* what would they be *if without it?*"

Franklin's Religion. Benjamin Franklin is not usually thought of as a religious figure. He never joined a church and never publicly identified himself with any one religious group. Nevertheless, Franklin is an excellent example of the effect of rationalism on American religion and the ways that many Americans held what seem to be conflicting ideas about religion. Franklin is often thought to have been one of the few true deists in America and to have left Christianity behind in his thinking in favor of the purest faith in reason. Yet he supported any number of Christian projects. In a well-known incident recorded in his *Autobiography* (1868) Franklin describes how he came to give money to George Whitefield, the English evangelical, swayed by the power of his preaching and convinced of the virtue of his several efforts to improve society, if not of the Christian truth behind that work. The notions of experiment and virtue are the keys to understanding Franklin's religious thought. Virtue was a frequent preoccupation of his. He brought his pragmatism and utilitarianism to the question of how best to promote virtuous behavior, all in the hope of improving society. Personal morality was of less concern to him, and he had little of the traditional Christian sense of sinfulness. Instead, Franklin supported religion as a form of experiment in virtuous behavior, social reform, and humanitarianism. In this way Franklin saw religion as important for the establishment of the kind of republic he hoped America would become. If a Christian preacher could bring this about efficiently, Franklin did not mind, as he considered the Christian aspects of the preaching to be incidental to the primary message urging the formation of the good society. So at various times in his life Franklin would write both a deist tract denying the immortality of the soul and a new version of the Lord's Prayer, updating Christian imagery for the new age. And in 1787 he proposed that the members of the Constitutional Convention pray together each morning before beginning their work. Franklin would try anything once to achieve his larger public goals. Franklin was careful with his public statements about his personal beliefs about God and the soul, never wanting to "shock the Professors" of any particular belief and considering his own beliefs to be "the Essentials of every known Religion," as he stated in his *Autobiography*. In this he shared the Enlightenment faith that all humans were rational and through the use of their minds must ultimately agree on all essential truths, whatever different external forms of religion they might follow. Despite their radical rejection of traditional Christian doctrines, in this way rationalists and deists shared the hope and optimism that animated their more-orthodox neighbors, all of whom were working to establish the American republic.

Sources:

Alfred Aldridge, *Benjamin Franklin and Nature's God* (Durham: Duke University Press, 1967);

Daniel Boorstin, *The Lost World of Thomas Jefferson* (Boston: Beacon Press, 1964);

Henry F. May, *The Enlightenment in America* (New York: Oxford University Press, 1976);

Kerry S. Walters, *Rational Infidels: The American Deists* (Durango, Colo.: Longwood Academic, 1992);

Robert J. Wilson III, *The Benevolent Deity* (Philadelphia: University of Pennsylvania Press, 1984).

REVIVAL AND RENEWAL

Great Awakening. One of the most important developments in eighteenth-century American religion was the emergence of a widespread religious revival, or awakening, as it was called by the people of the time. Periods of intense religious feeling, marked by large numbers of people joining churches or renewing their ties to their religious groups, were a feature of American religion almost from the beginning of English settlement. The ministry of John Cotton is said to have sparked such a period of renewal among Boston's Puritan settlers as early as 1633. About a hundred years later a series of revivals swept through all of Britain's American colonies and had a lasting influence. These revivals of the 1730s and 1740s came to be known as the first Great Awakening. They were supported in part by the work of George Whitefield, an English minister who visited America seven times between 1738 and 1770. Whitefield was an itinerant preacher. He had no settled parish in America but traveled from place to place, drawing huge crowds to his highly emotional message of Christian renewal.

Whitefield was a model for a new kind of American minister, one not tied to any one community. Such men were able to take the spark of renewal from one place to another. The specific message they preached might vary a great deal from town to town, especially as such men were not under the constraints a community could place on their settled minister. Although the Great Awakening declined after 1745, it never disappeared, even during the years of the American Revolution. Revivalism was a permanent feature of American religion.

Revival Meetings. There were important common themes in the faith that emerged from the revival meetings, whether in the North or South, in the cities or on the frontier. Revivalists preached a great deal about the spirit and tried to bring their listeners to an awareness of God's presence in their lives. They preached about sin and tried to awaken the congregants to their own sinfulness and the need for repentance. They wanted to bring people to a "new birth" by getting them to acknowledge their inability to earn their salvation and accept the gift of God's grace, which was the only way to heaven. Revivalists often got the response they wanted, as people emotionally embraced a new life during long church meetings attended by neighbors from miles around. In this setting the emotions of one convert could feed those of the sinners sitting nearby and bring them along to Christ also. Ecstatic behavior was common, as people felt the spirit moving within them, leading them to faint or cry out. The revivals of the revolutionary period were not as large or as carefully organized as the huge camp meetings of the early 1800s, nor were the emotional outpourings as intense. These earlier efforts paved the way for one of the most characteristic features of American Protestantism, as the personal experience of renewal through conversion to Christ became a common sight across America from the 1740s onward.

Jonathan Edwards. The leader of the revivals in New England was Jonathan Edwards, the minister of the church in Northampton, Massachusetts, from 1726 to 1750. Edwards was a major intellectual figure, trained at Yale College in the latest theology and philosophy. His sermons were learned, and his thinking was complicated. Yet he had the ability to reach the masses. His vivid descriptions of hell enthralled his listeners, and he kept their attention as he described the intense emotional reaction to God's grace that he considered to be the basis of true religious experience. His listeners followed where he led, and his preaching and that of his associates brought hundreds of new members into the churches of the Connecticut River valley in the 1740s. From 1750 to 1758 he moved to an Indian mission in Stockbridge on the Massachusetts frontier. There he produced a series of books that developed a theology that backed up the experience of grace and renewal that his preaching had prompted in the pews of his church. These books described in great detail the feelings associated with true religion and attributed them to God's powerful love breaking in to the world of the human sinners. Edwards argued that these experiences should draw people out of the world and they should begin their lives anew with a "new birth in the spirit." He gave special attention to the idea of human free will, which was gaining greater acceptance by the 1750s but which ran against the Calvinist doctrine of predestination. Edwards argued that humans could make free choices, but only within a world created and ordered by God. In that world, because of original sin, human choices did not have the total freedom that God's own choices would enjoy, and humans would always be sinful by nature. Only God, the original creator, could break humans out of the cycle of sin. Edwards argued forcefully that the only godly choice was acceptance of grace, if God saw fit to offer it, which in practice meant rejecting sin at every opportunity. This kind of submission to God's power, as realized in human experience, was the heart of the revivalistic religion that gained adherents throughout the revolutionary period.

Aftermath. In the 1750s and 1760s the mass experience of revivalism was not as common as it had been during the heyday of the early revivals. Yet this kind of emotional religion remained the ideal for many Christians. People joined churches while under the sway of heartfelt pain at their own sinfulness and offered complete submission to God. Only through God's grace, as exemplified in the Bible's account of Christ's crucifixion and resurrection, could humans be saved and have hope of reaching heaven. Revivalism was not a simple phenomenon, however, as later experience showed. One important consequence of the revivals was social disorder. In the revolutionary era in New England this was marked by dissension among many Protestants who had formerly worshiped together and in many cases by the actual division of churches. These divisions could mean bitter disputes. North Stonington, Connecticut, is an example of how divisive the revival experience could be. The minister there, Joseph Fish, had supported the revivals in the 1740s, although quickly regretted it when part of his congregation left in 1746. Fish did not abandon revivalistic preaching, but he continued to lose members. In 1765 there was another defection, and this time a new Baptist congregation was the result. Fish estimated then that some two-thirds of his people had separated and joined the new groups and that many of those still left were also inclined to extreme ideas about the need for purity in the church and so were likely to separate as well. Fish was dismayed at the freedom people felt to challenge the traditional social order in this way even though they did so for God. He quoted one man who left as saying to the pastor, "My God commanded me to go from you, and I know it, and that is all my reason." In addition to rifts in congregations, many ministers were troubled by more-general attacks. Radical revivalists argued that only a truly converted minister could bring others to Christ and criticized ministers who were not fully supportive of the revivals as unfit for the pulpit. This was shocking in a period when service to the church was a highly regarded profession. Divisions among the clergy and laity led to serious splits, and by the end of the Revolution, New England Congregationalism had split into

REVIVALS AND SOCIAL CONFLICT

The revivals sparked conflicts that marked other social divisions, as backcountry revivalists challenged the power and style of the elites who looked down on the behavior of upstart evangelicals. In Virginia, James Ireland, a young man of genteel origins, had to give up dancing and other forms of polite social intercourse when he experienced the revival in the late 1760s. His friends tried to persuade him to abandon his new religious feelings and attend a ball. Ireland's record of the encounter suggests two very different cultures uneasily existing side by side. Ireland wrote that

When I viewed [my friend] riding up, I never beheld such a display of pride in any man, . . . arising from his deportment, attitude and jesture; he rode a lofty elegant horse . . . his countenance appeared to me as bold and daring as satan himself, and with a commanding authority [he] called upon me, if I were there to come out, which I accordingly did, with a fearful and timorous heart. But O! how quickly can God level pride. . . . For no sooner did he behold my disconsolate looks, emaciated countenance and solemn aspect, than he . . . was riveted to the beast he rode on. . . . As soon as he could articulate a little his eyes fixed upon me, and his first address was this; 'In the name of the Lord, what is the matter with you?'"

The emotions of the revival were strong enough that they sometimes spilled over into violence. This 1771 diary entry records an attack by Anglican gentry on a Baptist meeting in Virginia:

Brother Walker Informed us . . . [that] about 2 Weeks ago on the Sabbath day Down in Caroline County he Introduced the Worship of God by Singing. . . . While he was Singing the Parson of the Parish [who had ridden up with his clerk, the sheriff, and some others] would Keep Running the End of his Horsewhip in [Waller's] Mouth, Laying his Whip across the Hym Book, &c. When done Singing [Waller] proceeded to Prayer. In it he was Violently Jerked off of the Stage, [they] Caught him by the Back part of his Neck, Beat his head against the ground, some Times up Sometimes down, they Carried him through a Gate that stood some Considerable Distance, where a Gentleman Give him . . . Twenty Lashes with his Horse Whip. . . . Then Brother Waller was Released, Went Back Singing praise to God, Mounted the Stage & Preached with a Great Deal of Liberty.

Source: Rhys Isaac, *The Transformation of Virginia, 1740–1790* (Chapel Hill: University of North Carolina Press, 1982), pp. 161–163.

New England families going to church services in 1776 (Library of Congress)

liberal, moderate, and revivalistic wings. Some of this social disruption was productive, however. The revival experience made many people more willing to think in new ways about questions of behavior and justice, to question authority, and to value the freedom of religious expression. In these ways the revivals contributed significantly to the larger revolutionary spirit of the age.

Theological Tensions. In addition to social problems revivalism posed difficult intellectual problems. Although the basis of revivalistic religion was complete submission to God's almighty power, the experience of submission was intensely individual. Each convert to Christ had to come to his or her particular awareness of his of her sinfulness and make a free decision in his or her heart to come to God and reject sin. This individualism was not always compatible with the mass experience of revivals that produced each person's special reaction and feelings. Further, the emphasis on the free acceptance of God's grace brought another complication. From the days of the first American Puritans ministers taught that humans did not earn their salvation. Rather it was a gift from God, who had decided at the beginning of time who would be saved. This doctrine was called predestination. Nothing humans could do really affected whether they went to heaven, although the Bible insisted that all humans should obey moral laws such as the Ten Commandments and so behave as if they deserved heaven. The revivalists' stress on the free acceptance of grace in the emotions of the conversion experience opened the door to some new thinking about this doctrine. Slowly the notion that humans had free will and could effectively choose faith came to be more widely accepted. If so, they could be said to earn their salvation by

this act of faith, if not technically by their good deeds. This was a challenge to older beliefs, which no revivalist minister was willing to acknowledge. Whitefield and other revivalists always insisted that they were strict Calvinists. Whatever they said, people heard them differently and found themselves comfortable with a faith that affirmed the ability of humans to affect their fate. This kind of faith seemed natural to Americans, who were accustomed to overcoming hardship and fending for themselves in a harsh world. The result was a reinterpretation of the Calvinist beliefs that were the basis for much American Protestantism in the colonial period. The process did not reach its full flowering until the coming of a second period of revivals in the 1820s. But the seeds were laid in the revolutionary era for a revolution in the relations of Americans to God as well as to King George.

Presbyterians. In the Middle colonies of New York, New Jersey, and Pennsylvania the revivals were led by the Presbyterians. Presbyterians differed from most other early American Protestants only in the ways they organized their church, not in matters of belief or practice. Presbyterian churches were governed by a hierarchy of regional bodies called presbyteries, synods, and assemblies. These bodies were composed of ministers and church elders who set policies for the entire church and settled disputes. Thus, Presbyterian congregations were not fully independent as were Baptist and Congregational churches of the time. More-centralized control did not prevent the disruptions of the revivals from affecting the Presbyterians. Gilbert Tennent, hailing from New Jersey, was the leading Presbyterian revivalist and after Edwards and Whitefield, the best-known figure of the movement across the colonies. The preaching of Tennent and his supporters stressed the immediate experience of grace, as did the New England revivals, and this touched off a fight with other Presbyterians more concerned with standardizing beliefs in the church. Revivalist "New Side" Presbyterians were ejected from the Synod of Philadelphia by their "Old Side" rivals in 1741 and joined the Synod of New York in 1745. The schism in American Presbyterianism lasted until 1758, when the enormous growth of the New Side allowed for the reunion of New York and Philadelphia on revivalistic terms. Division threatened the Presbyterians several more times during the revolutionary era, but with this base of agreement, they were poised for the rapid growth they experienced on the Western frontier in the years after the war ended.

Scots-Irish Religion. The growth of revivalistic Presbyterianism was fueled in part by the emigration of Protestants from northern Ireland, called the Scots-Irish, because many had come to Ireland from Scotland in the seventeenth century. Some fifty thousand Scots-Irish arrived in Pennsylvania in the 1770s. These people were especially attuned to the emotional religion of the revival, coming from a strong Calvinist background, and conditions in the Appalachian frontier where they settled were ideal for the revival's success. Living at great distances from each other and isolated from most churches and other social institutions, the itinerant revivalist was the only kind of minister most saw. They also drew on the Presbyterian tradition of the yearly administration of the sacrament of the Lord's Supper, or the love feast, as it was sometimes called. Held in the late summer or the early fall, these sacramental occasions became chances for far-flung neighbors to meet, socialize, settle differences, and renew their faith. A typical example was led by Reverend John Cuthbertson on the Pennsylvania frontier from 13 August to 17 August 1761. Hundreds of people gathered from the surrounding countryside, and Cuthbertson spent the rest of the year serving as an itinerant minister. They stayed in tents and heard Cuthbertson preach during the first two days, fasting at the same time. At the end of the second day those who felt renewed in the spirit received tokens, small pieces of lead that would admit them to the communion feast the next day. The third day those with tokens would sit at tables where they would receive the sacramental bread and wine while the others gathered around this group and shared in the preaching, prayer, and hymn singing. The fourth day was marked with more sermons and hymns and the departure for home. This ritual was an opportunity to bring a season of renewal into the rhythms of life and became a model for the huge revival meetings on the nineteenth-century frontier.

New Divinity. Just as the New Side Presbyterians consolidated their power and ended the schism with their antirevivalist Old School rivals, the College of New Jersey, the intellectual center of revivalism, called Ed-wards away from New England to be its president. Edwards accepted and looked forward to a new field of influence, but he died from a smallpox inoculation within a month of assuming the post in March 1758. He left behind a group of his students, who carried revivalism forward through the revolutionary period and became known as New Divinity men, as they shaped a revivalistic theology for a new nation. Two leaders of the New Divinity were Joseph Bellamy of Connecticut and Samuel Hopkins of Rhode Island. Both of these men had been students of Edwards and had fully supported the revivals. As the Great Awakening faded, however, they tried to develop new ways of thinking about it that would move it forward. Both emphasized God's absolute power and the need for humans to submit to it, in hope of redemption from sin. They also emphasized moral behavior, not as something that would earn salvation but as something that flowed from the experience of God's grace. They differed on this point from the liberal rationalists who had opposed the emotionalism of the revivals. Those men, such as Charles Chauncy and Jonathan Mayhew, had also emphasized morality but saw it as something rational humans ought to do for their own sake rather than for the glory of God. Their views flowed from their belief that humans had free will and could choose their fate. The New Divinity men disagreed, but as part of their own sense of God's presence in the world, worked tirelessly to make the world a more moral place. Many of them, such as Bellamy, supported the independence movement in the 1770s, as they became convinced that England's government was unjust and should be resisted.

Disinterested Benevolence. Samuel Hopkins, minister in Newport, Rhode Island, took up an even more radical stand, based on his hope for a better world. He was one of the first ministers to speak out against slavery, urging his people to put aside their commercial interests in favor of doing God's will. In his many writings Hopkins developed the idea of "disinterested benevolence," which was the heart of the New Divinity. He argued that truly godly people aspired to be completely disinterested in the things of this world and behaved well only for the sake of honoring God. They even should be willing to be damned, if God ordained it, since even that would honor God by being part of the world he had ordered. These seem like difficult ideas to accept, but the New Divinity men were concerned with expressing the glory of God's power in every possible way. This was the central theme of the evangelical form of Protestantism that was accepted by the vast majority of Americans in the nineteenth century.

Southern Revivals. Revivalism lasted longer in the Southern colonies, persisting well into the 1770s and with even more-significant social effects. The Southern frontier was thinly settled during this period, with few established churches. Frequent military conflicts during the Seven Years' War and the Revolution made life there

George Whitefield, the great itinerant minister, traveled the length of the colonies in his seven trips to America between 1739 and 1770. He was the first person to be well known throughout America and succeeded in bringing probably thousands of individuals to Christ through his powerfully emotional preaching. Many early Americans recorded their impressions of Whitefield. One was Olaudah Equiano, an African slave. In his autobiography he remembered hearing Whitefield when their paths overlapped in Savannah, Georgia, in 1765:

I came to a church crowded with people; the church-yard was full likewise, and a number of people were even mounted on ladders, looking in at the windows. I thought this a strange sight, as I had never seen churches, either in England or the West Indies, crowded in this manner before. I therefore made bold to ask some people the meaning of all this, and they told me that the Rev. George Whitefield was preaching. I had often heard of this gentleman, and had wished to see and hear him; but I had never before had an opportunity. I now therefore resolved to gratify myself with the sight, and pressed in amidst the multitude. When I got into the church I saw this pious man exhorting the people with the greatest fervour and earnestness, and sweating as much as ever I did while in slavery on Montserrat beach. I was very much struck and impressed with this; I thought it strange I had never seen divines exert themselves in this manner before, and was no longer at a loss to account for the thin congregations they preached to.

In a different vein Benjamin Franklin was also moved by his encounter with Whitefield in Philadelphia in the 1740s while Whitefield was raising money for an orphanage he wanted to build in Georgia. Franklin wrote that he

happened soon after to attend one of his Sermons, in the Course of which I perceived he intended to finish with a Collection, & I silently resolved he should get nothing from me. I had in my Pocket a Handful of Copper Money, three or four silver Dollars, and five Pistoles in Gold. As he proceeded I began to soften, and concluded to give the Coppers. Another Stroke of his Oratory made me asham'd of that, and determin'd me to give the Silver; & he finish'd so admirably, that I empty'd my Pocket wholly into the Collector's Dish, Gold and all. At this Sermon there was also one of our Club, who being of my sentiments respecting the Building in Georgia, and suspecting a Collection might be intended, had by Precaution emptied his Pockets before he came from home; towards the Conclusion of the Discourse however, he felt a strong Desire to give, and apply'd to a Neighbour who stood near him to borrow some Money for the Purpose. The Application was unfortunately to perhaps the only Man in the Company who had the firmness not to be affected by the Preacher. His Answer was, At any other time, Friend Hopkinson, I would lend to thee freely; but not now; for thee seems to be out of thy right senses.

Sources: Olaudah Equiano, *The Interesting Narrative and Other Writings*, edited by Vincent Carretta (New York: Penguin Books, 1995), p. 132;

Benjamin Franklin, *The Autobiography*, edited by Louis Masur (Boston: Bedford Books, 1993), pp. 108–109.

---

even more precarious. Over the period all the major Protestant groups sent ministers into this area, in what was essentially a missionary effort to the settlers there. These preachers brought with them the styles of the revivals of the Northern colonies, and their form of evangelical religion prevailed in the area. In some respects this minimized the differences among the Presbyterians, Baptists, Congregationalists, and even Anglicans who crossed paths in the backcountry, although religious conflicts were present there too, within these groups as well as between them. Presbyterians often led the way, for example, with the ministry of Samuel Davies, one of the best-known figures in early Southern revivalism. Davies centered his work in Hanover County, just west of the more-settled Tidewater region of Virginia, but traveled throughout the colony reaching people of all kinds. From the early 1750s Davies's work represented a serious challenge to the Anglican Church, whose authorities worried about people being drawn away to Davies's more enthusiastic faith. That challenge led to a long debate in Virginia about religious toleration, a difficult issue in this

colony, where the Anglican Church was sponsored by the government and supported with taxes. Davies carried the day on this issue in 1755, with the help of the English courts, which upheld the rights of non-Anglican or dissenting ministers to preach and form new congregations in the colonies. This small step was a symbol of one of the most significant contributions of revivalism, which often challenged more-established religious authority and ended up encouraging greater diversity of religious practice and belief. It was also a sign of the strength of the common folk, who in this case successfully resisted the power of the Anglican gentry and took a first step at establishing a more democratic society. Davies claimed the right to preach mainly because the people wanted to hear him, and he addressed their needs directly in a way that Anglican priests never did. Instead of abstract theological sermons, for example, he talked to his listeners clearly about their lives and their relationships with God. He taught people the rules for living a godly life and offered an alternative to the gentry culture that controlled Southern life in the 1750s. Davies and other evangelical preachers replaced social hierarchies with distinctions based on religious commitment, potentially turning the world upside down. In the South the work of the revival began with the Presbyterians but was taken up in the 1760s by the Baptists and the revival wing of Anglicanism, which became the separate Methodist church after the Revolution.

PHILLIS WHEATLEY ON WHITEFIELD'S DEATH

Phillis Wheatley was born in Africa and spent most of her short life as a slave in Boston. She became a literary wonder when her book, *Poems on Various Subjects, Religious and Moral,* was published in London in 1773. The poems were quite conventional, but that they were written at all amazed her readers. Despite her circumstances, Wheatley had managed to learn to read and write and had mastered poetic forms and could even read Latin. Few white women could match her accomplishments. She had also become a deeply committed Christian, under the influence of her owners, the Wheatleys. One of her most famous poems was "On the Death of the Rev. Mr. George Whitefield, 1770." It suggests both Wheatley's own spiritual life as well as the huge influence of the English preacher in America.

Hail, happy saint, on thine immortal throne,
Possessed of glory, life, and bliss unknown;
We hear no more the music of thy tongue,
Thy wonted auditories cease to throng.
Thy sermons in unequaled accents flowed,
And every bosom with devotion glowed;
Thou didst in strains of eloquence refined
Inflame the heart, and captivate the mind.

He freely offered to the numerous throng,
That on his lips with listening pleasure hung.
'Take Him, ye wretched, for your only good,
Take Him my dear Americans,' he said,
'Ye thirsty, come to this life-giving stream,
Ye preachers, take Him for your joyful theme;
Take Him my dear Americans,' he said,
'Be your complaints on His kind bosom laid:
Take Him, ye Africans, He longs for you,
Impartial Savior is His title due:
Washed in the fountain of redeeming blood,
You shall be son, and kings, and priests to God.'

Yet let us view him in the eternal skies,
Let every heart to this bright vision rise;
While the tomb safe retains its sacred trust,
Till life divine re-animates his dust.

Source: *The Poems of Phillis Wheatley,* edited by Julian D. Mason Jr. (Chapel Hill: University of North Carolina Press, 1966), pp. 9–10.

Pietism. Another element contributing to the revivalistic Protestantism that emerged in the revolutionary era was pietism. Pietism might best be described as an emphasis within traditional Christianity on intense spiritual experiences and on the importance of sensing the presence of the Holy Spirit in one's life. These were obviously basic ideas behind the revivals across the colonies, which also focused on the heartfelt experience of religion, but in the Middle colonies especially they took on characteristic forms thanks to the influence of a number of German immigrant groups. These are the people remembered today as the Pennsylvania Dutch, and throughout the 1700s they streamed into the backcountry of Pennsylvania and from there moved north and south along the Appalachian frontier. This area became a home to many sects, including the Mennonites, the Dunkers, the Schwenckfelders, and the Moravians. Pietists stressed purity and fidelity to the ideals of the first Christians, as represented in the Bible and revealed through the action of the Holy Spirit. These ideas led them in some cases to reach out to other people to convince them of the need for reform and in other cases to withdraw from the world and its sinful ways. The Moravians, led by founder Count Nicholaus Ludwig Zinzendorf, were the most important of the pietistic sects. Moravians had an intense devotion to the passion and suffering of Christ. They brought with them a spiritualism that had a social dimension, as the Holy Spirit prompted them to work to reform the world around them from within. Their pioneering missionary efforts to Native Americans were one manifestation of this. Another was their communalism, and many Moravians and pietists lived in small utopian communities, where they tried to realize the kingdom of God on earth. The most famous of these in the revolutionary era was the Ephrata Community, founded by Dunker Conrad Beissel. Ephrata residents sought spiritual purity by setting up a monastic economy, segregating the sexes, and worshipping on Saturday rather than Sunday. Ephrata folded after Beissel's death but was a model for hundreds of religious utopian ventures of the nineteenth century. Pietists offered other kinds of idealism as well. The Swedish scientist, philosopher, and mystic Emanuel Swedenborg, whose writings were beginning to be known in America in the 1770s and 1780s, drew heavily on the pietistic tradition in developing his own theories that exploration of the material world could lead to awareness of higher, spiritual truths and even a self-conscious dwelling in the spiritual realm. Swedenborg was later an important influence on Ralph Waldo Emerson's Transcendentalism. Emerson was no Protestant revivalist, but his interest in these related ideas shows how important they were to American culture as a whole. These were all movements aimed at spiritual renewal, and it was a fine line between renewal along orthodox Christian lines and renewal of a more radical sort, made possible by the reliance on the spirit. In their revolutionary-era efforts pietists were yet another representation of the power of an awakened religious spirit.

Transatlantic Revivals. An important aspect of the revivalism that developed in revolutionary-era America was that it was an international event. The influence of German pietists was one example of this. Whitefield was another, more important one. Whitefield's trips throughout the colonies in the revolutionary period brought him into contact with ministers of all types. Many of these remained in touch with him after he left their towns. Whitefield also had a wide circle of friends in Britain, and he was an initial point of contact for many transatlantic friendships. During the 1740s and well into the 1750s Scotland was swept by revivals much like those in the American colonies. News reports of awakenings in both areas found their way rapidly back and forth across the ocean. Whitefield himself often served as an evangelical mailman, taking trunkloads of letters and reports to England or America for circulation or sometimes publication, especially in the newly formed evangelical newspapers. These letters were often the basis for sermons designed to prompt further revivals. Many other ministers participated as well, including Edwards, John Erskine of Scotland, and Isaac Watts, the famous English hymnist. These people not only shared news of awakenings and related events but also tried to experience the revival through their letters. They used their correspondence to organize "concerts of prayer" where people on both sides of the ocean would set specific times each week and several days a year when they would join in fasting and prayer together in an effort to approximate the feeling of a universal Christian church. This arrangement continued from the 1740s into the 1760s and was revived after the end of the Revolution. During the war years the communications networks that began by transmitting religious news continued to function, now sending political and military news as well. This system of disseminating information was an important help in connecting people during these unsettled years, whether they favored or opposed independence.

Whitefield's Death. Whitefield died in the small town of Newburyport, Massachusetts, on 30 September 1770 in the midst of his seventh trip to Britain's colonies. His death was widely noted, but he was not praised universally. It brought his critics forward in a way that demonstrated again how revivalism not only renewed American Protestantism but also divided it. The clearest sign of this came with the burial of Whitefield's body. The funeral was reportedly attended by thousands of spectators. Moderates and liberals such as Stiles found this hard to believe, given how small and remote Newburyport was, and in any case thought it an unseemly display of emotion. Even more seriously they considered the emphasis on Whitefield as a saintly figure akin to superstition or to Roman Catholicism's veneration for its saints. As the years passed there was even more basis for this criticism. In 1775 an army chaplain and a group of officers including Benedict Arnold entered Whitefield's tomb to view his body. They commented upon its state of decomposition and passed around the clerical collar and wristbands for closer examination. This viewing of the body happened repeatedly into the early nineteenth century by Christians desiring closer contact with the minister most closely associated with the origins of the revival. Ironically, as critics claimed, honoring a man this way contradicted the focus on God which Whitefield had preached so relentlessly. It also suggested how traditional beliefs in saints and superstitions survived not only the coming of Protestantism but also the renewal of purity that the revivals of the revolutionary period successfully prompted. Revivalism was indeed a complex force in American culture.

Sources:

Jon Butler, *Awash in a Sea of Faith* (Cambridge, Mass.: Harvard University Press, 1990);

Edwin S. Gaustad, *The Great Awakening in New England* (New York: Harper, 1957);

Wesley M. Gewehr, *The Great Awakening in Virginia, 1740–1790* (Durham: Duke University Press, 1930);

C. C. Goen, *Revivalism and Separatism in New England, 1740–1800* (New Haven: Yale University Press, 1962);

William G. McLoughlin, *Revivals, Awakenings, and Reform* (Chicago: University of Chicago Press, 1978);

Susan O'Brien, "A Transatlantic Community of Saints: The Great Awakening and the First Evangelical Network, 1735–1755," *American Historical Review*, 91 (1986): 811–832;

Leigh Schmidt, *Holy Fairs* (Princeton, N.J.: Princeton University Press, 1989);

Harry S. Stout, *The Divine Dramatist: George Whitefield and the Rise of Modern Evangelicalism* (Grand Rapids, Mich.: W. B. Eerdmans, 1991);

Leonard J. Trinterud, *The Forming of an American Tradition* (Philadelphia: Westminster Press, 1949).

SECTARIANISM

Sectarian Impulse. The revolutionary era saw the beginnings of a more diverse religious society than America or Europe had ever known. The basis of the religious pluralism of the United States today lay in the new religious movements of the 1770s and 1780s. Even earlier, groups of revivalists had broken away from the established churches of New England and the Chesapeake Bay area to form new religious communities. But these groups of Virginia Baptists or New Light Congregationalists did not reject the basic Calvinist theology that most English settlers had brought with them to the New World. During the revolutionary years a few new groups made a more radical attack on those Calvinist premises. In doing this they exhibited one of the most common features of Protestantism, the tendency of some people to break away from the dominant church and form a new group, or sect. This sectarian impulse had its roots in the Protestant belief that all individuals are able to read and interpret the Bible for themselves. This belief made the formation of new, individualized religious groups possible. In addition the lack of central authority in Calvinism made it difficult to control the possibility of new, unor-

Title page for *Book of Psalms*, a German-language edition published in Pennsylvania

coastal areas, where the danger of attack was great, into the relatively undeveloped interior areas of what is today Maine, New Hampshire, Vermont, and western Massachusetts. Here they experienced the privations of life on a frontier, as they struggled to clear land, start farms, and build a new society. These unsettled people also experienced one of the periodic episodes of religious revival that marked eighteenth-century life. As early as 1778 western and northern New England began to exhibit the signs of a significant religious revival, which came to be known as the New Light Stir. The New Light Stir continued into the mid 1780s, as the Baptists came to dominate the area and displace the Congregationalists as the leading denomination.

New Sects. The Baptists were the main beneficiaries of the New Light Stir, which was thus part of that group's longer-term growth across America. Yet some settlers in these areas developed even more-radical positions on religion, and at least three groups sprang up that had a lasting influence on American religion despite their relatively small size. In each case the unsettled conditions of life on the frontier led a visionary leader to develop a more radical view of religion and society. These groups rejected many traditional Christian beliefs in favor of a variety of new thoughts about the Bible, God, and the end of the world. In doing this they also reconsidered the way society should be organized, and in this respect they were participating in the main social project of the revolutionary era and helping to frame the new nation. Socially and politically this area became a hotbed of anti-Federalist feeling, home to the people most suspicious of schemes of big government and organized economic development. The religious parallel was a highly individualized spiritualism, emphasizing the direct access of believers to God. Many people considered this to be a clear challenge to more-traditional religious institutions and to the society those institutions upheld.

Shakers. Probably the best known today of these new groups was the Shakers, or the Believers in Christ's Second Appearing, as they called themselves. The Shakers began in England as an enthusiastic offshoot of a group of Quakers. They got their name from the shaking they experienced when moved by the spirit during worship. The Shakers came to America in 1774, when a group led by Ann Lee arrived in New York. Lee's spirituality had become increasingly intense over the course of a difficult life that included sickness, unhappy marriage, and even prison. She turned to increasingly radical ideas about God, ideas that she continued to develop in America. In 1776 Lee led her small group of followers to the village of Niskeyuna in the hill country north of Albany, New York. The group began to recruit converts from the area and from northern New England and slowly grew. Lee preached enthusiastically about the coming end of the world and encouraged her followers to establish a new society to prepare for the final judgment. That new society included sexual purity and the public confession of

thodox beliefs developing as people thought for themselves about religion. In colonial America religion was primarily congregational, even in the South, where Anglicanism was established, since there were no bishops or other strong central authorities. It is no surprise then, that sectarianism took hold.

Social Factors. Sectarianism is often linked to social disruption, something else that early America had in abundance. The revivals of the Great Awakening and the years after were just one sign of the social tensions that could be expressed in religious forms. Opponents of the revivals, such as Boston minister Charles Chauncy, complained about the disruptive forces let loose on society by the revivals, which they feared radically undermined the social order. In the 1770s, as the war spread through the colonies, there were other challenges to settled life, creating the conditions for new religious experiences and developments. One case occurred in rural New England. During the war years many people moved away from the

A Gothic-type baptismal wish for Stovel Ehmrich, born 23 January 1771. It reads: "Oh dear child, you were baptized into the death of Christ, who purchased you from Hell, which is blood. As a reminder of this and as a constant memorial. I gave you this drawing after your baptism. Awake to God's honor and your parents' joy, to your neighbors' benefit and bliss." (Henry Francis du Pont Winterthur Museum, Winterthur, Delaware)

sin and then the taking up of a reformed, simpler life. Eventually, Lee came to believe that the judgment day had already come and that Christ had returned to earth in her own body. The Shakers came to consider Lee the embodiment of sinless perfection and as Christ's fulfillment in a female counterpart. As recruits arrived, Lee began to envision a community organized on her principles, where all members would be celibate and share their goods and lives equally and peacefully. Lee's doctrine of pacifism combined with news of this radical lifestyle to get the attention of the authorities in Albany. In July 1780 she and six other Shakers were jailed as "enemies to the country." Lee was released the following December and in 1781 started a tour of New England that extended over two years. By that time the Shakers were beginning to establish their first settlements where they could live apart from the world and pursue their lives in their distinctive style while they awaited the fulfillment of the millennial visions Lee had found inspiration for in the Bible. The first lasting Shaker village was in New Lebanon, New York, founded in 1785. It was the model for Shaker towns that would dot New England and New York in the coming decades and that can still be visited today.

Universalists. The Universalists did not take up celibacy or believe that the end of the world had already come, but their faith that God had saved all humans from damnation was just as radical, in the context of the time. Unlike other sects, the Universalists had a presence in urban areas as well as on the frontier. English revivalist John Murray arrived in New Jersey on 21 July 1770 after being awakened to God by revivals in his home country. He became an itinerant preacher and soon became well known in the coastal towns in the Middle colonies and in New England. In 1775, following the logic of his own reading of the Scripture and of the revivalists' emphasis on the free acceptance of God that was potentially available to all, he publicly took up Universalism. In 1779 he established one of the earliest American Universalist congregations in Gloucester, Massachusetts. He persevered in his ministry despite being at times arrested, stoned by mobs, and threatened with deportation. His influence extended mainly to city dwellers, especially those already drawn to the ideas about human nature and the benevolent deity that were attractive to people there in touch with the latest European thinking.

Rural Growth. At the same time in the New England backcountry, a homegrown version of Universalism was taking hold, again as an outgrowth of the revivals. There three prophetic men led the way, Isaac Davis, Adams Streeter, and Caleb Rich. Davis preached in the Connecticut River valley, honing in on the story of how

There were probably only about 1,000 Jews in revolutionary America. Despite their small numbers, they were beginning to make their presence felt. They were also feeling the pressures of needing to acculturate to a Christian society, something that burdened the American Jewish community well into the twentieth century. One of the most important early communities was in Newport, Rhode Island. Drawn by the colony's tradition of religious freedom, the first Jews arrived there in the 1680s. Most successfully participated in the shipping and commerce of this important port city. By 1763 Congregationalist Ezra Stiles counted 15 Jewish families, with about 80 individuals. That number had grown to about 125 by 1774. The Newport Jews mostly came from the Mediterranean area, although by the Revolution some had arrived from Germany. In 1763 the community dedicated their first permanent home, a building today called the Touro Synagogue, named in honor of Isaac Touro, the lay leader of the group. The synagogue was designed by Peter Harrison, who had earlier designed the home of Newport's Redwood Library, one of America's first private libraries. Harrison gave the community a synagogue in the Palladian style, then popular in England. The building was elegantly proportioned, symmetrically arranged, and detailed with classical elements. The interior was modeled after the synagogue of a wealthy London community and while arranged in the traditional form also conformed to the neoclassical style. The building captured the desire of this community to be true to their distinct heritage, as well as to conform to the standards of their Christian neighbors. The balance the Newport Jewish community tried to strike between their past and America's future was precarious and short lived, however. Many of the Jews sided with the British during the war, drawn to them through the commercial connections of their families. The long British occupation of Newport and the eventual American victory were serious blows to the Jewish community. By the early 1800s the community had completely collapsed.

Source: Eli Faber, *A Time for Planting: The First Migration, 1654–1820* (Baltimore: Johns Hopkins University Press, 1992), pp. 84–88.

Christ's suffering and death atoned for the sin of Adam once and for all. As early as 1775 a number of Davisonians withdrew to form a Universalist congregation in Oxford, Massachusetts. Adams may have been influenced by Davis, as he passed from being a Separate Congregationalist, then a Baptist, to finally a Universalist, taking over Davis's leadership role. Rich had the widest influence of the three. Long-term religious conflict in his family in the 1760s and early 1770s led Rich to a series of visions, in which a "still small voice" led him to accept Universalist principles, and an angel presented him with biblical texts with which to instruct others. Rich was attacked as a heretic by his Baptist neighbors, but in 1773 he and a few others formed a separate religious society and started attracting new members. Further visions of angels and even of Christ himself in 1778 pushed Rich to an even more radical position, as he now came to preach about the imminent end of the world as well. Rich was also impressed by Christ's easy manner with him during his vision, which emphasized the dignity of all humans since all had been saved equally, and he began to add a call for egalitarianism to his ministry as well.

Freewill Baptists. This group traced its start to the death of George Whitefield, the English evangelist of the Great Awakening. Whitefield's death in 1770 greatly moved Benjamin Randel, who had heard Whitefield preach a week before and had found him a "worthless, noisy fellow." Changing his first opinion while thinking of Whitefield in heaven and himself on the way to hell, Randel fell into a spiritual despair that ended with a profound experience of a new birth through the spirit. He continued to struggle with his faith, which he felt needed to be stricter, and in 1776 became a Baptist. He became an itinerant preacher and faced stonings, mobbings, and other abuses for his increasingly radical ideas. A failed attempt to settle at a church in New Hampshire led to another period of doubt and further revelations from God, who demanded even greater efforts to purity from Randel. The visions he had while praying in a cornfield in 1779 led him to reject family and congregation in favor of itinerant preaching. He spoke about the coming judgment day, about the need for Christian perfection, and most importantly about the free will humans had to accept Christ. This last point especially was a departure from the orthodox Calvinism of the Congregationalists and Baptists of the area. Randel faced down the opposition with a complete reliance on God. "I makes no odds with he who disowns me," he said, "so long as I know the Lord owns me." The first Randelite congregation formed in Strafford, New Hampshire, in August 1780, and the sect grew over the next two decades to become one of the largest groups on the Northern frontier, with more than 150 congregations by 1815.

Shared Characteristics. None of these groups was ever large or long lived, although a few Shakers still survive today. Yet their experiences have been a model for many Americans of later times. The sectarian impulse has emerged repeatedly in American history, sometimes in tiny movements that soon disappear and sometimes in movements that result in huge new religions, such as the Mormons. All of these movements have some of the elements that were shared by these three original American sects. They were each founded by a charismatic leader, one who had visions and was able to translate them into preaching that excited others to follow them. The death of these leaders created problems in how to carry on the group, which in each case involved giving the sect a more carefully considered set of beliefs and practices that could be taught to others in an organized way. Other characteristics made stability hard to achieve. The sects placed no restrictions on lay preaching, which left them open to new ideas and influences that clergy trained in seminaries or colleges would never have entertained. Many of the people joining sects were people who moved from one religious group to another frequently throughout their lives, always searching for a more perfect expression of their ideas about God. Sects drew converts from all levels of society, although in the revolutionary period they were much less prominent in the coastal cities. The notion of a pure community and the emphasis on sin and repentance was often at the forefront of sectarianism. Because of this, such groups tended to withdraw from the wider world, as the Shakers did, and form communities of their own with limited exposure to the profane ways of others. In these separate places sectarians were free to pursue an ideal world that would be a heaven on earth. These perfectionist communities often brought larger social conflicts to the surface, as they divided existing churches and even families and challenged the existing social and religious order. Emotions often ran high in these communities, founded as they were on intensely personal experiences of God's spirit. In this sense many sects had close ties to the evangelical Protestantism that was the heart of American religion in the nineteenth century even if many sects were extreme versions of tendencies within the larger denominations. Part of that extreme behavior was linked to a prevalent feeling in many sects that the end of the world was at hand. Such dire circumstances called for extreme expressions of reform and love and contributed as well to the willingness of many to reject the world.

Dissent. Finally sectarianism drew on at least one important aspect of American religion that has become a cherished part of our national identity. This is the tradition of religious dissent. Ann Lee, John Murray, Caleb Rich, and Benjamin Randel each departed from the mainstream of American religious thought and practice. Being an outsider was a basic part of their religious identity and of the identity of the groups they formed. Over the years since, strong individuals who stand up for what they believe is right against all opposition have become important symbols of American culture. Dissent is also an important means by which religion has developed in America, as freethinkers such as these sectarians have broken away from old traditions to start new ones with greater meaning for their own times. These people struggled against the opposition of their neighbors to find a way to express their ideas about God that were relevant to the unsettled conditions of life in revolutionary-era America. This process is so fundamental to American so-

ciety that after the end of the Revolution, it became embedded in the First Amendment to the Constitution, which protected dissent by guaranteeing freedom of speech and freedom of religion.

Sources:

Stephen A. Marini, *Radical Sects of Revolutionary New England* (Cambridge, Mass.: Harvard University Press, 1982);

Sidney E. Mead, *The Lively Experiment* (New York: Harper & Row, 1963);

R. Laurence Moore, *Religious Outsiders and the Making of Americans* (New York: Oxford University Press, 1986);

Stephen J. Stein, *The Shaker Experience in America* (New Haven, Conn.: Yale University Press, 1992).

SLAVERY AND AFRICAN AMERICAN RELIGION

Christianization. One of the most important developments in African American culture in this era was the spread of Christianity within both the slave and free black communities. In the Southern colonies, where most American slaves lived, Anglican missionaries led the way. Their efforts were directed at both white and black populations, as preachers tried to bring all Americans to Christ. Slavery was an important feature of this religious task. Part of the groundwork for this development was in the preaching of George Whitefield, the English revivalist who visited America seven times between 1738 and 1770. Whitefield called for the conversion of the slaves. He considered it the duty of slave owners to bring their slaves to Christ. Whitefield and his colleagues stressed the duties of masters to care for their slaves in a humane way and developed an ethic of Christian paternalism that was a basic tenet of the American slave system. In exchange for this care preachers told their slave converts that they owed absolute obedience to their owners, just as they did to God. This worked to the slaves' disadvantage, on the whole, as religion offered support for punishment of slaves' misdeeds. The cruelty of slave owners was much less likely to be punished, nor did the missionaries question the justice of the slave-holding system. Anglican missionaries worked especially hard to ensure that their religion supported the orderly, hierarchical world of slave labor, meeting the needs of their white planter supporters. But the relation between Christianity and slavery was uneasy. Whitefield brought many Americans to Christ during his visits, and his followers brought even more into the fold as they began preaching a more evangelical and emotional form of Christianity than had existed in America before the 1750s. During the revolutionary era Christianity would come to challenge slavery as well as support it.

Evangelicalism's Challenge. The introduction of slaves to Christianity was feared by many European Americans, however. They recognized that Christianity, especially in the evangelical form coming into prominence in the mid 1700s, provided a basis for antislavery feelings. They feared that slaves brought to the freedom of Christianity would begin agitating for freedom from

SLAVES AND CHRISTIAN FREEDOM

One of the earliest petitions from African Americans seeking their freedom came from a group of slaves in Massachusetts. In 1774 they petitioned the Massachusetts legislature for their liberty in a document that shows how political freedom and religious freedom mingled together for at least some early Americans. That only some understood this link is shown by Massachusetts's failure to respond to the plea of these men; slavery began to end in the state only after a judicial decision against it in the early 1780s.

Your Petitioners apprehind we have in common with all other men a naturel right to our freedoms without Being depriv'd of them by our fellow men as we are a freeborn Pepel and have never forfeited this Blessing by aney compact or agreement whatever. But we were unjustly dragged by the cruel hand of power from our dearest frinds and sum of us stolen from the bosoms of our tender Parents and from a Populous Pleasant and plentiful country and Brought hither to be made slaves for Life in a Christian land. Thus we are deprived of every thing that hath a tendency to make life even tolerable, the endearing ties of husband and wife we are strangers to. . . . By our deplorable situation we are rendered incapable of shewing our obedience to Almighty God how can a slave perform the duties of a husband to a wife or parent to his child How can a husband leave master and work and cleave to his wife How can the wife submit themselves to there husbands in all things. How can the child obey thear parents in all things. There is a grat number of us sencear . . . members of the Church of Christ how can the master and the slave be said to fulfill that command Live in love let Brotherly Love contuner and abound Beare ye onenothers Bordenes. How can the master be said to Beare my Borden when he Beares me down whith the Have chanes of slavery and oppression against my will?

Source: "To Gov. Thomas Gage and the Massachusetts General Court, May 25, 1774," *Collections of the Massachusetts Historical Society*, 5th ser. 3 (1877), pp. 432–433.

bondage as well. The dramatic experiences of some Christians during the revivals of the Great Awakening of the 1740s and 1750s brought this danger home. For example, Hugh Bryan, a South Carolina slave owner, became caught up in the religious enthusiasm that followed a visit from Whitefield in 1740. Whitefield took a stand against slavery, and Bryan soon followed him and began preaching against slavery as a sin warning about God's coming punishment. Significantly he raised the threat of slave uprisings, hitting a nerve in the colony that had recently experienced the Stono Rebellion, the most serious slave insurrection in colonial times. Bryan then began to preach to the slaves themselves. He cast himself as a new Moses who would lead the slaves to freedom as the biblical Moses led the Israelites from captivity in Egypt.

Bryan was an extremist who symbolized the fears of many Americans about the overenthusiasm of revivalistic Christianity. His ministry had little practical effect, as over time Bryan abandoned his antislavery position and took up life once again as a respectable planter and slaveholder. Yet his brief career as a Christian abolitionist demonstrated that African American Christianity was a potentially significant threat to the established order of society and religion.

Christian Egalitarianism. In addition to individual preachers who argued that slaveholding was sinful, there was an antislavery message embedded within the forms of Christianity that spread in the revivals from the 1740s on. The key idea was the equality of all believers in Christ. Evangelicals preached that Christ called all humans to repentance for their sins and to faith in God's saving power. There was no different treatment for blacks and whites. They preached the power of the conversion moment as an intense realization of the truth of these statements in experience. Preachers worked to produce these conversion experiences in all their listeners, white and black. Both groups responded, sharing the emotions and the ecstatic behaviors of people coming together to Christ, and blacks as well as whites left these experiences feeling they had the ability to preach to others about them in turn. As the revivals spread throughout the South in the 1750s and 1760s, the power and challenge of Christian equality became apparent. In Maryland and Virginia, for example, this racial equality within religious experience presented a direct challenge to the prevailing order. The established Anglican religion was marked by much more formality and distance between minister and laity, between whites and blacks. Anglicanism's decline was in part due to the appeal of the new evangelicalism to people, such as slaves, who had felt excluded from the old order. One revivalist preacher noted in 1757 the appeal of his kind of emotional, freewheeling religion for slaves especially, in a way that suggested the revolutionary potential of this faith. He wrote that "Many of them only seem to desire to be, they know not what: they feel themselves uneasy in their *present* condition, and therefore desire a *change*." The rebirth, or renewal, slaves found in revivalistic Christianity was just one sign of a broader rebirth in freedom that many hoped to share.

Slavery and Methodism. Some Baptists drew on their own egalitarian tradition to oppose slavery, but it was the Methodists who took the evangelical challenge to slavery to the furthest extreme in the revolutionary era. At this time the Methodists were a reform movement within the Anglican Church. As it became a separate group with the coming of war and the disestablishment of the Anglicans, it was centrally organized, following Anglican tradition. Policies set by the group's leaders were harder to ignore at the local level than for the Baptists who let each congregation govern itself. English Methodists such as John Wesley joined American followers such as Francis

Asbury and Thomas Coke in condemning slavery as evil and un-Christian. Freeborn Garrettson, a Methodist minister and former slaveholder, was struck one day while singing a hymn about Christian freedom by the contradiction of holding fellow humans in bondage. He claimed the experience of conversion had changed his life so much that it was as if he had never owned slaves, so free from his earlier sin he felt. Other early American Methodists agreed, and the denomination's governing body, the Methodist Conference, took stands against slavery and the slave trade in its meetings in 1780, 1783, and 1784. Methodist revivalists such as Thomas Rankin often preached to large crowds of blacks and whites meeting together, and they noted with approval the special enthusiasm of their African American converts. Rankin described a 1776 meeting where feelings were so high he begged people to compose themselves. "But they could not," he wrote, "some on their knees, and some on their faces, were crying mightily to God all the time I was preaching. Hundreds of Negroes were among them, with the tears streaming down their faces." Methodism was a Southern religion, however, and as the egalitarian ideals of the Revolutionary War period faded a bit, the intransigence of slaveholders increased. Faced with outspoken objections to their policies, Methodist leaders abandoned their antislavery positions beginning in 1785 although they continued to try to convert slaves.

Christian Runaways. These lessons were not lost on African Americans themselves, who took matters into their own hands when possible. Notices about runaway slaves often blamed religion for their disobedience. In 1767 the Virginian owner of the runaway Jupiter described him as "a great Newlight preacher" who had fled when his master had punished him for "stirring up the Negroes to insurrection." Five years later another Virginian advertised the escape of Primus, who had "been a Preacher ever since he was sixteen Years of Age, and has done much Mischief in his Neighborhood." Likewise another slave named Sam came to flee bondage after being "raised in a family of religious persons, commonly called Methodists;" he had "lived with some of them . . . on terms of perfect equality." Colonial newspapers were filled with such accounts, which were warnings against the bad effects of Christianizing blacks.

Black Preachers. African Americans slowly began to take leadership positions in their religious lives, roles that would lead to other forms of leadership and protest, just as so many European Americans feared. They pursued their opportunities in the face of strong and direct opposition from white leaders throughout the colonies, and the coming of the Revolution did little to ease that opposition. Once again they were helped in this by the evangelical emphasis on conversion. With experience as the basis of religious authority, being educated was not a requirement for preaching, and slaves could start their own ministries. In 1776 an Anglican attacked this trend, criticizing his evangelical rivals because the "most illiter-

<table>
<tr><td>

AN EVANGELIST REACHES OUT TO SLAVES

Samuel Davies was a leader of the Presbyterian revivals in rural Virginia in the 1750s. Like many other revivalists, Davies was interested in bringing African slaves to Christ, along with their white masters. In 1757 and 1761 he and some other likeminded ministers published a series of letters in London describing their efforts with America's slave population with an eye to encouraging English aid. Davies supported his efforts, noting that African Americans seemed to want the benefits of the revival experience. "Many of them," he wrote, "only seem to desire to be, they know not what: they feel themselves uneasy in their *present* condition, and therefore desire a *change*." Change did come to some. "There is a general alteration among them for the better. The sacred hours of the Sabbath, that used to be spent in frolicking, dancing, and other profane courses, are now employed in attending upon public ordinances, in learning to read at home, or in praying together, and singing the praises of God and the Lamb." Davies knew well the differences between his white and black adherents. He baptized them only "after they had been Catechumens for some time, and given credible evidence, not only of their acquaintance with the important doctrines of the Christian religion, but also of a deep sense of these things upon their spirits, and a life of the strictest Morality and Piety. As they are not sufficiently polished to dissemble with a good grace, they express the sensations of their minds so much in the language of simple nature, and with such genuine indications of Sincerity, that it is impossible to suspect the possession of some of them." Davies praised their religious fervor and hoped that the "poor African slaves will be made the Lord's free men."

Sources: Samuel Davies, *Letters* (London, 1761), p. 15;

Mechal Sobel, *The World They Made Together* (Princeton, N.J.: Princeton University Press, 1987), pp. 181, 183–184.

</td></tr>
</table>

ate among them are their Teachers even Negroes speak in their meetings." By the end of the 1700s there was a significant group of black preachers, especially among the Baptists. One early example was Lewis, a slave in Northern Virginia, who in 1782 was preaching to crowds as large as four hundred people. Sometimes black preachers spoke to white or mixed audiences, but their most important work was among other black slaves, whom few white preachers cared to address.

Slave Churches. Black ministers were crucial figures in the development of African American religion and culture. They were uniquely situated to combine elements of European Christianity, African rituals and traditions, and the actual experience of the slaves. Over time slave communities began to establish congregations, served by local slave preachers, or itinerant free black preachers. One example was the success of an independent black church in the neighborhood of Jamestown, Virginia. Led by a man named Gowen, in 1781 it numbered some two hundred members. Probably the first such congregation was founded in the early 1770s in Silver Bluff, South Carolina, close to Savannah, Georgia. This congregation began when a white Baptist converted eight slaves owned by George Galphin. One was named David George, and he became a gifted preacher. When the white minister fled as the British occupied Savannah in 1778, George became the congregation's minister, but this was only the first step in his independent career. As the war continued he eventually moved on to Charleston, South Carolina, and in 1782 left for Nova Scotia, founding a church for black refugees there. The 1790s brought him to Sierra Leone, where he founded yet another Baptist congregation. Jesse Galphin and George Liele were two more preachers who got their starts in Silver Bluff. Galphin became an itinerant based in his First African Church in Augusta, Georgia. Liele ended up leading a church with more than 350 members in Jamaica, but not before he had converted a slave named Andrew Bryan around 1780. Bryan was owned by the brother of Hugh Bryan, the early antislavery evangelist. During the 1780s Andrew Bryan gathered a black Baptist church in Savannah that had more than two hundred communicants in 1790. These examples show the highly personal networks through which Christianity spread among African Americans. It was only after the revolutionary era that black Christianity would come into full flower, but the seeds were planted in the important and difficult work of men such as David George and Andrew Bryan.

African Traditions. Africans brought to America as slaves came with their own religious beliefs and practices. The concerted effort to make slaves Christians combined with the dispersal of the African population across the colonies to break down these religions as organized systems. But elements of many African practices and beliefs survived among Africans and were passed on to later generations. These practices merged with Christian beliefs in many cases to form a distinctive and highly varied African American Christianity. The full development of this religion would await the growth of the large plantations in the South between the Revolution and the Civil War. Yet there is evidence, however scarce, that the pieces were present in this earlier time. Beliefs in magical powers and in the ability of certain people to "conjure" or invoke the spirits in various ways seem to have prevailed among many African Americans. Many also seem to have practiced special rituals related to healing physical and emotional sickness, with amulets, foods, and spells that supposedly could help friends or hurt enemies. Special burial rituals were also practiced, especially for slaves who never became Christians. They might be buried in carefully arranged ways, with valued objects to help them on their journeys. African Americans were by no means alone in having these beliefs in this time; many whites had similar ideas about witchcraft and magic and practiced their own versions of healing rituals. Traditional African practices could easily overlap Christian rituals, as the ecstatic visions of ancestors in the spirit world could correspond to the emotional outpourings of the Holy Spirit during a revival. Many European Americans even took up African beliefs, in modified forms. Such exchanges were never truly free or equal, however. Even in the realm of religion, blacks and whites might share a faith and even a meetinghouse, but whites always came first. In 1762, when Whitefield visited Virginia, the church quickly filled with an overflow crowd of both races. An observer noted, "Mr. Whitefield was obliged to make the negroes go out to make room for the white people."

Sources:

Jon Butler, *Awash in a Sea of Faith* (Cambridge, Mass.: Harvard University Press, 1990);

Sylvia R. Frey, *Water from the Rock: Black Resistance in a Revolutionary Age* (Princeton, N.J.: Princeton University Press, 1991);

Albert J. Raboteau, *Slave Religion: The "Invisible Institution" in the Antebellum South* (Oxford: Oxford University Press, 1978);

Leigh Eric Schmidt, "'The Grand Prophet,' Hugh Bryan: Early Evangelicalism's Challenge to the Establishment and Slavery in the Colonial South," in *Colonial America*, edited by Stanley Katz and others, 4th edition (New York: McGraw-Hill, 1993), pp. 604–616;

Mechal Sobel, *The World They Made Together* (Princeton, N.J.: Princeton University Press, 1987).

WOMEN AND RELIGION

Women in Church. Eighty years before the American Revolution began, the Puritan minister Cotton Mather observed that "there are far more godly women in the world than there are godly men." Mather's statement is one of the basic facts of the social history of American religion. In every religion, in almost every time and place, women outnumber men as church members. The support of women for organized religion in the revolutionary period was crucial even though they rarely had public roles to play. During this period women made up an increasingly large proportion of church members. Membership patterns in the Congregational churches of New England demonstrate this. During the entire revolutionary era women consistently made up more than half of most congregations. From 1730 to 1770 an average of 59 percent of all new church members were women. From 1770 to 1800 that number rose to 64 percent, and after 1800 it would grow again, to 69 percent. People at the time were well aware of this trend, given women's presence at the revivals of the era. In 1767 minister John Cleaveland of Ipswich, Massachusetts, reported on a revival that began during a meeting of a "considerable Number of the Youth, chiefly Females," and led to the conversion of ninety new church members, two-thirds of them women. These statistics reveal important develop-

Tapestry depicting a New England wedding in 1765 (Old North Church, Boston)

ments in the shaping of American religious culture. The stories of individual women, however, bring such statistics to life.

Faith Robinson Trumbull. Faith Trumbull was a pious Congregationalist and the daughter and great-granddaughter of ministers. She was also the wife of Connecticut's governor Jonathan Trumbull, the only colonial governor who supported the independence movement. Her son, John Trumbull, would aid the new nation by becoming one of its most prominent painters, taking the battles and heroes of the Revolution as his frequent topics. Faith Trumbull combined some of the attributes of her husband and son, expressing her political feelings in artistic form. Significantly it was religion that made it possible for her, a woman with no public role as a politician or artist, to do this. Sometime between the Stamp

Act crisis of 1765 and the onset of the Revolutionary War in 1775, she produced a piece of needlework depicting a scene from the Bible that was an allegory for the political events of her time. The scene was the death of Absalom, a son of King David who had rejected his father's authority and led a revolution against Israel's leader. Absalom suffered for his sin as he became caught in the branches of a tree and died from hanging. Many ministers, as well as Faith Trumbull, used this story to comment on America's rebellion against its king and figurative father, George III. David, like George, was noted for his interest in centralizing power over his subjects and the immorality of his court. He was also genuinely esteemed by his people, something that captures the difficulty many Americans had reconciling desire for freedom with sincere reverence for their legitimate king. The notion of the rebellious son resonated with many

Americans in this period. Absalom's tragic death was at once a warning to Americans to proceed carefully, as well as a hopeful sign of possible reconciliation since in the biblical story Absalom's death causes the grieving king to forgive his wayward son. In this small piece of cloth Trumbull used an art form practiced almost exclusively by women to express this complex political stance that was simultaneously an endorsement of revolutionary feeling and a caution against going too far with it. The work is filled with symbols combining political and religious feelings. A dove stands for peaceful relations and the Holy Spirit; Absalom is figured as a martyred rebel and the crucified Christ. Unlike her husband, Trumbull had few opportunities to express her political feelings and here found a homely means to do so in a way appropriate for the women's roles of the period. That she used religion to do so shows that women, like men, found a close correspondence between their faith and their revolution, even if they expressed themselves differently.

Patriotic Spinning. Trumbull's political statement was itself a religious activity, something true for other women as well. During the 1760s and 1770s resistance to British rule took the form of economic measures such as the nonimportation movement of 1769. Women had an important role in this movement because they were the ones able to produce what was no longer being imported. In many cases women came to this patriotic duty with a sense of religious obligation. Ezra Stiles, one of the ministers of Newport, Rhode Island, encouraged the linking of politics and religious feeling in his female congregants. He hosted a spinning bee at his home in 1769, during which women used thirty-seven spinning wheels to produce ninety-four skeins of valuable linen yarn. The women made a gift of their labor and the yarn to the church, and Stiles saw that it was used patriotically. Spinning bees continued yearly until war broke out, with up to seventy wheels spinning in Stiles's home. Similar bees were held throughout New England, at least thirty in 1769 alone. On one Sunday in November 1775 the minister of Litchfield, Connecticut, told his congregation about the suffering of American troops in Canada. The women of the church responded by spinning and knitting for the men all afternoon even though no work was to be done on Sunday, except for truly religious purposes. Clearly ministers successfully cast such work as a virtuous service to God and country. These meetings foreshadowed the vast religious humanitarian movement that emerged in the early national period, an effort largely undertaken and funded by women. In the revolutionary era, spinning meetings were a chance for women to be patriotic, public, and pious all at once.

Mary Gould Almy. Religion was a resource available to women on both sides of the political issues of the revolutionary period. Mary Gould married Benjamin Almy in 1762 in Newport, Rhode Island. Both hailed from families that had once been Quaker but now worshiped at a variety of Newport's many churches. Benjamin was a member of the Second Congregational Church, led by liberal Stiles, while his wife was a lifelong member of Trinity Church, Newport's Anglican community. Liberal Congregationalism shared many features with Anglicanism in the years leading up to the American Revolution, but the politics of the two churches could not be more different. Because they belonged to Britain's state church, headed by the king, the Anglicans generally resisted the independence movement and were the core of the Loyalist groups in most of the colonies. Mary Almy was no exception and remained a Loyalist throughout the war. Her husband was a Patriot and fought for the American side when the conflict broke open in 1775. This was not an easy situation for the Almys since it meant that Mary was rejecting her husband's authority in favor of her own interpretation of God's will, something that was not lightly done by an eighteenth-century woman. Some of her anxiety over this choice emerged in a letter she wrote her husband in 1778. While Benjamin was off fighting, Mary was left in Newport during the British occupation and was there to face the French-American invasion of the city in late July. When it was over she wrote to her husband, criticizing the French allies and asserting her continuing support for British rule. Yet she was also concerned for Benjamin's fate even though he fought for the other side, and she turned to God to ensure her husband's safety. "At last I shut myself from the family," she wrote, "to implore Heaven to protect you, and keep you from imprisonment and death." Prayer was the only way to reconcile the political and religious conflict that divided her family. She was not alone in this. Perhaps a third of Newport's families were divided religiously, and as churches divided on the political issues of the day, so too did families. The burden of this division necessarily fell on the mothers and wives of the day.

Mary Silliman. One woman who recorded her struggle to understand God's will for her life during the revolutionary conflict was Mary Silliman of Fairfield, Connecticut. Silliman's husband, Gold Selleck Silliman, was a prominent member of the Connecticut militia and the state's attorney in his town at the outbreak of war. He was instrumental in convicting local Tories of disloyalty. In retaliation Silliman was kidnapped and held by the British authorities for almost a year, leaving his wife, pregnant at the time, to manage the farm, raise the children, and endure the sacking of the village by the British. Religion helped Mary endure this and other wartime problems, and she mingled pious and military images in her writing. In 1776 she described to her husband a day of prayer and fasting she kept as "wrestling for you and our bleeding land," and she hoped that she had "in some measure acted the heroine as well as my dear Husband the Hero." Mary persevered, aided by a strong sense of the duty owed by women to submit to the judgment of men and by all humans to acknowledge the power of God. It was this religious doctrine, learned from her father, who was a minister, and from the pious woman who taught the school she attended, that sustained her during these times. Her letters and journal indicate that it was a powerful doctrine for her but also one with which she struggled. She resented the tests she had to endure but found meaning and comfort in what she called "the way of duty." In the end she agreed with her father, who wrote to ask "Where should our Friends be, and where are they safest, but there, where the Lord calls them, where their Duty lies? There only may we hope for & expect protection, even where we are serving God."

Women in Ministry. Very few women in the revolutionary era were able to become religious authorities in their own right, transcending at least in the sphere of religion the strictures on women's public lives that most early Americans took for granted. One example was Sarah Osborn, another woman from Newport, Rhode Island. Osborn was touched by the revivals of the Great Awakening and for the rest of her life sought to bring that experience to others in her congregation. In the course of this work she became the true center of that church, and even her minister credited her efforts as at least as important as his own. An even more dramatic example is Quaker Elizabeth Ashbridge. Women had greater freedom among the Quakers, at least as far as being religious leaders went, since that group had no ordained ministers and their participatory style of worship left room for women as well as men to speak publicly. Ashbridge endured an unusually harsh life, even by the standards of eighteenth-century women. She was widowed at an early age after marrying against her father's wishes and emigrated to America only to be unjustly placed into indentured servitude for four years. She was briefly an actor and dancer in New York. A second marriage brought no more happiness, as her husband abused her frequently, in part because she had become a convert to Quakerism. She also became a minister and traveled from place to place across Pennsylvania and New Jersey, speaking at Quaker meetings about God's presence. She drew directly from her experiences as a woman to do this, although that experience was hardly limited to the domestic sphere. Ashbridge provided a model for godliness in a way that expanded women's roles, even as it spoke to how those roles were limited by the American conditions she knew too well. She had an expansive vision of her ministry as well and in 1753 asked to be allowed to go to Ireland and pursue her preaching vocation there. She left behind an account of her life, first published in 1774, which enabled her work to continue after her death. Even though eighteenth-century women could not be ministers in the formal sense, examples such as Osborn and Ashbridge show they pursued a ministry of just as much value to the church and the nation.

Female Virtue. Religious women contributed in one other way to America's revolutionary history despite their limited public lives in this era. They provided a way of talking about what made America different from the rest of the world, and in doing this, religion helped women to contribute significantly to independence. The republican language that lay behind the speeches, pamphlets, songs, and sermons of the revolutionary era centered on the discussion of virtue. The civic virtue of caring about the country enough to serve it in politics or war would make the new nation prosper. While the military and political worlds were male worlds, virtue in this period was also a concept closely associated with women, especially religious women. The revivalistic preaching of the revolutionary era strongly emphasized the connection between virtue and God's grace. Only the reception of grace could produce true virtue, the disinterested benevolence that evangelical Protestants such as Jonathan Edwards and Samuel Hopkins talked about. That disinterested benevolence was the religious corollary to the ideal of civic service, for the sake of the country, not from self-interest. In making this connection religious thinkers of the period argued that religion was an essential support for the nation. Women were the key link in the chain, something increasingly made clear in the sermons and other writings of the 1770s and 1780s. For example, the sermon preached in New Haven, Connecticut, for Mary Clap's funeral in 1769 stressed her piety as a feminine virtue, one that led to a seemingly blameless and selfless life of service to others. Women were seen by many people of the time as especially open to the work of the spirit, and their growing dominance of the churches and revival meetings confirmed this idea. Women raising sons were also the people most responsible for training the next generation of leaders. Pious women could receive the gift of virtue from God and teach children how to do the same and so insure the safety of the republic. For many religious Americans the Revolution was a matter of reformed behavior as well as a new political order. While it was not a public effort, women had the leading roles in that campaign.

Sources:

Joy and Richard Buel, *The Way of Duty* (New York: Norton, 1984);

Elaine Forman Crane, "Religion and Rebellion: Women of Faith in the American War for Independence," in *Religion in a Revolutionary Age*, edited by Ronald Hoffman and Peter J. Albert (Charlottesville: University Press of Virginia, 1994);

Cristine Levenduski, *Peculiar Power: A Quaker Woman Preacher in Eighteenth-Century America* (Washington: Smithsonian Institution Press, 1996);

Richard D. Shiels, "The Feminization of American Congregationalism, 1730–1835," *American Quarterly*, 33 (1981): 46–62;

Laurel Thatcher Ulrich, "'Daughters of Liberty': Religious Women in Revolutionary New England," in *Women in the Age of the American Revolution*, edited by Hoffman and Albert (Charlottesville: University Press of Virginia, 1989).

HEADLINE MAKERS

JOSEPH BELLAMY

1719-1790
NEW DIVINITY LEADER

Local Origins. Although he became one of early America's most widely known religious figures, Joseph Bellamy spent most of his life working in rural Connecticut. He was born in Wallingford, Connecticut, on 20 February 1719. Bellamy was raised on a farm, yet attended Yale College, graduating at the age of sixteen in 1735. From Yale he became an informal student of Jonathan Edwards, who was the minister of Northampton, Massachusetts, and the most sophisticated theologian of eighteenth-century America. Edwards was a leader of the revivals of the Great Awakening, and Bellamy followed him in promoting that work. In November 1758 Bellamy became the minister of a newly formed church in Bethlehem, in rural Litchfield County on the Connecticut frontier. He remained in that pulpit for the rest of his life, although he preached widely in Connecticut, bringing his fervent preaching about the "new birth" that was the center of the emerging evangelical wing of New England Congregationalism to many people.

Consistent Calvinism. Bellamy's great contribution to American culture was the development of the New Divinity theology, or Consistent Calvinism, as its adherents called it. Bellamy built on the thinking of his teacher, Edwards, whose work allowed old ideas to speak to a new generation. In a series of books published in the 1740s and 1750s Edwards had revitalized traditional New England Puritanism by blending its core ideas drawn from the work of the sixteenth-century Protestant Reformer John Calvin, with the psychology and philosophy developed by John Locke at the end of the 1600s. Bellamy continued this work. In his own preaching and writing he continued to emphasize the central tenets of traditional Calvinism, including the ideas of natural human depravity, God's predestination of the elect for salvation, and the necessity of conversion to Christ. But he developed the notion of God as a moral governor, in response to the eighteenth-century Enlightenment emphasis on reason and fairness in the governance of the universe. He explained the presence of sin in moral terms, as something that God permitted in order to allow for the exercise of justice and forgiveness rather than as something actively caused by God as punishment for Adam's fall from grace. Christ's death, therefore, was not meant to satisfy God's anger but to express God's love for his straying children. Bellamy saw these ideas as consistent with the religion of his Puritan forebears, but in fact they were important modifications of the orthodox Calvinism that had prevailed in New England to that time.

Social Theology. Bellamy also went further; he was especially concerned with the social aspects of religion and considered Edwards's thought lacking in its ability to address the complex moral problems of the revolutionary era. Bellamy's preaching emphasized God's law and the responsibility of his listeners to honor God by obeying it. But instead of obeying the moral law in order to earn their salvation, Bellamy argued that true Christians would obey the law because they had already been saved by God, or regenerated. For him, part of his religious work was to spread morality, and so he came to focus on promoting the godly society, as well as encouraging the individual conversions that were behind that society. For example, while his sermons tried to convince the individuals in his church of their need to reject sin and embrace God, he also founded one of the first regular Sunday schools in order to teach morality to the entire community. He argued that the emerging market economy encouraged selfishness and sinfulness. He praised thrifty yeoman farmers, who were more interested in a stable family life than in amassing a fortune, and offered a vision of a new economy based on love of God, not greed. As Bellamy became a socially and politically important figure in Connecticut, he expanded his ideas to include government, which he thought also should have the moral order as its goal. This position led Bellamy to support the independence movement in 1776, when he concluded that British rule only encouraged immorality and injustice. From this time on he added republican language to his sermons, painting the new nation as a just and moral society organized on godly principles. He and his colleagues praised liberty, but it was a liberty that existed within the order established by God. As Americans established their own government and society, Bellamy was not afraid to criticize them for departing from God's way, even as he praised them for departing from England's way. Doing this, Bellamy laid a groundwork for the social reform efforts of American Protestants in the nineteenth century, one of the principal legacies of the New Divinity movement.

Later Career. Bellamy's ideas became influential even though he rarely left his own pulpit in Connecticut. In 1750 he published *True Religion Delineated,* a huge book outlining his ideas and describing the way to come to Christ. In many reprints, it became one of the steady sellers of early America, found in many families' homes. Bellamy was also an educator, beginning a seminary of sorts in his own home, taking in college-age men and newly established preachers, teaching them about "true religion" and how ministers could promote it. He taught many of the leading ministers of the late 1700s, including Jonathan Edwards Jr., Nathaniel Niles, John Smalley, and David Austin. These men in turn reached others and together formed the core of an important group of evangelical Protestants that came to dominate American religion through the revivals of the 1800s. Between 1765 and 1783 Bellamy's students took more than half of the parish appointments available in New England, and the New Divinity dominated the sermons heard by people in the interior of New England. Stiles recognized Bellamy's importance when he termed him the "Pope of Litchfield County" and worked to prevent the spread of his ideas at liberal Yale College. Bellamy died on 6 March 1790.

Source:
Mark Valeri, *Law and Providence in Joseph Bellamy's New England* (New York: Oxford University Press, 1994).

CHARLES CHAUNCY

1705-1787
LIBERAL CONGREGATIONALIST

Boston Roots. Charles Chauncy spent most of his life in Boston, becoming a leader of the liberal wing of New England Congregationalism from his post as pastor of the city's leading church. He was born on 1 January 1705 into a prominent family, the son of a leading merchant and great-grandson of the second president of Harvard College. After attending Boston Latin School he too graduated from Harvard, in 1721. Chauncy settled into the pastorate of Boston's First Congregational Church on 25 October 1727, where he stayed for sixty years. This position, combined with his intellectual power and strongly held opinions, enabled him tobecome the most prominent preacher in eighteenth-century Boston.

Old Lights. Chauncy became best known for his leadership of the Old Light Party of Congregationalism. This group formed in opposition to the religious upheavals of the Great Awakening of the 1730s and 1740s. Chauncy and his followers objected mainly to the open emotionalism of the revivals being led by evangelical preachers such as Jonathan Edwards and George Whitefield. Chauncy was especially dismayed by the emotional preaching of James Davenport, an itinerant preacher who openly criticized ministers more wary of the new revivals and who left divided churches wherever he preached. Edwards and other leaders of the awakenings tried to distance themselves from the excesses of men such as Davenport, but Chauncy saw all participation in the revivals as dangerous to religion and social order. His 1743 book, *Seasonable Thoughts on the State of Religion in New England,* exhaustively documented these dangers and was an important statement of the principles of the emerging liberal wing of New England Congregationalism.

Rationalism. At the heart of the Old Light thinking was a faith in reason that Chauncy and his followers got from thinkers active in the Enlightenment taking shape in Europe during the 1700s. Chauncy was drawn to reason as a way of integrating experience and faith into an orderly whole. His objection to the revivals was that they gave too much sway to the emotions as the basis of faith and of one's knowledge of God, thus overemphasizing the irrational part of religious life. Unlike some believers in the power of reason, Chauncy never drifted away from Christianity toward deism. He believed in the Bible and explained it tirelessly to his parishioners as a rational exploration of the truth about God.

Universalism. Chauncy's most radical contribution to American religion was in his thinking about salvation. As early as 1762 Chauncy began to think that Christ's death had saved all humans, not only an elect few, as orthodox Calvinists believed. His reading of the Bible brought him to a belief in a benevolent, loving God, who wanted people to be happy and would never condemn humans to an eternity in hell. There would be punishment for sin, he thought, but only in proportion to the crime, and over time it would cleanse the soul and prepare it for an eventual entry into heaven. These were extremely radical ideas for the time, and he explored them cautiously, through letters and private papers exchanged with friends. He published his views only anonymously near the end of his life. Chauncy died on 10 February 1787.

Sources:
Edward M. Griffin, *Old Brick: Charles Chauncy of Boston, 1705–1787* (Minneapolis: University of Minnesota Press, 1980);

Charles H. Lippy, *Seasonable Revolutionary: The Mind of Charles Chauncy* (Chicago: Nelson-Hall, 1981).

DEVEREUX JARRATT

1733-1801
EVANGELICAL EPISCOPALIAN

Conversion. Devereux Jarratt reached his widest fame as a leader of the Great Awakening in Virginia during the 1760s and 1770s. Surprisingly he participated in this revivalist movement as an Anglican and later an Episcopalian minister. Jarratt was born near Richmond, Virginia, on 17 January 1733 and raised in the Church of England. Like many Anglican families in colonial Virginia, the Jarratts were not especially religious, and Devereux lacked any strong feelings about God until he reached adulthood. Pursuing a career as a schoolteacher, Jarratt found himself a tutor to the sons of John Cannon, an evangelical Presbyterian. He felt the first stirring of religious belief while listening to Cannon's wife read pious tracts to her children. After this first step Jarratt learned from local Presbyterian ministers already engaged in the work of religious revival. They taught him about traditional Calvinistic beliefs such as predestination, the depravity of human nature, and the need for personal salvation by God. Jarratt saw himself as called by God to preach a "vital religion" to "unawakened" people such as the religiously complacent Virginians who had raised him. He decided to become a minister.

Ministry. Jarratt traveled to England in 1762 and was ordained in the Church of England even though he had been converted by Presbyterians. He returned to Virginia in 1763 and began preaching at the church in Bath, a town in the southern reaches of the colony. His powerful, musical voice together with his intensely emotional preaching brought large crowds to his church, and his ministry rapidly expanded. He added a traveling, itinerant ministry to his regular parish duties and for more than two decades preached tirelessly across the countryside of southern Virginia and into North Carolina. Jarratt preached at large outdoor gatherings on all days of the week and was extremely popular among Virginia's lower classes, who were most likely to be drawn into this revivalist religion. He was not such a favorite of the Virginia gentry and the established Anglican ministry, whom he criticized for their licentious lifestyle and lack of attention to piety. Jarratt rarely attended clerical meetings, and the one time he preached to an Anglican convention, he took the opportunity to lecture his colleagues for being "cold and languid, slothful and vicious."

Conflict with Methodism. If Jarratt found little encouragement for his efforts from within the established Anglican Church, he was supported by a growing evangelical wing of that church, people known as the Methodists. Methodism began as a revival movement within Anglicanism. Methodist leaders such as Francis Asbury and Thomas Coke worked alongside Jarratt, and Jarratt even converted to Christ the father of Jesse Lee, later one of the most famous Methodist preachers on the nine-teenth-century frontier. Asbury, the first American Methodist bishop, credited Jarratt in 1781 with saving more souls in Virginia than any other preacher. In the years after the American Revolution the Anglicans, now called Episcopalians, fell into general disfavor for their religious coldness and their failure to support the republican cause during the war. The Methodists formed a separate denomination, and Jarratt never forgave their lack of loyalty even though he was drawn to their religious practices more than most Episcopalians. Jarratt was a proud man, and his outspokenness on Methodist failings alienated many former supporters. Several Methodists also objected to Jarratt's slaveholding. He continued to preach into the 1800s, but to ever-smaller groups. The decline in his work mirrored the decline of Episcopalianism in the South. Jarratt died in Bath from cancer on 29 January 1801. After his death his work continued with the publication of his *Autobiography* in 1806, which he had written as a model for leading a Christian life and as a last effort to bring people to the true God.

Source:
The Life of the Reverend Devereux Jarratt: An Autobiography, edited by David L. Holmes (Cleveland: Pilgrim Press, 1995).

JONATHAN MAYHEW

1720-1766
CONGREGATIONAL REVOLUTIONARY

Early Training. Jonathan Mayhew was born on the small island of Martha's Vineyard, off the Massachusetts coast, on 8 October 1720. His father, Experience Mayhew, was the missionary to the Indians there, a post the Mayhew family had filled since 1641. The Vineyard mission was one of the few successful English ventures to Christianize Native Americans, and during Jonathan's youth the Chilmark congregation, as it was called, was a peaceful church, although its numbers were declining as the Indian population decreased. Experience nurtured his converts faithfully, defending them against spurious land claims and the rigors of orthodox Calvinism, which he came to see as too harsh a system of religion for Indians and whites alike. He struggled to obtain adequate funds to support his work. Jonathan's elder brother Nathan was marked to attend college and follow in his father's footsteps as a missionary, but his early death left Jonathan to assume this family duty.

Reason. Mayhew kept his father's liberal religious ideas with him as he attended Harvard College, graduating in 1744. There he embraced the rationalist Congregationalism that was a hallmark of the training Harvard offered at that time. Particularly important was the teaching of Professor Edward Wigglesworth, a leading spokesman for rational religion and against the emotionalism of the revivals of the 1730s and 1740s. In 1742 Mayhew briefly turned to revivalism after hearing the great evangelical preacher George Whitefield, but he soon rejected that kind of religion as "low, confused, puerile, conceited, ill-natur'd, [and] enthusiastik," as he wrote to his father. In 1747 Mayhew became the minister of Boston's West Congregational Church, where he worked for the rest of his life. From this pulpit Mayhew preached a rational religion that evolved into something quite different from its Puritan roots. Mayhew became an outspoken advocate of free rational inquiry into religious truth and argued that humans had the natural ability to come closer to God through that inquiry. He was a true Enlightenment figure, thinking of the practice of Christianity as a kind of science and even reading the radical French philosophers Voltaire and Jean-Jacques Rousseau. Mayhew ended by rejecting the orthodox beliefs in the three persons of God and in the predestination of a select few for salvation in favor of a faith in a universally benevolent God who loved all humans.

Controversies. Mayhew frequently came into conflict with others over religion, politics, and even social matters. An early sign was his lateness in marrying, unusual for a young minister with a good position. Instead of settling down, Mayhew enjoyed an active social life of dining out, hunting, and fishing, although he did not attend theatrical performances, which he considered immoral. His congregation's criticism of this lifestyle ended when he married nine years after assuming his pulpit, but more serious opposition came from theological and political figures. Mayhew's rational religion took him into public debates with John Cleaveland, a leading revivalist, and Samuel Hopkins, one of Jonathan Edwards's students and a major figure in the New Divinity movement. Mayhew's temper often got the better of him in these controversies, which fostered more bad feeling than mutual understanding. As early as 1754 Mayhew began another long conflict. This time his opponent was the Society for the Propagation of the Gospel, the leading sponsor of Indian missions in colonial America. He criticized the society for using its resources in parts of New England that needed no missionaries and so failing to bring Native Americans to Christ, reflecting on the difficulties of his own family's experiences with that task.

Politics. Criticism of Anglican missions brought Mayhew to a deeper skepticism about relations between England and America, coincided with the first political tensions between the two. Mayhew spoke out against rumors that the Anglican Church was preparing to send a bishop to America to better support its efforts there. Mayhew saw this effort as a significant threat to American religious liberty as it had existed in New England since the days of the Puritan founders. He recalled for his listeners and readers the sacrifices of English Puritans during their own revolution of the 1640s, as they opposed the tyranny of King Charles I and his bishops and struggled to worship God in accordance with their consciences. He argued that the English Puritans were right to oppose their king because he was unjust. This was a much more positive view of the English revolution than Americans had heard up to this period. Over time Mayhew expanded his thoughts to criticize the current English monarchy and its representatives in New England. Mayhew was never fully allied with American political leaders such as Samuel Adams and John Hancock, and he opposed the mobs who demonstrated against the Stamp Act. Yet Mayhew's thoughts about religious freedom supported their emerging notions of political liberty. He preached his most famous sermon, "The Snare Broken," in celebration of the repeal of the Stamp Act. In it he criticized mob violence but also spoke against England's exploitation of America, setting the tone for the revolutionary era. He failed to see that emerge, however, having a stroke soon after this success and dying on 9 July 1766.

Sources:

Charles W. Akers, *Called Unto Liberty: A Life of Jonathan Mayhew, 1720–1766* (Cambridge, Mass.: Harvard University Press, 1964);

John Corrigan, *The Hidden Balance: Religion and the Social Theories of Charles Chauncy and Jonathan Mayhew* (New York: Oxford University Press, 1987).

JUNIPERO SERRA

1713-1784

CATHOLIC MISSIONARY

Early Zeal. As the leader of the Spanish missionary effort in California, Junipero Serra laid the foundation for a strong Roman Catholic presence in the early American religious landscape. Serra was born on 24 November 1713 on the island of Majorca, in the Mediterranean Sea off the Spanish coast. Serra was baptized with the name Miguel Jose but changed it to Junipero in 1731, when he became a member of the community of religious men, originally called friars, founded by St. Francis of Assisi. As a Franciscan brother, Serra pledged complete obedience to the Roman Catholic Church, and promised to live a life of poverty and chastity devoted to God. He was well educated at a Spanish university and became a professor of philosophy. His intense piety left him feeling dissatisfied with an academic career, however, and in 1750 he arrived in Mexico to take up missionary work among the Indians there.

Indian Missions. Once in the Americas, Serra joined a huge effort of countless priests and monks who worked to bring Christianity as well as the benefits of European civilization to the Native American population. The Spanish missions had their most direct effects on the Indians who came to live beside European settlers and adopt their religion and culture. The missionary effort centered on establishing permanent settlements of Indians, who would take up agriculture and abandon their nomadic hunting customs. They would also take up Catholicism. The spiritual effort led many Southwestern Indians to take up at least elements of the Catholic faith, often in combination with their traditional beliefs and practices. The complex and lively religious culture that emerged was undermined by other aspects of the mission effort that included the military conquest of the lands controlled by the Indians and the often-harsh repression of the rights of the native population. World politics also had a part to play in this religious effort. A series of struggles between the Roman Catholic Church and various European countries led to the removal of the members of the Jesuit order from Spanish missions in 1767. The Franciscans were ready to take up the work begun by the Jesuits, and Serra was appointed superintendent of the Mexican mission efforts, at that time centered in the area that is today Baja, California. At the same time the arrival of Russian and English explorers along the upper California coast made Spain eager to expand the Franciscan missionary effort and extend the reach of its control northward.

California. Serra obliged his church and his nation by joining a Spanish expedition headed north into Califor-

nia in 1769. That same year he founded his first new mission, in San Diego. Eventually twenty-one missions were settled in the American Southwest, nine of them founded by Serra personally. These survive today as some of California's leading cities, including Santa Clara and San Francisco, as well as San Diego. The missions prospered under Serra's leadership. They became economic and military posts, as well as religious centers, identified by their distinctive buildings made of adobe, connected by arcades that protected walkers from the sun. Serra visited the settlements repeatedly and on many occasions spoke out against the abuse of Indian rights. Serra claimed to have baptized more than six thousand Native Americans and brought many of those into the shelter of the towns that surrounded each Spanish mission. He never understood how destructive the resettlement of Native Americans into the missions was, however, as these towns became centers of disease, as well as of farming, leading to the decline of the Indian groups. Serra died on a pastoral visit to the mission in Monterey, California, on 28 August 1784.

Sources:

Omer Englebert, *The Last of the Conquistadors: Junipero Serra, 1713–1784* (New York: Harcourt, Brace, 1956);

Maynard J. Geiger, *The Life and Time of Fray Junipero Serra, O. F. M.* (Washington, D.C.: Academy of American Franciscan History, 1959).

PUBLICATIONS

Elizabeth Ashbridge, *Some Account of the Fore Part of the Life of Elizabeth Ashbridge* (Nantwich, England, 1774)—an autobiography of an American Quaker female minister;

Isaac Backus, *An Appeal to the Public for Religious Liberty* (Boston: John Boyle, 1773)—influential statement of the principles of the separation of church and state, from New England's leading evangelical Baptist preacher;

Backus, *A History of New-England with Particular Reference to the Denomination of Christians Known as Baptists*, 3 volumes (Boston: Edward Draper, 1777–1796)—the story of the rise of the Baptist denomination in America, cast as an account of the gradual emergence of freedom of religious expression in the British colonies;

Joseph Bellamy, *Sermons upon the Following Subjects, viz, The Divinity of Jesus Christ, the Millennium, the Wisdom of God in the Permission of Sin* (Boston: Edes & Gill, 1758)—defense of Bellamy's New Divinity form of trinitarian Christianity, prompted by Jonathan Mayhew's outspoken criticism of orthodoxy, and an important step in the split between evangelical and liberal Congregationalism. He argues in part that God not only ordained but also permitted sin as a means to glorify himself by allowing greater exercise of forgiveness;

Anthony Benezet, *A Caution and Warning to Great-Britain and Her Colonies, in a Short Representation of the Calamitous State of the Enslaved Negroes* (Philadelphia: Henry Miller, 1766)—an argument on religious grounds against slavery, by a leading Quaker humanitarian and reformer, which had a significant effect on the emerging antislavery movement on both sides of the Atlantic;

William Billings, *The Singing Master's Assistant, or Key to Practical Music* (Boston: Draper & Folsom, 1778)—an early American hymnal, including Billings's original religious and patriotic songs, as well as popular hymns of Isaac Watts, compiled by the first professional American church musician;

Thomas Bradbury Chandler, *An Appeal to the Public, in Behalf of the Church of England in America* (New York: James Parker, 1767)—an argument for sending an Anglican bishop to establish religious order in the American colonies, written by a leading Anglican missionary;

Charles Chauncy, *A Compleat View of Episcopacy* (Boston: Daniel Kneeland, 1771)—an argument against the introduction of Anglican bishops to the American colonies;

Chauncy, *Salvation for All Men* (Boston: T. & J. Fleet, 1782)—an early statement of the doctrine of universal atonement, that Christ died to save all humans, rather than just an elect few, as traditional Calvinists believed;

Chauncy, *Twelve Sermons* (Boston: D. & J. Kneeland, 1765)—a series of sermons exemplifying the rationalism and optimism about human nature and God's love characteristic of the liberal wing of New England Congregationalism, which Chauncy led;

John Cleaveland, *An Essay to Defend Some of the Most Important Principles* (Boston: D. & J. Kneeland, 1763)—a defense of the New Light revivalist theology, in opposition to the preaching of the universal benevolence of God of Jonathan Mayhew and other Boston liberals;

Cleaveland, *A Short and Plain Narrative of the Late Work of God's Spirit* (Boston: Z. Fowle, 1767)—an account of revivals north of Boston in the 1760s, indicating that the religious fervor of the earlier Great Awakening continued through the revolutionary period;

Jonathan Edwards, *A Careful and Strict Inquiry into the Modern Prevailing Notions of that Freedom of the Will* (Boston: S. Kneeland, 1754)—a defense of the Calvinist doctrine of predestination, by describing the world as fully ordered by God and attacking the liberal emphasis on the power of humans to gain salvation through the exercise of the will;

Edwards, *The Great Christian Doctrine of Original Sin Defended* (Boston: S. Kneeland, 1758)—a defense of the Calvinist view of original sin of Adam, as initiating the depraved state of human nature, which could only be overcome with God's help, attacking liberal teachings that humans could affect their chances for salvation by their actions;

Edwards, *A History of the Work of Redemption* (Edinburgh: W. Gray; London: J. Buckland & G. Keith, 1774)—a sermon series placing the revivalistic religion promoted by Edwards during and after the Great Awakening in the context of the biblical story of the end of the world and the judgment of God and an example of how strongly attracted many revivalists were to millennial thinking;

Edwards, *Two Dissertations, [including] The Nature of True Virtue* (Boston: S. Kneeland, 1765)—a discussion of virtue as a willing consent to the sinfulness of the human condition, honoring God by attributing everything in life to his grace;

Ebenezer Gay, *Natural Religion as Distinguish'd from Revealed* (Boston: John Draper, 1759)—a liberal statement of the agreements between Christian scripture and the reasonable order of nature;

John Gillies, ed., *Works of the Reverend George Whitefield* (London: Edward & Charles Dilly, 1771–1772)—volumes one and two contain a collection of sermons of the famed English revivalist, including his extensive correspondence with important ministers on both sides of the Atlantic, which was itself an important means of furthering the work of revival;

Jonathan Mayhew, *Observations on the Charter and Conduct of the Society for the Propagation of the Gospel in Foreign Parts* (Boston: Richard & Samuel Draper, 1763)—a critique of Anglicans for using their missionary efforts in New England to covert Congregationalists to Anglicanism rather than Indians to Christianity;

Mayhew, *Sermons upon the Following Subjects* (Boston: Richard Draper, 1755)—a series of sermons outlining Mayhew's brand of liberal Congregationalism, including an attack on the doctrine of the trinity, which led to an uproar against Mayhew's unorthodox preaching;

Mayhew, *The Snare Broken* (Boston: R. & S. Draper, 1766)—a sermon preached after Parliament's repeal of the Stamp Act and defending the colonies' right to self-government, based on the natural law of self-preservation in the face of English oppression;

Samson Occom, *A Choice Selection of Hymns and Spiritual Songs* (New London: Timothy Green, 1774)—an Indian hymnal collected by a native American missionary;

Occom, *Sermon Preached at the Execution of Moses Paul, an Indian* (New Haven: T. & S. Green, 1772)—a plea for temperance from an Indian missionary and the first work published by a Native American writing in English;

Sarah Osborn, *Nature, Certainty, and Evidence of True Christianity* (Boston: S. Kneeland, 1755)—spiritual advice from a pious woman to a friend and an important example of the significance of women's religious lives in eighteenth-century America;

Philadelphia Yearly Meeting of the Society of Friends, *An Epistle of Caution and Advice, Concerning the Buying and Keeping of Slaves* (Philadelphia: James Chattin, 1754)—the first official condemnation of slavery from an American religious group;

Joseph Priestley, *A History of the Corruptions of Christianity* (Birmingham, U.K.: Piercy & Jones, 1782)—a critical examination of traditional Christian beliefs by an English Unitarian and supporter of American independence, read by Thomas Jefferson, who found it confirming his deistic beliefs and his interest in Christ as a moral teacher;

Valentine Rathbun, *An Account of the Matter, Form, and Manner of a New and Strange Religion* (Providence, R.I.: Bennett Wheeler, 1781)—an early account of the beliefs and practices of the Shakers, written by a former member of the group, and an important source for understanding sectarianism in early America;

Emanuel Swedenborg, *The New Jerusalem and Its Heavenly Doctrine* (London: J. Lewis, 1758)—the first edition of principles of biblical interpretation by an influential Swedish pietistic mystic;

William White, *The Case of the Episcopal Churches in the United States Considered* (Philadelphia: David C. Claypoole, 1782)—an effort to reorganize the colonial Anglican Church on democratic principles after the disruptions of the American Revolution;

John Woolman, *Some Considerations on the Keeping of Negroes* (Philadelphia: James Chattin, 1754)—an influential early antislavery tract by a Quaker reformer;

Woolman, *Works . . . in Two Parts* (Philadelphia: Joseph Crukshank, 1774)—writings of a New Jersey Quaker who became a model for the reform movement that emerged among the Society of Friends during the 1750s, including his journal that remained popular for decades as a devotional text.

Interior view of Touro Synagogue, Newport, Rhode Island, built in 1763

CHAPTER ELEVEN

SCIENCE, AND MEDICINE

by LEN TRAVERS

CONTENTS

1754

- King's College is founded in New York City; it becomes Columbia University after the Revolutionary War.

1755

18 Nov.
An earthquake strikes the Boston area of Massachusetts. Afterwards the Reverend Thomas Prince reprints his 1727 sermon *Earthquakes, the Works of God and Tokens of His Displeasure.* Meanwhile Harvard College astronomer and mathematician John Winthrop publishes his scientific observations in *Lectures on Earthquakes.*

1756

- Yale College president Thomas Clap advances the theory of three "terrestrial comets" in orbit around the earth.
- Benjamin Franklin is elected a fellow of the Royal Society of London.

1759

- John Winthrop publishes "Two Lectures on Comets."

3 Apr.
Halley's Comet reappears as predicted.

1760

- In an effort to regulate the medical profession, New York requires all doctors and surgeons to obtain a license by first passing a test.
- Jared Eliot, Connecticut clergyman and physician, publishes *Essays Upon Field Husbandry in New England.*

1761

- Inspired by new agricultural practices in Britain, Virginia planter George Washington starts to try crop rotation and soil fertilization at his estate Mount Vernon.

6 June
John Winthrop and a small group of Americans in Newfoundland observe the transit of Venus.

1762

- *Flora Virginica* (Virginia Plant Life) goes into a second edition using the new classification system of Swedish botanist Carl Linnaeus.
- Ethan Allen establishes an ironworks in Connecticut.

1763

- The first American medical society is founded in New London, Connecticut.

1764

- A smallpox epidemic in the Boston area prompts the establishment of two new inoculation hospitals.

24 Jan. A fire on the campus of Harvard College destroys Harvard Hall along with all of the scientific equipment housed there.

1765

- Philadelphia physician John Morgan establishes the first American medical school at the College of Philadelphia.

23 May Benjamin Gale, a Connecticut physician, writes a paper titled "Historical Memoirs relating to . . . Inoculation for the Small Pox, in the British American Provinces," which advocates using mercury in preventing the disease.

8 Dec. Eli Whitney, inventor of the cotton gin, is born in Westboro, Massachusetts.

1766

- John Morgan establishes the Philadelphia Medical Society.

1767

- David Rittenhouse, a Philadelphia astronomer, builds a sophisticated and accurate orrery, a model of the solar system.

- King's College, New York, opens the second medical school in America.

1768

- South Carolina naturalist Alexander Garden discovers the Congo snake, a previously unknown American species.

- The medical school at the College of Philadelphia graduates its first class of doctors.

1769

- Abel Buell, a silversmith from Connecticut, develops the first type fonts for printing made in America. Previously, all type was imported from Britain.

2 Jan. The American Philosophical Society is revitalized in Philadelphia. Benjamin Franklin is elected its president, a position he holds until his death in 1790.

June The last transit of Venus observable from earth for 105 years is witnessed by American scientists.

1770

- Benjamin Rush, a Philadelphia physician, publishes the first American chemistry textbook: *A Syllabus of a Course of Lectures on Chemistry.*

1771

- Pennsylvania physician and mathematics professor Hugh Williamson publishes "An Essay on the Use of Comets."

Feb. The American Philosophical Society publishes the first issue of its journal, *Transactions*.

1772

- Judge Andrew Oliver of Salem, Massachusetts, publishes *An Essay on Comets, in Two Parts*.

- William DeBrahm, a Dutch emigrant to Georgia and surveyor general for the southern district, publishes *The Atlantic Pilot, a guide for seafarers*.

1773

- The first mental hospital in America opens in Williamsburg, Virginia.

- Delaware inventor Oliver Evans proposes a steam-powered wagon.

- Benjamin Franklin is elected an associate of the Academie Royale des Sciences in France.

3 May The Virginia Society for Promoting Useful Knowledge is founded. It awards its first gold medal to John Hobday for his threshing machine.

1774

- Philadelphia physician Benjamin Rush writes an essay describing Native American healing practices and rituals.

- Abraham Chovet, a surgeon and recent immigrant from Jamaica, establishes an anatomical wax museum in Philadelphia as a teaching tool for medical students.

1775

- David Bushnell, Connecticut inventor, designs and builds a workable submarine, the *American Turtle*, for use by the American military.

- Alexander Garden writes a treatise on electric eels for the Royal Society of London.

17 Oct. John Morgan becomes director-general of hospitals and physician-in-chief for the Continental Army.

1776

- Dr. Lionel Chalmers publishes *An Account of the Weather and Diseases in South-Carolina*.

7 Sept. David Bushnell's *American Turtle* makes the first submarine attack in history by attempting to attach a torpedo to a British warship in New York harbor.

15 Sept. British troops capture New York and loot the library and scientific laboratories of King's College.

1777

- George Washington orders the Continental Army to be inoculated against smallpox.

9 Jan.   Amid political intrigue, Congress dismisses John Morgan as director-general of hospitals and physician-in-chief of the Continental Army.

1778

- Lutheran clergyman Gotthilf H. Muhlenberg begins a lifelong, systematic study of American plants.

- Dr. William Brown of Virginia publishes his *Pharmacopoeia.*

1779

- The College of William & Mary in Virginia establishes a school of medicine.

1780

- The American Academy of Sciences is instituted in Boston, Massachusetts.

- Philadelphia physicians establish the Philadelphia Humane Society to teach first aid, primarily for drowning victims.

1781

- Dartmouth College Medical School is founded.

- Rhode Island farmer and inventor Jeremiah Wilkinson devises a machine for making nails cut from iron plate.

1 Nov.   Massachusetts physician Cotton Tufts helps create the Massachusetts Medical Society.

1782

- Dr. William Shippen offers private lectures on birthing practices, signaling a shift from the use of midwives to doctors in childbirth.

- Hugh Martin, a Continental Army surgeon, concocts a "secret" cure for cancer.

1783

- Abel Buell prints the first map of the new United States.

- Josiah Flagg opens the first American dentistry practice in Boston, Massachusetts.

May   Harvard Medical School opens.

OVERVIEW

Franklin's Vision. In 1743 Benjamin Franklin considered America's prospects for the pursuit of science: "The first drudgery of settling new colonies which confines the attention of people to mere necessaries is now pretty well over; and there are many in every province in circumstances that set them at ease, and afford leisure to cultivate the finer arts and improve the common stock of knowledge." Franklin could have been writing about his own life: a successful Philadelphia printer after years of disciplined work, he was preparing an early retirement, hoping to devote the rest of his life to the "finer arts." Particularly, he wanted to see cooperative, intercolonial promotion of "natural science," the study of the physical world, the universe, and the forces in it.

American Backwardness. To most other Americans Franklin may have seemed overly optimistic. How could America support the kind of activity Franklin proposed? Europe was enjoying the scientific revolution known today as the Enlightenment, but where was America's place in that great intellectual awakening? When Franklin wrote of his hopes, the most established institution of higher learning, Harvard College, was only a century old, the next oldest, the College of William and Mary, less than half that. Neither had rich libraries, nor were there private scientific libraries in America of any great importance. America had no great scientific centers, no counterpart to England's prestigious Royal Society. No wealthy gentlemen supported the sciences as many did in Europe. There was no longstanding tradition of scientific pursuit in America upon which to build and no obvious financial gain from scholarly study that might in turn support more study. Most of the learned minds in America were those of the clergy, and while some of these made significant contributions to science and technology, most had only a limited use for the study of nature for its own sake. Science, wrote one commentator, was "a child of a thousand years," one that "approaches slowly to Maturity." As Franklin himself realized, there was a direct correlation between a society's maturity and its capacity to advance science. A traveler named Andrew Burnaby rendered this verdict in 1759: in America the arts and sciences were "just dawning."

Emphasis on Practicality. Because few colonists could afford to devote themselves to purely theoretical science, there was a utilitarian temperament toward scientific studies amounting almost to prejudice in America. There was no such thing as a professional "scientist." The term was not commonly used; since one studied "natural philosophy," eighteenth-century people used the term "philosopher" instead, and this word suggested a person's interest rather than his employment. For example, astronomer John Winthrop was a professor at Harvard; balloon enthusiast John Jeffries was a doctor, as was naturalist Alexander Garden. The attitude that science should have some practical application hardened in the years before the Revolution as Americans sought to distinguish themselves from Britons in every way possible. One patriot commented: "Rome was never wiser or more virtuous, than when moderately learned, and meddled with none but the useful Sciences. Athens was never more foolish than when it swarmed with Philosophers. . . . Use," he concluded, "is the Soul of Study." Ironically Benjamin Franklin, an American, would not have agreed with this opinion. Although known for such practical inventions as bifocal spectacles and the wood-burning stove that bears his name, Franklin's most important scientific investigations (concerning electricity) were not begun with any practical objective. In such cases Franklin worked on the assumption that understanding was in itself useful.

American Flora. It was in the area of natural history—the study of plant and animal life—that American "philosophers" began to form connections among themselves and with colleagues in Europe. Although America had been known to Europeans for two and one-half centuries, it was still an exotic place filled with flora and fauna unknown to Europeans. Some were important as food sources, Indian corn for example, but others became sources for new vegetable remedies. John Tennent of Virginia endorsed Seneca snakeroot, first as a cure for rattlesnake bite (only a problem in America), then for a variety of European ills. It was partly for this reason that a 1739 book published in Holland called *Flora Virginica* (Virginia Plant Life), based on the botanical collections of Englishman John Clayton, was popular with medical doctors and apothecaries.

The Rage to Classify. Enlightenment thinkers believed that every thing and phenomenon could be known and understood. This rationalist approach demanded a systematic classification of everything in the known world. Carl Linnaeus, the famous Swedish botanist, devised the binomial (two-name) system, still used today, for identifying and classifying every plant and animal. Using Latin terminology (the international language of the learned), Linnaeus categorized subjects by genus and species. For example, the maple tree that grows in Great Britain is *acer campestris* while the American sugar maple is also genus *acer*, but with the descriptive species name *saccharum* (sweet). Linnaeus's rational, descriptive method inspired botanical gardens throughout Europe, especially at Kew and Oxford. These soon set aside space for American plants. The Chelsea Apothecaries Company imported more than two hundred American plants, and one private gardener, an English lord, claimed to have ten thousand American plants. European philosophers scrambled to classify all these new and exotic specimens. When the second edition of *Flora Virginica* appeared in 1762, the American plants were all identified using the now-familiar Linnaean method.

The British Connection. Most of the plant and animal specimens turning up in European gardens and zoos were first collected and shipped by American naturalists. Some, such as Dr. Alexander Garden of South Carolina, were recent British emigrants fascinated with their new surroundings. Others, such as John Bartram of Pennsylvania, were native-born. They collected plants, fish, reptiles, and insects for British correspondents who were unable to come to America for study. Ironically it was often through these foreign associations that American naturalists discovered other interested colleagues in the colonies. This intercolonial fellowship of naturalists was the beginning of the first scientific community in America.

Imagining the Universe. Americans also showed interest in explaining and understanding the cosmos. Englishmen Edmund Halley and Sir Isaac Newton produced revolutionary observations and theories of physical laws and planetary movement. Thanks to them the universe was no longer considered a semireligious mystery that discouraged scrutiny. For Newton and his followers the universe ran like an amazingly huge and ornate clockwork mechanism: complicated, but fully understandable. Of all eighteenth-century sciences astronomy attracted the most attention because of the central position it occupied in Enlightenment thought and because of its visibility. When Halley's Comet, last seen in 1682, reappeared as predicted in 1759, it was a spectacular vindication of the predictable, measurable Newtonian universe.

Astronomy in America. The theories of the English astronomers found receptive audiences in America. Harvard College's John Winthrop and Philadelphia's David Rittenhouse were America's premier astronomers, but American interest in the heavens went well beyond the academy. Although the return of Halley's Comet inspired some lively debate on the nature of comets, the transits of Venus in 1761 and 1769, which promised to throw new light on the extent of the earth's solar system, commanded a surprising amount of attention from the general public. Astronomy also had two practical applications of great importance to Americans: navigation and surveying. Overseas trade was vital to America's economy, and shipmasters found their way across the oceans by their knowledge of astronomy and mathematics. On land Americans surveyed vast inland tracts using celestial positioning. The most famous American survey line, the Mason-Dixon line that separates Pennsylvania and Maryland, was laid out from 1763 to 1768 by English astronomers Charles Mason and Jeremiah Dixon.

Science and Religion. While the Newtonian view of the universe diminished the immediate, interventionist role of God in celestial events (comets as divine messages, for example), celestial theorists did not reject God as the creator of the universe. Rather they imagined a supremely rational, benign deity who designed the universe as a vast, clockwork-like device that ran according to physical laws that even He would not change. This more distant, less personal conception of God came to be known as deism, and clergymen in both Europe and America understandably abhorred it. Most eighteenth-century philosophers, however, had little trouble adapting religion to science. David Rittenhouse saw no problem in expressing his astronomical interest in religious terms when he declared: "All yonder stars innumerable, with their dependencies, may perhaps compose but the leaf of a flower in the creator's garden, or a single pillar in the immense building of the divine architect. Here is ample provision made for the all-grasping mind of man!"

Electrical Science. It was Benjamin Franklin who made the only truly revolutionary contribution from America to western science during this period. Electricity was the nuclear science of the eighteenth century. When Franklin took up its study at the age of forty, there was already a widely accepted hypothesis on the nature of electricity. According to this hypothesis, put forth in 1733, there were actually two distinct electricities, or types of electrical "fluids." Neutral or uncharged bodies contained equal amounts of both fluids—that was why they were neutral. When electrically charged, as by rubbing a glass rod with cloth, the glass lost one type of electric fluid and gained the other: the glass was charged by having a superabundance of one kind of fluid. Further, the hypothesis went, bodies charged with differing electricities attracted each other, but bodies charged with the same fluid were repelled. This was why some objects, such as gold foil, when charged by touching the charged glass rod, bent away from the rod afterwards (it had absorbed the same kind of fluid) but was attracted to a piece of charged amber, which presumably possessed the opposite type of fluid. This two-fluid hypothesis had the virtue of explaining electrical attraction and repulsion. It also happened to be wrong.

Franklin's Theories. In 1746 European scientists stumbled upon the principle of the electrical condenser. They discovered that a glass jar partially filled with water and with a wire projecting through both sides of the jar's stopper could store large charges of electricity. These "Leyden jars" produced long, visible sparks and audible cracks, which not only were a source of amusement at the courts of Europe but also made possible some truly impressive electrical demonstrations, as when 180 French soldiers, joining hands in one long line, were made to jump simultaneously as an electric current passed through them. Traveling demonstrators crisscrossed Europe and America, entertaining and lecturing. One of the many who paid to see electrical demonstrations was Franklin, who instantly became fascinated with electricity and began his own experiments. In a few short years, encouraged by English correspondents who publicized his work, Franklin destroyed the European two-fluid hypothesis, substituting a modern, single-fluid theory that explained all known electrical phenomena and proved conclusively that lightning was a form of electricity.

Medical Science. Medicine made few real advances during this period. The practice of healing was a hodgepodge of ancient Greek theory, folk remedies, modern practices, and trial and error. The causes of most diseases, and of infection, were unknown. Epidemic diseases—smallpox, diphtheria, and yellow fever—periodically swept through entire regions with little that doctors could do about them. The most significant medical development in this period was the movement toward professionalizing medicine. This was done through the establishment of medical schools in New York, Boston, and Philadelphia; the founding of medical societies for professionals; and attempts to license anyone practicing medicine. These actions helped promote a disciplined approach to medicine that eventually brought about improvements in medical science, but it would take time for these results to have any real impact. By the time of the Revolution, America still had no medical journals, and little more than 10 percent of its medical practitioners were licensed professionals. One other significant trend was in the area of obstetrics. Childbearing had long been the responsibility of midwives, local women who aided deliveries and often dispensed folk medicine as well; doctors (all of whom were male) were called only in cases of difficult or dangerous birth. Toward the end of the Revolution male doctors began to study fetal development and birthing practice, and to take over the midwives' traditional role. This change, however, did not immediately result in any material improvements to women's health.

Agriculture, Industry, and the Future. Science had not yet reached a point at which it might be of significant benefit to farmers, merchants, or artisans in their work. New farming techniques developed in Britain promised real benefits to farmers in terms of efficient land use, soil nutrition, new crops, and cattle breeding, but these did not translate well to America. Although America boasted abundant water power for manufacturing mills, British commercial regulation forbade most kinds of manufacturing in the colonies, so technological development in that regard received no encouragement. One major exception to British restrictions was iron production, and that industry grew rapidly, especially in Pennsylvania and New Jersey. American interest in manufactures increased with the Revolutionary movement, but America's chronic lack of capital, made worse by an economy ruined by a war for independence, precluded any industrial progress. Nevertheless, signs of a manufacturing future existed: by the time the new United States won its independence from Great Britain, American inventors had built prototypes of harvesting and threshing machines, developed crude mass-production technology, and designed water-powered spinning mills. The American scientific and technological renaissance came in the next century, but the Revolutionary period produced ample evidence of both native ability and commitment.

TOPICS IN THE NEWS

AMERICAN INVENTION

Potential. Revolutionary-period America was hardly a technologically advanced society. Nevertheless, several inventors proposed or produced ingenious innovations that foretold the "know-how" that later became Americans' famous reputation. Just before the Revolutionary War, John Hobday of Virginia designed and built a machine for threshing wheat, ordinarily a laborious and time-consuming task that separated the kernels from the chaff. A farmer usually beat no more than a few bushels of wheat in a day; Hobday's threshing machine could beat sixty bushels in the same time. What was more, Hobday claimed that his invention would cost only fifteen pounds to duplicate, easily affordable by wealthy planters such as George Washington who had turned from tobacco to wheat agriculture. In Connecticut at about the same time silversmith Abel Buell developed the first type fonts made in America. The colonial printers, who had presses in virtually every major urban center, produced regular issues of newspapers, almanacs, and books, but they had to import type from Britain. Buell's work presaged the end of that dependence.

Science at War. During the Revolutionary struggle patriotic men of science put their minds to inventions to aid the war effort. David Bushnell built a submarine designed to attack British warships. Clockmaker David Rittenhouse tried to develop a rifled cannon and collaborated with painter Charles Wilson Peale on a telescopic sight to make America's famous rifles even more deadly. None of these inventions had any real effect on the war though all would have a serious and profound impact on future conflicts.

Mass Production. Although Americans imported most of their clothing, many, especially in rural areas, produced wool for homespun clothes. To do this, however, required that the wool first be "carded," or combed between paddle-shaped "cards" hand-set with hundreds of wire teeth. Around 1780 Oliver Evans of Delaware (who would build America's first steam engines after the war) invented a machine that inserted the wire teeth into cards at the rate of three thousand per minute. Although he had developed the technology of mass production, the process was never a success; the finished cards were simply not as good quality as the handmade kind, "owing to the shape & largeness of the pierced holes in the leather & consequent looseness of the teeth." Jeremiah Wilkinson of Rhode Island developed

another manufacturing process in 1781: a machine that cut nails from an iron plate far more quickly than any blacksmith could forge them. As with other scientific and technological efforts in America, factory production would get its real start after the war.

Sources:

Silvio A. Bedini, *Thinkers and Tinkers: Early American Men of Science* (New York: Scribners, 1975);

Brooke Hindle, *The Pursuit of Science in Revolutionary America 1735–1789* (Chapel Hill: University of North Carolina Press, 1956).

DAVID RITTENHOUSE'S "ORRERY"

New discoveries concerning planetary orbits inspired gifted artisans to build orreries, clockwork or hand-cranked models of the solar system used as teaching aids. Several English and American examples were already in the colonies in 1767 when David Rittenhouse, a Pennsylvania clock maker and amateur astronomer, began one of his own. Rittenhouse wanted to make a name for himself in the scientific community: what he had in mind was something not to instruct beginners but, as he put it, "to astonish the skillful." He succeeded admirably with an orrery exceeding any other in sophistication. Not only did it properly simulate the elliptical (not perfectly circular) orbits of the planets, it even incorporated a "curious contrivance" for illustrating the appearance of a solar eclipse from any point on earth. So meticulous was Rittenhouse's mechanism that his orrery could display the relative positions of the planets for any time over a five thousand-year period, with a margin of error of less than one degree. After Thomas Jefferson had seen the device, he commented that if Rittenhouse had not actually created a world, then he had "by imitation approached nearer its Maker than any man who has lived." Two of Rittenhouse's orreries survive; one at the Franklin Institute in Philadelphia and the other at Princeton University in New Jersey.

Source: Howard C. Rice Jr., *The Rittenhouse Orrery* (Princeton, N.J.: Princeton University Press, 1954).

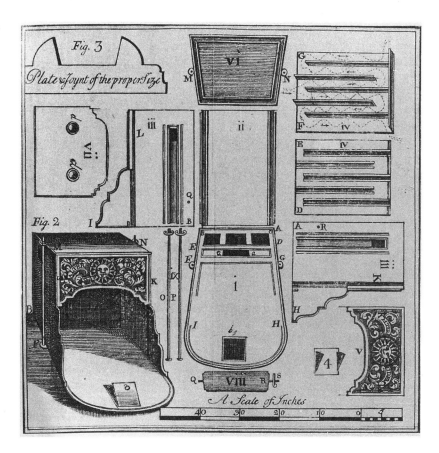

A diagram of Benjamin Franklin's stove

David Rittenhouse's 1767 model showing relative movement of bodies in the solar system (Princeton University, N.J.)

BLEEDING

Cure or Killer? In January 1765 twenty-six-year-old George III was suffering from fever, restlessness, nausea, and chest pains. On the thirteenth of the month his doc-

tors, completely stumped, reported "a violent cold, a restless night, complained of [pains] in his breast." They did the only thing they could agree on: "His Majesty was blooded 14 ounces." His Majesty eventually recovered. Thirty-four years later, the king's old nemesis, George Washington, lay sick with what may have been diphtheria. He had already been bled once by his plantation overseer, and two of his three doctors repeated the process three more times. Despite (or because of) their ministrations, Washington died the next night.

Approved Practice. What was good enough for a British king and an American president was considered good enough for everyone else. Exsanguination, or bleeding, was an almost universally approved treatment for a vast array of illnesses. The practice hearkened back to medieval Europe and was constructed on the belief that blood was one of the body's four "humors"—blood, phlegm, bile, and black bile—which had to maintain proper balance within the body for good health. Like the other humors, blood could become excessive in the body, resulting in various symptoms, fever among them. The obvious remedy was to restore the humoral balance by drawing off the excess blood.

Applications. The theory made so much sense and the treatment was so simple that the practice was applied to all sorts of situations. While breathing deeply and coughing, a patient with pleurisy—a respiratory inflammation—could expect the doctor or surgeon to draw

LEECHES, LANCETS, AND SCARIFICATORS

Bleeding was one of the most common medical practices in the eighteenth-century western world, and the tools for the job ranged from the ancient to the most modern. Doctors and surgeons often kept jars of leeches ready for use. Using leeches for bleeding had advantages: the amount of blood taken could be easily controlled; they could be applied anywhere on the body; and no incision was required. But it was a slow process. Bleeding by incision required more skill and judgment but could remove blood more quickly, and for this the surgeon's lancet was simple and effective. Indeed the lancet was undoubtedly the most used tool in a surgeon's kit. Incisions were more painful, however, and doctors generally recommended leeches for children and the faint of heart. To overcome a patient's fear of the lancet, doctors who could procure one used a "scarificator," a handheld device that was pressed against the patient's skin, and when a small trigger was released, a set of spring-loaded blades pierced the vein to a precise depth, making several incisions at once. The patient felt only a momentary pang.

Source: J. Worth Estes, "Therapeutic Practice in Colonial New England," in *Medicine in Colonial Massachusetts, 1620–1820* (Boston: Colonial Society of Massachusetts, 1980).

twelve ounces of blood from his or her jugular vein. If symptoms persisted after twenty-four hours, another bleeding followed. The particular place on the body from which the blood was drawn was often as important as the amount of blood taken. For rheumatic patients, for example, the bloodletter was supposed to draw ten ounces from the aching area. Patients submitted willingly to the procedure, many even considering regular bleeding part of a sensible health regimen; the lightheadedness that followed bloodletting was taken as a positive sign. For such all-purpose bleeding, the customary (and easiest) point of access was the inside of the patient's arm. The great advantage of the practice of bleeding was that it could be performed almost anywhere, and with only a simple lancet. The disadvantage, of course, was that it almost never did any real good. By the time George Washington died in 1799, the practice was already being criticized by some doctors. After centuries of widespread use bleeding was virtually abandoned in the early nineteenth century.

Sources:

Don Cooke, *The Long Fuse: How England Lost the American Colonies* (New York: Atlantic Monthly Press, 1995);

James Thomas Flexner, *Washington: The Indispensible Man* (Boston: Little, Brown, 1974);

Harold L. Peterson, *The Book of the Continental Soldier* (Harrisburg, Penn.: Stackpole, 1968).

THE EARTHQUAKE OF 1755: SCIENCE V. RELIGION

"A Great Shaking." It was still dark on the morning of 18 November 1755, when Harvard professor John Winthrop was jolted awake by the shaking motion of his house. He knew it was an earthquake: he had felt similar tremors in 1727, when he was thirteen, but these were more violent and longer-lasting. He kept to his bed while the house continued to shake around him, and objects fell from their places. When the shocks eventually subsided, Winthrop leapt from his bed and struck a light. His pendulum clock said the time was 4:11, but it had stopped, thrown off balance by the first shock. He then looked at his pocket watch, and it was nearly four minutes farther along. The earthquake had lasted about three and a half minutes, but it had been long enough and strong enough to do considerable damage: some fifteen hundred chimneys had been toppled or damaged, and the gable ends of some of the brick houses had collapsed. The quake was felt up and down the east coast. In the days immediately following the earthquake Winthrop learned of a two-foot-wide, thousand-foot-long fissure that had opened in New Hampshire and of ash gushing from cracks in the earth that had opened in a nearby coastal town. At his home Winthrop set to work recording all he could observe of the quake's effects: he calculated the vertical and lateral velocity of objects that had been pitched from his mantle and from the top of his chimney; from the direction they had fallen he ascertained the direction from which the earthquake had come. Most importantly, when he experienced an aftershock several days later (this time in daylight), he noticed the bricks in his fireplace moving upward, one after another, and immediately dropping back into place. As he described it, the motion was not "of the whole hearth together," whether from side to side or up and down, "but of each brick moving separately by itself": it was as if there were a "wave of earth rolling along." Neither Winthrop nor anyone else fully comprehended the implication of this observation; today the wavelike quality of seismic motion is basic to the understanding of earthquakes.

An Unscientific Response. Soon Bostonians learned of the devastating earthquake felt in Europe and North Africa only seventeen days before, which had killed more than sixty thousand people in Lisbon, Portugal, and virtually destroyed the city. In an age when earthquakes were little understood (Winthrop's systematic analysis was exceptional) and in which people accepted that nothing happened without God's knowledge and approval, it was natural to look for meaning in what modern people consider natural occurrences. Soon Boston's pulpits rang with sermons warning that these earthquakes were indications of God's anger. One minister, the Reverend Thomas Prince, republished "Earthquakes, the Works of God and Tokens of his Just Displeasure," a sermon he had written on the occasion of the 1727

FRANKLIN'S LIGHTNING ROD

The success of Benjamin Franklin's "Philadelphia Experiment" had a practical application that found instant popularity. Lightning was a serious hazard that frequently shattered chimneys and church steeples, set houses and barns ablaze, and killed people even inside their homes. Franklin first recommended the widespread use of lightning rods in his *Poor Richard's Almanack* for 1753. Curiously, Europeans were slow to adopt their use, but Americans embraced the novelty wholeheartedly. In only two years there were so many lightning rods on the houses and public buildings of Boston that one man blamed them for provoking the 1755 earthquake, in the belief that they directed too many lightning bolts into the ground. Fortunately few agreed with this position; in 1772 Franklin could report that "pointed conductors to secure buildings from Lightning have now been in use near 20 Years in America, and are there become so common, that Numbers of them appear on private Houses in every Street of the principal Towns, besides those on Churches, public Buildings, Magazines of Powder, and Gentlemen's Seats in the Country."

Source: Carl Van Doren, *Benjamin Franklin* (New York: Viking, 1938).

quake. The title suggests its content, but added to the recycled sermon was new information that made Winthrop bristle. Ever since Benjamin Franklin's famous experiments in electricity, men of science sought electrical influence in almost every field of inquiry. Franklin had even postulated that electricity had a hand in causing earthquakes, a belief enthusiastically seconded by the Reverend Prince, who suggested that the earthquake may actually have been induced by electricity attracted by Boston's many lightning rods. (Ironically the lightning rod had been invented by Franklin).

Winthrop Attacks. This was too much for Winthrop, who felt that Prince was mixing theology with "junk science." In response Winthop published "Two Lectures on Earthquakes," amounting to a direct attack on the orthodox relationship of God and the universe. Winthrop did not accept the widely held belief that God frequently intervened directly in the physical world by manifesting His anger through natural disasters. Winthrop believed instead that God had built an amazingly complex universe that then ran by itself, like a perpetual clock. This universe was absolutely governed by immutable physical laws, laws which could be learned and understood by humans. Thus earthquakes were forces of nature, not "scourges in the hand of the Almighty."

Appealing to the Public. The public interest in this thorny issue was so great that the Reverend Prince was able to publish his reply on the front page of the *Boston Gazette,* opening a month-long public debate in that newspaper. Prince responded gently enough, but too condescendingly for the prickly Winthrop's liking, who came back with a caustic, no-holds-barred reply, ruthlessly taking Prince's faulty theories to pieces. "Since the earthquake," claimed Winthrop, "our pulpits have generally rung with terror." He accused the clergy of exploiting earthquakes, comets, and "other terrifying phenomena . . . to keep up in mankind a reverent sense of the deity." Winthrop let his passion for rational science get the better of him, but there was no denying his data, and Prince publicly conceded Winthrop's points, with somewhat more grace than the younger man had shown in his attacks. Winthrop's challenge to a centuries-old interpretation of the natural world showcased the scientific method to which he had devoted his life and brought the science-versus-religion debate out of the academy and before an attentive public.

Source:
Bryce Walker, *Earthquake* (Alexandria, Va.: Time-Life Books, 1982).

A HOSPITAL FOR THE "DISTRACTED"

Beliefs and Attitudes. Mental illness was even less well understood than the physical sort in the eighteenth century. The medieval notion that insanity, or "distraction," was inflicted by God on account of the victim's or someone else's sins, died hard, especially when medical science offered little by way of explanation or cure. In the first century of English settlement the mentally ill were either humored or ignored if deemed harmless or shunned, restrained, or imprisoned if feared violent. Little attempt was made to understand the cause of the victim's condition (God's will could not be questioned), and even less effort was given to therapy. The stigma that mental illness carried with it meant that harsh discipline and corporal punishment were legitimate means to at least enforce obedience.

Problem of Treatment. Enlightenment-era thinking demanded a more rational explanation for insanity than an angry and capricious God. Doctors postulated that insanity was a disease, perhaps an imbalance of the body's "humors" that affected the brain, and therefore capable of a cure. Unfortunately the sort of humoral therapies with which doctors were familiar—bleedings, blisterings, and purges—were no more likely to cure the insane than to cure a cold. As often as not, doctors took on insane patients to experiment with a new remedy, or with variations on an old one. But there was no institution in America dedicated to the treatment of the mentally ill; unless the subject was homeless or considered a threat to the community, the care of the distracted person was entirely the responsibility of his or her family.

Ornamental grillwork made by a colonial ironworker

Asylum. In 1766 Gov. Francis Fauquier of Virginia proposed to change this. He proposed that public money be used for a building to house "these miserable Objects, who cannot help themselves." Fauquier probably had in mind something like London's famous Bethlehem (pronounced "Bedlam") Hospital, which had long been used to incarcerate some of England's insane. If so he presumably intended a more benign institution than the notoriously filthy, overcrowded prison that Bedlam had become. The House of Burgesses enacted the legislation and voted for the funds in 1770. The Public Hospital, as it was to be known, was to be situated in Williamsburg, Virginia's capital, and so was intended to be an architectural showpiece, a symbol of the Enlightenment in the colony. The building committee turned to Philadelphia's Robert Smith, who had designed that city's famous Carpenter's Hall and Walnut Street Jail. The result, completed in 1773, was a long, handsome, two-storied brick building with hipped roof and cupola.

Step Forward. Perhaps the inmates of the new hospital appreciated the architecture, but their fate was still fairly grim by modern standards. Medical science was no closer to curing mental illness in 1773 than it had ever been, and inmates, prisoners in all but name, were still subject to restraints and discipline. Nevertheless, the intention of the Public Hospital was not simply to shut away social misfits but to encourage doctors to study the puzzling disorders of the mind and to provide care for patients who might one day be cured. The Public Hospital represented a giant leap in perspective on the nature of mental illness and of a society's obligation to treat it.

Source:
George Humphrey Yetter, *Williamsburg Before and After* (Williamsburg, Va.: Colonial Williamsburg Foundation, 1980).

IRONMAKING

American Production. Extracting iron from ore in the eighteenth century was a process that combined sophisticated water-power technology with the science of metallurgy. English colonists began casting iron in the mid seventeenth century. These were mostly small operations; America had an abundance of raw materials, but ironmaking on a large scale required heavy investments of capital, which the colonies habitually lacked. By 1700 American iron production amounted to no more than 1 percent of the estimated world production. Seventy-five years later, however, that figure had risen to almost 15 percent. What had happened to produce this dramatic change?

British Encouragement. Britain's growing empire was built largely on its manufactures, which British merchants exchanged for the exotic commodities so much in demand in Europe and America. Britain had been largely stripped of forest, from which charcoal, the required fuel for iron production, was made. On the other hand, American forests seemed endless, and with the discovery

DEATH FROM BELOW: THE AMERICAN TURTLE

David Bushnell's submarine the *American Turtle* had a "shell" of solid oak, carefully caulked and pitched to be watertight. Its shape was roughly that of a top, with the pointed end weighted so that it floated upright. A small, windowed cupola on top served for a "conning tower," allowing the operator to see where he was going. For controls, an operator had two screw-type, hand-cranked propellers for horizontal and vertical travel and a rudder, all operated from within the shell. A foot-operated valve allowed water into a compartment for descent while hand pumps served to discharge the same water for surfacing. Instrumentation consisted of a water gauge depth indicator and a compass, both lighted with phosphorus to save air consumption. For armament the *Turtle* carried an underwater bomb called a "torpedo." The torpedo, located just over the rudder of the *Turtle*, had a sharp screw attached, pointing upward, and the entire bomb was spun by another interior hand crank. To deploy the torpedo the operator dove the boat under a ship's hull, then fastened the bomb to the underside of the hull by turning the crank, which screwed the bomb to the hull. As the boat then pulled away, a clockwork-driven time fuse ignited the torpedo after a set amount of time, blowing a fatal hole in the ship's hull.

Source: Frederick Wagner, *Submarine Fighter of the American Revolution: The Story of David Bushnell* (New York: Dodd, Mead, 1963).

---

bushels of charcoal and three tons of ore were required to produce one ton of iron. Once begun an ironmaking "campaign" might last thirty or forty weeks, nonstop. Obviously fuel and ore had to be constantly on hand, and gangs of men tended the furnace in shifts. Twice a day the crucible at the bottom of the furnace was tapped, and the molten iron ran out into prepared shallow ditches in the ground, where it sputtered and cooled into one-hundred-pound pigs of raw cast iron. Brittle and full of impurities, the pigs then went to the forge, itself a masterpiece of waterwheel-driven technology. There the pigs were heated again, almost to melting, and beaten into squared bars with half-ton mechanical hammers, squeezing out the impurities with each deafening blow. The entire process called for men with physical strength, skill, and judgment.

The Impact of Revolution. Ironmaking at this scale was an industry, employing men from all over the region to cut wood, make charcoal, mine the ore, tend the furnace, operate the forge, furnish transport, and manage the whole operation. Like any industry, an ironworks changed its community for both better and worse. Forests were quickly cut away to supply the ravenous furnaces, and slag heaps soon piled up around the operations. On the other hand, ironworks frequently invested in local road improvement and supplied relatively well-paying employment. When the Revolution came, American ironworks were able to supply most military needs, but the loss of British investment and markets for American iron put the industry into a decline from which it did not recover until the mid nineteenth century.

Sources:
Silvio A. Bedini, *Thinkers and Tinkers: Early American Men of Science* (New York: Scribners, 1975);

E. N. Hartley, *Ironworks on the Saugus* (Norman: University of Oklahoma Press, 1957).

NAVIGATION: THE SCIENCE OF COMMERCE

Practicality. The majority of European Americans in the eighteenth century lived within one hundred miles of the seacoast. Virtually everyone living there was linked inescapably to the great Atlantic commercial routes, from the urban merchants to the inland farmers, from governors to slaves. Manufactures of every sort—clothing, tools, pottery—came from Europe, paid for with American timber, tobacco, fish, and grain. And none of this extensive trade could take place without the ability to get a ship safely and efficiently across three thousand miles of trackless ocean. The science of navigation made American trade possible. It was an ancient art, but significant advances in astronomy and instrumentation in the eighteenth century transformed it into a science, one in which mathematics and the latest astronomical information were tools of the trade.

One's Place in the World. For centuries seafarers had used maps that placed the known world on a grid of imaginary lines, one set running east-west, parallel to the

---

of good-quality ore deposits in Connecticut, northern New Jersey, and Pennsylvania all that was lacking was money and management. Britain supplied much of both, forming companies of investors to raise capital and sending English, Dutch, and German experts to America to erect and manage large-scale operations. British legislation such as the Iron Acts of 1750 and 1757 encouraged American production of raw pig iron but at the same time forbade American production of finished iron goods. The idea behind this legislation was to create a dependable American supply of iron while protecting British manufacturers of iron and steel products. British money and imported expertise gave colonial ironmaking the boost it needed: while smaller, all-American operations continued, large-scale ironworks grew in the middle colonies and Maryland. The largest of these was Peter Hasenclever's ironworks in New Jersey, which in the 1760s ran six great blast furnaces smelting ore into pig iron and seven water-powered forges beating the metal into semifinished bars ready for export.

Making Iron. Even one twenty-foot-high furnace required enormous amounts of fuel, ore, and labor—265

equator, and another set running north-south, converging at the north and south poles—the lines of latitude and longitude. Even before the first settlement of America, mariners knew how to find their latitude thanks to the never-moving North Star at night and the Sun's zenith position at noon every day. Determining longitude, however, was always more complicated. By the mid eighteenth century making one's "westing" accurately required solving the "celestial triangle." One point of this triangle was formed by the north or south pole. The second point was a position on earth directly under another known star; this was determined from published astronomical tables. The last point was the ship's (unknown) degree of longitude. To solve the triangle the navigator had to make careful measurement of the angle of the known star and know the time as accurately as possible. Using spherical trigonometry the navigator could then determine the final point of the triangle and thus his position at sea.

Improvements. For measuring angles above the horizon crude cross staffs and plumb-line contrivances gave way to sophisticated optical instruments. About 1731 the navigator's quadrant made possible much more accurate measurements of angles above the horizon, and later the sextant refined measurements still further. As warships extended the British empire around the world, they brought back data that aided in making accurate astronomical tables for every season in every ocean. Perhaps most importantly, Englishman John Harrison developed the chronometer, essentially a highly accurate seaborne clock, with intricate mechanisms to compensate for a ship's movement, changes in temperature and humidity, dust, and other variations. Chronometers were expensive, as were sextants, but the advantage they gave American shipmasters made them prized possessions. But whether equipped with the latest English instruments or the more common quadrant and hourglass, American trade undoubtedly benefited from the great improvements in astronomical measurement, and the value they placed on learning the science of navigation is suggested by the frequent advertisements in colonial newspapers for training in celestial navigation.

Sources:

Brian Lavery, *Nelson's Navy: The Ships, Men, and Organization, 1793–1815* (Annapolis, Md.: Naval Institute Press, 1994);

Dava Sobel, *Longitude* (New York: Walker, 1995).

NOT-SO-REVOLUTIONARY MEDICINE

An Unprecedented Problem. In the last two centuries times of war have often seen great advances in medicine. This was decidedly not the case in the Revolutionary War. The eight-year conflict was America's first experience with large-scale treatment of sick and wounded over a protracted period. The colonies were woefully unprepared for a long war in this as in so many other areas. The Continental Congress learned about providing medical care for its troops "on the job," giving much of its effort

an inefficient quality. Lack of funds, problems of supply, and the limitations of eighteenth-century medicine made medical delivery to the needy soldier problematic. At any one time throughout the war an average of 18 percent of the Continental Army—almost one-fifth—was ill, and of course this number rose dramatically when epidemic diseases swept the army.

Medical Staff. Each regiment had a surgeon to attend to its soldiers. Ideally surgeons were trained doctors, but with these often in short supply, the army was glad to get anyone with some medical experience. The surgeon was supported by several surgeon's mates. James Thacher of Plymouth, Massachusetts, was probably a fairly typical surgeon's mate. He had apprenticed for some time under an established doctor, and when the war began, he wanted to serve as a medical officer. He and fifteen other candidates were examined by the Massachusetts medical board: "This business occupied about four hours; the subjects were anatomy, physiology, surgery, and medicine. . . . The examination was in a considerable degree close and severe." When it was over, ten out of the sixteen passed, including young Thacher, and received appointments as surgeon's mates.

Seeing the Doctor. When a soldier felt sick enough to seek medical attention, his first stop was his regimental

TO "BITE THE BULLET"

The term "to bite the bullet," meaning to bear hardship stoically, is commonly thought to have derived from eighteenth-century military surgery practices. The patient, about to undergo an agonizing operation with no anesthetic, was supposedly given a soft lead musket bullet to bite upon, to stifle his screams and prevent severing his own tongue with his teeth. This does not seem to have been the case; patients instead bit a stick of wood or a leather pad, these being both easier on the teeth and incapable of being swallowed while reclining on an operating table. The term more likely originates in military punishment; soldiers about to be flogged for some infraction were expected to take their punishment "like men" and not cry out. A bullet held in the back teeth enabled the victim to "bite back" the pain of the whip's impact without the visible aid of a wooden or leather gag. One further use of bitten or chewed bullets in this period does not relate directly to "biting the bullet" as defined here. Some soldiers deliberately chewed their musket balls in the knowledge that irregular or cut bullets would create more ragged wounds in their enemies. Several such bullets have been discovered at Revolutionary War battle sites.

Source: Roger R.P. Dechame, "To 'Bite the Bullet,'" *The Bulletin of the Fort Ticonderoga Museum*, 15 (1993): 403-406.

A 1768 drawing by Lorenz Heister of amputation procedures (Royal Society of Medicine, London)

hospital. If his regiment was in a town or city, the hospital might be located in a private home (often that of an absent Loyalist); during long winter encampments such as those at Valley Forge and Morristown the hospital might be in three-hut complexes built to house twenty-five patients. In either case the sick soldier met with the regimental surgeon or one of his mates. The surgeon knew that any soldier out of action due to wounds or sickness was worse than useless; he was a drain on meager supplies, personnel, and payroll. Depending on the ailment, the surgeon or his mates would either treat the sufferer and send him back to duty or confine him to the regimental hospital. If the case proved serious or epidemic, the surgeon would send the soldier on to the general hospital for more-specialized care or for discharge from the army. The general hospitals were usually commandeered private homes and barns or public buildings such as churches or colleges. The only advantages to these structures was their size; they were generally too cramped, cold, or dirty for the purpose of restoring sick men to health. Many soldiers who technically should have gone to a general hospital remained with their regiment, however, due to lack of transportation.

Dubious Drugs. Assuming the regimental surgeon considered the soldier's problem treatable with drugs, he turned to the contents of the regiment's medicine chest. More than likely it was seriously short of the eighty-one different medicines it was supposed to contain, for before the war most medical supplies had come from England, and, of course, that source was no longer available. Medicines trickled in from ships braving the Royal Navy's blockade, but the supply in America soon ran low; private doctors and apothecaries were increasingly un-

willing to take wildly inflated Continental money for their precious stores of drugs. Only after the French alliance in 1778 did medical supplies arrive at the hospitals in decent quantities. American doctors and surgeons tended to rely on relatively few "standby" drugs, anyway. "Peruvian bark" was a favorite and may actually have done some good; it was from this source that quinine, the answer to malaria, was later developed. Other choices were less effective and almost universally unpleasant. Great store was put in purgatives, either tartar emetic to induce vomiting or concoctions of ipecac, rhubarb, and other agents swallowed to "cleanse" the body by defecation. Venereal diseases might be treated with a drink made of spring water, sumac roots, and gunpowder. If that did not work (and it is difficult to imagine that it did) the patient took a stronger dose of mineral salts and turpentine. For snakebites the surgeon sometimes applied a mercury-based ointment accompanied by doses of olive oil. Kidney problems sometimes required an elixir of horseradish roots, mustard seeds, and gin. Narcotics in the form of gum opium or laudanum (a tincture of opium) deadened the pain of toothaches and especially of surgery, for there were no effective anesthetics.

Battlefield Surgery. When on campaign, American armies included "flying," or mobile, hospitals housed in tents or huts. These contained operating tables for the gruesome work of treating bayonet or gunshot wounds. Musket bullets, three-quarters of an inch in diameter, often created shocking wounds. If the bullet was lodged in the body, long probes located it while retractors held the skin and muscle apart, and extractors drew the bullet and bits of clothing from the wound. The skin was then stitched back together. If the ball had struck bone, the

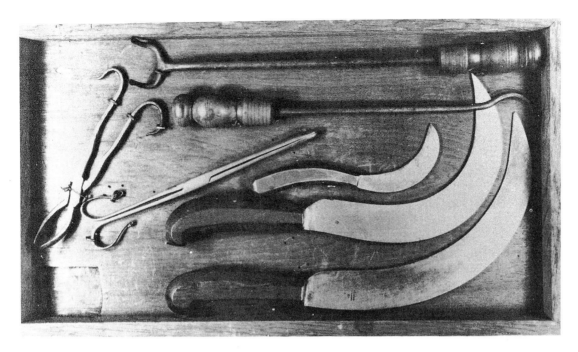

A field operating kit of the Revolutionary War; the instruments included are forceps, a bullet extractor, two retractors, and three amputating knives (Armed Forces Institute of Pathology, Washington, D.C.)

bone was often shattered beyond saving, and amputation was the only alternative. For this grisly job the surgeon's kit contained tourniquets, forceps, surgical knives, bone saws, and usually a few opiates. The patient was strapped or held down and the operation carried out as quickly as possible. Shock was the primary danger in any amputation, so speed was essential. In this American doctors could learn much from the enemy, as Thacher discovered when he observed the great "skill and dexterity" of British surgeons operating on their own wounded after the Battle of Bemis Heights in 1777. If the patient survived the operation, however, the greatest concern was infection. In an age before tools and bandages were sterilized, when doctors had little idea how infection worked, even flesh wounds could be as life-threatening as highly intrusive operations such as amputations.

Sanitation. Hygienic conditions in American camps were often deplorable, even by the standards of the time. European soldiers understood that it was important to keep latrines far away from tents and drinking water. Americans had little experience with army camps before the Revolution; during the French and Indian War, British officers were scandalized by the filth and disorder of American camps, and when Washington took command of the Continental Army in 1775, he had much the same reaction. These conditions were perfect for contracting and spreading disease among a closely packed population of soldiers. Some American doctors strove to improve camp conditions. One, Hugh Willamson, conducted an "experiment" with American soldiers encamped in the Great Dismal Swamp of North Carolina and Virginia after the battle of Camden in 1780. Williamson wondered

if strict attention to cleanliness in dress and lodging, a wholesome diet, and good camp drainage would reduce the incidence of sickness. His findings were encouraging: out of a force ranging from five hundred to twelve hundred men, only two died in six months, an incredible survival rate for the time. Sadly, Williamson's experiment was not tried elsewhere, and disease continued to be the great killer of American soldiers. Statistically a Revolutionary soldier had a 98 percent chance of survival on the battlefield; that chance dropped to 75 percent the moment he entered a hospital—small wonder that soldiers often preferred to suffer in silence rather than face dubious remedies, bloodletting, and hospitalization.

Sources:

Harold L. Peterson, *The Book of the Continental Soldier* (Harrisburg, Pa.: Stackpole, 1968);

James Thacher, *Military Journal of the American Revolution* (New York: Arno, 1969).

REBIRTH OF THE AMERICAN PHILOSOPHICAL SOCIETY

A Tale of Two Societies. Shortly after the Stamp Act unrest in 1765, a group of Philadelphians revived the idea of Benjamin Franklin's famous "junto," a gathering of artisans and gentlemen interested in all aspects of natural philosophy. The American Society, as the new association was called, emphasized the application of science to economic improvement—agriculture, navigation, industry—in the American colonies. At about the same time another group in the same city proposed reviving the American Philosophical Society, which Franklin had founded in 1743 but which had languished in inactivity. Neither society had intended to compete with the

JEFFRIES'S HIGH-ALTITUDE EXPERIMENTS

John Jeffries's balloon flights were not mere joyrides; on his first ascent he took with him a carefully selected array of instruments, intending to collect scientific data, the first attempt of its kind. He brought a thermometer and a barometer for measuring temperature and air pressure at different heights, a hygrometer for humidity, and an "electrometer," apparently an experimental device for measuring atmospheric electricity. Additionally he brought a telescope, a compass, ribbons to throw out to help determine his flight direction and speed, and six four-ounce bottles filled with distilled water. The bottles were to be emptied and then stoppered at various heights to obtain air samples for chemical analysis. During the flight the electrometer proved useless, Jeffries reporting that he "could never discover it to be affected." Nevertheless Jeffries made twelve observations of temperature, air pressure, and humidity up to a height of 9,309 feet above sea level, and the data he collected agrees closely with that obtained from modern observations.

Source: Mary Beth Norton, "America's First Aeronaut: Dr. John Jeffries," *History Today*, 18 (October 1968): 722–729.

other, but they soon found themselves rivals. Both aspired to become great scientific societies and were at the same stage of development. Each society embarked on aggressive membership drives, especially for political allies. The Philosophical Society courted Pennsylvania's executive faction, and when Gov. John Penn became a patron of the society, the members easily got permission to hold their meetings in the State House (for free) while their rivals were forced to rent space elsewhere. Sensing its strength, the Philosophical Society tried to amalgamate the American Society by electing its members en masse to the Philosophical Society. American Society members regarded the Philosophical Society's attempt at unification as a highhanded and hostile takeover, and the competition continued.

Playing to the Public. As it happened, competition had positive side effects, for it brought issues of science and its pursuit in America to public attention. In order to attract interested candidates the rival societies printed essays on science and technology in Philadelphia's newspapers. The papers also advertized membership drives. Predictably the newspapers championing one society or the other were rivals too; the Philosophical Society regularly used the *Pennsylvania Chronicle* while the American Society favored the *Pennsylvania Gazette*. Anyone comparing newspapers would soon discover that the two societies were not clones by any means. The Philosophical Society sought to advance theoretical knowledge in the

tradition of the prestigious Royal Society and accordingly attracted more of the elite. The more technology-minded American Society tended to get a greater share of merchants, artisans, and professionals, especially physicians. In January 1768 the Philosophical Society reprinted Franklin's original proposal of 1743 in the *Pennsylvania Chronicle* as a statement of its objectives as well as an obvious attempt to co-opt the image of their famous founder. The American Society fought back by showcasing articles on American natural history, inventions, wine production, and other patriotic subjects, such as Lionel Chalmers' observations on South Carolina weather and its medical effects. The 1769 transit of Venus gave the Philosophical Society, always less impressed with gadgets or inventions, a tremendous boost over its rival. The much anticipated and publicized event played to the Philosophical Society's decided advantage in astronomical knowledge; its members used public enthusiasm over the celestial phenomenon to successfully raise money for expensive observation equipment. (The colonial legislature eventually raised £200 of public money). The American Society was unable to match the deeper pockets of the Philosophical Society, but it scored heavily in November 1768 when its members persuaded Benjamin Franklin to be their president.

E Duo, Unum. By the end of the year, however, members of the two societies wished to stop the feud and voted to negotiate a union. Committees settled major differences, and on 20 December each society met and agreed to the terms of the union. Membership lists were exchanged, and the first meeting of the united society occurred on 2 January 1769. The members adopted the cumbersome hybrid title of the American Philosophical Society, Held at Philadelphia, for Promoting Useful Knowledge, but in practice it was always shortened to the American Philosophical Society, the name it retains today. In the election for officers that followed, Franklin was confirmed as president, a position he held until his death in 1790. His election was a good move: Franklin was internationally known, and his prestige gave the new American Philosophical Society instant credibility (the French referred to it as "Franklin's Society"). With broader membership and proven fund-raising skills, the American Philosophical Society set about the important work of publishing the first volume of its journal, *Transactions*, in 1771, which was enthusiastically received in Europe and "much sought after by the Literati in London." Franklin's dream of a distinguished American scientific society had finally come to pass.

Source:
Brooke Hindle, *The Pursuit of Science in Revolutionary America 1735–1789* (Chapel Hill: University of North Carolina Press, 1956).

A SCIENCE OF AGRICULTURE

A Growing Discipline. Only about 10 percent of the American population lived in towns or cities during this

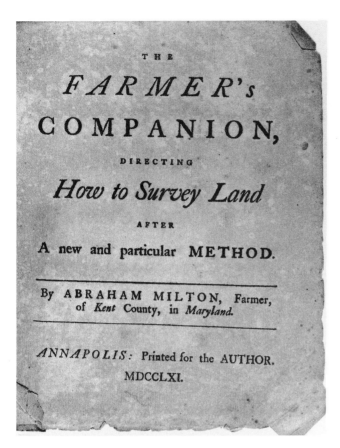

Title page for a 1761 manual on surveying, the first of its kind in the Middle colonies (Maryland Historical Society, Baltimore)

period; the rest lived and worked on farms. Agriculture was by far the primary American employment, but it was in dire need of improvement. Whether the crop was for export, like tobacco, or for home consumption, like corn, American farmers tended to work the same land over and over again until it was exhausted and then clear new lands. In England, where farmers did not have extensive land to use in the American manner, gentleman farmers experimented with techniques for getting the most out of their land for as long as possible: crop rotation, soil enhancement by fertilizing, more efficient use of cattle, and employing new and better farming implements. They discovered that agriculture could benefit a great deal from more scientific farming methods.

American Application. Some informed Americans advocated the new techniques in the colonies. In 1758 the *American Magazine* suggested that townspeople form "companies or societies" to discuss agricultural improvement and to make new experiments. Unfortunately little was done to introduce English practices in America. Some newspapers advertised new implements and marl (calcium-rich clay for enhancing depleted soil) and instructions on its use. Enthusiasts tried out new plow designs and seed drills, and a few put their minds to designing harvesting and threshing machines to improve production. Even so, the practices of everyday farmers were not much affected. Part of the problem was that English practices could not always apply to colonial conditions: America had a wide range of different soils, and its thousand-mile Atlantic coastline comprised several climates. Jared Eliot's *Essays on Field Husbandry,* published in 1760 and based on his own experiments in Killingworth, Connecticut, was a serious attempt to modify English techniques to American climate, but he was the only colonial to write extensively on the subject of agricultural improvement. Perhaps the main reason for America's slow progress in this regard was its persistent problem with labor. Many of the new practices required more hands to make them productive, and the cost of labor in America—free, indentured, or slave—had always been high. Many planters did not see the point to harvesting and threshing more grain if they could not afford to clear, plant, and cultivate the additional land required. As late as 1775 one author still saw wasteful practices everywhere and argued for an American association, on the model of the American Philosophical Society, dedicated to encouraging agricultural improvement. Such a society might "settle a plan of operations, which would, in a few years, by means of an annual subscription . . . alter the face of things. They might reduce these doubtful points to a certainty; they might introduce a better system of rural economy and be in a few years of infinite service to their country." However, no such effort was made, and only a relative few experimented seriously with scientific agriculture: well-to-do planters such as Thomas Jefferson and George Washington in Virginia, William Allen in Pennsylvania, and Benjamin Gale in Connecticut. Wherever land remained plentiful and labor dear, the great majority of Americans had few inducements to explore the science of agriculture.

Source:

Brooke Hindle, *The Pursuit of Science in Revolutionary America 1735–1789* (Chapel Hill: University of North Carolina Press, 1956).

SMALLPOX AND REVOLUTION

Dreaded Disease. Before the nineteenth century smallpox swept eastern North America in recurrent epidemics. Unlike malaria or yellow fever, which kept mostly to the southern half of the eastern seaboard, smallpox could break out anywhere. For any early American its appearance in his or her neighborhood was an ever-present possibility, and there was even an atmosphere of inevitability about its arrival, much as there is about the flu today. "It is the opinion of some very observent men," according to a contemporary, "that there are few persons but what have the Small-pox at some period of their lives." It was a killer and was feared not only because it could spread like wildfire but also because it was an ugly, disfiguring disease. One writer concluded "there is no disease so universal, and at the same time so mortal."

Characteristics. The onset of smallpox was signaled by fatigue, high fever, and aching. Since these could be

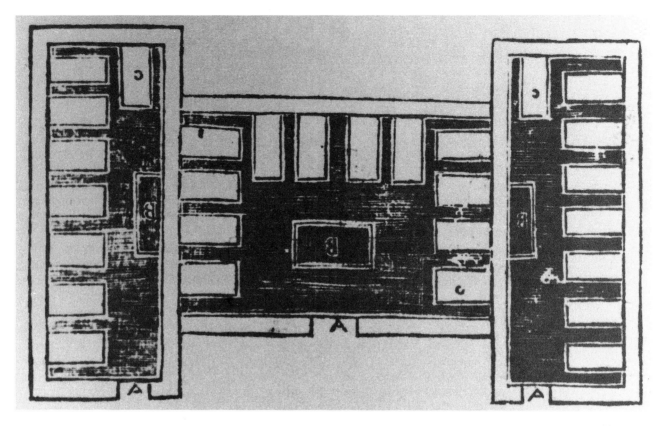

Plan of a hospital from James Tilton's *Economical Observations on Military Hospitals* (1813)

A DIFFICULT DECISION

People who had never had smallpox tended to avoid inoculating themselves and their children until a crisis appeared. After all, the procedure involved deliberate exposure to the disease, with the certainty of a period of sickness and the possibility of death. When smallpox struck a community, people were forced to make painful choices. Contracting the disease "in the natural way" was terrible even to contemplate, but the uncertainty of inoculation could be even more frightening. Sally Fisher of Philadelphia was "very anxious, about my little Boy what to do for the best, whether to Inoculate him or not." She decided in favor of the procedure. Her son survived, and when smallpox revisited the city two years later, she had her daughter inoculated also. Women often had to make these choices in the absence of their husbands. Lucy Knox, whose husband Henry was a general in the American army, placed herself and their baby daughter in a Boston smallpox hospital to receive the treatment. Henry approved of the decision but confessed "my heart palpitates at the thought of my Lucy being in the least danger, May God preserve and carry you and our dear babe safe through it." Abigail Adams likewise

made the decision without her Congressman husband John, but as she left the inoculation hospital in Boston, she was able to report that "all my treasure of children have passed thro one of the most terrible Diseases to which human nature is subject, and not one of us is wanting." Those who were reluctant to choose inoculation, however, ran a great risk. Even Benjamin Franklin hesitated, and it cost him dearly: his four-year-old son died in 1736, "by the Small Pox taken in the common way." Many years later he confessed in his *Autobiography* (1868): "I long regretted bitterly and still regret that I had not given it to him by Inoculation. This I mention for the Sake of parents, who omit that Operation on the Supposition that they should never forgive themselves if a child died under it; my Example showing that the Regret may be the same either way, and that therefore the safer should be chosen."

Sources: Mary Beth Norton, *Liberty's Daughters: The Revolutionary Experience of American Women, 1750–1800* (Ithaca, N.Y.: Cornell University Press, 1996);

Benjamin Franklin, *The Autobiography of Benjamin Franklin*, edited by Leonard W. Labaree, Ralph L. Ketcham, and others (New Haven: Yale University Press, 1964).

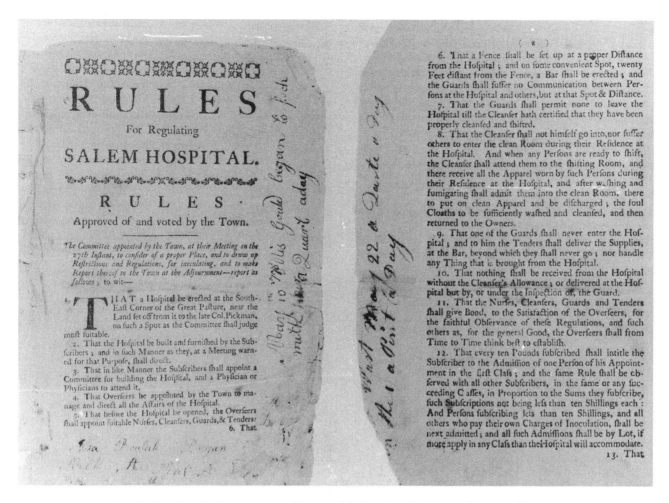

RULES

For Regulating

SALEM HOSPITAL.

RULES.

Approved of and voted by the Town.

The Committee appointed by the Town, at their Meeting on the 27th Instant, to consider of a proper Place, and to draw up Restrictions and Regulations, for inoculating, and to make Report thereof to the Town at the Adjournment—report as follows; to wit—

1. THAT a Hospital be erected at the South-East Corner of the Great Pasture, near the Land set off from it to the late Col. Pickman, on such a Spot as the Committee shall judge most suitable.

2. That the Hospital be built and furnished by the Subscribers; and in such Manner as they, at a Meeting warned for that Purpose, shall direct.

3. That in like Manner the Subscribers shall appoint a Committee for building the Hospital, and a Physician or Physicians to attend it.

4. That Overseers be appointed by the Town to manage and direct all the Affairs of the Hospital.

5. That before the Hospital be opened, the Overseers shall appoint suitable Nurses, Cleaners, Guards, & Tenders.

6. That

6. That a Fence shall be set up at a proper Distance from the Hospital; and on some convenient Spot, twenty Feet distant from the Fence, a Bar shall be erected; and the Guards shall suffer no Communication between Persons at the Hospital and others, but at that Spot & Distance.

7. That the Guards shall permit none to leave the Hospital till the Cleanser hath certified that they have been properly cleansed and shifted.

8. That the Cleanser shall not himself go into, nor suffer others to enter the clean Room during their Residence at the Hospital. And when any Persons are ready to shift, the Cleanser shall attend them to the shifting Room, and there receive all the Apparel worn by such Persons during their Residence at the Hospital, and after washing and fumigating shall admit them into the clean Room, there to put on clean Apparel and be discharged; the foul Cloaths to be sufficiently washed and cleansed, and then returned to the Owners.

9. That one of the Guards shall never enter the Hospital; and to him the Tenders shall deliver the Supplies, at the Bar, beyond which they shall never go; nor handle any Thing that is brought from the Hospital.

10. That nothing shall be received from the Hospital without the Cleanser's Allowance; or delivered at the Hospital but by, or under the Inspection of, the Guard.

11. That the Nurses, Cleaners, Guards and Tenders shall give Bond, to the Satisfaction of the Overseers, for the faithful Observance of these Regulations, and such others as, for the general Good, the Overseers shall from Time to Time think best to establish.

12. That every ten Pounds subscribed shall intitle the Subscriber to the Admission of one Person of his Appointment in the first Class; and the same Rule shall be observed with all other Subscribers, in the same or any succeeding Classes, in Proportion to the Sums they subscribe, such Subscriptions not being less than ten Shillings each: And Persons subscribing less than ten Shillings, and all others who pay their own Charges of Inoculation, shall be next admitted; and all such Admissions shall be by Lot, if more apply in any Class than the Hospital will accommodate.

13. That

Regulations for administering a smallpox ward (Massachusetts Historical Society, Boston)

symptoms of any number of ailments, the victim could easily spread the illness before breaking out with the definitive pock marks. These were blisters, often large, which filled with pus as the sickness progressed. If the sufferer survived, the eruptions eventually subsided but left permanent scars. George Washington contracted smallpox as a young man, and although his eruptions were not severe, his face bore the scars to the end of his life. A community's first and best defense was to quarantine the afflicted person and anyone who had had recent contact with him. Even so, sometimes the disease was too widespread to contain, and it became epidemic, especially in urban centers such as Philadelphia or New York. When that occurred, the mortality rate could be high. Cotton Mather, a Boston minister, compiled statistics during the 1720–1721 outbreak there, noting that 15 percent of uninoculated smallpox victims had died of the disease.

Debatable Safeguard. Fortunately those who contracted smallpox and survived never had to go through the ordeal again: they were now immune. In addition some victims seemed to have much milder cases and yet were also immune thereafter. A procedure originating in the Orient slowly made its way into Europe and America

that seemed to promise relief. If a small incision was made in the skin of a healthy person, and the wound was dabbed with the pus, or "matter," from a smallpox victim, the healthy person then contracted a mild form of the disease and was thereafter immune. The procedure still carried risk—according to Mather's study, 3 percent of those thus inoculated died anyway—but the odds of escaping death and disfigurement improved dramatically. Many opposed inoculation, however, as untrustworthy and too dangerous, believing that it actually spread the disease. In 1774 concerned citizens in Philadelphia formed a Society for Inoculating the Poor, which unfortunately foundered during the Revolution, but this was an exceptionally foresighted effort. Resistance to the procedure was still high a year later, when the Revolutionary War began; several colonies passed laws forbidding its practice within their borders.

Epidemic. Armies and cities under siege were ideal breeding grounds for diseases of all sorts. In 1776 New England was struck with a smallpox epidemic directly related to the Revolutionary War. British troops had just evacuated Boston after a ten-month siege, leaving an outbreak of smallpox behind them (Americans accused them of deliberately spreading the disease). At nearly the same time some New England soldiers returning from the failed Canada expedition brought smallpox back with them: of the eight thousand men who marched to Canada, two thousand fell ill with the disease. George Washington knew from firsthand experience what smallpox could do. Fearing an outbreak that would cripple his main army, he ordered a general inoculation for his troops and made the procedure available to civilians as well. The experiment-by-necessity was a resounding success; physician Benjamin Gale compiled statistics from Boston to show that only one person out of one hundred inoculated died—a great improvement over Mather's 3 percent a half century before. One might think that the benefits of inoculation could no longer be doubted, but that would be to underestimate conservative resistance to the procedure. New York still outlawed the practice, so Washington was forced to suspend inoculation while his army operated there and even to threaten punishment for any soldier or officer undergoing the procedure. As a result smallpox outbreaks continued throughout the war.

Sources:

Harold L. Peterson, *The Book of the Continental Soldier* (Harrisburg, Pa.: Stackpole, 1968);

Ola Elizabeth Winslow, *A Destroying Angel: The Conquest of Smallpox in Colonial Boston* (Boston: Houghton Mifflin, 1974).

THE TRANSIT OF VENUS

A Celestial Event. In 1716 Englishman Edmund Halley (for whom the comet is named) described a procedure for using observations of the "transit" of the planet Venus across the face of the Sun to determine the solar parallax—an angle calculated from two positions on Earth—and hence the distance from the Earth to the Sun. Astronomers were eager to know this distance because it would enable them to calculate more accurately the distances of the other known planets from the Sun. They knew the relative distances of the planets from one another, but they could not determine accurately the solar system's size without learning the Earth's distance from the Sun. And there was a problem: transits occurred rarely; before 1761, the last transit of Venus had been in 1639. The transit was expected again in 1761 and 1769, but after that not for another 105 years. Clearly the opportunity to make precise observations had to be siezed, for the chance would not come again for anyone then living. The entire scientific world focused on the approaching events.

The Requirements. A proper calculation of the parallax required at least three observation points on the Earth, each with precisely measured longitude and latitude. Each observer had to know the exact local time of day when the transit began (as well as the time at that same moment at the Royal Observatory in Greenwich, England), and then had to measure the length of time of the transit from start to finish with the same pinpoint accuracy. The most powerful telescopes and the most exact

TRANSIT AND PARALLAX

The planet Venus moves in an orbit closer to the Sun than that of the Earth, and it completes its orbit sooner. This means that Venus periodically passes between the Earth and the Sun: for a few hours these three bodies are almost directly aligned. When this happens, Venus can be seen from the Earth, appearing as a small, dark disc moving across the face of the Sun. When this "transit" is viewed from different points on earth, careful calculations yield the Sun's "parallax"—the angle of the Sun made by a change in the position of the observer on earth. The parallax is a key factor for determining the Earth's distance from the Sun at the time the transit was observed. In turn that distance helps resolve the size of the entire solar system, and the relative distances of the other planets in it from the Sun and from each other.

Source: Silvio A. Bedini, *Thinkers and Tinkers: Early American Men of Science* (New York: Scribners, 1975).

timekeeping intruments would be required for the transit when it came. Clear weather was also a necessity.

American Science. Those colonials interested in developing the sciences recognized the advantages of American involvement in these celestial events: "It would be a great honour," wrote one, "to our young Colleges in America if they forthwith prepared themselves with a proper apparatus for that Observation & made it." However, almost nothing was done in America for the 1761 transit. John Winthrop of Harvard was the only American astronomer with a European reputation at the time; equipment was lacking; and few provincial legislatures wished to spend public money to fund scientific observations. Massachusetts was the only province that made any real effort, and the results had not been entirely satisfactory.

One Last Opportunity. The last chance for any living person came eight years later in 1769. For the newly revitalized American Philosophical Society, and for the reputation and promotion of scientific endeavor in America generally, the 1769 transit was an opportunity that the scientific community could not afford to miss. And this time American observations were considered vital. Only the beginning of the transit would be visible in Europe, but most of it would be observable in the North American colonies; in fact, astronomers calculated that the area around Lake Superior was one of the few spots on Earth where the full transit could be seen. Due to its changed political situation, Massachusetts would not spend the money to support the observations this time. The American Philosophical Society in Philadelphia raised public money by somewhat untruthfully declaring the observations to be "an Object, on which the Promotion of Astronomy and Navigation, and consequently of Trade and Commerce so much depends." In fact the transit was of only marginal importance to navigation and trade, but some people who would willingly support efforts to boost commerce would not contribute to purely scientific knowledge.

Preparations. The American observers employed the most sophisticated instruments available to them. Near Philadelphia, master clockmaker David Rittenhouse used his own specially built timepiece, a 144-power refracting telescope, and an equal-altitude instrument. In Cambridge, Massachusetts, John Winthrop had the use of Harvard's eight-foot telescope and exceptionally accurate pendulum clock and an astronomical quadrant he borrowed from Boston's collector of customs. Other observations points were set up in Rhode Island, New York, New Jersey, and Virginia. In all, at least twenty-two official observations were made in North America. Popular enthusiasm grew; nonacademics gathered smoked glasses to use with their less powerful telescopes and pocket watches. They knew little about what was going on but realized that it was big and wanted to be part of it.

Success. When the day came that June, the weather was clear in virtually every place where an observation was made. In the cities crowds gathered in hushed respect to watch the observers. Rittenhouse, peering expectantly through his telescope, became so excited at the moment of contact that he actually forgot to report it for several seconds (in a situation when every second made a huge difference in the final calculations). When it was all over, the American Philosophical Society printed several observations. The quality of these varied considerably, but all were sought out, for it was felt that a greater number of variations would ultimately yield a more accurate mean. The European scientists seemed pleased with the American efforts; one Swedish scientist declared that they had given "infinite satisfaction to our astronomers." The data gained was a triumph in itself; although several American astronomers and mathematicians tackled the painstaking math, only one attempt to calculate the parallax was actually published in America, and that was after some of the European results were already known. Comparing Pennsylvania and Greenwich observations, Rittenhouse and a compatriot reckoned the distance from the Earth to the Sun at about 93 million miles—close to today's accepted figure. The transit of Venus gave not only public attention and a much-needed stimulus to scientific pursuit in America, the observations brought international attention. One enthusiast undoubtedly spoke for many when he declared that the transit of Venus "hath done a Credit to our Country which would have been cheaply purchased for twenty times the Sum!"

Sources:

Brooke Hindle, *The Pursuit of Science in Revolutionary America 1735–1789* (Chapel Hill: University of North Carolina Press, 1956);

Harry Wolfe, *The Transits of Venus: A Study of Eighteenth-century Science* (Princeton, N.J.: Princeton University Press, 1959).

WAR AND THE DECLINE OF SCIENCE

English Connection. The Revolutionary War had immediate and overwhelmingly negative effects on the pursuit of science and technological improvement in America. Perhaps most obviously, many of the professional connections with British men of science, so slowly and painstakingly cultivated by men such as Benjamin Franklin, John Winthrop, and Alexander Garden, were irretrievably lost when the fighting began (some correspondence resumed, however, after the peace). Also, not all Americans were revolutionary. The rebellious colonies lost perhaps a third of their doctors and scientists in a Loyalist "brain drain." John Jeffries and Alexander Garden, for example, fled their homes in America—Garden never returned.

Arrested Development. The war interrupted efforts at scientific and technological improvements that would have advanced learning, public health, and productivity. Plans for a public observatory near Philadelphia, headed by David Rittenhouse, were dashed by the opening of hostilities—there was simply no public money available for anything that did not directly benefit the war effort. A New York City plan for a public water system, delivered through hollowed logs, was curtailed for the same reason and then stopped altogether when the British occupied that city. For obvious reasons the revolutionary movement sparked interest in American manufactures, which had been long discouraged by British imperial

ONE DOCTOR'S ARMY EXPERIENCE

After the battles of Saratoga, New York, in the autumn of 1777, the American, British, and German wounded were sent to nearby Albany for treatment. James Thacher, of the American army, recorded that "not less than one thousand wounded and sick are now in this city; the Dutch Church, and several private houses are occupied as hospitals." Thacher and his colleagues had much to do: "I am obliged to devote the whole of my time, from eight o'clock in the morning to a late hour in the evening, to the care of our patriots. . . . Amputating limbs, trepanning fractured skulls, and dressing the most formidable wounds, have familiarized my mind to scenes of woe." He added, bitterly, "here is a fine field for professional improvement [employment]."

Source: James Thacher, *Military Journal of the American Revolution* (New York: Arno, 1969).

A painting of David Bushnell's submarine the *American Turtle* after its abortive attempt to sink HMS *Eagle* in New York Harbor (Wide World Photos)

economy. Just before the war began, a plan for a water-powered spinning mill was presented to the American Philosophical Society, two decades before Samuel Slater built his famous mill in Pawtucket, Rhode Island. But building factories for pottery, finished iron goods, and especially textiles, required large outlays of capital, not to mention overseas markets for finished products not consumed at home. America's great manufacturing potential would have to wait for realization. Private efforts to encourage useful technology also suffered setbacks. Virginia's Society for the Promotion of Useful Knowledge, founded in 1773, gave its first gold medal to John Hobday for his threshing machine, but it did little else. It might have if the imperial crisis had not intervened, but the society declined during the war and never recovered.

Higher Learning. America's fledgling centers of science and learning were located mainly in its cities. Several of these were occupied by the British in the course of the war, and others suffered from friend and foe alike. Early in the fighting Harvard College was forced to close when the American army used its buildings as barracks. New York's King's College was looted by British troops in 1776, its instruments and books sold off by the soldiers for drinking money. The College of Philadelphia had its halls used as barracks by Americans and later as hospitals by British troops. Rhode Island College (later Brown University) was a barracks during most of the war, first for American and then French soldiers. Princeton College in New Jersey actually became a battleground: Nassau Hall still bears the scars made by American cannons against redcoats who barricaded themselves inside.

Conclusion. Whatever America's triumphs in the conflict with Britain, the war was a severe setback for American science. Nearly all the gains made in the previous decades were compromised by the consequences of a long war with the former colonies' chief patron of the sciences. Together with the damage done to higher learning institutions, the loss of talented Loyalists, and the disruption of the economy, the scientific community required great efforts to repair itself in the postwar years.

Source:
Brooke Hindle, *The Pursuit of Science in Revolutionary America 1735–1789* (Chapel Hill: University of North Carolina Press, 1956).

HEADLINE MAKERS

DAVID BUSHNELL

1742?-1824
INVENTOR

Background. David Bushnell must have seemed an unlikely student when he entered Yale College in 1771. For one thing, he was almost thirty—twice as old as the other students. He and his only brother had worked on their father's secluded Saybrook, Connecticut, farm until the senior Bushnell's death in 1769, when David was around twenty-seven. David, however, had had enough of farming. He sold his share of the farm, moved to New Haven, and secured a tutor to help him "catch up" academically and to prepare for entrance to Yale. It was a bold move for him. Bushnell had spent his youth almost entirely on the family farm, where he had devoted all his leisure time to reading, which fueled his desire for knowledge but alienated him from social contact. At college he remained something of an introvert, animated by a simple desire for "something more." Despite the much-acclaimed benefits of a country life, Bushnell's health was never robust.

A Peculiar Interest. Whatever drew Bushnell to pursue an advanced education, it was clearly physical science that fascinated him. While still a student, Bushnell became involved in a purely theoretical discussion over whether or not gunpowder could explode underwater. Many believed that the lack of an atmosphere and the suffocating properties of water would prevent explosion. Bushnell disagreed and settled the debate by a small demonstration. He must have been working on this and related problems for some time, for in 1775, the year he graduated, he completed his masterpiece, a one-man submarine capable of underwater attack, which he named the *American Turtle*.

Revolution. By the time Bushnell completed the *Turtle*, the war between the colonies and Great Britain was already in progress. He demonstrated his invention before the Connecticut Committee of Safety, which approved the use of the *Turtle* against British warships at the first opportunity. The chance came in 1776, when a British armada descended on New York harbor; on a

September night, the *Turtle* made the first submarine attack in history. Bushnell, however, found himself unequal to the physical effort required to pilot the *Turtle*, which was powered by human muscle. As a result he found a volunteer, Sgt. Ezra Lee, to pilot the boat. In the waters off New York, with currents and tides to contend with, simply getting from place to place was strenuous. The operator needed to be skillful as well as strong to submerge far enough away from the target to be unseen, find the ship underwater, dive under the hull, attach an underwater bomb called a "torpedo," and then escape before his air ran out or the torpedo exploded.

Eagle. The target was H.M.S. *Eagle*, the British fleet's flagship. The *Turtle's* pilot managed to get the submarine under the *Eagle's* hull, but he could not attach the torpedo. After several tries, his air running out and perhaps fearful that he had triggered the bomb's timer too soon, Lee abandoned the attempt. The torpedo drifted away on the tide. Its explosion did no damage but caused a minor panic among the British fleet, which then moved to new anchorages. The *Turtle* made another unsuccessful attempt the next year in the Delaware River. Failure cost Bushnell what support he had; without the means to continue his work and amid general ridicule, he gave up his submarine project. However, he continued to work for the American cause, joining the Continental Army as an officer of engineers. He was stationed at West Point when the war ended in 1783, and once again chose a new life. He opted to receive five years' pay for his military services, instead of half-pay for life, and with this money reportedly went to France. There Bushnell witnessed the early years of the French Revolution. In 1795 he reappeared in Georgia, earning a modest living as a schoolteacher, then as the head of a private school. He changed professions once more, practicing medicine in Warrentown, Georgia, until his death in January or February 1826. Apparently solitary to the end, he never married. Bushnell was not a first-rate scientist. He was a talented technician who set his mind to particular problems and found specific solutions to them. Although he was not able to prove the worth of the *Turtle* in combat, he nevertheless designed and built the first viable submarine in history and proved its potential as a military weapon. Bushnell's technical achievement was unmatched until the Civil War, nearly a century later.

Source:

Frederick Wagner, *Submarine Fighter of the American Revolution: The Story of David Bushnell* (New York: Dodd, Mead, 1963).

ALEXANDER GARDEN

1730?-1791
NATURALIST

Origins. To a student of natural science born and raised in cold and rugged Scotland the lush forests and semitropical coastal lands of South Carolina must have seemed a kind of paradise. Alexander Garden emigrated there in his early twenties, shortly after completing his studies in the great intellectual center of Edinburgh and receiving his M.D. degree in 1753. In Prince William County, South Carolina, he entered practice as a physician to wealthy planters.

New Surroundings. Garden was enthralled by his new home. Virtually every plant and animal was new to the young doctor, and he was eager to share his interests and discoveries with a wider intellectual world than South Carolina offered. Opportunity came disguised as adversity. New emigrants to the American South typically underwent a period of adjustment—then known as "seasoning"—to the often fierce climate. Garden's seasoning apparently went badly, for after a year's residence he traveled northward for his health. He quickly made contacts with some of the leading lights of America's growing scientific community. In New York he met with Lt. Gov. Cadwallader Colden, also an avid botanist. Through Colden's impressive library, Garden first became acquainted with Carl Linnaeus's new system for classifying the world's flora and fauna. Returning to South Carolina via Philadelphia, Garden conferred with the renowned Quaker botanist John Bartram.

Linnaeus. Back in South Carolina in 1755, Garden got the chance to see yet another facet of America's natural variety. He accompanied an expedition to secure Cherokee support at the outset of the French and Indian War, penetrating as far as the Blue Ridge Mountains. Determined to live no longer in scientific isolation, he reported his observations from this trip to acquaintances in Britain and even attempted to open a correspondence with Linnaeus himself. Three years and several unanswered letters later, Garden finally received a reply from the great man. The ice broken, Garden and Linnaeus corresponded voluminously thereafter. To Linnaeus and to his faraway friends, Garden sent specimens of American animals and plants, proposing many new species that were often rejected by his European colleagues. Garden was not simply being a nuisance; in the world of natural science, discovering hitherto unknown species was the way to publication, recognition, and fame. He fared better with exotic reptiles and amphibians—the Congo snake and the mud eel are two of Garden's "discoveries"—and achieved fame when a British colleague named a previously unclassified flower after him (*Gardenia*). Linnaeus also had Garden elected to the Swedish Royal Society of Upsala in 1763. British recognition came a decade later: in 1773 Garden was elected to the Royal Society of London. His scientific paper on the mysterious electric eel was read before the society in 1775. But by then the real news in London was of the outbreak of war in the colonies.

Loyalist. Garden was a Loyalist, but he managed at first to avoid undue attention from South Carolinian rebels. His son Alexander, at school in Britain, staunchly supported American independence, but Garden forbade his return. When the main theater of war turned to South Carolina in 1780, neither father nor son could maintain neutrality. Dr. Garden openly sided with the British, and Alexander Jr. came back against his father's will and served the American army. When the war ended, Garden Sr. was exiled and his property confiscated by the victorious Americans. Although later granted permission to return with most of his property restored, Garden refused to go back to America. He had suffered severely from seasickness on his return to England, made worse by the tuberculosis that would eventually kill him. He sought relief by traveling through Europe, and he ended his days in London on 15 April 1791. His exile and illness were made more bearable by the honors he received from the scholarly company he so craved.

Source:

Brooke Hindle, *The Pursuit of Science in Revolutionary America 1735–1789* (Chapel Hill: University of North Carolina Press, 1956).

JOHN JEFFRIES

1745-1819
PHYSICIAN AND BALLOONIST

Boston. John Jeffries, born on 5 February 1745, probably never dreamed that he would be the first American to fly. Jeffries was a thirty-two-year-old Boston physician when the Revolutionary War began in 1775. He was also a Loyalist in a place where loyalty to America's last king was not only unpopular but also dangerous. He had graduated from Harvard twelve years earlier and had continued his studies in England and Scotland. Returning to Boston, he married, became assistant surgeon on a British naval vessel, and settled into the predictable and profitable life of a doctor. Boston was a hotbed of anti-British sentiment during the imperial crisis of the 1760s and early 1770s, but Jeffries never embraced the radical cause although his father was an avowed Patriot. He does not appear to have made many enemies, however, a fact that benefited him after the war.

Exile. Jeffries and his family, along with some fifteen hundred other Loyalists, remained in Boston during the American siege of that town and evacuated with the British forces in 1776. Jeffries worked as a surgeon in the British military hospital in Halifax, Nova Scotia, until 1779, when he moved his family to London so he could lobby for a more permanent position in the medical service. He got the position he wanted in New York (then in British hands), and set sail for America to prepare the way for his family. In his absence his wife died. Heartbroken, Jeffries resigned his commission and returned to London to join the growing community of exiled Americans there.

Balloon Experiments. He was more fortunate than many exiles, for he was able to support himself and his children by setting up a small medical practice, but an event changed the direction of his life yet again. In May 1783 the Montgolfier brothers had launched the first successful but unmanned hot-air balloon in France. More trials followed until, on 21 November, a French balloonist made the first free flight over the cheering crowds of Paris. Four days later Jeffries attended an unmanned British experiment in London and was immediately enthralled. After watching the first manned, freeflight ascensions in England the next year, Jeffries decided no longer to be merely a spectator. Seduced by the lure of flight, and recognizing the balloon's potential for conducting atmospheric experiments, he begged French balloonist Pierre Blanchard to take him along on his next flight. The Frenchman obliged, provided that Jeffries cover virtually all expenses. Jeffries quickly agreed.

First Flight. On 29 November 1784, despite the sobs of his children and several female admirers who begged him not to take the risk, Jeffries boarded Blanchard's "flying boat." While London's "four millions of others (Idlers, thieves, Pickpockets, Princes royal, Nobles &c)" looked on, Blanchard and Jeffries rose quickly above the city. The earth "appeared to run away from us," he later wrote, and, rising above the low clouds, the ground reminded him of "a beautiful coloured map . . . not having the least appearance of hill, elevation . . . or inequality of surface whatsoever." After a somewhat hazardous landing some seventeen miles away in Dartford, Kent, Jeffries returned to a hero's welcome in London.

Crossing the Channel. His taste for flight was by no means satisfied, however; Blanchard planned to make his way home in the next month or so by flying his balloon across the English Channel, and Jeffries was determined to go with him. On 7 January 1785 he got his wish, and the two now-famous aeronauts took off from Dover, wafting on the cold breeze toward Calais. This time the two had brought books, instruments, food, and heavy clothing for the trip, and the extra weight was almost their undoing. The balloon began losing altitude before they were a third of the way across, and part of the balloon even collapsed, threatening to drop them into the frigid Channel far below. The balloonists responded by throwing everything they could spare over the side; first all the ballast, then the books, food, anchors, most of the scientific equipment, and even their outer clothing. It was all to no avail; the balloon was little more than one hundred yards from the water and still four miles from land when a sudden low-pressure pocket lifted them clear of the sea and over the low hills of coastal France. They had another hazardous landing, this time in a forest, but they had made it—the first men to cross the English Channel by air.

Return Home. Jeffries enjoyed the next two months as the toast of Paris, receiving an interview with King Louis XVI and even dining with Benjamin Franklin and John Paul Jones. Jeffries retained his interest in balloon flight but never flew again. He was allowed to return to his homeland, the new United States, in 1789, and he resumed a profitable practice in Boston. For the rest of his days he lead the relatively quiet life he had no doubt expected before the Revolution intervened, and with it the train of events that had brought him fame. He died on 16 September 1819.

Sources:

Mary Beth Norton, "America's First Aeronaut: Dr. John Jeffries," *History Today*, 18 (October 1968): 722–729;

L. T. C. Rolt, *The Aeronauts: A History of Ballooning, 1783–1903* (New York: Walker, 1966).

JOHN WINTHROP

1714-1779

ASTRONOMER

Family. Before the Revolution, Harvard College ranked its freshmen according to family status, a practice often yielding embarrassing results. Coming from one of New England's most famous and influential families, John Winthrop, born on 19 December 1714, was placed at the head of his class when he entered Harvard at age fourteen. He soon made it clear that in his case the honor was fully justified. Devoting himself to science and mathematics, Winthrop developed a rational, methodical, and critical mind that made him America's preeminent academic scientist. He also developed a habit of independent thinking and an impatience for unscientific argument that frequently placed him at odds with more conservative classmates.

Professorship. His ability and reputation were such that in 1738, when he was only twenty-four, he was elected Hollis professor of mathematics and natural philosophy at his alma mater, the second one to receive that honor. He was a controversial choice, not only on account of his known religious liberality but, because of his youth. A rival for the post who had once been his tutor protested that "that Boy . . . knew no more of Philosophy than a Fowl," and that "I could teach him his A.B.C. in the Mathematicks." As Winthrop's career was to prove, that claim was unjustified.

Astronomy. Winthrop's particular delight was astronomy. His first work was on the nature of sunspots, and he later wrote and lectured on comets, but he became better known for his celestial observations of planetary transits across the Sun. These events, such as the transit of Mercury in 1740 and the transits of Venus in 1761 and 1769, were important to the scientific community because accurate measurements made during their observation could yield clues to the size and nature of the solar system, still something of a mystery. In these events all eyes looked to Winthrop, for he was an acknowledged master of the methods and mathematics necessary for accurate computations.

Popular Academic. He held lectures for the public as well as for Harvard's students, and in 1746 he established the first experimental laboratory of its kind at the college, for both instruction and research. One of the laboratory's prize possessions was an electrical battery built by Winthrop's famous correspondent, Benjamin Franklin. To some students, particularly new ones, Winthrop seemed overwhelming. One student later wrote of Winthrop's lectures: "he touched on a few matters rapidly; the subjects were of course very familiar to him—but to the novitiates, 'it was all Greek.' We derived no benefit from his remarks." On the other hand, more advanced students thought he had "a happy talent of communicating his ideas in the easiest and most elegant manner."

Religion v. Science. Winthrop's highest public visibility came in 1755, when a violent earthquake struck America's eastern seaboard. Many ministers interpreted the quake as a sign of God's displeasure and a warning to the faithful and preached and published copiously to that effect. Winthrop, disgusted by the providential and pseudoscientific explanations for what he considered a strictly natural phenomenon, published some of his lectures on the subject. One minister in particular carried the debate into Boston's newspapers, a venue that Winthrop entered with pleasure. In the month-long, sometimes acrimonious debate that followed, Winthrop got the upper hand and in the process brought the science-versus-religion issue into public discourse.

Honors. By the time of the American Revolution, Winthrop was renowned in the scientific communities of America and Europe and had received virtually every accolade his profession could bestow. He was made a fellow of the Royal Society of London in 1766, elected a member of the American Philosophical Society three years later, and received an honorary L.L.D. from Edinburgh in 1771 and from Harvard in 1773. Preferring the pursuit of science to administrative duties, he twice refused the presidency of his college. He was an ardent supporter of independence but did not live to see the end of the war that established it, dying on 3 May 1779. His son James was considered for Harvard's chair of mathematics and natural philosophy, but his uneven temperament cost him that position.

Assessment. Benjamin Franklin is the best-known of America's early scientists today, but Winthrop was perhaps better qualified to be America's premier natural philosopher. Unlike the many-faceted Franklin, who focused more and more on his political career in the 1750s, Winthrop remained immersed in scientific study almost to the exclusion of all other interests for all of his life. He lacked Franklin's intuitive genius (and his talent for self-promotion), but he shared Franklin's capacity for independent thought and had the advantage of superior education, access to the resources of a top intellectual institution, and a first-rate, analytical mind that could grapple with questions of cosmic consequences. Ezra Stiles, the Connecticut minister and scientist, eulogized Winthrop with words that few contemporaries would have disputed. "In Mathematics and natural Philosophy," he wrote, "I believe he had not his equal in Europe."

Source:
Silvio A. Bedini, *Thinkers and Tinkers: Early American Men of Science* (New York: Scribners, 1975).

PUBLICATIONS

William Brown, *Pharmacopoeia Simpliciorum* (Philadelphia: Styner & Cist, 1778)—a comprehensive directory of current medicine and drugs, with recommended dosages. This book was entirely in Latin and not intended for laymen;

Lionel Chalmers, *An Account of the Weather and Diseases of South-Carolina* (London: E. C. Dilly, 1776)—a two-volume effort to systematically determine the effects of climate on health. It includes carefully collected records of weather observations and data on epidemics;

Thomas Clap, *Conjectures upon the Nature and Motion of Meteors* (Norwich, Conn.: Trumbull, 1781)—published posthumously. Although now proven mostly erroneous, Clap's hypotheses were generally well received during his time;

William Gerar DeBrahm, *The Atlantic Pilot* (London: T. Spilsbury, 1772)—the first guide for mariners based on careful surveys of the southeasten Atlantic coast and Florida;

Jared Eliot, *Essays Upon Field Husbandry in New England* (Boston: Edes & Gill, 1760)—advocates the use of the latest agricultural techniques in Britain, adapted to New England's soils and climate;

Flora Virginica (Leiden, 1762)—based on botanical discoveries of John Clayton in Virginia. This was the second edition of a 1739 work, incorporating the new classification system of Swedish botanist Carl Linnaeus;

Benjamin Franklin, *Experiments and Observations on Electricity, made at Philadelphia in America . . .* , fifth edition (London: F. Newbery, 1774)—an illustrated volume of Franklin's letters describing his theories and experiments in electricity;

Benjamin Gale, "Historical Memoirs, relating to the Practice of Inoculation for the Small Pox, in the British American Provinces, particularly in New England," in *Transactions of the American Philosophical Society*, volume 55, 1766—Gale championed inoculation to a still-skeptical public;

Hugh Martin, *A Narrative of a Discovery of a Sovereign Specific for the Cure of Cancers* (Philadelphia: Robert Aitken, 1782)—an example of plausible quackery, Martin's "secret" concoction contained arsenic, actually a popular contemporary medicinal ingredient. He sought endorsement from George Washington, who replied that "recommendations from those who have been restored to health by the efficacy of your medicine would be vastly more pertinent";

John Morgan, *A Recommendation of Inoculation, According to Baron Dimsdale's Method* (Boston: J. Gill, 1776)—when smallpox broke out in the Boston area after British troops left, American officials advised a general inoculation. Morgan wrote this pamphlet both to advise medical officials and to quiet the fears of the populace;

Andrew Oliver, *An Essay on Comets, in Two Parts* (Salem, Mass.: Samuel Hall, 1772)—suggesting something akin to "solar wind," Oliver argued that the direction of comets' tails was caused by the pressure of the sun's atmosphere;

Benjamin Rush, *Experiments and Observations on the Mineral Waters of Philadelphia, Abington, and Bristol* (Philadelphia: James Humphries, 1773)—a comparative study of the supposed medicinal efficacy of mineral springs that describes careful tests of water samples;

Rush, *A Syllabus of a Course of Lectures on Chemistry* (Philadelphia: Robert Aitken, 1770);

Hugh Williamson, "An Essay on the Use of Comets," *Transactions of the American Philosophical Society*, volume 1, 1771—along with a discussion of cosmic data gained from observing comets, the author suggests that comets are in fact solid heavenly bodies, and probably inhabited;

John Winthrop, *Two Lectures on Comets* (Boston: Russell & Henchman, 1759)—the return of Halley's Comet in 1758 confirmed Sir Isaac Newton's "mechanical" view of the universe. Winthrop's lectures provided the American reader with the most up-to-date theories and hypotheses concerning comets at the time;

Winthrop, *Two Lectures on the Parallax and Distance of the Sun as Deducible from the Transit of Venus* (Boston: Edes & Gill, 1769)—the leading American astronomer presents findings based on his observations during the recent transit of Venus.

George Washington's pocket knife and field compass (George Washington Birthplace National Monument, Virginia)

Title page for a popular almanac (Massachusetts Historical Society, Boston)

CHAPTER TWELVE

SPORTS AND RECREATION

by ROBERT J. ALLISON

CONTENTS

OVERVIEW
370

Sidebars and tables are listed in italics.

A 1769 cartoon depicting the raucous crowd at a Pope's Day parade

OVERVIEW

Introduction. The fertile North American continent provided its inhabitants with much free time for recreation and leisure. Colonists had brought with them European games and sports such as bowling, football, cricket, quoits, and cards. Some of these activities, such as cricket and football, fell out of use as they did not require the kinds of skills the colonists needed in their everyday lives. Colonists continued to enjoy other sports as the century progressed. Hunting and fishing, which had been necessary to sustain life, became recreational activities, and shooting contests, which had been features of militia musters, became sporting activities in their own right.

Native American Sports. Long before the Europeans arrived, Native Americans engaged in a variety of fierce athletic competitions. In addition to hunting, fishing, and war, native societies played games that helped develop their skills in these activities. The native men played a game the French called lacrosse because the stick resembled a bishop's crozier. The Iroquois called this game *O-ta-da-jish-qua-age,* and the Cherokee called it "little brother war." Teams composed of between five and one hundred men tried to throw a ball (*ga-ne-a,* in Iroquois) into the other one's goal using only a five-foot netted stick . These competitions could last for days and often involved extremely high stakes. It is said that the 1654 war between the Senecas and Eries resulted from bad faith that the Eries showed after losing a ball game. This sport could be a spectacle or a way to resolve differences between villages or tribes. Among the Iroquois different clans would compete against one another, one team being the Wolf, Bear, Turtle, or Beaver clan to compete against the Deer, Snipe, Heron, or Hawk clan.

Gambling. The native people gambled heavily on these and other sporting activities. While the European colonists did not take up lacrosse, they gambled on virtually everything. In 1752 William Stith preached a sermon before Virginia's general assembly on "The sinfulness and pernicious nature of gaming." In 1765, William Byrd, one of the colonies' richest men, had to sell four hundred slaves to cover his gambling debts. Colonists gambled on horses, cockfights, fistfights, and cards.

Horse Racing. Horses were the essential means of transportation, but they also became an important form of recreation. British aristocrats had made horse racing a form of competition; in the colonies after 1730 wealthy men began importing race horses for breeding purposes. Unlike

A drawing from an instruction book on dancing, circa 1770 (Library Company of Philadelphia)

British races, which typically were run on a long, straight track, colonists built oval tracks to accommodate large crowds of spectators. In this way American horse races became an activity involving entire communities. In the Chesapeake Bay area the summer racing season began in March and lasted until June, while the fall races lasted from September to November. Every week a different community would hold races. In South Carolina the races became a fixture of colonial life, with the newspapers after 1763 publishing race results and the odds on each horse.

Cockfights. In addition to horse races, the colonies south of New York had chickens that were raised for their fighting ability. Poet Francis Hopkinson wrote of a 1770 match fought in Germantown, Pennsylvania, between chickens belonging to New Yorker James DeLancey and Philadelphian Timothy Matlack, saying that, "Chickens

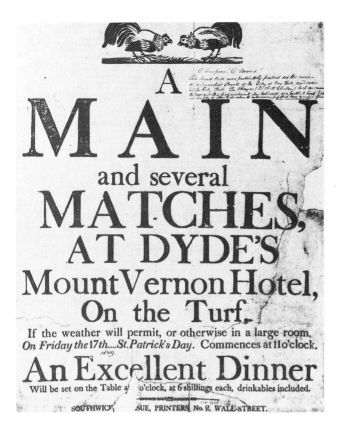

A New York handbill for a cockfight

ticular, was famous for its shooting matches. Bowling had been brought from Europe, and it was easy for a tavern to provide a lawn area for knocking over pins. Quoits, a game similar to horseshoes, and card games, which became a colonial obsession, were also played in taverns.

Pope's Day. Taverns were also meeting places for colonists sharing social or political views. In the mid eighteenth century, colonists began organizing wild celebrations on 5 November, the anniversary of an attempt in 1605 by Catholic conspirators to blow up Parliament. In Boston, mobs of sailors, dock workers, and laborers of all races would organize parades each carrying effigies of the Pope, the devil, and the Stuart pretender to the British throne. In 1745 Boston was the scene of a major riot as these different mobs converged in the center of town. The town then tried to rein in these activities, forbidding them to take place at night. By the 1750s Pope's Day had become an all-day holiday in Massachusetts, New York, and other colonies involving parades, fireworks, drinking, and rioting, anticipating the kinds of popular demonstrations of the Revolutionary period.

Dancing. Perhaps the most common form of physical activity in colonial America was dancing. Almost all Americans danced as a form of exercise as well as a form of social activity. People of different social classes would hold their own dances, with wealthier colonists attending more

yet unhatched shall curse D[eLancey]'s name." Typically the fighting cocks would be armed with steel or other sharp implements on their legs and the match would end when one of them was either dead or unable to get up. These matches would be fought in special pits below an area for spectators who, of course, would gamble on the outcome. Taverns would accommodate these matches as well as other sporting activities such as bull or bear baiting, which had been outlawed in Massachusetts in 1631 but continued to be practiced.

Fighting. In England boxing was becoming refined in the eighteenth century as Jack Broughton (champion from 1734 to 1750) made the first rules for exhibition bareknuckle boxing. Rounds would last until a man fell; there was no hitting below the belt or while a man was down. In America fighting matches had less delicacy and colonists referred to the sport as "rough and tumbling." Taverns also drew great crowds to these matches. In America one of the objects of a fight was to gouge the opponent in the genitals with waxed fingernails especially grown for the purpose. While in some cases fighting was simply a way to resolve differences or a result of the colonists large appetite for alcohol, these matches also provided spectators with entertainment and potential for wagering.

Tavern Activities. Taverns provided a venue for blood sports as well as more genteel sporting activities. Benjamin Berry's tavern in what is today Berryville, Virginia, hosted so many sporting activities that the village was nicknamed "Battletown." Taverns also became sites for shooting contests or target practice, and Hagerstown, Maryland, in par-

---

BOXING MATCH

Olaudah Equiano was an African enslaved when he was eleven years old. He was bought in 1757 by an English sea captain and served for much of the Seven Years' War in the British navy. Here he recounts an incident on the British warship *Roebuck*.

When I went on board this large ship, I was amazed indeed to see the quantity of men and the guns. . . . There was a number of boys on board, which still made it more agreeable; for we were always together, and a great part of our time was spent in play.

I remained in this ship a considerable time, during which we made several cruises, and visited a variety of places; among others we were twice in Holland, and brought over several persons of distinction from it, . . . On the passage, one day, for diversion of those gentlemen, all the boys were called on the quarter-deck, and were paired proportionably, and then made to fight; after which the gentlemen gave the combatants from five to nine shillings each. This was the first time I ever fought with a white boy; and I never knew what it was to have a bloody nose before. This made me fight most desperately, I suppose considerably more than an hour; and at last, both of us being weary, we were parted. I had a great deal of this kind of sport afterwards, in which the captain and the ship's company used very much to encourage me.

Source: Olaudah Equiano, *The Interesting Narrative of Olaudah Equiano (1789)*, edited by Robert J. Allison (Boston: Bedford Books, 1995).

formal affairs, while people of less status and slaves would also enjoy their own dances. In Charleston, New York, Boston, and Philadelphia formal dances formed a vital part of the social season. In 1768, Boston's Patriot leaders boycotted the dancing assembly to avoid the royal officials and British military officers attending. That same year, New York's Dancing Assembly witnessed a less political but as bitter quarrel between the wives of Gen. Thomas Gage and New York governor Sir Henry Moore, each believing she should be first in a country dance.

Fishing and Hunting. The American landscape provided excellent opportunities for fishing and hunting, which were not only sources of food. In 1732 the Schuylkill Fishing Company, a private club for fishermen, drew up rules for fishing. The sport of fishing had become popularized in England in the seventeenth century with a publication of Isaak Walton's *Compleat Angler*. Other fishing clubs were formed throughout the colonies, and they occasionally engaged in cricket and other athletic competitions with other rival companies. The society of Fort St. David, another Pennsylvania fishing club, also housed a museum of native American artifacts and curiosities. Charleston, South Carolina, had two hunting clubs that merged in 1761. In 1776, Pennsylvania's new state constitution guaranteed citizens the right to "fowl and hunt" on all open land, and to fish "in all boatable waters," providing a liberty restricted in England by the feudal privileges of aristocrats.

Water Sports. In New England colonists raced sailing sloops or rowboats, and in the Chesapeake colonists raced canoes and sometimes galleys rowed by slaves. South Carolina planters who spent their summer months in Rhode Island enjoyed the pleasures of sailing. New Yorkers raced yachts, which were a Dutch innovation (the word *yacht* comes from a Dutch word for hunting boat). In addition to sailing, many Americans also swam. Benjamin Franklin, who learned to swim in Boston Harbor, at one point considered traveling through Europe as a swimming instructor.

Card Playing. The most popular card game of the eighteenth century was whist. Edmond Hoyle's 1742 *Short Treatise on Whist* codified the rules for this game similar to today's bridge. Charleston had a weekly "Whist Club," and in Boston a "Card Assembly" met every Thursday evening. Cribbage, invented in the seventeenth century, had also become popular, and German and French colonists played a game derived from the Italian *tremonta,* a game played with three cards. This game required bluffing one's opponents; the Germans played it with five cards and called it *pochen* (meaning to bluff). The French called it *poque,* which the Americans mispronounced as poker. In 1765 the Stamp Act taxed playing cards, requiring a revenue stamp to be placed on the Ace of Spades. Taxing playing cards may have been the most unpopular feature of this act.

Evolution of American Sports. Though the American colonists did not continue the British sports of cricket or football, they did begin to develop other sports imported

---

SHIPBOARD RECREATION

John Adams sailed to France in 1778 and recorded this episode of shipboard life.

MARCH 7. SATURDAY

We have passed all the Dangers of the American Coast. Those of the Bay of Biscay, remain. God grant Us, an happy Passage through them all.

This Morning the Captain ordered all Hands upon Deck and took an account of the Number of Souls on board which amounted to 172. Then he ordered the Articles of War to be read to them—after which he ordered all Hands upon the Forecastle and then all Hands upon the Quarter deck, in order to try Experiments, for determining whether any difference was made in the Ships sailing, by the Weight of the Men being forward or abaft. Then all Hands were ordered to their Quarters to exercise them at the Guns. Mr. Barron [the captain] gave the Words of Command and they spent an Hour perhaps in the Exercise, at which they seemed tolerably expert. Then the Captain ordered a Dance, upon the Main Deck, and all Hands, Negroes, Boys and Men were obliged to dance. After this the old Sailors set on Foot another Frolic, called the Miller, or the Mill. I will not spend Time to describe this odd Scene: but it ended in a very high frolic, in which almost all the Men were powdered over, with Flour, and wet again to the Skin.—Whether these whimsical Diversions are indulged, in order to make the Men wash themselves, and shift their Cloaths, and to wash away Vermin I dont know. But there is not in them the least Ray of Elegance, very little Wit, and a humour of the coarsest Kind. It is not superior to Negro and Indian Dances.

Very likely the dance was not done to clean the men's clothes but to relax them before they faced the dangers of the Bay of Biscay. Within two weeks the ship would have fought two battles and Captain Barron would lose first his leg and then his life.

Source: John Adams, *Diary and Autobiography of John Adams*, volume 2, *1771–1781*, edited by Lyman H. Butterfield (Cambridge, Mass.: Harvard University Press, 1961).

---

from Europe that better suited their character and environment. In 1762 a British book reprinted in New York showed a batter, catcher, and pitcher with two bases marked by poles. In 1778 soldiers in George Washington's army were reported to be "playing at base" at Valley Forge. In 1787 Princeton, New Jersey, forbade local college students to "play with balls and sticks" on the Common. In April 1779 Philadelphia printer James Rivington advertised golf clubs and the "veritable Caledonian BALLS" for sale in his print shop. Baseball and golf in the next century would become important American sports. Like the other forms of recreation enjoyed by colonial Americans, these emphasized individual skills in the wide-open American environment.

GENERAL REFERENCES

GENERAL

Bernard Bailyn, *The Peopling of British North America: An Introduction* (New York: Knopf, 1986);

Daniel Boorstin, *The Americans: The Colonial Experience* (New York: Random House, 1958);

Jacob Ernest Cooke, ed., *Encyclopedia of the North American Colonies*, 3 volumes (New York: Scribners, 1993);

Jack P. Greene and J. R. Pole, eds., *Colonial British America: Essays in the New History of the Early Modern Era* (Baltimore: Johns Hopkins University Press, 1984);

Richard Middleton, *Colonial America: A History, 1585–1776*, second edition (Oxford: Blackwell, 1996).

ARTS

Emory Elliot, ed., *Columbia Literary History of the United States* (New York: Columbia University Press, 1988);

Robert Ferguson, *The American Enlightenment, 1750–1820* (Cambridge, Mass.: Cambridge University Press, 1997);

Jay Fliegelman, *Declaring Independence: Jefferson, Natural Language, and the Culture of Performance* (Stanford, Cal.: Stanford University Press, 1994);

J. Meredith Neill, *Toward a National Taste: America's Quest for Aesthetic Independence* (Honolulu: University Press of Hawaii, 1975);

Kenneth Silverman, *A Cultural History of the American Revolution* (New York: Columbia University Press, 1987).

BUSINESS AND THE ECONOMY

Thomas M. Doerflinger, *A Vigorous Spirit of Enterprise: Merchants and Economic Development in Revolutionary Philadelphia* (Chapel Hill: University of North Carolina Press, 1986);

Robert A. East, *Business Enterprise in the American Revolutionary Era* (New York: Columbia University Press, 1938);

E. James Ferguson, *The Power of the Purse: A History of American Public Finance, 1776–1790* (Chapel Hill: University of North Carolina Press, 1961);

John J. McCusker and Russell R. Menard, *The Economy of British America, 1607–1789* (Chapel Hill: University of North Carolina Press, 1985);

Edwin J. Perkins, *The Economy of Colonial America* (New York: Columbia University Press, 1980).

COMMUNICATIONS

Bernard Bailyn and John B. Hench, eds., *The Press and the American Revolution* (Worcester, Mass.: American Antiquarian Society, 1980);

Richard D. Brown, *Revolutionary Politics in Massachusetts: The Boston Committee of Correspondence and the Towns, 1772–1774* (Cambridge, Mass.: Harvard University Press, 1970);

Catherine S. Crary, ed., *The Price of Loyalty: Tory Writings from the Revolutionary Era* (New York: McGraw-Hill, 1973);

Philip Davidson, *Propaganda and the American Revolution, 1763–1783* (Chapel Hill: University of North Carolina Press, 1941);

Richard B. Kielbowicz, *News in the Mail: The Press, Post Office, and Public Information, 1700–1860s* (Westport, Conn.: Greenwood, 1989);

Arthur M. Schlesinger, *Prelude to Independence: The Newspaper War on Britain, 1764–1776* (New York: Knopf, 1957);

Francis G. Walett, *Patriots, Loyalists, and Printers: Bicentennial Essays on the American Revolution* (Worcester, Mass.: American Antiquarian Society, 1976).

EDUCATION

Bernard Bailyn, *Education in the Forming of American Society: Needs and Opportunities for Study* (Chapel Hill: University of North Carolina Press, 1960);

Lawrence Cremin, *American Education: The Colonial Experience, 1760–1783* (New York: Harper & Row, 1970);

Robert Middlekauf, *Ancients and Axioms: Secondary Education in Eighteenth-Century New England* (New Haven: Yale University Press, 1963);

Barbara Solomon, *In the Company of Educated Women: A History of Women and Higher Education in America* (New Haven: Yale University Press, 1985);

Julia Cherry Spruill, *Women's Life and Work in the Southern Colonies* (Chapel Hill: University of North Carolina Press, 1938).

GOVERNMENT AND POLITICS

Bernard Bailyn, *Faces of Revolution: Personalities and Themes in the Struggle for American Independence* (New York: Vintage, 1992);

Bailyn, *Ideological Origins of the American Revolution* (Cambridge, Mass.: Harvard University Press, 1967);

Lawrence Henry Gipson, *The Coming of the Revolution, 1763–1775* (New York: Harper, 1954);

Jack Rakove, *The Beginnings of National Politics: An Interpretive History of the Continental Congress* (Baltimore: Johns Hopkins University Press, 1979);

Gordon S. Wood, *Creation of the American Republic, 1776–1787* (Chapel Hill: University of North Carolina Press, 1969).

LAW AND JUSTICE

Willi Paul Adams, *The First American Constitutions* (Chapel Hill: University of North Carolina Press, 1980);

Lawrence Friedman, *A History of American Law* (New York: Simon & Schuster, 1985);

Lawrence Henry Gipson, *The Coming of the Revolution, 1763–1775* (New York: Harper, 1954);

Bernard Schwartz, *Thomas Jefferson and* Bolling v. Bolling: *Law and the Legal Profession in Pre-Revolutionary America* (San Marino, Cal.: Huntington Library, 1997).

LIFESTYLES, SOCIAL TRENDS, AND FASHION

Bernard Bailyn, *The Peopling of British North America: An Introduction* (New York: Knopf, 1986);

Ronald Hoffman, ed., *Economy of Early America: The Revolutionary Period, 1763–1790* (Charlottesville: University Press of Virginia, 1988);

Richard J. Hooker, *Food and Drink in America: A History* (Indianapolis & New York: Bobbs-Merrill, 1981);

Alice Hanson Jones, *The Wealth of a Nation to Be: The American Colonies on the Eve of the Revolution* (New York: Columbia University Press, 1980);

Sidney Kaplan, *The Black Presence in the Era of the American Revolution, 1770–1800* (New York: New York Graphic Society, 1973);

Gary Nash, *Forging Freedom: The Formation of Philadelphia's Black Community, 1720–1840* (Cambridge, Mass.: Harvard University Press, 1988);

Nash, *The Urban Crucible: Social Change, Political Consciousness, and the Origins of the American Revolution* (Cambridge, Mass.: Harvard University Press, 1979).

MILITARY

Arthur Bowler, *Logistics and the Failure of the British Army in America, 1775–1783* (Princeton, N.J.: Princeton University Press, 1975);

Don Higginbotham, *The War of American Independence: Military Attitudes, Policies, and Practice, 1763–1789* (New York: Macmillan, 1971);

Piers Mackesy, *The War for America, 1775–1783* (Cambridge, Mass.: Harvard University Press, 1964);

John S. Pancake, *This Destructive War: The British Campaign in the Carolinas, 1780–1782* (Tuscaloosa: University of Alabama Press, 1985);

John Shy, *A People Numerous and Armed: Reflections on the Military Struggle for American Independence* (New York: Oxford University Press, 1976);

Christopher Ward, *War of the Revolution,* 2 volumes (New York: Macmillan, 1952).

RELIGION

Jon Butler, *Awash in a Sea of Faith* (Cambridge, Mass.: Harvard University Press, 1990);

Alan Heimert, *Religion and the American Mind, From the Great Awakening to the Revolution* (Cambridge, Mass.: Harvard University Press, 1966);

William G. McLoughlin, *Isaac Backus and the American Pietistic Tradition* (Boston: Little, Brown, 1970);

Harry Stout, *The Divine Dramatist: George Whitefield and the Rise of Modern Evangelicism* (Grand Rapids, Mich.: W. B. Eerdmans, 1991).

SCIENCE AND MEDICINE

Silvio A. Bedini, *Thinkers and Tinkers: Early American Men of Science* (New York: Scribners, 1975);

Brooke Hindle, *The Pursuit of Science in Revolutionary America, 1735–1789* (Chapel Hill: University of North Carolina Press, 1956).

SPORTS AND RECREATION

Carl Bridenbaugh, *Cities in Revolt: Urban Life in America, 1743–1776* (New York: Knopf, 1955);

Bruce C. Daniels, *Puritans at Play: Leisure and Recreation in Colonial New England* (New York: St. Martin's Press, 1955);

Nancy L. Struna, *People of Prowess: Sport, Leisure, and Labor in Early Anglo-America* (Urbana: University of Illinois Press, 1996).

CONTRIBUTORS

THE ARTS

BUSINESS & THE ECONOMY

COMMUNICATIONS

EDUCATION

GOVERNMENT & POLITICS

LAW & JUSTICE

LIFESTYLES & SOCIAL TRENDS

MILITARY

RELIGION

SCIENCE & MEDICINE

SPORTS & RECREATION

THOMAS E. AUGST
University of Minnesota

ROWENA OLEGARIO
University of Michigan

ANTHONY J. SCOTTI
Manly, Inc.

BARBARA DEWOLFE
Harvard University

ROBERT J. ALLISON
Suffolk University

ELI C. BORTMAN
Winchester, Massachusetts

PAUL FOOS
Suffolk University

JOSEPH M. MCCARTHY
Suffolk University

JOHN T. O'KEEFE
Harvard University

LEN TRAVERS
Massachusetts Historical Society

ROBERT J. ALLISON
Suffolk University

GENERAL INDEX

A

Abercrombie, Gen. James   265,   277
Abolition   144, 209, 230, 311, 326
Abolition Society of Philadelphia   120, 125
Academie Royale des Sciences   342
Academy and Charitable School of Philadelphia   118, 126–127, 140
Acadians   198, 229, 264
An Account of the Weather and Diseases in South-Carolina (Chalmers)   342
Act for Establishing Religious Freedom in Virginia   297, 305
Adams, Abigail Smith   74, 124, 241, 358
Adams, Elizabeth Wells   186
Adams, John   35, 70, 74, 78, 80–81, 92, 93, 99, 110, 121, 124, 134, 157, 160, 162–164, 166–167, 174, 176, 178–180, 185, 187–188, 190, 195, 200, 203–205, 215–218, 220, 223, 225, 239, 241, 243, 291, 299, 303–304, 372
Adams, Mary Checkley   185, 186
Adams, Samuel   16, 88, 94, 110, 154, 163, 166, 174–176, 178, 184–185, 186, 188, 191–192, 195, 203, 260, 335
Adams, Susanna Boylston   217
Addison, Joseph   33
Administration of Justice Act   156
The Adulateur (Warren)   18
Advertisements   34, 136, 140, 146
Advice to a Young Tradesman (Franklin)   15
African American churches   241
African American dancing   238
African American education   124, 130, 144
African American poetry   43
African American schools   118–121, 125
African Lodge Number One of Freemasons   230
African Methodist Episcopal Church   295
The Age of Reason (Paine)   195

Agrippina Landing at Brundisium with the Ashes of Germanicus (West)   16, 26
Agrarian Justice (Paine)   195
Agriculture   124, 126–128, 340, 357
Aikman, William   134
Aitken Bible   20
Aitken, Robert   194
An Alarm to the Unconverted (Alleine)   146
Albany Congress   165, 167, 191, 198
Albany Plan   152, 166, 167
Alexander, James   64
Alexander, Mary   64
Algonquian tribe   166
Alison, Francis   123
Alleine, Joseph   146
Allen, Col. Ethan   19, 267, 280, 288, 340
Allen, Richard   242, 295
Allen, William   357
Allston, Washington   27
Almy, Benjamin   330
Almy, Mary Gould   330
America (Dwight)   19
America, A Poem (Martin)   16
America: Or, a Poem on the Settlement of the British Colonies (Livingston)   17
American Academy of Arts and Sciences   121, 343
American Booksellers Association   112
The American Cock Robin: Or, A choice collection of English Songs…agreeable to the North-American Taste   15
American Company of Comedians   30
American Congregational churches   17
The American Crisis (Paine)   89–90, 92, 110, 194
The American Magazine and Monthly Chronicle   14, 17, 109–110, 228, 357
American Manufactory of Woolens, Linens, and Cottons   49
American Methodist Episcopal Church   296
The American Mock-bird. A Collection of the most familiar Songs now in vogue   15
American Philosophical Society   120, 341–342, 355–357, 360, 362, 366

American Philosophical Society Held at Philadelphia for Promoting Useful Knowledge   120
American Romanticism   38
American Society for Promoting and Propagating Useful Knowledge Held at Philadelphia   120
American Spelling Book (Webster)   20
The American Times (Odell)   39
American Turtle   342, 352, 363
The American Village, A Poem (Freneau)   17, 38
American Weekly Mercury   109
American Whig Society   38
Amherst, Gen. Jeffrey   265–266, 277
André, Maj. John   98, 288
Angell, Abigail   113
Anglican Church   125, 130, 215, 295–299, 301–302, 309, 314, 316, 319, 334
Anglican Society for the Propagation of the Gospel in Foreign Parts   123
Annapolis Convention   220
"An Anthem for Easter" (Billings)   41
Anthony, Susanna   146
Anthracite coal   46, 48
Antiproprietary petition   219
Anti-tea declaration   49
Anza, Juan Bautista de   157
Apo   242
An Appeal to the Public for Religious Liberty (Backus)   306
Apprenticeships   59, 128–129
Apthorp, Rev. East   303
Arabian Nights   136
Arcadia: or the Shepard's Wedding (Lloyd)   15
Architecture   18, 23–24, 140, 324
Architecture (Greek)   251
Architecture (Roman)   251
Ariosto, Ludovico   41
Aristotle   162
Arithmetic   123, 132, 140, 142
Arnold, Benedict, Gen.   98, 159, 194, 268, 270, 280, 282–283, 286, 288–289, 321
Arnold, Peggy Shippen   288
Articles of Confederation   81–82, 158–159, 164, 168, 200–201, 220
Artisans   61
The Arts   13–43

Asbury, Francis   296, 302, 327, 334
Ashanti tribe   242
Ashbridge, Elizabeth   294, 331
Associates of Dr. Bray   118–119, 130
Astronomical tables   353
Astronomy   126, 341, 345, 347, 352, 356, 360, 366
Asylums   351
The Atlantic Pilot (DeBrahm)   342
Auctions   86
Austin, David   333
Austin, George   79
Autobiography (Adams)   204
Autobiography (Franklin)   22, 314, 358
Autobiography (Jarratt)   334

B

Bache, Richard   105
Backus, Isaac   294, 297–298, 306
Bacon, Sir Francis   123
Ball, Eleanor   79
Ballooning   356, 365
Bank of North America   50, 60, 67, 70, 76–77, 81, 159, 170, 195
Bank of the United States   78
Banking systems   48
Banks, John   15
Baptist Church   215, 241, 259, 294, 295–299, 303–306, 308, 316–317, 319, 321, 324
Baptist Warren Association   297
Barford, Richard   15
Barlow, Joel   14, 19, 39
Barnes, Edward   230
Barometer   356
Barre, Col. Isaac   181
Barry, John   40
Barton, Andrew   16
Bartram, John   345, 364
The Basset-Table: A Comedy (Centlivre)   15
The Bastille   195, 289
Battles—
—Alamance Creek (1771)   267
—Bemis Heights (1777)   269, 282–283, 355
—Bennington (1777)   269
—Brandywine (1777)   269, 284, 289, 299
—Bunker Hill (1775)   167, 177, 260, 267, 279–280
—Bushy Run (1763)   267
—Camden (1780)   270, 285, 355
—Concord (1775)   39, 79, 89, 103–104, 115, 163, 177, 220, 267, 279–280
—Cowpens (1781)   100, 270, 286
—Eutaw Springs (1781)   271, 286
—Fort Ninety-Six (1781)   286
—Freeman's Farm (1777)   269, 282–283, 288
—Golden Hill (1770)   154, 267
—Guilford Courthouse (1781)   270, 286
—Harlem Heights (1776)   268

—Hobkirk's Hill (1781)   270, 286
—King's Mountain (1780)   270
—Lake George (1755)   264, 276
—Lexington (1775)   79, 81, 89, 103–104, 115, 163, 177, 187, 194, 220, 267, 279, 280
—Long Island (1776)   268, 280–281
—Minden (1759)   289
—Monmouth Courthouse (1778)   96, 269, 284, 289
—the Monongahela (1755)   264, 273–275, 291
—Moore's Creek Bridge (1776)   268
—Oriskany (1777)   259, 268
—Plains of Abraham (1759)   266, 277–278
—Point Pleasant (1774)   267
—Princeton (1777)   110
—Ticonderoga (1758)   265, 277
—Trenton (1776)   268
—Valcour Island (1776)   268
—White Plains (1776)   253
—Yorktown (1781)   115, 286, 289
Battle of Bunkers-Hill (Brackenridge)   18
"The Battle of the Kegs" (Hopkinson)   19
Bay Psalm Book   36
Bayley, Daniel   15
Bear baiting   238, 371
Beaujeu, Capt. Daniel   274
Beaumarchais, Pierre-Augustin Caron de   188
"The Beauties of Santa Cruz" (Freneau)   18
Beekman, James   67
Behrent, John   18
Beissel, Conrad   296, 320
Believers in Christ's Second Appearing. *See* Shakers.
Bell, Robert   99, 134
Bellamy, Joseph   33, 318, 332
Benezet, Anthony   118, 120, 136, 142, 144, 242, 261, 294, 311
Benezet, Jean Etienne   144
Benezet, Judith   144
Bentham, Jeremy   176
Berkeley, George   21
Bernard, Gov. Francis   43, 110, 154, 173, 182, 185, 191, 203, 224
Berry, Benjamin   371
Bethabara, North Carolina   142
Bethania, North Carolina   142
Bethlehem Hospital   351
Bethlehem, Pennsylvania   142
Bettering House   250, 251
Bible   20, 44, 90, 134–138, 143, 146–147, 205, 306, 308, 309, 314, 333
Bifocal spectacles   344
"A Bill Concerning Slaves" (Jefferson)   121
"Bill for the More General Diffusion of Knowledge" (Jefferson)   121
Bill of Rights   164, 192–193, 218, 222
Billings, William   17, 19, 36–37, 40, 310
Binney, Barnabas   259

Birthing practices   343, 346
Black Prince   75
Black Princess   75
Blacksmithing   129
Blackstone, Sir William   206
Blair, John   122
Blanchard, Pierre   365
Bland, Robert   41
Bleeding   348, 349, 355
The Blind Beggar of Bethal Green (Dodsley)   19
The Blockade of Boston   18
The Blockheads: Or, the Affrighted Officers. A Farce (Warren)   18
Blood, Caleb   307
Bolling, Robert   41
Bolton, John   96
Bonaparte, Napoleon   289
Bonhomme Richard (ship)   284
Boone, Daniel   49, 89, 92, 108
Boscawen, Adm. Edward   277
Boston Committee of Correspondence   95
Boston Evening Post   66, 228
Boston Gazette   17, 88–89, 110–111, 229, 350
Boston Gazette and Country Journal   40, 86, 92, 99, 107, 110, 140
Boston Journal   115
Boston Latin School   333
Boston Magazine   20
Boston Massacre   17, 31, 78, 88, 110, 154, 162, 173, 199, 202–204, 217, 223, 260, 267
Boston News-Letter   137
Boston Port Bill   80, 156, 184
Boston Public Library   133
Boston Society for Encouraging Industry and Employing the Poor   48
Boston Tea Party   29, 43, 48, 54, 80, 88, 95, 111, 155–156, 163, 173, 184, 187, 192, 200, 260, 306
Botany   340, 343, 345
Boudinot, Elias   168
Bowdoin, James   121, 175
Bowling   370, 371
Bownas, Samuel   14
Boxing   29, 371
Boy with Squirrel (Copley)   16, 42
Boycotts   22, 30, 47–48, 119, 121, 132, 190, 202–203, 212, 236, 250, 252, 256–257, 309, 372
Brackenridge, Hugh Henry   17, 18, 19, 22, 38
Braddock, Maj. Gen. Edward   92, 108, 152, 264, 274–275, 291, 307, 309
Bradford, Andrew Sowle   109
Bradford, Rachel Budd   109
Bradford, Thomas   99, 110, 134
Bradford, William III   86, 87, 89, 99, 102, 107, 109, 113
Bradstreet, Anne   14
Bradstreet, Col. John   265, 277
Brant, Joseph (Thayendanegea)   253, 258
Brant, Mary (Molly)   253, 258

Bray, Dr. Thomas   125, 130, 135
Bremer, James   15
Brewster, Caleb   97
Brewster, Martha   14
Bridge building   195
A Brief Narrative of the Revival of Religion in Virginia (Jarratt)   231
British Army   66, 247, 260
British Board of Trade   165
British Coffee House   225
British Constitution   186
British Legion   93
Broadwater, Charles   193
Brooker, William   110
Broughton, Jack   371
Brown University. *See* College of Rhode Island.
Brown, Charles Brockden   17, 35
Brown, Dr. William   35, 343
Brown, John   14
Brownson, Oliver   20
Bryan, Andrew   328
Bryan, Hugh   326, 328
Bryant, William Cullen   38
Bucarely y Ursua, Antonio Maria   154
Buckland, William   23, 192
Buell, Abel   341, 343, 347
Bull baiting   371
Bull, Lt. Gov. William   107
Bunyan, John   16
Burgoyne, Gen. John   19, 22, 103, 268, 279, 281, 284, 288
Burke, Edmund   49, 53, 80, 176, 184–185, 195
Burnaby, Rev. Andrew   228, 344
Bushnell, David   268, 342, 347, 352, 363
Business and the Economy   45–84
Butler, Samuel   39
Byrd, William   370
Byrd, William II   42, 134

C

Calvin, John   332
Calvinist Church   39, 301, 305, 316, 318, 321, 324, 332, 334
Cambridge University   124
Cameron, Duncan   14
Campbell, Col. Sir Archibald   269, 285
Campbell, Gen. John, Earl of Loudon   137, 265, 276
Canajoharie   258
Candle making   129, 195
Cannon manufacturing   50
Cannon, John   334
Cannons   272, 280–281, 347
"A Canzonet" (Bolling)   41
Capital offenses   214
Card playing   238, 370–371, 372
Carleton, Guy   268
Carlisle Peace Commission   101
Carpenter's Hall   351
Carpentry   129
Carroll, Charles   296, 307
Carson, Jemmy   15

Case, Wheeler   19
"The Case of the Officers of the Excise" (Paine)   88
Caspipina's Letters (Duché)   18
Catholic Church   23, 156
Cato (Addison)   19
Cato's Letters (Gordon and Trenchard)   21
Caucus Club   176, 186
A Caution to Great Britain and Her Colonies, in a Short Representation of the Calamitous State of the Enslaved Negroes in the British Dominion (Benezet)   144
Cayuga tribe   165
Celestial navigation   345, 353
Celestial theorists   345
Centlivre, Susannah   15
Ceramics   54
Chalmers, Dr. Lionel   342, 356
Chaloner, John   66
Chambers of Commerce   46
Charles I, king of England   161, 335
Charles, Carroll   206
Charleston Library Society   118
Charter of Liberties   219
Chase, Samuel   167
Chauncy, Charles   313, 318, 322, 333
Checkley, Mary Cranston   147
Chelsea Apothecaries Company   345
Cherokee tribe   253, 290, 364, 370
Chesapeake gentry   238
"Chester" (Billings)   40, 310
Chiabrera, Gabriello   41
The Child of Nature, a Philosophical Novel   18
Child rearing   252, 257
Chillicothe   244
Chilmark congregation   334
Chiswell scandal   41
The Choice: A poem, after the manner of Mr. Pomfret (Church)   14
The Chorister's Companion Or, Church Music Revised (Jocelin)   20
Chovet, Abraham   342
Christ Church   24
Christian Hymns, Poems, and Spiritual Songs (J. and J. Relly)   20
The Christian Soldier's Duty briefly Delineated   100
Chronometer   353
Church membership   304
Church of England   301, 302, 334
Church of the Brethren. *See* Dunkers.
Church, Benjamin   14, 95
Churchill, Charles   39
Churchman, John   310
Cicero   38
Cincinnatus   291
Civic virtue   22
"Civil Dudgeon" (Bolling)   41
Civil law   217
Clap, Mary   331
Clap, Nathaniel   146
Clap, Thomas   119, 340
Clarissa (Richardson)   35
Clark, George Rogers   269

Clarke, Jonathan   184
Clarkson, Thomas   144
Classical education   123, 127, 131
Classical languages   123
Clayton, John   120, 344
Cleaveland, John   328, 335
Clinton, Gen. Sir Henry   94, 98, 231, 247, 268–269, 279, 284, 286, 288, 291
Clock making   347
Clothing   236
Cobbett, William   195
Cockfighting   29, 31, 238, 370
Coercive or Intolerable Acts of 1774   95–96, 163, 200, 297
Coke, Sir Edward   206, 221
Coke, Thomas   327, 334
Colden, Lt. Gov. Cadwallader   206, 364
A Collection of Designs in Architecture (Swann)   18
A Collection of Hymns, for Social Worship (Madan)   16
A Collection of Psalm Tunes, with a few anthems and Hymns (Hopkinson)   15
A Collection of the Best Psalm Tunes (Flagg)   15
A Collection of the Most Approved Tunes and Anthems, for the Promotion of Psalmody   19
College degrees   133
Collège du Plessis   289
College of New Jersey   118–119, 121, 122, 124–125, 128, 132–134, 294–295, 318
College of Philadelphia   119, 121, 124, 128, 131, 133–134, 341, 362
College of Rhode Island   119, 120, 124, 132–133, 147, 239, 252, 295, 306, 362
College of William and Mary   124–125, 130, 133–134, 222, 239, 343–344
Colonial trade   182, 183
Columbia University. *See* King's College.
A Commentary upon Littleton (Coke)   221
Commentaries on the Laws of England (Blackstone)   206
Commercial banks   70, 78
Committee of Commerce   81
Committee of Observation and Inspection   241
Committees of safety   95, 193
Committee of Secret Correspondence   81
Committee on Foreign Affairs   90, 188, 195
Committees of correspondence   88, 94, 96, 102, 105, 113, 154–155, 184, 186, 203
Common law   212, 217, 243
Common Sense (Paine)   33, 89, 92, 102–103, 164, 167, 179, 194, 200, 210, 246
Communications   85–115
Compass   356

INDEX OF PHOTOGRAPHS